Lecture Notes in Computer Science 2830
Edited by G. Goos, J. Hartmanis, and J. van Leeuwen

Springer
*Berlin
Heidelberg
New York
Hong Kong
London
Milan
Paris
Tokyo*

Frank Pfenning   Yannis Smaragdakis (Eds.)

Generative Programming and Component Engineering

Second International Conference, GPCE 2003
Erfurt, Germany, September 22-25, 2003
Proceedings

Series Editors

Gerhard Goos, Karlsruhe University, Germany
Juris Hartmanis, Cornell University, NY, USA
Jan van Leeuwen, Utrecht University, The Netherlands

Volume Editors

Frank Pfenning
Carnegie Mellon University
Department of Computer Science
Pittsburgh, PA 15213, USA
E-mail: fp@cs.cmu.edu

Yannis Smaragdakis
Georgia Institute of Technology
College of Computing
Atlanta, GA 30332, USA
E-mail: yannis@cc.gatech.edu

Cataloging-in-Publication Data applied for

A catalog record for this book is available from the Library of Congress.

Bibliographic information published by Die Deutsche Bibliothek
Die Deutsche Bibliothek lists this publication in the Deutsche Nationalbibliografie;
detailed bibliographic data is available in the Internet at <http://dnb.ddb.de>.

CR Subject Classification (1998): D.2, D.1, D.3, K.6

ISSN 0302-9743
ISBN 3-540-20102-5 Springer-Verlag Berlin Heidelberg New York

This work is subject to copyright. All rights are reserved, whether the whole or part of the material is concerned, specifically the rights of translation, reprinting, re-use of illustrations, recitation, broadcasting, reproduction on microfilms or in any other way, and storage in data banks. Duplication of this publication or parts thereof is permitted only under the provisions of the German Copyright Law of September 9, 1965, in its current version, and permission for use must always be obtained from Springer-Verlag. Violations are liable for prosecution under the German Copyright Law.

Springer-Verlag Berlin Heidelberg New York
a member of BertelsmannSpringer Science+Business Media GmbH

http://www.springer.de

© Springer-Verlag Berlin Heidelberg 2003
Printed in Germany

Typesetting: Camera-ready by author, data conversion by Olgun Computergrafik
Printed on acid-free paper   SPIN: 10955727   06/3142   5 4 3 2 1 0

Preface

This volume constitutes the proceedings of the second International Conference on Generative Programming and Component Engineering (GPCE 2003), held September 22–25, 2003, in Erfurt, Germany, sponsored by the NetObjectDays German industrial software development event, in cooperation with the ACM SIGPLAN and SIGSOFT societies. GPCE was created as an effort to bring together researchers working on both the programming languages and the software engineering side of program generation and component engineering. The common theme of program generation and component engineering is the domain-specific nature of both approaches. Depending on the characteristics of a domain, either a generative or a compositional technical solution may be appropriate.

In just its second year, GPCE has shown a lot of promise for building a strong community. The response to the call for papers was excellent, with 62 submissions to the technical program, 2 of which were later withdrawn. Each paper received between three and five reviews, many of them quite thorough and hopefully valuable to all authors. The electronic meeting allowed for in-depth discussions of all submissions, often to a much greater extent than possible in a physical PC meeting. As a result, 21 papers were selected for presentation at the conference and are included in this volume, together with abstracts for the invited talks by Olivier Danvy and Peri Tarr. Of the accepted papers, 3 are co-authored by PC members (from a total of 5 PC submissions). We tried hard to ensure fairness and hold PC submissions to a high standard.

The EDAS conference submission system was used to manage the paper submissions. Our EDAS installation was supported by Blair MacIntyre, who was particularly helpful in resolving technical issues with the system. Our thanks also go to Jennifer Landefeld for her work in editing the proceedings contributions.

Finally, we would like to thank the conference chair, Krzysztof Czarnecki, and all program committee members for their hard work. The GPCE technical program was possible only because of their dedication and outstanding reviewing work.

July 2003

Frank Pfenning
Yannis Smaragdakis

Program Chairs

Frank Pfenning, Carnegie Mellon University
Yannis Smaragdakis, Georgia Institute of Technology

Program Committee

Giuseppe Attardi, University of Pisa
Don Batory, University of Texas
Ira Baxter, Semantic Designs
Ted Biggerstaff, softwaregenerators.com
Shigeru Chiba, Tokyo Institute of Technology
Rowan Davies, University of Western Australia
Premkumar Devanbu, University of California, Davis
Ulrich W. Eisenecker, University of Applied Sciences, Kaiserslautern
Robert Glueck, Waseda University
Trevor Jim, AT&T Labs Research
Gregor Kiczales, University of British Columbia
Kai Koskimies, Tampere University of Technology
Julia Lawall, University of Copenhagen
Eugenio Moggi, University of Genova
Jim Neighbors, Bayfront Technologies
Calton Pu, Georgia Institute of Technology
Olin Shivers, Georgia Institute of Technology
Clemens Szyperski, Microsoft Research
Peter Thiemann, University of Freiburg
Eelco Visser, Utrecht University

External Reviewers

Antonio Brogi, Giovanni Cignoni, Antonio Cisternino,
Krzysztof Czarnecki, Simon Helsen, Douglas Schmidt

General Chair

Krzysztof Czarnecki, University of Waterloo

Organizing Committee

Workshop Chair:	Kasper Østerbye, IT University of Copenhagen
Tutorial Chair:	Gerd Frick, FZI Karlsruhe
Demonstration Chair:	Markus Voelter
Poster Chair:	Jorn Bettin, SoftMetaWare
Industrial Chair:	Ulrich W. Eisenecker, University of Applied Sciences, Kaiserslautern
Publicity Chair:	Akos Ledeczi, Vanderbilt University

Table of Contents

Domain-Specific Languages

Spidle: A DSL Approach to Specifying Streaming Applications............ 1
   Charles Consel, Hedi Hamdi, Laurent Réveillère, Lenin Singaravelu, Haiyan Yu, and Calton Pu

TDL: A Hardware Description Language
for Retargetable Postpass Optimizations and Analyses................. 18
   Daniel Kästner

Hume: A Domain-Specific Language for Real-Time Embedded Systems ... 37
   Kevin Hammond and Greg Michaelson

Staged Programming

Implementing Multi-stage Languages
Using ASTs, Gensym, and Reflection................................. 57
   Cristiano Calcagno, Walid Taha, Liwen Huang, and Xavier Leroy

On Stage Ordering in Staged Computation 77
   Zhenghao Wang and Richard R. Muntz

Staged Notational Definitions....................................... 97
   Walid Taha and Patricia Johann

Invited Talk

A Journey from Interpreters to Compilers and Virtual Machines 117
   Olivier Danvy

Modeling to Code

DAOP-ADL: An Architecture Description Language
for Dynamic Component and Aspect-Based Development 118
   Mónica Pinto, Lidia Fuentes, and Jose María Troya

ANEMIC: Automatic Interface Enabler for Model Integrated Computing.. 138
   Steve Nordstrom, Shweta Shetty, Kumar Gaurav Chhokra, Jonathan Sprinkle, Brandon Eames, and Akos Ledeczi

Aspect-Orientation

An Approach for Supporting Aspect-Oriented Domain Modeling 151
  *Jeff Gray, Ted Bapty, Sandeep Neema, Douglas C. Schmidt,
  Aniruddha Gokhale, and Balachandran Natarajan*

The Convergence of AOP and Active Databases:
Towards Reactive Middleware 169
  Mariano Cilia, Michael Haupt, Mira Mezini, and Alejandro Buchmann

A Selective, Just-in-Time Aspect Weaver 189
  Yoshiki Sato, Shigeru Chiba, and Michiaki Tatsubori

Meta-programming and Language Extension

An Extension to the Subtype Relationship in C++ Implemented
with Template Metaprogramming 209
  István Zólyomi, Zoltán Porkoláb, and Tamás Kozsik

Concept-Controlled Polymorphism 228
  Jaakko Järvi, Jeremiah Willcock, and Andrew Lumsdaine

Component-Based DSL Development 245
  Thomas Cleenewerck

Invited Talk

Towards a More Piece-ful World 265
  Peri Tarr

Automating Design-to-Code Transitions

A Generative Approach to Framework Instantiation 267
  *Vaclav Cechticky, Philippe Chevalley, Alessandro Pasetti,
  and Walter Schaufelberger*

Making Patterns Explicit with Metaprogramming 287
  Daniel von Dincklage

Principled Domain-Specific Approaches

Generating Spreadsheet-Like Tools from Strong Attribute Grammars 307
  João Saraiva and Doaitse Swierstra

SynchNet: A Petri Net Based Coordination Language
for Distributed Objects 324
  Reza Ziaei and Gul Agha

Partial Evaluation of MATLAB 344
  Daniel Elphick, Michael Leuschel, and Simon Cox

Generation and Translation

An Easy-to-Use Toolkit for Efficient Java Bytecode Translators 364
  Shigeru Chiba and Muga Nishizawa

A Case for Test-Code Generation in Model-Driven Systems 377
  Matthew J. Rutherford and Alexander L. Wolf

Author Index 397

Spidle: A DSL Approach to Specifying Streaming Applications

Charles Consel[1], Hedi Hamdi[1], Laurent Réveillère[1],
Lenin Singaravelu[2], Haiyan Yu[1,*], and Calton Pu[2]

[1] INRIA/LaBRI
ENSEIRB 1, avenue du docteur Albert Schweitzer
Domaine universitaire - BP 99, F-33402 Talence Cedex, France
{consel,hamdi,reveillere}@labri.fr
http://compose.labri.fr
[2] College of Computing, Georgia Institute of Technology
801 Atlantic Drive, NW, Atlanta, GA 30332-0280, USA
{calton,lenin}@cc.gatech.edu
http://www.cc.gatech.edu

Abstract. Multimedia stream processing is a rapidly evolving domain which requires much software development and expects high performance. Developing a streaming application often involves low-level programming, critical memory management, and finely tuned scheduling of processing steps.

To address these problems, we present a domain-specific language (DSL) named *Spidle*, for specifying streaming applications. Spidle offers high-level and declarative constructs; compared to general-purpose languages (GPL), it improves robustness by enabling a variety of verifications to be performed.

To assess the expressiveness of Spidle in practice, we have used it to specify a number of standardized and special-purpose streaming applications. These specifications are up to 2 times smaller than equivalent programs written in a GPL such as C.

We have implemented a compiler for Spidle. Preliminary results show that compiled Spidle programs are roughly as efficient as the compiled, equivalent C programs.

1 Introduction

The development of multimedia streaming applications is becoming an increasingly important software activity to account for frequently changing requirements. More and more new formats compete to structure the main media types, creating an explosion in format converters. The need for continuous innovation in the multimedia device industry has shifted an increasing part of stream processing from hardware to software, to shorten the time-to-market [12].

---

* Author's current address: Institute of Computing Technology, Chinese Academy of Sciences. P.O.Box 2704, 100080, Beijing, China. E-mail: yuhaiyan@ict.ac.cn

Fortunately, the development of streaming applications relies on well understood libraries of operations for filtering, converting or degrading multimedia streams (*e.g.*, Sox [13]). Furthermore, to account for various application requirements, many implementation variants of common stream operations are often available.

Yet, due to the lack of programming language support, the development of streaming applications tends to be labor-intensive, cumbersome and error-prone: it involves low-level manipulation to cope with bit-level data layout of stream formats, complicated plumbing of components, critical memory management, and meticulous scheduling of processing steps. These difficulties are compounded by the performance critical nature of most streaming applications. As a result, streaming programs are typically manually-optimized for time, and often for space in the case of embedded systems.

This Paper

This paper introduces a domain-specific language (DSL) [1, 2] named Spidle, for developing streaming applications. This language enables high-level and declarative programming of streaming applications without performance loss. Domain-specific verifications are performed on Spidle programs to enhance their robustness.

Domain Specific. The design and development of Spidle is based on a thorough analysis of the domain of streaming applications. This analysis has included the study of various specifications of standardized streaming applications [4, 7] as well as typical streaming programs.

High Level. Spidle offers high-level constructs and data types that enable programmers to concisely express stream processing. Domain-specific data types and attributes capture dedicated aspects of some values. Domain-specific constructs abstract over common program patterns.

Declarative. A Spidle programmer need only specify the treatment of a given stream; the compiler then maps the specification into an efficient implementation. Information required to trigger domain-specific optimizations is captured in the Spidle program.

Robust. Spidle is safer than a general-purpose language because its syntax and semantics enable domain-specific verifications. In particular, the Spidle compiler checks the consistency of component composition and memory behavior.

The idea of a language dedicated to stream processing has already been discussed in existing literature. Nevertheless, existing approaches are either limited to introducing a language for gluing components of a stream library [19], or geared towards exploiting the features of a specific hardware platform [5, 6].

Contributions

This paper makes the following contributions:

- We have identified common aspects and key concepts used in the development of streaming applications, based on a close examination of various streaming programs as well as specifications of standardized streaming applications.
- We present the definition of Spidle, a high-level and declarative language dedicated to the specification of streaming applications. The language is strongly typed and enables various consistency checks. The resulting degree of robustness of a Spidle program goes beyond what can be achieved with an equivalent program written in a general-purpose language.
- We show that Spidle is highly expressive. It has been used to describe a wide range of streaming applications (see our web site [14]), including traditional ones like a GSM encoder, a GSM decoder, and an MPEG-1 audio encoder as well as special-purpose streaming applications such as Earwax effect, which adjusts CD-audio to headphones [3], and Audio Mixer, which mixes two stereo audio streams into one mono stream [13].
- We demonstrate that Spidle is concise. Our Spidle programs are up to 2 times smaller than equivalent C programs.
- We have implemented a compiler for Spidle programs. The generated code is as efficient as equivalent programs written in C.

Paper Overview

Section 2 presents the difficulties involved in developing a streaming application. Section 3 introduces the Spidle language, focusing on the main language abstractions. Section 4 gives an overview of the compilation process, and lists the main verifications and optimizations performed on a Spidle program. Section 5 assesses the approach. Section 6 presents the related work, and Section 7 concludes the paper and discusses future work.

2 Difficulties in Developing a Streaming Application

In this section, we discuss the issues involved in developing a streaming application and illustrate them with two working examples, namely, GSM encoding and usage of the Sox library. We first briefly introduce these examples.

2.1 Working Examples

GSM transcoding (the process of coding and decoding) enables speech to be transmitted to a digital cellular telecommunication system. The speech signal is compressed before its transmission, thus reducing the size of its digital representation while keeping an acceptable quality of the decoded output. The GSM coder works on a 13-bit uniform pulse-code modulation (PCM) speech input signal, sampled at 8KHz. The input is processed on a frame-by-frame basis, with a frame duration of 20 ms (160 samples). The full rate encoder [4] presented in this paper transforms a frame of 160 samples into a block of 260 bits, leading to a bit rate of 13 Kbps.

Sox is a library of audio stream processing components. It offers a command line interface that enables an audio file to be converted from one format to another. Various effects and filters can be inserted in the conversion process. Examples include adding an echo, swapping channels, and band pass/reject filters. Additionally, the command line interface enables audio files to be recorded and played.

2.2 The Difficulty of Mapping a Streaming Specification into a Program

A streaming application is often specified informally using a graph-like notation. A node represents a stream filter which transforms particular parts of a stream item. An edge defines the flow of the stream items. Although this notation is convenient at a conceptual level, it can be complex to map such a specification into an implementation. While a specification typically describes some stream tasks as being performed in parallel, an implementation needs to invoke the corresponding components sequentially. This mapping needs to take into account implementation details of the stream tasks involved, such as the possibility of side-effects to a global state. Individual stream tasks require specific data layouts, which entail data conversion. Parts of a stream item may correspond to bit fragments, which must be accessed using low-level bit operators.

Example. A simplified version of the standardized GSM full-rate speech encoding diagram [4] is depicted in Figure 1. The input speech frame is first preprocessed to produce an offset-free signal, which is then subjected to a first order pre-emphasis filter ("Preprocess" in the figure). The 160 samples obtained are then analysed to determine the coefficients for the short term analysis filter (LPC). These parameters are then used to filter the 160 samples. The result is 160 samples of the short term residual signal (STA). For the remaining operations, the speech frame is divided into 4 sub-frames each containing 40 samples of the short term residual signal. Each sub-frame is processed by the subsequent functional elements – we refer to these elements as "Sub-Frame Processing".

Although this is a simplified view of the GSM encoding process, it shows the tangled paths and stages involved in forming the 260-bit encoded block: stream items need to be split, merged and shared across various stages. These intricacies require special care to be mapped into an efficient implementation.

2.3 The Need to Manually Optimize a Streaming Program

The high volume of stream items to process and the stringent real-time constraints to satisfy translate into high-performance expectations when developing

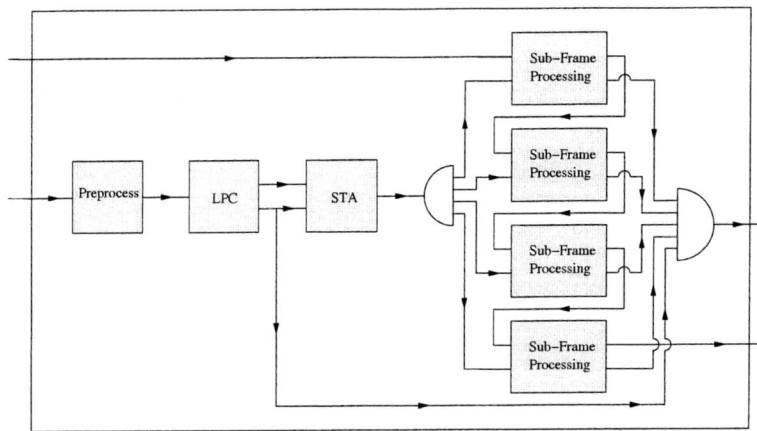

Fig. 1. GSM RPE-LTP Speech Encoding Diagram

a streaming program. As a result, the programmer has to manually perform a number of optimizations, until the performance and resource usage goals are attained. A streaming program not only requires local optimizations, such as loop transformations, but it also relies on global optimizations mostly centered around memory management.

Example. The implementation of GSM full-rate speech encoding, as provided by Jutta and Carsten [8], contains a number of manual optimizations such as code inlining.

2.4 The Need to Manually Optimize Memory Management

Streaming applications typically minimize data copying to reduce the cost of memory management. To apply this strategy, two major aspects need to be taken into account: (1) For efficiency reasons, an implementation of a stream filter often performs side-effects and expects a specific data layout. (2) Most streaming applications not only transform the contents of a stream item but they also change its layout incrementally as it gets processed (*e.g.*, the size of a data fragment expands when it is decompressed).

Two strategies are commonly used to improve the memory usage of a streaming application. One strategy is to schedule stream filters in a particular order depending on their side-effects so as to minimize copying. The other strategy is to allocate memory according to the output data layout, as early as possible in the streaming process, to reduce temporary memory fragments.

Example. The implementation of the GSM encoder is optimized to minimize copying, minimize allocation of temporary buffers and maximize data locality. For example, consider the Sub-Frame Processing filter shown in Figure 1. The components making up this filter are depicted in Figure 2. The 40-bit residual signal calculated by the long term predictor (LTP) filter is fed to the regular pulse excitation (RPE) filter as a 50-bit signal where the five highest and lowest bits have been padded with zeroes. Memory usage is reduced by propagating the need for a 50-bit buffer backward, to the filter that allocates the incoming 40-bit buffer. This strategy eliminates one memory allocation and one memory copy.

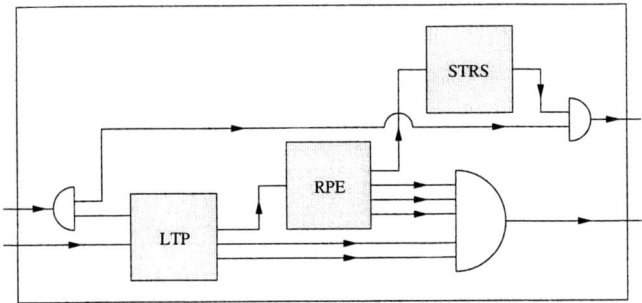

Fig. 2. Sub-Frame Processing

2.5 Error-Prone Re-use of Stream Filter Implementations

The expected data layout of a stream filter may be incompatible with the one at the current stream stage. This situation requires rewriting a portion of the streaming program, or function wrapping of the stream filter. Although there are many libraries of stream filters, the expertise required for their use often goes beyond the synopsis provided by the library manual. The side-effects of a filter need to be carefully studied to avoid an unexpected data modification at a given streaming stage that corrupts subsequent processing.

Example. Sox filters can be classified based on the type of stream (stereo or mono) they work on. Consider a configuration where the audio stream passes exclusively through stereo filters. Adding a new filter that operates on a mono stream requires a wrapper function that separates the left and right streams before applying the filter and recomposes the stream once the filter is done.

2.6 The Difficulty of Managing Low-Level Code

The need to reduce memory usage implies that very compact data layouts are typically used for stream items. Consequently, accessing individual fields of a stream item often requires low-level bit operations. Such code is known to be hard to develop and to maintain.

Example. Table 1 shows an excerpt of the structure of a 260-bit encoded block generated by the GSM encoder. This description clearly illustrates that compactness of data representation translates into bit-level data layout.

Table 1. Data Layout of the Encoded Blocks of the GSM Encoder

Parameter	Number of bits	Bit n°	Parameter	Number of bits	Bit n°
LARc[0]	6	1 .. 6	xmc[13]	3	110 .. 112
LARc[1]	6	7 .. 12	xmc[14]	3	113 .. 115
LARc[2]	5	13 .. 17	...	3	...
LARc[3]	5	18 .. 22	xmc[25]	3	146 .. 148
LARc[4]	4	23 .. 26	Nc[2]	7	149 .. 155
LARc[5]	4	27 .. 30	bc[2]	2	156 .. 157
LARc[6]	3	31 .. 33	Mc[2]	2	158 .. 159
LARc[7]	3	34 .. 36	xmaxc[2]	6	160 .. 165
Nc[0]	7	37 .. 43	xmc[26]	3	166 .. 168
bc[0]	2	44 .. 45	xmc[27]	3	169 .. 171
Mc[0]	2	46 .. 47	...	3	...
xmaxc[0]	6	48 .. 53	xmc[38]	3	202 .. 204
xmc[0]	3	54 .. 56	Nc[3]	7	205 .. 211
xmc[1]	3	57 .. 59	bc[3]	2	212 .. 213
...	3	...	Mc[3]	2	214 .. 215
xmc[12]	3	90 .. 92	xmaxc[3]	6	216 .. 221
Nc[1]	7	93 .. 99	xmc[39]	3	222 .. 224
bc[1]	2	100 .. 101	xmc[40]	3	225 .. 227
Mc[1]	2	102 .. 103	...	3	...
xmaxc[1]	6	104 .. 109	xmc[51]	3	258 .. 260

3 The Spidle Language

Based on the domain analysis of stream processing, we have identified the following key requirements for a language dedicated to this domain. The language should be flow-based to describe the paths through which stream items are propagated and processed by stream tasks; it should include stream-specific declarations to enable dedicated verifications and optimizations to be performed; it should be module-based to enable a streaming application to be decomposed into manageable components; it should include an interface language to enable disciplined re-use of existing stream filter libraries.

3.1 An Overview of Spidle

A Spidle program essentially defines a network of *stream tasks*. *Flow declarations* specify how stream items flow within stream tasks (nodes) and across stream tasks (edges), as well as the types of these stream items.

A stream task can either be a *connector* or a *filter*. Connectors represent common patterns of value propagation. Filters correspond to transducers; they can either be *primitive* or *compound*. A primitive filter refers to an operation implemented in some other programming language. This facility enables existing filter libraries to be re-used. A compound filter is defined as a composition of stream filters and connectors. This composition is achieved by *mapping* the output stream of a task to the input stream of another task.

Let us now present the abstractions offered by Spidle in detail.

3.2 Flow Declarations

Two abstractions address the flow aspects of a streaming application: a *stream* specifies the flow aspects at the task level; a *mapping* specifies how stream items flow across tasks.

Streams. A stream task declares streams using the type constructor `stream`. A stream declaration defines what type of items flow in a stream and their direction. The first aspect is addressed by an appropriate type language. The second aspect defines how items flow. A stream task can declare a stream to be an input stream, to be an output stream, or both. An input-only stream contains values that flow in, but not out, of the stream task. An output-only stream describes values that are created in the stream task. An input-output stream contains values that are propagated through a stream task.

An example of a stream is displayed below.

```
stream inout int16[40] e;
```

This declaration is extracted from the Spidle definition of the filter `RPE_Encoding` of the GSM encoder. It specifies that values of type `int16[40]` flow both in and out of the filter `RPE_Encoding`.

The stream declarations of a stream task are grouped in a clause named `interface`, as illustrated later in stream task examples.

Mappings. A mapping defines how stream items flow from one stream task to another. Mapping declarations of a stream task are grouped into a clause called `map`. A mapping can either be (1) one-one, (2) one-many or (3) many-one. The first kind is the most common; it connects the output of one stream task to the input of another one. An example of such a mapping is displayed below. It specifies that the value of stream `so` is obtained by padding 5 zero-bits on both sides of stream `si`.

```
map {
    {0,0,0,0,0} # si # {0,0,0,0,0} -> so;
}
```

This `map` clause consists of a single mapping declaration. The left-hand side of the "`->`" sign defines the source stream of the mapping; the right-hand side names the destination stream. As shown in the example, the source stream is represented by a *stream expression*, that is, an expression that constructs a stream value by applying the concatenation operator "`#`" to constants and stream variables.

The one-many mapping is required when the processing of one item produces many items, which are then processed sequentially. This situation is illustrated by the MPEG-1 audio encoder shown in Figure 3. In this encoder, a buffer of PCM samples is split into 24 blocks, each of which is processed by the SubbandBlock filter.

A many-one mapping is used when a stream task needs a collection of items before performing an operation. This situation is again exemplified by the MPEG-1 audio encoder (see Figure 3) where the ScaleFactorCalculator filter expects to receive all the samples produced by the SubbandBlock filter as a single input stream item.

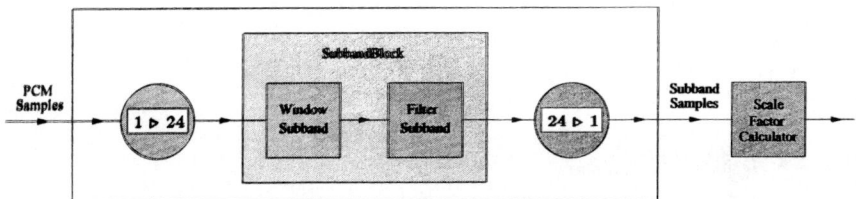

Fig. 3. MPEG Subband Filter for Stereo Streams

We have not found any use for a many-many mapping, except in cases that can be re-expressed using a one-one mapping.

3.3 Stream Tasks

A stream task can either be a connector or a filter. The difference between these two kinds of tasks is that a connector propagates stream items in a fixed way and is guaranteed not to modify their value, beyond what a stream expression enables. These restrictions do not apply to filters.

Spidle offers a type constructor for connectors and one for filters. These type constructors enable the programmer to define a task type. Instances of a new task type can then be created throughout a Spidle program. To improve re-use, a task type can be instantiated with respect to both compile-time and run-time arguments. An example of such instantiation is presented in the filter section below.

Connectors. There are two kinds of connectors: mergers and splitters. A merger fuses independent input streams into a single output stream. A splitter performs the opposite operation. Because a connector can only be used to link stream tasks, a connector declaration only contains an interface clause and a map clause. An example of a declaration of a merger from the GSM specification is given below.

```
merger Frame_Merger {
   interface {
      stream in  bit[7]  nc;
      stream in  bit[2]  bc;
      stream in  bit[2]  Mc;
      stream in  bit[13][3] xMc;
      stream in  bit[6]  xmaxc;
      stream out bit[56] bits;
   }
   map {
      nc # bc # Mc # xmaxc # xMc -> bits;
   }
}
```

This connector merges input streams `nc`, `bc`, `Mc`, `xMc` and `xmaxc` into the single output stream `bits`.

Filters. A filter can either be compound, when it combines a set of stream tasks, or primitive, when it refers to an operation implemented in some foreign programming language.

Compound Filters. A compound filter defines a combination of other stream tasks. As a result, besides the `interface` and `map` clauses, a compound filter consists of an `import` clause referring to the Spidle files defining the needed stream tasks. Since a compound filter imports task types, it also needs an `instantiate` clause to define task instances with respect to a specific context. An example of a declaration of a compound filter from the MPEG-1 audio encoder specification follows.

```
filter SubbandBlock(int stereo) {
   interface {
      stream in  int16[2][384] buffer;
      stream out float64[32]   sample;
   }
   instantiate {
      WindowSubband(stereo) ws;
      FilterSubband fs;
   }
   map {
      buffer -> ws.buffer;
      ws.Z -> fs.Z;
      fs.sb_sample -> sample;
   }
}
```

This filter has a formal parameter, `stereo`, which is given a value at run time, when the filter is instantiated. This value is also used to instantiate the filter `WindowSubband`, as shown in the `instantiate` clause of `SubbandBlock`.

Primitive Filters. A primitive filter enables existing library code to be imported into Spidle. Like the compound filter, a primitive filter includes an `import` clause, but this clause refers to files written in some other programming language. Both functions and types can be imported, thus allowing Spidle to propagate foreign values from one primitive filter to another one.

Because a primitive filter provides an interface to a foreign function, it does not include an `instantiate` clause. Instead, it consists of a `run` clause that invokes the foreign function.

The foreign function invoked in a primitive filter may also modify the contents of the buffer attached to an input-only stream using, for example, previously read locations as temporary storage. Spidle requires that the declaration of each input-only stream that is passed to the foreign function specify the effects of this function on the stream items. A stream can be declared to be read by the foreign function (default behavior) or both read and written to by the foreign function. This critical information is later used to optimize memory management.

Let us examine an example of a primitive filter from the GSM specification.

```
filter Weighting {
  interface {
    stream in  bit[50][16] e;
    stream out bit[40][16] x;
  }
  import {
    func Weighting_filter from "rpe.c";
  }
  run {
    Weighting_filter (e, x);
  }
}
```

This filter only reads input stream e, and writes output stream x. These streams are passed to the foreign function `Weighting_filter` defined in file `rpe.c`. Here, the C programming language is assumed to be the foreign language used in the `run` clause.

3.4 Advanced Features

A network of stream tasks may contain loopbacks (cycles) when a path connects the output of one stream task to one of its inputs. Such a network has special semantics since some items are unavailable as inputs when processing begins.

Spidle offers a built-in task type named *delay* for introducing loopbacks in a network. This specific task simply propagates items from its input stream to its output stream. Such a task type requires at least one compile-time argument at the time of instantiation. This parameter enables the programmer to define how many initial items have to be produced on the output stream before looking for items on the input stream. In addition, a delay task can also be instantiated with respect to appropriate values of the initial items.

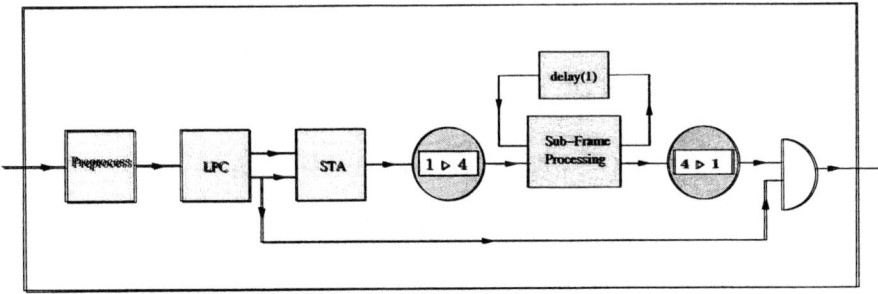

Fig. 4. GSM Speech Encoding Diagram with Loopback

The GSM full-rate speech encoding diagram depicted in Figure 4 illustrates the use of the built-in task delay. In this modified version of the GSM encoding diagram shown in Figure 1, the 160 samples of the short term residual signal are first split into 4 sub-frames before being processed sequentially by the Sub-Frame Processing filter. One of the output streams of this filter is connected to one of its input streams through a delay filter. This task has been instantiated with the value 1 to indicate that it produces a value with a one-step delay. Since no initial value has been defined for this delay task, the first item provided to the Sub-Frame Processing filter is 0. Following items are obtained by looking at the output stream of previous iterations. When all the required items are available, they are merged to form the 260-bit encoded block.

4 Compilation

We now present a preliminary design of the Spidle compilation process. This process consists of the following steps. First, dependencies between stream tasks are collected and represented as a graph. Second, this graph is annotated with effects and memory management information. Third, the resulting graph is used to schedule stream tasks. Fourth, the memory layout of stream items at each stage of the streaming process is computed. Lastly, code is generated.

Dependency Graph. Given a Spidle program, the compiler computes the transitive closure of the referred stream tasks by examining the `instantiate` and `import` clauses. The resulting information is represented as a dependency graph.

Effects. This pass determines the effects of each compound filter based on the effects of the primitive filters it references.

Memory Management. This analysis annotates the graph of stream tasks with information describing the lifetime of memory fragments. This information is computed using the stream declarations. Specifically, for an output-only stream, memory needs to be allocated to store the value of a stream item. Conversely, for an input-only stream, the memory used for the stream item is not needed beyond the execution of the stream task.

Task Scheduling. Most Spidle programs have more than one possible schedule for their stream tasks. In our current design, the scheduling strategy focuses on the choice points represented by splitters. Spidle chooses a schedule that minimizes memory copies, using effect information.

Memory Layout. A streaming application often transforms values from one format to another. The transformation is carried out incrementally as the item gets propagated through the various steps of the stream process. This situation introduces temporary memory fragments. To remedy this potential source of inefficiency, our compiler attempts to allocate space eagerly. That is, when the size of an item grows as it gets processed, its final size is used for the initial allocation. Of course this optimization cannot always be applied; for example, when non-contiguous data from input streams are processed, replacing the allocated buffers of input streams by the final buffer may not be allowed.

Currently, Spidle has only been interfaced with C and C++ languages. These are the programming languages used by most stream libraries, mainly for efficiency reasons.

4.1 Verifications

Because of its domain-specific nature, the Spidle compiler can perform a number of verifications that are beyond the reach of a compiler for a general-purpose language. These verifications focus on the composition of stream tasks, the propagation of stream items, and the usage of foreign libraries.

Composition of Stream Tasks. Stream declarations are checked to ensure that types and directions of stream items are compatible when stream tasks are combined. Inconsistent combinations of effects and directions are detected.

Propagation of Stream Items. Mappings are inspected to find unconnected streams and input streams connected to more than one output stream. Also, omitted or double definitions can be detected. For example, one and only one mapping declaration must specify how the value of a bit of an output stream is obtained.

Usage of Foreign Libraries. External function declarations are analyzed to ensure that the types of the actual parameters they accept are equivalent to types specified in the stream declarations that use them.

4.2 Optimizations

In fact, most streaming applications are targeted for use in embedded systems. Such systems usually have moderately powered processors, minimal amounts of memory and limited battery. To stay within these limitations, streaming programs are typically optimized manually.

The domain-specific constructs of Spidle open up opportunities for various optimizations that are not possible when using a general-purpose language. The goals of these optimizations are to reduce the number of memory copy operations, to reduce memory usage, to improve data and code locality, and to reduce the size of the resulting code. The order of this list reflects roughly the order of the significance of these optimizations, although it may vary considerably in certain scenarios depending on their specific requirements.

For example, in embedded systems, it is often more desirable to keep memory utilization below a certain threshold than to minimize it as much as possible.

In contrast with manual optimizations dedicated to a given architecture and a specific streaming application, the Spidle compiler automatically performs global optimizations that are not possible locally. Because the engine is parametrized, optimizations are retargetable without any additional effort to a new system that has different resource constraints, such as memory usage and cache sizes.

5 Assessment

The assessment our language is a crucial step of the DSL approach. In our experience [16–18, 11, 10], a DSL should be assessed with respect to three pragmatic criteria: expressiveness, conciseness, and performance.

Expressiveness. Assessing the expressiveness of a DSL in practice requires to use it for a variety of non-trivial applications. We have used Spidle to express a GSM encoder, a GSM decoder and an MPEG-1 audio encoder. These applications must satisfy industrial-strength standards, and are commonly mentioned as reference cases to assess work in the domain of stream processing (*e.g.*, [19, 15]). We have also specified other, more dedicated, streaming applications referenced in various libraries, toolkits and middleware for stream processing.

Conciseness. Because Spidle offers domain specific abstractions and constructions, it enables the programmer to concisely define a streaming application. We found that Spidle programs are up to 2 times smaller than equivalent version written in C.

Performance. Our performance measurements of the compiled code of Spidle programs show that, at worst, there is a negligeable loss of performance (around 4%) compared with the equivalent C-compiled code written by an outside expert. These results are preliminary and should improve as our compiler gets further developed.

6 Related Work

StreamIt [19] is certainly the work most related to Spidle. It is a Java extension that provides the programmer with constructs to assemble stream components.

While StreamIt and Spidle share the same goals, their approaches vary considerably. StreamIt is essentially a GPL that offers extensions corresponding to common program patterns and an interface to library components. Because it is a superset of Java, performance of compiled StreamIt code is as good as what existing Java compilers produce, which is currently much slower than compiled equivalent C code. Indeed, Java has some intrinsic overhead (*e.g.*, memory management and object layout) that may not be easy to work around. Lastly, because a StreamIt program is intertwined with Java code, verification is very local to the domain-specific constructs, unlike what can be done in Spidle.

The Infopipes system [9] is a middleware abstraction for describing information flow in the case of distributed streaming applications. The goal of Infopipes is to expose the underlying communication layer to the application so that it can adapt dynamically to changing network or processing conditions. The Infopipes system offers distributed versions of our splitters, mergers and filters. In contrast, Spidle is limited to local stream processing, and focuses on performance and verification.

Stream-C [5] and Sassy [6] are two stream-oriented languages used to describe hardware circuits. The aim of these languages is to represent circuits with higher level abstractions like processes, streams and signals with the emphasis on reducing the clock rate and the board area occupied by the generated circuit. Spidle operates in a different domain. While it might be possible to write a compiler for Stream-C or Sassy dedicated to streaming applications, their constructs are not well suited to this domain.

7 Conclusions and Future Work

Stream processing is a rapidly evolving field which requires much software development with high-performance expectations. To address these requirements, we have developed a domain-specific, high-level and declarative language named Spidle, for specifying streaming applications.

We have used Spidle to write a variety of industry-standardized streaming applications as well as special-purpose ones. These specifications have experimentally validated the expressiveness of our language. Spidle programs were up to 2 times smaller than equivalent programs written in C.

We have implemented a compiler for Spidle. Preliminary experiments show that compiled Spidle programs have performance that is roughly comparable to compiled equivalent C programs.

Our implementation of the Spidle compiler is preliminary, and there is a number of optimizations that need to be explored. In particular, we plan to optimize locality by taking into account processor features, such as data cache and instruction cache, when determining a scheduling for stream tasks. We also want to study the performance impact of buffering input stream items before firing the stream process. These ideas are examples of highly domain-specific optimizations that can be enabled by the presence of more explicit information at the language level, and can be factorized into a compiler.

Another track of research aims to go beyond local stream processing to tackle the distributed case. To do so, we are studying ways to integrate Spidle into a middleware for distributed streaming. In particular, we are working on Infopipes [9], partly developed by one of the authors.

Finally, we are working on a graphical representation for Spidle. A visual version of Spidle seems quite a natural step to take considering that the graph-like notation is commonly used in the field. Toward this end, we first plan to build a tool capable of visualizing Spidle programs as a graph of stream tasks.

Acknowledgment

We thank Julia Lawall, Anne-Françoise Le Meur and the other members of the Compose group for helpful comments and discussions on earlier versions of this paper. We also thank the anonymous reviewers for their valuable inputs.

This research has been partially funded by Conseil Régional d'Aquitaine, DARPA/IXO (PCES program), National Science Foundation grants numbered CCR-9988452, ITR-0121643, ITR-0219902, and 0208953, and Georgia Tech Foundation through the John P. Imlay, Jr. Chair endowment.

References

1. C. Consel and R. Marlet. Architecturing software using a methodology for language development. In C. Palamidessi, H. Glaser, and K. Meinke, editors, *Proceedings of the 10th International Symposium on Programming Language Implementation and Logic Programming*, number 1490 in Lecture Notes in Computer Science, pages 170–194, Pisa, Italy, September 1998.
2. A. Van Deursen, P. Klint, and J. Visser. Domain-specific languages: An annotated bibliography. *ACM SIGPLAN Notices*, 35(6):26–36, June 2000.
3. Earwax effect. http://www.geocities.com/beinges/works.htm.
4. European Telecommunications Standards Institute, 650, route des Lucioles F-06921 Sophia-Antipolis Cedex – France. *GSM full speech transcoding 06.10*, Nov 2000. REN/SMG-110610Q8R1.
5. M. Gokhale, J. Stone, J. Arnold, and M. Kalinowski. Stream-oriented FPGA computing in the Streams-C high level language. In *IEEE Symposium on Field-Programmable Custom Computing Machines*, pages 49–59, Apr 2000.
6. J. P. Hammes, B. A. Draper, and A. P. Willem Boehm. Sassy: A language and optimizing compiler for image processing on reconfigurable computing systems. *Lecture Notes in Computer Science*, 1542:83–97, 1999.
7. International Organisation for Standardisation, 1, rue de Varembé, Case postale 56 CH-1211 Geneva 20, Switzerland. *Moving Picture Experts Group (MPEG-1 audio) Specifications*, 1993. ISO/IEC 11172-3:1993.
8. D. Jutta and B. Carsten. C implementation of GSM 06.10 RPELTP coder and decoder. http://kbs.cs.tu-berlin.de/ jutta/toast.html, Nov 1994.
9. R. et al. Koster. Infopipes for composing distributed information flows. In *Proceedings of the ACM Multimedia Workshop on Multimedia Middleware*, Oct 2001.
10. F. Mérillon, L. Réveillère, C. Consel, R. Marlet, and G. Muller. Devil: An IDL for Hardware Programming. In *4th Symposium on Operating Systems Design and Implementation (OSDI 2000)*, pages 17–30, San Diego, California, October 2000.

11. L. Réveillère, F. Mérillon, C. Consel, R. Marlet, and G. Muller. A DSL approach to improve productivity and safety in device drivers development. In *Proceedings of the 15th IEEE International Conference on Automated Software Engineering (ASE 2000)*, pages 101–109, Grenoble, France, September 2000. IEEE Computer Society Press.
12. L. Rizzo. On the feasibility of software FEC. Technical Report LR-970131, Dip. di Ingegneria dell'Informzione, Università di Pisa, Jan 1997.
13. Sox sound exchange. http://www.spies.com/Sox.
14. Spidle home page. http://compose.labri.fr/prototypes/spidle.
15. R. Stephens. A survey of stream processing. *Acta Informatica*, 34(7):491–541, 1997.
16. S. Thibault and C. Consel. A framework of application generator design. In M. Harandi, editor, *Proceedings of the Symposium on Software Reusability*, pages 131–135, Boston, Massachusetts, USA, May 1997. Software Engineering Notes, 22(3).
17. S. Thibault, C. Consel, and G. Muller. Safe and efficient active network programming. In *17th IEEE Symposium on Reliable Distributed Systems*, pages 135–143, West Lafayette, Indiana, October 1998.
18. S. Thibault, R. Marlet, and C. Consel. A domain-specific language for video device driver: from design to implementation. In *Proceedings of the 1st USENIX Conference on Domain-Specific Languages*, Santa Barbara, California, October 1997.
19. W. Thies, M. Karczmarek, and S. P. Amarasinghe. Streamit: A language for streaming applications. In *International Conference on Compiler Construction*, Lecture Notes in Computer Science, pages 179–196. Springer-Verlag, 2002.

TDL: A Hardware Description Language for Retargetable Postpass Optimizations and Analyses

Daniel Kästner

Universität des Saarlandes &
AbsInt Angewandte Informatik GmbH
Saarbrücken, Germany
kaestner@absint.com

Abstract. The hardware description language TDL has been designed with the goal to generate machine-dependent postpass optimizers and analyzers from a concise specification of the target processor. TDL is assembly-oriented and provides a generic modeling of irregular hardware constraints that are typical for many embedded processors. The generic modeling supports graph-based and search-based optimization algorithms. An important design goal of TDL was to achieve extendibility, so that TDL can be easily integrated in different target applications. TDL is at the base of the PROPAN system that has been developed as a retargetable framework for high-quality code optimizations at assembly level. For two contemporary microprocessors, the Analog Devices SHARC 2106x, and the Philips TriMedia TM1000, significant improvements of the code produced by production-quality compilers could be achieved with short retargeting time. TDL has also been used for implementing postpass optimizations for the Infineon C16x/ST10 processor that are part of a commercial postpass optimizer. TDL specifications are concise and can be produced in short time.

1 Introduction

During the past years, the markets for telecommunication, embedded systems, and multimedia applications have been growing rapidly. Real-time applications, which are part of many embedded systems, impose stringent performance requirements. Cost constraints and performance requirements have led to the development of irregular hardware architectures specially designed for real-time applications and digital signal processing. For this type of architecture the quality of the code generated by traditional high-level language compilers is often not satisfactory [36, 22]. Generating efficient code for irregular architectures requires sophisticated optimization techniques exploiting specific hardware features of the target processor. The shortcomings of available compilers have resulted in many applications being developed in assembly language, or at least in part. Due to the growing complexity of embedded applications and the shrinking design cycles of embedded products the usage of high-level programming languages is becoming increasingly imperative. There is an urgent need for *retargetable* code generation and optimization techniques that can be quickly adapted to different target architectures, e.g. by deriving machine-specific properties from a dedicated hardware description. At the same time these techniques must be able to produce high-quality code for the modeled architectures.

The PROPAN system [19, 16, 17] has been developed as a retargetable framework for high-quality code optimizations and machine-dependent program analyses at assembly level. In the past, research on retargetability has mainly focused on closed compilation systems. Examples for retargetable research compilers are, e.g. CHESS[21], RECORD[22], AVIV[12], SPAM [32], or EXPRESS[11]. Using such a system in industry however mostly requires replacing the existing compiler infrastructure which causes high costs. Thus the use of retargetable compilers in industry is rare. Due to the postpass orientation, PROPAN can be integrated in existing tool chains with moderate effort and allows to improve the code quality of existing compilers. Thus the costs associated with changing the compiler infrastructure in a company can be avoided.

The retargetability concept of PROPAN is based on a combination of generic and generative mechanisms. The machine description language TDL (*Target Description Language*) allows to specify the hardware resources of the target processor, its instruction set, irregular hardware constraints and the assembly language in a concise way [15]. Irregular hardware constraints are modeled in a generic way enabling them to be exploited in generic graph-based and search-based optimization algorithms. TDL offers a hierarchical structuring of operation semantics specification, and semantical consistency checks.

The article is structured as follows: after a brief overview of related work in Sec. 2, the basic design principles and the most important language elements of TDL are described in Sec. 3. To illustrate the usage of TDL, the PROPAN-framework is sketched in Sec. 4. Sec. 5 summarizes experimental results gained with applications of TDL. Sec. 6 contains a summary and gives an outlook to future work.

2 Related Work

Hardware description languages are used for a variety of application areas: for architectural synthesis, hardware simulation, code generation and program analysis. In consequence, a large number of different hardware description formalisms has been developed. In the area of processor modeling and simulating, widely used languages are VHDL [23] and Verilog [34]; well-known approaches used in code generation are ISPS [3], MARIL [6, 5], the MIMOLA language [27], the SALTO language [4], SLED [30], and nML [8]. Languages currently under development are LISA [28] aiming at generating cycle-accurate simulators for architectures with complex pipelines, ISDL [10], EXPRESSION [11], and λ−RTL [7].

Hardware description languages can be categorized as behavioral, structural or mixed behavioral/structural languages [25]. A behavioral description specifies the instruction set of the target processor and focuses on the semantics, i.e. the behavior of the machine operations. Structural specifications typically are close to the gate-level and describe the hardware modules of the processor with their interconnections. Many hardware description languages used for code generation incorporate aspects of both views and are classified as mixed-level approaches.

An assembly-oriented architecture description language is used in the SALTO system [4]. SALTO has been designed to support analyses and transformations of low-level code. The architecture specification covers the hardware resources and the instruction set, but without means for specifying detailed operation semantics. Complex interactions among operations or interdependencies between scheduling and allocation decisions cannot be modeled.

ISDL [10] has been designed to support a wide range of tools, from code generators, disassemblers up to instruction set simulators. Since assemblers and disassemblers are automatically generated, ISDL can make simplifying assumptions on the structure of the assembly language. Structural information is restricted to the declaration of storage resources; behavioral components are the specification of the instruction set and a mechanism for specifying constraints on operation combinations. Since only storage resources can be declared the problem of functional unit binding cannot be addressed with an ISDL description. The constraint mechanism is purely syntactical and does not exploit structural and semantical information from other specification parts. There is no semantical analysis of the machine description itself.

nML [8] is used in the retargetable code generator CBC, the retargetable compiler CHESS and the instruction set simulator CHECKERS [21]. The instruction set is modeled as an attribute grammar; each terminal of the grammar corresponds to a valid instruction. Structural information is provided by declaring the available storage resources. Specifying the timing of machine operations, irregular hardware constraints, and building long instruction words from independent operations, i. e. the VLIW execution model, is not explicitly supported. Since nML has not been designed for processing assembly files, specifying the syntax of assembly expressions, comments, or directives is not supported.

SLED [30] is part of the CSDL (*Computer Systems Description Languages*) language family [7]. SLED focuses on instruction decoding and encoding; for specifying the semantics of machine operations a dedicated language called λ-RTL has been developed [7]. λ-RTL is a higher-order functional language, based on SML. The effect of each machine operation is specified as a register-transfer list (RTL) that describes the change to the machine state induced by the operation. A detailed specification of the timing behavior of operations is not directly supported.

EXPRESSION [11] is a mixed-level language for supporting architectural design space exploration and automatic generation of compilers and simulators. Structural information is given by specifying the hardware resources of the architecture, including its memory hierarchy, the pipeline mechanism, and the data transfer paths. However, the assembly syntax cannot be specified and the modeling of irregular hardware characteristics seems to be restricted. As an example it is not clear whether encoding restrictions limiting instruction word packing can be specified. In [11, 9] no information about the specification of the detailed semantics of machine operations is given.

3 TDL

TDL (*Target Description Language*) is a descriptive language that allows to concisely specify the hardware resources and the assembly language of the processor to be modeled. A TDL specification provides all information about the target architecture that can influence program analyses and optimizations. This includes the properties of the relevant hardware resources, the syntax and semantics of the machine operations and additional information as, e. g., timing characteristics. TDL offers a generic modeling of irregular hardware constraints and a hierarchical structuring of the instruction set specification. TDL is easily extendible and flexible in use which is a presupposition for modeling a wide range of target architectures and for supporting different kinds of optimizations and analyses.

TDL can be classified as a mixed structural/behavioral description formalism [25]. The resources are declared in a structural style while the machine operations are mainly described from the view of the operation behavior, i. e. their semantics. A TDL description has a modular structure. It can comprise a specification of the hardware resources, a description of the instruction set, a constraint section, and an assembly section. Specification parts that are not needed for the target applications can be omitted. Each TDL description is checked for semantical consistency so that input errors and inconsistencies in the machine description are detected early.

In the remainder of this chapter, the different sections of a TDL description are presented.

3.1 Resource Specification

Hardware-sensitive program analyses and optimizations require knowledge about the hardware resources of the target processor. This includes, e. g., its functional units, and the available register sets, memories and caches. As a rule of thumb, all hardware components that are important for the target application have to be declared as resources in the TDL description. TDL offers a set of predefined resource types whose properties can be described by a predefined set of attributes. The predefined resource types comprise functional units, register sets, memories and caches. Attributes are available to describe the bit width of registers, their default data type, the size of a memory, its access width, alignment restrictions, etc. The designer can extend the domain of the predefined attributes and declare user-defined attributes if additional properties have to be taken into account. It is also possible to declare user-defined resource types which allows for maximum flexibility with respect to the range of supported hardware architectures and target applications. Those declarations are used during the semantical analysis of the machine description. Different views of hardware resources are supported in TDL by a dedicated alias mechanism. As an example, in the Analog Devices

ADSP-2106x [2] the same register file is used as integer and as floating-point register file. One view is associated with fixed-point operations, the other with floating-point operations; the assembly representation of both views differs.

An implicit assumption of the machine model of TDL is that all resources of different types can work in parallel. If there are functional unit types with multiple instances it is assumed that those can work in parallel, too. This way, the VLIW machine model is supported. Architectures without instruction-level parallelism can be considered as a special case of VLIW architectures where only one execution unit is available. Most architectures do not have a fully orthogonal instruction set, i.e. the parallelism of functional units is restricted. Such restrictions of the parallelism can be modeled in the constraint section. Currently TDL cannot be used to completely specify architectures with complex superscalar pipelines. However there is ongoing work to develop a specification mechanism for complex superscalar pipelines and integrate it into TDL.

```
Resources Section
...
FuncUnit ALU replication=2;
Register gpr "r%d" [0:31] size=32, type=signed<32>;
SetProperties gpr[30] usage=SP;
RegisterAlias dreg "d%d" gpr mapping=[2:1],
   type=float<56,8>;
Memory DM type=data, align=16, access=32;
DefineAttribute Replacement {"LRU","FIFO"}
   associated to Cache;
Cache InstrCache assoc=2, size=256, linesize=32,
   type=instr, Replacement = LRU;
```

Fig. 1. Example of a Resource Section.

An example of a resource section is shown in Fig. 1. First a functional unit type *ALU* is declared of which two instances exist. This means that the target architecture disposes of two functionally equivalent ALUs that do not have to be distinguished during analyses and optimizations. Subsequently a register file named *gpr* is declared that consists of thirty-two 32-bit registers. The width of the element registers is given by the predefined attribute `size`; the value of the predefined attribute `type` indicates that by default the registers are used to store 32-bit two's complement numbers. The assembly representation of each element register is declared in the notation of C format strings; in the example the element registers of *gpr* are represented by r0,..., r31. The `SetProperties` statement allows to modify or extend the attribute setting of previously declared resources. In the example, the register *gpr*[30] is declared as the stack pointer. Subsequently the alias mechanism is used to declare another view of the register file *gpr*. Two successive integer registers are combined to form one 64-bit floating-point register. The assembly representation of the combined registers is declared as d0, ..., d15. The following declaration introduces a data memory named *DM*

that supports 32-bit accesses that have to be aligned on 16-bit boundaries. The
example concludes with declaring a two-way set-associative instruction cache
with 256 lines of 32 byte length. The replacement strategy is an example of a
user-defined attribute: its domain consists of the two strings *LRU* and *FIFO*
and its scope is the resource type `Cache`.

3.2 Specification of the Instruction Set

The central part of a TDL specification is the description of the instruction set of
the target processor. The assembly representation of all machine operations, their
timing behavior and their semantics have to be known and the specification of
additional information must be supported. As already mentioned the execution
model of TDL corresponds to that of a VLIW architecture. Each instruction can
be composed of several machine operations that are executed in parallel.

The definition of the instruction set is given in the form of an attribute grammar [35]. Each operation is represented by a rule of this grammar; orthogonal
operation parts are encapsulated in rules of their own. The terminals of the
grammar represent the feasible machine operations.

```
DefineOp IAdd "%!(optguard) %s = %s + %s"
  {dst1="$2" in {gpr}, src2="$3" in {gpr},
   src3="$4" in {gpr}},
  {ALU(exectime=1, latency=1);},
  {extern unsigned<1> gval;
   if (((guarded=true)&&(gval<0>=1))||(guarded=false))
     { dst1:=src2+src3;}};
OpNT optguard "if %s"
    {src1="$1" in {gpr}, guarded=true},{;},
    {unsigned<1> gval; gval:=src1<0>;}
  | "if !%s" {src1="$1" in {gpr}, guarded=true},{;},
    {unsigned<1> gval; gval:=!src1<0>;}
  | "" {guarded=false},{;},{};
```

Fig. 2. Example Operation Declaration.

An example for an operation declaration is shown in Fig. 2 where a machine
operation with unambiguous name `IAdd` is declared. This name is followed by
the definition of the assembly representation of the operation. The assembly
representation is specified in a syntax similar to C format strings. The expression `%!(optguard)` represents an occurrence of the non-terminal `optguard`. The
productions for non-terminals are introduced by a dedicated keyword *OpNT* in
order to distinguish them from complete operations. In the definition of the assembly representation, the `%s` directive represents a sequence of characters. The
expression `dst1 = "$2" in {gpr}` specifies that the first occurrence of `%s` in
the format string (the second placeholder) denotes the destination register of
the operation which has to be a register from register file `gpr`. This way the

information of the resource section is reused in the instruction set description. The resource section can be viewed as a special part of the attribute grammar for the instruction set that contains rules for representing the resources of the target processor. As a consequence the description is shortened and, more importantly, a semantical analysis of the operation definitions becomes possible. It is checked that all referenced resources have been declared and that the semantical specification is type-correct.

The other operands are declared as source operands by using the attributes src1, src2, src3. The attribute guarded is used as a flag indicating whether the operation is guarded by an additional source operand (predicated execution). The operation part corresponding to the optional guard is represented by the non-terminal optguard. If a condition register is specified (with a leading exclamation mark) the operation is executed only if the least significant condition bit has the value 1 (0).

The subsequent two blocks represent the timing and the semantics of the operation. The reservation table specification of Fig. 2 indicates that the operation IAdd is executed by an instance of the resource type ALU and that both execution time and functional unit latency take one clock cycle.

The attribute mechanism plays an important role in supporting different views of the instruction set. When computing the data dependences of an input procedure, it must be known for each operation which storage locations are read and which ones are modified. It is not necessary to know how storage locations are modified, the information that they are modified is sufficient. If the machine description is used as the basis of a value analysis, or constant propagation, the information about how the result of an operation is computed is essential. Finally, if an instruction set simulator is to be generated from the machine description, it must additionally be known at which clock cycles the effects of an operation take place. All those views are supported by TDL in an efficient way. As an example, the calculation of the generic data dependence graph is based on the values of the attribute instances of the operation instances of the input program as, e.g., dst_i and src_i. It is not necessary to interpret the detailed specification of the operation semantics.

Specifying the Semantics. The semantics of an operation describes how the execution of the operation affects the machine state. Components of the machine state are the storage resources of the processor, i.e. memory and register cells, condition codes, etc. In TDL the semantics is specified by a dedicated register transfer language (RTL) that is similar to the mechanism of register transfer lists (cf. [8, 10, 7]). A register transfer represents the transfer of a value into a storage location and thus a change of the machine state. Register transfers contained in the same list are assumed to take simultaneously effect.

The register transfer language of TDL is statement-oriented. The main reason is to retain the flexibility for generating cycle-accurate instruction set simulators. Statements can be grouped; each group of statements is assumed to take simultaneously effect. Thus the execution of an operation can be viewed as a sequence

RTLPrg	→ (*RTLStat*)*
RTLStat	→ *RTLAsgn* | *RTLIfStat* | *RTLForStat* | *RTLWhileStat*
	| *RTLSwitchStat* | *RTLVStorageDecl* | *RTLPreFunc*
	| *RTLCanFunc* | *RTLBlock*
RTLBlock	→ { *RTLStat* }
RTLAsgn	→ *AsgnLHS* := *RTLExpr* ;
IfStat	→ if (*RTLExpr*) *RTLBlock* [else *RTLBlock*] ;
ForStat	→ for (*RTLStat* ; *RTLExpr* ; *RTLStat*) *RTLBlock* ;
WhileStat	→ while (*RTLExpr*) *RTLBlock* ;
SwitchStat	→ switch (*RTLExpr*) { *SwitchCaseList SwitchOptDef* };
RTLExpr	→ *RTLExpr BinOp RTLExpr* | *UnOp RTLExpr*
	| *RTLCanFunc* | *RTLPreFunc* | *IntConst*
	| *FloatConst* | *StorageRef* | *AttribRef*;
BinOp	→ || | && | | | ^ | % | == | != | < | > | <= | >=
	| << | >> | + | - | * | /
UnOp	→ - | ~ | !
RTLCanFunc	→ *ID* (*RTLParalist*)

Fig. 3. Skeleton of the RTL grammar in BNF form.

of effects spanning several control steps. All effects can be explicitly assigned to the appropriate control step. A skeleton of the RTL grammar is shown in Fig. 3 in BNF form; the complete definition is given in [15].

The semantics of each machine operation is specified by an RTL program consisting of a sequence of statements. The RTL program may contain declarations of virtual storage locations that are helpful in describing the semantics of complex operations. The scope of virtual storage declarations is the complete RTL program, i.e. the complete specification of the semantics of one machine operation. Feasible statements comprise assignments, conditional statements, loops, and function calls. Statements can be grouped to blocks. Values are computed by expressions without side effects. This means that there are no implicit modifications of storage locations; all changes have to be explicitly given. Expressions may be numerical or string constants, attribute values, references to storage locations, or applications of operators or RTL functions to expressions. All storage resources that are referenced in RTL statements must have been declared in the resource section or by preceding virtual storage declarations in the same RTL program. The operators include the set of arithmetic and logical operators known from the C language. Those are assumed to produce no side effects. Additionally there is a set of predefined RTL-functions for common functions that offer the possibility of explicitly specifying side effects, as e.g. the setting of condition codes, overflow flags, etc.

The designer also has the possibility of declaring user-defined "canonical" functions. This way the specification can be modularized and shortened. All parameters passed to functions can be thought of bit sequences with optionally a given type constructor. In the declaration of the formal parameters it must be annotated whether the parameters are read-only, or can be modified within the body of the function.

RTL expressions are typed. This facilitates analyzing properties of machine operations and is helpful in finding bugs in the machine description. Since register transfers represent operations on machine level, the basic data types of RTL are bit sequences of a given length, denoted by the keyword `storage`. When specifying the semantics of an operation it must be clear how the contents of a storage location are to be evaluated. Often the type of a storage location depends on special conditions or mode settings. As an example the contents of the same register might be interpreted as signed integer in two's complement representation, as unsigned integer, as a fractional value or even a floating-point number. In order to allow for maximum flexibility, RTL provides the possibility of annotating a type to each storage location. These annotations do not represent conversion functions but can be seen as explicit type constructors. The basic data types of RTL are the following:

- `signed<n>` denotes an n-bit signed integer in two's complement representation.
- `unsigned<n>` denotes an n-bit unsigned integer.
- `float<m,n>` denotes an IEEE floating point value with an m-bit mantissa and an n-bit exponent.
- `fract<n>` denotes fractional values. Let $a = (a_0, a_1, \ldots, a_{n-1})$ be an n-bit number of type `fract<n>`. Then its value is defined as $\langle a \rangle = -2^0 + \sum_{i=1}^{n-1} a_i \cdot 2^{-i}$
- `storage<n>` denotes a storage location of length n whose type can be any of the previously mentioned.

TDL uses a polymorphic type inference algorithm; if an explicit type constructor is used, the inferred type is overridden. An example is the expression `_signed(dst1, 32)` that requires the destination to be interpreted as a 32-bit two's complement value. The polymorphism of the RTL language is restricted; it is similar to the subtype rule in object-oriented languages. If the formal parameter of a function has been declared to be of type `storage`, it is also feasible to pass storage locations whose contents have been inferred to be of `signed` or `unsigned` type. In most cases the polymorphism is concerned with the width of storage locations. As an example consider the predefined function `_iabs` that has the following prototype:

`signed<T> _iabs (signed<T>, unsigned<1>, unsigned<1>*)`.

The first parameter can be a signed integer of any length; then the result is a signed integer of the same length. If the bit passed as second parameter has the value 1, saturation is performed; then in the case of positive (negative) overflow the largest positive (smallest negative) number of the appropriate bit width is returned. If an overflow occurs, the bit passed as third parameter is set to 1. All parameters except the last are read-only parameters; the symbol * indicates that this parameter is modified by the function.

The RTL operators as, e. g., *, +, -, & are provided as default operators; they are overloaded. Special attention has to be paid for constants. Integer constants are always treated as 32-bit two's complement values, floating-point constants as 32-bit numbers with 24-bit mantissa and 8-bit exponent. If another representation is required, this must be explicitly annotated by an appropriate type constructor. Binary and hexadecimal values are always exactly represented.

3.3 Constraint and Assembly Specification

In the constraint section of TDL, restrictions of instruction-level parallelism and resource usage as well as interdependencies between scheduling and allocation are modeled by specifying a set of *rules*. The rules are composed from boolean expressions that refer to the properties of the hardware resources and machine operations specified in the preceding sections of a TDL description. The rules are independent from the assembly syntax and allow a semantical analysis of the machine description. The resulting representation is more concise, more flexible and less error prone than in previous approaches, e. g. [10], and it allows modeling resource and encoding restrictions in a uniform way. The most important property of the rule-based approach of TDL is that the specified rules can be automatically transformed into C functions for generic graph-based optimizers (e. g. list scheduling) and in integer linear constraints for generic search-based optimizers. This way, irregular hardware properties can be modeled in a completely generic way.

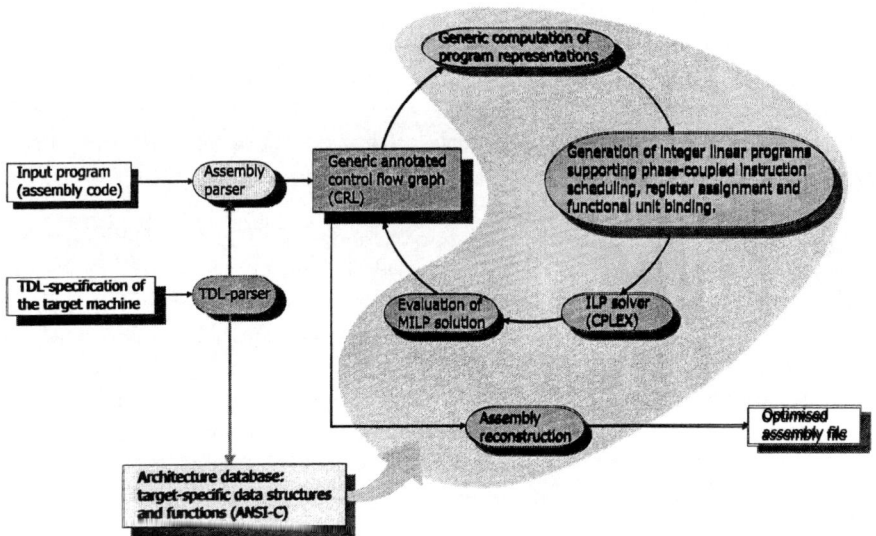

Fig. 4. The PROPAN system.

The constraint section of TDL can be viewed as a constraint store containing the specified rules. The rules represent conditions that have to be respected to preserve correctness during program transformations. Each rule is composed of a *premise* and a *consequent*. The premise is a boolean expression that can be statically evaluated, i. e. when the TDL description is processed. It represents the condition under which the boolean expression of the consequent must be satisfied. The condition specified in the premise must describe operation properties that are invariant with respect to scheduling and allocation decisions. An example is a test whether an operation belongs to a certain operation class. The consequent represents a condition that must be dynamically evaluated, i.e. during the runtime of the optimization phases. Since the focus is on instruction scheduling, register assignment and functional unit allocation, this includes conditions over the usage of storage resources or execution units, parallel execution of operations, and operation sequencing. In order to support additional optimizations to be based on TDL, it is also possible to incorporate conditions that are static with respect to instruction scheduling, register assignment and functional unit allocation. During these phases the conditions are treated as static information. The TDL parser checks whether the premise can be statically evaluated; if this is not the case an error is reported.

From the constraint section, C functions are generated that can be invoked by the target application in a generic way in order to take into account the specified architectural restrictions. For each rule, two functions are generated, one for the use in ILP-based optimization, the other for the use in a generic list scheduling algorithm. The first function traverses the operations of each input program in a nested loop and for each set of operations that satisfy the condition of the premise, ILP constraints that are equivalent to the consequent of the rule are generated. This way, additional hardware-specific information can be flexibly incorporated into the integer linear programs. The second function is a support function for generic list scheduling algorithms that is called in order to decide whether the scheduling of an operation to a given control step does not violate irregular hardware properties. Additional user-supplied optimization phases have to individually analyses the representation of the rules and extract the information relevant for them.

The syntax of the constraint language is shown in Fig. 5 in BNF form. The constraint section is introduced by the keyword Constraint-Section and consists of a set of rules. Each rule consists of two boolean expressions separated by a colon. These expressions represent the premise and the consequent of the rule. In the premise unbound variables for operations can be introduced. These variables are bound to operation instances of each input program during the runtime of the generated optimizers. The boolean expressions are constructed by the boolean operators disjunction, conjunction, and negation from a predefined set of atomic expressions. The atomic expressions describe relations between the resource usage and scheduling properties of machine operations. Atomic expressions are available to check whether an operand is located in a given set of storage locations, whether an operation belongs to a given operation class, whether two operations are executed in parallel, and whether one operation is executed exactly (at least) n cycles after another. Additionally the values of operation attributes can be compared; the feasible comparisons depend on the type of the attribute values (character strings and resource references can only compared for (in)equality, numerical values also for the relations $<, >, \geq, \leq$).

$$
\begin{array}{rl}
CRule & \to CExpr : CExpr \ ; \\
CExpr & \to CExpr \mid CTerm \mid CTerm \\
CTerm & \to CTerm \ \& \ CFactor \mid CFactor \\
CFactor & \to \mid \ !(CExpr) \mid (\ CExpr \ ) \\
 & \mid ResAttribref \ \text{in} \ ResRefs \\
 & \mid id \ \text{in} \ OpOrOpClassList \\
 & \mid id \ \&\& \ id \mid id \ \text{->}(n) \ id \mid id \ \text{->>}(n) \ id \\
 & \mid COpnd \ CRel \ COpnd \\
CRel & \to == \mid \ != \mid > \mid < \mid <= \mid >= \\
COpnd & \to id.AttribName \mid Const \\
ResAttribRef & \to id \ \texttt{.src1} \mid id \ \texttt{.src2} \mid \ldots \\
 & \mid id \ \texttt{.dst1} \mid id \ \texttt{.dst2} \mid \ldots \mid id \ \texttt{. exec}
\end{array}
$$

Fig. 5. Excerpt of the grammar of the constraint language in BNF form.

```
Constraints-Section

op in {C0}: op.dst1 = op.src1;
op1 in {C1} & op2 in {C2}: !(op1 && op2);
(op1 in {AluOps} & op2 in {MulOps}):
 (op1 && op2) -> ((op1.src1 in {GroupA})
  & (op1.src2 in {GroupB})
  & (op2.src1 in {GroupC})
  & (op2.src2 in {GroupD}));
```

Fig. 6. Exemplary constraint section.

Some exemplary rules are shown in Fig. 6. The first one enforces the first source operand to be identical to the destination operand for all operations of the operation class $C0$. The second rule prevents any operation of operation class $C1$ to be executed in parallel with an operation of operation class $C2$. The last rule models the restricted parallelism of ALU and multiplier of the digital signal processor Analog Devices ADSP-2106X SHARC[2]. Some operations can only be executed in parallel if all operands reside in uniquely defined register groups within the heterogeneous register file. If other registers are used, the operations still are feasible but cannot be executed in parallel [19, 17].

The assembly section deals with syntactic details of the assembly language such as instruction or operation delimiters, assembly directives, assembly expressions, etc. In order to perform semantic-preserving transformations of an assembly program it must be possible to distinguish between machine operations and assembly directives. Among the existing machine specification languages, the only approach that supports this distinction is the description language of the SALTO system [4]. While the specification of the syntax of assembly directives would also be possible in other languages as, e.g. nML [8], those could not be distinguished from regular machine operations. An example of a simple directive declaration in TDL is shown in the following; more details can be found in [15, 17].

```
DefineDirective DirGlobVar ".global %s;"
  {type = GlobalDecl, name="$1"};
```

4 The PROPAN Framework

The PROPAN system (*Postpass-oriented Retargetable Optimizer and Analyzer*) [19, 16, 17] has been developed as a retargetable framework for high-quality code optimizations and machine-dependent program analyses at assembly level. An overview of PROPAN is shown in Fig. 4.

PROPAN combines the issues of machine description driven retargetability and of search-based postpass optimisations to improve the quality of machine code especially for irregular hardware architectures.

The retargetability concept of PROPAN is based on the combination of generic and generative techniques. *Generic* program parts are independent from the target architecture and can be used for different processors without any modification. Hardware-specific information is retrieved in a standardized way from an architecture 'database' which is *generated* from the TDL-description.

The input of PROPAN consists of a TDL-description of the target machine and of the assembly programs that are to be analysed or optimized. The TDL specification is processed once for each target architecture; from the TDL description a parser for the specified assembly language and an architecture database are generated. The architecture database consists of a set of ANSI-C files where data structures representing all specified information about the target architecture and functions to initialise, access and manipulate them are defined. The core system of PROPAN is generic; if hardware-specific knowledge is required the architecture database is referenced. For each target architecture, the generic core system is linked with the generated files yielding a dedicated hardware-sensitive postpass optimizer.

The generated assembly parser reads the input programs and reconstructs their control flow graphs [20]. From the control flow graph, other required program representations as, e. g., the data dependence and the control dependence graphs are calculated. The optimizations are based on integer linear programming (ILP) and allow a phase-coupled modeling of instruction scheduling, register assignment and resource allocation taking precisely into account the hardware characteristics of the target architecture [16, 17]. The generated integer linear programs can be solved exactly, or by using novel ILP-based approximations. The approximations allow the calculation time for both models to be drastically reduced while obtaining a solution quality that is superior to conventional graph-based approaches [18]. The optimization scope is not restricted to basic blocks: a dedicated superblock concept allows the optimization scope to be extended across basic block and loop boundaries. The superblock mechanism also allows the ILP-based high-quality optimizations to be combined with fast graph-based heuristics. This way, ILP optimizations can be restricted to frequently used code sequences like inner loops, providing for computation times that are acceptable for practical use [17].

5 Experimental Results

This section focuses on the experience gained with TDL and PROPAN to illustrate the design goals and the application field of the TDL description language.

The PROPAN framework has been retargeted to several different target architectures. It has been used to generate ILP-based postpass optimizers for two widely used contemporary digital signal processors with considerably different hardware characteristics, the Analog Devices ADSP-2106X SHARC [2] and the Philips TriMedia TM1000 [29].

All hardware characteristics of the ADSP-2106X SHARC and the TriMedia TM1000 that have to be known for phase-coupled code optimization are provided by the TDL-descriptions. This especially includes constraints for modelling irregular restrictions of instruction-level parallelism. The SHARC-optimizer performs integrated instruction scheduling and register assignment; the TM1000 optimizer couples instruction scheduling and functional unit binding. In Sec. 5.1 and Sec. 5.2 the experimental evaluation of both optimizers is shortly summarized. The evaluation shows that using the hardware description language TDL enables significant improvements of the code produced by production-quality compilers to be achieved with short retargeting time.

PROPAN has also been used as a platform to implement hardware-specific postpass optimizations for the Infineon C16x [31] microprocessor family that are part of a commercial postpass optimizer [1]. TDL descriptions also exist for the Infineon TriCore μC/DSP [14], the Motorola Coldfire 5307 [26] and the TI320C6x [33].

Including comments, the TDL files contain between 1000 and 3000 lines; by using the cpp preprocessor the size can be further reduced. The time to develop and test a TDL description for a new architecture ranges from two weeks for an experienced user to two months for unexperienced users.

5.1 The ADSP-2106x SHARC

The ADSP-2106X SHARC is a digital signal processor with irregular architecture and restricted instruction-level parallelism. It has a VLIW execution model: several machine operations can be grouped to long instructions and be executed in parallel. Two memory banks are available that can be configured as program and data memory where program memory can be used to store instructions and data. Data accesses to program memory and data memory can be executed in parallel for a restricted set of addressing modes, if specific address registers are used. Many arithmetic operations can be executed in parallel to memory accesses and some control flow operations can be executed in parallel to arithmetic operations. Additionally there is a restricted parallelism between ALU and multiplier. Some ALU and multiplier operations can be combined to a multifunctional instruction and can then be executed in parallel. A presupposition is that each of the four input operands is located in a register from a specific register group within the heterogeneous general purpose register file. If any operand is located in a register from another group, the operation is feasible but cannot be part of a multifunctional instruction (cf. Sec. 3.3). Thus, generating high-quality code requires a phase-coupled modeling of instruction scheduling and register assignment.

The experiments have been performed under SunOS 5.7 on a SPARC Ultra-Enterprise 10000; the generated integer linear programs are solved by the

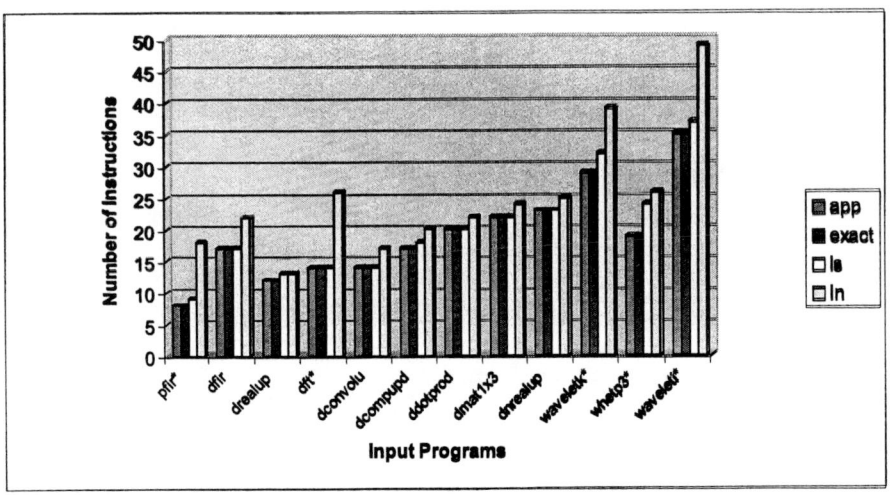

Fig. 7. Optimization Results (ADSP-2106X SHARC).

CPLEX library [13]. The investigated input programs are typical applications of digital signal processing. They comprise the computation routines of the Dsp-Stone benchmark [36] and some hand-written assembly programs. The input programs from the DspStone benchmark [36] have been compiled to assembly code by the gcc-based g21k compiler. The hand-crafted assembly programs have been explicitly sequentialized so that in the input programs the available instruction-level parallelism is not exploited. The input programs contain between 14 and 55 microoperations.

An overview of the results for some representative input programs is given in Fig. 7. In Fig. 7 a comparison of code quality is shown; the number of compacted instructions in the exact, i.e., provably optimal ILP-based solution (exact) is compared to the result of the fastest ILP-based approximation (app) [17], a generic list scheduling algorithm with highest-level-first heuristic (ls) and to the schedule of the input programs (in). In order to ensure a conservative comparison, an optimal register assignment is given as an input to the list scheduling algorithm while it is explicitly computed by the ILP-based methods. The programs marked with an asterisk are the sequentialized hand-crafted assembly programs; for those programs the number of instructions in the input program corresponds to the number of microoperations.

In most cases the ILP-based approximations [18] produce optimal results; the optimal number of instructions was only exceeded in 5 of 108 approximative computations. The computation time of the ILP-based approximations ranges from a few seconds up to 15 minutes for input programs containing up to 30 – 50 instructions. The superblock mechanism allows to combine them with fast heuristic methods to generate highly optimized code for hotspots, i.e. important and often executed code sequences like inner loops within acceptable computation time.

Although the register assignment in the input programs for the list scheduling algorithm is always optimal, its code quality is lower than that of the ILP-based methods. The largest deviation in the investigated programs is 21.05%; with a suboptimal register assignment of the input program this difference can grow significantly larger. The code produced by the gcc-based g21k compiler exceeds the optimal number of instructions on average by 8.2%.

5.2 The Philips TriMedia TM1000

The TriMedia TM1000 is a multimedia processor with a VLIW architecture where the instruction scheduling interacts with the *slot allocation problem*. Each long instruction word is composed of five microoperations that are issued simultaneously. All operations have to be assigned to issue slots in the instruction word and the assignment of operations to issue slots is restricted. The assignment to issue slots also determines which operations can be executed in parallel. Moreover, the operations have to be synchronized with respect to the write-back bus; no more than five operations may write their result simultaneously on the bus. Since different operations have different execution times, this is a non-trivial problem.

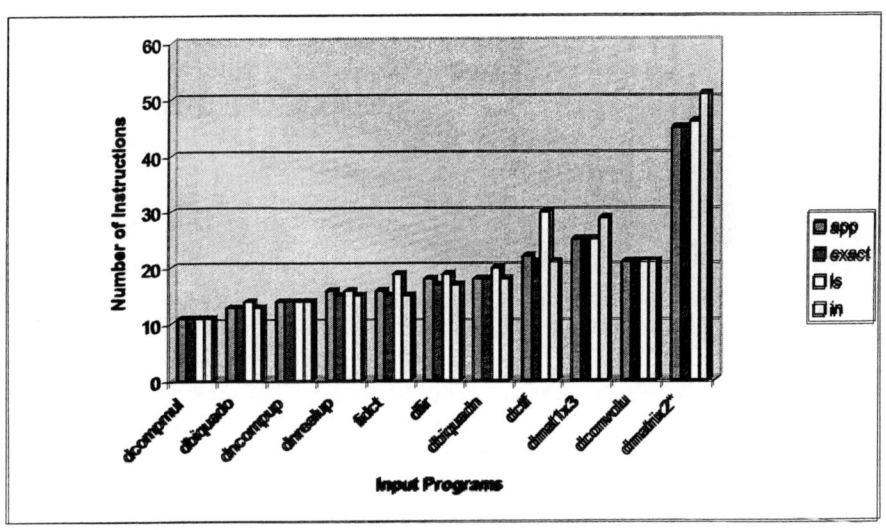

Fig. 8. Optimization Results (TM1000).

An overview of the results for some representative input programs is presented in Fig. 8. The input programs have been generated with the highly optimizing Philips tmcc compiler. In Fig. 8 the number of compacted instructions in the exact, i.e., provably optimal ILP-based solution (exact) is compared to the result of the fastest ILP-based approximation (app), of a generic list scheduling algorithm with highest-level-first heuristic that performs resource allocation on the fly (ls) [17] and to the schedule of the input programs (in). In most cases the tmcc compiler produces optimal results, but for some input programs the code can be improved significantly. The code quality of the ILP-based approximation is high. For 18 of 26 investigated programs it produces an optimal result; for the remaining programs, the optimal number of instructions is exceeded only by one. The computation time ranges from a few seconds up to 9 minutes for input programs containing up to 70 – 100 instructions. Again the superblock mechanism allows to combine them with fast heuristic methods to generate highly optimized code for hotspots within acceptable computation time.

The schedule produced by the generic list scheduling algorithm exceeds the optimal number of instructions on average by 7.29%. The two hand-crafted assembly programs (fidct, dctf) offer a high level of parallelism and make use of special DSP operations that can only be assigned to few issue slots. For those programs, the interaction between instruction scheduling and resource allocation has a significant effect which becomes apparent in the result of the list scheduling algorithm. Here the optimal number of instruction is exceeded by more than 25% respectively more than 42%.

6 Conclusion and Outlook

In this article the machine description language TDL has been presented. TDL has been designed to support generating machine-dependent postpass optimizers and program analyzers on assembly level. The focus is on embedded processors and irregular hardware architectures for which traditional code generation and optimization techniques fail to achieve a satisfactory code quality. TDL is assembly-oriented and provides a generic modeling of irregular hardware constraints that allows them to be exploited in generic graph-based and search-based optimization algorithms. The extendibility of TDL and dedicated abstraction mechanisms provide for an easy integration of TDL in different target applications. It is used within the PROPAN system that has been developed as a retargetable framework for high-quality code optimizations and machine-dependent program analyses at assembly level. PROPAN allows machine-specific postpass optimizers to be automatically generated from a TDL specification. The optimizers generated can be based on heuristic algorithms as well as exact or approximative ILP-based methods. With short retargeting time significant improvements of the code produced by production-quality compilers can be achieved.

TDL has also been used for implementing hardware-sensitive postpass optimizations based on the PROPAN framework that are part of a commercial postpass optimizer. TDL descriptions have been written for various contemporary embedded processors; the specifications are concise and can be produced in short time.

Future research aims at different directions. There is ongoing work to extend the TDL language by a modeling of superscalar architectures with complex pipelines. The generation of cycle-accurate instruction set simulators from the TDL specification is another goal. Moreover there is ongoing work to develop an interface between TDL and the program analyzer generator PAG [24]. This allows to use the same program analyzer specification to generate hardware-sensitive program analyzers for different target architectures. Examples are value analyses that allow to disambiguate memory accesses and remove spurious data dependences in guarded code. Furthermore, the modeling of additional processors is planned.

References

1. AbsInt Angewandte Informatik GmbH. *aiPop166. Code Compaction for the C166/ST10. User Documentation – Version 1.0*, 2000. http://www.absint.com.
2. Analog Devices. *ADSP-2106x SHARC User's Manual*, 1995.
3. M. Barbacci. Instruction Set Processor Specifications (ISPS): The Notation and Its Applications. *IEEE Transactions on Computers*, C-30(1):24–40, Jan. 1981.
4. F. Bodin, Z. Chamski, E. Rohou, and A. Seznec. *Functional Specification of SALTO: A Retargetable System for Assembly Language Transformation and Optimization, rev. 1.00 beta*. INRIA, 1997.
5. D. Bradlee. Retargetable Instruction Scheduling for Pipelined Processors. Phd thesis, Technical Report 91-08-07, University of Washington, 1991.
6. D. Bradlee, R. Henry, and S. Eggers. The Marion System for Retargetable Instruction Scheduling. *Proceedings of the PLDI*, pages 229–240, 1991.
7. J. Davidson and N. Ramsey. Machine Descriptions to Build Tools for Embedded Systems. In *Proceedings of the ACM SIGPLAN Workshop on Languages, Compilers and Tools for Embedded Systems*, pages 172–188. Springer LNCS, Volume 1474, June 1998.
8. A. Fauth, J. Van Praet, and M. Freericks. Describing Instruction Set Processors Using nML. In *Proceedings of the European Design and Test Conference*, pages 503–507. IEEE, 1995.
9. P. Grun, A. Halambi, A. Khare, V. Ganesh, N. Dutt, and A. Nicolau. EXPRESSION: An ADL for System Level Design Exploration. Technical Report 1998-29, University of California, Irvine, 1998.
10. G. Hadjiyiannis. ISDL: Instruction Set Description Language Version 1.0. Technical report, MIT RLE, Apr. 1998.
11. A. Halambi, P. Grun, V. Ganesh, A. Khare, N. Dutt, and A. Nicolau. EXPRESSION: A Language for Architecture Exploration through Compiler/Simulator Retargetability. *Proceedings of the DATE99*, 1999.
12. S. Hanono and S. Devadas. Instruction Scheduling, Resource Allocation, and Scheduling in the AVIV Retargetable Code Generator. In *Proceedings of the Design Automation Conference 1998*, San Francisco, California, 1998. ACM.
13. ILOG S.A. *ILOG CPLEX 6.5. User's Manual*, 1999.
14. Infineon, http://www.infineon.com. *TriCore v1.3. Architecture Manual*, 2000.
15. D. Kästner. TDL: A Hardware and Assembly Description Language. Technical Report TDL1.3, Transferbereich 14, Saarland University, 1999.
16. D. Kästner. PROPAN: A Retargetable System for Postpass Optimisations and Analyses. *Proceedings of the ACM SIGPLAN Workshop on Languages, Compilers and Tools for Embedded Systems*, June 2000.

17. D. Kästner. *Retargetable Code Optimisation by Integer Linear Programming*. PhD thesis, Saarland University, 2000.
18. D. Kästner. ILP-based Approximations for Retargetable Code Optimization. *International Conference on Optimization: Techniques and Applications (ICOTA01)*, 2001.
19. D. Kästner and M. Langenbach. Code Optimization by Integer Linear Programming. In S. Jähnichen, editor, *Proceedings of the 8th International Conference on Compiler Construction CC99*, pages 122–136. Springer LNCS 1575, Mar. 1999.
20. D. Kästner and S. Wilhelm. Generic Control Flow Reconstruction from Assembly Code. *Proceedings of the ACM SIGPLAN Joined Conference on Languages, Compilers, and Tools for Embedded Systems (LCTES'02) and Software and Compilers for Embedded Systems (SCOPES'02)*, June 2002.
21. D. Lanneer, J. Van Praet, A. Kifli, K. Schoofs, W. Geurts, F. Thoen, and G. Goossens. CHESS: Retargetable Code Generation For Embedded DSP Processors. In *[25]*, pages 85–102. Kluwer, 1995.
22. R. Leupers. *Retargetable Code Generation for Digital Signal Processors*. Kluwer Academic Publishers, 1997.
23. R. Lipsett, C. Schaefer, and C. Ussery. *VHDL: Hardware Description and Design*. Kluwer Academic Publishers, 12. edition, 1993.
24. F. Martin. *Generation of Program Analyzers*. PhD thesis, Saarland University, 1999.
25. P. Marwedel and G. Goossens. *Code Generation for Embedded Processors*. Kluwer, Boston; London; Dortrecht, 1995.
26. Motorola Inc. *MCF5307 ColdFire Integrated Microprocessor User's Manual*, Aug. 2000. MCF5307UM/D, Rev. 2.0.
27. L. Nowak. Graph Based Retargetable Microcode Compilation in the MIMOLA Design System. *20th Annual Workshop on Microprogramming*, pages 126–132, 1987.
28. S. Pees, A. Hoffmann, V. Zivojnovic, and H. Meyr. LISA: Machine Description Language for Cycle-Accurate Models of Programmable DSP Architectures. *Proceedings of the Design Automation Conference*, 1999.
29. Philips Electronics North America Corporation. *TriMedia TM1000 Preliminary Data Book*, 1997.
30. N. Ramsey and M. Fernandez. Specifying Representations of Machine Instructions. *ACM Transactions on Programming Languages and Systems*, 19(3):492–524, May 1997.
31. Siemens. *C165/C163 User's Manual 10.96 Version 2.0*. Siemens AG, 1996. http://www.infineon.com.
32. SPAM Research Group, http://www.ee.princeton.edu/spam. *SPAM Compiler User's Manual*, Sept. 1997.
33. Texas Instruments. *TMS320C62xx Programmer's Guide*, 1997.
34. D. Thomas and P. Moorby. *The Verilog Hardware Description Language*. Kluwer Academic Publishers, 2. edition, 1995.
35. R. Wilhelm and D. Maurer. *Compiler Design*. Addison-Wesley, 1995.
36. V. Zivojnovic, J. Velarde, C. Schläger, and H. Meyr. DSPSTONE: A DSP-Oriented Benchmarking Methodology. In *Proceedings of the International Conference on Signal Processing Applications and Technology*, 1994.

Hume: A Domain-Specific Language for Real-Time Embedded Systems*

Kevin Hammond[1] and Greg Michaelson[2]

[1] School of Computer Science
University of St Andrews, St Andrews, Scotland
kh@dcs.st-and.ac.uk
Tel: +44-1334-463241, Fax: +44-1334-463278
[2] Dept. of Mathematics and Computer Science
Heriot-Watt University, Edinburgh, Scotland
greg@macs.hw.ac.uk
Tel: +44-131-451-3422, Fax: +44-131-451-3327

Abstract. This paper describes Hume: a novel domain-specific language whose purpose is to explore the expressibility/costability spectrum in resource-constrained systems, such as real-time embedded or control systems. Hume provides a number of high level features including higher-order functions, polymorphic types, arbitrary but sized user-defined data structures, asynchronous processes, lightweight exception handling, automatic memory management and domain-specific metaprogramming features, whilst seeking to guarantee strong space/time behaviour and maintaining overall determinacy.

1 Essential Language Properties in the Real-Time Embedded System Domain

Embedded systems are becoming increasingly prevalent in everyday life. From a computer science perspective such systems represent a software/hardware blend at a much lower level of abstraction than usual. They also introduce strict cost-driven requirements on system capabilities. Adapting general purpose languages for such a domain often leads to a poor fit between the language features and the implementation requirements. Domain-specific language designs such as Hume allow low-level system requirements to guide the design of the high level language features we desire. We can identify a number of essential or desirable properties for a language that is aimed at real-time embedded systems [20].

– *determinacy* – the language should allow the construction of determinate systems, by which we mean that under identical environmental constraints, all executions of the system should be *observationally equivalent*;

---

* This work is generously supported by a grant from the UK's Engineering and Physical Sciences Research Council.

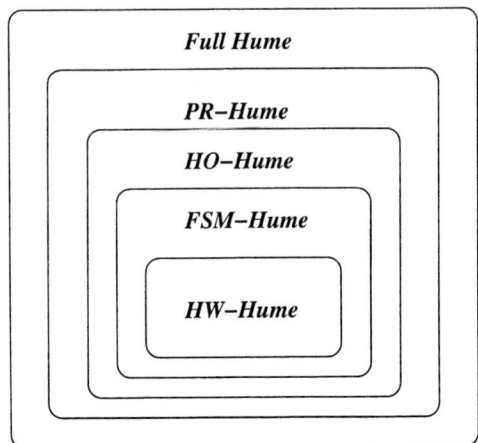

Fig. 1. Hume Design Space

- *bounded time/space* – the language must allow the construction of systems whose resource costs are statically bounded – so ensuring that *hard real-time* and *real-space* constraints can be met;
- *asynchronicity* – the language must allow the construction of systems that are capable of responding to inputs as they are received without imposing total ordering on environmental or internal interactions;
- *concurrency* – the language must allow the construction of systems as communicating units of independent computation;
- *correctness* – the language must allow a high degree of confidence that constructed systems meet their formal requirements [1].

Our goal with the Hume design is to allow as high a level of program abstraction as possible whilst still maintaining these properties. For example, we provide exception handling, automatic memory management, higher-order functions, polymorphism and recursion in different levels of the language. In each case, the requirement for transparent time and space costing has been paramount in formulating the language design.

1.1 The Hume Design Model

We have designed Hume as a three-layer language: an outer (static) declaration/metaprogramming layer, an intermediate coordination layer describing a static layout of dynamic processes, and an inner layer describing each process as a dynamic mapping from patterns that match inputs to expressions that produce outputs. Rather than attempting to apply cost modelling and correctness proving technology to an existing language framework either directly or by altering the language to a greater or lesser extent (as with e.g. RTSj [6]), our approach

$program ::=$	$decl_1$; ... ; $decl_n$	$n \geq 1$
$decl ::=$	**box** | **function** | **datatype** | **exception** | **wire** | **device**	
$datatype ::=$	**data** id α_1 ... α_m = $constr_1$ | ... | $constr_n$	$n \geq 1$
$constr ::=$	**con** τ_1 ... τ_n	$n \geq 1$
$exception ::=$	**exception** id [:: τ]	
$wire ::=$	**wire** $link_1$ **to** $link_2$ [**initially** $cexpr$]	
$link ::=$	$connection$ | $deviceid$	
$connection ::=$	$boxid$. $varid$	
$box ::=$	**box** id ins $outs$ **fair**/**unfair** $matches$ [**handle** $exnmatches$]	
$ins/outs/ids ::=$	(id_1 , ... , id_n)	
$matches ::=$	$match_1$ | ... | $match_n$	$n \geq 1$
$match ::=$	(pat_1 , ... , pat_n) $\to$ $expr$	
$expr ::=$	**int** | **float** | **char** | **bool** | **string** | **var** | *****	
	| **con** $expr_1$ ... $expr_n$	$n \geq 0$
	| ($expr_1$, ... , $expr_n$)	$n \geq 2$
	| **if** $cond$ **then** $expr_1$ **else** $expr_2$	
	| **let** $valdecl_1$; ...; $valdecl_n$ **in** $expr$	
	| $expr$ **within** ($time$ | $space$)	
$function ::=$	**var** $matches$	
$valdecl ::=$	$id = expr$	
$pat ::=$	**int** | **float** | **char** | **bool** | **string** | **var** | **_** | ***** | **_***	
	| **con** var_1 ... var_n	$n \geq 0$
	| (pat_1 , ... , pat_n)	$n \geq 2$
$device ::=$	(**stream** | **port** | **fifo** | **memory** | **interrupt**) $devdesc$	
$devdesc ::=$	id (**from** | **to**) $string$ [**within** $time$ **raising** id]	

Fig. 2. Hume Syntax (Simplified)

is to design Hume in such a way that we are certain that formal models and proofs can be constructed. We envisage a series of overlapping Hume language levels as shown in Figure 1, where each level adds expressibility to the expression semantics, but either loses some desirable property or increases the technical difficulty of providing formal correctness/cost models. Figure 2 shows the syntax of Hume. We use a rule-based design, with a functional expression notation (*match, function, exception*) embedded in an asynchronous process model (*box*, *wire, device*). This simplifies both correctness proofs and the construction of cost models at the expression level. Process abstractions ("boxes") specify an asynchronous and stateless mapping of inputs to outputs. These abstractions can be seen as stateless objects with a rigid communication structure, which both assists process/communication costing and simplifies the construction of deadlock/termination proofs. Boxes are wired explicitly into a static process network, using *wires* to link *boxes* and *devices*, (again simplifying both correctness and costing) using a single-buffer approach. Single-buffering allows tight controls over buffer sizes based on the types of values that are communicated, gives a simple easily-implemented semantics, and can be extended to multiple buffering stages by using additional intermediary boxes. The metaprogramming layer (Section 3) introduces polymorphic templates for box construction, allows wiring macros to simplify descriptions of process networks, incorporates abstractions to deal with repetitive situations, and provides macros to calculate compile-time constant values that may be shared between the coordination and computation layers.

1.2 The Evolution of the Hume Design

As a research language, Hume has undergone a number of changes, reflecting increased maturity in understanding the requirements of the real-time systems domain, in improved cost technology, and in our implementations. Our initial design [11] was for a synchronous subset of the language, for which we produced a formal dynamic semantics [12]. We subsequently extended Hume to include asynchronous constructs and metaprogramming features, separating the design into the layers described here, introduced strong space modelling for the FSM-Hume subset [14], developed a number of exemplars (e.g. [13]), and produced a real-time implementation based on a high-level abstract machine design. This new paper describes how Hume matches domain-specific requirements, covers our layered design approach, introduces our metaprogramming constructs (Section 3), provides a detailed description of our scheduling algorithm, and describes timing and device issues for the first time (Section 4).

2 Boxes and Coordination

A box is an abstraction of a finite state machine. An output-emitting Moore machine has transitions of the form: (*old state, input symbol*) $\rightarrow$ (*new state, output symbol*). We observe that (*oldstate, inputsymbol*) is like a tuple pattern, to match the current state and input symbol, and that (*newstate, outputsymbol*) is like a tuple expression, returned from the result of processing given the current state and input symbol. Thus, we generalise Moore machine transitions to: *pattern* $\rightarrow$ *function(pattern)* where *pattern* is based on arbitrarily nested constants, variables and data structures and *function* is an arbitrary recursive function over *pattern* written in the *expression language*. Here the *pattern* on the left matches the inputs, binding variables which are then processed by the *function* on the right to generate the outputs. By controlling the types that are permissible in *pattern* and the constructs that are usable in *function*, the expressibility and hence formal properties of Hume may be altered.

Although the body of a box is a single function, the process defined by a box will iterate indefinitely, effectively calling the function repeatedly on the changing inputs. Since a box is stateless, information that is preserved between box iterations must be passed explicitly between those iterations through some *wire* (Section 2.1). This roughly corresponds to tail recursion over a stream in a functional language, as used by RT-FRP, for example, to control resource bounds [30]. In the Hume context, this design allows a box to be implemented as an uninterruptible thread, taking its inputs, computing some result values and producing its outputs. Moreover, if a bound on dynamic memory usage can be predetermined, a box can execute with a fixed size stack and heap without requiring garbage collection.

2.1 Wiring

Boxes are connected using wiring declarations to form a static process network. A wire provides a mapping between an output link and an input link, each of which may be a named box input/output, a port, or a stream. For example, wire x.o to y.i connects the output x.o to the input x.i. Initial values may be specified. For example, initial x.o = 1 specifies that the initial value of the wire connected to x.o is 1.

2.2 Box and Wiring Example

The Hume code for a simple even parity checking box is shown below. The inputs to the box are a bit (either 0 or 1) and a boolean value indicating whether the system has detected even or odd parity so far. The output is a string indicating whether the result should be even ("true") or odd ("false") parity.

```
type bit = word 1;  type parity = boolean;

box even_parity
in   ( b  :: bit,    p  :: parity )
out  (p'  :: parity, show :: string)
unfair
   ( 0, true  ) -> ( true,  "true"  )
|  ( 1, true  ) -> ( false, "false" )
|  ( 0, false ) -> ( false, "false" )
|  ( 1, false ) -> ( true,  "false" );
```

The corresponding wiring specification connects the bit stream to the input source and the monitoring output to standard output. Note that the box output p' is wired back to the box input p as an explicit state parameter, initialised to true. The box will run continuously, outputting a log of the monitored parity.

```
stream input from "/dev/sensor";
```

```
stream output to    "std_out";

wire input                to even_parity.b;
wire even_parity.p'       to even_parity.p     initially true;
wire even_parity.show to output;
```

2.3 Coordination

The basic box execution cycle is:

1. check input availability for all inputs and latch input values;
2. match inputs against rules in turn;
3. consume all inputs;
4. bind variables to input values and evaluate the RHS of the selected rule;
5. write outputs to the corresponding wires.

A key issue is how input and output values are managed. In the Hume model, there is a one-to-one correspondance between input and output wires, and these are single-buffered. In combination with the fixed size types that we require, this ensures that communications buffers are bounded size, whilst avoiding the synchronisation problems that can occur if no buffering is used. In particular, a box may write an output to one of its own inputs, so creating an explicit representation of state, as shown in the example above.

Values for available inputs are latched atomically, but not removed from the buffer (consumed) until a rule is matched. Consuming an input removes the lock on the wire buffer, resetting the availability flag. Output writing is atomic: if any output cannot be written to its buffer because a previous value has not yet been consumed, the box blocks. This reduces concurrency by preventing boxes from proceeding if their inputs could be made available but the producer is blocked on some other output. However, it improves strong notions of causality: if a value has appeared as input on a wire the box that produced that input has certainly generated all of its outputs. Once a cycle has completed and all outputs have been written to the corresponding wire buffers, the box can begin the next execution step. This improves concurrency, by avoiding unnecessary synchronisation. Individual boxes never terminate. Program termination occurs when no box is runnable.

2.4 Asynchronous Coordination Constructs

The two primary coordination constructs that are used to introduce asynchronous coordination are to *ignore* certain inputs/outputs and to introduce *fair matching*. The basic box execution cycle is altered as follows (changes are italicised):

1. check input availability *against possible matches* and latch *available* inputs;
2. match *available* inputs against rules in turn;
3. consume *those inputs that have been matched and which are not ignored in the selected rule*;
4. bind variables to input values and evaluate the RHS of the selected rule;

5. write *non-ignored* outputs to the corresponding wires;
6. *reorder match rules according to the fairness criteria.*

Note that: i) inputs are now consumed after rules have been selected rather than before; ii) only some inputs/outputs may be involved in a given box cycle, rather than all inputs/outputs being required; and iii) rules may be reordered if the box is engaged in fair matching. This new model in which inputs can be ignored in certain patterns or in certain output positions can be considered to be equivalent to non-strictness at the box level.

We use the accepted notion of *fairness* whereby each rule will be used equally often given a stream of inputs that match all rules [2]. *Channel fairness* is not enforced, however: it is entirely possible, for example, for a programmer to write a sequence of rules that will treat the input from different sources unfairly. It is the programmer's responsibility to ensure that channel fairness is maintained, if required. For example, a fair merge operator can be defined as:

```
box merge
in  ( xs  :: int 32, ys :: int 32)
out ( xys :: int 32)
fair
  (x, *) -> x  |  (*, y) -> y;
```

The *-pattern indicates that the corresponding input position should be ignored, that is the pattern matches any input, without consuming it. Such a pattern must appear at the top level. Note the difference between *-patterns and wildcard/variable patterns: in the latter cases, successful matching will mean that the corresponding input value (and all of that value) is removed from the input buffer. For convenience, we also introduce a hybrid pattern: _*. If matched, such patterns will consume the corresponding input value *if one is present*, but will ignore it otherwise. Note that this construct cannot introduce a race condition that might affect the meaning of a box, since the availability status for each input is latched at the start of each box execution cycle rather than checked during each individual pattern match. Ignored values can also be used as dynamic outputs. In this case no output is produced on the corresponding wire, and consequently the box cannot be blocked on that output.

2.5 Thread Scheduling

The prototype Hume Abstract Machine implementation maintains a vector of threads (*thread*), one per box, each with its own *thread state record*, containing state information and links to input/output wires. Each wire comprises a pair of a value (*value*) and a validity flag (*available*) used to ensure correct locking between input and output threads. The flag is atomically set to *true* when an output is written to the wire, and is reset to *false* when an input is consumed.

Threads are scheduled under the control of a built-in scheduler, which currently implements round-robin scheduling. A thread is deemed to be *runnable* if all the required inputs are available for any of its rules to be executed (Figure 3). A compiler-specified matrix is used to determine whether an input is needed: for

```
for i = 1 to nThreads do
    runnable := false;
    for j = 1 to thread[i].nRules do
        if ¬ runnable then
            runnable := true;
            for k = 1 to thread[i].nIns do
                runnable &= thread[i].required[j, k] ⇒ thread[i].ins[k].available
            endfor
        endif
    endfor
    if runnable then schedule (thread[i]) endif
endfor
```

Fig. 3. Hume Abstract Machine Thread Scheduling Algorithm

some thread t, $thread[t].required[r, i]$ is true if input i is required to run rule r of that thread. Since wires are single-buffered, a thread will consequently block when writing to a wire which contains an output that has not yet been consumed. In order to ensure a consistent semantics, a single check is performed on all output wires immediately before any output is written. No output will be written until all the input on all output wires has been consumed. The check ignores * output positions.

3 The MetaProgramming Layer

The Hume metalanguage is designed to simplify the construction of boxes and wiring by creating abstractions that can be instantiated at compile-time. The metalanguage supports box templates which may be instantiated to one or more boxes; defined constants used as identifiers both in expressions and in the metalanguage; macro expressions and parameterised macros which may be used in the metalanguage, in declarations, and in expressions; and abstract wiring/initial declarations. The syntax of the metalanguage is shown in Figure 4: *cexpr* indicates a statically computable expression that is evaluated at compile-time.

3.1 Box Templates

A box template can be defined to give the structure of a box, which is then instantiated to produce one or more boxes. Such templates are polymorphic. For convenience, we also allow boxes to be replicated but the box copies all have the same monomporphic type as the original box. A box/template may optionally be replicated/instantiated a number of times. For example, `instantiate t as b * 4` will introduce boxes b1, b2, b3 and b4.

In the second, more substantial, example, we generate a `Track` template which is then instantiated to give 16 `Ring` boxes, named `Ring1` to `Ring16`, and four `ByPass` boxes, named `ByPass1` to `ByPass4`. This example forms part of an example model railway track layout defined by Roscoe to illustrate deadlock

$$
\begin{array}{rl}
meta ::= & \textbf{constant}\ id\ =\ cexpr \\
 & |\ \textbf{template}\ templateid\ prelude\ body \\
 & |\ \textbf{instantiate}\ templateid\ \textbf{as}\ boxid\ [\ *\ intconst\ ] \\
 & |\ \textbf{replicate}\ boxid\ \textbf{as}\ boxid\ [\ *\ intconst\ ] \\
 & |\ \textbf{macro}\ mid\ ids\ =\ cexpr \\
 & |\ wiredecl \\
 & |\ \textbf{for}\ id\ =\ cexpr\ \textbf{to}\ cexpr\ [\ \textbf{except}\ excepts\ ]\ meta \\
\\
excepts ::= & (\ cexpr_1\ ,\ \ldots\ ,\ cexpr_n\ ) \hspace{4em} n \geq 1 \\
\\
wire ::= & \textbf{wire}\ boxid\ sources\ dests \\
 & |\ \textbf{wire}\ wmacid\ (\ id_1\ ,\ \ldots\ ,\ id_n\ )\ =\ wireid\ sources\ dests \\
 & |\ \textbf{wire}\ wmacid\ args \\
\\
sources/dests/args ::= & (\ linkspec_1\ ,\ \ldots\ ,\ linkspec_n\ ) \hspace{4em} n \geq 0 \\
\\
linkspec ::= & link\ [\ \textbf{intially}\ cexpr\ ]
\end{array}
$$

Fig. 4. Hume MetaProgramming Constructs

issues in CSP. The layout comprises two loops of track with a common section. The `ByPass` creates a short circuit of the track by forking from the `Ring` at some point (`ForkPos`) and joining it at a later point (`JoinPos`). The `Fork` and `Join` boxes are also template instantiations. Note the reuse of the same input/output names in the different templates. This is used to assist abstraction.

```
template Track
in  ( value  :: State,  inp    :: Channel,  outctl :: Ctl        )
out ( value' :: State,  inctl  :: Ctl ,     outp   :: Channel )
...

constant RingSize =  16;
instantiate Track as Ring*RingSize;
instantiate Track as Bypass*4;

template SyncMerge
in  ( value  :: State,  in1, in2      :: Channel,  outctl :: Ctl        )
out ( value' :: State,  in1ctl, in2ctl :: Ctl,      outp   :: Channel )
...

template SyncSplit
in  ( value  :: State,  inp    :: Channel,  out1ctl, out2ctl :: Ctl        )
out ( value' :: State,  inctl  :: Ctl ,     out1, out2       :: Channel )
...

instantiate SyncMerge as Join;
instantiate SyncSplit as Fork;
```

3.2 Macro Expressions and Definitions

Macro expressions are quoted using "{"..."}", and have integer types. They may appear as basic expressions, be used to qualify identifiers in any layer, or used in positions requiring an integer constant. Basic arithmetic, conditional and macro call operations are supported. Parameterised macro definitions are also supported: these can be used in any macro position.

```
macro predR pos = (pos - 1) mod RingSize;
macro succR pos = (pos + 1) mod RingSize;

constant BeforeFork  = { predR(ForkPos) };
constant AfterFork   = { succR(ForkPos) };
constant BeforeJoin  = { predR(JoinPos) };
constant AfterJoin   = { succR(JoinPos) };
```

3.3 Wiring Macros

Wiring macros are introduced by associating a wiring definition with a name and set of parameter names. These parameters textually substitute the corresponding concrete links. For example,

```
wire Track ( this, prev, next ) =
    wire {this} ( {this}.value', {prev}.outp,  {next}.inctl )
                ( {this}.value,  {prev}.outctl, {next}.inp   );
```

declares a macro to wire the box called this to the prev and next boxes. The full input/output names are derived textually from the arguments. So for example,

```
wire Track ( Ring{0}, Ring{RingSize-1}, Ring{1} );
```

is equivalent to:

```
wire Ring{0}.value'         to Ring{0}.value;
wire Ring{RingSize-1}.outp  to Ring{0}.inp;
wire Ring{1}.inctl          to Ring{0}.outctl;
wire Ring{0}.value'         to Ring{0}.value;
wire Ring{0}.inctl          to Ring{RingSize-1}.outctl;
wire Ring{0}.outp           to Ring{RingSize-1}.inp;
```

Since the Fork and Join boxes reuse the same names for equivalent inputs/outputs, the Track wiring macro can also be used to wire general Ring boxes to these special boxes. For example,

```
wire Track ( Ring{BeforeFork}, Ring{predR(BeforeFork)}, Fork );
```

3.4 Repetition

In order to further improve abstraction, meta-level declarations can be repeated under the control of a variable (optionally omitting certain values). The repetition variable may be used within the wiring declation (enclosed within braces), where it takes on each iterated value. For example,

```
for i =  0 to RingSize-1 except (ForkPos, JoinPos)
 instantiate Track as Ring{i};

for i = 1 to RingSize-2
 except ( ForkPos, JoinPos, BeforeFork, AfterFork, BeforeJoin, AfterJoin )
 wire Track ( Ring{i}, Ring{predR(i)}, Ring{succR(i)} );
```

generates `RingSize` boxes from the `Track` template, and wires them in a ring, leaving holes for the `Fork` and `Join` boxes. Note the use of the loop variable i within the macros. Loops may be nested as required.

4 Exceptions, Timing and Devices

4.1 Exceptions

Exceptions are raised in the expression layer and handled by the surrounding box. In order to ensure tight bounds on exception handling costs and to allow a direct implementation, exception handlers are not permitted within expressions. Consequently, we avoid the (difficult to cost) chains of dynamic exception handlers that can arise when using non-real-time languages such as standard Java or Concurrent Haskell.

The following (trivial) example shows how an exception that is raised in a function is handled by the calling box. Since each Hume process instantiates one box, the exception handler is fixed at the start of each process and can therefore be called directly. A static analysis is used to ensure that all exceptions that could be raised are handled by each box.

```
exception Div0 :: string 10

f n = if n == 0 then raise Div0 "f" else (n / 0) as string 10;

box example in  (c :: char) out (v :: string 29) handles Div0
unfair n  -> f n
handle Div0 x -> "Divide by zero in: " ++ x;
```

4.2 Timing

Hume uses a hybrid static/dynamic approach to modelling time. Expressions and boxes are costed statically using the defined time analysis. Since this may be inadequate to ensure the required timing properties, dynamic time requirements can be introduced at the expression or at the coordination level. Inside expressions, the `within` construct is used to limit the time that can be taken by an expression. Where an expression would exceed this time, a `timeout` exception is raised. A fixed time exception result is then used instead. In this way we can provide a hard guarantee on execution time. At the coordination level, timeouts can be specified on both input and output wires, and on devices. Such timeouts are also handled through the exception handler mechanism at the box level. This allows hard real-time timing constraints to be expressed, such as a requirement to read a given input within a stated time of it being produced.

```
box b   in ( v :: int 32 ) out ( v' :: int 32 )
unfair x -> complex_fn x within 20ns
handle Timeout -> 0;
```

4.3 Device Declarations

Five kinds of device are supported: buffered streams (files), unbuffered fifo streams, ports, memory-mapped devices, and interrupts. Each device has a directionality (which can only be input for interrupts), an operating system designator, and an optional time specification. The latter can be used to enable periodic scheduling or to ensure that critical events are not missed. Devices may be wired to box inputs or outputs using normal wiring declarations. For example, an operation that reads a mouse periodically, returning true if the mouse button is down could be specified as:

```
exception Timeout_mouseport;
port mouseport from "/dev/mouse" within 1ms raising Timeout_mouseport;

box readmouse in ( mousein :: bool ) out ( clicked :: bool )
unfair m -> m;
handle Timeout_mouseport -> false;

wire mouseport to readmouse.mousein;
wire readmouse.clicked to mouseuser.mouse;
```

5 Modelling Space Costs

A major goal of the Hume project is to provide good cost models for Hume programs. We have defined a simple space cost model for FSM-Hume that predicts upper bound stack and space usage with respect to the prototype Hume Abstract Machine (pHAM) [14]. The stack and heap requirements for the boxes and wires represent the only dynamically variable memory requirements: all other memory costs can be fixed at compile-time based on the number of wires, boxes, functions and the sizes of static strings. In the absence of recursion, we can provide precise static memory bounds on rule evaluation. Predicting the stack and heap requirements for an FSM-Hume program thus provides complete static information about system memory requirements.

$$
\begin{array}{c}
\text{(1)} \quad \dfrac{E \vdash^{space} exp \Rightarrow Cost, Cost}{E \vdash^{space} n \Rightarrow \mathcal{H}_{int32}, 1}
\end{array}
$$

...

$$
\text{(2)} \quad \dfrac{E\,(var) = \langle h, s \rangle \qquad \forall i.\ 1 \leq i \leq n,\ E \vdash^{space} exp_i \Rightarrow h_i, s_i}{E \vdash^{space} var\ exp_1\ \ldots\ exp_n \Rightarrow \sum_{i=1}^{n} h_i + h,\ \underset{i=1}{\overset{n}{max}}\ (s_i + (i-1)) + s}
$$

$$
\text{(3)} \quad \dfrac{\forall i.\ 1 \leq i \leq n,\ E \vdash^{space} exp_i \Rightarrow h_i, s_i}{E \vdash^{space} con\ exp_1\ \ldots\ exp_n \Rightarrow \sum_{i=1}^{n} h_i + n + \mathcal{H}_{con},\ \underset{i=1}{\overset{n}{max}}\ (s_i + (i-1))}
$$

$$
\text{(4)} \quad \dfrac{E \vdash^{space} exp_1 \Rightarrow h_1, s_1 \quad E \vdash^{space} exp_2 \Rightarrow h_2, s_2 \quad E \vdash^{space} exp_3 \Rightarrow h_3, s_3}{E \vdash^{space} \textbf{if}\ exp_1\ \textbf{then}\ exp_2\ \textbf{else}\ exp_3 \Rightarrow h_1 + max(h_2, h_3),\ max(s_1, s_2, s_3)}
$$

$$
\text{(5)} \quad \dfrac{E \vdash^{decl} decls \Rightarrow h_d, s_d, s'_d, E' \qquad E' \vdash^{space} exp \Rightarrow h_e, s_e}{E \vdash^{space} \textbf{let}\ decls\ \textbf{in}\ exp \Rightarrow h_d + h_e,\ max(s_d, s'_d + s_e)}
$$

Fig. 5. Space cost axioms for expressions

5.1 Space Cost Rules

Figure 5 gives cost rules for a representative subset of FSM-Hume expressions, based on an operational interpretation of the pHAM implementation. Heap and stack costs are each integer values of type Cost, labelled h and s, respectively. Each rule produces a pair of such values representing an independent upper bound on the stack and heap usage. The result is produced in the context of an environment, E, that maps function names to the space (heap and stack) requirements associated with executing the body of the function. This environment is derived from the top-level program declarations plus standard prelude definitions. Rules for building the environment are omitted here, except for local declarations, but can be trivially constructed.

The heap cost of a standard integer is given by $\mathcal{H}_{int32}$ (rule 1), with other scalar values costed similarly. The cost of a function application is the cost of evaluating the body of the function plus the cost of each argument (rule 2). Each evaluated argument is pushed on the stack before the function is applied, and this must be taken into account when calculating the maximum stack usage. The cost of building a new data constructor value such as a user-defined constructed type (rule 3) is similar to a function application, except that pointers to the arguments

box	predicted heap	actual heap	excess	predicted stack	actual stack	excess
airflow	16	16	0	10	10	0
carbonmonoxide	16	16	0	10	10	0
environ	37	35	2	27	26	1
logger	144	104	40	25	25	0
methane	16	16	0	10	10	0
operator	38	29	9	23	23	0
pump	51	42	9	21	18	3
supervisor	29	29	0	20	20	0
water	54	54	0	20	20	0
(wires)	96	84	8	0	0	0
TOTAL	483	425	68	166	162	4

Fig. 6. Heap and stack usage in words for boxes in the mine drainage control system

must be stored in the newly created closure (one word per argument), and fixed costs $\mathcal{H}_{con}$ are added to represent the costs of tag and size fields. The heap usage of a conditional (rule 4) is the heap required by the condition part plus the maximum heap used by either branch. The maximum stack requirement is simply the maximum required by the condition and either branch. Case expressions (omitted) are costed analogously. The cost of a let-expression (rule 5) is the space required to evaluate the value definitions (including the stack required to store the result of each new value definition) plus the cost of the enclosed expression. The local declarations are used to derive a quadruple comprising total heap usage, maximum stack required to evaluate any value definition, a count of the value definitions in the declaration sequence (used to calculate the size of the stack frame for the local declaratons), and an environment mapping function names to heap and stack usage. The body of the let-expression is costed in the context of this extended environment.

6 The Mine Drainage Control System

In order to illustrate cost modelling and the use of real-time features in Hume, we will use a simple control application with strong real-time requirements, a simplified pump control system, which is to be used to drain water from a mine shaft. This application has previously been studied in the context of a number of other languages, including Ada with real-time extensions [8]. It was originally constructed as a realistic exemplar for control applications and comprises 750 lines of Ada or about 250 lines of (FSM-)Hume, of which the functional core is about 100 lines. We have also constructed a Java version.

6.1 Space Analysis of the Mine Drainage Example

The cost rules specified in Section 5 have been extended to cover all of FSM-Hume [14] and implemented as a 200-line Haskell [22] module which is integrated into the pHAM compiler. Figure 6 reports predicted and actual maximum stack and heap usage for each box for 12,000,000 iterations of the box scheduler under the prototype Hume Abstract Machine Interpreter.

The results in Figure 6 show completely accurate cost predictions for the majority of boxes, with more serious variations for the heap usage of the *logger*, *operator* and *pump* boxes. All three boxes are relatively complex with many alternative choices (for which the worst case must be assumed even if it is not used). These boxes are asynchronous and may therefore become active when only a few inputs are available: hence, for correctness it is necessary to reserve space for the unavailable inputs, since they could be present in other dynamic contexts. Finally, the *logger* function makes extensive use of string append. Since the size of the result varies dynamically in some cases and a conservative estimate has been used, the heap usage consequently has been overestimated slightly. Overall, the space requirements of the boxes have been overestimated by 72 words or 11% of the total actual dynamic requirement. Since precise analysis is, in general, undecidable, we conclude that this represents a good static estimate of dynamic space usage.

In order to verify that the pHAM can yield constant space requirements in practice, the pump application has been run continuously on a 1GHz Pentium III processor under RTLinux, kernel version 2.4.4. RTLinux [4] is a realtime microkernel operating system, which supports multiple realtime threads and runs a modified Linux system as a separate non-realtime thread. Realtime threads communicate with non-realtime Unix tasks using realtime FIFOs which appear as normal Unix devices, and which are the only I/O mechanism available to realtime threads other than direct memory-mapped I/O. The system guarantees a $15\mu s$ worst-case thread context-switch time for realtime threads.

Our measurements show that the total memory requirements of the pump application amount to less than 62KB. These include heap and stack overheads as calculated here, *RTLinux operating system code and data*, Hume runtime system code and data, and the abstract machine instructions. RTLinux itself accounts for 34.4KB of this total. Since little use is made of RTLinux facilities, and there is scope for reducing the sizes of the prototype abstract machine runtime code, abstract machine instructions, and data representation, we conclude that it should be possible to construct full Hume applications requiring much less than 32Kbytes of memory, including runtime system support, for bare hardware as found in typical embedded systems. The total dynamic memory usage for the pump application amounts to approximately 9KB on RTLinux, comprising 2KB for C stack and runtime initialisation, 4KB for process data structures (including runtime statistics monitoring accounting for about 2KB of this figure), and 3KB for application stack and heap space as costed above.

6.2 Timing Behaviour under RTLinux

In order to confirm that our system can also meet real-time requirements, we have run the mine drainage control system continuously for a period of about 6 minutes under RTLinux on the same 1GHz Pentium III processor (effectively locking out all Linux processes during this period). At this point, the simula-

	complete program		pump process	
	(loc)	(object code – bytes)	(loc)	(object code – bytes)
Ada	?	?	206	12045
Java	867	18136	234	7360
Hume	251	7991	51	2003

Fig. 7. Source and object code sizes for the mine drainage control system (Linux)

tion has run to completion. Clock timings have been taken using the RTLinux system clock, which is accurate to the nanosecond level. The primary real-time constraint on the mine drainage control system is that the methane alarm request generated by the `environ` box is serviced within 3ms. In fact, we have measured this delay to be approx. 150μs (20 times faster than required). Moreover, over the 6 minute time period, the *maximum delay* in servicing *any* wire is approximately 2.2ms (for the simulated operator input, which is often locked out by more important and therefore higher priority inputs). The maximum delay on any other wire is less than 1.1ms (`environ.meth_reply` in the `pump` box). Clearly, it is necessary to adjust for the lower speed processors found in typical embedded systems, but these figures demonstrate that it is possible to meet hard real-time constraints *in practice* using the Hume abstract machine implementation given suitable hardware. Moreover, in order to improve confidence in its correctness, the implementation deliberately follows the formal translation rules precisely, without optimisation. We estimate that a factor of 2-3 performance improvement can be gained through bytecode optimisations, for example, and that significantly better performance can be achieved using threaded interpretation.

6.3 Comparison with Ada and Java Implementations

The Ada implementation is unfortunately restricted to the pump process, and we have therefore been unable to execute it or to provide code size comparisons with the complete Hume application. In order to provide a good basis for comparison, we have therefore constructed a Java implementation for the full system. We have used the Hume implementation to guide the Java design including the correct use of threads, but have used normal Java features including iterative loop constructs, assignment etc. as would be expected. This should not fundamentally change the language basis of comparison [7] but allows us to conduct a direct comparison of the quality of the Hume bytecode against that of the equivalent Java. The advantage of a bytecode representation over machine code is compactness, an attractive property for embedded systems. The disadvantage is that there is usually a high performance cost.

Figure 7 shows source and object code sizes for the three languages. We used the `gnat` Ada compiler, and Sun's `javac` Java compiler on Linux, choosing options to minimise object code size. The Hume bytecode compiler is a small refinement of the RTLinux version, and the code size is therefore smaller than reported earlier (8KB versus 20KB). The Hume program is both considerably shorter, and produces smaller object code than either the Java or Ada programs.

This reflects the use of high-level concurrency features in Hume, and the higher-level (and thus more compact) bytecode format.

It might be expected that use of a lower-level abstract machine code as in the JVM would yield performance advantages over the higher-level code used in the pHAM. However, we have found that the performance of the pHAM is consistently 9-12 times that of the standard JVM on various testbeds, including simple tests such as loop iteration. This is exacerbated by conventional embedded implementations of Java such as Sun's KVM, whose performance is only 30%-80% that of the standard machine [24]. Partial explanations for this difference are that fewer abstract machine instructions are executed by the pHAM, there is no runtime type checking in Hume, the JVM performs dynamic consistency checking, garbage collection is trivial in the pHAM, and that Java uses dynamic method dispatch rather than static function call. The conventional answer to performance problems in Java is to use more sophisticated compilation techniques such as just-in-time compilation. However, such techniques also carry a fixed runtime space penalty, which may render them unsuitable for use in embedded systems. For example, Shaylor has implemented a small-footprint just-in-time compiler based on the KVM [25], which speeds execution by a factor of 5.7-10.7 over the KVM. This is still rather slower than the interpreted pHAM implementation. Moreover, the code footprint for this RTS is 60K bytes on the ARM, compared with less than 30K bytes for the pHAM on RTLinux. We conclude that the basic implementation of the pHAM is highly competitive with current Java virtual machine implementations for embedded systems.

7 Related Work

Accurate time and space cost-modelling is an area of known difficulty for functional language designs [23]. Hume is thus, as far as we are aware, unique both in being a practical language based on strong automatic cost models, and in being specifically designed to allow straightforward space- and time-bounded implementation for hard real-time systems, those systems where tight real-time guarantees must be met. A number of functional languages have, however, looked at *soft* real-time issues [3, 29, 30], there has been work on using functional notations for hardware design (essentially at the HW-Hume level) [15, 9, 21], and there has been much recent theoretical interest both in the problems associated with costing functional languages [23, 17, 10, 27] and in bounding space/time usage [18, 26, 16, 30], including work on statically predicting heap and stack memory usage [28]. There is, however, a considerable gap between this work and current implementation practice as exemplified by e.g. the Glasgow Haskell Compiler (GHC) or Standard ML of New Jersey, where space and heap consumption is often measured in tens of Mbytes (compared with less than ten Kbytes for the pHAM), and no strong attempt is made to bound resource usage.

In a wider framework, two extreme approaches to real-time language design are exemplified by SPARK Ada [5] and the real-time specification for Java (RTSJ) [6]. The former epitomises the idea of language design by elimination of unwanted behaviour from a general-purpose language, including concurrency.

The remaining behaviour is guaranteed by strong formal models. In contrast, the latter provides specialised runtime and library support for real-time systems work, but makes no absolute performance guarantees. Thus, SPARK Ada provides a minimal, highly controlled environment for real-time programming emphasising *correctness by construction* [1], whilst Real-Time Java provides a much more expressible, but less controlled environment, without formal guarantees. Our objective with the Hume design is to maintain correctness whilst providing high levels of expressibility.

8 Conclusions and Further Work

This paper has introduced the novel Hume language, a concurrent functional language aimed at resource-limited systems such as the real-time embedded systems domain. We achieve the combination of a high level of programming abstraction with strong properties included bounded time and space behaviour through synthesising recent advances in theoretical computer science into a coherent pragmatic framework. Our empirical results suggest that hard real-time functional programming may be highly practical, provided that good design and implementation practice is adopted. We are in the process of extending our cost models to cover higher-order polymorphic functions and primitive recursion (i.e. HO-Hume and PR-Hume). Once complete, these cost models will be adapted to also cover concrete time costs for specific architectures.

Hume incorporates high-level metaprogramming features as an essential part of the design. Box templates and wiring macros have proved to be good abstraction mechanisms for dealing with larger or more complex applications such as Roscoe's model of a simple rail network. Our metaprogramming constructs allow the encapsulation of repetitive wiring and box definitions, provide "polymorphism" at the box level, and allow abstraction over manifest constants defining the structure of the process network etc. We are now investigating structured forms of template (a "box calculus") to capture higher levels of process and wiring abstraction. This will allow us to capture common patterns of box composition, permitting the construction of *libraries* of box constructors etc.

References

1. P. Amey, "Correctness by Construction: Better can also be Cheaper", *CrossTalk: the Journal of Defense Software Engineering*, March 2002, pp. 24–28.
2. K.R. Apt and E.-R. Olderog, *Verification of Sequential and Concurrent Programs*, 2nd Edition, Springer Verlag, 1997.
3. J. Armstrong, S.R. Virding, and M.C. Williams, *Concurrent Programming in Erlang*, Prentice-Hall, 1993.
4. M. Barabanov, *A Linux-based Real-Time Operating System*, M.S. Thesis, Dept. of Comp. Sci., New Mexico Institute of Mining and Technology, June 97.
5. J. Barnes, *High Integrity Ada: the Spark Approach*, Addison-Wesley, 1997.
6. G. Bollela et al. *The Real-Time Specification for Java*, Addison-Wesley, 2000.

7. B. Brosgol and B. Dobbing, "Real-Time Convergence of Ada and Java", *Proc. ACM SIGAda Annual Intl. Conf.*, Bloomington MN, Sept-Oct 2001, pp. 11–26.
8. A. Burns and A. Wellings, *Real-Time Systems and Programming Languages* (Third Edition), Addison Wesley Longman, 2001, Chapter 17, pp. 653–684.
9. K. Claessen and M. Sheeran, "A Tutorial on Lava: a Hardware Description and Verification System", Tech. Rept., Chalmers Univ. of Tech., Sweden, Aug. 2000.
10. R. Burstall, "Inductively Defined Functions in Functional Programming Languages", Dept. of Comp. Sci., Univ. of Edinburgh, ECS-LFCS-87-25, April, 1987.
11. K. Hammond, "Hume: a Bounded Time Concurrent Language", *Proc. IEEE Conf. on Electronics and Control Systems (ICECS '2K)*, Kaslik, Lebanon, Dec. 2000, pp. 407–411.
12. K. Hammond, "The Dynamic Properties of Hume: a Functionally-Based Concurrent Language with Bounded Time and Space Behaviour", *Proc. Impl. of Funct. Langs. (IFL 2000)*, Springer-Verlag LNCS 2011, pp. 122-139, 2001.
13. K. Hammond and G.J. Michaelson "The Mine Drainage Control System in Hume", http://www.hume-lang.org/examples/pump, January 2003.
14. K. Hammond and G.J. Michaelson "Predictable Space Behaviour in FSM-Hume", To appear in *Proc. 2002 Intl. Workshop on Impl. Functional Langs. (IFL '02)*, Madrid, Spain, Springer-Verlag LNCS 2670, 2003.
15. J. Hawkins and A. Abdallah "An Overview of Systematic Development of Parallel Systems for Reconfigurable Hardware", *Proc. EuroPar 2002*, Paderborn, Germany, Springer-Verlag LNCS 2400, 2002, pp. 615–619.
16. M. Hofmann, "A Type System for Bounded Space and Functional In-Place Update", *Proc. European Symposium on Programming — (ESOP 2000)*, Springer-Verlag LNCS, 2000.
17. R.J.M. Hughes, L. Pareto, and A. Sabry. "Proving the Correctness of Reactive Systems Using Sized Types", *Proc. POPL'96 — ACM Symp. on Principles of Programming Languages*, St. Petersburg Beach, FL, Jan. 1996.
18. R.J.M. Hughes and L. Pareto, "Recursion and Dynamic Data Structures in Bounded Space: Towards Embedded ML Programming", *Proc. 1999 ACM Intl. Conf. on Functional Programming (ICFP '99)*, Paris, France, pp. 70–81, 1999.
19. T. Lindholm and F. Yellin, *The Java Virtual Machine Specification*, Second Edition, Addison-Wesley, April 1999.
20. J. McDermid, "Engineering Safety-Critical Systems", I. Wand and R. Milner(eds), *Computing Tomorrow: Future Research Directions in Computer Science*, Cambridge University Press, 1996, pp. 217–245.
21. J.L. Matthews, J. Launchbury and B. Cook, "Microprocessor Specification in Hawk", *Proc. Intl. Conf. on Computer Science*, Chicago, 1998.
22. S.L. Peyton Jones (ed.), L. Augustsson, B. Boutel, F.W. Burton, J.H. Fasel, A.D. Gordon, K. Hammond, R.J.M. Hughes, P. Hudak, T. Johnsson, M.P. Jones, J.C. Peterson, A. Reid, and P.L. Wadler, *Report on the Non-Strict Functional Language, Haskell (Haskell98)* Yale University, 1999.
23. A.J. Rebón Portillo, K. Hammond, H.-W. Loidl and P. Vasconcelos, "Automatic Size and Time Inference", To appear in *Proc. Intl. Workshop on Impl. of Functional Langs. (IFL 2002)*, Madrid, Spain, Sept. 2002, Springer-Verlag LNCS 2670, 2003.
24. T. Sayeed, N. Shaylor and A. Taivalsaari, "Connected, Limited Device Configuration (CLDC) for the J2ME Platform and the K Virtual Machine (KVM)", *Proc. JavaOne – Sun's Worldwide 2000 Java Developers Conf.*, San Francisco, June 2000.
25. N. Shaylor, "A Just-In-Time Compiler for Memory Constrained Low-Power Devices", *Proc. 2nd Usenix Symposium on Java Virtual Machine Research and Technlog (JVM '02)*, San Francisco, August 2002.

26. M. Tofte and J.-P. Talpin, "Region-based Memory Management", *Information and Control*, **132**(2), 1997, pp. 109–176.
27. D.A. Turner, "Elementary Strong Functional Programming", *Proc. Symp. on Funct. Prog. Langs. in Education*, Springer-Verlag LNCS No. 1022, Dec. 1995.
28. L. Unnikrishnan, S.D. Stoller and Y.A. Liu, "Automatic Accurate Stack Sapce and Heap-Space Analysis for High-Level Languages", *Technical Report TR-538*, Dept. of Comp. Sci., Indiana University, 2000.
29. M. Wallace and C. Runciman, "Extending a Functional Programming System for Embedded Applications", *Software: Practice & Experience*, **25**(1), January 1995.
30. Z. Wan, W. Taha and P. Hudak, "Real-Time FRP", *Proc. Intl Conf. on Funct. Prog. — ICFP '01*, Firenze, Italy, 2001.

Implementing Multi-stage Languages Using ASTs, Gensym, and Reflection*

Cristiano Calcagno[1], Walid Taha[2], Liwen Huang[3], and Xavier Leroy[4]

[1] Imperial College London, UK
ccris@doc.ic.ac.uk
[2] Rice University, Houston, TX, USA
taha@cs.rice.edu
[3] Yale University, New Haven, CT, USA
liwen.huang@yale.edu
[4] INRIA, Roquencourt, France
Xavier.Leroy@inria.fr

Abstract. The paper addresses theoretical and practical aspects of implementing multi-stage languages using abstract syntax trees (ASTs), gensym, and reflection. We present an operational account of the correctness of this approach, and report on our experience with a bytecode compiler called MetaOCaml that is based on this strategy. Current performance measurements reveal interesting characteristics of the underlying OCaml compiler, and illustrate why this strategy can be particularly useful for implementing domain-specific languages in a typed, functional setting.

1 Introduction

Program generation, partial evaluation (PE) [22], dynamic compilation, and runtime code generation (RTCG) [24] are all techniques to facilitate writing generic programs without unnecessary runtime overheads. These systems have proven effective in challenging domains including high-performance operating systems [36, 9, 8]. Multi-stage languages have been developed as a uniform, high-level, and semantically-based view of these diverse techniques. These languages provide three simple annotations to allow the programmer to distribute a computation into distinct stages [46, 40, 48].

1.1 Multi-stage Basics

Multi-stage programming languages provide a small set of constructs for the construction, combination, and execution of delayed computations. Program-

---
* Funded by NSF ITR-0113569.

ming in a multi-stage language such as MetaOCaml [29] can be illustrated with
the following classic example[1]:

```
let even n = (n mod 2) = 0
let square x = x * x
let rec power n x = (* int -> .<int>. -> .<int>. *)
  if n=0 then .<1>.
    else if even n
         then .<square .~(power (n/2) x)>.
         else .<.~x * .~(power (n-1) x)>.
let power72 =                          (* int -> int *)
  .! .<fun x -> .~(power 72 .<x>.)>.
```

Ignoring the type constructor .<t>. and the three staging annotations brackets
.<e>., escapes .~e and run .!, the above code is a standard definition of a function that computes x^n, which is then used to define the specialized function x^{72}.
Without staging, the last step just produces a closure that invokes the power
function every time it gets a value for x. The effect of staging is best understood
by starting at the end of the example. Whereas a term fun x -> e x is a value,
an annotated term .<fun x -> .~(e .<x>.)>. is not. Brackets indicate that
we are constructing a future stage computation, and an escape indicates that we
must perform an immediate computation *while* building the bracketed computation. The application e .<x>. has to be performed even though x is still an
uninstantiated *symbol*. In the power example, power 72 .<x>. is performed immediately, once and for all, and not repeated every time we have a new value for
x. In the body of the definition of the power function, the recursive applications
of power are also escaped to make sure that they are performed immediately.
The run .! on the last line invokes the compiler on the generated code fragment,
and incorporates the result of compilation into the runtime system.

1.2 Problem

Filinski [15, 14] presented a denotational account of the correctness of using abstract syntax trees (ASTs) and gensym to implement two-level languages. We are
currently developing a multi-stage extension of OCaml [26] called MetaOCaml
[29]. This setting requires previous results to be extended to include:

1. allowing multiple levels instead of two
2. allowing cross-stage persistence
3. allowing the execution of dynamically generated code (from within the language)

Without such a generalization we cannot be confident that results established
with respect to the substitution semantics of multi-stage languages (most notably

---

[1] Dots are used around brackets and escapes to disambiguate the syntax in the implementation. They are dropped when we talk about the underlying calculus rather
than the implementation.

type safety [12, 40, 42, 43, 32, 45]) are relevant to an implementation that employs this strategy.

Compared to two-level languages, multi-stage languages are generalized to multiple levels. More significantly, multi-stage languages allow computations in any stage to refer to values from previous stages, and provide a facility for executing future-stage computations. Unfortunately, denotational models are currently available only for restricted versions of multi-stage languages [3, 15, 14, 30, 31][2].

1.3 Contributions

This paper presents an operational account of the correctness of implementing multi-stage languages using ASTs, gensym, and reflection. The key technical challenge in achieving this result lies in devising an appropriate notion of "decompilation" to relate the semantics of both the source (surface) and target (implementation) languages. This notion allows us to formally state that evaluating a multi-stage program can be achieved by translating it into a mostly standard single-stage language, evaluating that program, and then decompiling the result. The single-stage language is somewhat non-standard because it supports an eval-like construct (modeling runtime compilation and execution of code) that itself refers to the compilation strategy that we have set out to verify.

The correctness result shows that with the implementation strategy presented here any free variables contained in dynamically executed code are handled in a manner consistent with the substitution semantics for multi-stage languages. The result also justifies various subtle choices in the translation, such as why runtime calls to the compiler are passed the empty environment, and exactly when freshly generated names can be safely viewed as variables. By separating the correspondence between variables and names from the other concerns we were able to easily formalize and prove correctness of execution of open code.

Although the formal development is carried out with a minimal calculus, the strategy has been used to implement a multi-stage extension of the OCaml language (called MetaOCaml). The paper reports on our experience so far with this implementation. Current findings indicate that gains from staging can be less in some typed functional settings than when partially evaluating other programming languages such as C. At the same time, significant gains (in the typed functional setting) are possible when the implementation strategy studied here is used in conjunction with runtime source-to-source transformations such as tag elimination.

1.4 Organization of This Paper

Section 2 introduces the syntax and semantics of a multi-stage calculus. Section 3 defines a minimal single-stage language with minimal support for ASTs, a

---
[2] Reflective towers often come with a denotational model [37, 38, 10, 27]. But a reflective tower is a sequence of one language interpreting the next, and are quite different from multi-stage languages in terms of formal meta-theory. Specifically, core issues of interest to this paper, such as evaluation under lambda, have not been addressed in studies on reflective towers.

$$\frac{}{\alpha \stackrel{n}{\hookrightarrow} \alpha} \qquad \frac{}{\lambda x.e \stackrel{0}{\hookrightarrow} \lambda x.e} \qquad \frac{e_1 \stackrel{0}{\hookrightarrow} \lambda x.e \quad e_2 \stackrel{0}{\hookrightarrow} v_1 \quad e[x := v_1] \stackrel{0}{\hookrightarrow} v_2}{e_1\,e_2 \stackrel{0}{\hookrightarrow} v_2}$$

$$\frac{e \stackrel{0}{\hookrightarrow} \langle v_1 \rangle \quad v_1 \stackrel{0}{\hookrightarrow} v_2}{!\,e \stackrel{0}{\hookrightarrow} v_2} \qquad \frac{}{x \stackrel{n+1}{\hookrightarrow} x} \qquad \frac{e \stackrel{n+1}{\hookrightarrow} v}{\lambda x.e \stackrel{n+1}{\hookrightarrow} \lambda x.v}$$

$$\frac{e_1 \stackrel{n+1}{\hookrightarrow} v_1 \quad e_2 \stackrel{n+1}{\hookrightarrow} v_2}{e_1\,e_2 \stackrel{n+1}{\hookrightarrow} v_1\,v_2} \quad \frac{e \stackrel{n+1}{\hookrightarrow} v}{\langle e \rangle \stackrel{n}{\hookrightarrow} \langle v \rangle} \quad \frac{e \stackrel{0}{\hookrightarrow} \langle v \rangle}{\tilde{\ } e \stackrel{1}{\hookrightarrow} v} \quad \frac{e \stackrel{n+1}{\hookrightarrow} v}{\tilde{\ } e \stackrel{n+2}{\hookrightarrow} \tilde{\ } v} \quad \frac{e \stackrel{n+1}{\hookrightarrow} v}{!\,e \stackrel{n+1}{\hookrightarrow}\, !\,v}$$

Fig. 1. Big-Step Semantics for CBV λ-U

weak gensym operation, and reflection. Section 4 presents the translation from the multi-stage language to the minimal single stage language, as well as the de-compilation strategy. Section 5 develops the correctness result for the translation. Section 6 discusses practical aspects of using this strategy to implement a multi-stage extension of the OCaml language, and reports on our experience with this effort. Section 7 reviews related work, and Section 8 concludes.

2 A Multi-stage Source Language

The formal development is based on a variant of the λ-U calculus [40, 42] as the source language. The syntax for this variant is as follows:

$$e \in E ::= \alpha \mid x \mid e\,e \mid \lambda x.e \mid \langle e \rangle \mid \tilde{\ } e \mid !\,e$$

Terms $e \in E$ are built using two disjoint sets: variables $x, y \in \mathcal{V}$ and constants $\alpha \in \mathcal{A}$. The constants α are an addition to the standard λ-U. They are included because they make defining a de-compilation function convenient. In the target language, these constants will be used to represent dynamically generated names. We write $FV(e)$ for the set of variables occurring free in e, and $FA(e)$ for the set of names occurring in e.

To ensure that we work only with terms where there is a sensible correspondence between escapes and brackets, the development does not refer directly to the set E, but rather, to the following families of expressions E^n and values V^n:

$$\begin{aligned}
e^0 &\in E^0 &&::= \alpha \mid x \mid \lambda x.e^0 \mid e^0\,e^0 \mid \langle e^1 \rangle \mid !\,e^0 \\
e^{n+1} &\in E^{n+1} &&::= \alpha \mid x \mid \lambda x.e^{n+1} \mid e^{n+1}\,e^{n+1} \mid \langle e^{n+2} \rangle \mid \tilde{\ } e^n \mid !\,e^{n+1} \\
v^0 &\in V^0 &&::= \alpha \mid \lambda x.e^0 \mid \langle v^1 \rangle \\
v^{n+1} &\in V^{n+1} &&= E^n
\end{aligned}$$

The call-by-value big-step semantics for the language is presented in Figure 1.

Lemma 1. $e \in E^n$ and $e \stackrel{n}{\hookrightarrow} v$ implies $v \in V^n$.

$$A, \lambda x.e' \hookrightarrow \lambda x.e' \qquad \dfrac{A, e'_1 \hookrightarrow \lambda x.e' \quad A, e'_2 \hookrightarrow v'_1 \quad A, e'[x := v'_1] \hookrightarrow v'_2}{A, e'_1\, e'_2 \hookrightarrow v'_2}$$

$$\dfrac{}{A, \alpha \hookrightarrow \alpha} \qquad \dfrac{\alpha \notin A \quad A\alpha, e'[x := \alpha] \hookrightarrow v'}{A, \text{let } x = \text{gensym}\,()\text{ in Lam}\,(x, e') \hookrightarrow \text{Lam}\,(\alpha, v')} \qquad \dfrac{A, e' \hookrightarrow v'}{A, c\,e' \hookrightarrow c\,v'}$$

$$\dfrac{A, e'_1 \hookrightarrow v'_1 \quad A, e'_2 \hookrightarrow v'_2}{A, c\,(e'_1, e'_2) \hookrightarrow c\,(v'_1, v'_2)} \qquad \dfrac{A, e' \hookrightarrow c\,v'}{A, \text{unc}\,e' \hookrightarrow v'} \qquad \dfrac{A, e' \hookrightarrow \text{Mrk}\,v'_1 \quad A, \left[\!\left[|v'_1|^1_\emptyset\right]\!\right]^0_\emptyset \hookrightarrow v'_2}{A, \text{mor}\,e' \hookrightarrow v'_2}$$

Fig. 2. Semantics of target language

3 A Single-Stage Target Language

The target language has the following syntax:

$$e' \in E' ::= \alpha \mid x \mid \lambda x.e' \mid e'e' \mid \text{let } x = \text{gensym}()\text{ in Lam}\,(x, e')$$
$$\mid c\,e' \mid c\,(e', e') \mid \text{unc}\,e' \mid \text{mor}\,e'$$

It contains lambda terms, names α, a gensym construct, unary and binary AST constructors, de-constructors and a run construct. A term $c\,e'$ is an application of a value constructor (or attachment of a "union type" tag) c to the result of the expression e'. The essential feature of a de-constructor is that $\text{unc}(c\,e)$ evaluates to the result of e. For example, if Mrk is a constructor then unMrk is the corresponding de-constructor. The MetaOCaml Run (mor) construct represents the action of the overall implementation of MetaOCaml on a program.

Staging constructs are translated into operations on ASTs. The constructors are as follows:

$$c \in C ::= \text{Var} \mid \text{Lam} \mid \text{App} \mid \text{Brk} \mid \text{Esc} \mid \text{Run} \mid \text{Csp} \mid \text{Mrk}$$

Intuitively, the constructors will mimic an ML datatype:

```
type exp = Var of const | App of exp * exp | Lam of const * exp | Brk of exp
         | Esc of exp | Run of exp | Csp of exp | Mrk of exp
```

where each variant (respectively) represents a production in the syntax E of the *source* language. The first three are for standard lambda terms. Note that the value carried by the Var and the first value carried by Lam construct will be a constant α representing a name. The next three capture the rest of the syntax in the source language. Csp and Mrk are technical devices that do not occur in the source language, but which will be explained in more detail in the next section.

The set of values that can result from evaluation is defined as follows:

$$v' \in V' ::= \lambda x.e' \mid c\,v' \mid c\,(v', v') \mid \alpha$$

The big-step semantics for the target language is presented in Figure 2. The semantics is given by a judgment $A, e' \hookrightarrow v'$ where A is a finite set of names.

$\boxed{[\bullet]_\tau^n : E \to E'}$ $\qquad$ $\boxed{|\bullet|_\tau^n : E' \to E}$

$[x]_{\tau,x^t}^0 = x$ $\qquad$ $|x|_{\tau,x^t}^0 = x$

$[\lambda x.e]_\tau^0 = \lambda x.[e]_{\tau,x^0}^0$ $\qquad$ $|\lambda x.e'|_\tau^0 = \lambda x.|e'|_{\tau,x^0}^0$

$[e_1\ e_2]_\tau^0 = [e_1]_\tau^0\ [e_2]_\tau^0$ $\qquad$ $|e_1'\ e_2'|_\tau^0 = |e_1'|_\tau^0\ |e_2'|_\tau^0$

$[\langle e \rangle]_\tau^0 = \mathsf{Mrk}\ [e]_\tau^1$ $\qquad$ $|\mathsf{Mrk}\ e'|_\tau^0 = \langle\, |e'|_\tau^1\, \rangle$

$[!\,e]_\tau^0 = \mathsf{mor}\ [e]_\tau^0$ $\qquad$ $|\mathsf{mor}\ e'|_\tau^0 = !\ |e'|_\tau^0$

$[\alpha]_\tau^0 = \alpha$ $\qquad$ $|\alpha|_\tau^0 = \alpha$

$[x]_{\tau,x^+}^{n+1} = \mathsf{Var}\ x$ $\qquad$ $|\mathsf{Var}\ x|_{\tau,x^+}^{n+1} = x$

$[x]_{\tau,x^0}^{n+1} = \mathsf{Csp}\ x$ $\qquad$ $|\mathsf{Csp}\ x|_{\tau,x^0}^{n+1} = x$

$\qquad\qquad\qquad\qquad\qquad\qquad$ $|\mathsf{Csp}\ v'|_\tau^{n+1} = |v'|_\tau^0$

$[\lambda x.e]_\tau^{n+1} = \begin{cases} \mathsf{let}\ x = \mathsf{gensym}\ () \\ \mathsf{in}\ \mathsf{Lam}\ (x, [e]_{\tau,x^+}^{n+1}) \end{cases}$ $\qquad$ $\left|\begin{array}{l}\mathsf{let}\ x = \mathsf{gensym}\ () \\ \mathsf{in}\ \mathsf{Lam}\ (x, e')\end{array}\right|_\tau^{n+1} = \lambda x.|e'|_{\tau,x^+}^{n+1}$

$\qquad\qquad\qquad\qquad\qquad\qquad$ $|\mathsf{Lam}\ (\alpha, v')|_\tau^{n+1} = \lambda x.(|v'|_\emptyset^{n+1}\ [\alpha := x])$

$[e_1\ e_2]_\tau^{n+1} = \mathsf{App}\ ([e_1]_\tau^{n+1}, [e_2]_\tau^{n+1})$ $\qquad$ $|\mathsf{App}\ (e_1', e_2')|_\tau^{n+1} = |e_1'|_\tau^{n+1}\ |e_2'|_\tau^{n+1}$

$[\langle e \rangle]_\tau^{n+1} = \mathsf{Brk}\ [e]_\tau^{n+2}$ $\qquad$ $|\mathsf{Brk}\ e'|_\tau^{n+1} = \langle\, |e'|_\tau^{n+2}\, \rangle$

$[\tilde{}\,e]_\tau^1 = \mathsf{unMrk}\ [e]_\tau^0$ $\qquad$ $|\mathsf{unMrk}\ e'|_\tau^1 = \tilde{}\,|e'|_\tau^0$

$[\tilde{}\,e]_\tau^{n+2} = \mathsf{Esc}\ [e]_\tau^{n+1}$ $\qquad$ $|\mathsf{Esc}\ e'|_\tau^{n+2} = \tilde{}\,|e'|_\tau^{n+1}$

$[!\,e]_\tau^{n+1} = \mathsf{Run}\ [e]_\tau^{n+1}$ $\qquad$ $|\mathsf{Run}\ e'|_\tau^{n+1} = !\ |e'|_\tau^{n+1}$

$[\alpha]_\tau^{n+1} = \mathsf{Var}\ \alpha$ $\qquad$ $|\mathsf{Var}\ \alpha|_\tau^{n+1} = \alpha$

Fig. 3. Translation and De-compilation Functions

We have chosen to use a "weak gensym" instead of one where a name-state A is threaded through the semantics. Our semantics of gensym picks a name non-deterministically. It is weak in the sense that it does not restrict the set of names that can be picked as much as the name-state gensym would. It is nevertheless sufficient to prove the correctness result presented here. This choice both simplifies presentation and provides a slightly stronger result.

The special construct mor (short for "MetaOCaml's run") is the operation that is intended to implement the more abstractly-specified construct run. Because defining the semantics of this construct itself depends on the definition of the translation, it is explained in Section 4.

4 Translation from Source to Target

This section presents the definition for both the translation and de-compilation functions. Whereas the translation is used to implement multi-stage languages using a single-stage language, the de-compilation function is purely a mathematical construction used to prove the soundness of the translation.

To define the translation, we need to associate variables to times and instantiate names with variables:

$$\begin{aligned}
\text{Times} & \quad t \in T ::= 0 \mid + \\
\text{Binding times} & \quad \tau \in B ::= \emptyset \mid \tau, x^t \\
\text{Instantiations} & \quad \rho \in R ::= [\alpha_i := x_i]
\end{aligned}$$

Notation 1 *Instantiations are substitutions where any variables or names (be it an "x" or an "α") occurring anywhere in them must be distinct: they form a one-to-one correspondence between variables and names.*

Definition 1. *The application of an instantiation to a source language expression, written $e[\alpha_i := x_i]$ denotes the result of performing the multiple substitutions (without capturing any x_i).*

Note that bound variables are not captured by substitutions and instantiations. However, there are no binders for names, so for instance $\mathsf{Lam}\,(\alpha,x)[x := \alpha] = \mathsf{Lam}\,(\alpha,\alpha)$.

The left hand side of Figure 3 defines the **translation** function $[\bullet]_\tau^n : E \to E'$, where n is a natural number called the *level* of the term, and τ is an environment mapping free variables to binding times. Intuitively, the level of the term will just be the number of surrounding brackets less the number of surrounding escapes. The result of the translation consists mostly of either unchanged programs, operations to build ASTs (using constructors like Var, Lam, etc), or the use of the two functions gensym and mor. At level 0, the translation $[\bullet]_\tau^0$ does essentially nothing but traverse the term. At levels $n+1$, for the most part, the translation takes a term and generates a new term that represents that first one.

There are two cases for variables at level $n+1$, depending on whether the variable was bound at level 0 or any other level. If the variable was bound at level zero, then we construct a marker around it as a cross-stage persistent (CSP) constant, otherwise it is treated as expected. The next interesting case is that of a lambda abstraction, where the essential trick is to use a fresh-name function to generate a new name so as to avoid accidental name capture. Such a function is used in the translation by Gomard and Jones [20] and before that in hygienic macro systems [25, 13]. This trick is used only in the implementation and it is completely invisible to the user. Relieving the programmer from having to explicitly ensure that accidental capture is avoided is an important feature of multi-stage languages, from both the programmer's and the language designer's point of view (c.f. [16] for an example of the latter).

From the practical point of view, an important feature of the translation is that it does not need a substitution function (which is costly) or a complex environment. The key idea is to use the same name for variables that are used in the input in the output. The types of these variables certainly change (in the input the type can vary, but in the output it is always of "identifier"). Care must be taken, however, to make sure that the scoping of these variables in the original program is not accidentally modified (we give an example of this in section 6.1).

For example, if the translation encounters the term $(\lambda x.x)\ (\lambda y.y)$ at level 1, it generates the term

$$\mathsf{App}(\mathsf{let}\ x = \mathsf{gensym}()\ \mathsf{in}\ \mathsf{Lam}(x, \mathsf{Var}\ x), \mathsf{let}\ y = \mathsf{gensym}()\ \mathsf{in}\ \mathsf{Lam}(y, \mathsf{Var}\ y))$$

At level $n+1$ the source-to-source translation roughly generates the AST for an expression which will construct at runtime the AST for the specialized program that will be passed to the runtime compiler and evaluator (mor). For Brackets and Escapes, we always adjust the level parameter. There is no case for Esc at level 0 (such terms are rejected by the expression families). When the translation finds a Bracket, the level is raised by one. Note that at the lowest levels the translation for Brackets generates Mrk and the translation for escape generates unMrk. While it may seem unnecessary to do that, it simplifies the formal treatment of this translation. Without Mrk and unMrk, terms such as $\tilde{}\langle e \rangle$, for example, would have the same translation as e. If this were the case, then the translation would have no functional inverse. Having such a functional inverse (de-compilation) is instrumental for the formal development presented here.

At level 0, Run is replaced by an application of the constant mor. Recall the formal semantics of mor in Figure 2. The de-compilation $|\bullet|^1_\emptyset$ corresponds to passing to the compiler a value representing source code, since the ASTs used in the implementation are those used by the compiler to represent ASTs. However, this de-compilation produces a source language term that contains constructs such as $\langle \bullet \rangle$ and $\tilde{}\bullet$ that the target language does not understand. Thus, it is necessary to apply the very translation that we are presenting here once again: $[\bullet]^0_\emptyset$. It is useful to note that, in the big-step semantics for Run, de-compilation treats the term as a level 1 term, but translation treats it as a level 0 term. This is justified by the fact that, in the source language, $E^n = V^{n+1}$.

The right hand side of Figure 3 defines the **de-compilation** function. For all the forms *produced* by the translation, the de-compilation function simply tries to invert the translation by producing something of the same form as the translation using the de-compilation of the sub-terms. The interesting cases in the de-compilation function are the ones that take as input forms not directly generated by the translation, but which arise during the evaluation of a term produced by the translation. In fact, in what follows we show that the de-compilation function deals with *all* the new forms generated during evaluation in the target. There are only two new forms that arise: one for cross-stage persistent (CSP) variables at level $n+1$, and abstractions at level $n+1$. For CSP variables, we need a more general form which is closed under substitution. Also, we know that these variables are only ever substituted by level 0 values, so, we decompile these values at that level. Level $n+1$ abstractions were the most subtle to deal with and are probably the most interesting case in the de-compilation function. Once the form generated by the translation (let x =gensym()...) is evaluated, it causes all the occurrences of the variable x to be replaced by a fresh name α. This is the only case where instantiation $[\alpha := x]$ is used. Thus, it is only at that point that a dynamically generated name is viewed as a variable name. The fact that the translation of the sub-term in this case is carried out in the empty environment will be essential for the correctness proof. The definition is justified by the observation that the target semantics produces new names but no new free variables during evaluation (and that evaluation begins with a closed term).

Whereas translation is total, de-compilation is partial. The following definition will be convenient for denoting the domain of the de-compilation function:

Definition 2. *We write $\tau \overset{n}{\vdash} e'$ when $|e'|_\tau^n$ is defined.*

Lemma 2 (Basic Properties). $\tau \overset{n}{\vdash} e'$ *implies that*

1. $FV(|e'|_\tau^n) \subseteq dom(\tau)$, *and*
2. $|e'|_\tau^n \in E^n$, *and*
3. $e' \in V'$ *implies* $|e'|_\tau^n \in V^n$.

5 Correctness

The compilation function does not introduce any information loss:

Lemma 3 (Inversion). $e \in E^n$ *and* $FV(e) \subseteq dom(\tau)$ *implies* $e = |[e]_\tau^n|_\tau^n$.

Thus $|e'|_\tau^n$ is surjective, which makes it possible (in the main theorem) to quantify over all n, e', and τ to cover the set of all source programs E.

The above property is the only one that we establish about translation. In the rest of the development, all the work goes into establishing properties of the de-compilation function.

Lemma 4 (Weakening). $\tau \overset{n}{\vdash} e'$ *and* $x \notin \tau$ *implies* $|e'|_\tau^n = |e'|_{\tau, x^t}^n$.

Lemma 5 (Substitution). *There are two distinct cases:*

1. $\tau, x^0 \overset{n}{\vdash} e'$ *and* $\tau \overset{0}{\vdash} v'$ *and* $v' \in V'$ *implies*

$$|e'|_{\tau, x^0}^n \left[x := |v'|_\tau^0\right] = |e'[x := v']|_\tau^n$$

2. $\tau, x^+ \overset{n}{\vdash} e'$ *implies*

$$|e'|_{\tau, x^+}^n [x := \alpha] = |e'[x := \alpha]|_\tau^n$$

Proof. Both cases are by induction on the structure of e'. The most interesting case for part 2 is Lam (α, e'), where there is a possibility of introducing a name capture: this does not happen because de-compilation uses $|e'|_\emptyset^{n+1}$ which implies $FV(e') = \emptyset$ so that substitution has no effect. (This is also why the first part of the lemma holds for Lam .) □

Two examples illustrate why we need two separate cases. First, $|\mathsf{Var}\,(x)|^1_{x+}$ is defined but not $|\mathsf{Var}\,(\lambda y.y)|^1_\emptyset$. Second, $|\mathsf{Lam}\,(\alpha,x)[x := \alpha]|^1_\emptyset$ is defined but $|\mathsf{Lam}\,(\alpha,x)|^1_{x+}$ is not.

The key observation about names is the following:

Lemma 6 (Subject Reduction w.r.t. $FA(|-|^n_\emptyset)$). *For all $\emptyset \overset{n}{\vdash} e'$, whenever $A, e' \hookrightarrow v'$ then $\emptyset \overset{n}{\vdash} v'$ and $FA(|v'|^n_\emptyset) \subseteq FA(|e'|^n_\emptyset)$.*

In particular, names are generated dynamically in the target language, so, we certainly cannot say that the result of evaluation has no more names than the input to evaluation. What we can say, however, is that viewed as source language terms, the result of evaluation contains no more names than the term that evaluation starts of with. Having a formal notion of de-compilation is what allows us to make this statement formally.

Theorem 1 (Main). *For all $\emptyset \overset{n}{\vdash} e'$, whenever $|e'|^n_\emptyset \rho \overset{n}{\hookrightarrow} v$ and $\mathrm{dom}(\rho) \cup FA(|e'|^n_\emptyset) \subseteq A$, there exists v' such that $A, e' \hookrightarrow v'$ and $|v'|^n_\emptyset \rho = v$.*

Proof. By case analysis on e' and n, and by induction on the derivation of $|e'|^n_\emptyset \rho \overset{n}{\hookrightarrow} v$.

From inversion and the main theorem it is easy to see that

Corollary 1 (Simulation). *If $e \in E^n$ and $FV(e) = \emptyset$ and $FA(e) \subseteq A$ and $e \overset{n}{\hookrightarrow} v$, then there exists v' such that $A, [e]^n_\emptyset \hookrightarrow v'$ and $|v'|^n_\emptyset = v$.*

6 Implementation

This section gives a more detailed description of the implementation, reports measurements on performance gains from staging and tag elimination on small example programs, and discusses expectations for performance in the native code compiled setting.

6.1 Overview

The MetaOCaml implementation is currently a modified OCaml bytecode compiler[3]. Minor changes are made to the parser and type-inference/check to accommodate the three staging annotations and a parametric type constructor (to distinguish code values from regular values). Because these changes are very localized and are done by direct analogy with other constructs in the language, error reporting continues to be reliable and accurate (good error reporting is particularly hard in typed functional languages based on Hindley-Milner inference).

---
[3] OCaml also has a native code compiler, and modifying the native code compiler is still work in progress.

The bulk of the work in developing MetaOCaml is in the addition of a source-to-source translation phase right after type-inference/checking. Because we use a functional language with pattern matching to implement the translation, the implementation follows closely the formal definition presented above. The ASTs are the ones used internally by the compiler. In addition to sheer size of the AST datatype for the full language, the implementation is complicated by the fact that OCaml propagates source code file information in each construct, for very accurate error messages. In addition, the type of the AST changes during type-checking (from an AST without explicit typing annotations to a different AST with typing information), raising the need to work with two different representations. Finally, constructing ASTs that represent other ASTs is not only tedious, but type systems of languages like ML (which do not provide the necessary dependent typing structure) do not help in this regard. This problem has been a significant practical challenge for our work.

Binding Constructs. In principle, once we have addressed lambda at levels higher than 1 correctly, we have captured the essence of how all binding constructs should be handled. In practice, some care is still needed when dealing with syntactic sugar for other binding constructs. For example, it is tempting to translate let as follows:

$$[\text{let } x = e_1 \text{ in } e_2]_\tau^{n+1} = \begin{cases} \text{let } x = \text{gensym } () \\ \text{in Let } (x, [e_1]_\tau^{n+1}, [e_2]_{\tau;x \mapsto (n+1)}^{n+1}) \end{cases}$$

Whereas an x in e_1 would have been bound somewhere completely outside this expression, in the new term, we are replacing it every time by a completely new fresh name that is not bound in the scope of e_2. The correct translation is as follows:

$$[\text{let } x = e_1 \text{ in } e_2]_\tau^{n+1} = \begin{cases} \text{let } z = [e_1]_\tau^{n+1} \\ \quad x = \text{gensym } () \\ \text{in Let } (x, z, [e_2]_{\tau;x \mapsto (n+1)}^{n+1}) \end{cases}$$

Datatypes and Exceptions. In OCaml, datatype constructors as well as case-statements are partially interpreted (or "compiled") during the type-checking phase. The reason is that runtime values of datatypes do not contain constructor names, but instead integer tags[4] identifying the constructors, and determined during type-checking by examination of the datatype declaration to which the constructors belong. Thus it would be incorrect to build a code fragment that uses just constructor names. If this is done, and the code is type-checked and executed in the context of another declaration for another datatype that happens to use the same constructor name, the representation of that constructor would be determined in the wrong typing environment (dynamic scoping), and type safety would also be violated. This issue would arise with the program:

---

[4] Note that the use of "tag" here and in "tag elimination" are (again) different. Here a tag is an integer, there a tag is a constructor.

type t = C of int;; let v = ⟨C 7⟩;; type t = C of string;; !v;;

The correct implementation would allow us to execute the last statement safely. To deal with this problem, we interpret all constructors and case-statements when we type-check the source program for the first time (in this case, our implementation is doing a simple kind of staged compilation). In addition, the AST datatype is extended for these two cases with an extra field that tells us if these constructs have been interpreted before or not. The first time they are type-checked, their interpretation is recorded. If they are type-checked again, they are not re-interpreted, but rather, their original interpretation is used directly. This treatment parallels the implementation of CSP which allows us to incorporate pointers to previously compiled (and even executed) values in ASTs.

We expected exceptions to be similar to datatypes. But because there is only one global name space for exceptions, and they are represented at runtime by their names, the treatment of exceptions is in fact simpler than for datatypes: all that needs to be done is to construct a code fragment that carries the name of the exception.

Cross-Stage Persistence (CSP). Cross-stage persistence on ground values is known as lifting [22]. For literals, a simple optimization on the basic scheme is quite desirable, namely, simply producing an AST that would later just compile to that literal. Doing this has two advantages: First, a pointer de-reference is eliminated, making such constants a bit more efficient. Second, it enables further optimizations such as constant propagation and strength reduction, which would otherwise be blocked.

Run. In the implementation, assuming that native-run is the existing compilation routine, mor is defined as:

$$\text{mor p} = \text{native-run env0 } ([p]_\emptyset^0)$$

Where env0 is the empty environment except for pervasive constants. The compiler (composed with a jump to the compiled code) denoted here by native-run corresponds to the evaluation relation $\hookrightarrow$.

6.2 Performance Gains from Staging

One of the key goals behind developing MetaOCaml is to collect concrete data about multi-stage programming. At this point, we have only collected preliminary data on a number of small examples. Larger and more extensive studies are under way. In this section, we present our findings on these small examples. For the most part they are encouraging and are consistent with the experience of other researchers with PE and RTCG systems. The data points to the utility of multi-stage languages for building simple yet efficient DSLs, and also highlights some peculiarities of both the OCaml bytecode setting.

Name	Run	Generate	Compile	Run (2)	Factor	BEP
power	$(7.44s/10^6)$=1x	2.65x	336x	0.18x	5.43	416
dot	$(2.14s/10^5)$=1x	39.4x	3490x	0.80x	1.25	17500
dotU	$(1.68s/10^5)$=1x	49.1x	4360x	0.72x	1.40	15400
eval "fib 15"	$(6.48s/10^3)$=1x	0.00529x	0.348x	0.235x	4.25	1
TE(eval "fib 15")	$(6.48s/10^3)$=1x	0.00338x	0.348x	0.0225x	44.4	1
rewrite	$(6.61s/10^6)$=1x	13.2x	1200x	0.90x	1.11	12100
rewriteCPS	$(7.42s/10^6)$=1x	5.69x	229x	0.08x	13.1	255
chebyshev	$(1.37s/10^4)$=1x	8.03x	1010x	0.32x	3.08	1510
chebyshevU	$(1.37s/10^4)$=1x	8.39x	1050x	0.32x	3.12	1550

Fig. 4. Speedup Factors and Break-even Points (BEPs) with Staging

What Is Measured. Figure 4 tabulates the timings for a set of small benchmarks, and two metrics based on the raw data. The first column, **Run**, contains a pair (t/n) where t is the total time in seconds for n runs of an unstaged version of the program at hand. The number of n is chosen so as to 1) be at least 10, and 2) so that the total time is at least 0.5 seconds[5]. The rest of the timings are for a staged version of the program, but are all normalized with respect to the time of the unstaged program. **Generate** is the time needed to perform the first stage of the staged program, which involves the generation of a code fragment. **Compile** is the time needed to compile that fragment using the .! construct. **Run (2)** is the time needed to run the code that results from compiling that fragment. The next two columns are computed from the first four. **Factor** is the first run time divided by the second run time. This is an indicator of the improvement when generation and compilation times can be amortized. **Break-even point (BEP)** is the number of times the program must be run before the total time of running the staged version (including a one-time generation and compilation cost) would be greater than the time of running the unstaged version. This is an alternative measure of the effectiveness of staging.

6.3 Experiments

We have considered the following programs:

- <u>power</u>: The example described in Section 1. The staged version runs about 5.4 times as fast as the unstaged program. The gain of performance comes from moving the recursion and function calls from runtime to code generation time.
- <u>dot</u>: Dot product turns out to be a poor example for staging, not because of the small performance gains, but rather the very large compilation times.

---

[5] Measurements collected on a P-III 900M machine with 128MB of main memory running Red Hat Linux 6.1 using the MetaOCaml timing function found in the Trx module. The benchmarks instrumented with the measuring functions are part of the distribution in the mex/benchmark1/ directory. The MetaOCaml_302_alpha_002 distribution is used, and is available online [29].

Compilation times are large because the code generated by the first stage is essentially a long sequence of multiplication and addition expressions (linear in the size of the array). This situation does not improve significantly even with RTCG [34].

Nevertheless, this example points out the issue of how many garbage-collected languages deal with arrays, because our gains were slightly lower than those reported in Tempo [34]. In the setting of Tempo, when the array and the index are both known at RTCG time, the computation of the address of the array element can be done entirely, resulting in a constant address being put in the generated code. For garbage-collected languages such as OCaml, arrays are dynamically managed by the garbage collector, which might even relocate them, so it is not possible to treat the array pointer as a constant. It is still possible to exploit the knowledge of the array index and the array size to 1) simplify the address computation, and 2) eliminate the runtime bound check (like Java, OCaml enforces array bounds checking). The OCaml native-code compiler implements some of these optimizations, but the bytecode compiler that MetaOCaml uses does not. Because of the overhead involved in interpreting bytecode, in our setting, the specialization of array accesses does not improve performance significantly. Switching off bounds checking in our experiment does not improve runtimes significantly.

- **eval "fib 15"**: The eval function is an interpreter for a lambda calculus with recursion, arithmetic, and conditionals. It is a particularly good example of staging. This can be seen both by the relatively high speedup, but more importantly, by the optimal break-even point.

- **TE(eval "fib 15")**: This is exactly the same example as above, but with tag elimination [44] performed on the result of the first stage. The speed up is substantially higher. Note also that compilation times are lower, because tag elimination generally reduces the size of the program. Tag elimination is discussed in the next section.

- **rewrite**: This is a matching function that takes a left-hand side of a rule and a term and returns either the same term or the corresponding right-hand side [40, 48]. Staging this program directly produces mediocre results, but staging it after it is CPS-converted produces significantly better results. Rewriting a program into CPS is one of many "binding-time improvements" that can make programs more amenable to staging [22].

- **chebyshef**: This is an example from a study on specializing scientific programs by Glück et al. [19]. Although we achieve some speedup, our results are weaker on this example than those achieved by others [19, 34]. We suspect that the reason is again the issue with array lookups in OCaml. chebyshefU is without bounds checks.

Experience with Tempo on specializing small programs indicates performance gains between 1.42 to 12.17 times [34]. In this light, the speedups achieved using staging in MetaOCaml are reasonable, although we have discussed above

eval "..."	n	R	R1	R2	R/R1	R1/R2	R/R2
arithmetic	10^7	19.4s	10.4 s	3.20s	1.87	3.25	6.06
fact 0	10^7	23.8s	5.62s	3.51s	4.23	1.60	6.78
fact 5	10^6	22.9s	4.19s	0.87s	5.47	4.82	26.3
fact 10	10^6	43.3s	7.71s	1.32s	5.62	5.84	32.8
fib 1	10^7	29.3s	7.94s	3.93s	3.69	2.02	7.46
fib 5	10^6	47.1s	11.3 s	1.39s	4.17	8.13	33.9
fib 10	10^5	58.5s	13.9 s	1.36s	4.21	10.2	43.0
fib 15	10^4	65.9s	15.6 s	1.48s	4.22	10.5	44.5

Fig. 5. The Effect of Staging and Tag Elimination on Runtimes

the typed functional settings may not be the best suited for certain kinds of computations.

6.4 Performance Gains from Tag Elimination

The previous section mentioned tag elimination, and it was seen that it can produce a significant speedup when applied to the eval example. Tag elimination is a recently-proposed source-to-source transformation that can be applied to dynamically generated code to remove typed coercions (referred to as tagging and untagging operations) that are no longer needed [44]. Tag elimination solves a long-standing problem in effectively staging (or partially evaluating) interpreters written in typed functional languages [44].

Figure 5 summarizes experiments carried out to assess tag elimination. The rows in the table correspond to different inputs to the eval function. The term arithmetic is a simple arithmetic expression (with no conditionals or recursion). The functions fact and fib are the standard factorial and Fibonacci functions. The number n is the number of times each computation is repeated so that the total time for the repetitions (**R**, **R1**, and **R2**) is a value that is easy to measure accurately. The time for running unstaged eval is **R**. The time for running the code generated by the staged interpreter is **R1**. The time for running the code generated by applying tag elimination to the result of the staged interpreter is **R2**.

In the absence of iteration or recursion, the overall gain (**R/R2**) is only 6-7 times. With iteration, overall gains are (at least in this set of examples) over 20 times. The overall gains for the Fibonacci example are the highest, and a large portion of that overall gain is due to tag elimination. Previous estimates of the potential gains from tag elimination were around 2-3 times [44]. Here it seems that tag elimination has additional benefits, probably because of enabling the compiler to perform more optimizations on the code being compiled.

6.5 Bytecode vs. Native Code Compilers

Bytecode interpreters do not have the same timing characteristics as real processors. Bytecode interpreters cannot execute several instructions in parallel, and incur an interpretation overhead on each instruction (fetching, decompiling, and branching to the appropriate piece of code to perform the instruction) that accounts for approximately half of the total execution time. Thus, in a bytecode interpretation setting, most of the benefits of runtime code specialization comes from the reduction in the number of instructions executed, e.g. when eliminating conditional branches, or removing the loop overhead by total unrolling.

In contrast, as we mentioned in the case of arrays, specializing the arguments to a bytecode instruction gains little or nothing. A typical example is that of an integer multiplication by 5. A native code compiler might replace the multiplication instruction by a shift and an add. In a bytecode setting, this kind of strength reduction is not beneficial: the overhead of interpreting two instructions instead of one largely offsets the few cycles saved in the actual computations.

For these reasons, we believe that using a native code compiler instead of a bytecode compiler and interpreter would result in higher speedups (of staged code w.r.t. unstaged code), because this would take advantage of instruction removal and of argument specialization. On the other hand, runtime compilation times could be significantly higher, especially if the native code compiler performs non-trivial optimizations, resulting in higher break-even points. The effect of moving to the native code compiler on the break-even point, however, is much less predictable. In particular, the native code compiler can be ten times slower, and code generated by that compiler can be ten times faster. If we assume that the speedup will be constant in the native code setting (which is a pessimistic approximation), then the estimated break-even point in the native code compiler jumps up by a factor of 40 times for many of the cases above. The notable exceptions, however, are the interpreter examples, where the break-even point remains unchanged at 1. For these reasons we expect that, after analyzing the performance in the native compiler setting, staging combined with tag elimination will remain a viable approach for building staged interpreters.

7 Related Work

Kohlbecker, Friedman, Felleisen, and Duba seem to have been the first to give a formal treatment of hygiene, which is what gives rise to the need for dynamic renaming. They introduce a formal renaming system and prove that in their system hygiene (defined as a HC/ME criterion) is preserved. Their system assumes that all syntactic transform functions are known before the macro-expand process commences (no macro can create macros). Clinger and Rees's [7] follow-up on this work with two improvements. First, they show that the performance of Kohlbecker's algorithm can be improved, from quadratic down to linear. Furthermore, they generalize the Kohlbecker algorithm to handle macros that can generate macros. No formal notion of correctness is given.

The notion of two-level languages originated in work of Jones on a different kind of two-level language developed primarily to model the internal workings of PE systems [20, 23], which were in turn inspired by quasi-quotes in LISP and to Quine's corners ⌜•⌝ [40]. (Bawden[1] gives a detailed historical review of the history of quasi-quotations in LISP.) Glück and Jørgensen [17, 18] were the first to generalize the techniques of two-level languages to a multi-level setting. Over the last six years, significant efforts have been invested in the development of a theory of multi-stage computation, starting from the work of Davies on linear temporal logic [11] and Moggi on functor-category and topos-theoretic semantics [30, 31], then continuing as various studies on the semantics [43, 2, 40] and type systems for MetaML [32, 6, 4, 5].

Significant effort has also been put in studying staging interpreters. Thibault, Consel, Lawall, Marlet, and Muller [49] and Hasuhara and Yonezawa [28] study the staging (via partial evaluation) of byte-code interpreters, and deal with many technical problems that arise in this setting. These efforts investigate real-world interpreters (such as the OCaml and Java bytecode interpreters), and it would be interesting future work to reproduce these results in MetaOCaml and to see the impact of using tag elimination (which was not available at the time of these works) in that setting.

A number of extensions of C [8, 21, 39] can be viewed as two-level languages. In these languages, delayed computations are not implemented by parse trees, but rather, directly by low-level code that is dynamically constructed at runtime (one system [8] supports both strategies). In future work we will study how this alternative strategy can be used for multi-level languages.

8 Conclusions

This paper presents an operational account of the correctness of using ASTs, gensym, and reflection to implement a multi-stage calculus on top of a single-stage calculus. The paper also reports on experience with putting this strategy to work in the context of extending the OCaml language with multi-stage constructs. On the positive side, we find that using this strategy in conjunction with transformations such as tag elimination yields significant performance improvement for concise definitional interpreters written in OCaml. On the negative side, we find that for certain applications that involve numerical computation written in OCaml, the gains obtained are not as much as those achieved by staging (or partially evaluating) programs written in C.

The present work focuses on effect-free multi-stage programming. Big-step semantics exist for multi-stage programming in the imperative setting, but can be quite involved [6, 5]. Future work will focus on studying the soundness of the strategy studied here in this more challenging setting.

MetaOCaml has been used for instruction in two graduate courses on multi-stage programming (c.f. [33]). MetaOCaml distributions are publicly available online [29].

Acknowledgments

Oleg Kiselyov pointed out a technical oversight and corrected us on related work. Antoney Courtney, Stephan Ellner, Bill Harrison, Julia Lawall, Eugenio Moggi,

Henrik Nilsen, Matthai Philipose, Andrew Tolmach, and Zhanyong Wan read and commented on drafts of this paper.

References

1. BAWDEN, A. Quasiquotation in LISP. In *Proceedings of the Workshop on Partial Evaluation and Semantics-Based Program Manipulation* (San Antonio, 1999), O. Danvy, Ed., University of Aarhus, Dept. of Computer Science, pp. 88–99. Invited talk.
2. BENAISSA, Z. E.-A., MOGGI, E., TAHA, W., AND SHEARD, T. Logical modalities and multi-stage programming. In *Federated Logic Conference (FLoC) Satellite Workshop on Intuitionistic Modal Logics and Applications (IMLA)* (1999).
3. CALCAGNO, C., AND MOGGI, E. Adequacy and correctness for two-level languages. (Unpublished manuscript), 1998.
4. CALCAGNO, C., AND MOGGI, E. Multi-stage imperative languages: A conservative extension result. In *[41]* (2000), pp. 92–107.
5. CALCAGNO, C., MOGGI, E., AND SHEARD, T. Closed types for a safe imperative MetaML. *Journal of Functional Programming* (2003). To appear.
6. CALCAGNO, C., MOGGI, E., AND TAHA, W. Closed types as a simple approach to safe imperative multi-stage programming. In *the International Colloquium on Automata, Languages, and Programming (ICALP '00)* (Geneva, 2000), vol. 1853 of *Lecture Notes in Computer Science*, Springer-Verlag, pp. 25–36.
7. CLINGER, W., AND REES, J. Macros that work. In *In proceedings of the ACM Symposium on Principles of Programming Languages (POPL)* (Orlando, 1991), ACM Press, pp. 155–162.
8. CONSEL, C., AND NOËL, F. A general approach for run-time specialization and its application to C. In *In proceedings of the ACM Symposium on Principles of Programming Languages (POPL)* (St. Petersburg Beach, 1996), pp. 145–156.
9. CONSEL, C., PU, C., AND WALPOLE, J. Incremental specialization: The key to high performance, modularity, and portability in operating systems. In *Proceedings of the Symposium on Partial Evaluation and Semantics-Based Program Manipulation* (New York, 1993), ACM Press, pp. 44–46.
10. DANVY, O., AND MALMKJÆR, K. Intensions and extensions in a reflective tower. In *Proceedings of the 1988 ACM Conference on LISP and Functional Programming* (1988), ACM Press, pp. 327–341.
11. DAVIES, R. A temporal-logic approach to binding-time analysis. In *the Symposium on Logic in Computer Science (LICS '96)* (New Brunswick, 1996), IEEE Computer Society Press, pp. 184–195.
12. DAVIES, R., AND PFENNING, F. A modal analysis of staged computation. In *the Symposium on Principles of Programming Languages (POPL '96)* (St. Petersburg Beach, 1996), pp. 258–270.
13. DYBVIG, R. K., HIEB, R., AND BRUGGEMAN, C. Syntactic abstraction in Scheme. *Lisp and Symbolic Computation 5*, 4 (Dec. 1992), 295–326.
14. FILINSKI, A. A semantic account of type-directed partial evaluation. In *Principles and Practice of Declarative Programming (PPDP)* (1999), vol. 1702 of *Lecture Notes in Computer Science*, Springer-Verlag, pp. 378–395.
15. FILINSKI, A. Normalization by evaluation for the computational lambda-calculus. In *Typed Lambda Calculi and Applications: 5th International Conference (TLCA)* (2001), vol. 2044 of *Lecture Notes in Computer Science*, Springer-Verlag, pp. 151–165.

16. GANZ, S., SABRY, A., AND TAHA, W. Macros as multi-stage computations: Type-safe, generative, binding macros in MacroML. In *the International Conference on Functional Programming (ICFP '01)* (Florence, Italy, September 2001), ACM.
17. GLÜCK, R., AND JØRGENSEN, J. Efficient multi-level generating extensions for program specialization. In *Programming Languages: Implementations, Logics and Programs (PLILP'95)* (1995), S. D. Swierstra and M. Hermenegildo, Eds., vol. 982 of *Lecture Notes in Computer Science*, Springer-Verlag, pp. 259–278.
18. GLÜCK, R., AND JØRGENSEN, J. Fast binding-time analysis for multi-level specialization. In *Perspectives of System Informatics* (1996), D. Bjørner, M. Broy, and I. V. Pottosin, Eds., vol. 1181 of *Lecture Notes in Computer Science*, Springer-Verlag, pp. 261–272.
19. GLÜCK, R., NAKASHIGE, R., AND ZÖCHLING, R. Binding-time analysis applied to mathematical algorithms. In *System Modelling and Optimization* (1995), J. Doležal and J. Fidler, Eds., Chapman & Hall, pp. 137–146.
20. GOMARD, C. K., AND JONES, N. D. A partial evaluator for untyped lambda calculus. *Journal of Functional Programming 1*, 1 (1991), 21–69.
21. HORNOF, L., AND JIM, T. Certifying compilation and run-time code generation. *Higher-Order and Symbolic Computation 12*, 4 (Dec. 1999), 337–375.
22. JONES, N. D., GOMARD, C. K., AND SESTOFT, P. *Partial Evaluation and Automatic Program Generation*. Prentice-Hall, 1993.
23. JONES, N. D., SESTOFT, P., AND SONDERGRAARD, H. An experiment in partial evaluation: The generation of a compiler generator. In *Rewriting Techniques and Applications*, J.-P. Jouannaud, Ed., vol. 202 of *Lecture Notes in Computer Science*. Springer-Verlag, 1985, pp. 124–140.
24. KEPPEL, D., EGGERS, S. J., AND HENRY, R. R. A case for runtime code generation. Tech. Rep. 91-11-04, University of Washington, 1991.
25. KOHLBECKER, E. E. *Syntactic Extensions in the Programming Language Lisp*. PhD thesis, Indiana University, Bloomington, Indiana, 1986.
26. LEROY, X. Objective Caml, 2000. Available from http://caml.inria.fr/ocaml/.
27. MALMKJÆR, K. On some semantic issues in the reflective tower. In *Mathematical Foundations of Programming Semantics. (Lecture Notes in Computer Science, vol. 442)* (1989), M. Main, A. Melton, M. Mislove, and D. Schmidt, Eds., pp. 229–246.
28. MASUHARA, H., AND YONEZAWA, A. Run-time bytecode specialization. *Lecture Notes in Computer Science 2053* (2001), 138–??
29. MetaOCaml: A compiled, type-safe multi-stage programming language. Available online from http://www.cs.rice.edu/~taha/MetaOCaml/, 2003.
30. MOGGI, E. A categorical account of two-level languages. In *Mathematics Foundations of Program Semantics* (1997), Elsevier Science.
31. MOGGI, E. Functor categories and two-level languages. In *Foundations of Software Science and Computation Structures (FoSSaCS)* (1998), vol. 1378 of *Lecture Notes in Computer Science*, Springer Verlag.
32. MOGGI, E., TAHA, W., BENAISSA, Z. E.-A., AND SHEARD, T. An idealized MetaML: Simpler, and more expressive. In *European Symposium on Programming (ESOP)* (1999), vol. 1576 of *Lecture Notes in Computer Science*, Springer-Verlag, pp. 193–207.
33. Multi-stage programming. http://www.cs.rice.edu/~taha/teaching/02F/511, 2003.
34. NOËL, F., HORNOF, L., CONSEL, C., AND LAWALL, J. L. Automatic, template-based run-time specialization: Implementation and experimental study. In *Proceedings of the 1998 International Conference on Computer Languages* (1998), IEEE Computer Society Press, pp. 132–142.

35. Oregon Graduate Institute Technical Reports. P.O. Box 91000, Portland, OR 97291-1000,USA. Available online from ftp://cse.ogi.edu/pub/tech-reports/README.html. Last viewed August 1999.
36. Pu, C., AND WALPOLE, J. A study of dynamic optimization techniques: Lessons and directions in kernel design. Tech. Rep. CSE-93-007, Oregon Graduate Institute, 1993. Available from [35].
37. SMITH, B. C. *Reflection and Semantics in a Procedural Language*. PhD thesis, Massachusetts Institute of Technology, 1982.
38. SMITH, B. C. Reflection and semantics in LISP. In *ACM Symposium on Principles of Programming Languages* (1984), pp. 23–35.
39. SMITH, F., GROSSMAN, D., MORRISETT, G., HORNOF, L., AND JIM, T. Compiling for template-based run-time code generation. *Journal of Functional Programming* (2002). To appear.
40. TAHA, W. *Multi-Stage Programming: Its Theory and Applications*. PhD thesis, Oregon Graduate Institute of Science and Technology, 1999. Available from [35].
41. TAHA, W., Ed. *Semantics, Applications, and Implementation of Program Generation* (Montréal, 2000), vol. 1924 of *Lecture Notes in Computer Science*, Springer-Verlag.
42. TAHA, W. A sound reduction semantics for untyped CBN multi-stage computation. Or, the theory of MetaML is non-trivial. In *Proceedings of the Workshop on Partial Evaluation and Semantics-Based Program Manipulation (PEPM)* (Boston, 2000), ACM Press.
43. TAHA, W., BENAISSA, Z.-E.-A., AND SHEARD, T. Multi-stage programming: Axiomatization and type-safety. In *25th International Colloquium on Automata, Languages, and Programming (ICALP)* (Aalborg, 1998), vol. 1443 of *Lecture Notes in Computer Science*, pp. 918–929.
44. TAHA, W., MAKHOLM, H., AND HUGHES, J. Tag elimination and Jones-optimality. In *Programs as Data Objects* (2001), O. Danvy and A. Filinksi, Eds., vol. 2053 of *Lecture Notes in Computer Science*, pp. 257–275.
45. TAHA, W., AND NIELSEN, M. F. Environment classifiers. In *The Symposium on Principles of Programming Languages (POPL '03)* (New Orleans, 2003).
46. TAHA, W., AND SHEARD, T. Multi-stage programming with explicit annotations. In *Proceedings of the Symposium on Partial Evaluation and Semantic-Based Program Manipulation (PEPM)* (Amsterdam, 1997), ACM Press, pp. 203–217.
47. TAHA, W., AND SHEARD, T. MetaML and multi-stage programming with explicit annotations. Tech. Rep. CSE-99-007, Department of Computer Science, Oregon Graduate Institute, 1999. Extended version of [46]. Available from [35].
48. TAHA, W., AND SHEARD, T. MetaML: Multi-stage programming with explicit annotations. *Theoretical Computer Science 248*, 1-2 (2000). Revision of [47].
49. THIBAULT, S., CONSEL, C., LAWALL, J. L., MARLET, R., AND MULLER, G. Static and dynamic program compilation by interpreter specialization. *Higher-Order and Symbolic Computation 13*, 3 (Sept. 2000), 161–178.

On Stage Ordering in Staged Computation*

Zhenghao Wang and Richard R. Muntz

Computer Science Department, University of California Los Angeles

Abstract. A staged computation is a computation organized in a cascade of stages: each stage produces code for its successive stage; the final stage produces the desired output. An off-line procedure called binding time analysis (BTA) is often used to pre-convert unstaged code into staged code, i.e., code annotated with stage labels, which can guide online staged computation. For dynamic re-optimization purposes, it is advantageous for the order of stages in the cascade to change during runtime; however, the staged code may not support all permutations of stage sequences. Thus, it is both a and practical question to efficiently decide whether a specific stage sequence is valid for a staged code.

Our approach is to encode the set of valid stage sequences for a staged code off-line in a *stage ordering language* (SOL) to facilitate fast online decision. Contrary to the intuition that we only need a single generic SOL (such as the language of posets of stage labels) to sufficiently and efficiently encode the set of valid stage sequences for any staged code in any staged language, we may need different SOLs for different staged languages. We analyze several staged languages and then present a metatheory on validating a SOL for a given staged language. Our result reveals the relationship between SOLs and semantic properties of staged languages, and can influence the design of staged languages and BTA.

1 Introduction

A staged computation is a computation organized in a cascade of stages: each stage produces code for its successive stage; the final stage produces the desired output. Each stage may also be associated with an input whose value has to be known in order to carry out the computation of that stage. The major benefit of staging a computation is to reuse the intermediate code from an earlier stage when inputs of the later stages change, so as to avoid repeating part of the computation and increase run-time performance. It exists more or less explicitly in various forms in the area of programming languages, e.g., compilation, partial evaluation [4], multi-level partial evaluation [2], multi-stage programming [10, 9], and run-time code generation [5, 1, 3].

Given an unstaged code in some (unstaged) programming language, an off-line procedure called binding-time analysis (BTA) is often used to derive a staged version with annotations of stage labels, which serve as guidelines for online

---

* This material is based upon work supported by the National Science Foundation under Grant Nos. 0086116, 0085773, and 9817773.

staged computation [4, 2]. The staged version is called a *staged code*; corresponding to the unstaged language, the pieces of staged code form a *staged language*. It is also possible to manually write staged code [10, 9].

The current state of the art BTA has a presumption on the order of stages to be followed by the online staged computation (the cascade of stages). This is even reflected in the design of staged languages, e.g., [10, 9], which has a built-in assumption of a fixed stage sequence. We will argue that it is beneficial for a staged language to allow a staged code to support multiple stage sequences, and there is a need to efficiently decide whether a specific stage sequence is valid for a staged code online.

For example, consider the following staged code in the simple staged language of arithmetic expressions ($\mathcal{L}_1$):

$$(v_a -_b v_b) +_c v_c,$$

where subscripts $a, b, \ldots$ are stage labels, $v_a, v_b, \ldots$ are placeholders for the inputs of the corresponding stages $a, b, \ldots$, and the informal semantics is that an annotated operator such as $-_b$ means that the operation "$-$" *should and must* be carried out in stage b. It can be easily verified that $\langle a, b, c \rangle$ is the only valid stage order for the above staged code:

$$(v_a -_b v_b) +_c v_c, 4 \stackrel{\langle a \rangle}{\Longrightarrow} (4 -_b v_b) +_c v_c,$$
$$(4 -_b v_b) +_c v_c, 5 \stackrel{\langle b \rangle}{\Longrightarrow} (-1) +_c v_c,$$
$$(-1) +_c v_c, 6 \stackrel{\langle c \rangle}{\Longrightarrow} 5.$$

However, for the same semantics, the following staged code

$$(v_a -_b v_b) +_d (v_c \times_d v_d),$$

has three valid stage sequences, namely $\langle a, b, c, d \rangle$, $\langle a, c, b, d \rangle$, $\langle c, a, b, d \rangle$.

To see why it is beneficial for a staged code to support multiple stage sequences, we need to see that the runtime efficiency of a stage sequence depends not only on the cost of each stage but also on the relative frequencies of changes to the input of each stage. Intuitively but not absolutely, one stage sequence is better than another if the input that belongs to an earlier stage changes less frequently than that of a later stage. Thus if a staged code supports multiple stage sequences, it is possible to dynamically re-optimize the stage sequence during runtime without re-doing BTA during runtime.

To facilitate efficient online decision of whether a specific stage sequence is valid for a staged code online, we propose to encode the set of valid stage sequences for a piece of staged code off-line in a *stage ordering language* (SOL). A term in a SOL denotes a set of stage sequences, and there should be an efficient algorithm to decide whether a stage sequence *conforms to* a SOL term, i.e., whether it is in the set of stage sequences denoted by a SOL term.

For example, we may use the language of partially ordered sets (posets) of stage labels as the SOL for $\mathcal{L}_1$. A stage sequence conforms to a SOL term (a poset) if it is a topological sort of the poset. Then the SOL term for $(v_a -_b v_b) +_c v_c$ is $(\{a, b, c\}, \sqsubseteq)$, where $a \sqsubseteq b \sqsubseteq c$. It can be verified that the only topological sort of this poset is $\langle a, b, c \rangle$. Similarly, the SOL term for $(v_a -_b v_b) +_d (v_c \times_d v_d)$ is $(\{a, b, c, d\}, \sqsubseteq)$, where $a \sqsubseteq b \sqsubseteq d$ and $c \sqsubseteq d$, as the three possible topological sorts of this poset are $\langle a, b, c, d \rangle$, $\langle a, c, b, d \rangle$, $\langle c, a, b, d \rangle$.

It would be nice if there were a single generic SOL that is sufficient and necessary for all staged languages. However, as we will show later, this is not possible. There do exist generic SOLs that are sufficient, like the trivial language of enumerated sets of stage sequences: $\{\langle a, b, c \rangle\}$ and $\{\langle a, b, c, d \rangle, \langle a, c, b, d \rangle, \langle c, a, b, d \rangle\}$. However, they can be very inefficient. For example, while the size of a poset is $O(n^2)$ for n stage labels, the size of an enumerated set of stage sequences is $O(n!)$. This inefficiency is due to the fact that these generic SOLs can encode more stage sequences than possibly valid in a given staged language. For example, we will show that it is impossible for any staged code in $\mathcal{L}_1$ to have exactly the following set of valid stage sequences $\{\langle a, b, c \rangle, \langle a, c, b \rangle, \langle b, a, c \rangle, \langle b, c, a \rangle\}$, and there are far too many such sets.

In this paper, we will analyze several staged languages to show that they require different SOLs. Then, we present a metatheory that can be used to validate a SOL as both sufficient and efficient for staged languages whose semantics have certain properties[1]. The metatheory is applied to the previous several staged languages to validate their corresponding SOLs. Although we do not provide a prescriptive approach to design a SOL for a given staged language, which seems to be very hard to us, our result reveals the relationship between SOLs and semantic properties of staged languages. Our result not only helps a creative language designer to design SOLs for staged languages, but also can influence the design of staged languages and even BTA itself.

2 Related Work

In existing staged languages [6, 2, 9], an annotated program only describes one particular stage sequence. For example, in the 2-level language[6] used in code generation, the cascade of stages is always $\langle c, r \rangle$, where c and r signify compile-time and run-time respectively. In MetaML[9], the nesting level of meta-brackets minus that of escapes is essentially the natural number stage label, and the cascade of stages is always $\langle 1, 2, \ldots, n \rangle$.

Nielson and Nielson have proposed to extend their 2-level language to multi-level languages [6]. They have proposed that the well-formedness rules of multi-level (types and) expressions in a particular language have characteristics that can be described by a structure on levels. Such a structure can be given in the form of a partial order [6], the signature of a many-sorted algebra [7,8], etc.

While similar, our work is different from Nielson and Nielson's multi-level languages. The most significant difference is that in the framework of multi-level languages [6–8], the structure on stages is an a priori property of the multi-level

---
[1] Our informal notion of efficiency is weaker than necessity, in that impossible stage orderings are allowed—the fewer the more efficient.

language being designed. In other words, the structure on levels is fixed for all expressions in one language, and is the basis for both the static semantics (e.g., well-formedness) and the dynamic semantics of that language. For example, a linear order such as $1 < 2 < 3 < \ldots$ makes $e_0 \stackrel{\langle 1 \rangle}{\Longrightarrow} e_1 \stackrel{\langle 2 \rangle}{\Longrightarrow} e_2 \stackrel{\langle 3 \rangle}{\Longrightarrow} e_3 \ldots$ the only cascading staged evaluation sequence. The language MetaML [9], as an example, has this restriction tightly built in its syntax as well as its semantics.

In contrast, we do not define a structure on stages a priori. Stage ordering is rather a property of each staged code. What kind of mathematical structure can be used to encode stage orderings is an issue whose answer depends on the semantics of the staged language under consideration. Therefore, we try to let each staged code describe as many cascades of stages as allowed by its semantics.

3 Case Study of Several Staged Languages

3.1 Some Notations and Definitions

Let us describe the semantics of staged computation with an operational semantics formalism. Suppose that we have a set of stage labels $\langle lbl \rangle$, and the metavariable s ranges over it. The "big-step" staged evaluation relation $e, input_s \stackrel{\langle s \rangle}{\Longrightarrow} e'$ relates a staged code e, an input to stage s $input_s$ to the outcome of this stage e'. For simplicity, we will often drop $input_s$ in the above relation: $e \stackrel{\langle s \rangle}{\Longrightarrow} e'$.

Given an expression e, we denote the set of stage labels that occurs in it as $S(e)$. A (finite) sequence of distinct stages $\langle s_1, \ldots, s_n \rangle$ is also denoted as $\langle s_i \rangle_{i=1..n}$. We use the metavariable σ to range over stage sequences, and use the metavariable Σ to range over sets of stage sequences. Our notation also includes: $\sigma_1 \cdot \sigma_2$ denotes the concatenation of σ_1 and σ_2; $s \in \sigma$ denotes that s occurs in σ, i.e., $\sigma = \langle \ldots, s, \ldots \rangle$; $s \to s' \prec \sigma$ denotes that $s \to s'$ is *compatible with* σ, i.e., if $s' \in \sigma$ then $\sigma = \langle \ldots, s, \ldots, s', \ldots \rangle$ or $\sigma = \langle \ldots, s = s', \ldots \rangle$. Analogous to $S(e)$, we define $S(\sigma) = \{s | s \in \sigma\}$.

Definition 1 (Valid Stage Sequence) $\langle s_i \rangle_{i=1..n}$ *is a* valid stage sequence *for* e, *denoted as* $\langle s_i \rangle_{i=1..n} \propto e$, *if there exist* $e_1, \ldots, e_n$ *s.t.*[2] $e \stackrel{\langle s_1 \rangle}{\Longrightarrow} e_1 \ldots \stackrel{\langle s_n \rangle}{\Longrightarrow} e_n$.

Definition 2 (Stage Ordering) *The* stage ordering *of* e, *denoted as* $\mathcal{O}(e)$, *is the set of all valid stage sequences for* e, *i.e.*, $\mathcal{O}(e) = \{\sigma | \sigma \propto e\}$.

Definition 3 (SOL Conformance) *A* stage ordering language *(SOL)* Ψ *is composed of a) a grammar whose set of terminals includes* $\langle lbl \rangle$, *and b) possibly a set of well-formedness rules. We use the metavariable* ψ *to vary over terms in* Ψ. *A SOL conformance relation* $\triangleright$ *is a relation between stage sequences and terms in* Ψ. *That a stage sequence* σ *conforms to a SOL term* ψ *is denoted as* $\sigma \triangleright \psi$. *The set of all stage sequences that conform to* ψ *is denoted as* $\mathcal{C}(\psi)$, *i.e.*, $\mathcal{C}(\psi) = \{\sigma | \sigma \triangleright \psi\}$.

---

[2] s.t. = such that

$$\frac{}{n',n \overset{\langle s \rangle}{\Longrightarrow} n'} \quad \frac{}{\mathsf{v}_s, n \overset{\langle s \rangle}{\Longrightarrow} n} \quad \frac{(s' \neq s)}{\mathsf{v}_{s'}, n \overset{\langle s \rangle}{\Longrightarrow} \mathsf{v}_{s'}} \quad \frac{e_0, n \overset{\langle s \rangle}{\Longrightarrow} n_0 \quad e_1, n \overset{\langle s \rangle}{\Longrightarrow} n_1}{e_0 \; o_s \; e_1, n \overset{\langle s \rangle}{\Longrightarrow} f_o(n_0, n_1)} \quad \frac{e_0, n \overset{\langle s \rangle}{\Longrightarrow} e'_0 \quad e_1, n \overset{\langle s \rangle}{\Longrightarrow} e'_1}{e_0 \; o_{s'} \; e_1, n \overset{\langle s \rangle}{\Longrightarrow} e'_0 \; o_{s'} \; e'_1} \; (s' \neq s)$$

Fig. 1. Formal semantics for $\mathcal{L}_1$. Here f_o is the mathematical function for o.

3.2 Staged Arithmetic Expressions $\mathcal{L}_1$

The (abstract) syntax of our first staged language $\mathcal{L}_1$ is as follows:

$$s \in \langle lbl \rangle ::= \mathsf{a} | \mathsf{b} | \mathsf{c} | \ldots$$
$$n \in \langle num \rangle ::= \ldots | -2 | -1 | 0 | 1 | 2 | \ldots$$
$$o \in \langle op \rangle ::= + | - | \times | \div$$
$$e \in \langle \mathcal{L}_1 \rangle ::= n | \mathsf{v}_s | e_0 \; o_s \; e_1.$$

Informally, the annotated variable v_s is the placeholder for the input of stage s, i.e., input$_s$ will substitute v_s in stage s; the annotated operator o_s means that the operation *should and must* be carried out in stage s. The formal semantics that reflects the informal "should and must" condition is shown in Fig. 1.

To obtain the stage ordering $\mathcal{O}(e)$, we note that any subexpression $e_0 \; o_s \; e_1$ in e imposes a constraint on a valid stage sequence σ such that all stage label in $S(e_0) \cup S(e_1)$ should occur before or at the same position as s in σ, i.e., for each $s' \in S(e_0) \cup S(e_1)$, we have $s' \to s \prec \sigma$. Thus, by examining all subexpressions of e, we obtain a set of constraints, each of which looks like $s' \to s \prec \sigma$. $\mathcal{O}(e)$ is the set of solutions that satisfy all the constraints.

Example 4 *Let $e = (\mathsf{v}_\mathsf{a} -_\mathsf{b} \mathsf{v}_\mathsf{b}) +_\mathsf{c} \mathsf{v}_\mathsf{c}$. By examining all subexpressions, we obtain the following set of constraints:*

$$\mathsf{a} \to \mathsf{b} \prec \sigma \quad \mathsf{b} \to \mathsf{b} \prec \sigma \quad \mathsf{a} \to \mathsf{c} \prec \sigma \quad \mathsf{b} \to \mathsf{c} \prec \sigma \quad \mathsf{c} \to \mathsf{c} \prec \sigma.$$

The solutions are $\sigma_0 = \langle \rangle$, $\sigma_1 = \langle \mathsf{a} \rangle$, $\sigma_2 = \langle \mathsf{a}, \mathsf{b} \rangle$, and $\sigma_3 = \langle \mathsf{a}, \mathsf{b}, \mathsf{c} \rangle$, and $\mathcal{O}(e) = \{\sigma_0, \sigma_1, \sigma_2, \sigma_3\}$.

Example 5 *Let $e = (\mathsf{v}_\mathsf{a} -_\mathsf{b} \mathsf{v}_\mathsf{b}) +_\mathsf{d} (\mathsf{v}_\mathsf{c} \times_\mathsf{d} \mathsf{v}_\mathsf{d})$. By examining all subexpressions, we obtain the following set of constraints:*

$$\mathsf{a} \to \mathsf{b} \prec \sigma \quad \mathsf{b} \to \mathsf{b} \prec \sigma \quad \mathsf{a} \to \mathsf{d} \prec \sigma \quad \mathsf{b} \to \mathsf{d} \prec \sigma \quad \mathsf{c} \to \mathsf{d} \prec \sigma \quad \mathsf{d} \to \mathsf{d} \prec \sigma.$$

It can be solved that $\mathcal{O}(e) = \{\langle \mathsf{a}, \mathsf{b}, \mathsf{c}, \mathsf{d} \rangle, \langle \mathsf{a}, \mathsf{c}, \mathsf{b}, \mathsf{d} \rangle, \langle \mathsf{c}, \mathsf{a}, \mathsf{b}, \mathsf{d} \rangle, prefixes\}$ [3].

Observing that the stage orderings of staged code in $\mathcal{L}_1$ are closely related to posets of stage labels, we can define the notion of poset conformance as follows:

Definition 6 (Poset Conformance) *Given a poset of stage labels $\psi = (S, \sqsubseteq)$, σ conforms to ψ, denoted as $\sigma \triangleright \psi$, if for each $s, s' \in S$, $s \sqsubseteq s'$ implies $s \to s' \prec \sigma$.*

---

[3] "prefixes" means prefixes of previous sequences: $\langle \rangle, \langle \mathsf{a} \rangle, \langle \mathsf{c} \rangle, \langle \mathsf{a}, \mathsf{b} \rangle, \langle \mathsf{a}, \mathsf{c} \rangle, \langle \mathsf{c}, \mathsf{a} \rangle$, $\langle \mathsf{a}, \mathsf{b}, \mathsf{c} \rangle, \langle \mathsf{a}, \mathsf{c}, \mathsf{b} \rangle, \langle \mathsf{c}, \mathsf{a}, \mathsf{b} \rangle$.

$$\frac{}{n',n \overset{\langle s \rangle}{\Longrightarrow} n'} \quad \frac{}{v_s, n \overset{\langle s \rangle}{\Longrightarrow} n} \quad \frac{(s' \neq s)}{v_{s'}, n \overset{\langle s \rangle}{\Longrightarrow} v_{s'}} \quad \frac{e_0, n \overset{\langle s \rangle}{\Longrightarrow} n_0 \quad e_1, n \overset{\langle s \rangle}{\Longrightarrow} n_1}{e_0 \, o \, e_1, n \overset{\langle s \rangle}{\Longrightarrow} f_o(n_0, n_1)} \quad \frac{e_0, n \overset{\langle s \rangle}{\Longrightarrow} e_0' \quad e_1, n \overset{\langle s \rangle}{\Longrightarrow} e_1'}{e_0 \, o \, e_1, n \overset{\langle s \rangle}{\Longrightarrow} e_0' \, o \, e_1'} \text{ (otherwise)}$$

Fig. 2. Formal semantics for $\mathcal{L}_2$.

Without proving it for the time being, we conjecture that the SOL made of posets is sufficient for $\mathcal{L}_1$:

Proposition 7 (Sufficient SOL for $\mathcal{L}_1$) *For each staged code e in $\mathcal{L}_1$, there exists a poset ψ s.t. $\mathcal{C}(\psi) = \mathcal{O}(e)$.*

The poset ψ for e can be obtained by the following procedure: first make a directed graph of the constraints we have obtained for e, and then remove all stage labels involved in any cycle (except self-loops); the result is a directed acyclic graph (DAG) representing the poset ψ for e.

Example 8 *Following the above procedure, we obtain that the poset for $(v_a -_b v_b) +_c v_c$ is $(\{a,b,c\}, \sqsubseteq)$, where $a \sqsubseteq b \sqsubseteq c$. Similarly, the poset for $(v_a -_b v_b) +_d (v_c \times_d v_d)$ is $(\{a,b,c,d\}, \sqsubseteq)$, where $a \sqsubseteq b \sqsubseteq d$ and $c \sqsubseteq d$.*

3.3 Staged Arithmetic Expressions $\mathcal{L}_2$

$\mathcal{L}_2$ is a slight variance of $\mathcal{L}_1$:

$$e \in \langle \mathcal{L}_2 \rangle ::= n | v_s | e_0 \, o \, e_1.$$

$\mathcal{L}_2$ is different from $\mathcal{L}_1$ in that operators are no longer annotated with stages[4]; accordingly, the informal semantics differs in that an operation should be carried out *as soon as* its operands are reduced to numerical values, i.e., it is not limited to a particular stage. The formal semantics that reflects the above informal "as soon as" condition is shown in Fig. 2.

Obviously, all permutations of stage sequences are valid for a given staged code in $\mathcal{L}_2$, i.e., $\mathcal{O}(e) = \{\sigma | \sigma$ is any stage sequence$\}$. For example, for $e = (v_a - v_b) + v_c$, the following are all valid staged evaluation sequences:

$$e, 4 \overset{\langle a \rangle}{\Longrightarrow} (4 - v_b) + v_c, 5 \overset{\langle b \rangle}{\Longrightarrow} (-1) + v_c, 6 \overset{\langle c \rangle}{\Longrightarrow} 5;$$

$$e, 4 \overset{\langle a \rangle}{\Longrightarrow} (4 - v_b) + v_c, 6 \overset{\langle c \rangle}{\Longrightarrow} (4 - v_b) + 6, 5 \overset{\langle b \rangle}{\Longrightarrow} 5;$$

$$e, 5 \overset{\langle b \rangle}{\Longrightarrow} (v_a - 5) + v_c, 4 \overset{\langle a \rangle}{\Longrightarrow} (-1) + v_c, 6 \overset{\langle c \rangle}{\Longrightarrow} 5;$$

$$e, 5 \overset{\langle b \rangle}{\Longrightarrow} (v_a - 5) + v_c, 6 \overset{\langle c \rangle}{\Longrightarrow} (v_a - 5) + 6, 4 \overset{\langle a \rangle}{\Longrightarrow} 5;$$

$$e, 6 \overset{\langle c \rangle}{\Longrightarrow} (v_a - v_b) + 6, 4 \overset{\langle a \rangle}{\Longrightarrow} (4 - v_b) + 6, 5 \overset{\langle b \rangle}{\Longrightarrow} 5;$$

$$e, 6 \overset{\langle c \rangle}{\Longrightarrow} (v_a - v_b) + 6, 5 \overset{\langle b \rangle}{\Longrightarrow} (v_a - 5) + 6, 4 \overset{\langle a \rangle}{\Longrightarrow} 5.$$

The SOL for $\mathcal{L}_2$ contains only a dumb term $\bot$, and any σ conforms to it: $\sigma \triangleright \bot$. The following is then trivially true:

---
[4] Essentially, there is a vacuous BTA in this case.

[VarN] $\dfrac{}{v \stackrel{\langle s \rangle}{\Longrightarrow}_N v}$ [VarF] $\dfrac{}{v \stackrel{\langle s \rangle}{\Longrightarrow}_F v}$ [AbsF] $\dfrac{e \stackrel{\langle s \rangle}{\Longrightarrow}_F e'}{\lambda v.e \stackrel{\langle s \rangle}{\Longrightarrow}_F \lambda v.e'}$

[AbsN] $\dfrac{}{\lambda v.e \stackrel{\langle s \rangle}{\Longrightarrow}_N \lambda v.e}$ [Ap1aF] $\dfrac{e_0 \stackrel{\langle s \rangle}{\Longrightarrow}_N \lambda v.e_0' \quad [e_1/v]\, e_0' \stackrel{\langle s \rangle}{\Longrightarrow}_F e'}{e_0 \,{}^{\langle s \rangle}\, e_1 \stackrel{\langle s \rangle}{\Longrightarrow}_F e'}$

[Ap1aN] $\dfrac{e_0 \stackrel{\langle s \rangle}{\Longrightarrow}_N \lambda v.e_0' \quad [e_1/v]\, e_0' \stackrel{\langle s \rangle}{\Longrightarrow}_N e'}{e_0 \,{}^{\langle s \rangle}\, e_1 \stackrel{\langle s \rangle}{\Longrightarrow}_N e'}$ [Ap1bF] $\dfrac{e_0 \stackrel{\langle s \rangle}{\Longrightarrow}_N e_0' \quad e_0' \stackrel{\langle s \rangle}{\Longrightarrow}_F e_0'' \quad e_1 \stackrel{\langle s \rangle}{\Longrightarrow}_F e_1'}{e_0 \,{}^{\langle s \rangle}\, e_1 \stackrel{\langle s \rangle}{\Longrightarrow}_F e_0''\,{}^{\langle s \rangle}\, e_1'}\; e_0' \neq \lambda v.e$

[Ap1bN] $\dfrac{e_0 \stackrel{\langle s \rangle}{\Longrightarrow}_N e_0'}{e_0 \,{}^{\langle s \rangle}\, e_1 \stackrel{\langle s \rangle}{\Longrightarrow}_N e_0' \,{}^{\langle s \rangle}\, e_1}\; e_0' \neq \lambda v.e$ [Ap2F] $\dfrac{e_0 \stackrel{\langle s \rangle}{\Longrightarrow}_F e_0' \quad e_1 \stackrel{\langle s \rangle}{\Longrightarrow}_F e_1'}{e_0 \,{}^{\langle s' \rangle}\, e_1 \stackrel{\langle s \rangle}{\Longrightarrow}_F e_0' \,{}^{\langle s' \rangle}\, e_1'}\; s' \neq s$

[Ap2N] $\dfrac{}{e_0 \,{}^{\langle s' \rangle}\, e_1 \stackrel{\langle s \rangle}{\Longrightarrow}_N e_0 \,{}^{\langle s' \rangle}\, e_1}\; s' \neq s$ (b) $\stackrel{\langle s \rangle}{\Longrightarrow}_F$

(a) $\stackrel{\langle s \rangle}{\Longrightarrow}_N$

[EV] $\dfrac{e \stackrel{\langle s \rangle}{\Longrightarrow}_F e'}{e \stackrel{\langle s \rangle}{\Longrightarrow} e'}\; e'$ is a stage-s value

(c) $\stackrel{\langle s \rangle}{\Longrightarrow}$

Fig. 3. Formal semantics for $\mathcal{L}_3$. $\stackrel{\langle s \rangle}{\Longrightarrow}_N$ and $\stackrel{\langle s \rangle}{\Longrightarrow}_F$ are two auxiliary relations.

Proposition 9 (Sufficient SOL for $\mathcal{L}_2$) *For each staged code e in $\mathcal{L}_2$, there exists a ψ, which is $\bot$, s.t. $\mathcal{C}(\psi) = \mathcal{O}(e)$.*

3.4 $\mathcal{L}_3$-Calculus

Our third staged language $\mathcal{L}_3$-calculus is based on λ-calculus[5]:

$$s \in \langle lbl \rangle \qquad v \in \langle var \rangle \qquad e \in \langle \mathcal{L}_3 \rangle ::= v \mid \lambda v.e \mid e_0 \,{}^{\langle s \rangle}\, e_1,$$

where $\langle var \rangle$ is the set of variables; the change from λ-calculus is the stage label s in the application $e_0 \,{}^{\langle s \rangle}\, e_1$. The definitions of free variables ($FV(e)$), substitution ($[e'/v]\,e$), and α-equivalence ($e \equiv e'$) are analogous to those in λ-calculus.

We also define the following concepts. A *stage-s β-redex* is an expression of the form $(\lambda v.e) \,{}^{\langle s \rangle}\, e'$; a *stage-$s$ normal form* is an expression without any stage-s β-redex; a *stage-s value* is an expression free of stage label s.

The informal semantics of $\mathcal{L}_3$-calculus is that all stage-s applications s *should and must* be β-reduced in stage s. The formal semantics that reflects this "should and must" condition is shown in Fig. 3[6],[7]. The evaluation is normal order; it proceeds under abstractions, which reflects the essence of program generation.

Example 10 *For the expression $e = (\lambda x.(\lambda y.x \,{}^{\langle a \rangle}\, y) \,{}^{\langle b \rangle}\, z) \,{}^{\langle a \rangle}\, (\lambda w.w)$, we have:*

$$e \stackrel{\langle a \rangle}{\Longrightarrow} (\lambda y.y) \,{}^{\langle b \rangle}\, z \stackrel{\langle b \rangle}{\Longrightarrow} z \quad \text{and} \quad e \stackrel{\langle b \rangle}{\Longrightarrow} (\lambda x.x \,{}^{\langle a \rangle}\, z) \,{}^{\langle a \rangle}\, (\lambda w.w) \stackrel{\langle a \rangle}{\Longrightarrow} z$$

---

[5] To disambiguate concrete syntax into the abstract syntax, we adopt the common convention that application is left associative and that e in $\lambda v.e$ extends to the first unmatched ")" or the end of the whole expression.

[6] As a result of the simplification of $\mathcal{L}_3$, no input is associated with a stage; the essence of our work is not affected.

[7] The correctness of Fig. 3 can be formalized and proved with similar ideas used to prove Church-Rosser and Standardization Theorems of λ-calculus.

Therefore $\mathcal{O}(e) = \{\langle\rangle, \langle a\rangle, \langle b\rangle, \langle a,b\rangle, \langle b,a\rangle\}$.

Example 11 *For the expression* $e = (\lambda v.(\lambda x.v)\,^{\langle b\rangle}\,(v\,^{\langle c\rangle}\,w))\,^{\langle a\rangle}\,(\lambda z.z)$, *we have only the following valid stage sequences (and their prefixes):*

$e \xRightarrow{\langle a\rangle} (\lambda x.\lambda z.z)\,^{\langle b\rangle}\,((\lambda z.z)\,^{\langle c\rangle}\,w) \xRightarrow{\langle b\rangle} \lambda z.z \xRightarrow{\langle c\rangle} \lambda z.z$

$e \xRightarrow{\langle a\rangle} (\lambda x.\lambda z.z)\,^{\langle b\rangle}\,((\lambda z.z)\,^{\langle c\rangle}\,w) \xRightarrow{\langle c\rangle} (\lambda x.\lambda z.z)\,^{\langle b\rangle}\,w \xRightarrow{\langle b\rangle} \lambda z.z$

$e \xRightarrow{\langle b\rangle} (\lambda v.v)\,^{\langle a\rangle}\,(\lambda z.z) \xRightarrow{\langle a\rangle} \lambda z.z \xRightarrow{\langle c\rangle} \lambda z.z$

$e \xRightarrow{\langle b\rangle} (\lambda v.v)\,^{\langle a\rangle}\,(\lambda z.z) \xRightarrow{\langle c\rangle} (\lambda v.v)\,^{\langle a\rangle}\,(\lambda z.z) \xRightarrow{\langle a\rangle} \lambda z.z$

Therefore $\mathcal{O}(e) = \{\langle a,b,c\rangle, \langle a,c,b\rangle, \langle b,a,c\rangle, \langle b,c,a\rangle, \text{prefixes}\}$.

The last example can be used to show that the poset SOL introduced in Sec. 3.2 is no longer sufficient for $\mathcal{L}_3$-calculus: it is impossible to find a poset ψ so that $\mathcal{C}(\psi) = \{\langle a,b,c\rangle, \langle a,c,b\rangle, \langle b,a,c\rangle, \langle b,c,a\rangle, \text{prefixes}\}$.

Finding a sufficient yet efficient SOL for $\mathcal{L}_3$-calculus turns out to be a nontrivial task; we were able to find one only after we had developed the metatheory to be discussed in Sec. 4. Let us call the SOL $\Psi_\diamond$. The grammar of $\Psi_\diamond$ is

$$s \in \langle lbl \rangle$$
$$S \in \langle label\text{-}set \rangle ::= \{s_1, \ldots, s_m\}$$
$$d \in \langle diamond \rangle ::= S \diamond S'$$
$$\psi \in \Psi_\diamond ::= \{d_1, \ldots, d_n\}.$$

The intuition is that a stage ordering is described by a set of "diamonds"; each diamond is a hypercube with a starting vertex described by S and a set of edges along dimensions described by S'. The well-formedness rules are:

$$\frac{S \cap S' = \{\} \quad |S'| \geq 1}{\vdash_\diamond S \diamond S'} \qquad \frac{\vdash_\diamond d_i (i = 1..n)}{\vdash \{d_1, \ldots, d_n\}},$$

and the SOL conformance relation $\triangleright$ is defined by the following rules:

$$[\text{DMD Empty}] \; \frac{\vdash \psi}{\langle\rangle \triangleright \psi} \qquad [\text{DMD Grow1}] \; \frac{\sigma \triangleright \psi \quad S(\sigma) \diamond S \in \psi \quad s \in S}{\sigma \cdot \langle s\rangle \triangleright \psi} \quad (1)$$

$$[\text{DMD Grow2}] \; \frac{\sigma_2 \cdot \langle s\rangle \triangleright \psi \quad \sigma_2 \cdot \langle s'\rangle \triangleright \psi \quad \sigma_1 \triangleright \psi \quad S(\sigma_2 \cdot \langle s'\rangle) = S(\sigma_1) \quad s \neq s'}{\sigma_1 \cdot \langle s\rangle \triangleright \psi}.$$

We will prove later using the metatheory that $\Psi_\diamond$ is a sufficient SOL for $\mathcal{L}_3$-calculus:

Proposition 12 (Sufficient SOL for $\mathcal{L}_3$-calculus) *For each staged code e in $\mathcal{L}_3$, there exists a term $\psi \in \Psi_\diamond$ s.t. $\mathcal{C}(\psi) = \mathcal{O}(e)$.*

Example 13 *The SOL term for* $(\lambda x.(\lambda y.x\,^{\langle a\rangle}\,y)\,^{\langle b\rangle}\,z)\,^{\langle a\rangle}\,(\lambda w.w)$ *in Example 10, is* $\{\{\} \diamond \{a,b\}\}$. *Similarly, the SOL term for* $(\lambda v.(\lambda x.v)\,^{\langle b\rangle}\,(v\,^{\langle c\rangle}\,w))\,^{\langle a\rangle}\,(\lambda z.z)$ *in Example 11 is* $\{\{\} \diamond \{a,b\}, \{a\} \diamond \{c\}, \{b\} \diamond \{c\}\}$.

4 Metatheory on Proving Sufficient SOL Propositions

In the last section, we proposed several sufficient SOL propositions for various staged languages (Propositions 7, 9, 12). In this section, we present a metatheory that can be used to prove these sufficient SOL propositions and indirectly show the efficiency of SOLs. The taste of the metatheory is like the principle of mathematical/structural/well-founded induction, in that it transforms such a proof into a more tractable procedure.

The first step is to come up with and formally prove some properties of the semantic relation $\stackrel{\langle s \rangle}{\Longrightarrow}$ that are related to stage sequences. Such a property has the flavor of the following example:

If $e_0 \stackrel{\langle s \rangle}{\Longrightarrow} e_1 \stackrel{\langle s' \rangle}{\Longrightarrow} e_2$, then there exist e_1' and e_2' s.t. $e_0 \stackrel{\langle s' \rangle}{\Longrightarrow} e_1' \stackrel{\langle s \rangle}{\Longrightarrow} e_2'$.

Follow a mechanical procedure to turn these semantic properties into inference rules about valid sequences. For example, the above example property is turned into the following inference rule:

$$\frac{\sigma \cdot \langle s, s' \rangle \propto e}{\sigma \cdot \langle s', s \rangle \propto e}. \qquad (2)$$

Let us denote the set of all proven semantic properties expressed in such inference rules as $\mathcal{P}$.

On the other side, specify the grammar of the target SOL Ψ formally with BNF-like grammar and, optionally, well-formedness rules. Then define the conformance relation $\sigma \triangleright \psi$ formally using inference rules. (See the example specification of $\Psi_\diamond$ in Sec. 3.4.)

The metatheory contains a meta-theorem (Theorem 20) that can be used to prove that a SOL Ψ is sufficient for a staged language, given that the semantics of the staged language satisfies properties $\mathcal{P}$. As we will see later, this meta-theorem, similar to the meta-theorem that validates well-founded induction, turns the problem into a tractable proof using standard structural/well-founded induction techniques.

The metatheory contains another meta-theorem (Theorem 21) that can be used to indirectly show that a SOL Ψ is efficient. This meta-theorem can be used to prove that the semantics of a staged language must satisfy certain properties if a SOL Ψ is sufficient for it, which is the inverse of what the other meta-theorem (Theorem 20) helps to prove. In general, the more efficient a SOL is, the less generic it is, i.e., it contains fewer stage orderings. Thus the more properties the semantics of the staged language must have if the SOL is sufficient for it. If the semantics of a staged language satisfies a property that cannot be proved using the meta-theorem w.r.t. a SOL that is sufficient for it, the SOL is probably not the most efficient SOL. Therefore, to show that a SOL is quite efficient for a staged language, we can indirectly show that many semantic properties of the staged language can be proved by the fact that the SOL is sufficient.

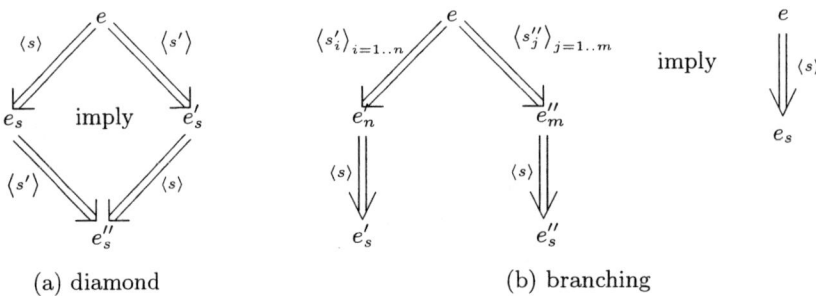

Fig. 4. The diamond and branching properties.

4.1 Properties of Staged Computation Semantics

First let us define some properties and check them against the semantics of the three staged languages we have introduced in Sec. 3

Definition 14 (Free Property) *For any e, s, there exists e_s s.t. $e \stackrel{\langle s \rangle}{\Longrightarrow} e_s$.*

Definition 15 (Diamond Property) *If $e \stackrel{\langle s \rangle}{\Longrightarrow} e_s$ and $e \stackrel{\langle s' \rangle}{\Longrightarrow} e'_s$ ($s \neq s'$), then there exists e''_s s.t. $e_s \stackrel{\langle s' \rangle}{\Longrightarrow} e''_s$, as illustrated in Fig. 4(a).*

Definition 16 (Branching Property) *If $e \stackrel{\langle s'_1 \rangle}{\Longrightarrow} \ldots \stackrel{\langle s'_n \rangle}{\Longrightarrow} e'_n \stackrel{\langle s \rangle}{\Longrightarrow} e'_s$ and $e \stackrel{\langle s''_1 \rangle}{\Longrightarrow} \ldots \stackrel{\langle s''_m \rangle}{\Longrightarrow} e''_m \stackrel{\langle s \rangle}{\Longrightarrow} e''_s$, where $\{s'_1, \ldots, s'_n\} \cap \{s''_1, \ldots, s''_m\} = \{\}$, then there exists e_s s.t. $e \stackrel{\langle s \rangle}{\Longrightarrow} e_s$, as illustrated in Fig. 4(b).*

Definition 17 (Weak Convergence Property) *If $e \stackrel{\langle s_{i_1} \rangle}{\Longrightarrow} e_{i_1} \stackrel{\langle s_{i_2} \rangle}{\Longrightarrow} \ldots \stackrel{\langle s_{i_n} \rangle}{\Longrightarrow} e_{i_n} \stackrel{\langle s_{n+1} \rangle}{\Longrightarrow} e_{i_{n+1}} \stackrel{\langle s_{n+2} \rangle}{\Longrightarrow} \ldots \stackrel{\langle s_m \rangle}{\Longrightarrow} e_{i_m}$ and $e \stackrel{\langle s_{j_1} \rangle}{\Longrightarrow} e_{j_1} \stackrel{\langle s_{j_2} \rangle}{\Longrightarrow} \ldots \stackrel{\langle s_{j_n} \rangle}{\Longrightarrow} e_{j_n}$, where $\langle i_1, i_2, \ldots, i_n \rangle$ and $\langle j_1, j_2, \ldots, j_n \rangle$ are permutations of $\langle 1, 2, \ldots, n \rangle$, then there exist $e_{j_{n+1}}, \ldots, e_{j_m}$ s.t. $e_{j_n} \stackrel{\langle s_{n+1} \rangle}{\Longrightarrow} e_{j_{n+1}} \stackrel{\langle s_{n+2} \rangle}{\Longrightarrow} \ldots \stackrel{\langle s_m \rangle}{\Longrightarrow} e_{j_m}$.*

The following two trivial properties are satisfied by all staged languages.

Definition 18 (Empty Sequence Property) $\langle \rangle \propto e$.

Definition 19 (Prefix Property) *If $\langle s_i \rangle_{i=1..n} \propto e$, then $\langle s_i \rangle_{i=1..n-1} \propto e$.*

Using standard structural induction techniques or counter-examples, we can obtain the satisfiability matrix between these properties and the semantics of the three staged languages in Sec. 3 in Table 1. Equivalent inference rules for these properties involving only $\propto e$ are also shown in the table.

Table 1. Satisfiability matrix and inference rules of some semantic properties.

	$\mathcal{L}_1$	$\mathcal{L}_2$	$\mathcal{L}_3$	inference rule
Free		✓		$\dfrac{\sigma \propto e}{\sigma \cdot \langle s \rangle \propto e}$
Diamond	✓	✓	✓	$\dfrac{\sigma \cdot \langle s \rangle \propto e \quad \sigma \cdot \langle s' \rangle \propto e \quad s \neq s'}{\sigma \cdot \langle s, s' \rangle \propto e}$
Branching	✓	✓		$\dfrac{\sigma \cdot \sigma_1 \cdot \langle s \rangle \propto e \quad \sigma \cdot \sigma_2 \cdot \langle s \rangle \propto e \quad S(\sigma_1) \cap S(\sigma_2) = \{\}}{\sigma \cdot \langle s \rangle \propto e}$
Weak Convergence	✓	✓	✓	$\dfrac{\sigma_1 \cdot \sigma \propto e \quad \sigma_2 \propto e \quad S(\sigma_1) = S(\sigma_2)}{\sigma_2 \cdot \sigma \propto e}$
Empty Sequence	✓	✓	✓	$\overline{\langle \rangle \propto e}$
Prefix	✓	✓	✓	$\dfrac{\sigma \cdot \langle s \rangle \propto e}{\sigma \propto e}$

4.2 Two Meta-theorems

Given a staged language with semantics $\overset{\langle s \rangle}{\Longrightarrow}$ and a SOL Ψ, we wish to relate two propositions:

- Proposition A: $\overset{\langle s \rangle}{\Longrightarrow}$ satisfies a set of properties $\mathcal{P}$;
- proposition B: Ψ is sufficient, i.e., for each staged code e in the stage language, there exists a term $\psi \in \Psi$ s.t. $\mathcal{C}(\psi) = \mathcal{O}(e)$.

We have the following two meta-theorems:

Theorem 20 *The "sufficient condition" part (i.e., $A \Rightarrow B$) holds, if there exists a function p that maps a set of sequences Σ to a term in Ψ: $\psi = p(\Sigma)$, s.t. a) for each Σ, $\sigma \in \Sigma$ implies $\sigma \triangleright p(\Sigma)$, and b) for each Σ that satisfies $\mathcal{T}_{\propto e \to \in \Sigma}(\mathcal{P})$, $\sigma \triangleright p(\Sigma)$ implies $\sigma \in \Sigma$. Here $\mathcal{T}_{\propto e \to \in \Sigma}(\mathcal{P})$ is the set of inference rules obtained by replacing $\propto e$ in $\mathcal{P}$ with $\in \Sigma$.*

PROOF Condition a) means that $\forall \Sigma . \Sigma \subseteq \{\sigma | \sigma \triangleright p(\Sigma)\}$, while condition b) means that $\forall \Sigma$ satisfying $\mathcal{T}_{\propto e \to \in \Sigma}(\mathcal{P}) . \{\sigma | \sigma \triangleright p(\Sigma)\} \subseteq \Sigma$. Thus

$$\exists p. \forall \Sigma \text{ satisfying } \mathcal{T}_{\propto e \to \in \Sigma}(\mathcal{P}) . \{\sigma | \sigma \triangleright p(\Sigma)\} = \Sigma.$$

On the other hand, if $\propto$ is a relation that satisfies $\mathcal{P}$, then $\Sigma(e) = \{\sigma | \sigma \propto e\}$ is a set of sequences that satisfies $\mathcal{T}_{\propto e \to \in \Sigma}(\mathcal{P})$. Therefore we have:

$$\exists p. \forall e. \{\sigma | \sigma \triangleright p(\{\sigma | \sigma \propto e\})\} = \{\sigma | \sigma \propto e\},$$

which implies Proposition B.

□

Theorem 21 *The "necessary condition" part (i.e., $B \Rightarrow A$) holds, if all rules in $\mathcal{T}_{\propto e \to \triangleright \psi}(\mathcal{P})$ are sound w.r.t. the definition of $\triangleright$, where $\mathcal{T}_{\propto e \to \triangleright \psi}(\mathcal{P})$ is the set of inference rules obtained by replacing $\propto e$ in $\mathcal{P}$ with $\triangleright \psi$.*

Table 2. $\mathcal{T}_{\propto e \to \in \Sigma}$ and $\mathcal{T}_{\propto e \to \rhd \psi}$ on the earlier properties.

	$\mathcal{L}_1$	$\mathcal{L}_2$	$\mathcal{L}_3$	$\mathcal{T}_{\propto e \to \in \Sigma}$	$\mathcal{T}_{\propto e \to \rhd \psi}$
Free		✓		$\dfrac{\sigma \in \Sigma}{\sigma \cdot \langle s \rangle \in \Sigma}$	$\dfrac{\sigma \rhd \psi}{\sigma \cdot \langle s \rangle \rhd \psi}$
Diamond	✓	✓	✓	$\dfrac{\sigma \cdot \langle s \rangle \in \Sigma \quad \sigma \cdot \langle s' \rangle \in \Sigma \quad s \neq s'}{\sigma \cdot \langle s, s' \rangle \in \Sigma}$	$\dfrac{\sigma \cdot \langle s \rangle \rhd \psi \quad \sigma \cdot \langle s' \rangle \rhd \psi \quad s \neq s'}{\sigma \cdot \langle s, s' \rangle \rhd \psi}$
Branching	✓	✓		$\dfrac{\sigma \cdot \sigma_1 \cdot \langle s \rangle \in \Sigma \quad \sigma \cdot \sigma_2 \cdot \langle s \rangle \in \Sigma \quad \sigma_1 \cap \sigma_2 = \{\}}{\sigma \cdot \langle s \rangle \in \Sigma}$	$\dfrac{\sigma \cdot \sigma_1 \cdot \langle s \rangle \rhd \psi \quad \sigma \cdot \sigma_2 \cdot \langle s \rangle \rhd \psi \quad \sigma_1 \cap \sigma_2 = \{\}}{\sigma \cdot \langle s \rangle \rhd \psi}$
Weak Convergence	✓	✓	✓	$\dfrac{\sigma_1 \cdot \sigma \in \Sigma \quad \sigma_2 \in \Sigma \quad S(\sigma_1) = S(\sigma_2)}{\sigma_2 \cdot \sigma \in \Sigma}$	$\dfrac{\sigma_1 \cdot \sigma \rhd \psi \quad \sigma_2 \rhd \psi \quad S(\sigma_1) = S(\sigma_2)}{\sigma_2 \cdot \sigma \rhd \psi}$
Empty Sequence	✓	✓	✓	$\dfrac{}{\langle \rangle \in \Sigma}$	$\dfrac{}{\langle \rangle \rhd \psi}$
Prefix	✓	✓	✓	$\dfrac{\sigma \cdot \langle s \rangle \in \Sigma}{\sigma \in \Sigma}$	$\dfrac{\sigma \cdot \langle s \rangle \rhd \psi}{\sigma \rhd \psi}$

PROOF According to Defs. 2,3, Proposition B can be rephrased as:

$$\forall e. \exists \psi. \{\sigma \mid \sigma \rhd \psi\} = \{\sigma \mid \sigma \propto e\},$$

which implies that, given e, we can always find $\psi(e)$ s.t. $\sigma \propto e$ iff $\sigma \rhd \psi(e)$.

Thus, if all inference rules in $\mathcal{T}_{\propto e \to \rhd \psi}(\mathcal{P})$ are sound, i.e., they are valid for each ψ, Proposition B implies that they must also be valid for $\psi = \psi(e)$ for each e. We can further replace $\rhd \psi(e)$ by $\propto e$ as the two are equivalent under Proposition B; what we obtain is the original set $\mathcal{P}$ of inference rules containing $\propto e$. To summarize, if all inference rules in $\mathcal{T}_{\propto e \to \rhd \psi}(\mathcal{P})$ are sound, then B $\Rightarrow$ A. □

For readers' convenience, we list the results of applying $\mathcal{T}_{\propto e \to \in \Sigma}$ and $\mathcal{T}_{\propto e \to \rhd \psi}$ to the properties in Table 1 together with satisfiability matrix again in Table 2.

5 Application of Metatheory

5.1 $\mathcal{L}_1$

First, let us define the SOL $\Psi_\sqsubseteq$ of posets formally. Posets can be represented by *directed acyclic graphs* (DAGs)[8]. The grammar for directed graphs is

$$s \in \langle lbl \rangle$$
$$S \in \langle vertices \rangle ::= \{s_1, \ldots, s_n\}$$
$$E \in \langle edges \rangle ::= \{s_1 \to s'_1, \ldots, s_m \to s'_m\}$$
$$\psi \in \Psi_\sqsubseteq ::= (S, E).$$

The well-formedness rules for DAGs are:

[DAG Empty] $\dfrac{}{\vdash (\{\}, \{\})}$ [DAG Grow] $\dfrac{\vdash (S, E) \quad s_i \in S \ (i = 1..k) \quad s \notin S}{\vdash (S \cup \{s\}, E \cup \{s_1 \to s, \ldots, s_k \to s\})}$.

The SOL conformance relation $\rhd$ between stage sequences and DAGs is defined by the following "DAG conformance rules:"

---

[8] Note that the same poset may be represented by several different DAGs.

$$[\text{DC Empty}] \; \frac{\vdash \psi}{\langle\rangle \triangleright \psi}$$

$$[\text{DC Grow}] \; \frac{\sigma \triangleright (S,E) \quad s \notin \sigma \quad s \in S \quad \{s'|s' \to s \in E\} \subseteq S(\sigma)}{\sigma \cdot \langle s \rangle \in (S,E)}. \quad (3)$$

To show that $\Psi_{\sqsubseteq}$ is sufficient (i.e., Proposition 7), we can use Theorem 20. According to Table 2, $\mathcal{T}_{\propto e \to \in \Sigma}(\mathcal{P}_{\mathcal{L}_1})$ contains:

$$[\mathcal{T}_{\propto e \to \in \Sigma}(\text{Diamond})] \; \frac{\sigma \cdot \langle s \rangle \in \Sigma \quad \sigma \cdot \langle s' \rangle \in \Sigma \quad s \neq s'}{\sigma \cdot \langle s, s' \rangle \in \Sigma}$$

$$[\mathcal{T}_{\propto e \to \in \Sigma}(\text{Branching})] \; \frac{\sigma \cdot \sigma_1 \cdot \langle s \rangle \in \Sigma \quad \sigma \cdot \sigma_2 \cdot \langle s \rangle \in \Sigma \quad S(\sigma_1) \cap S(\sigma_2) = \{\}}{\sigma \cdot \langle s \rangle \in \Sigma}$$

$$[\mathcal{T}_{\propto e \to \in \Sigma}(\text{Weak Convergence})] \; \frac{\sigma_1 \cdot \sigma \in \Sigma \quad \sigma_2 \in \Sigma \quad S(\sigma_1) = S(\sigma_2)}{\sigma_2 \cdot \sigma \in \Sigma}$$

$$[\mathcal{T}_{\propto e \to \in \Sigma}(\text{Empty Sequence})] \; \frac{}{\langle\rangle \in \Sigma} \qquad [\mathcal{T}_{\propto e \to \in \Sigma}(\text{Prefix})] \; \frac{\sigma \cdot \langle s \rangle \in \Sigma}{\sigma \in \Sigma}. \quad (4)$$

Let us define the following function p:

$$p(\Sigma) = (S_\Sigma, E_\Sigma), \text{ where}$$
$$S_\Sigma = \bigcup_{\sigma \in \Sigma} S(\sigma),$$
$$E_\Sigma = \bigcup_{s \in S_\Sigma} \left(\bigcap_{\sigma_1 \cdot \langle s \rangle \cdot \sigma_2 \in \Sigma} \{s' \to s | s' \in \sigma_1\} \right). \quad (5)$$

Thus, we end up to show that:

- If $\sigma \in \Sigma$, then $\sigma \triangleright p(\Sigma)$;
- Given a Σ that satisfies the rules in Eq. (4), if $\sigma \triangleright p(\Sigma)$, then $\sigma \in \Sigma$.

The proofs are shown in detail in Appendix A.1.

To show that $\Psi_{\sqsubseteq}$ is efficient, we can use Theorem 21. $\mathcal{T}_{\propto e \to \triangleright \psi}(\mathcal{P}_{\mathcal{L}_1})$ contains[9]:

$$[\mathcal{T}_{\propto e \to \triangleright \psi}(\text{Diamond})] \; \frac{\sigma \cdot \langle s \rangle \triangleright \psi \quad \sigma \cdot \langle s' \rangle \triangleright \psi \quad s \neq s'}{\sigma \cdot \langle s, s' \rangle \triangleright \psi}$$

$$[\mathcal{T}_{\propto e \to \triangleright \psi}(\text{Branching})] \; \frac{\sigma \cdot \sigma_1 \cdot \langle s \rangle \triangleright \psi \quad \sigma \cdot \sigma_2 \cdot \langle s \rangle \triangleright \psi \quad S(\sigma_1) \cap S(\sigma_2) = \{\}}{\sigma \cdot \langle s \rangle \triangleright \psi}$$

$$[\mathcal{T}_{\propto e \to \triangleright \psi}(\text{Weak Convergence})] \; \frac{\sigma_1 \cdot \sigma \triangleright \psi \quad \sigma_2 \triangleright \psi \quad S(\sigma_1) = S(\sigma_2)}{\sigma_2 \cdot \sigma \triangleright \psi}$$

$$[\mathcal{T}_{\propto e \to \triangleright \psi}(\text{Empty Sequence})] \; \frac{}{\langle\rangle \triangleright \psi} \quad \text{if } \vdash \psi \qquad [\mathcal{T}_{\propto e \to \triangleright \psi}(\text{Prefix})] \; \frac{\sigma \cdot \langle s \rangle \triangleright \psi}{\sigma \triangleright \psi}. \quad (6)$$

Thus, to show that $\Psi_{\sqsubseteq}$ enforces $\mathcal{P}_{\mathcal{L}_1}$, it is enough to show that the above rules in Eq. (6) are sound w.r.t. the definition of $\triangleright$ in Eq. (3), as detailed in Appendix A.2.

5.2 $\mathcal{L}_2$

First, the syntax of SOL $\Psi_\perp$ is trivial: $\psi \in \Psi_\perp ::= \perp$, with the trivial SOL conformance relation $\triangleright$:

$$\frac{}{\sigma \triangleright \perp}. \quad (7)$$

---
[9] We added a side condition ($\vdash \psi$) to the $[\mathcal{T}_{\propto e \to \triangleright \psi}(\text{Empty Sequence})]$ rule for clarity.

To show that $\Psi_\perp$ is sufficient (i.e., Proposition 9), we can use Theorem 20. According to Table 2, $\mathcal{T}_{\alpha e \to \in \Sigma}(\mathcal{P}_{\mathcal{L}_2})$ contains all six inference rules in the $\mathcal{T}_{\alpha e \to \in \Sigma}$ column of Table 2. We define the following trivial function p:

$$p(\Sigma) = \perp.$$

Thus, we end up to show that:

- If $\sigma \in \Sigma$, then $\sigma \triangleright p(\Sigma)$;
- Given a Σ that satisfies all six rules in the $\mathcal{T}_{\alpha e \to \in \Sigma}$ column of Table 2, if $\sigma \triangleright p(\Sigma)$, then $\sigma \in \Sigma$.

The first point is obvious; the second point is true because such a Σ must contain all stage sequences due to $\mathcal{T}_{\alpha e \to \in \Sigma}(\text{Free})$ and $\mathcal{T}_{\alpha e \to \in \Sigma}(\text{Empty Sequence})$.

To show that $\Psi_\perp$ is efficient, we can use Theorem 21. $\mathcal{T}_{\alpha e \to \triangleright \psi}(\mathcal{P}_{\mathcal{L}_2})$ contains all six inference rules in the $\mathcal{T}_{\alpha e \to \triangleright \psi}$ column of Table 2. Thus, to show that $\Psi_\perp$ enforces $\mathcal{P}_{\mathcal{L}_2}$, it is enough to show that the six rules in the $\mathcal{T}_{\alpha e \to \triangleright \psi}$ column of Table 2 are all sound w.r.t. Eq. (7), which is obvious as $\forall \sigma . \sigma \triangleright \psi = \perp$.

5.3 $\mathcal{L}_3$

We have already defined the SOL $\Psi_\diamond$ and its conformance relation $\triangleright$ in Sec. 3.4.

To show that $\Psi_\diamond$ is sufficient (i.e., Proposition 12), we can use Theorem 20. According to Table 2, $\mathcal{T}_{\alpha e \to \in \Sigma}(\mathcal{P}_{\mathcal{L}_3})$ contains:

$$[\mathcal{T}_{\alpha e \to \in \Sigma}(\text{Branching})] \quad \frac{\sigma \cdot \sigma_1 \cdot \langle s \rangle \in \Sigma \quad \sigma \cdot \sigma_2 \cdot \langle s \rangle \in \Sigma \quad S(\sigma_1) \cap S(\sigma_2) = \{\}}{\sigma \cdot \langle s \rangle \in \Sigma}$$

$$[\mathcal{T}_{\alpha e \to \in \Sigma}(\text{Weak Convergence})] \quad \frac{\sigma_1 \cdot \sigma \in \Sigma \quad \sigma_2 \in \Sigma \quad S(\sigma_1) = S(\sigma_2)}{\sigma_2 \cdot \sigma \in \Sigma}$$

$$[\mathcal{T}_{\alpha e \to \in \Sigma}(\text{Empty Sequence})] \quad \overline{\langle \rangle \in \Sigma} \qquad [\mathcal{T}_{\alpha e \to \in \Sigma}(\text{Prefix})] \quad \frac{\sigma \cdot \langle s \rangle \in \Sigma}{\sigma \in \Sigma}. \quad (8)$$

We define the following function p:

$$p(\Sigma) = \bigcup_{\sigma \in \Sigma} \{ S(\sigma_1) \diamond s | \sigma = \sigma_1 \cdot \langle s \rangle \cdot \sigma_2 \}. \quad (9)$$

Thus, we end up to show that:

- If $\sigma \in \Sigma$, then $\sigma \triangleright p(\Sigma)$;
- Given a Σ that satisfies the rules in Eq. (4), if $\sigma \triangleright p(\Sigma)$, then $\sigma \in \Sigma$.

The proofs are shown in detail in Appendix B.1.

To show that $\Psi_\diamond$ is efficient, we can use Theorem 21. $\mathcal{T}_{\alpha e \to \triangleright \psi}(\mathcal{P}_{\mathcal{L}_3})$ contains:

$$[\mathcal{T}_{\alpha e \to \triangleright \psi}(\text{Branching})] \quad \frac{\sigma \cdot \sigma_1 \cdot \langle s \rangle \triangleright \psi \quad \sigma \cdot \sigma_2 \cdot \langle s \rangle \triangleright \psi \quad S(\sigma_1) \cap S(\sigma_2) = \{\}}{\sigma \cdot \langle s \rangle \triangleright \psi}$$

$$[\mathcal{T}_{\alpha e \to \triangleright \psi}(\text{Weak Convergence})] \quad \frac{\sigma_1 \cdot \sigma \triangleright \psi \quad \sigma_2 \triangleright \psi \quad S(\sigma_1) = S(\sigma_2)}{\sigma_2 \cdot \sigma \triangleright \psi}$$

$$[\mathcal{T}_{\alpha e \to \triangleright \psi}(\text{Empty Sequence})] \quad \overline{\langle \rangle \triangleright \psi} \quad \text{if} \vdash \psi \qquad [\mathcal{T}_{\alpha e \to \triangleright \psi}(\text{Prefix})] \quad \frac{\sigma \cdot \langle s \rangle \triangleright \psi}{\sigma \triangleright \psi}. \quad (10)$$

Thus, to show that $\Psi_\diamond$ enforces $\mathcal{P}_{\mathcal{L}_3}$, it is enough to show that the above rules in Eq. (10) are sound w.r.t. the definition of $\triangleright$ in Eq. (1). The proof is shown in detail in Appendix B.2.

6 Conclusion

We have studied the problem of how to encode stage orderings of staged code in staged languages. The stage ordering language (SOL) of a staged language is key for efficient on-line re-optimization of stage sequences, because the structure of the SOL can lead to well-organized and efficient search for an optimal stage sequence. By analyzing several staged languages, we have shown that no single generic SOL exists that is both sufficient (stage orderings of all staged code can be encoded) and necessary (no redundant term exists that encodes stage ordering of no staged code) for any staged language. We have related the design and validation of a SOL with semantic properties of a staged language, by developing a metatheory about sufficient and efficient SOLs.

There are many interesting possibilities for future work. Firstly, although the metatheory provides a way to transform the validation of a SOL to simpler theorem-proving tasks, there is no prescriptive method to develop a SOL in the first place. This first step relies on human intelligence; automation or guidelines in this step are worth exploring. Secondly, we did not study the problem of normal form encoding. Both $\Psi_{\sqsubseteq}$ and $\Psi_{\diamond}$ allow multiple terms to encode the same stage ordering; it may be useful to define normal forms that uniquely represent different stage orderings. Thirdly, it is desirable that the validation phase be automated. The biggest obstacle seems to be the construction of the function p.

Beyond the technical aspects, it is even more worthwhile to explore how this work will influence the design of staged languages and even BTA itself. This is similar to the case of past research in type systems: at first type systems are installed to existing languages, but later on types become a vital basis in designing new languages. Example challenges include whether we can do BTA with a less restricted stage ordering than a linear ordering.

References

1. C. Consel and F. Noël. A general approach for run-time specialization and its application to C. In *Proc. of the 23th ACM Symposium on Principles of Programming Languages*, pages 145–156, 1996.
2. R. Glück and J. Jørgensen. Efficient multi-level generating extensions for program specialization. In *Programming Languages: Implementations, Logics and programs (PLILP'95)*, volume 982 of *LNCS*, pages 259–278. Springer, 1995.
3. B. Grant, M. Mock, M. Philipose, C. Chambers, and S. Eggers. DyC: An expressive annotation-directed dynamic compiler for C. *Theoretical Computer Science*, 248(1-2):147–199, Oct. 2000.
4. N. D. Jones, C. K. Gomard, and P. Sestoft. *Partial Evaluation and Automatic Program Generation*. Prentice Hall International, Englewood Cliffs, NJ, 1993.
5. P. Lee and M. Leone. Optimizing ML with run-time code generation. In *Proc. of Programming Language Design and Implementation Conf.*, pages 137–148, 1996.
6. F. Nielson and H. R. Nielson. *Two-Level Functional Languages*. Cambridge University Press, 1992.
7. F. Nielson and H. R. Nielson. *Multi-level lambda-calculi: an algebraic description*, pages 338–354. Lecture Notes in Computer Science. Springer-Verlag, 1996.

8. F. Nielson and H. R. Nielson. A prescriptive framework for designing multi-level lambda-calculi. In *Proc. of the 1997 ACM Symposium on Partial Evaluation and Semantics-based Program Manipulation*, pages 193–202, June 1997.
9. W. Taha. *Multi-Stage Programming: Its Theory and Applications*. PhD thesis, Oregon Graduate Institute of Science and Technology, Nov. 1999.
10. W. Taha and T. Sheard. Multi-stage programming with explicit annotations. In *Proc. of the 1997 ACM Symposium on Partial Evaluation and Semantics-based Program Manipulation*, pages 203–217, June 1997.

A Proofs for $\mathcal{L}_1$

A.1 The Sufficient Part

We need to show that: a) if $\sigma \in \Sigma$, then $\sigma \triangleright p(\Sigma)$, where p is defined in Eq. (5); b) given a Σ that satisfies the rules in Eq. (4), if $\sigma \triangleright p(\Sigma)$, then $\sigma \in \Sigma$.
a) We need the following lemmas.

Lemma 22 *If $\vdash (S, E)$ and $E' \subseteq E$, then $\vdash (S, E')$.*

PROOF By a simple structural induction on the proofs of $\vdash (S, E)$.

Lemma 23 $\vdash p(\Sigma)$.

PROOF By mathematical induction on the size of Σ.

- Base case: $\Sigma = \{\}$. $p(\Sigma) = (\{\}, \{\})$, so $\vdash p(\Sigma)$ with the [DAG Empty] rule.
- Induction step: $\Sigma = \Sigma' \cup \{\sigma\}$ ($\sigma \notin \Sigma'$). Let $p(\Sigma) = (S_\Sigma, E_\Sigma)$ and $p(\Sigma') = (S_{\Sigma'}, E_{\Sigma'})$. According to induction hypothesis, $\vdash (S_{\Sigma'}, E_{\Sigma'})$. We also define

$$E_{\Sigma',\sigma} \stackrel{\text{def}}{=} \bigcup_{s \in S_{\Sigma'}} \left(\bigcap_{\sigma_1 \cdot \langle s \rangle \cdot \sigma_2 \in \Sigma' \cup \{\sigma\}} \{s' \to s | s' \in \sigma_1\} \right).$$

Observe $E_{\Sigma',\sigma} \subseteq E_{\Sigma'}$, so we can apply Lemma 22 and obtain $\vdash (S_{\Sigma'}, E_{\Sigma',\sigma})$. Now let us divide $\sigma = \sigma_1 \cdot \langle s_1 \rangle \cdot \sigma_2 \cdot \ldots \cdot \langle s_m \rangle \cdot \sigma_{m+1}$, where $s_1, \ldots, s_m$ are those stage labels not in $S_{\Sigma'}$. We also define S_i and $E_i (i = 0..m)$ iteratively:

$$S_0 = S_{\Sigma'} \qquad S_{i+1} = S_i \cup \{s_{i+1}\}$$
$$E_0 = E_{\Sigma',\sigma} \qquad E_{i+1} = E_i \cup \{s \to s_{i+1} | s \in \sigma_1 \cdot \langle s_1 \rangle \cdot \ldots \cdot \langle s_i \rangle \cdot \sigma_{i+1}\}.$$

Observe that for each $s \in \sigma_1 \cdot \langle s_1 \rangle \cdot \ldots \cdot \langle s_i \rangle \cdot \sigma_{i+1}$, $s \in S_i$ and $s_{i+1} \notin S_i$, so we have if $\vdash (S_i, E_i)$, then $\vdash (S_{i+1}, E_{i+1})$, according to the [DAG Grow] rule. As we have already shown $\vdash (S_0, E_0)$, we obtain that $\vdash (S_i, E_i)$ $(i = 1..m)$. Finally, it can be verified that $S_m = S_\Sigma$ and $E_m = E_\Sigma$, so that $\vdash (S_\Sigma, E_\Sigma)$.

□

Now we are ready to prove that $\sigma \in \Sigma$, then $\sigma \triangleright p(\Sigma)$. Let us denote $p(\Sigma) = (S_\Sigma, E_\Sigma)$, $\sigma = \langle s_j \rangle_{j=1..k}$, and define $\sigma_i = \langle s_j \rangle_{j=1..i}$. As $s_{i+1} \notin \sigma_i$, $s_{i+1} \in S_\Sigma$, and

$$\{s'|s' \to s_{i+1} \in E_\Sigma\} = \bigcap_{\sigma_a \cdot \langle s_{i+1} \rangle \cdot \sigma_b \in \Sigma} \{s'|s' \in \sigma_a\}$$
$$\subseteq \{s'|s' \in \sigma_a, \text{ where } \sigma_a \cdot \langle s_{i+1} \rangle \cdot \sigma_b = \sigma\} = \{s'|s' \in \sigma_i\},$$

we can apply the [DC Grow] rule to obtain that if $\sigma_i \triangleright p(\Sigma)$, then $\sigma_{i+1} \triangleright p(\Sigma)$.

On the other hand, we have $\vdash p(\Sigma)$ according to Lemma 23, and thus $\sigma_0 = \langle \rangle \triangleright p(\Sigma)$ according to the [DC Empty] rule.

Now we can obtain $\sigma_i \triangleright p(\Sigma)(i = 0..k)$. As $\sigma_k = \sigma$, we conclude that $\sigma \triangleright p(\Sigma)$.

b) We need the following lemmas. In the following, Σ satisfies the rules in Eq. (4).

Lemma 24 *If $\sigma \cdot \sigma_1 \cdot \langle s \rangle \cdot \sigma_2 \in \Sigma$ and $\sigma \cdot \langle s \rangle \in \Sigma$, then $\sigma \cdot \langle s \rangle \cdot \sigma_1 \cdot \sigma_2 \in \Sigma$.*

PROOF Let us denote $\sigma_1 = \langle s_i \rangle_{i=1..l}$ and define

$$\sigma_{pk} = \sigma \cdot \langle s_i \rangle_{i=1..k} \cdot \langle s \rangle \qquad \sigma_{qk} = \sigma \cdot \langle s \rangle \cdot \langle s_i \rangle_{i=1..k} \qquad (k = 0..l)$$

We wish to show that $\sigma_{pk} \in \Sigma$ and $\sigma_{qk} \in \Sigma$ imply $\sigma_{pk+1} \in \Sigma$ and $\sigma_{qk+1} \in \Sigma$. Firstly, $\sigma \cdot \sigma_1 \cdot \langle s \rangle \cdot \sigma_2 \in \Sigma$ and the $[\mathcal{T}_{\infty e \to \in \Sigma}(\text{Prefix})]$ rule can give us $\sigma \cdot \langle s_i \rangle_{i=1..k+1} \in \Sigma$. Together with $\sigma_{pk} \in \Sigma$, we can apply the $[\mathcal{T}_{\infty e \to \in \Sigma}(\text{Diamond})]$ rule and obtain that $\sigma_{pk+1} \in \Sigma$ and $\sigma_{pk} \cdot \langle s_{k+1} \rangle \in \Sigma$. Then we can apply the $[\mathcal{T}_{\infty e \to \in \Sigma}(\text{Weak Convergence})]$ rule to $\sigma_{pk} \cdot \langle s_{k+1} \rangle \in \Sigma$, $\sigma_{qk} \in \Sigma$, and $\{s | s \in \sigma_{pk}\} = \{s | s \in \sigma_{qk}\}$ and obtain that $\sigma_{qk+1} \in \Sigma$.

As $\sigma_{p0} = \sigma_{q0} = \sigma \cdot \langle s \rangle \in \Sigma$, we have $\sigma_{pk}, \sigma_{qk} \in \Sigma$. Thus $\sigma_{ql} = \sigma \cdot \langle s \rangle \cdot \sigma_1 \in \Sigma$. Together with $\sigma \cdot \sigma_1 \cdot \langle s \rangle \cdot \sigma_2 \in \Sigma$, $\{s | s \in \sigma \cdot \sigma_1 \cdot \langle s \rangle\} = \{s | s \in \sigma_{ql}\}$, and the $[\mathcal{T}_{\infty e \to \in \Sigma}(\text{Weak Convergence})]$ rule, we conclude $\sigma_{ql} \cdot \sigma_2 = \sigma \cdot \langle s \rangle \cdot \sigma_1 \cdot \sigma_2 \in \Sigma$. □

Let $\sigma - \sigma'$ denote a sequence obtained by removing stage labels in σ' from σ.

Corollary 25 *If $\sigma, \sigma' \in \Sigma$ and $\{s | s \in \sigma'\} \subseteq \{s | s \in \sigma\}$, then $\sigma' \cdot (\sigma - \sigma') \in \Sigma$.*

Lemma 26 *If $\sigma_1 \in \Sigma$, $\sigma_2 \in \Sigma$, $\{s | s \in \sigma_1\} \cap \{s | s \in \sigma_2\} = \{s_1, \ldots, s_l\}$, and $\sigma_1 = \sigma_{11} \cdot \langle s_1 \rangle \cdot \ldots \cdot \langle s_l \rangle \cdot \sigma_{1l+1}$, then $\langle s_i \rangle_{i=1..l} \in \Sigma$.*

PROOF Let us define $\sigma_{pk} = \langle s_i \rangle_{i=1..k}$ $(k = 0..l)$. We wish to obtain that if $\sigma_{pk} \in \Sigma$ then $\sigma_{pk+1} \in \Sigma$. We can apply Coro. 25 to obtain that $\sigma_{pk} \cdot (\sigma_1 - \sigma_{pk}) \in \Sigma$ and $\sigma_{pk} \cdot (\sigma_2 - \sigma_{pk}) \in \Sigma$, where $\sigma_1 - \sigma_{pk} = \sigma_{11} \cdot \ldots \cdot \sigma_{1k} \cdot \langle s_{k+1} \rangle \cdot \ldots \cdot \langle s_l \rangle \cdot \sigma_{l+1}$. Using the $[\mathcal{T}_{\infty e \to \in \Sigma}(\text{Prefix})]$ rule, we obtain $\sigma_{pk} \cdot \sigma_{11} \cdot \ldots \cdot \sigma_{1k} \cdot \langle s_{k+1} \rangle \in \Sigma$ and $\sigma_{pk} \cdot \sigma_{2k} \cdot \langle s_{k+1} \rangle \in \Sigma$ for some σ_{2k} that satisfies $\{s | s \in \sigma_{2k} \cdot \langle s_{k+1} \rangle\} \subseteq \{s | s \in \sigma_2\}$. It can be verified that $\{s | s \in \sigma_{11} \cdot \ldots \cdot \sigma_{1k}\} \cap \{s | s \in \sigma_{2k}\} = \{\}$, so we can apply the $[\mathcal{T}_{\infty e \to \in \Sigma}(\text{Branching})]$ rule to obtain that $\sigma_{pk+1} = \sigma_{pk} \cdot \langle s_{k+1} \rangle \in \Sigma$.

Using the $[\mathcal{T}_{\infty e \to \in \Sigma}(\text{Empty Sequence})]$ rule, we have $\sigma_{p0} = \langle \rangle \in \Sigma$. Therefore, we obtain $\sigma_{pk} \in \Sigma(k = 0..l)$. Finally $\sigma_{pl} = \langle s_i \rangle_{i=1..l} \in \Sigma$. □

Corollary 27 *If $\sigma_k \in \Sigma(k = 1..l)$, $\bigcap_{k=1}^{l} \{s | s \in \sigma_k\} = \{s_1, \ldots, s_l\}$, and $\sigma_1 = \sigma_{11} \cdot \langle s_1 \rangle \cdot \ldots \cdot \langle s_l \rangle \cdot \sigma_{1l+1}$, then $\langle s_i \rangle_{i=1..l} \in \Sigma$.*

Lemma 28 *If $\sigma \cdot \sigma_1 \in \Sigma$ and $\sigma \cdot \langle s \rangle \in \Sigma$, then $\sigma \cdot \sigma_1 \cdot \langle s \rangle \in \Sigma$.*

PROOF Actually, we already proved this lemma in the proof of Lemma 24.

Lemma 29 *If $\sigma \in \Sigma$, $s \notin \sigma$, $s \in S_\Sigma$, and $\{s' | s' \to s \in E_\Sigma\} \subseteq \{s' | s' \in \sigma\}$, then $\sigma \cdot \langle s \rangle \in \Sigma$.*

PROOF   Let $\{\sigma_1 \cdot \langle s \rangle \cdot \sigma'_1, \ldots, \sigma_l \cdot \langle s \rangle \cdot \sigma'_l\} = \{\sigma | \sigma \in \Sigma \text{ and } s \in \sigma\}$. Using the [$\mathcal{T}_{\infty e \to \in \Sigma}$(Prefix)] rule, we have $\sigma_k \cdot \langle s \rangle \in \Sigma (k = 1..l)$. It can also be shown that $\bigcap_{k=1}^{l} \{s' | s' \in \sigma_k \cdot \langle s \rangle\} = \{s' | s' \to s \in E_\Sigma\} \cup \{s\}$. Now we can apply Coro. 27 and obtain that there exists σ' s.t. $\{s' | s' \in \sigma'\} = \{s' | s' \to s \in E_\Sigma\}$ and $\sigma' \cdot \langle s \rangle \in \Sigma$.

By [$\mathcal{T}_{\infty e \to \in \Sigma}$(Prefix)] rule, $\sigma' \in \Sigma$. Together with $\sigma \in \Sigma$ and $\{s' | s' \in \sigma'\} = \{s' | s' \to s \in E_\Sigma\} \subseteq \{s' | s' \in \sigma\}$, we get $\sigma' \cdot (\sigma - \sigma') \in \Sigma$ using Coro. 25. Together with $\sigma' \cdot \langle s \rangle \in \Sigma$, we further get $\sigma' \cdot (\sigma - \sigma') \cdot \langle s \rangle \in \Sigma$ using Lemma 28.

Finally, observe that $\{s' | s' \in \sigma' \cdot (\sigma - \sigma')\} = \{s' | s' \in \sigma\}$, we can conclude that $\sigma \cdot \langle s \rangle \in \Sigma$ using the [$\mathcal{T}_{\infty e \to \in \Sigma}$(Weak Convergence)] rule.   □

Now we are ready to prove that if $\sigma \triangleright p(\Sigma)$, then $\sigma \in \Sigma$, by structural induction on the proofs of $\sigma \triangleright p(\Sigma)$.

- Case [DC Empty]. $\sigma = \langle \rangle \in \Sigma$ by the [$\mathcal{T}_{\infty e \to \in \Sigma}$(Empty Sequence)] rule.
- Case [DC Grow]. Suppose $\sigma \triangleright p(\Sigma)$ is derived as:

$$\frac{\sigma_r \triangleright (S_\Sigma, E_\Sigma) \quad s \notin \sigma_r \quad s \in S_\Sigma \quad \{s' | s' \to s \in E_\Sigma\} \subseteq \{s' | s' \in \sigma_r\}}{\sigma = \sigma_r \cdot \langle s \rangle \triangleright (S_\Sigma, E_\Sigma) = p(\Sigma)}.$$

By induction hypothesis, we have $\sigma_r \in \Sigma$. Then it is straightforward to apply Lemma 29 and obtain that $\sigma = \sigma_r \cdot \langle s \rangle \in \Sigma$.

A.2   The Efficient Part

We need to show that the five rules in Eq. (6) are sound w.r.t. the definition of $\triangleright$ in Eq. (3).

The [$\mathcal{T}_{\infty e \to \triangleright \psi}$(Empty Sequence)] rule is equivalent to the [DC Empty] rule.

The [$\mathcal{T}_{\infty e \to \triangleright \psi}$(Prefix)] rule can be proved by a straightforward structural induction on the proofs of $\sigma \cdot \langle s \rangle \triangleright \psi$.

The [$\mathcal{T}_{\infty e \to \triangleright \psi}$(Weak Convergence)] rule can be proved by a mathematical induction on the lengths of σ; the induction step needs the [$\mathcal{T}_{\infty e \to \triangleright \psi}$(Prefix)] rule and the following lemma:

If $\sigma_1 \cdot \{s\} \triangleright \psi$, $\sigma_2 \triangleright \psi$, and $\{s | s \in \sigma_1\} = \{s | s \in \sigma_2\}$, then $\sigma_2 \cdot \{s\} \triangleright \psi$,

which can be proved by by structural induction on the proofs of $\sigma_1 \cdot \{s\} \triangleright \psi$:

- Case [DC Empty]. $\sigma_1 \cdot \langle s \rangle \triangleright \psi$ cannot be derived by this rule.
- Case [DC Grow]. Suppose $\sigma \cdot \langle s \rangle \triangleright \psi$ is derived as:

$$\frac{\sigma_1 \triangleright (S, E) \quad s \notin \sigma_1 \quad s \in S \quad \{s' | s' \to s \in E\} \subseteq \{s' | s' \in \sigma_1\}}{\sigma_1 \cdot \langle s \rangle \in (S, E) = \psi}.$$

As $\{s | s \in \sigma_1\} = \{s | s \in \sigma_2\}$, $s \notin \sigma_1$ and $\{s' | s' \to s \in E\} \subseteq \{s' | s' \in \sigma_1\}$ is equivalent to $s \notin \sigma_2$ and $\{s' | s' \to s \in E\} \subseteq \{s' | s' \in \sigma_2\}$ respectively. In addition, we have $\sigma_2 = \psi = (S, E)$ and $s \in S$. Now we can apply the [DC Grow] rule and obtain that $\sigma_2 \cdot \langle s \rangle \triangleright (S, E) = \psi$.

The [$\mathcal{T}_{\infty e \to \rhd \psi}$(Diamond)] rule can be proved by a structural induction on the proofs of $\sigma \cdot \langle s' \rangle \rhd \psi$:

- Case [DC Empty]. $\sigma \cdot \langle s' \rangle \rhd \psi$ cannot be derived by this rule.
- Case [DC Grow]. Suppose $\sigma \cdot \langle s' \rangle \rhd \psi$ is derived as:

$$\frac{\sigma \rhd (S, E) \quad s' \notin \sigma \quad s' \in S \quad \{s_r | s_r \to s' \in E\} \subseteq \{s_r | s_r \in \sigma\}}{\sigma \cdot \langle s' \rangle \in (S, E) = \psi}.$$

From the premises of the [$\mathcal{T}_{\infty e \to \rhd \psi}$(Diamond)] rule, we have $\sigma \cdot \langle s \rangle \rhd \psi = (S, E)$ and $s \neq s'$. $s' \notin \sigma$ and $s \neq s'$ imply $s' \notin \sigma \cdot \langle s \rangle$. $\{s_r | s_r \to s' \in E\} \subseteq \{s_r | s_r \in \sigma\} \subset \{s_r | s_r \in \sigma \cdot \langle s \rangle\}$. Now we can apply the [DC Grow] rule and obtain that $\sigma \cdot \langle s, s' \rangle = (\sigma \cdot \langle s \rangle) \cdot \langle s' \rangle \rhd (S, E) = \psi$.

The [$\mathcal{T}_{\infty e \to \rhd \psi}$(Branching)] rule can be proved by a structural induction on the proofs of $\sigma \cdot \sigma_1 \cdot \langle s \rangle \rhd \psi$:

- Case [DC Empty]. $\sigma \cdot \sigma_1 \cdot \langle s \rangle \rhd \psi$ cannot be derived by this rule.
- Case [DC Grow]. Suppose $\sigma \cdot \sigma_1 \cdot \langle s \rangle \rhd \psi$ is derived as:

$$\frac{\sigma \cdot \sigma_1 \rhd (S, E) \quad s \notin \sigma \cdot \sigma_1 \quad s \in S \quad \{s' | s' \to s \in E\} \subseteq \{s' | s' \in \sigma \cdot \sigma_1\}}{\sigma \cdot \sigma_1 \cdot \langle s' \rangle \in (S, E) = \psi}.$$

As $\sigma \cdot \sigma_1 \rhd (S, E)$, we have $\sigma \rhd (S, E)$ according the [$\mathcal{T}_{\infty e \to \rhd \psi}$(Diamond)] rule. $s \notin \sigma \cdot \sigma_1$ implies $s \notin \sigma$.
From the premises of the [$\mathcal{T}_{\infty e \to \rhd \psi}$(Branching)] rule, we have $\sigma \cdot \sigma_2 \cdot \langle s \rangle \rhd \psi = (S, E)$, which can only be derived by the [DC Grow] rule as:

$$\frac{\sigma \cdot \sigma_2 \rhd (S, E) \quad s \notin \sigma \cdot \sigma_2 \quad s \in S \quad \{s' | s' \to s \in E\} \subseteq \{s' | s' \in \sigma \cdot \sigma_2\}}{\sigma \cdot \sigma_2 \cdot \langle s' \rangle \in (S, E) = \psi}.$$

Thus $\{s' | s' \to s \in E\} \subseteq \{s' | s' \in \sigma \cdot \sigma_2\}$. Together with $\{s' | s' \to s \in E\} \subseteq \{s' | s' \in \sigma \cdot \sigma_1\}$, we obtain that $\{s' | s' \to s \in E\} \subseteq \sigma \cdot \sigma_1 \cap \sigma \cdot \sigma_2$, where we have abused the notation of $\sigma \cdot \sigma_1 \cap \sigma \cdot \sigma_2$ to really mean $\{s | s \in \sigma \cdot \sigma_1\} \cap \{s | s \in \sigma \cdot \sigma_2\}$. Again from the premises of the [$\mathcal{T}_{\infty e \to \rhd \psi}$(Branching)] rule, $\sigma_1 \cap \sigma_2 = \{\}$, so $\sigma \cdot \sigma_1 \cap \sigma \cdot \sigma_2 = \sigma$. Thus we have $\{s' | s' \to s \in E\} \subseteq \{s' \in \sigma\}$. Now we can apply the [DC Grow] rule and obtain that $\sigma \cdot \langle s \rangle \rhd (S, E) = \psi$.

B Proofs for $\mathcal{L}_3$

B.1 The Sufficient Part

a) We can show the following lemmas by structural induction on the appropriate structure in each lemma:

- $\vdash p(\Sigma)$;
- $\sigma \rhd \{S(\sigma_1) \diamond s | \sigma = \sigma_1 \cdot \langle s \rangle \cdot \sigma_2\}$;
- If $\sigma \rhd \psi$, $\vdash \psi'$, and $\psi \subseteq \psi'$, then $\sigma \rhd \psi'$.

Then we can show assertion a) holds easily.
b) By structural induction on the proofs of $\sigma \triangleright p(\Sigma)$:

- Case [DMD Empty]. $\sigma = \langle \rangle \in \Sigma$ by the $\mathcal{T}_{\infty e \to \in \Sigma}$(Empty Sequence) rule.
- Case [DMD Grow1]. Suppose $\sigma \triangleright p(\Sigma)$ is derived as:

$$\frac{\sigma_r \triangleright p(\Sigma) \quad S(\sigma_r) \diamond S \in p(\Sigma) \quad s \in S}{\sigma = \sigma_r \cdot \langle s \rangle \triangleright p(\Sigma)}.$$

According to Eq. (9), $S(\sigma_r) \diamond S \in p(\Sigma)$ means that there exists $\sigma_p \in \Sigma$ s.t. $S(\sigma_r) \diamond S \in \{S(\sigma_{p1}) \diamond s | \sigma_p = \sigma_{p1} \cdot \langle s \rangle \cdot \sigma_{p2}\}$. As $s \in S$, this means there exists $\sigma_{p1} \cdot \langle s \rangle \cdot \sigma_{p2} \in \Sigma$, s.t. $\{s|s \in \sigma_{p1}\} = \{s|s \in \sigma_r\}$. From $\sigma_{p1} \cdot \langle s \rangle \cdot \sigma_{p2} \in \Sigma$, we can obtain $\sigma_{p1} \cdot \langle s \rangle \in \Sigma$ using the [$\mathcal{T}_{\infty e \to \in \Sigma}$(Prefix)] rule. From $\sigma_r \triangleright p(\Sigma)$, we can obtain $\sigma_r \in \Sigma$ by induction hypothesis. Now we can apply the [$\mathcal{T}_{\infty e \to \in \Sigma}$(Weak Convergence)] rule to $\sigma_{p1} \cdot \langle s \rangle \in \Sigma$, $\sigma_r \in \Sigma$, and $\{s|s \in \sigma_{p1}\} = \{s|s \in \sigma_r\}$ and obtain that $\sigma = \sigma_r \cdot \langle s \rangle \in \Sigma$.
- Case [DMD Grow2]. Suppose $\sigma \triangleright p(\Sigma)$ is derived as:

$$\frac{\sigma_2 \cdot \langle s \rangle \triangleright p(\Sigma) \quad \sigma_2 \cdot \langle s' \rangle \triangleright p(\Sigma) \quad \sigma_1 \triangleright p(\Sigma) \quad \{s|s \in \sigma_2 \cdot \langle s' \rangle\} = \{s|s \in \sigma_1\}}{\sigma = \sigma_1 \cdot \langle s \rangle \triangleright p(\Sigma)}.$$

By applying the induction hypothesis to $\sigma_2 \cdot \langle s \rangle \triangleright p(\Sigma)$, $\sigma_2 \cdot \langle s' \rangle \triangleright p(\Sigma)$, and $\sigma_1 \triangleright p(\Sigma)$, we obtain $\sigma_2 \cdot \langle s \rangle \in \Sigma$, $\sigma_2 \cdot \langle s' \rangle \in \Sigma$, and $\sigma_1 \in \Sigma$. Using the [$\mathcal{T}_{\infty e \to \in \Sigma}$(Diamond)] rule, $\sigma_2 \cdot \langle s \rangle \in \Sigma$ and $\sigma_2 \cdot \langle s' \rangle \in \Sigma$ imply $\sigma_2 \cdot \langle s', s \rangle \in \Sigma$. Together with $\sigma_1 \in \Sigma$ and $\{s|s \in \sigma_2 \cdot \langle s' \rangle\} = \{s|s \in \sigma_1\}$, we can apply the [$\mathcal{T}_{\infty e \to \in \Sigma}$(Weak Convergence)] rule and obtain that $\sigma = \sigma_1 \cdot \langle s \rangle \in \Sigma$.

B.2 The Efficient Part

The [$\mathcal{T}_{\infty e \to \triangleright \psi}$(Empty Sequence)] rule is equivalent to the [DMD Empty] rule; the [$\mathcal{T}_{\infty e \to \triangleright \psi}$(Prefix)] rule can be proved by a straightforward structural induction on the proofs of $\sigma \cdot \langle s \rangle \triangleright \psi$; the [$\mathcal{T}_{\infty e \to \triangleright \psi}$(Diamond)] rule is a corollary of the [DMD Grow2] rule. The [$\mathcal{T}_{\infty e \to \triangleright \psi}$(Weak Convergence)] rule is the interesting one. It can be proved by mathematical induction on the lengths of σ. The induction step needs the [$\mathcal{T}_{\infty e \to \triangleright \psi}$(Prefix)] rule and the following lemma:

If $\sigma_1 \cdot \langle s \rangle \triangleright \psi$, $\sigma_2 \triangleright \psi$, and $\{s|s \in \sigma_1\} = \{s|s \in \sigma_2\}$, then $\sigma_2 \cdot \langle s \rangle \triangleright \psi$,

which can be proved by structural induction on the proofs of $\sigma_1 \cdot \langle s \rangle \triangleright \psi$:

- Case [DMD Empty]. $\sigma_1 \cdot \langle s \rangle \triangleright \psi$ cannot be derived by this rule.
- Case [DMD Grow1]. Suppose $\sigma_1 \cdot \langle s \rangle \triangleright \psi$ is derived as:

$$\frac{\sigma_1 \triangleright \psi \quad \{s|s \in \sigma_1\} \diamond S \in \psi \quad s \in S}{\sigma_1 \cdot \langle s \rangle \triangleright \psi}$$

$\{s|s \in \sigma_1\} = \{s|s \in \sigma_2\}$ and $\{s|s \in \sigma_1\} \diamond S \in \psi$ imply $\{s|s \in \sigma_2\} \diamond S \in \psi$. Together with $\sigma_2 \triangleright \psi$, $s \in S$ and the [DMD Grow2] rule, we obtain $\sigma_2 \cdot \langle s \rangle \triangleright \psi$.
- Case [DMD Grow2]. Similar to case [DMD Grow1].

Staged Notational Definitions

Walid Taha[1,*] and Patricia Johann[2]

[1] Department of Computer Science, Rice University
taha@cs.rice.edu
[2] Department of Computer Science, Rutgers University
pjohann@crab.rutgers.edu

Abstract. Recent work proposed defining type-safe macros via interpretation into a multi-stage language. The utility of this approach was illustrated with a language called MacroML, in which all type checking is carried out before macro expansion. Building on this work, the goal of this paper is to develop a macro language that makes it easy for programmers to reason about terms locally. We show that defining the semantics of macros in this manner helps in developing and verifying not only type systems for macro languages but also equational reasoning principles. Because the MacroML calculus is sensetive to renaming of (what appear locally to be) bound variables, we present a calculus of staged notational definitions (SND) that eliminates the renaming problem but retains MacroML's phase distinction. Additionally, SND incorporates the generality of Griffin's account of notational definitions. We exhibit a formal equational theory for SND and prove its soundness.

1 Introduction

Macros are powerful programming constructs with applications ranging from compile-time configuration and numeric computation packages to the implementation of domain-specific languages [14]. Yet the subtlety of their semantics has long been the source of undeserved stigma. As remarked by Steele and Gabriel,

> "Nearly everyone agreed that macro facilities were invaluable in principle and in practice but looked down upon each particular instance as a sort of shameful family secret. If only the Right Thing could be found!" [15].

Recently, a promising approach to the semantics of generative macros has been proposed. This approach is based on the systematic formal treatment of macros as multi-stage computations [7]. Some of its benefits were illustrated with MacroML, an extension of ML which supports inlining, parametric macros, recursive macros, and macros that define new binding constructs, and in which all type-checking is carried out before macro expansion.

Interpreting macros as multi-stage computations avoids some technical difficulties usually associated with macro systems (such as hygiene and scoping issues). But while MacroML is capable of *expressing* staged macros, it is not

---

* Funded by NSF ITR-0113569.

well-suited to *reasoning* about them. This is in part because MacroML does not allow general alpha-conversion, and thus requires a non-standard notion of substitution as well.

Our goal in this paper is to demonstrate that interpreting macros as multi-stage computations facilitates both the development of type systems *and* the verification of formal reasoning principles for macro languages. More specifically, we aim to formalize staged macros in a way that makes it possible for programmers to reason effectively about programs which use them.

1.1 Contributions

To this end we define SND, a calculus of staged notational definitions that reforms and generalizes the formal account of MacroML. SND combines the staging of MacroML with a staged adaptation of Griffin's formal development of notational definitions in the context of logical frameworks [8]. The former provides the phase distinction [3] expected from macro definitions, and ensures that SND macro expansion takes place before regular computation. The latter captures precisely how parameters need to be passed to macros. A novel notion of signature allows us to express in the term language the information needed to pass macro parameters to macros correctly. The signatures are expressive enough to allow defining macros that introduce new binding constructs.

The semantics of SND is defined by interpreting it into a multi-stage language. By contrast with both Griffin's notational definitions and MacroML, the interpretation and formal equational theory for SND are developed in an untyped setting. The interpretation of SND is defined in a compositional and context-independent manner. This makes possible the main technical contribution of this paper, namely showing that the soundness of SND's equational theory can be established directly from the equational properties of the multi-stage language used for interpretation. Our soundness result is obtained for untyped SND, and so necessarily holds for *any* typed variant of that calculus. We develop a simply typed variant of SND, prove that it is type-safe, and exhibit a sound embedding of MacroML in it.

An alternative to the approach to "macros as multi-stage computations" presented here is to define the semantics of the macro language by interpretation into a domain-theoretic or categorical model[1]. But the CPO model of Filinski [5,6] would be too intensional with respect to second stage (i.e., run-time) computations, and so additional work would still be needed to demonstrate that equivalence holds in the second stage. This is significant: Even when languages are extended with support for macros, the second stage is still considered the primary stage of computation, with the first stage often regarded as a pre-processing stage. Categorical models can, of course, be extensional [10, 2], but they are currently fixed to specific type systems and specific approaches to typing multi-level languages. By contrast, interpreting a macro language in the term-model of a

---

[1] In this paper the word "interpretation" is used to mean "translation to give meaning" rather than "an interpreter implementation".

multi-stage language constitutes what we expect to be a widely applicable approach.

1.2 Organization of This Paper

Section 2 reviews MacroML, and illustrates how the absence of alpha-conversion can make reasoning about programs difficult. Section 3 reviews key aspects of Griffin's development of notational definitions, and explains why this formalism alone is not sufficient for capturing the semantics of macros. Section 4 reviews λ^U, the multi-stage calclus which will serve as the interpretation language for SND. Section 5 introduces the notion of a staged notational definition and the macro language SND which supports such definitions. It also defines the interpretation of SND into λ^U, and uses this to show how SND programs are executed. Section 6 presents a formal equational theory for SND and shows that the soundness of this theory be established by reflecting the equational theory for the interpretation language through the interpretation. Section 7 presents an embedding of MacroML into SND along with a soundness result for the embedding. Section 8 concludes.

2 Renaming in MacroML

New binding constructs can be used to capture shorthands such as the following:

letopt $x = e_1$ in e_2 $\stackrel{\text{def}}{=}$ case e_1 of Just$(x) \to e_2$ | Nothing $\to$ Nothing

Such notational definitions frequently appear in research papers (including this one). The intent of the definition above is that whenever the pattern defined by its left-hand side is encountered, this pattern should be read as an instance of the right-hand side.

In MacroML, the notation defined above is introduced using the declaration

```
let mac (let opt x=e1 in e2) = case e1 of Just x -> e2
                                        | Nothing -> Nothing
```

Unfortunately, the programmer may at some point choose to change the name of the bound variable in the right-hand side of the above definition from x to y, thus rewriting the above term to

```
let mac (let opt x=e1 in e2) = case e1 of Just y -> e2
                                        | Nothing -> Nothing
```

Now the connection between the left- and right-hand sides of the definition is lost, and the semantics of the new term is, in fact, not defined. This renaming problem is present even in the definition of letopt above, and it shows that general alpha-conversion is not sound in MacroML.

The absence of alpha-conversion makes it easy to introduce subtle mistakes that can be hard to debug. In addition, since the notion of substitution depends on alpha-conversion, MacroML necessarily has a non-standard notion of substitution. Having a non-standard notion of substitution can significantly complicate the formal reasoning principles for a calculus.

The SND calculus presented here avoids the difficulties associated with alpha-conversion. It regains the soundness of alpha-conversion by using a *convention* associated with higher-order syntax. This convention is distinct from higher-order syntax itself, which is already used in MacroML and SND. It goes as far back as Church at the meta-theoretic level, and is used in Griffin's formal account of notational definitions [8], and by Michaylov and Pfenning in the context of LF [9]. It requires that whenever a term containing free variables is used, that term must be *explicitly* instantiated with the local names for those free variables.

According to the convention, we would write the example above as

$$\text{letopt } x = e_1 \text{ in } e_2^x \stackrel{\text{def}}{=} \text{case } e_1 \text{ of } \text{Just}(x) \to e_2^x \mid \text{Nothing} \to \text{Nothing}$$

It is now possible to rename bound variables without confusing the precise meaning of the definition. Indeed, the meaning of the definition is preserved if we use alpha-conversion to rewrite it to

$$\text{letopt } x = e_1 \text{ in } e_2^x \stackrel{\text{def}}{=} \text{case } e_1 \text{ of } \text{Just}(z) \to e_2^z \mid \text{Nothing} \to \text{Nothing}$$

In SND (extended with a case construct and datatypes) the above definition can be written with the following concrete syntax:

```
let mac (let opt x=e1 in ~(e2 <x>)) =   case ~e1 of
                                          Just x   -> ~(e2 <x>)
                                        | Nothing -> Nothing
```

By contrast with MacroML, when a user defines a new variant of an existing binding construct with established scope in SND, it is necessary to indicate on the left-hand side of the mac declaration which variables can occur where.

Previous work on MacroML has established that explicit escape and bracket constructs can be used to control the unfolding of recursive macros [7]. In this paper we encounter additional uses for these constructs in a macro language. The escape around e1 indicates that e1 is a macro-expansion-time value being inserted into the template defined by the right-hand side of the macro. The escapes around the occurrences of e2 <x>, on the other hand, indicate an instantiation to the free variable x of a macro argument e2 containing a free variable.

3 Griffin's Notational Definitions

Like Griffin's work, this paper is concerned with the formal treatment of new notation. Griffin uses a notion of term pattern to explicitly specify the binding structure of, and name the components of, the notation being defined. His formal account of notational definitions provides the technical machinery needed to manage variable bindings in patterns, including binding patterns that themselves contain bindings. A staged version is used in Section 5 to indicate precisely how parameters should be passed to macros in order to ensure that the standard notion of alpha-conversion remains valid for SND.

SND is concerned with definitions akin to what Griffin calls Δ-equations. The above example would be written in the form of a Δ-equation as:

$$\mathsf{opt}\ (e_1, \lambda x.e_2) \stackrel{\Delta}{=} \mathsf{case}\ \tilde{}e_1\ \mathsf{of}\ \mathsf{Just}(x) \to \tilde{}(e_2\ \langle x \rangle)\ |\ \mathsf{Nothing} \to \mathsf{Nothing}$$

Δ-equations can be incorporated into a lambda calculus as follows[2]:

$$p \in P_{ND} ::= x\ |\ (p,p)\ |\ \lambda x.p$$
$$e \in E_{ND} ::= x\ |\ \lambda x.e\ |\ e\ e\ |\ (e,e)\ |\ \pi_i\ e\ |\ \mathsf{let\text{-}delta}\ x\ p \stackrel{\Delta}{=} e\ \mathsf{in}\ e$$

Here P_{ND} is the set of *patterns* and E_{ND} is the set of *expressions*. The pattern $\lambda x.p$ denotes a pattern in which x is bound. A well-formed pattern can have at most one occurrence of any given variable, including binding occurrences. Thus, $Vars(p_1) \cap Vars(p_2) = \emptyset$ for the pattern (p_1, p_2), and $x \notin Vars(p)$ for $\lambda x.p$.

Griffin shows how the let-delta construct can be interpreted using only the other constructs in the language. To define the translation, he uses two auxiliary functions. The first computes the binding environments of pattern terms.

$$\begin{aligned}
\mathsf{scope}^z_z(p) &= [\,] \\
\mathsf{scope}^{(p_1,p_2)}_z(p'_1, p'_2) &= \mathsf{scope}^{p_i}_z(p'_i), \quad z \in FV(p_i) \\
\mathsf{scope}^{\lambda y.p_1}_z(\lambda x.p) &= x :: \mathsf{scope}^{p_1}_z(p)
\end{aligned}$$

The second computes, for a pattern p, each variable z occurring free in p, and each expression e, the subterm of e which occurs in the same pattern context in which z occurs in p.

$$\Phi^z_z(e) = e, \quad \Phi^{(p_1,p_2)}_z(e) = \Phi^{p_i}_z(\pi_i\ e)\ \text{where}\ z \in FV(p_i), \quad \Phi^{\lambda y.p}_z(e) = \Phi^p_z(e\ y)$$

We write let $x = e_1$ in e_2 to mean $(\lambda x.e_2)\ e_1$, and let $x_i = e_i$ in e to denote a sequence of multiple simultaneous let bindings. With this notation, Δ-equations can be interpreted in terms of the other constructs of the above calculus by

$$[\![\mathsf{let\text{-}delta}\ f\ p \stackrel{\Delta}{=} e_1\ \mathsf{in}\ e_2]\!] = \begin{cases} \mathsf{let}\ f = \lambda x.\ \mathsf{let}\ v_i = \lambda \mathsf{scope}^p_{v_i}(p).\Phi^p_{v_i}(x) \\ \quad \mathsf{in}\ [\![e_1]\!] \\ \mathsf{in}\ [\![e_2]\!]\ \mathrm{where}\ \{v_i\} = FV(p) \end{cases}$$

The construction $\lambda \mathsf{scope}^p_{v_i}(p).\Phi^p_{v_i}(x)$ is a nesting of lambdas with $\Phi^p_{v_i}(x)$ as the body. In $\lambda \mathsf{scope}^p_{v_i}(p).\Phi^p_{v_i}(x)$ it is critical that all three occurrences of p denote the same pattern. Note that $\lambda [\,].y = y$ where $[\,]$ is the empty sequence.

Griffin's translation performs much of the work that is needed to provide a generic account of macros that define new binding constructs. What it does not

---

[2] Throughout this paper we adopt Barendregt's convention of assuming that the set of bound variables in a given formula is distinct from the set of free variables.

provide is the phase distinction. Griffin's work is carried out in the context of a strongly normalizing typed lambda calculus where order of evaluation is provably irrelevant. In the context of programming languages, however, expanding macros before run-time can affect both the performance and the semantics of programs. This point is discussed in detail in the context of MacroML in [7].

4 A Multi-stage Language

The semantics of SND is given by interpretation into λ^U, a multi-stage calculus. This section presents λ^U together with the results on which the rest of the paper builds.

The syntax of λ^U is defined as follows:

$$e \in E_{\lambda^U} ::= x \mid \lambda x.e \mid e\ e \mid (e,e) \mid \pi_i\ e \mid \text{letrec } f\ x = e \text{ in } e \mid \langle e \rangle \mid \,\tilde{}\,e \mid \text{run } e$$

To develop an equational theory for λ^U, it is necessary to define a level classification of terms that keeps track of the nesting of escaped expressions $\tilde{}\,e$ and bracketed expressions $\langle e \rangle$. We have

$$\begin{aligned}
e^0 \in E_{\lambda^U}^0 ::= &\ x \mid \lambda x.e^0 \mid e^0\ e^0 \mid (e^0,e^0) \mid \pi_i\ e^0 \\
&\mid \text{letrec } f\ x = e^0 \text{ in } e^0 \mid \langle e^1 \rangle \mid \text{run } e^0 \\
e^{n+1} \in E_{\lambda^U}^{n+1} ::= &\ x \mid \lambda x.e^{n+1} \mid e^{n+1}\ e^{n+1} \mid (e^{n+1},e^{n+1}) \mid \pi_i\ e^{n+1} \\
&\mid \text{letrec } f\ x = e^{n+1} \text{ in } e^{n+1} \mid \langle e^{n+2} \rangle \mid \,\tilde{}\,e^n \mid \text{run } e^{n+1} \\
v^0 \in V_{\lambda^U}^0 ::= &\ \lambda x.e^0 \mid (v^0,v^0) \mid \langle v^1 \rangle \\
v^{n+1} \in V_{\lambda^U}^{n+1} =\ & E^n
\end{aligned}$$

Above and throughout this paper, the level of a term is indicated by a superscript, e and its subscripted versions to denote arbitrary λ^U expressions, and v and its subscripted versions indicate λ^U values. Values at level 0 are mostly as would be expected in a lambda calculus. Code values are not allowed to carry arbitrary terms, but rather only level 1 values. The key feature of level 1 values is that they do not contain escapes that are not surrounded by matching brackets. It turns out that this is easy to specify for λ^U, since values of level $n+1$ are exactly level n expressions.

Figure 1 defines the big-step semantics for λ^U. This semantics is based on similar definitions for other multi-stage languages [4, 12, 18]. There are two features of this semantics worthy of special attention. First, it makes evaluation under lambda explicit. This shows that multi-stage computation often violates one of the most commonly made assumptions in programming language semantics, namely that attention can, without loss of generality, be restricted to closed terms. Second, using just the standard notion of substitution [1], this semantics captures the *essence* of static scoping. As a result, there is no need for additional machinery to handle renaming at run-time.

The big-step semantics for λ^U is a family of partial functions $\_ \stackrel{n}{\hookrightarrow} \_ : E_{\lambda^U} \to E_{\lambda^U}$ from expressions to answers, indexed by level. Focusing on reductions at

$$\frac{e_1 \stackrel{0}{\hookrightarrow} e_3 \quad e_2 \stackrel{0}{\hookrightarrow} e_4}{(e_1, e_2) \stackrel{0}{\hookrightarrow} (e_3, e_4)} \quad \frac{e \stackrel{0}{\hookrightarrow} (e_1, e_2)}{\pi_i \, e \stackrel{0}{\hookrightarrow} e_i} \quad \frac{}{\lambda x.e \stackrel{0}{\hookrightarrow} \lambda x.e}$$

$$\frac{e_1 \stackrel{0}{\hookrightarrow} \lambda x.e \quad e_2 \stackrel{0}{\hookrightarrow} e_3 \quad e[x := e_3] \stackrel{0}{\hookrightarrow} e_4}{e_1 \, e_2 \stackrel{0}{\hookrightarrow} e_4}$$

$$\frac{e_2[f := \lambda x.e_1[f := \text{letrec } f \, x = e_1 \text{ in } f]] \stackrel{0}{\hookrightarrow} e_3}{\text{letrec } f \, x = e_1 \text{ in } e_2 \stackrel{0}{\hookrightarrow} e_3} \quad \frac{e_1 \stackrel{0}{\hookrightarrow} \langle e_2 \rangle \quad e_2 \stackrel{0}{\hookrightarrow} e_3}{\text{run } e_1 \stackrel{0}{\hookrightarrow} e_3}$$

$$\frac{e_1 \stackrel{n+1}{\hookrightarrow} e_2}{\pi_i \, e_1 \stackrel{n+1}{\hookrightarrow} \pi_i \, e_2} \quad \frac{e_1 \stackrel{n+1}{\hookrightarrow} e_3 \quad e_2 \stackrel{n+1}{\hookrightarrow} e_4}{(e_1, e_2) \stackrel{n+1}{\hookrightarrow} (e_3, e_4)} \quad \frac{}{x \stackrel{n+1}{\hookrightarrow} x} \quad \frac{e_1 \stackrel{n+1}{\hookrightarrow} e_2}{\lambda x.e_1 \stackrel{n+1}{\hookrightarrow} \lambda x.e_2}$$

$$\frac{e_1 \stackrel{n+1}{\hookrightarrow} e_3 \quad e_2 \stackrel{n+1}{\hookrightarrow} e_4}{e_1 \, e_2 \stackrel{n+1}{\hookrightarrow} e_3 \, e_4} \quad \frac{e_1 \stackrel{n+1}{\hookrightarrow} e_3 \quad e_2 \stackrel{n+1}{\hookrightarrow} e_4}{\text{letrec } f \, x = e_1 \text{ in } e_2 \stackrel{n+1}{\hookrightarrow} \text{letrec } f \, x = e_3 \text{ in } e_4} \quad \frac{e_1 \stackrel{n}{\hookrightarrow} \langle e_2 \rangle}{\langle e_1 \rangle \stackrel{n}{\hookrightarrow} \langle e_2 \rangle}$$

$$\frac{e_1 \stackrel{n+1}{\hookrightarrow} e_2}{\text{run } e_1 \stackrel{n+1}{\hookrightarrow} \text{run } e_2} \quad \frac{e_1 \stackrel{n+2}{\hookrightarrow} e_2}{\tilde{\,} e_1 \stackrel{n+2}{\hookrightarrow} \tilde{\,} e_2} \quad \frac{e_1 \stackrel{0}{\hookrightarrow} \langle e_2 \rangle}{\tilde{\,} e_1 \stackrel{1}{\hookrightarrow} e_2}$$

Fig. 1. λ^U Big-Step Semantics

level 0, we see that the third and fourth rules correspond to the rules of a CBV lambda calculus. The rule for **run** at level 0 says that an expression is run by first evaluating it to get an expression in brackets, and then evaluating that expression. As a special case of the rule for evaluating bracketed expressions, we see that an expression $\langle e_1 \rangle$ is evaluated at level 0 by rebuilding e_1 at level 1. The semantics of pairing and recursive unfolding at level 0 is standard.

Rebuilding, i.e., evaluating at levels higher than 0, is intended to eliminate level 1 escapes. Rebuilding is performed by traversing the expression while correctly keeping track of levels. It simply traverses a term, without performing any reductions, until a level 1 escape is encountered. When an escaped expression $\tilde{\,} e_1$ is encountered at level 1, normal (*i.e.*, level 0) evaluation is performed on e_1. In this case, evaluating e_1 must yield a bracketed expression $\langle e_2 \rangle$, and then e_2 is returned as the value of $\tilde{\,} e_1$.

In this paper we prove the soundness of the equational theory for SND by building on the following results for λ^U [17] leading upto Theorem 1:

Definition 1 (λ^U Reductions). *The notions of reduction of λ^U are:*

$$\pi_i \, (v_1^0, v_2^0) \rightarrow_{\pi_U} v_i^0$$

$$(\lambda x.e_1^0) \, v_2^0 \rightarrow_{\beta_U} e_1^0[x := v_2^0]$$

$$\text{letrec } f \, x = e_1^0 \text{ in } e_2^0 \rightarrow_{rec_U} e_2^0[f := \lambda x.e_1^0[f := \text{letrec } f \, x = e_1^0 \text{ in } f]]$$

$$\tilde{\,}\langle v^1 \rangle \rightarrow_{esc_U} v^1$$

$$\text{run } \langle v^1 \rangle \rightarrow_{run_U} v^1$$

We write $\rightarrow_{\lambda^U}$ for the compatible extension of the union of these rules.

Definition 2 (Level 0 Termination). $\forall e \in E^0 . e \Downarrow \equiv (\exists v \in V^0 . e \overset{0}{\hookrightarrow} v)$

Definition 3 (Context). *A* context *is an expression with exactly one hole* $[\,]$.

$$C \in \mathbb{C} ::= [\,] \mid (e, C) \mid (C, e) \mid \pi_i\, C \mid \lambda x.C \mid C\, e \mid e\, C$$
$$\mid \mathsf{letrec}\ f\ x = C\ \mathsf{in}\ e \mid \mathsf{letrec}\ f\ x = e\ \mathsf{in}\ C \mid \langle C \rangle \mid {\tilde{\ }} C \mid \mathsf{run}\ C$$

We write $C[e]$ for the expression resulting from replacing ("filling") the hole $[\,]$ in the context C with the expression e.

Definition 4 (Observational Equivalence). *The relation* $\approx_n\, \subseteq E^n \times E^n$ *is defined by:* $\forall n \in \mathbb{N}.\, \forall e_1, e_2 \in E^n.$

$$e_1 \approx_n e_2 \equiv \forall C \in \mathbb{C}.\, C[e_1], C[e_2] \in E^0 \implies (C[e_1]\Downarrow \iff C[e_2]\Downarrow)$$

Theorem 1 (Soundness). $\forall n \in \mathbb{N}.\, \forall e_1, e_2 \in E^n.\, e_1 \to_{\lambda^U} e_2 \implies e_1 \approx_n e_2.$

A simple type system can be defined for λ^U using the following types:

$$t \in T_{\lambda^U} ::= \mathsf{nat} \mid t * t \mid t \to t \mid \langle t \rangle$$

Here nat is a type for natural numbers, pair types have the form $t_1 * t_2$ and function types have the form $t_1 \to t_2$. The λ^U code type is denoted by $\langle t \rangle$.

The rules of the type system are presented in Figure 2. The type system for λ^U is defined by a judgment of the form $\Gamma \vdash^n e : t$. The natural number n is defined to be the *level* of the λ^U term e. The typing context Γ is a map from identifiers to types and levels, and is represented by the term language $\Gamma ::= [\,] \mid \Gamma, x : t^n$. In any valid context Γ there should be no repeating occurrences of the same variable name. We write $x : t^n \in \Gamma$ if $x : t^n$ is a subterm of a valid Γ.

The first six rules of the type system are standard typing rules, except that the level n of each term is recorded in the typing judgments. In the rules for abstractions and recursive functions, the current level is taken as the level of the bound variable when it is added to the typing context.

The rule for brackets gives $\langle e \rangle$ type $\langle t \rangle$ whenever e has type t and e is typed at the level one greater than the level at which $\langle e \rangle$ is typed. The rule for escape performs the converse operation, so that escapes undo the effect of brackets. The level of a term thus counts the number of surrounding brackets minus the number of surrounding escapes. Escapes can only occur at level 1 and higher.

The rule for run e is rather subtle. We can run a term of type $\langle t \rangle$ to get a value of type t. We must, however, be careful to check that the term being run can be typed under an appropriate extension Γ^+ of the current type context Γ, rather than simply in Γ itself. The type context Γ^+ has exactly the same variables and corresponding types as Γ, but the level of each is incremented by 1. Without this level adjustment, the type system is unsafe [18, 12, 16].

The soundness of this type system has already been established [18, 12, 16]. While this type system is not the most expressive one available for λ^U (c.f. [19]), it is simple and sufficient for our purposes.

$$\frac{x:t^n \in \Gamma}{\Gamma \vdash^n x:t} \quad \frac{\Gamma \vdash^n e_1:t_1 \quad \Gamma \vdash^n e_2:t_2}{\Gamma \vdash^n (e_1,e_2):t_1 * t_2} \quad \frac{\Gamma \vdash^n e:t_1 * t_2}{\Gamma \vdash^n \pi_i\, e:t_i} \quad \frac{\Gamma, x:t_1^n \vdash^n e:t_2}{\Gamma \vdash^n \lambda x.e:t_1 \to t_2}$$

$$\frac{\Gamma \vdash^n e_1:t_2 \to t \quad \Gamma \vdash^n e_2:t_2}{\Gamma \vdash^n e_1 e_2:t}$$

$$\frac{\Gamma, f:(t_1 \to t_2)^n, x:t_1^n \vdash^n e_1:t_2 \quad \Gamma, f:(t_1 \to t_2)^n \vdash^n e_2:t_3}{\Gamma \vdash^n \text{letrec } f\, x = e_1 \text{ in } e_2:t_3} \quad \frac{\Gamma \vdash^{n+1} e:t}{\Gamma \vdash^n \langle e \rangle:\langle t \rangle} \quad \frac{\Gamma \vdash^n e:\langle t \rangle}{\Gamma \vdash^{n+1} \tilde{\ } e:t} \quad \frac{\Gamma^+ \vdash^n e:\langle t \rangle}{\Gamma \vdash^n \text{run } e:t}$$

Fig. 2. λ^U Type System

5 Staged Notational Definitions

We begin with the syntax of SND. This extension of Griffin's notational definitions has all the usual expressions for a CBV language, together with the previously described letmac construct for defining macros, pattern-bound expressions for recording macro binding information, and the explicit staging annotations $\tilde{\ } e$ and $\langle e \rangle$ of λ^U for controlling recursive inlining. SND is defined by:

$$p \in P_{SND} ::= x \mid \tilde{\ } x \mid (p,p) \mid \lambda x.p$$
$$q \in Q_{SND} ::= * \mid \tilde{\ } * \mid (q,q) \mid \lambda q$$
$$e \in E_{SND} ::= x \mid \lambda x.e \mid e\,e \mid (e,e) \mid \pi_i\, e \mid \text{letrec } y\, x = e_1 \text{ in } e_2$$
$$\mid p.e \mid e_q\, e \mid \text{letmac } f\, p\ = e_1 \text{ in } e_2 \mid \langle e \rangle \mid \tilde{\ } e$$

Elements of P_{SND} are called *patterns*. An SND pattern can be either a regular macro parameter x, an early macro parameter $\tilde{\ } x$, a pair (p_1, p_2) of patterns, or a pair $\lambda x.p$ of a bound variable and a pattern. Early parameters represent regular values which are available at macro-expansion time; they appear as escaped variables, which ensures that the arguments replacing them in a macro call are evaluated during macro expansion. Binder-bindee pairs represent subterms of new binding constructs. Like patterns in Griffin's notational definitions, an SND pattern can contain at most one occurrence of any given variable.

Elements of Q_{SND} are called *signatures*. Signatures capture the structure of the elements of P_{SND} as defined by the following function:

$$\overline{x} = * \qquad \overline{\tilde{\ } x} = \tilde{\ } * \qquad \overline{(p_1,p_2)} = (\overline{p_1}, \overline{p_2}) \qquad \overline{\lambda x.p} = \lambda \overline{p}$$

Signatures play an essential role in defining an untyped semantics for SND. They capture precisely how parameters need to be passed to macros, and do this without introducing additional complexity to the notion of alpha-conversion.

Elements of E_{SND} are SND *expressions*. Of particular importance are SND macro abstractions and applications, i.e., expressions of the form $p.e$ and $e'_q\, e''$, respectively. Intuitively, a macro expression is a first-class value representing a Δ-equation. Such a value can be used in any macro application. In a macro application $e'_q\, e''$, the expression e'_q is a computation that should evaluate to a macro abstraction $p.e$. Because the way in which parameters are passed to a macro depends on the pattern used in the macro abstraction, the pattern p in $p.e$ must have the signature q indicated at the application site in $e'_q\ e''$.

The definition of substitution for SND is standard (omitted for space).

Because of the non-standard interdependence between names of bound variables in MacroML, it is not clear how to define the notion of alpha-conversion (and, in turn, substitution) in that setting. The same difficulties do not arise for SND because alpha-conversion is valid for SND.

Although a type system is not necessary for defining the semantics of SND, certain well-formedness conditions are required. Intuitively, the well-formedness conditions ensure that variables intended for expansion-time use are only used in expansion-time contexts, and similarly for variables intended for run-time use. The well-formedness conditions also ensure that an argument to a macro application has the appropriate form for the signature of the macro being applied. A system similar to that below has been used in the context of studies on monadic multi-stage languages [11].

Well-formedness of SND expressions requires consistency between binding levels and usage levels of variables. Thus, to define the well-formedness judgment for SND, we first need to define a judgment capturing variable occurrence in patterns. In the remainder of this paper, $m \in \{0, 1\}$ will range over evaluation levels 0 and 1. Level 0 corresponds to what is traditionally called macro-expansion time, and level 1 corresponds to what is traditionally called run-time.

Lookup of a variable x in a level-annotated pattern p is given by the judgment $p \vdash^m x$ defined as follows:

$$\frac{}{x^m \vdash^m x} \qquad \frac{}{(\tilde{\ }x)^0 \vdash^0 x} \qquad \frac{p_i^0 \vdash^0 x}{(p_1, p_2)^0 \vdash^0 x} \qquad \frac{p^0 \vdash^0 x}{(\lambda y.p)^0 \vdash^0 x}$$

If P is a set of level-annotated patterns, write $P \vdash^m x$ to indicate that x occurs at level m in (at least) one of the patterns in P.

We now define the *well-formedness judgments* $P \vdash^m e$ and $P \vdash^q e$ for SND expressions. Here, the context P ranges over sets of level-annotated patterns in which any variable occurs at most once. Well-formedness must be defined with respect to a context P because we need to keep track of the level at which a variable is bound to ensure that it is used only at the same level.

$$\frac{p^m \vdash^m x}{P, p^m \vdash^m x} \qquad \frac{P \vdash^m e_1 \quad P \vdash^m e_2}{P \vdash^m (e_1, e_2)} \qquad \frac{P \vdash^m e}{P \vdash^m \pi_i e} \qquad \frac{P, x^m \vdash^m e}{P \vdash^m \lambda x.e}$$

$$\frac{P \vdash^m e_1 \quad P \vdash^m e_2}{P \vdash^m e_1\ e_2} \qquad \frac{P, y^m, x^m \vdash^m e_1 \quad P, y^m \vdash^m e_2}{P \vdash^m \text{letrec } y\ x = e_1 \text{ in } e_2}$$

$$\frac{P, p^0 \vdash^1 e}{P \vdash^0 p.e} \qquad \frac{P \vdash^0 e_1 \quad P \vdash^q e_2}{P \vdash^1 (e_1)_q\ e_2} \qquad \frac{P, p^0, f^0 \vdash^1 e_1 \quad P, f^0 \vdash^1 e_2}{P \vdash^1 \text{letmac } f\ p\ = e_1 \text{ in } e_2} \qquad \frac{P \vdash^1 e}{P \vdash^0 \langle e \rangle}$$

$$\frac{P \vdash^0 e}{P \vdash^1 \tilde{\ }e} \qquad \frac{P \vdash^1 e}{P \vdash^* e} \qquad \frac{P \vdash^0 e}{P \vdash^{\tilde{\ }*} e} \qquad \frac{P \vdash^{q_1} e_1 \quad P \vdash^{q_2} e_2}{P \vdash^{(q_1, q_2)} (e_1, e_2)} \qquad \frac{P, y^1 \vdash^q e}{P \vdash^{\lambda q} \lambda y.e}$$

As is customary, we write $\vdash^m e$ for $\emptyset \vdash^m e$.

$[\![x]\!]^m = x$, $\quad [\![(e_1, e_2)]\!]^m = ([\![e_1]\!]^m, [\![e_2]\!]^m)$, $\quad [\![\pi_i\ e]\!]^m = \pi_i\ [\![e]\!]^m$, $\quad [\![\lambda x.e]\!]^m = \lambda x.[\![e]\!]^m$,
$[\![e_1\ e_2]\!]^m = [\![e_1]\!]^m\ [\![e_2]\!]^m$, $\quad [\![\text{letrec } y\ x = e_1 \text{ in } e_2]\!]^m = \text{letrec } y\ x = [\![e_1]\!]^m \text{ in } [\![e_2]\!]^m$,
$[\![p.e]\!]^0 = \lambda x.\text{let } v_i = \lambda \text{scope}^p_{v_i}(p).\varPhi^p_{v_i}(x) \text{ in } \langle [\![e]\!]^1 \rangle \text{ where } \{v_i\} = FV(p)$,
$[\![(e_1)_q\ e_2]\!]^1 = \tilde{\ }([\![e_1]\!]^0\ [\![e_2]\!]^q)$

$[\![\text{letmac } f\ p = e_1 \text{ in } e_2]\!]^1 = \begin{cases} (\text{letrec } f\ x = \text{ let } v_i = \lambda \text{scope}^p_{v_i}(p).\varPhi^p_{v_i}(x) \\ \qquad\qquad\qquad\qquad \text{ in } \langle [\![e_1]\!]^1 \rangle \\ \text{ in } \langle [\![e_2]\!]^1 \rangle) \text{ where } \{v_i\} = FV(p) \end{cases}$

$[\![\langle e \rangle]\!]^0 = \langle [\![e]\!]^1 \rangle$, $\quad [\![\tilde{\ }e]\!]^1 = \tilde{\ }[\![e]\!]^0$

$[\![e]\!]^* = \langle [\![e]\!]^1 \rangle$, $\quad [\![e]\!]^{\tilde{\ }*} = [\![e]\!]^0$, $\quad [\![(e_1, e_2)]\!]^{(q_1, q_2)} = ([\![e_1]\!]^{q_1}, [\![e_2]\!]^{q_2})$,
$[\![\lambda x.e]\!]^{\lambda q} = \lambda x.[\![e]\!]^q[x := \tilde{\ }x]$

Fig. 3. Interpretation of SND in λ^U

In the untyped setting, the signature q at the point where a macro is applied is essential for driving the well-formedness check for the argument to the macro. As will be seen later in the paper, the signature q also drives the typing judgment for the argument in a macro application. In source programs, if we restrict e_q in a macro application to the name of a macro, then the signature q can be inferred from the context, and does not need to be written explicitly by the programmer. At the level of the calculus, however, it is more convenient to make it explicit.

The expected weakening results hold, namely, if $P \vdash^n e$ then $P, p^m \vdash^n e$, and if $P \vdash^q e$ then $P, p^m \vdash^q e$. Substitution is also well-behaved:

Lemma 1 (Substitution Lemma).

1. If $p^n \vdash^n x$, $P, p^n \vdash^m e_1$, and $P \vdash^n e_2$, then $P, p^n \vdash^m e_1[x := e_2]$.
2. If $p^n \vdash^n x$, $P, p^n \vdash^q e_1$, and $P \vdash^n e_2$, then $P, p^n \vdash^q e_1[x := e_2]$.

5.1 Semantics of SND

The only change we need to make to Griffin's auxiliary functions to accommodate staging of notational definitions is a straightforward extension to include early parameters:

$\text{scope}^z_z(p) = \text{scope}^{\tilde{\ }z}_z(\tilde{\ }p) = [\,]$, $\quad \text{scope}^{(p_1, p_2)}_z(p'_1, p'_2) = \text{scope}^{p_i}_z(p'_i)$, $z \in FV(p_i)$,
$\text{scope}^{\lambda y.p_1}_z(\lambda x.p) = x :: \text{scope}^{p_1}_z(p)$

$\varPhi^z_z(e) = \varPhi^{\tilde{\ }z}_z(e) = e$, $\quad \varPhi^{(p_1, p_2)}_z(e) = \varPhi^{p_i}_z(\pi_i\ e)$, $z \in FV(p_i)$, $\quad \varPhi^{\lambda y.p}_z(e) = \varPhi^p_z(e\ y)$

The interpretation of SND in λ^U is given in Figure 3. It is well-behaved in the sense that, for all m, and for all signatures q and expressions e, if $P \vdash^m e$ then $[\![e]\!]^m$ is defined and is in $E^m_{\lambda U}$, and if $P \vdash^q e$ then $[\![e]\!]^q$ is defined and is in $E^0_{\lambda U}$. It is also substitutive:

Lemma 2. *For all m and n, and for all patterns p, signatures q, sets P and P' of patterns, and expressions e_1 and e_2,*

1. *If $p^n \vdash x$, if $P, P', p^n \vdash^m e_1$, and if $P \vdash^n e_2$, then $[\![e_1]\!]^m[x := [\![e_2]\!]^n] = [\![e_1[x := e_2]]\!]^m$.*
2. *If $p^n \vdash x$, if $P, P', p^n \vdash^q e_1$, and if $P \vdash^n e_2$, then $[\![e_1]\!]^q[x := [\![e_2]\!]^n] = [\![e_1[x := e_2]]\!]^q$.*

Note that no analogue of Lemma 2 holds for the interpretation of MacroML.

5.2 Executing SND Programs

After translation into λ^U, SND programs are executed in exactly the same way as MacroML programs. The result of running a well-formed SND program $\vdash^1 e$ is obtained simply by evaluating the λ^U term run $e \langle [\![\vdash^1 e]\!] \rangle$. A finer-grained view of the evaluation of $[\![\vdash^1 e]\!]$ can be obtained by observing that evaluating proceeds in two distinct steps, namely

1. macro expansion, in which the SND program e is expanded into the λ^U program e'_1 for which $\langle [\![\vdash^1 e]\!] \rangle \xrightarrow{0} e'_1$.
2. regular execution, in which the λ^U expansion e'_1 of e is evaluated to obtain the value e'_2 for which run $e'_1 \xrightarrow{0} e'_2$.

The following examples illustrate SND program execution. They assume a hypothetical extension of our calculus in which arithmetic expressions have been added in a standard manner, such as using Church numerals.

Example 1 (Direct Macro Invocation). In SND, the level 1 term $(x.\tilde{\ }x + \tilde{\ }x)_* (2+3)$ represents a direct application of a macro $x.\tilde{\ }x + \tilde{\ }x$ to the term $2+3$. The macro itself simply takes one argument and constructs a term that adds this argument to itself. The result of applying the translation to this macro is

$$[\![(x.\tilde{\ }x + \tilde{\ }x)_* (2+3)]\!]^1$$
$$= \tilde{\ }([\![(x.\tilde{\ }x + \tilde{\ }x)_*]\!]^0 [\![2+3]\!]^*)$$
$$= \tilde{\ }(\lambda y.\text{let } x = y \text{ in } \langle [\![(\tilde{\ }x + \tilde{\ }x)]\!]^1 \rangle \langle [\![2+3]\!]^1 \rangle)$$
$$= \tilde{\ }(\lambda y.\text{let } x = y \text{ in } \langle (\tilde{\ }x + \tilde{\ }x) \rangle \langle 2+3 \rangle)$$

The result is a level 1 λ^U term which, if rebuilt at level 1, produces the term $(2+3)+(2+3)$. That is, $\tilde{\ }(\lambda y.\text{let } x = y \text{ in } \langle (\tilde{\ }x + \tilde{\ }x) \rangle \langle 2+3 \rangle) \xrightarrow{1} (2+3)+(2+3)$.

Example 2 (First Class Macros). This example demonstrates that macros can be passed around as values, and then used in the context of a macro application. The level 0 SND term let $M = x.\tilde{\ }x + \tilde{\ }x$ in $\langle M_* (2+3) \rangle$ binds the variable M to the macro from the above example, and then applies M (instead of directly applying

Staged Notational Definitions   109

the macro) to the same term seen in Example 1. The result of translating this SND term is

$$[\![\text{let } M = x.\tilde{\ }x + \tilde{\ }x \text{ in } \langle M_* \ (2+3) \rangle]\!]^0$$
$$= \text{let } M = \lambda y.\text{let } x = y \text{ in } \langle [\![(\tilde{\ }x + \tilde{\ }x)]\!]^1 \rangle \text{ in } \langle [\![M_* \ (2+3)]\!]^1 \rangle$$
$$= \text{let } M = \lambda y.\text{let } x = y \text{ in } \langle \tilde{\ }x + \tilde{\ }x \rangle \text{ in } \langle \tilde{\ }(M \ [\![2+3]\!]^*) \rangle$$
$$= \text{let } M = \lambda y.\text{let } x = y \text{ in } \langle \tilde{\ }x + \tilde{\ }x \rangle \text{ in } \langle \tilde{\ }(M \ \langle 2+3 \rangle) \rangle$$

When the resulting level 0 λ^U term is evaluated at level 0, the term $\langle (2+3)+(2+3)\rangle$ is produced. If we had put an escape $\tilde{\ }$ around the original SND expression, then it would have been a level 1 expression. Translating it would thus have produced a level 1 λ^U term which, if rebuilt at level 1, would give exactly the same result produced by the term in Example 1.

Example 3 (Basic Macro Declarations).

$$[\![\text{letmac } M \ x = \tilde{\ }x + \tilde{\ }x \text{ in } M_* \ (2+3)]\!]^1$$
$$= \tilde{\ }(\text{letrec } M \ y = \text{let } x = y \text{ in } \langle [\![\tilde{\ }x + \tilde{\ }x]\!]^1 \rangle \text{ in } \langle [\![M_* \ (2+3)]\!] \rangle)$$
$$= \tilde{\ }(\text{letrec } M \ y = \text{let } x = y \text{ in } \langle \tilde{\ }x + \tilde{\ }x \rangle \text{ in } \langle \tilde{\ }(M \ \langle 2+3 \rangle) \rangle)$$

Example 4 (SNDs). Consider the following SML datatype:

```
datatype 'a C = C of 'a
fun unC (C a) = a
```

The SND term $(x, \lambda y.z).(\lambda y.\tilde{\ }(z \ \langle y \rangle))(\text{unC } \tilde{\ }x)$ defines a "monadic-let" macro for this datatype.

$$\begin{bmatrix} \text{letmac } L \ (x, \lambda y.z) = (\lambda y.\tilde{\ }(z \ \langle y \rangle))(\text{unC } \tilde{\ }x) \\ \text{in } L_{(*,\lambda*)} \ (\text{C } 7, \lambda x.\text{C } (x+x)) \end{bmatrix}^1$$

$$= \begin{cases} \tilde{\ }(\text{letrec } L \ x' = \\ \quad \text{let } x = \lambda \text{scope}_x^{(x,\lambda y.z)}(x, \lambda y.z).\Phi_x^{(x,\lambda y.z)}(x') \\ \quad \text{let } z = \lambda \text{scope}_z^{(x,\lambda y.z)}(x, \lambda y.z).\Phi_z^{(x,\lambda y.z)}(x') \\ \quad \text{in } \langle [\![(\lambda y.\tilde{\ }(z \ \langle y \rangle))(\text{unC } \tilde{\ }x)]\!]^1 \rangle \\ \text{in } \langle [\![L_{(*,\lambda*)} \ (\text{C } 7, \lambda x.\text{C } (x+x))]\!]^1 \rangle) \end{cases}$$

$$= \begin{cases} \tilde{\ }(\text{letrec } L \ x' = \\ \quad \text{let } x = \pi_1 \ x' \\ \quad \text{let } z = \lambda y.((\pi_2 \ x')y) \\ \quad \text{in } \langle (\lambda y.\tilde{\ }(z \ \langle y \rangle))(\text{unC } \tilde{\ }x) \rangle \\ \text{in } \langle \tilde{\ }(L \ ([\![\text{C } 7]\!]^*, [\![\lambda x.\text{C } (x+x)]\!]^{\lambda*}))) \rangle \end{cases}$$

$$= \begin{cases} \tilde{\ }(\text{letrec } L \ x' = \\ \quad \text{let } x = \pi_1 \ x' \\ \quad \text{let } z = \lambda y.((\pi_2 \ x')y) \\ \quad \text{in } \langle (\lambda y.\tilde{\ }(z \ \langle y \rangle))(\text{unC } \tilde{\ }x) \rangle \\ \text{in } \langle \tilde{\ }(L \ (\langle \text{C } 7 \rangle, \lambda x.\langle \text{C } (\tilde{\ }x + \tilde{\ }x) \rangle))))) \end{cases}$$

Evaluating the final term according to the standard λ^U semantics at level 1 yields $(\lambda y.\text{C } (y+y)) \ (\text{unC } (\text{C } 7))$.

6 Reasoning about SND Programs

A reasonable approach to defining observational equivalence on SND terms is to consider the behavior of the terms generated by the translation.

Definition 5. *Two SND expressions e_1 and e_2 are* observationally equivalent *if there exists a P such that both $P \vdash^m e_1$ and $P \vdash^m e_2$ are derivable, and $[\![e_1]\!]^m$ and $[\![e_2]\!]^m$ are observationally equivalent level m λ^U terms.*

We write $e_1 \approx_m e_2$ when e_1 and e_2 are observationally equivalent SND terms.

To specify the equational theory for SND and show that it has the desired properties, we use the following five sets to categorize the syntax of SND terms after the macro expansion phase has been completed. All are subsets of E_{SND}.

Definition 6.

$$e^m \in E_{SND}^m = \{\, e \mid \exists P.\ P \vdash^m e \,\}$$
$$e^p \in E_{SND}^p = \{\, e \mid \exists P.\ P \vdash^{\bar{p}} e \,\}$$
$$v^0 \in V_{SND}^0 ::= \lambda x.e^0 \mid (v^0, v^0) \mid p.e^1 \mid \langle v^1 \rangle$$
$$v^1 \in V_{SND}^1 ::= x \mid \lambda x.v^1 \mid v^1\, v^1 \mid (v^1, v^1) \mid \pi_i\, v^1 \mid \textsf{letrec}\ y\ x = v^1\ \textsf{in}\ v^1$$
$$v^p \in V_{SND}^p = \{\, v \mid \exists P.\ P \vdash^{\bar{p}} v \,\}$$

The set V_{SND}^1 is a subset of E_{SND}, but it does not allow for escapes, macros, or brackets in terms. The interpretation of SND in λ^U preserves syntactic categories, i.e., $[\![v^m]\!]^m \in V_{\lambda^U}^m$ and $[\![v^p]\!]^{\bar{p}} \in V_{\lambda^U}^0$.

Definition 7 (SND Reductions). *The relation $\rightarrow$ is defined as the reflexive transitive closure of the compatible extension of the following notions of reduction defined on SND terms:*

$$\pi_i\, (v_1^0, v_2^0) \rightarrow_\pi v_i^0$$
$$(\lambda x.e_1^0)v_2^0 \rightarrow_\beta e_1^0[x := v_2^0]$$
$$\textsf{letrec}\ f\ x = e_1^0\ \textsf{in}\ e_2^0 \rightarrow_{rec} e_2^0[f := \lambda x.e_1^0[f := \textsf{letrec}\ f\ x = e_1^0\ \textsf{in}\ f]]$$
$$(p.e_1^0)_{\bar{p}}\, v_2^p \rightarrow_\mu e_1^0[v_i = \lambda scope_{v_i}^p(p).\Theta_{v_i}^p(v_2^p)],\ \{v_i\} = FV(p)$$
$$\tilde{}\langle v^1 \rangle \rightarrow_{esc} v^1$$
$$\textsf{letmac}\ fp = e_1^1\ \textsf{in}\ e_2^1 \rightarrow_{mac} \begin{cases} \tilde{}(\textsf{letrec}\ f\ x = \\ \quad \textsf{let}\ v_i = \lambda scope_{v_i}^p(p).\Phi_{v_i}^p(x) \\ \quad \textsf{in}\ \langle e_1^1 \rangle \\ \textsf{in}\ \langle e_2^1 \rangle)\ \textsf{where}\ \{v_i\} = FV(p) \end{cases}$$

Here,

$$\Theta_z^z(e) = \langle e \rangle$$
$$\Theta_z^{\tilde{}z}(e) = e$$
$$\Theta_z^{\lambda y.p}(\lambda x.e) = \Theta_z^p(e[x := \tilde{}y])$$
$$\Theta_z^{(p_1, p_2)}((e_1, e_2)) = \Theta_z^{p_i}(e_i),\quad z \in FV(p_i)$$

Note that $\Phi_z^p(\llbracket e^p \rrbracket^{\overline{p}}) = \llbracket \Theta_z^p(e^p) \rrbracket^0$ shows that the use of signatures is implicit in the definition of $\Theta_z^p(e)$.

Theorem 2 (Soundness of SND Reductions).
If $P \vdash^m e_1$ and $P \vdash^m e_2$ then $e_1 \to e_2 \implies e_1 \approx_m e_2$.

6.1 A Type System for SND

The development so far shows that we can define the semantics for untyped SND, and that there is a non-trivial equational theory for this language. These equalities will hold for *any* typed variant of SND. To illustrate how such a type system is defined and verified, this section presents a simply typed version of SND and proves that it guarantees type safety.

The set of type terms is defined by the grammar:

$$t \in T_{SND} ::= \mathsf{nat} \mid t * t \mid t \to t \mid \langle t \rangle$$

Here, nat is representative for various base types, $t_1 * t_2$ is a type for pairs comprising values of types t_1 and t_2, $t_1 \to t_2$ is a type for partial functions that take a value of type t_1 and return a value of type t_2, and $\langle t \rangle$ is the type for a next-stage value of type t.

To define the typing judgment, a notion of type context is needed. Type contexts are generated by the following grammar, with the additional condition that any variable name occurs exactly once in any valid context Γ.

$$\Gamma \in G_{SND} ::= [\,] \mid \Gamma, x : t^m \mid \Gamma, \underline{x} : t^1 \mid \Gamma, p : t^0$$

The case of $\underline{x} : t^1$ is treated just like that of $x : t^m$ by the type system. The distinction is useful only as an instrument for proving type safety. Figure 4 presents a type system for SND and various auxiliary judgments needed in defining it.

6.2 Type Safety for SND

Type safety for SND is established by showing that the interpretation maps well-typed SND terms to well-typed λ^U terms (which themselves are known to be type-safe). SND types map unchanged to λ^U types. The translation on type contexts "flattens" the $p : t^0$ bindings into bindings of the form $x : t^0$. This translation also transforms bindings of the form $\underline{y} : t^0$ to ones of the form $y : \langle t \rangle$. Formally, the translation interprets each binding in a type context Γ as follows:

$$\llbracket x : t^m \rrbracket = x : t^m, \quad \llbracket \underline{x} : t^1 \rrbracket = x : \langle t \rangle^0,$$
$$\llbracket \tilde{x} : t^0 \rrbracket = x : t^0, \quad \llbracket (p_1, p_2) : (t_1, t_2)^0 \rrbracket = (\llbracket p_1 : t_1^0 \rrbracket, \llbracket p_2 : t_2^0 \rrbracket),$$
$$\llbracket (\lambda x.p) : (\langle t_1 \rangle \to t_2)^0 \rrbracket = \{x_i : (\langle t_1 \rangle \to t_i)^0\} \text{ where } \{x_i : t_i^0\} = \llbracket p : t_2 \rrbracket$$

The translation of SND into λ^U preserves types in the following sense. Suppose $\llbracket \Gamma \rrbracket$ is well-defined and y_i are the underlined variables in Γ. If $\Gamma \vdash^m e : t$ is a valid SND judgment, then $\llbracket \Gamma \rrbracket \vdash^m \llbracket e \rrbracket^m [y_i = \tilde{y}_i] : t$ is a valid λ^U judgment. Similarly,

$$\overline{\vdash * : \langle t \rangle} \quad \overline{\vdash \tilde{*} : t} \quad \frac{\vdash q_1 : t_1 \quad \vdash q_2 : t_2}{\vdash (q_1, q_2) : t_1 * t_2} \quad \frac{\vdash q : t_2}{\vdash \lambda q : \langle t_1 \rangle \to t_2} \quad \overline{x : t^m \vdash^m x : t}$$

$$\overline{(\tilde{x} : t)^0 \vdash^0 x : t} \quad \frac{p_i : t_i^0 \vdash^0 x : t}{(p_1, p_2) : (t_1, t_2)^0 \vdash^0 x : t} \quad \frac{p : t_2^0 \vdash^0 x : t_3}{(\lambda y.p) : (t_1 \to t_2)^0 \vdash^0 x : t_1 \to t_3}$$

$$\frac{p : t_1^m \vdash^m x : t_2}{\Gamma, p : t_1^m, \Gamma' \vdash^m x : t_2} \quad \frac{}{\Gamma, \underline{y} : t^1, \Gamma' \vdash^1 y : t} \quad \frac{\Gamma \vdash^m e_1 : t_1 \quad \Gamma \vdash^m e_2 : t_2}{\Gamma \vdash^m (e_1, e_2) : t_1 * t_2}$$

$$\frac{\Gamma \vdash^m e : t_1 * t_2}{\Gamma \vdash^m \pi_i e : t_i} \quad \frac{\Gamma, x : t_1^m \vdash^m e : t_2}{\Gamma \vdash^m \lambda x.e : t_1 \to t_2} \quad \frac{\Gamma \vdash^m e_1 : t_1 \to t_2 \quad \Gamma \vdash^m e_2 : t_1}{\Gamma \vdash^m e_1 \, e_2 : t_2}$$

$$\frac{\Gamma, p : t_1^0 \vdash^1 e : t_2 \quad \vdash \overline{p} : t_1}{\Gamma \vdash^0 p.e : t_1 \to \langle t_2 \rangle}$$

$$\frac{\Gamma, y : t_1 \to t_2^m, x : t_1^m \vdash^m e_1 : t_2 \quad \Gamma, y : t_1 \to t_2^m \vdash^m e_2 : t_3}{\Gamma \vdash^m \mathsf{letrec} \, y \, x = e_1 \, \mathsf{in} \, e_2 : t_3}$$

$$\frac{\Gamma \vdash^0 e_1 : t_1 \to \langle t_2 \rangle \quad \vdash q : t_1 \quad \Gamma \vdash^q e_2 : t_1}{\Gamma \vdash^1 (e_1)_q \, e_2 : t_2}$$

$$\frac{\Gamma, p : t_1^0, f : t_1 \to \langle t_2 \rangle^0 \vdash^1 e_1 : t_2 \quad \vdash \overline{p} : t_1 \quad \Gamma, f : t_1 \to \langle t_2 \rangle^0 \vdash^1 e_2 : t_3}{\Gamma \vdash^1 \mathsf{letmac} \, f \, p = e_1 \, \mathsf{in} \, e_2 : t_3}$$

$$\frac{\Gamma \vdash^1 e : t_1}{\Gamma \vdash^0 \langle e \rangle : \langle t_1 \rangle} \quad \frac{\Gamma \vdash^0 e : \langle t_1 \rangle}{\Gamma \vdash^1 \tilde{e} : t_1} \quad \frac{\Gamma \vdash^1 e_1 : t_1}{\Gamma \vdash^* e_1 : \langle t_1 \rangle} \quad \frac{\Gamma \vdash^0 e : t_1}{\Gamma \vdash^{\tilde{*}} e : t_1}$$

$$\frac{\Gamma \vdash^{q_1} e_1 : t_1 \quad \Gamma \vdash^{q_2} e_2 : t_2}{\Gamma \vdash^{(q_1, q_2)} (e_1, e_2) : t_1 * t_2} \quad \frac{\Gamma, \underline{y} : t_1^1 \vdash^q e : t_2}{\Gamma \vdash^{\lambda q} \lambda y.e : \langle t_1 \rangle \to t_2}$$

Fig. 4. Type System for SND

if $\Gamma \vdash^q e : t$ is a valid SND judgment, then $[\![\Gamma]\!] \vdash^0 [\![e]\!]^q [y_i = \tilde{y}_i] : t$ is a valid λ^U judgment. Comparing this result to the corresponding one for MacroML, we notice that: 1) types require no translation, 2) the translation operates directly on the term being translated and not on the typing judgment for that term, and 3) each part of the lemma requires that $[\![\Gamma]\!]$ is well-defined. This last condition is vacuously true for the empty type context (which is what is needed for type safety). In the general case, this condition simply means that any binding $p : t^m$ occurs at level $m = 0$ and satisfies the well-formedness condition $\vdash \overline{p} : t$.

Theorem 3 (Type Safety). *If $\vdash^m e : t$ is a valid SND judgment, then translating e to λ^U yields a well-typed λ^U program, and executing that program does not generate any λ^U run-time errors.*

7 Embedding of MacroML in SND

Embedding MacroML into SND requires a minor modification to the original definition of how MacroML is interpreted in a multi-stage language. In particular,

$$\frac{x : t^m \in \Gamma}{\Sigma; \Delta; \Pi; \Gamma \vdash^m x : t} \quad \frac{x : t \in \Pi \text{ or } \underline{x} : t \in \Pi}{\Sigma; \Delta; \Pi; \Gamma \vdash^1 x : t} \quad \frac{x_2 : [x_1 : t_1]t_2 \in \Delta \quad x_1 : t_1^1 \in \Gamma}{\Sigma; \Delta; \Pi; \Gamma \vdash^1 x_2 : t_2}$$

$$\frac{\Sigma; \Delta; \Pi; \Gamma, x : t_1^m \vdash^m e : t_2}{\Sigma; \Delta; \Pi; \Gamma \vdash^m \lambda x.e : t_1 \to t_2} \quad \frac{\Sigma; \Delta; \Pi; \Gamma \vdash^m e_1 : t_2 \to t \quad \Sigma; \Delta; \Pi; \Gamma \vdash^m e_2 : t_2}{\Sigma; \Delta; \Pi; \Gamma \vdash^m e_1 e_2 : t}$$

$$\frac{\begin{array}{c} \Gamma' \equiv \Gamma, f : (t_1 \to t_2 \to t_3 \to t)^m \\ \Sigma; \Delta; \Pi; \Gamma', x_1 : t_1^m, x_2 : t_2^m, x_3 : t_3^m \vdash^m e_1 : t \\ \Sigma; \Delta; \Pi; \Gamma' \vdash^m e_2 : t_4 \end{array}}{\Sigma; \Delta; \Pi; \Gamma \vdash^m \mathsf{letrec}\ f\ x_1\ x_2\ x_3 = e_1\ \mathsf{in}\ e_2 : t_4} \quad \frac{\begin{array}{c} f : (t_1, t_2, [t_3]t_4) \Rightarrow t_5 \in \Sigma \\ \Sigma; \Delta; \Pi; \Gamma \vdash^0 e_1 : t_1 \\ \Sigma; \Delta; \Pi; \Gamma \vdash^1 e_2 : t_2 \\ \Sigma; \Delta; \Pi, \underline{x} : t_3; \Gamma \vdash^1 e_3 : t_4 \end{array}}{\Sigma; \Delta; \Pi; \Gamma \vdash^1 f(e_1, e_2, \lambda x.e_3) : t_5}$$

$$\frac{\begin{array}{c} \Sigma' \equiv \Sigma, f : (t_1, t_2, [t_3]t_4) \Rightarrow t_5 \\ \Sigma'; \Delta, x_2 : [x : t_3]t_4; \Pi, x_1 : t_2; \Gamma, x_0 : t_1^0 \vdash^1 e_1 : t_5 \\ \Sigma'; \Delta; \Pi; \Gamma \vdash^1 e_2 : t \end{array}}{\Sigma; \Delta; \Pi; \Gamma \vdash^1 \mathsf{letmac}\ f(\tilde{\ }x_0, (x_1, \lambda x.x_2)) = e_1\ \mathsf{in}\ e_2 : t} \quad \frac{\Sigma; \Delta; \Pi; \Gamma \vdash^1 e : t}{\Sigma; \Delta; \Pi; \Gamma \vdash^0 \langle e \rangle : \langle t \rangle}$$

$$\frac{\Sigma; \Delta; \Pi; \Gamma \vdash^0 e : \langle t \rangle}{\Sigma; \Delta; \Pi; \Gamma \vdash^1 \tilde{\ }e : t}$$

Fig. 5. MacroML Type System (with underlines)

MacroML macros have exactly three arguments (representative of the three possible kinds of arguments: early parameters, regular parameters, and new binding constructs). In the original definition of MacroML, these arguments are taken to be curried. It simplifies the embedding to modify the original definition to treat these three arguments as a tuple.

The type system of MacroML is virtually unchanged, and is reproduced in Figure 5. The modified interpretation of MacroML in λ^U is presented in Figure 7. The embedding of MacroML into SND is given in Figure 6.

Theorem 4 (Embedding). *Translating any well-formed MacroML term into SND and then into λ^U is equivalent to translating the MacroML term directly into λ^U. That is, If $\Sigma; \Delta; \{x_i : t_i\}; \Gamma \vdash^m e : t$ is a valid MacroML judgment, then $[\![[\![\Sigma; \Delta; \{x_i : t_i\}; \Gamma \vdash^m e : t]\!]^M]\!]^m [x_i := \tilde{\ }x_i] \approx_m [\![\Sigma; \Delta; \{x_i : t_i\}; \Gamma \vdash^m e : t]\!]$.*

8 Conclusions

Previous work demonstrated that the "macros as multi-stage computations" approach is instrumental for developing and verifying type systems for expressive macro languages. The present work shows that, for a generalized revision of the MacroML calculus, the approach also facilitates developing an equational theory for a macro language. Considering this problem has also resulted in a better language, in that the semantics of programs does not change if the programmer accidentally "renames" what she perceives is a locally bound variable. The work presented here builds heavily on Griffin's work on notational definitions, and extends it to the untyped setting using the notion of signatures.

Compared to MacroML, SND embodies a number of technical improvements in terms of design of calculi for modeling macros. First, it supports alpha-

Lambda Terms

$$\frac{x : t^m \in \Gamma}{[\![\Sigma; \Delta; \Pi; \Gamma \vdash^m x : t]\!]^M = x} \qquad \frac{[\![\Sigma; \Delta; \Pi; \Gamma, x : t_1^m \vdash^m e : t_2]\!]^M = e'}{[\![\Sigma; \Delta; \Pi; \Gamma \vdash^m \lambda x.e : t_1 \to t_2]\!]^M = \lambda x.e'}$$

$$\frac{[\![\Sigma; \Delta; \Pi; \Gamma \vdash^m e_1 : t_2 \to t]\!]^M = e_1' \quad [\![\Sigma; \Delta; \Pi; \Gamma \vdash^m e_2 : t_2]\!]^M = e_2'}{[\![\Sigma; \Delta; \Pi; \Gamma \vdash^m e_1 e_2 : t]\!]^M = e_1' e_2'}$$

$$\frac{\begin{array}{l}[\![\Sigma; \Delta; \Pi; \Gamma, f : (t_1 \to t_2 \to t_3 \to t)^m, x_1 : t_1^m, x_2 : t_2^m, x_3 : t_3^m \vdash^m e_1 : t]\!]^M = e_1' \\ [\![\Sigma; \Delta; \Pi; \Gamma, f : (t_1 \to t_2 \to t_3 \to t)^m \vdash^m e_2 : t_4]\!]^M = e_2'\end{array}}{[\![\Sigma; \Delta; \Pi; \Gamma \vdash^m \text{letrec } f \; x_1 \; x_2 \; x_3 = e_1 \text{ in } e_2 : t_4]\!]^M = \text{letrec } f \; x_1 = \lambda x_2.\lambda x_3.e_1' \text{ in } e_2'}$$

Macros

$$\frac{\underline{x} : t \in \Pi}{[\![\Sigma; \Delta; \Pi; \Gamma \vdash^1 x : t]\!]^M = x} \qquad \frac{x : t \in \Pi}{[\![\Sigma; \Delta; \Pi; \Gamma \vdash^1 x : t]\!]^M = \tilde{} x}$$

$$\frac{x_2 : [x_1 : t_1]t_2 \in \Delta \quad x_1 : t_1^1 \in \Gamma}{[\![\Sigma; \Delta; \Pi; \Gamma \vdash^1 x_2 : t_2]\!]^M = \tilde{}(x_2 \; \langle x_1 \rangle)}$$

$$\frac{\begin{array}{l}[\![\Sigma, f : (t_1, t_2, [t_3]t_4) \Rightarrow t_5; \Delta, x_2 : [x : t_3]t_4; \Pi, x_1 : t_2; \Gamma, x_0 : t_1^0 \vdash^1 e_1 : t_5]\!]^M = e_1' \\ [\![\Sigma, f : (t_1, t_2, [t_3]t_4) \Rightarrow t_5; \Delta; \Pi; \Gamma \vdash^1 e_2 : t]\!]^M = e_2'\end{array}}{\begin{array}{l}[\![\Sigma; \Delta; \Pi; \Gamma \vdash^1 \text{letmac } f(\tilde{}x_0, x_1, \lambda x.x_2) = e_1 \text{ in } e_2 : t]\!]^M \\ = \text{letmac } f(\tilde{}x_0, x_1, \lambda x.x_2) = e_1' \text{ in } e_2'\end{array}}$$

$$\frac{f : (t_1, t_2, [t_3]t_4) \Rightarrow t_5 \in \Sigma \quad [\![\Sigma; \Delta; \Pi; \Gamma \vdash^0 e_1 : t_1]\!]^M = e_1'}{[\![\Sigma; \Delta; \Pi; \Gamma \vdash^1 e_2 : t_2]\!]^M = e_2' \quad [\![\Sigma; \Delta; \Pi, \underline{x} : t_3; \Gamma \vdash^1 e_3 : t_4]\!]^M = e_3'}{[\![\Sigma; \Delta; \Pi; \Gamma \vdash^1 f(e_1, e_2, \lambda x.e_3) : t_5]\!]^M = (f_{(\tilde{}*, (*, \lambda *))} \; (e_1', (e_2', \lambda x.e_3')))}$$

Code Objects

$$\frac{[\![\Sigma; \Delta; \Pi; \Gamma \vdash^1 e : t]\!]^M = e'}{[\![\Sigma; \Delta; \Pi; \Gamma \vdash^0 \langle e \rangle : \langle t \rangle]\!]^M = \langle e' \rangle} \qquad \frac{[\![\Sigma; \Delta; \Pi; \Gamma \vdash^0 e : \langle t \rangle]\!]^M = e'}{[\![\Sigma; \Delta; \Pi; \Gamma \vdash^1 \tilde{}e : t]\!]^M = \tilde{}e'}$$

Fig. 6. Translation from MacroML to SND

equivalence. Second, its translation into λ^U is substitutive. Compared to notational definitions, SND provides the phase distinction that is not part of the formal account of notational definitions. Introducing the phase distinction means that macro application is no longer just function application. To address this issue, a notion of signatures is introduced, and is used to define an untyped semantics and equational theory for SND.

Previous work on MacroML indicated a need for making explicit the escape and bracket constructs in the language, so that unfolding recursive macros could be controlled. In the present work, escapes and brackets are found to be useful for specifying explicitly the instantiation of a macro parameter with free variables to specific variables inside the definition of the macro. These observations, as well as the results presented in this paper, suggest that macro languages may naturally and usefully be viewed as conservative extensions of multi-stage (or at least two-level) languages.

Type Contexts

$$[\![\emptyset]\!] = [\,]$$
$$[\![\Sigma, f : (t_1, t_2, [t_3]t_4) \Rightarrow t_5]\!] = [\![\Sigma]\!], f : (t_1 * (\langle t_2 \rangle * (\langle t_3 \rangle \to \langle t_4 \rangle)) \to \langle t_5 \rangle)^0$$
$$[\![\Delta, x_2 : [x_1 : t_1]t_2]\!] = [\![\Delta]\!], x_2 : (\langle t_1 \rangle \to \langle t_2 \rangle)^0$$
$$[\![\Pi, x : t]\!] = [\![\Pi]\!], x : \langle t \rangle^0$$
$$[\![\Pi, \underline{x} : t]\!] = [\![\Pi]\!], x : \langle t \rangle^0$$

Lambda Terms

$$\frac{x : t^m \in \Gamma}{[\![\Sigma; \Delta; \Pi; \Gamma \vdash^m x : t]\!] = x} \qquad \frac{[\![\Sigma; \Delta; \Pi; \Gamma, x : t_1^m \vdash^m e : t_2]\!] = e'}{[\![\Sigma; \Delta; \Pi; \Gamma \vdash^m \lambda x.e : t_1 \to t_2]\!] = \lambda x.e'}$$

$$\frac{[\![\Sigma; \Delta; \Pi; \Gamma \vdash^m e_1 : t_2 \to t]\!] = e_1' \quad [\![\Sigma; \Delta; \Pi; \Gamma \vdash^m e_2 : t_2]\!] = e_2'}{[\![\Sigma; \Delta; \Pi; \Gamma \vdash^m e_1 e_2 : t]\!] = e_1' e_2'}$$

$$\frac{[\![\Sigma; \Delta; \Pi; \Gamma, f : (t_1 \to t_2 \to t_3 \to t)^m, x_1 : t_1^m, x_2 : t_2^m, x_3 : t_3^m \vdash^m e_1 : t]\!] = e_1'}{[\![\Sigma; \Delta; \Pi; \Gamma, f : (t_1 \to t_2 \to t_3 \to t)^m \vdash^m e_2 : t_4]\!] = e_2'}$$
$$\frac{}{[\![\Sigma; \Delta; \Pi; \Gamma \vdash^m \text{letrec } f \ x_1 \ x_2 \ x_3 = e_1 \text{ in } e_2 : t_4]\!] = \text{letrec } f \ x_1 = \lambda x_2.\lambda x_3.e_1' \text{ in } e_2'}$$

Macros

$$\frac{x : t \in \Pi \text{ or } \underline{x} : t^m \in \Pi}{[\![\Sigma; \Delta; \Pi; \Gamma \vdash^1 x : t]\!] = \tilde{\ } x} \qquad \frac{x_2 : [x_1 : t_1]t_2 \in \Delta \text{ and } x_1 : t_1^1 \in \Gamma}{[\![\Sigma; \Delta; \Pi; \Gamma \vdash^1 x_2 : t_2]\!] = \tilde{\ }(x_2 \ \langle x_1 \rangle)}$$

$$\frac{[\![\Sigma, f : (t_1, t_2, [t_3]t_4) \Rightarrow t_5; \Delta, x_2 : [x : t_3]t_4; \Pi, x_1 : t_2; \Gamma, x_0 : t_1^1 \vdash^1 e_1 : t_5]\!] = e_1'}{[\![\Sigma, f : (t_1, t_2, [t_3]t_4) \Rightarrow t_5; \Delta; \Pi; \Gamma \vdash^1 e_2 : t]\!] = e_2'}$$
$$[\![\Sigma; \Delta; \Pi; \Gamma \vdash^1 \text{letmac } f(\tilde{\ } x_0, x_1, \lambda x.x_2) = e_1 \text{ in } e_2 : t]\!]$$
$$= \tilde{\ }(\text{letrec } f \ y = \begin{pmatrix} \text{let } x_0 = \pi_1 \ y \text{ in} \\ \text{let } x_1 = \pi_1(\pi_2 \ y) \text{ in} \\ \text{let } x_2 = \lambda x.(\pi_2(\pi_2 \ y))x \\ \text{in } \langle e_1' \rangle \end{pmatrix} \text{ in } \langle e_2' \rangle)$$

$$\frac{f : (t_1, t_2, [t_3]t_4) \Rightarrow t_5 \in \Sigma}{[\![\Sigma; \Delta; \Pi; \Gamma \vdash^0 e_1 : t_1]\!] = e_1'}$$
$$[\![\Sigma; \Delta; \Pi; \Gamma \vdash^1 e_2 : t_2]\!] = e_2'$$
$$[\![\Sigma; \Delta; \Pi, \underline{x} : t_3; \Gamma \vdash^1 e_3 : t_4]\!] = e_3'$$
$$\overline{[\![\Sigma; \Delta; \Pi; \Gamma \vdash^1 f(e_1, e_2, \lambda x.e_3) : t_5]\!] = \tilde{\ }(f \ (e_1', (\langle e_2' \rangle, \lambda x.\langle e_3' \rangle)))}$$

Code Objects

$$\frac{[\![\Sigma; \Delta; \Pi; \Gamma \vdash^1 e : t]\!] = e'}{[\![\Sigma; \Delta; \Pi; \Gamma \vdash^0 \langle e \rangle : \langle t \rangle]\!] = \langle e' \rangle} \qquad \frac{[\![\Sigma; \Delta; \Pi; \Gamma \vdash^0 e : \langle t \rangle]\!] = e'}{[\![\Sigma; \Delta; \Pi; \Gamma \vdash^1 \tilde{\ } e : t]\!] = \tilde{\ } e'}$$

Fig. 7. Modified Interpretation of MacroML in λ^U

Acknowledgments

Amr Sabry was the first to notice that alpha-conversion in the context of MacroML's `letmac` could be problematic. We thank the anonymous referees for their helpful and detailed comments, some of which we were not able to address fully due to space constraints. Stephan Ellner proofread a draft of the paper.

References

1. BARENDREGT, H. P. *The Lambda Calculus: Its Syntax and Semantics*, revised ed. North-Holland, Amsterdam, 1984.
2. BENAISSA, Z. E.-A., MOGGI, E., TAHA, W., AND SHEARD, T. Logical modalities and multi-stage programming. In *Federated Logic Conference Satellite Workshop on Intuitionistic Modal Logics and Applications* (1999).
3. CARDELLI, L. Phase distinctions in type theory. (Unpublished manuscript.) Available online from http://www.luca.demon.co.uk/Bibliography.html, 1988.
4. DAVIES, R. A temporal-logic approach to binding-time analysis. In *Symposium on Logic in Computer Science* (1996), IEEE Computer Society Press, pp. 184–195.
5. FILINSKI, A. A semantic account of type-directed partial evaluation. In *Principles and Practice of Declarative Programming* (1999), vol. 1702 of *LNCS*, pp. 378–395.
6. FILINSKI, A. Normalization by evaluation for the computational lambda-calculus. In *Typed Lambda Calculi and Applications: 5th International Conference* (2001), vol. 2044 of *LNCS*, pp. 151–165.
7. GANZ, S., SABRY, A., AND TAHA, W. Macros as multi-stage computations: Type-safe, generative, binding macros in MacroML. In *International Conference on Functional Programming* (2001), ACM.
8. GRIFFIN, T. G. Notational definitions — a formal account. In *Proceedings of the Third Symposium on Logic in Computer Science* (1988).
9. MICHAYLOV, S., AND PFENNING, F. Natural semantics and some of its meta-theory in Elf. In *Extensions of Logic Programming* (1992), L. Hallnäs, Ed., LNCS.
10. MOGGI, E. Functor categories and two-level languages. In *Foundations of Software Science and Computation Structures* (1998), vol. 1378 of *LNCS*.
11. MOGGI, E. A monadic multi-stage metalanguage. In *Foundations of Software Science and Computation Structures* (2003), vol. 2620 of *LNCS*.
12. MOGGI, E., TAHA, W., BENAISSA, Z. E.-A., AND SHEARD, T. An idealized MetaML: Simpler, and more expressive. In *European Symposium on Programming* (1999), vol. 1576 of *LNCS*, pp. 193–207.
13. Oregon Graduate Institute Technical Reports. P.O. Box 91000, Portland, OR 97291-1000,USA. Available online from ftp://cse.ogi.edu/pub/tech-reports/README.html.
14. SHEARD, T., AND PEYTON-JONES, S. Template meta-programming for Haskell. In *Proc. of the Workshop on Haskell* (2002), ACM, pp. 1–16.
15. STEELE, JR., G. L., AND GABRIEL, R. P. The evolution of LISP. In *Proceedings of the Conference on History of Programming Languages* (1993), R. L. Wexelblat, Ed., vol. 28(3) of *ACM Sigplan Notices*, ACM Press, pp. 231–270.
16. TAHA, W. *Multi-Stage Programming: Its Theory and Applications*. PhD thesis, Oregon Graduate Institute of Science and Technology, 1999. Available from [13].
17. TAHA, W. A sound reduction semantics for untyped CBN multi-stage computation. Or, the theory of MetaML is non-trivial. In *Proceedings of the Workshop on Partial Evaluation and Semantics-Based Program Maniplation* (2000), ACM Press.
18. TAHA, W., BENAISSA, Z.-E.-A., AND SHEARD, T. Multi-stage programming: Axiomatization and type-safety. In *25th International Colloquium on Automata, Languages, and Programming* (1998), vol. 1443 of *LNCS*, pp. 918–929.
19. TAHA, W., AND NIELSEN, M. F. Environment classifiers. In *The Symposium on Principles of Programming Languages (POPL '03)* (New Orleans, 2003).

A Journey from Interpreters to Compilers and Virtual Machines
Invited Talk

Olivier Danvy

BRICS*
Department of Computer Science, University of Aarhus
Ny Munkegade, Building 540, DK-8000 Aarhus C, Denmark
danvy@brics.dk

Abstract. We review a simple sequence of steps to stage a programming-language interpreter into a compiler and virtual machine. We illustrate the applicability of this derivation with a number of existing virtual machines, mostly for functional languages. We then outline its relevance for today's language development [5].
The work is joint with Mads Sig Ager, Dariusz Biernacki, and Jan Midtgaard [1–4].

References

1. Mads Sig Ager, Dariusz Biernacki, Olivier Danvy, and Jan Midtgaard. From interpreter to compiler and virtual machine: a functional derivation. Technical Report BRICS RS-03-14, DAIMI, Department of Computer Science, University of Aarhus, Aarhus, Denmark, March 2003.
2. Mads Sig Ager, Dariusz Biernacki, Olivier Danvy, and Jan Midtgaard. A functional correspondence between evaluators and abstract machines. Technical Report BRICS RS-03-13, DAIMI, Department of Computer Science, University of Aarhus, Aarhus, Denmark, March 2003. Accepted for presentation at PPDP 2003.
3. Mads Sig Ager, Olivier Danvy, and Jan Midtgaard. A functional correspondence between call-by-need evaluators and lazy abstract machines. Technical Report BRICS RS-03-24, DAIMI, Department of Computer Science, University of Aarhus, Aarhus, Denmark, June 2003.
4. Dariusz Biernacki and Olivier Danvy. From interpreter to logic engine: A functional derivation. Technical Report BRICS RS-03-25, DAIMI, Department of Computer Science, University of Aarhus, Aarhus, Denmark, June 2003. Accepted for presentation at LOPSTR 2003.
5. Charles Consel and Renaud Marlet. Architecturing software using a methodology for language development. In Catuscia Palamidessi, Hugh Glaser, and Karl Meinke, editors, *Tenth International Symposium on Programming Language Implementation and Logic Programming*, number 1490 in Lecture Notes in Computer Science, pages 170–194, Pisa, Italy, September 1998. Springer-Verlag.

---

* Basic Research in Computer Science (www.brics.dk),
funded by the Danish National Research Foundation.

DAOP-ADL: An Architecture Description Language for Dynamic Component and Aspect-Based Development[*]

Mónica Pinto, Lidia Fuentes, and Jose María Troya

Dpto. de Lenguajes y Ciencias de la Computación
University of Málaga, Málaga, Spain
{pinto,lff,troya}@lcc.uma.es

Abstract. Architecture description languages deal with the description, analysis and reuse of software architectures. This paper describes DAOP-ADL, a component- and aspect-based language to specify the architecture of an application in terms of components, aspects and a set of plug-compatibility rules between them. With the aim of connecting the specification of the application architecture to the implementation, we describe our language using XML and XML Schemas. The DAOP-ADL language was designed to be interpreted by DAOP, our own dynamic component- and aspect-oriented platform. DAOP provides a composition mechanism that plugs aspects into components dynamically at runtime. The software architect will use the DAOP-ADL language at design time to describe the architecture of the application. Later this architectural information is loaded into the DAOP platform, which needs it to establish the dynamic connections between autonomous components and aspects. Therefore, the use of DAOP-ADL closes the gap between design and implementation of component- and aspect-based applications.

1 Introduction

The emergence of Component-Based Software Engineering (CBSE) [1] imposes a new way of developing applications by plugging in standalone software components, rather than building them from scratch. In consequence, traditional methods provided by the Software Engineering should be adapted in order to evolve to more compositional architectures. The goal is the reduction of development times, costs, and efforts, while improving the flexibility, extensibility, and reusability of the final application due to the (re)use of software components already developed and verified.

However, everybody agrees that achieving an accurate functional decomposition of systems in context independent components is not a trivial task. Commonly, the same concern happens to be spread over different components creating undesirable dependencies among them. These dependencies make the functional decomposition of a system in autonomous components difficult. In this

---

[*] This research was funded by the CICYT under grant TIC2002-04309-C02-02

way, advanced separation of concerns is widely accepted as the most adequate approach to solve this problem, extending CBSE with new dimensions of concerns, beyond "objects" or "components". Aspect-Oriented Software Development (AOSD) [2] is a promising discipline based on the principle of separation of concerns. AOSD introduces a new dimension named *aspect*, which models those concerns presented along multiple components in a system that may change or evolve independently, resulting in more decoupled systems. Therefore, the techniques proposed by AOSD can be successfully applied in the context of CBSE, improving the modularity and in consequence the reusability and evolution of final applications. Our main goal is then, to combine CBSE and AOSD techniques to obtain all their mutual benefits.

Although aspects were originally defined only at the programming level [3], AOSD tries to cover all phases of the software development life-cycle, from requirements to implementation. Therefore, it is needed to define notations and languages that help software developers to specify and validate component- and aspect-based software architectures, enabling a more effective analysis and design of applications. Moreover, the resulting specification of the application architecture (AA) must be connected to the implementation to avoid inconsistencies and to promote software evolution.

Architecture Description Languages (ADLs) deal with the description, analysis and reuse of software architectures [4]. ADLs describe the structure of the system, which comprises software components, the externally visible properties of those components, and the relationships among them[5]. The purpose of this paper is to define a new ADL to specify the structure of a system in terms of components and aspects, and a set of composition rules. These composition rules will define how to plug software components among them and how and when to apply aspects to components to extend the system behavior with aspectual properties. Similar to other ADLs, our ADL is used to analyze and verify the correctness of a certain design, being possible to reason about the system structure and to evaluate different design possibilities, even before implementation.

While a number of different ADLs[4] have been defined, most of these languages have the problem of being loosely coupled to implementation languages, causing problems in the analysis, implementation, understanding, and evolution of software systems[6]. With the aim of avoiding this problem and facilitating the integration and interpretation of the information provided by the ADL at runtime (e.g. in a dynamic aspect platform), we describe our ADL using XML and XML Schemas. Most of the new ADLs are already using XML Schemas as the representation basis[8], as well as some of the existing ones such as Acme[7]. Our language (we call it DAOP-ADL), has been concretely designed to be "interpreted" by our own component- and aspect-based middleware platform (the "Dynamic Aspect-Oriented Platform", DAOP). The main characteristic of DAOP is that components and aspects are first-order entities that are dynamically composed at runtime. The DAOP platform and its supporting component and aspect model are described in detail in [9][10].

One of the main problems of current component platforms (e.g. CORBA, J2EE and .NET) is that the information about the AA is spread around a large number of classes [12] being difficult to verify the correctness of component composition. The DAOP platform copes with this problem by separating the information that describes the AA from the reusable components and aspects. In fact, the AA information that the platform consults at runtime is exactly the information generated using the DAOP-ADL language. With this approach we close the usual "gap", or loss of information, between the design and the implementation level - the information about the software architecture of an application is usually lost at implementation level.

The main focus of this paper is to present the XML Schemas used to specify a component- and aspect-based architecture and the role that DAOP-ADL plays at runtime in the DAOP platform. The DAOP platform will interpret a certain architectural description in DAOP-ADL, and will store this information as part of its internal data structures. The main benefit of using this approach is that components and aspects are really independent and autonomous entities, because the information about connections is not hard coded, it only resides inside the platform. The DAOP platform consults this information at runtime to perform dynamic weaving between components and aspects. Another important advantage is that the global configuration of the system is available throughout the software life cycle. So, apart from the analysis at design phase, the platform is able to detect at runtime if some component or aspect is violating some design rule. In order to simplify the software architect task, we provide a set of architecture description tools (DAOP-ADTools) that simplify the creation and verification of software architectures described with the DAOP-ADL language.

The structure of this paper is as follows. Firstly, in Section 2 we present some related work comparing our approach to other aspect-oriented systems. Then, Section 3 summarizes the main characteristics of our DAOP platform. Section 4 and Section 5 focus on the definition of the DAOP-ADL language and the creation and validation of a AA using the ADTools. Since we have experience in the implementation of virtual offices applications as part of a research project, we are going to use examples of collaborative applications throughout all the paper. Finally, in Section 6, we show how to integrate and use the AAs specified using the DAOP-ADL language in the DAOP platform.

2 Related Work

Aspects were introduced by [3] and are defined as system properties that tend to cut across functional components, resulting in more coupled systems (*code tangling*). AOSD technologies model components and aspects as two separate entities where the aspects are automatically weaved into the functional behavior of the system in order to produce the overall system.

In AOSD approaches, we can find different alternatives to tackle the separation of concerns issue, even though the final goal is the same. These approaches differ mainly as regards where the weaving information is placed (which aspects are applied to the primary code and when), and the phase in the software life cycle in which the weaving process is performed (statically during compilation or dynamically at runtime). The variety of AOSD approaches is so extensive that it is not possible to cover all of them in this section. Then, we are going to compare our approach with those that we consider more relevant in relation to our work. A complete description of AOSD technologies can be found in [2]. Firstly, some works define AO libraries [13], which are characterized by offering static weaving and in which the functional code must include some information dependent of the aspects applied.

AO languages are the most common approaches. A broadly used AO language is AspectJ [14], which uses a slightly modified form of Java providing a new construction similar to Java classes to implement aspects. In AspectJ, the aspect encapsulates join points that indicate weaving information and advices that indicate aspect behaviors. The weaving process in AspectJ is static, mixing component and aspect codes at compile-time. Static composition provides high performance but separation of concerns is lost at runtime. Other similar approaches are [15] [16].

Another option is to use AO frameworks that provide template classes for modelling components and aspects and a more or less dynamic composition mechanism. Recently, new proposals on AO frameworks have emerged to be used instead of aspect languages and static weaving. Dynamic weaving is much more flexible than static weaving because the separation of concerns remains through all phases of the software cycle, enabling in some cases the late binding between components and aspects. These approaches are based mainly on the reflection mechanism to achieve application adaptability. Most runtime reflective systems are based on the ability to modify the application semantics while the application is running. This adaptability is commonly achieved by implementing a Meta Object Protocol (MOP) as part of the language interpreter that specifies the way a program may be modified at runtime.

For instance, PROSE [17] is an AO platform with dynamic composition that uses MOP-reflective interpreters on its back-ends. Its main contribution is that the platform weaves and unweaves aspects directly in the Java Virtual Machine (JVM), so this work is valuable but only applicable to Java applications. In addition, join points and advices are implemented in PROSE in the class representing the aspect, with the drawback of reducing the use of aspects advices in different contexts.

Another similar approach is JAC [18], an AO framework that uses BCEL [19], a load-time reflective system for Java, for adding aspects with a reflection mechanism. Using this mechanism, aspects in JAC are dynamically deployed and undeployed on top of running application objects. In contrast with PROSE and some aspect language approaches, in JAC, join points are not specified as part of the aspect definition but in a third-party entity available at runtime, making aspects more reusable. Another important feature of JAC is that it provides a development environment to help in the construction of aspect-oriented applications in JAC. This environment generates aspect configuration files to configure aspects, and program descriptors files to describe which aspects must be applied to an application. These text files are loaded into the JAC architecture during application execution, and can be modified at runtime adapting the application functionality without code (re)compilation. In addition, JAC authors are working on a UML notation for aspect-oriented software design [20], although this UML design has not been connected with the JAC implementation yet. Basically, JAC is a client-server approach with all its advantages and disadvantages, and its main limitation is that it is again only applicable to Java applications.

Another proposal for load-time transformation of Java classes is JMangler [21]. JMangler is an AO framework which supports conflict-free composition of independently developed aspects. Aspects are implemented as JMangler transformer components and their main goal is to find an automatic way of combining black box components, avoiding unwanted side effects. Transformers are easy to configure in JMangler, as software developers can combine them just by editing a simple text file. JMangler supports all the transformations of class files that do not violate binary compatibility, for instance the addition of classes, interfaces, fields and methods, and it enables changing a method code. Similar to PROSE and JAC, JMangler modifies java classes when they are loaded in the Java Virtual Machine (JVM). However, JMangler modifies the base class of the Java class loader hierarchy, making the transformation independent of a specific class loader or JVM implementation. Its main limitations are again the dependency of the Java language and, like most dynamic approaches, its efficiency.

The Composition Filters (CFs) model [22] is another aspect-oriented programming technique where aspects are expressed in filters as declarative and orthogonal message transformation specifications. The CF model is a modular extension of the conventional object-based model. Therefore, all behavior is implemented by the manipulation of incoming and outgoing object messages. The main advantage of CFs are that filters are expressed using declarative specifications and, in consequence, they are not dependent of a specific implementation language. Secondly, the CF model provides the advantages of both static and dynamic approaches. Filters can be interpreted, providing runtime solutions, or they may be compiled, providing faster solutions.

Finally, current component platforms such as J2EE already offer a set of built-in services such as security, persistence and transaction services that can be incorporated to an application without programming effort. However, these services are limited to a predefined set and it cannot be considered that they fully support separation of any other concern at the application level. Some current approaches, such as the JBoss AOP framework [23], are trying to solve this limitation. Similar to PROSE, JAC and JMangler, the JBoss AOP framework supports load-time transformations of Java classes using Javassist, a load-time reflective system for Java that allows the modification of a class file before the JVM loads it. The JBoss AOP framework has been designed to be used on top of JBoss, which is a J2EE-based application server. They have developed several system-level aspects such as transaction, security and remoting, which use the "container" technology provided by J2EE.

Our approach is a sort of middleware AO framework. DAOP differs basically from other AO frameworks in that: (1) we define a new compositional model that overcomes the deficits of distributed component, mainly regarding the representation of the AA, while the rest of aspect approaches does not encompass components in the CBSE sense; (2) the platform performs dynamic composition instead of the static one, the most used in AOSD; (3) we specify component- and aspect-based software architectures using an ADL (the DAOP-ADL language) (4) the DAOP-ADL language closes the gap between design and implementation connecting the AA with the DAOP platform that loads it at runtime as part of its internal data structures (5) the contribution of our approach does not rely on taking advantage of a platform or programming language, for instance Java [18] [17] [21]. Although DAOP is currently developed using Java/RMI, the aspect-component model supported by this platform can be implemented in any general purpose language or component platform.

3 DAOP: Dynamic Aspect-Oriented Platform

In this section we summarize the main contributions of the DAOP platform. A complete description of our approach can be found in [9] [10].

Components and aspects exist at runtime. The DAOP platform is based on a component-aspect model where components and aspects are first order entities implemented in the same general purpose language. The composition between components and aspects is established during runtime interaction and is governed by a set of plug-compatibility rules in order to guarantee their correct interoperation. Although the model does not impose any restriction on the granularity of both entities, the way they are composed may impose may recommend not to define a few lines of code as components or aspects. The overhead normally introduced by dynamic composition moves us to consider both components and aspects as high-level, black-box, coarse-grained entities as in CBSE. This model is an extension of a previous work that only separates the coordination aspect [11].

The software architecture of an application (AA) is explicitly specified and stored in the platform. In our aspect-component model, the AA is described in terms of a set of components, aspects and the connections between them. The AA is defined by the software architect during the design phase, using the language to describe software architectures presented in next section, and it is stored in an application repository inside the DAOP server (see right side of Figure 1). More details about how the DAOP platform downloads the AA as part of the application launching are given in the last section of this paper.

Components and aspects have an unique and universal role name. Apart from the dynamic composition, another important contribution of DAOP is that the model detaches components and aspects interfaces from the final implementation classes. We use neither class names coupled to concrete implementations, or interface names as component and aspect identifiers. We assign a unique role name to reference both components and aspects. These role names are archi-

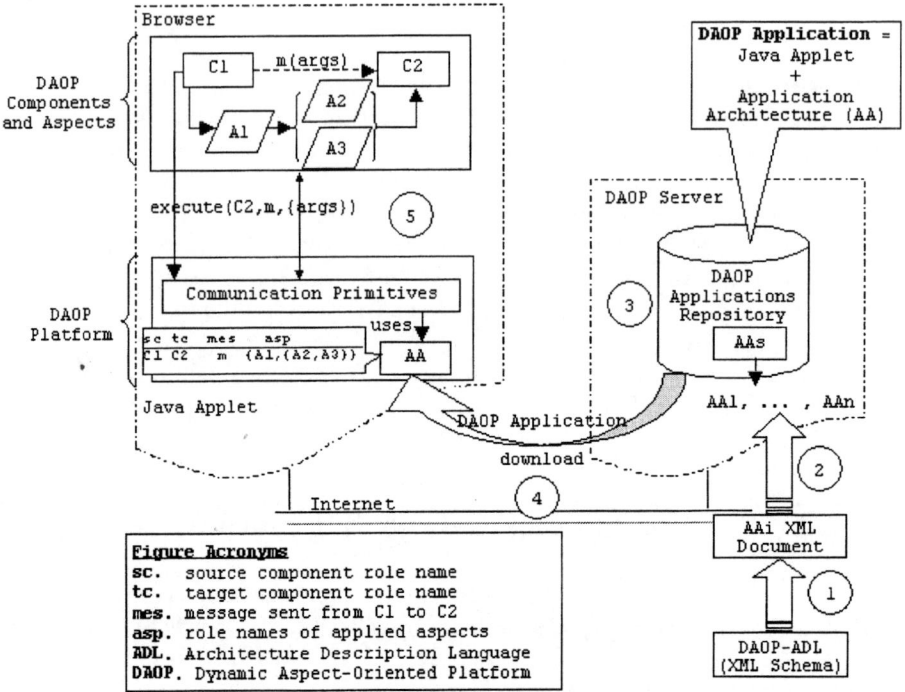

Fig. 1. Dynamic Aspect-Oriented Platform

tectural names that will be used for component and aspect composition and interaction, allowing loosely coupled communication among them - i.e., no hard-coded references need to be used for exchanging information, but just the role name of the target of a message. In addition, components can also be addressed by a unique component identifier that refers to a component instance, in case particular instances need to be addressed.

Component and aspect implementations can be modified at runtime without any code recompilation. By describing the AA in terms of role names, for instance components, are not enforced to implement a concrete implementation. We only require them to offer a set of methods. The benefits of this approach is that components or aspects with different interface and/or class names can play the same role name. Components and aspects with the same role name that are instantiated in different user sites provide the same behavior, so we are able to replace them by equivalent components or aspects according to their abstract definition inside the AA. This is very powerful, because different users of the same distributed application can collaborate through different implementations of, for example, a chat component. Furthermore, users may choose among a set of component implementations, the most appealing one.

Components do not have direct references among them. Another relevant feature of DAOP is that references between components are not hard coded inside them. Instead of that, components use the role name to specify the target of an output message. In consequence, components in our platform are loosely coupled.

Component interactions are performed through the platform. The DAOP middleware layer defines different communication primitives for components to send messages and events to other components. For instance, in Figure 1 the component with role name C1 sends the asynchronous message *m(args)* to the component with role name C2 by invoking the *execute* primitive. The platform checks in the AA which component instance plays the C2 architectural role name and which aspects (aspects with role name A1, A2 y A3 in Figure 1) need to be evaluated before and/or after the invocation of that method in the target component. This decouples the composition information from the implementation classes making the system more extensible and configurable. Likewise, if a component needs to send a synchronous message it will use the *execsync* primitive. The *broadcast* primitive is used to send a message to all the components with the same role name, and events are sent using the *event* primitive.

Components and aspects are independent. In order to achieve component and aspect independence, they do not have any information about how they are composed, providing a powerful mechanism for late binding among them. This information is explicitly stated in the platform and consulted at runtime after the invocation of the middleware communication primitives. This means that components have no knowledge about the aspects they are affected by and also that the number and type of aspects applied to a component can vary dynamically. For each component and each method inside a component, the platform stores the information about the sort of aspects to apply and the order in which they have to be applied. We want to point out that component and aspect join points are neither part of the aspect implementation, nor of the aspect interface. As we already mentioned, they are stated in the AA inside the platform, so the resulting aspects are more extensible and reusable in different contexts.

The DAOP platform applies aspects at message and event interception. The AOSD community offers different approaches for weaving aspects, depending on the points where the pointcuts can be placed. Some approaches support the definition of pointcuts at any place of the code (e.g., before, after, around, ...), mainly because they are based on code insertion. Other approaches use different kinds of message interception, so the aspect evaluation is triggered by the delivery of a message or an event. This allows aspects to be applied to blackbox components, closely to the CBSE philosophy. In the DAOP platform, aspects can be applied to the component's methods when a message or event is sent or received. We understand the meaning of messages and events in the CBSE sense, since events are messages with no information about the source and/or target component. In this case, the platform resolves the target component(s) by using a coordination aspect.

Context dependencies between components and aspects are solved defining properties. Since software components usually have some context dependencies,

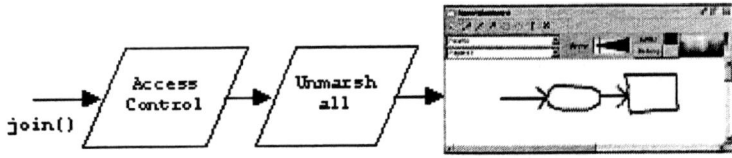

Figure 2.a. User joins the collaborative whiteboard application

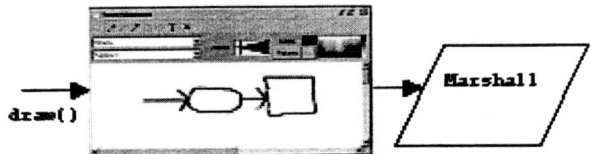

Figure 2.b. User draws in the collaborative whiteboard application

Fig. 2. Collaborative Whiteboard Application

i.e, sometimes they need to share data, the DAOP platform defines the concept of property, which it is an entity that encapsulates this kind of data dependency. Properties can also be used to solve dependencies between non-orthogonal aspects. For instance, if an aspect needs any information generated previously by another aspect, it will take this information from the DAOP platform. That is, aspect output information is stored inside the platform, ready to be retrieved by any other aspect that needs it.

Summing up, the use of DAOP results in software components and aspects more extensible and reusable in different contexts. These benefits lie in the dynamic composition of components and aspects at runtime and in the explicit definition of the AA. In the rest of the paper we describe an ADL to specify and analyze the software architecture of an application developed following the component-aspect model of the DAOP platform.

4 DAOP-ADL: The Architecture Description Language of DAOP

In this section we present DAOP-ADL, a language to specify the software architecture of any application running on top of the DAOP platform. We avoid using complex and in some contexts not very popular formalisms for DAOP-ADL, so we decided to use XML Schemas [24]. XML is the standard language to represent structured information. A major advantage of using XML is the range of XML tools that can be applied both to write XML documents and to validate and analyze their content.

The DAOP-ADL language consists of two parts: the description of the interfaces of components and aspects and the description of their relationships. We had to define a new ADL since the existing ones, like UNICON, Darwin and

Rapide, are not able to express the concepts of our composition model, such as the separation between components and aspects and the rules that define the component and aspect composition. We are going to introduce an example of a shared whiteboard that will be used throughout the paper to illustrate our proposal. Figure 2 shows a *user* that wants to join a *whiteboard* application. Before executing the *join()* method, the *access control* and *unmarshall* aspects are evaluated (Figure 2 .a). The *access control* aspect makes it sure that the user only joins the application if he or she has the right permissions. The *unmarshall* aspect retrieves the persistent state of the component from a store, for example a LDAP directory server or an Oracle database. This is useful for *latecomer* users that join the application once there are other users working on it. When the user is drawing on the whiteboard the method *draw()* is executed, and the *marshall* aspect is applied to make the component state for other users persistent. We are going to describe the AA of this system with the DAOP-ADL language.

4.1 Description of Components and Aspects

Our component-aspect model as well as DAOP-ADL, consider components and aspects as two separate entities. So in this section we are going to present how to describe components and aspects in DAOP-ADL.

Similar to other component models such as CORBA CCM [25] and EJB [26], we specify components by a set of public interfaces. Conforming to our DAOP model, components are referred by the role name that they play in the software architecture. Therefore, the DAOP-ADL language names components by a XML-attribute that represents DAOP role names. In AOSD, components represent the functional behavior of a system. Traditionally, components publish a *provided* interface that describes this behavior. However, in order to define and reason about the software architecture of an application, a component model needs to make other kind of interfaces explicit. Therefore, DAOP-ADL defines, in addition to the provided interface, a *required* interface for specifying the output messages or events that the component is able to send. Figure 3 shows a XML schema for a component *required* interface. The *required* interface describes the events that the component may throw and the output messages indicating the method name and optionally the return value and a set of parameter types. The message delivery may be asynchronous or synchronous. The target component of each message is identified by the role name played by that component.

Aspects are properties of a system whose evaluation is automatically added to a component behavior, during component communication. Instead of a *provided* interface as for components, aspects have an *evaluated* interface describing those messages that are able to evaluate. It is possible that the signature of messages being evaluated by an aspect may change during evaluation. This transformation is specified in the *evaluated* interface. More details about this transformation are showed through some examples in the next section. In addition, during aspect evaluations, aspects communicate with components using the communication mechanisms provided by the platform. This means that in the *required* interface of aspects also goes the specification of output messages and events. In addition,

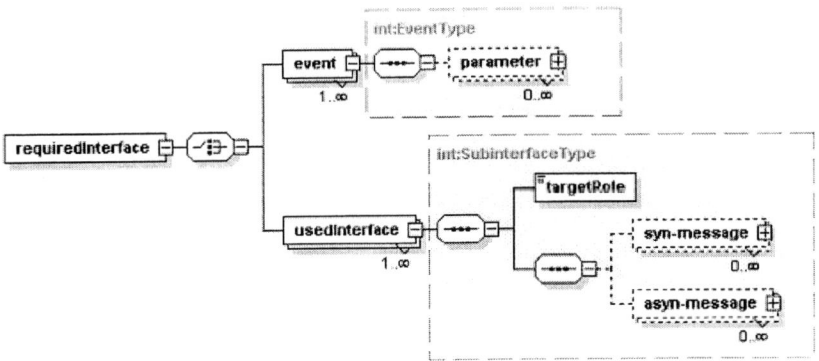

Fig. 3. DAOP-ADL Interfaces XML Schemas

aspects are able to handle events thrown by components, then they define a *target events* interface describing the events that they can capture.

Apart from the specification of abstract interfaces, the description of components and aspects includes other relevant information:

1. A list of possible *implementation classes*. Components that are candidate for playing a role name must implement the same *provided* interface for interoperability purposes. Likewise, aspect implementations of a certain role name must be able to evaluate all the messages described in the *evaluated* interface.
2. A list of input and/or output *properties*. Components and aspects can share information using these properties, which are stored into or retrieved from the platform. Each property is identified by a *name* and a *signature*. This is very useful, for instance, to solve parameter passing between independent aspects. They only have to know the public name of the property, and later they will be able to put a value in the platform or take it from the platform. The scope of these properties can be *usersite*, which means that the value is shared by all the components and aspects instantiated in the same middleware layer, and *serversite*, which means that the value is common to all the components and aspects that are part of the same distributed application.
3. A list of *dependencies*. Component and aspect dependencies are a list of names that match with the role names of the target components that appear in the *required* interface. Since components and aspects use role names to send messages in the implementation code, we use the dependency list for substituting formal parameters of role names by the actual ones.
4. In the aspects case, the software architect needs to specify if the platform has to create an instance of the aspect for each user or there must be a unique instance for that aspect in the application. In the latter case, the software architect may provide the URL where the aspect will be created.

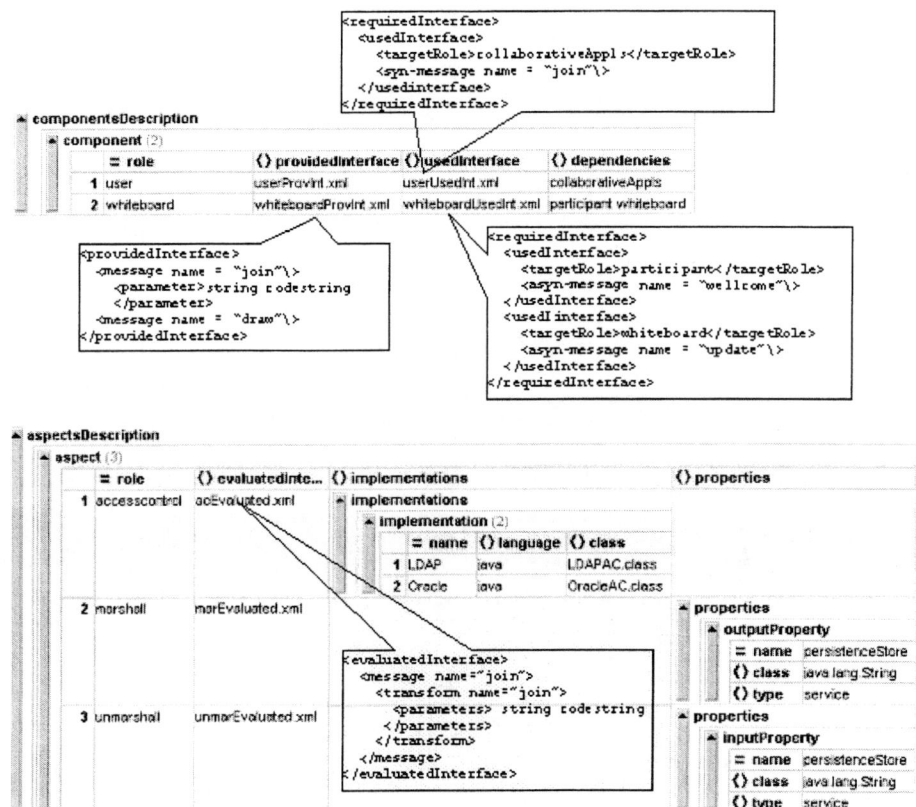

Fig. 4. Component and Aspect XML Description

An Example Figure 4 shows the description of the components and the aspects encoding the example presented in Figure 2. For clarity purposes we omit part of the description information for some of the components and aspects. There are two components in the system with role names *user* and *whiteboard*. We show the XML file describing the *provided* interface of the component with role name *whiteboard* having the *join* and *draw* methods. The *required* interface for the same component describes the output messages that are sent to interact with components with role names *participant* and *whiteboard*. These role names match the names in the *dependencies* list of the *whiteboard* component. The *whiteboard* component sends the asynchronous message *wellcome* to a participant that joins the application. Also, it will send the message *update* to other components with the same role name *whiteboard* to update the application state.

There are three aspects in the system with role names *accesscontrol*, *marshall* and *unmarshall*. In this example, the software architect provides two possible implementations of the *accesscontrol* aspect (based in LDAP or Oracle Database), the programming language (e.g. Java or CORBA), and the corresponding class

```
<compositionConstraints>
    <componentsCompositionRules>
        <componentRule role="user">
            <matchedPair>collaborativeAppls whiteboard
            </matchedPair>
        </componentRule>
        <componentRule role="whiteboard">
            <matchedPair>participant user
            </matchedPair>
            <matchedPair>whiteboard whiteboard
            </matchedPair>
        </componentRule>
        ...
    </componentsCompositionRules>

    <aspectsEvaluationRules>
        <aspectRule>
            <compRole>whiteboard</compRole>
            <inputAspects>
                <messages>joins</messages>
                <aspectlist>accesscontrol</aspectlist>
                <aspectList>unmarshall</aspectlist>
            </inputAspects>
            <outputAspects>
                <messages>draws</messages>
                <aspectList>marshall</aspectlist>
            </outputAspects>
        </aspectRule>
        ...
    </aspectsEvaluationRules>
</compositionConstraints>
```

Fig. 5. Description of Components and Aspects Composition

name. The *accesscontrol* aspect implementation may change even at runtime, since it is identified by a role name and never by anything related with implementation. The *evaluated* interface associated with the *accesscontrol* aspect says that this aspect transforms the message *join()* into *join(user,password)* upon evaluation. Also in the example, two aspects share the same property named *persistentStore*, containing the location of the persistent data associated with the collaborative application. *PersistentStore* is an output property for the aspect with role name *marshall*. This means that this aspect generates the value for this property and stores it in the platform. The *unmarshall* aspect uses the same property but as a consumer. This means that this aspect will obtain the value associated to this property from the platform. Although both aspects are related through the use of this property, they do not need to have any reference among them.

4.2 Description of the Component and Aspect Composition Rules

Using the first part of the DAOP-ADL language described above, the software architect describes all components and aspects that can be instantiated in the application. Now, we present the second part of the language that is used to express the relationships among components and aspects, and some information for adapting mismatched interfaces. As we told in the introduction, composition constraints are expressed in terms of a set of component composition rules and a set of aspect evaluation rules as showed in Figure 5.

Coming back to the example, component composition rules define the relationships between the *user* and *whiteboard* components described previously. Since component connections are established by mapping component role names, incompatibilities may appear as we mentioned in previous section. For each component we have to match role names used by those components in their interactions with role names assigned to components in the AA. The former role names are hard coded in the component implementations while the latter ones are established by the software architect. In Figure 4, in the *required* interface of the *whiteboard* component, the *participant* role name must be understood as a formal parameter that will be substituted by the platform with the *user* role name, that is, the actual parameter. In addition, you can notice that the *user* component sends the join message to a *collaborativeAppls* component, but again the platform will substitute this role name by the actual role name, that is *whiteboard*. Using the component composition rules in Figure 5, the platform will automatically adapt those role names at runtime.

On the other hand, aspect evaluation rules define when and how to apply aspects to components. There are three kind of aspects. *Input aspects* that are evaluated before the execution of a method in a component. *Output aspects* that are evaluated after the execution of a method in a component. And, *event aspects* that are evaluated when a component sends an event, needed to resolve which target components must receive the event. In Figure 5 we show the lists of input and output aspects for the *whiteboard* component. Before executing the *join* method in the component with role name *whiteboard* the aspects with role names *accesscontrol* and *unmarshall* are evaluated. Notice that there are two XML elements with the label *aspectlist*. This means that aspects contained in different *aspectlist* XML elements are evaluated sequentially, and those in the same list will be evaluated concurrently. After executing the *draws* method in the component with role name *whiteboard*, the DAOP platform will evaluate the aspect with role name *marshall* to make the drawing persistent.

Once again we want to highlight here that both component composition rules and aspect evaluation rules are expressed in terms of component and aspect role names, and we never use their interface or implementation classes. This is a relevant feature of our language because the AA of the running application can be adapted at runtime without code recompilation.

5 Analysis and Validation of the Application Architecture

Application developers need to understand the benefits of using aspects and how components and aspects interact and only after this they will be able to design their own component-aspect applications. Our approach provides some tools to guide designers through the development process of DAOP applications (Figure 6). We use the Xerces 2 Java parser [27], that is a fully conforming XML Schema processor, to parse the AAs described in DAOP-ADL. The Architecture Description and Validation Tool (DAOP-ADTool) of Figure 6 presents the typical functionality included in other development environments like visualCafe.

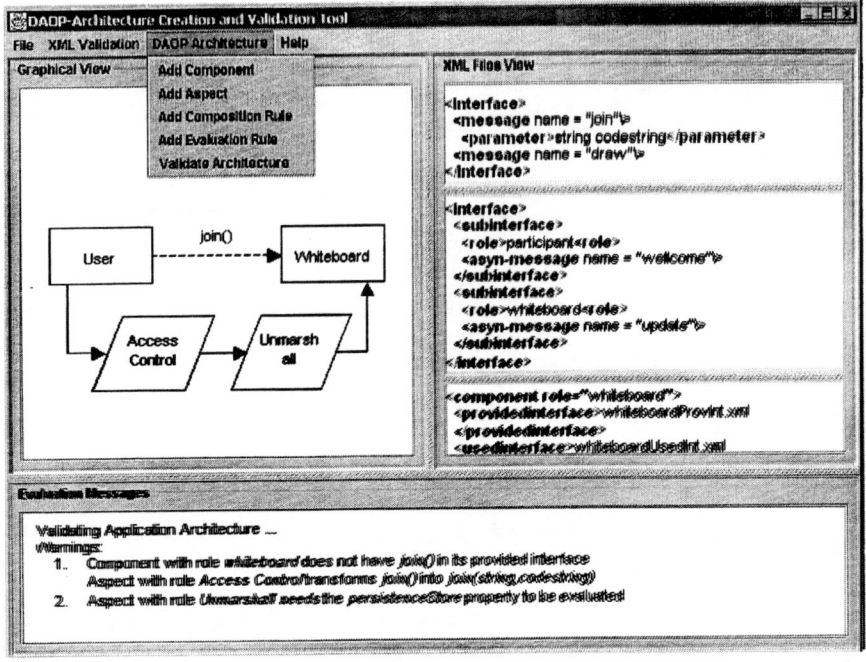

Fig. 6. DAOP Architecture Creation and Validation Tool

It has a visual editor for displaying available components and aspects and for interconnecting them. The DAOP-ADL (simply an XML Schema) serves as the back end of the visual representation.

We differentiate two levels of validation. Firstly, using the XML parser we check the well-formedness and validity of XML documents. An XML document is well-formed if it meets all the well-formedness constraints given in the XML 1.0 [28] specification. A well-formed XML document may in addition be valid if it has an associated XML Schema and if the document complies with the constraints expressed in it. Using the Schema formalism we can express syntactic, structural and value constraints applicable to the definition of XML documents describing AAs. The Schema formalism will allow a useful level of constraint, checking things like the type of the elements, the cardinality, default values, uniqueness, etc.

In addition, there are other constraints that the application must conform and cannot be expressed directly using an XML Schema. Then, the second level of validation is performed by our DAOP-ADTool. We classify the validation process according to the different parts of the DAOP-ADL language.

5.1 Validation of Component and Aspect Descriptions

The most relevant constraints checked by our DAOP-ADTool during the AA description process are related to the component and aspect *interfaces, implementations* and *properties*.

The software architect may propose different implementation classes for the same component or aspect. Component and aspect implementations are available through a *Component Repository* and an *Aspect Repository* respectively (as COTS components). The information needed to validate the correctness of the implementation list can be provided using different mechanisms. One of them is *introspection* as provided by JavaBeans [29]. Using introspection it is possible to recognize predefined patterns in method signatures and it is possible to *look inside* a component or an aspect to determine its properties and behavior. An alternative to introspection used by other component platform such as CCM and J2EE is packaging the component and the aspect with a set of XML description files that provide the same information obtained by introspection.

Using any of the above mechanisms we can validate that the interfaces implemented by classes conform the interfaces provided during components and aspects description. Other important constraints to validate are related to component and aspect properties.

DAOP-ADTool tool is able to verify that an aspect-component AA is correct by performing the following checks:

- Each component implementation class must implement at least the *provided* interface described for that component.
- The messages sent by an implementation class must all be described in the *required* interface for the component or the aspect. In addition, each message must be sent to the component that plays the appropriate role name in the AA. If the implementation class is able to send more messages than expected the tool will generate a warning. The software architect will decide wether this is critical or not. This is useful in an incremental development process and also when the designer really knows that a component will never send that critical message (for instance, it is a result of extra functionality)
- The *events* in the *required* interface must describe exactly the same events that the implementation class is able to throw. In other case, a warning will be generated, similarly to the last case.
- Each aspect implementation class must be able to evaluate at least all the messages described in the *evaluated* interface for that aspect.
- The component and aspect implementation classes must generate all the output properties described in the AA. If a component does not store in the platform an output property, an error message is generated. With input properties, we relax this constraint. The component could need or not the input properties described in the AA. In this case, only a warning message is generated by the validation tool.

Other constraints that are worthwhile to validate are the uniqueness of component and aspect role names and property names. The uniqueness of properties names means that two properties with the same name must have the same signature. In addition, for all input properties described in a component or aspect, there must exist another component or aspect that have the same property in its list of output properties. Otherwise, there would be at runtime a component or aspect needing a property that no other component or aspect will ever generate.

5.2 Validation of the Component Composition Rules

As explained before, component composition rules match role names used by components in their interactions with role names assigned to the components in the AA. We show the composition rules validation process through an example (see again Figure 5).

1. The formal parameters of role names must be in the *dependency* list of the component or aspect. The label *collaborativeAppls* must be in the *dependency* list of the component with role name *user*, and the same for the labels *participant* and *whiteboard* in the component with role name *whiteboard*.
2. The target component of output messages or events must exist inside the AA. There must be components with role names *user* and *whiteboard* in the AA description.
3. Given a formal role name for a target component in the *required* interface of a component or aspect, the set of messages associated with that role name must be contained in the *provided* interface of the component or aspect with the actual role name. For instance, the messages sent by the component with role name *user* to the component *collaborativeAppls* must be contained in the *provided* interface of the *whiteboard* component.

It is important to highlight the possibility of a mismatch between the *required* interface in the source component and the *provided* interface in the target component. This situation is showed in Figure 6, where the *user* component sends the *join()* message to the *whiteboard* component. However, the *whiteboard* components expects a message with the same name but the additional parameters *(string, codestring)* representing the user name and password. As showed in Figure 6 this provokes a warning message instead of an error message, because the validation tool is able to check that the *access control* aspect evaluated before executing *join(string, codestring)* transforms *join()* into *join(string, codestring)*.

5.3 Aspect Evaluation Rules Validation

A desirable feature of aspects is orthogonality. This means no dependencies among them. However, this is a hard task to achieve, and sometimes information generated during the evaluation of an aspect it is needed in the evaluation of following aspects. In DAOP we resolve this problem using input and output properties. With this mechanism of storing and retrieving properties from the platform, we achieve our goal of aspects independence. Dependent aspects do not interact directly, but through the platform using the same properties.

However, a set of aspects can be evaluated sequentially or concurrently depending on the information provided in the AA. When aspects are completely independent both approaches are valid. But, if there are dependencies among aspects, they must be evaluated sequentially. Otherwise, the platform cannot guarantee the correct behavior of the application. Then, if there is an aspect evaluation rule stating that two aspects will be evaluated concurrently, and those aspects share the same property, and it is an input property in one aspect and an output property in the other aspect, the validation tool will generate a warning notifying the problem.

6 Putting It All Together

In this section we briefly illustrate how we integrate the description of a AA written in the DAOP-ADL language into the DAOP platform, bridging the gap between design and implementation. As explained before AAs in DAOP are described using XML Schemas and XML documents. The DAOP-ADL language provides an XML Schema defining the structure of a DAOP application. Then, XML documents conforming that schema represent AA instances (AA1, ..., AAn of Figure 1) describing concrete applications (Figure 1, step 1). In DAOP it is expected that the software architect defines the AA during the design phase and afterwards the resulting XML file is stored in a repository as part of the application registration in the DAOP Server (Figure 1, step 2 and 3).

Users initiate DAOP applications from a browser by downloading a java applet that will retrieve a concrete AA. Therefore, when the user downloads the application applet from a web server (Figure 1, step 4), the AA is downloaded at the same time and it is stored in the instance of the DAOP platform created for that user (Figure 1, step 5) at the client side. The AA definition will drive the dynamic composition of components and aspects (Figure 1, step 6) throughout application execution.

7 Conclusions and Future Work

In this paper we highlight the importance of explicitly describing the software architecture of complex distributed system to increase their configurability and adaptability. We have presented an architecture description language to describe and validate software architectures that conform to the component-aspect model of the DAOP platform. We have used XML Schemas because XML is the standard language for representing structured information and provides appropriate mechanisms to validate the correctness of the AA.

The main contributions of our DAOP-ADL language proposal are the following: 1) It defines the AA independent from programming languages and component platforms. This means the language is general enough to be used in other contexts besides DAOP; 2) The definition of aspect information is optional. Then, it is possible to describe the AA of any component-based application, including aspects or not; 3) The dependencies between components and aspects are explicitly defined. This makes possible to reason about them and to analyze the impact of changing, modifying or adding new components and aspects both statically and dynamically at runtime; 4) It allows the use of validation tools to assure the correctness of components composition and aspect evaluation. This system is currently being used in a virtual office developed in the TRACOM project. Our next goal is to improve the DAOP-ADTool tools with code generation. Since the information that we specify in XML can be easily adapted to the UML language, we plan to use UML as the graphic notation. The AA defined now in UML could be stored according to our XML Schemas of the DAOP-ADL language, and then incorporated to the platform as we showed here.

Acknowledgment

The authors wish to thank Kim Mens for his insightful comments and suggestions in an initial version of this paper.

References

1. Heineman, G.T., Councill, W.T. Component-Based Software Engineering: Putting the Pieces Together. *Addison Wesley*, 1st Edition, 2001.
2. Aspect-Oriented Software Development Web Site. *http://www.aosd.net*.
3. Kiczales, G., Lamping, J., Mendhekar, A. et al. Aspect-Oriented Programming. In *Proceedings of the ECOOP'97*. June 1997.
4. Medvidovic, N., Taylor, R. A Classification and Comparison Framework for Software Architecture Description Languages. *IEEE Transaction on Software Engineering*, 26 (1), January 2000.
5. Garlan, D. Software Architecture. *Encyclopedia of Software Engineering*, J. Marciniak (Ed.), John Wiley & Sons, 2001.
6. Aldrich, J., Chambers, G., Notkin, D. ArchJava: Connecting Software Architecture to Implementation In *Proccedings of the ICSE'02*, May 2002.
7. xAcme: Acme Extension to xArch *http://www-2.cs.cmu.edu/ acme/pub/xAcme/*
8. Khare, R., Guntersdorfer, M., Oreizy, P., et al. xADL: Enabling Architecture-Centric Tool integration with XML In *Proceedings of the 34th Annual Hawaii ICSS'01*, January 2001.
9. Pinto, M., Fuentes, L., Fayad, M.E., Troya, J.M. Towards an Aspect-Oriented Framework in the Design of Collaborative Virtual Environments. In *Proceedings of the 8th IEEE Workshop on FTDCS'01*, November 2001.
10. Pinto, M., Fuentes, L., Fayad, M.E., Troya, J.M. Separation of Coordination in a Dynamic Aspect-Oriented Framework. In *Proceedings of the 1st International Conference on AOSD'02*, April 2002.
11. Fuentes, L., Troya, J.M. Coordinating Distributed Components on the Web: an Integrated Development Environment. *Software-Practice and Experience*, 31 (39), pp. 209-233, March 2001.
12. Krieger, D., Adler, R.M. The Emergence of Distributed Component Platforms. In *IEEE Computer*, 31 (3), pp. 43-53, March 1998.
13. Lieberherr, K., Orleans, D., and Ovlinger, J. Aspect-Oriented Programming with Adaptive Methods. *Communications of the ACM*, 44 (10), October 2001.
14. Kiczales, G., Hilsdale, E., Hugunin, J., et al. An overview of AspectJ. In *Proceedings of the ECOOP'01*, June 2001.
15. Wichman, J.C. ComposeJ: The Development of a Preprocessor to Facilitate Composition Filters in the Java Language. MSc. thesis, Dept. of Computer Science, University of Twente, December 1999.

16. Ossher, H., and Tarr, P. Multi-Dimensional Separation of Concerns and The Hyperspace Approach. *Proceedings of the Symposium on Software Architectures and Component Technology: The State of the Art in Software Development.* Kluwer 2000.
17. Popovici, A., Gross, T., Alonso, G. Dynamic Weaving for Aspect-Oriented Programming. In *Proceedings of the 1st International Conference on AOSD'02*, April 2002.
18. Pawlack, R., Seinturier, L., Duchien, L., Florin, G. Jac: A flexible and efficient framework for aop in java. In *Proceedings of Reflection'01*, September 2001.
19. Byte Code Engineering Library (BCEL). *http://jakarta.apache.org/bcel/*.
20. Pawlack, R., Duchien, L., Florin, G. A UML Notation for Aspect-Oriented Software Design. In *Proccedings of AO modeling with UML workshop at the AOSD'02 conference*, April 2002.
21. Kniesel, G., Constanza, P., and Austermann, M. JMangler - A Framework for Load-Time Transformation of Java Class Files *IEEE Workshop on SCAM'01*, November 2001.
22. Bergmans, L., and Aksit, M. Analyzing Multi-dimensional Programming in AOP and Composition Filters. *First Workshop on Multi-Dimensional Separation of Concerns in Object-oriented Systems (at OOPSLA '99)*, November 1999.
23. Burke, B., Brock, A. Aspect-Oriented Programming and JBoss. *http://www.onjava.com/pub/a/onjava/2003/05/28/aop_jboss.html*
24. XML Schema. *http://www.w3.org/XML/Schema*.
25. Wang, N., Schmidt, D.C., O'Ryan, C. Overview of the CORBA Component Model. In *Component-Based Software Engineering: Putting the Pieces Together*, Addison Wesley, Editors G.T. Heineman and W.T. Council. 2001.
26. Blevins, D. Overview of the Enterprise JavaBeans Component Model. In *Component-Based Software Engineering: Putting the Pieces Together*, Addison Wesley, Editors G.T. Heineman and W.T. Council. 2001.
27. The Xerces 2 Java Parser. *http://xml.apache.org/xerces2-j/index.html*.
28. Extensible Markup Language (XML) 1.0. *http://www.w3.org/TR/2000/REC-xml-20001006*.
29. JavaBeans Component Architecture Documentation. *http://java.sun.com/products/javabeans/docs/*.

ANEMIC: Automatic Interface Enabler for Model Integrated Computing

Steve Nordstrom, Shweta Shetty, Kumar Gaurav Chhokra, Jonathan Sprinkle, Brandon Eames, and Akos Ledeczi

Institute for Software Integrated Systems, Vanderbilt University
2015 Terrace Place, Nashville, TN 37235
{steve.nordstrom,shweta.shetty,kg.chhokra,
jonathan.sprinkle,b.eames,akos.ledeczi}@vanderbilt.edu
http://www.isis.vanderbilt.edu

Abstract. A domain-specific language provides domain experts with a familiar abstraction for creating computer programs. As more and more domains embrace computers, programmers are tapping into this power by creating their own languages fitting the particular needs of the domain. Graphical domain-specific modeling languages are even more appealing for non-programmers, since the modeling language constructs are automatically transformed into applications through a special compiler called a translator. The Generic Modeling Environment (GME) at Vanderbilt University is a meta-programmable model-ing environment. Translators written to interface with GME models typically use a domain-independent API. This paper presents a tool called ANEMIC that generates a domain-specific API for GME translators using the same metamodel that generates the language.

1 Introduction

One of the disadvantages of low-level coding is that a small change in the requirements of the program could necessitate drastic changes in the code. Consider the Y2K challenge of the late 1990s: the size of the requirement change - change the year representation from two digits to four - was small, yet a vast amount of effort was needed to correct this change. One solution that helps to alleviate the disparity between requirements change and implementation change is to generate the code of the final system from a centralized set of models. This technique, called Model-Integrated Program Synthesis (MIPS), is an application of Model-Integrated Computing (MIC) [1].

In order to generate final system code, several transformations take place. Typically, the set of models are examined and interrogated using a specialized high-level compiler (referred to in this paper as a *translator*) and the output of that translator is the final system code. However, the process of creating this translator is currently heavily dependent on the programmer and little advantage is taken of code generation. A great deal of the work that the programmer does can be streamlined and automated using user-defined macros and traditional "code-cloning", but this process is error prone, and inconsistent across users. Furthermore, the macros operate on the individual class level, and do not have a global view of the software architecture.

This paper presents a tool that automatically generates an appropriate domain-specific API from the metamodels that describe the domain specific modeling language.

2 Background

MIC is a framework for developing domain artifacts for computer-based systems. MIC depends on a model-based definition of the target system, and it integrates the created models when generating domain-specific artifacts. The same models are often used by external analysis and simulation tools to verify properties of the system under development. Example uses for MIC are the generation of real-time schedules from software models, creation of a configuration file to integrate distributed systems, or the generation of source code that is later compiled to execute within an embedded system.

MIC relies heavily on the use of domain-specific languages to describe the final system implementation. A domain-specific language allows a modeler to describe the system in terms of the domain rather than in terms of traditional computer languages. Domain-specific modeling environments (DSME's) are the interface for domain experts to program using a domain-specific modeling language (DSML). The DSME provides domain-specific constructs that are associated with one another to describe a computer-based system. For further explanation of this process please refer to [2].

However, modeling language development is not a trivial task. In addition to the development of the language ontology, syntax, well-formedness and semantics, there is also the question of representation and implementation.

2.1 Metamodeling

A technique called *metamodeling* can be used to rapidly describe the syntax and static semantics (well-formedness) of a language. The artifact of the metamodeling process - called the metamodel - is generally retained in an object database for further manipulation, and can later be modified to generate a new version of the domain-specific language.

The metamodel is a formalized description of a particular modeling language and is used to configure the Generic Modeling Environment (GME) (GME is a configurable toolset that supports the easy creation of domain-specific modeling and program-synthesis environments [3]). Here, we provide a brief overview of the metamodeling concepts. For a more in depth discussion, see [4].

Using essentially the UML class diagram and OCL syntax, metamodels describe the entities, their attributes, and inter-relationships that are available in the target modeling environment [5] [6] [7]. The DSML may be specified in terms of Models, Atoms, Connections, References, and Sets. Models are the centerpieces of the MIC environment. They are hierarchically decomposable objects

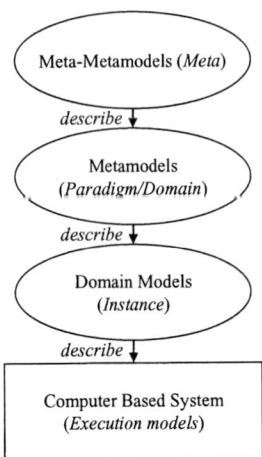

Fig. 1. The four layers of metamodeling

that may contain parts and inner structure. Atoms cannot be further decomposed. Associations between objects are captured by Connections, References, and Sets. References can be used to associate objects in different parts of the model hierarchy. All objects may be qualified by one or more Attributes: key-value pairs that capture non-structured information.

The metamodel in Figure 2 captures a language used to model the composition of neighborhoods. It shows that each Neighborhood may contain zero or more Buildings, where each Building may either be a House or a Store. Each House may contain Residents, and each Store may contain Patrons. The Neighborhood may also contain Walkways that connect the Buildings to each other.

Once a metamodel has been created and the domain-specific language generated, only a portion of the overall domain-specific environment is complete. Without a compiler, the domain-specific language is just pictures - the compiler gives semantics to the syntax specified by the metamodel. With respect to Figure 2, if we want to find all the instances of Walkways that connect one Building to another we would need to write a special kind of translation program to extract this information from the model.

In order to provide the semantics, syntax patterns are transformed into a domain artifact (e.g., glue code, configuration files) with a special compiler called a *translator* [1]. The translator provides the mapping from the domain-specification in the language to the domain-use in the application.

2.2 Language Translation

It is the translator that releases the full power of a domain-specific language. The translator abstracts away the mundane details of the implementation by encoding domain details that can be automatically generated rather than burdening the modeler with the task of manually implementing them. In this way,

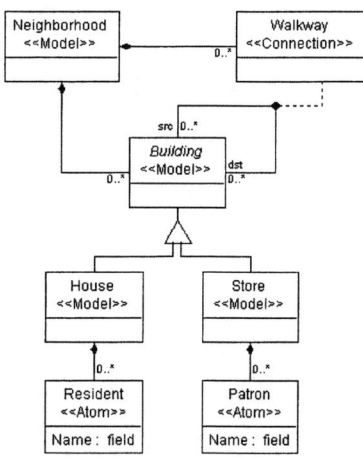

Fig. 2. A UML description of a domain-specific modeling language, used to model Neighborhoods. A Neighborhood may be modeled as one or more Buildings, connected by Walkways. The Houses or Stores (both being Buildings) may contain Residents or Patrons, respectively

models can be interpreted (translated) in more than one way, while the meaning of the models is captured only once. A good example of this is the generation of either C++ or Java classes from the same UML class diagram [8] or executable code from Statecharts [9].

The creation of the translator is strongly connected to the domain-specific modeling language that the translator compiles. Since the translator is the connection between the domain-specific implementation of the models and the (usually) domain-independent implementation of the computer based system (i.e., many computer-based systems are implemented in a programming language, such as C++ or Java, which require the management of details not important to the high-level design of the system) a great deal of domain knowledge must be present in the translator. For the GME, a translator is created in a standard language (VB, C++, C#, etc.) and operates on the models through a public interface that utilizes COM.

The translator takes as input a model database, and produces as output the appropriate domain-specific artifact. The translator can make execution decisions for generation through the types of models that it encounters by querying the runtime-types of the objects. These types are the same as those described by the metamodel of this domain-specific language. The next two sections describe the existing framework for interfacing with domain-independent model types, and the new framework for automatically generating specialized classes that extend these domain-independent model types to create domain-specific classes.

3 The Builder Object Network (BON)

As mentioned in the preceding section, the process of translation involves querying the model database for the types of entities defined and their relation (hierarchy, aggregation, association etc.). Figure 3 shows a schematic of GME's modular COM-based architecture; the GME core components (GModel and GMeta) expose a set of COM interfaces that facilitate model interrogation (For a more in-depth discussion of the architecture, refer to [2]).

While the COM interface provides the translator writer with all the functionality needed to access and manipulate the models, it entails using repetitious COM-specific querying, error checking and handling. To abstract these issues from the translator writer, GME provides a collection of C++ wrapper classes: the Builder Object classes.

The fundamental types of entities in GME (Atoms, Models, Sets, Connections and References) share common traits. Each modeling entity has an associated name, kind name, metamodel and type. They may, depending on the metamodel and the specific model being examined, each be qualified by one or more attributes, connected to one or more objects. The operations of querying and specifying such details are common to these entities and are thus abstracted in to a base class called CBuilderObject.

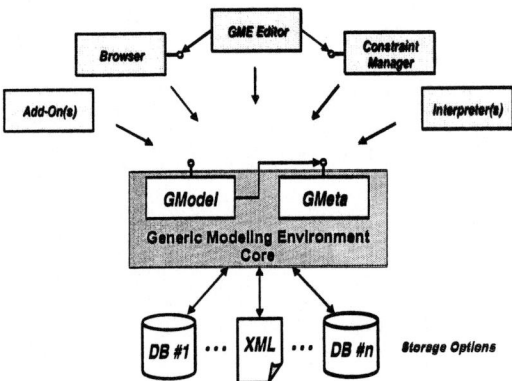

Fig. 3. GME Architecture provides a generic, meta-programmable modeling environment upon which domain-specific models can be created and examined

Many operations are consistent across all types of entities in the BON, which justifies the CBuilderObject base type. This important class serves as the base type for any BON class and provides a default implementation for the most common tasks. The corresponding classes for Atoms (CBuilderAtom), Models (CBuilderModel), Sets (CBuilderSet), Connections (CBuilderConnection) and References (CBuilderReference) specialize CBuilderObject via inheritance to provide relevant functionality. For example, CBuilderModel adds to

CBuilderObject the ability to query or create contained entities. Figure 4 illustrates the inheritance relationship between the various BON classes.

When the user initiates model translation, the component interface builds a graph mirroring the models: for each model, atom, reference, set and connection an object of the corresponding class is instantiated. We refer to this graph as the Builder Object Network and the infrastructure for creating it as the Builder Object Network API (BON). While the BON implements a corpus of access and manipulation methods, it must by design be generic: it has no knowledge of the attribute names, kind names or other qualifiers of the entities defined by the meta-model. Thus to access a particular attribute, say "Color", of an Atom, the translator writer provides the domain-specific intelligence via parameters to the appropriate method.

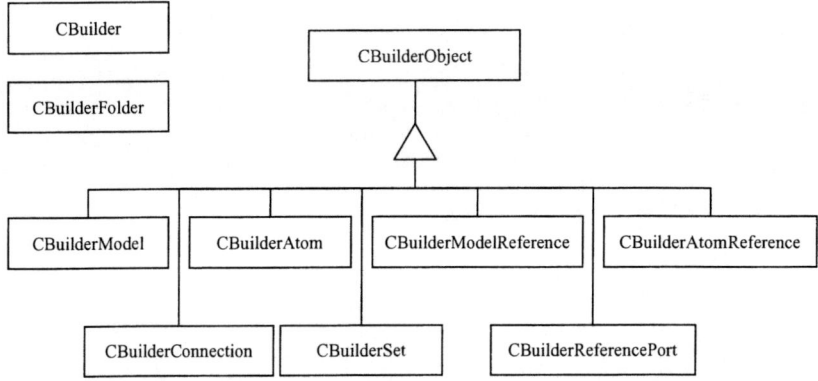

Fig. 4. Builder Object class hierarchy dictates that all Models, Atoms, Connections, and References inherit from the `CBuilderObject` class

To allow for domain specific information, the BON provides a mechanism for extending the general-purpose functionality of the `CBuilder` classes. For more functional components, the `CBuilder` classes can be extended by the programmer with inheritance [2]. By using a pair of supplied macros, the programmer can have the component interface instantiate these paradigm-specific classes instead of the default ones. This allows the programmer to have the implementation classes more closely mimic the properties of the metamodel.

Consider the metamodel presented in Figure 2. With the default BON methods, the following code would be needed to retrieve and iterate through a list of Residents given a House.

```
extern CBuilderModel *pHouse;
const CBuilderAtomList*pAtomResidents =
    pHouse->GetAtoms("Resident");
if(pAtomResidents && !pAtomResidents->IsEmpty()){
```

```
    POSITION pos = pAtomResdients->GetHeadPosition(pos);
    while(pos){
      CString haircolor;
      CBuilderAtom* pResident =
          pAtomResidents->GetNext(pos);
      VERIFY(*pResident.GetAttribute(
            "haircolor", haircolor));
    }
}
```

The programmer could specialize both House and Resident, such that the extension classes meet this requirement. Let `CSBuilderHouse` and `CSBuilderResident` extend `CBuilderModel` and `CBuilderAtom` via inheritance respectively. Thus the above code is transformed as follows:

```
extern CSBuilderHouse *pHouse;
const CSBuilderResidentList*pResidents =
    pHouse->GetResidents();
if(!pResidents && !pResidents->IsEmpty()){
    POSITION pos = pResidents->GetHeadPosition();
    while(pos){
        CSBuilderResident *pResident =
            pResidents->GetNext(pos);
        CString haircolor =
            pResident->GetAttribute_haircolor();
    }
}
```

From the above code, it is apparent that the extension leads to much smaller and more intuitive code. The extension eliminates the need for the programmer to concentrate on error checking and type manipulation code.

Moreover, the default access methods being generic in BON, do not provide specific type checking. For example, for the `GetInConnections(Cstring& name, CBuilerObjectList &list)` method, if the wrong name is provided or if the string name provided is case-incongruent with the name defined by the metamodel, the function returns an unexpected false. The translator writer must pay close attention to the correctness of the name and return value by either memorizing the metamodel, or constantly referring back to it. Such discrepancies manifest themselves as run-time errors (`VERIFY` failures), which are difficult to detect and debug. Furthermore, once a list of connections is retrieved, the programmer must manually implement repetitious code to distinguish the various connections found. By extending the default `CBuilder` classes, this onus of checking details may be moved from the programmer to the compiler by implementing a function `GetWalkwayInConnections()` that returns a valid list of only `CSBuilderWalkway` objects.

This ability to augment the default implementation with the desired functionality can be exploited by generating paradigm-specific extensions of the

BON. The translator writer typically generates customized BON classes using the metamodel as a source for architecture, naming convention, and as a reference for parameters to the generic BON. The automatic generation of such a class hierarchy directly from the metamodel would, therefore, facilitate creation of the language translator by decreasing the time spent in class construction, ensuring correctness of the extensions, and allowing the programmer to devote his creative energies towards the specification of semantics.

4 Domain Specific API Generation

The ANEMIC (Automatic Interface Enabler for Model Integrated Computing) tool was created to perform the automatic generation of the domain specific API used to create a language translator. ANEMIC generates C++ classes to implement this specialized BON class structure directly from the metamodel. The ANEMIC tool is itself a model translator that traverses the metamodel to produce a code framework for the domain translator, consisting of classes and methods corresponding to the entities captured in the metamodel, as well as the methods for traversing the domain models.

4.1 ANEMIC Translator Approach

The ANEMIC translator is a transformation program that traverses the network of objects in the metamodel. Figure 5 shows the decomposition of the ANEMIC translator. In [10] and [11], algorithms for writing structured model translators are discussed in detail.

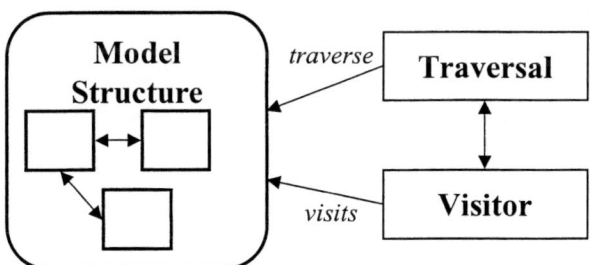

Fig. 5. Design of the ANEMIC translator includes automated visitor and traversal patterns for navigating the BON and collecting specialization information

- *Model Structure:* The model structure specification defines what classes of objects are available, and their inter-relations (compositions, hierarchies, associations, etc.). This information is captured in the metamodel being examined.
- *Traversal:* Traversal captures how the models should be traversed. The specification addresses the order of traversal, which can vary based on the type of

entities encountered. A breadth-first search strategy is used here, which is a graph search algorithm that tries all one step extensions of current paths before trying the larger extensions. The root is examined first, followed by the children of the root, and then the children of those nodes are examined, etc. This helps in keeping the class dependencies and also preserves the hierarchy information.
- *Visitor:* Visitors capture the actions to be taken when visiting an object of particular type. The different types of objects would be "Model", "Atom", "Reference", "Connection", "Attribute", "Inheritance" etc. The visitor considers - based on the type of the current object - what state information should be stored to produce an accurate architecture. ANEMIC gathers the structural (containment, hierarchy, connection, inheritance, etc.) and type (kind name, role name, attributes etc.) information for each entity defined.

For each entity defined, ANEMIC generates a corresponding extension class from the appropriate CBuilder class. ANEMIC preserves the inheritance relationships captured in the metamodel through the use of C++ inheritance structure in the generated output. If an object in the metamodel is defined abstract then, a corresponding abstract C++ class is created. This affords the programmer the ability to exploit, in code, the hierarchical relationships existing in the metamodel.

The attributes belonging to a particular entity (for example a Model or an Atom), appear as protected data members of the respective extension class. The following section elucidates this process with an example.

4.2 Class and Method Generation Using the ANEMIC Translator

Figure 6 shows the UML class diagram that represents a Resident, which has haircolor as an attribute. Notice that Resident is of type Atom. Consequently, the generated class CSBuilderResident extends CBuilderAtom. The extension is facilitated by the use of a pair of BON extension macros: DECLARE_CUSTOMATOM and IMPLEMENT_CUSTOMATOM. BON provides such extension macros for all entities defined in the GME meta-metamodel.

To enable easy identification of the generated class and eliminate naming conflicts with existing BON objects, the generated C++ class code adheres to a nomenclature where the generated classes are named as

CSBuilder{Name}

where Name is the name of the object in the metamodel. All default BON access methods, except those dealing with Connections, are specialized as

{return_value} {FUNCTION NAME}_{name}({parameters})

where FUNCTION NAME is the default BON method, parameters are appropriate arguments to the new method, and return_value is the data type of the corresponding attribute. Figure 7 shows the specialization of

```
bool CBuilderAtom::GetAttribute(CString &name,  CString &value)
```
as
```
CString GetAttribute_haircolor() const
```

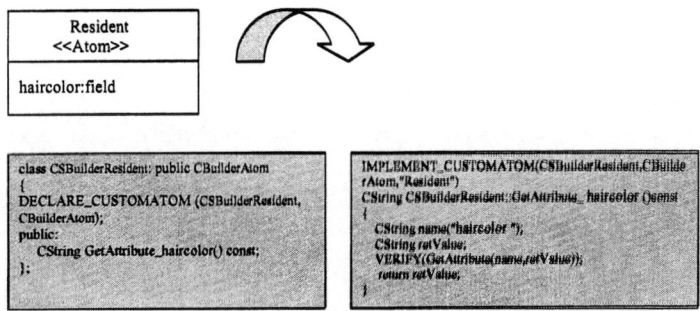

Fig. 6. ANEMIC exploits the generic `GetAttribute(name, value)` method to specifically access the attribute `haircolor`

BON methods dealing with Connections are specialized as

{terminator_list*}{Get|Set}{In|Out}{name}Connection()

where **terminator_list** is a typed list as specified by the metamodel and **name** is the name of this Connection.

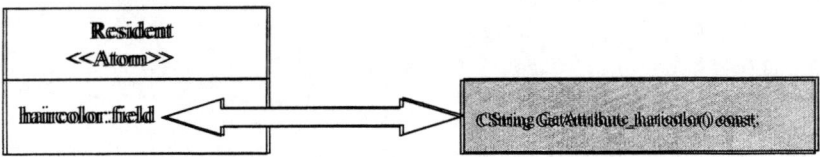

Fig. 7. Specialized methods for each attribute are generated by the ANEMIC translator using a predefined naming convention. Proper implementations for parent-class method wrappers are generated as well

The attributes of the specialized class can be of type `int`, `bool` or `CString` depending on the type specified by the user in the metamodel. Table 1 shows the mapping between GME attribute types and C++ data types.

5 Example Metamodel and Generation

Creation of a translator for the modeling language described in Figure 2 is possible with the domain independent BON API, but is now streamlined by using

Table 1. A mapping between GME attributes and generated C++ member variable types is generated by ANEMIC

Attribute Type	C++ type
<<FieldAttribute>>	CString
<<EnumAttribute>>	int
<<BoolAttribute>>	bool

the architecture of customized classes created by ANEMIC. By executing the API generation tool on the metamodel this required specialization takes place automatically resulting in a variety of specialized objects and methods. Two such objects are given below:

```
class CSBuilderBuilding : public CBuilderModel{
DECLARE_CUSTOMMODEL(CSBuilderBuilding, CBuilderModel)
public:
   virtual void Initialize();
   virtual ~CSBuilderBuilding();
   CSBuilderWalkwayList * GetOutWalkwayConnections();
   CSBuilderWalkwayList * GetInWalkwayConnections();
};

class CSBuilderHouse : public CSBuilderBuilding{
DECLARE_CUSTOMMODEL(CSBuilderHouse, CSBuilderBuilding) public:
   virtual void Initialize();
   virtual ~CSBuilderHouse();
   CSBuilderResidentList * GetResidents();
   CSBuilderResident * CreateNewResident();
};
```

These class definitions define the specialized BON interface to be used by the domain specific translator. Class hierarchy from the metamodel is preserved, and forward declarations are created. Also, typed lists for storing the new specialized objects and are generated. List types for containing specialized objects are also created.

```
typedef CTypedPtrList<CPtrList,
        CSBuilderWalkway *>CSBuilderWalkwayList;
typedef CTypedPtrList<CPtrList,
        CSBuilderResident *>CSBuilderResidentList;
```

Implementation of the specialized API is also generated from the metamodel by the ANEMIC tool. The following is an example method implementation from a specialized Store object, showing the generation of a proper wrapper for parent methods:

```
CSBuilderPatron * CSBuilderStore::CreateNewPatron(){
  return BUILDER_CAST(CSBuilderPatron,
         CBuilderModel::CreateNewModel("Patron"));
}
```

The automatic generation of the class definitions and method implementations now allow the domain-specific model translator to be created with much ease. For example,

`CBuilderConnectionList GetInConnections("Walkway");`

can be written using domain-specific methods and objects as

`CSBuilderWalkwayList GetInWalkways();`

By using the interface generated by ANEMIC, a translator can now be created with domain-specific objects and methods, using only a small amount of hand-written code.

6 Conclusions and Future Work

The work described in this paper significantly decreases the amount of overhead required to create an translator for a domain-specific modeling language. The domain-specific API generator can generate code that would take several days for one programmer to create, by using the metamodel that describes the language. It should be noted that the domain-specific API was typically hand created for every C++ translator before this generator was available.

In addition to the creation of the class structures, ANEMIC also takes advantage of the definition of abstract classes and inheritance hierarchies when generating the output classes. This allows translator programmers to maximize code reuse and minimize code duplication by using the same object-oriented approaches used to create the metamodels.

Future versions of this tool can be configurable by the user to follow naming conventions and personal preferences for class definition. Also, other versions of the tool that could generate an API for other languages would greatly reduce the amount of overhead for users that prefer an implementation language other than C++.

References

1. Sztipanovits J., Karsai G.: Model-Integrated Computing, IEEE Computer, vol. 30, no. 4, pp. 110-112, April (1997)
2. Ledeczi A., Maroti M., Bakay A., Nordstrom G., Garrett J., Thomason IV C., Sprinkle J., Volgyesi P.: GME 2000 Users Manual (v2.0), ISIS document, December 18, (2001)
3. Ledeczi A., Maroti M., Bakay A., Karsai G., Garrett J., Thomason IV C., Nordstrom G., Sprinkle J., Volgyesi P.: The Generic Modeling Environment, Workshop on Intelligent Signal Processing, accepted, Budapest, Hungary, May 17, (2001)

4. Sprinkle J., Karsai G., Ledeczi A., Nordstrom G.: The New Metamodeling Generation, IEEE Engineering of Computer Based Systems, Proceedings p.275, Washington, D.C., USA, April, 2001.
5. Karsai G., Nordstrom G., Ledeczi A., Sztipanovits J.: Specifying Graphical Modeling Systems Using Constraint-based Metamodels, IEEE Symposium on Computer Aided Control System Design, Conference CD-Rom, Anchorage, Alaska, September 25, (2000)
6. UML Summary, ver. 1.0.1, Rational Software Corporation, et al., Sept. (1997)
7. Object Constraint Language Specification, ver. 1.1, Rational Software Corporation, et al., Sept. (1997)
8. Jürjens J.: Formal Semantics for Interacting UML subsystems, Fifth International Conference on Formal Methods for Open Object-Based Distributed Systems (FMOODS 2002), Twente, March 20-22, (2002)
9. Harel D., Gery E.: Executable Object Modeling with Statecharts, IEEE Computer, vol. 30, no. 7, pp. 31-42, July (1997)
10. Karsai G.: Structured Specification of Model Interpreters, ECBS, pp 84-91, Nashville, TN, March, (1999)
11. Gamma E., Helm R., Johnson R.,Vlissides J.: Design Patterns: Elements of Reusable Object- Oriented Software, Addison-Wesley, (1995)

An Approach for Supporting Aspect-Oriented Domain Modeling

Jeff Gray[1], Ted Bapty[2], Sandeep Neema[2], Douglas C. Schmidt[2],
Aniruddha Gokhale[2], and Balachandran Natarajan[2]

[1] Dept. of Computer and Information Sciences, University of Alabama at Birmingham
Birmingham AL 35294-1170
gray@cis.uab.edu
http://www.gray-area.org

[2] Institute for Software Integrated Systems, Vanderbilt University
Nashville TN 37235
{bapty,sandeep,schmidt,gokhale,bala}@isis.vuse.vanderbilt.edu
http://www.isis.vanderbilt.edu

Abstract. This paper describes a technique for improving separation of concerns at the level of domain modeling. A contribution of this new approach is the construction of support tools that facilitate the elevation of crosscutting modeling concerns to first-class constructs in a type-system. The key idea is the application of a variant of the OMG Object Constraint Language to models that are stored persistently in XML. With this approach, weavers are generated from domain-specific descriptions to assist a modeler in exploring various alternative modeling scenarios. The paper examines several facets of Aspect-Oriented Domain Modeling (AODM), including: domain-specific model weavers, a language to support the concern separation, an overview of code generation issues within a meta-weaver framework, and a comparison between AODM and AOP. An example of the approach is provided, as well as a description of several future concepts for extending the flexibility within AODM.

1 Introduction

The benefits of performing refinements on non-code artifacts are well documented [3]. Our contribution to this area has been in Aspect-Oriented Domain Modeling (AODM), which represents the union of Aspect-Oriented Software Development (AOSD) [1] and Model-Integrated Computing (MIC) [34]. An AOSD approach can be beneficial at different stages of the software lifecycle and at various levels of abstraction. In particular, it can be advantageous to apply AOSD principles at levels closer to the *problem space*, e.g., architectural analysis [18], requirements engineering [30], and modeling [14], as well as the *solution space*, e.g, design [5, 10, 33], and implementation/coding [4, 19, 21, 36].

The advantages of applying AOSD to domain modeling are considerable. AODM assists a modeler in capturing concerns that were previously hard, if not impossible, to modularize (see the introductory example in Section 3). A key benefit is the ability to explore numerous scenarios by considering crosscutting modeling concerns, such as desired fault tolerance or latency levels, as aspects that can be inserted and removed from a model rapidly.

A growing area of research is concentrated on bringing aspect-oriented techniques into the purview of analysis and design (see [5, 10, 33] for examples of work in this area). A focal point of these efforts is the development of notational conventions that assist in the documentation of concerns that crosscut a design. These notational conventions advance the efficiency of expression of these concerns in the design. Moreover, they also have the important trait of improving the traceability from design to implementation. Although these current efforts do well to improve the cognizance of AOSD at the design level, they generally tend to treat the concept of aspect-oriented design primarily as a specification convention. This is to say that the focus has been on the graphical representation, semantical underpinnings, and decorative attributes concerned with aspects and their representation within UML. A contribution of this paper is to consider AODM more as an operational task by constructing executable model weavers. That is, we view AOSD as a mechanism to improve the modeling task itself by providing the ability to quantify properties across a model *during* the system modeling process. This action is performed by utilizing a weaver that has been constructed with the concepts of domain modeling in mind. A research effort that also appears to have this goal in mind can be found in [17], although this work seems more aimed at providing a transformation tool that reifies patterns at the level of object-oriented design.

The successful application of AODM necessitates the availability of weavers that understand the underlying modeling domain. These weavers process *models*, not source code, so programming language compilers like AspectJ [19] are not applicable due to the semantic mismatch of the abstraction level. Because the syntax and semantics of each modeling domain are unique, a different weaver is needed for each domain. To support this requirement, we have developed a meta-weaver framework to assist in the creation of new model weavers. We call this framework the Constraint-Specification Aspect Weaver (C-SAW) – (Note: the name is borrowed from the realization that a crosscutting saw, or c-saw, cuts across the grain of wood). This framework uses several code generators whose inputs are meta-level specifications, described in a Domain-Specific Language (DSL), which hide accidental complexities of interacting with XML and COM. The generators produce code that is merged into the C-SAW framework to instantiate a domain-specific weaver.

The remainder of this introduction provides the background information needed to understand the modeling context for the emergence of scattered constraints.

1.1 Model-Integrated Computing

Expressive power in software specification is often gained from using notations and abstractions that are aligned with the problem domain. This can be further enhanced when graphical representations are provided to model the domain abstractions. In our particular approach to domain-specific modeling, a design engineer describes a system by constructing a visual model using the terminology and concepts from a specific domain. Analysis can then be performed on the model, or the model can be synthesized into an implementation [20, 24, 34, 35].

Model-Integrated Computing (MIC) has been refined over many years to assist in the creation and synthesis of complex computer-based systems. A key application area for MIC is in those systems that have a tight integration between the computational structure of a system and its physical configuration (e.g., embedded systems)

[34]. In such systems, MIC has been shown to be a powerful tool for providing adaptability in changing environments [35].

The Generic Modeling Environment (GME) [20] is a meta-configurable modeling environment for realizing the principles of MIC. The GME provides meta-modeling capabilities that can be configured and adapted from meta-level specifications (representing the *modeling paradigm*) that describe the domain. There are several domains to which MIC and the GME have been successfully applied. The most notable evidence for the advantages of applying model-driven techniques is found in [22], where the documented benefits are described from the initiation of MIC into an automotive factory process.

1.2 Design Space Exploration in a Product-Line Architecture

A beneficial approach toward domain modeling considers the creation of a base model for representing a family of related systems, often called product-line architecture [6]. In such an approach, a design space corresponds to a set of implementation alternatives that are available within the product family. The selection of a fixed-point, among the set of possible alternatives from the base model, must be explored prior to model synthesis [23]. Design space exploration is an iterative process that selectively evaluates a set of constraints that are chosen by a modeler using a tool.

The exploration of a design space often requires the existence of constraints that are dispersed throughout a model [23]. Constraints codify properties of the model that must be satisfied during exploration. A modeler can specify constraints in the GME as model attributes that are then evaluated during design-space exploration. An example of a constraint is an assertion about the end-to-end latency within the flow of a sub-model. Each iteration of the exploration prunes the design space further. Focusing the exploration on different sets of constraints can lead the exploration and pruning algorithms along different elaborations of synthesis.

Although constraints are a necessary modeling construct for supporting design space exploration, the next section explains why constraints emerge as a crosscutting modeling entity.

2 Model Weavers for Separating Crosscutting Constraints

The primary goal of AOSD is to assist in modularizing crosscutting behavior [4, 19, 21, 36]. In the same manner that crosscutting code detracts from the cohesiveness of an implementation, the utility of specifying constraints within a model is often diminished due to their scattering throughout the model hierarchy [14]. It is often the case that the meta-model forces the emergence of a "dominant decomposition" (i.e., the primordial criteria for modular decomposition) [8, 36] that imposes the subjugation of other concerns, such as those captured by constraints.

In conventional system modeling tools, any change to the intention of a global property requires visiting and modifying each constraint, for every context, representing the property. This requires the modeler to "drill-down" (i.e., traverse the hierarchy by recursively opening, with the mouse, each sub-model), manually, to many locations of the model. It is common for a model in the GME to contain thousands of different modeling elements with hierarchies that are ten or more levels deep. The interdependent nature of each constraint makes change maintenance a daunting task for anything but a simple model. The benefits of a single model representation of a product family are nullified because the "Parnasian" objectives [27] of changeability, comprehensibility, and independent development are sacrificed in the presence of crosscutting constraints.

As models grow in size and complexity, it becomes unmanageable to view the contents of a model in its entirety because there are too many participating entities. The concept of viewpoints has been researched frequently as a topic within requirements engineering [25]. The GME supports the concept of a viewpoint as a first-class modeling construct, which assists a modeler in separating the concerns of multi-perspective views [20]. Each GME viewpoint describes a partitioning that selects a subset of entities as being visible.

Although they offer a powerful conceptualization for concern separation, GME's implementation of viewpoints, however, does not fit completely within the definition of aspects (at least in the way that they are defined within the AOSD community). Using only viewpoints, for example, a modeler cannot quantify over a model's join points and apply advice. The key parts of AOP, as enumerated in [19], are not fully present in many viewpoint-oriented implementations. Research into aspectual requirements also suggests that viewpoints alone are incapable of capturing many crosscutting concerns [30].

Because the current viewpoint implementation in most modeling tools does not adequately capture crosscutting concerns, a new extension to modeling tools is needed. We further motivate this need in the next section and provide an introduction to our approach for AODM.

2.1 The Need for Domain-Specific Model Weavers

Different domains typically will have different dominant decompositions and dissimilar crosscutting concerns. For instance, the adaptation of the frame rate or size of a visual display in an avionics system would have no counterpart in a domain that models an automotive factory. Consequently, because each new GME meta-modeling paradigm introduces different types of modeling elements, syntax, and semantics, different weavers are needed for each new modeling paradigm. The situation is similar to the reason that a different compiler is needed for a new programming language – the syntax and semantics typically vary too much between each language to permit a single instance of a generalized translator that compiles multiple languages. Thus, the domain for automotive manufacturing (e.g., a Saturn car) [22] needs its own specialized weaver, as does the BBN Unmanned Aerial Vehicle (UAV) domain [31], and the Boeing Bold Stroke domain [32].

```
<model id="id-05" kind="Component">
 <name>InertialSensor</name>
 <atom id="id-17" kind="ComputeMethod" role="ComputeMethod">
   <name>compute</name>
     <attribute kind="WCET">
       <value>2</value>
     </attribute>
```

Fig. 1. Bold Stroke XML Model

```xml
<model id="id-544975-39" kind="State">
  <name>frameRate</name>
<model id="id-544975-42" kind="State">
  <name>Range1-7</name>
<connection id="id-544975-63" kind="Transition">
  <name>Transition</name>
<connpoint role="dst" target="id-544975-42" />
<connpoint role="src" target="id-544975-46" />
  <attribute kind="Guard">
    <value>latency > 25</value>
  </attribute>
  <attribute kind="Action">
    <value>frameRate=4</value>
  </attribute>
```

Fig. 2. BBN/UAV XML Model

The GME has the capability to store models persistently using XML. To better understand the need for multiple weavers, consider the XML document in Figure 1. This represents a subset of a domain model description. The document has distinctly named regions with respect to the kind of elements being presented in the domain (e.g., "Component"), as well as roles (e.g., "ComputeMethod"), name, and even attributes (e.g., "WCET"). This is the meta-description of the Bold Stroke domain.

Further consider the XML fragment in Figure 2. It also has its own unique modeling entities (e.g., "State," "Transition," "Guard"). It should be noted that the same XML DTD is used in both Figures 1 and 2. However, the modeling concepts captured in each model are significantly different. The quoted strings in some of these models (e.g., the "kind" slots) show that something "meta" is truly happening.

Because of the diversity of domains, the ability to construct weavers for new domains is desired. The AODM approach that we are using can be summarized by the diagram in Figure 3. In this figure, new weavers are created by integrating domain-specific strategies into a meta-weaver framework (shown in the top-part of Figure 3). A *strategy* specifies a heuristic (e.g., processor assignment, as shown in the example in Section 3) for a specific modeling paradigm. Strategies are specified in a DSL called the Embedded Constraint Language (ECL), which is described in Section 4. A generator translates each strategy into C++, such that an instantiation of the meta-weaver framework is created (i.e., the generated C++ is in the middle of the framework). The instantiation of the framework (with a set of strategies) produces a new domain-specific weaver (middle of Figure 3). After a weaver is created for a specific domain, GME models (represented in that domain) can be woven with modeling pointcuts. A *modeling pointcut* identifies specific points in a model that are affected by a crosscutting modeling concern.

As mentioned earlier, the output of a domain-specific weaver is a new GME model that contains constraints that have been woven, i.e., the input to the weaver may be a base model that is void of any constraints, like the middle-right of Figure 3. The newly created constrained model can then be passed on to the design-space exploration tool, as mentioned previously in Section 1.2. The content inside the box of Figure 3 represents our contributions to AODM. The design space exploration research is a previous effort that provided the initial motivation for exploring this new area.

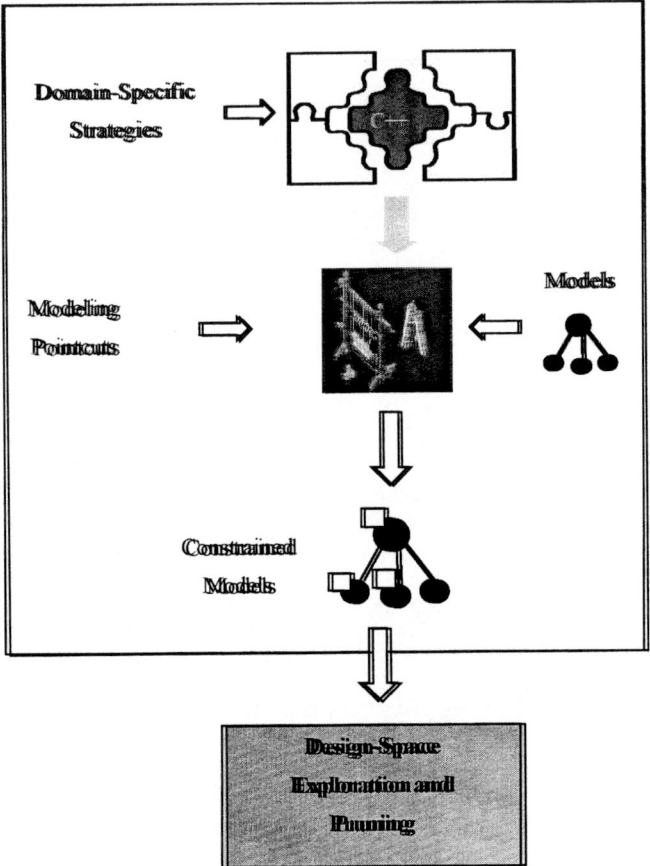

Fig. 3. Summary of AODM Process

3 Example

Bold Stroke is a product-line framework from Boeing for avionics navigation software [32]. In this section, an example crosscutting modeling concern is presented in a domain for modeling a subset of Bold Stroke applications and configurations.

Consider the requirements for a simple model that contains five software components representing a simplified scenario of an avionics mission program (see Figure 4). The first component is an inertial sensor. This sensor outputs, at a 100Hz rate, the position and velocity deltas of an aircraft. A second component is a position integrator. It computes the absolute position of the aircraft given the deltas received from the sensor. It must at least match the sensor rate such that there is no data loss. The weapon release component uses the absolute position to determine the time at which a weapon is to be deployed. It has a fixed period of 2Hz and a minimal-latency requirement. A mapping component is responsible for obtaining visual location information based on the absolute position. A map must be constructed such that the current absolute position is at the center of the map. A fifth component is responsible for displaying the map on an output device. Each of these components has distinct frequencies, latencies, and Worst Case Execution Times (WCET) [29]. The specific values of these properties will likely differ depending on the type of aircraft represented by the model, e.g., the latencies and WCETs for an F/A-18 fighter aircraft would most likely be lower than a helicopter. The core modeling components describe a product family with the values for each property indicating the specific characteristics of a member of the family.

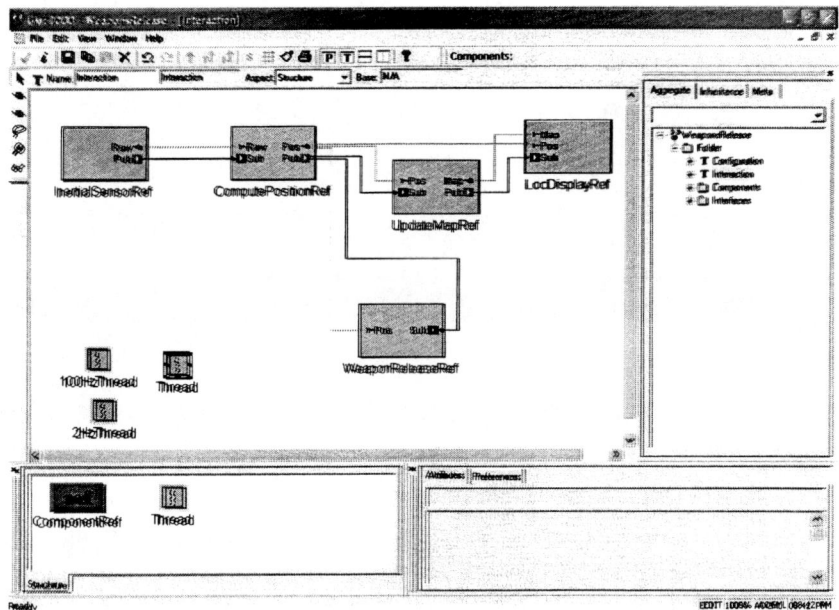

Fig. 4. Bold Stroke Component Interactions as Modeled in the GME

Figure 4 depicts the weapons deployment model represented within the GME. The model is an instance of the domain that was developed initially for modeling of Bold Stroke applications and component-based middleware. Each of the components in Figure 4 has internal details that also are modeled. For instance, the contents of the "Compute Position" component are rendered in Figure 5. As shown in the internals of this component, the series of interactions actually take place using a publish/subscribe model. The figure specifically highlights the attributes of a method called "compute" (see the bottom-right of the figure). The attributes provide the name of the method, the C++ source file that contains the method, and the method's estimated WCET.

3.1 Example Crosscutting Concern: Processor Assignment

Suppose that we wanted to model the processor assignment of each component. That is, based upon the expected WCET, the component methods are executed as tasks on various processors. A notation is needed to specify the assignment of component methods/tasks to processors. One way to accomplish this representation issue is to specify the processor assignment as a constraint of the component model.

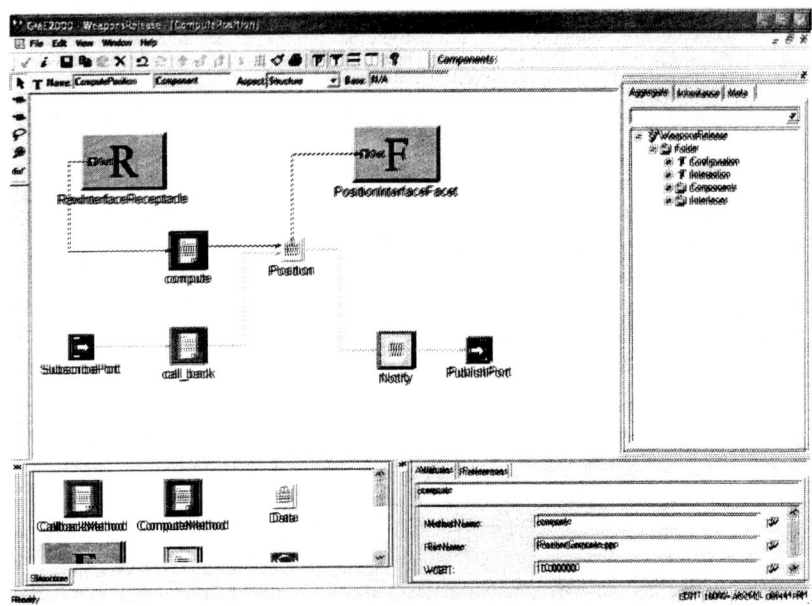

Fig. 5. A GME Model of the Internals of Compute Position

The way that processor assignment is typically modeled involves the application of a set of heuristics that globally assign tasks to processors based on specific properties of each component. In modeling, this often requires the modeler to visit each component, or task, in order to manually apply the heuristic. For a model with a large number of components, this can be a daunting task. It becomes increasingly unmanageable in situations where the modeler would like to play "what-if" scenarios. These "what-if" scenarios are used to drive the iterative evolution of the model, such that intermediate scenarios may even be discarded. This is helpful because a modeler may want to change the values of different properties, or even modify the details of the heuristic, in order to observe the effect of different scenarios. A manual application of a heuristic would require that the modeler re-visit every component and re-apply the rules of the heuristic.

An example of our approach for separating the concern of processor assignment can be found in Figures 6 and 7. The details of the language are defined elsewhere in the paper, but an outline of the meaning of these figures is offered here. The interpretation of the pointcut called ProcessorAssignment (Figure 7) is that a selection is specified over all of the modeling elements that are of type "Comp*" (note the use of the wildcard designator). Although not shown here, modeling pointcuts can also be formally named and composed with other pointcuts. It is not necessary that a pointcut be bound to a strategy, but the pointcut in Figure 7 is tied to a particular strategy called Assign (Figure 6). The combination of the pointcut and strategy invokes Assign on each of these modeling components (here, a parameter bound to the value 10 represents a threshold of the execution time for each processor load). The purpose of the Assign strategy is to look into the "compute" method of each component and find its WCET. The WCETs of each component are accumulated. Whenever this accumulated value reaches past the threshold, a new processor is created for component assignment. `Assign` will finally call another strategy, named `AddConstraint`, which will add a new constraint to the model. The new constraint, in this case, represents the processor assignment.

Note that the `ProcessorAssignment` pointcut could be modified so that a different strategy is invoked (i.e., some strategy other than `Assign`); or, a different parameter threshold could be provided that may result in a different set of constraints (i.e., the parameter to `Assign` may be changed from 10 to 20). The key advantage of this approach is realized in the observation that, from a change in *one* place, an entirely different set of constraints can be weaved into the model. This solves a serious scalability problem concerning maintenance issues, and the ability to change the constraints within a model.

```
defines AddConstraint, Assign, ProcessorAssignment;

strategy AddConstraint(constraintName, expression : string)
{
   addAtom("OCLConstraint", "Constraint",
           constraintName).addAttribute("Expression", expression);
}

strategy Assign(limit : integer)
{
   declare static accumulateWCET, processNum : integer;
   declare currentWCET : integer;
   declare aConstraint : string;

   self.compute.WCET.getInt(currentWCET);
   accumulateWCET := accumulateWCET + currentWCET;

   if (limit < accumulateWCET) then
      accumulateWCET := currentWCET;
      processNum := processNum + 1;
   endif;

   aConstraint = "self.assignTo() = processor" + processNum;
   AddConstraint("ProcessConstraint", aConstraint);
}
```

Fig. 6. Strategy for Processor Assignment

```
pointcut ProcessorAssignment
{
   models("")->select(m | m.kind() = "Comp*")->Assign(10);
}
```

Fig. 7. Pointcut Defining Model Locations for Applying the `Assign` Strategy

In comparison to the weaving performed at the coding level, as typified by AspectJ, the pointcut specification is encapsulated with the advice in order to describe where and when the aspect is to be applied. We took a different approach in the mechanism for specifying crosscutting modeling concerns. In our approach, the pointcut and strategies are often specified in separate files. This permits better reuse

160   Jeff Gray et al.

among the pointcuts and strategies (i.e., the pointcuts are more transparent to the individual strategy definitions).

Figure 8 shows the same component that was given in Figure 5. The only difference is that the component now contains a constraint that was added by the weaver as a result of applying the strategies described by the pointcut. Notice that the strategy has assigned this component to processor 0. An examination of all the other components involved in this interaction would reveal that different components are assigned to processors based on their WCET and the parameterized threshold.

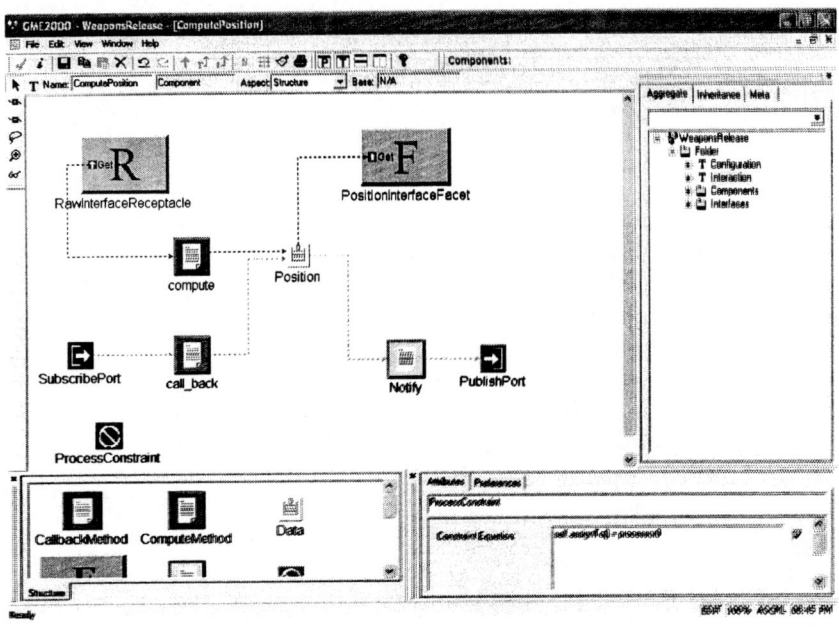

Fig. 8. Component with Weaved Constraint

4 Embedded Constraint Language

Model weavers are specified using the ECL - an extension (and subset) of the OMG Object Constraint Language (OCL) [37]. This language allows the weaver designer to specify the traversal of models, computations upon the model structure and attributes, and subsequent modifications to the models. In essence, the ECL is used to describe the transformations of an existing domain model that are needed to represent the crosscutting modeling concerns. Examples of the type of modifications that can be performed on models would be the addition of constraint objects, addition/modification of attributes to existing models, and addition of domain-specific modeling objects. A short description of the ECL follows.

The ECL supports many of the basic language constructs found in the OCL, as categorized in Table 1. The following capabilities distinguish ECL from OCL:

Table 1. Included OCL Operators

Arithmetic Operators
`+, -, *, /, =, <, >,`
`<=, >=, <>`

Logical Operators
`and, or, xor, not, implies, if/then/else`

Collection Operator & Property Operator
`->`
`.`

Standard OCL Collection Operators
`collection->size() : integer`
`collection->forAll(x | f(x) ) : Boolean`
`collection->select(x | f(x) ) : collection`
`collection->exists(x | f(x) ) : Boolean`

- ECL provides a set of operators to navigate the hierarchical structure of a model (see Table 2). These aggregate operators can be applied to first-class model objects (e.g., a container model or primitive model element) to obtain reflective information needed in either a strategy or modeling pointcut, such as `findModel`, `getID`, `findAttribute`. These operators are akin to the introspective operators in Java (e.g., `getName`, `getType`, `getInt`); i.e., they are reflective to the internal representation used in the GME. These operators, and the standard OCL selection operators, have similarities to the submitted OMG proposals to support Query/View/Transformations (QVT) [26] (e.g., CompuWare's TPL, and Rational XDE's pattern engine). In ECL, a query across the model can be specified using these navigational operators. The underlying XML representation of the model is searched by translating the ECL navigational statements into the XPath querying language.
- ECL also supports the "Transformation" idea of the OMG QVT. Traditionally, OCL has been used as a declarative language to specify properties of UML diagrams [37]. The use of ECL, however, requires the capability to introduce side-effects into the underlying XML model. This capability is needed because the strategies often specify transformations that must be performed on the model, which requires the ability to make modifications to the model as the strategy is applied. ECL therefore supports an imperative procedural style with numerous operations that can alter the state of the model, such as `addAtom`, `addAttribute`, `removeChild`. Because the underlying model hierarchy is stored as an XML file, these functions are often implemented as wrappers for the specific calls that are needed to use XPath and the XML Document Object Model (DOM).
- The procedural nature of ECL permits dependencies between strategies. Strategies can be chained together as procedure calls. Recursion is also supported in the ECL. Circular dependencies are possible (of course, the strategy must specify a termination condition for the strategy to complete its processing).

Table 2. ECL Model Operators

Aggregates
`folders, models, atoms, attributes, connections`
Connections
`connpoint, target, refs, resolveReferredID`
Transformation
`addAttribute, addAtom, addModel, addConnection, removeNode`
Selection
`findFolder, findModel, findAtom, findAttributeNode`
General
`id, parent, getID, getInt, getStr`

5   Comparison to AOP

Domain-specific weavers rely on modeling pointcuts and strategies to perform their responsibilities. Modeling pointcuts are used to describe *where* the concern will be applied in the model, and strategies describe *how* a concern is applied in the context of a particular node in the model. Several comparisons can be made between the approach to AODM described in this paper and traditional AOP.

Table 3 provides a comparison of the critical elements that make a system aspect-oriented, according to the definition provided in [19]; i.e., the join point model, the pointcut designator construct, and the concept of advice. The AODM approach presents a way to query and traverse over a large model space. As such, the approach has borrowed from the experience of traversal specifications as typified by work done in Demeter and Adaptive Programming techniques [21]. The crucial difference is that the implementations of Demeter have primarily focused on code-level traversals. Our models are graphical representations of a domain at a higher level of abstraction, thus necessitating a different focus.

Table 3. Comparison of AspectJ and AODM

	AspectJ	AODM
Join Point Model	Well-defined points in the execution of a program	Static points (nodes) in a model
Pointcut Designator	A declarative statement (formed from a set of primitives like `call`, `this`, and `target`) that describes a set of join points in a program	A declarative statement (formed from ECL collection operators) that identifies a set of locations within a model
Advice	A block of code that is executed at a join point	A strategy, or heuristic, for instrumenting a model with information related to a concern

The box in the bottom of Figure 9 represents a subset of a modeling pointcut. In the pointcut of Figure 9, a predicate within the select statement instructs the weaver to collect all nodes in the model that are of kind "StateFlow" and have a name that matches "Model*." Such a statement has a direct correspondence to a pointcut (as in AspectJ) that picks out specific points in the execution of a program satisfying some condition. The modeling pointcut also describes the strategy that is to be invoked on each node selected from the predicate. The effect of this association is the quantification of a concern over multiple join points [11]. As the strategy is applied at each node, the model is transformed according to the intent of the strategy, which has a direct correspondence to the association of pointcuts with advice in AspectJ, and how advice affects the execution of the program (of course, our models as represented in XML are static).

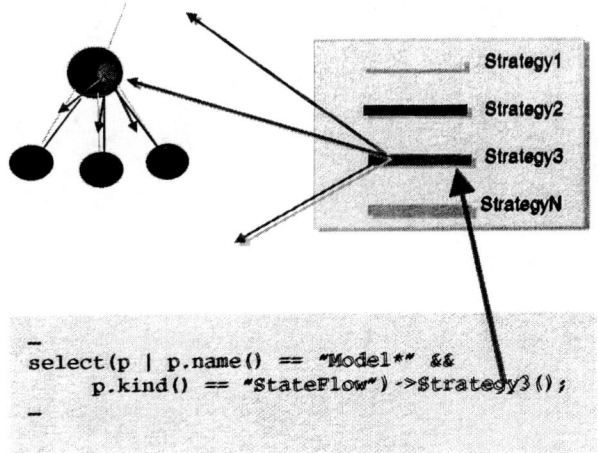

Fig. 9. Effects of the Coordination Between Modeling Pointcuts and Strategies

6 Code Generation

This section discusses issues related to the development of the ECL code generator. In particular, the benefits of using a domain-specific language (DSL) to isolate several accidental complexities (e.g., the lower-level XML DOM, and the COM data structures) are described.

The Strategy Code Generator (StratGen) tool translates strategies, as specified in the ECL, into C++ code that can be inserted into the meta-weaver framework (see the top of Figure 3). This sub-section provides an example of the translation approach used within StratGen.

```
components.models("")->select(c |
         c.id()==refID)->DetermineLaziness();
```

Fig. 10. Fragment of an EagerLazy Strategy

Figure 10 contains a statement from a strategy, described in [16], which is focused on eager/lazy evaluation for a CORBA event channel (this is just one of several lines found in that strategy – it is not meant to imply that this single line represents the entirety of the strategy). This statement finds all of the models that match a specific id and then calls the `DetermineLaziness` strategy on those selected nodes. The amount of C++ code that is generated by StratGen, however, is far from being concise or simple (see Figure 11). Much of the code for implementing this strategy statement is focused on iterating over a collection and selecting elements of the collection that satisfy the predicate. The ECL hides the accidental details that pertain to the fact that the underlying model is represented in XML. As such, the COM invocations of the lower-lever API calls to manipulate the XML DOM are concealed.

```
...
CComPtr<IXMLDOMNodeList> models0 = XMLParser::models(components, "");
nodeTypeVector selectVec1 = XMLParser::ConvertDomList(models0);
nodeTypeVector selectVecTrue1 = new std::vector<nodeType>;
vector<nodeType>::iterator itrSelect1;
for(itrSelect1 = selectVec1->begin();
    itrSelect1 != selectVec1->end(); itrSelect1++) {
  nodeType selectNode1 = (*itrSelect1);
  nodeType c;
  c = selectNode1;
  CComBSTR id0 = XMLParser::id(c);

  ClData varforward1(id0);
  ClData varforward2(referredID);
  bool varforward3 = varforward1 == varforward2;
  if(varforward3)
      selectVecTrue1->push_back(*itrSelect1);
}

vector<nodeType>::iterator itrCollCall1;
for(itrCollCall1 = selectVecTrue1->begin();
    itrCollCall1 != selectVecTrue1->end(); itrCollCall1++)
  DetermineLaziness::apply(...);
...
```

Fig. 11. Sample of Generated C++ Code

The code in Figure 11 contains a generic value class named `ClData`. It is in this class where the equality operator performs a special match for string wildcards. The C++ code calls an XML Parser wrapper class that retrieves a set of all models. An iteration over the list of models checks to see if the name of the node referenced by the current iterator matches the wildcard. The ECL was one of several candidate languages used in a study of the conciseness of DSLs [15]. In that study, the ECL was shown to be 3 times more concise than the representative C++.

7 Future Work

The ECL has truly been an evolving language – each new strategy that was created brought fresh insight into additional language constructs that would be beneficial. In the future, the ECL will continue to evolve to support additional features (e.g., support for a "cflow" or "dflow" modeling construct, similar to AspectJ). This section outlines some additional research objectives that will be explored in the immediate future.

A potentially rewarding subject for future investigation will be to subsume the textual descriptions formulated within the ECL into a graphical modeling language. This effort will investigate the expression of modeling pointcuts, and even strategies, using a graphical formalism similar to that of visual programming languages. This kind of visual aspect modeling would, of course, be perfectly suited for exploration from within the GME. The concept of generating weavers from visual formalisms (i.e., interpreting strategy specifications that are described visually) is also appealing.

The current version of C-SAW assumes that the separation of modeling concerns was being performed on models created with the GME. In fact, this assumption is built into the XML Parser within the weaver framework. The limitation imposed by this assumption precludes other modeling tools (that also can export models using XML) from being able to employ the benefits of an aspect weaver. In addition to the GME, other examples of domain-specific visual modeling tools are Honeywell's Domain Modeling Environment [9], and metaEdit+ (from metaCASE) [28]. It is possible that these, and other modeling tools could benefit from an aspect-oriented modeling approach. A new code generator could be inserted into the weaver framework in order to provide an added measure of variability. From the modeling tool's Document Type Definition (DTD), the functionality of the wrappers provided within the XML Parser can be generated. This would permit adaptability of the framework between domains (using the strategy code generator), and also adaptability between modeling tools, using Generative Programming [7] and invasive composition techniques [2].

A future goal of our project is to provide the capability for generating the configuration of Bold Stroke components from domain-specific models in such a way that specific parts of each component are weaved together as an aspect. For example, a base model can capture the infrastructure of a product-line with constraints representing specific configuration information for a particular product (e.g., for distributed real-time embedded systems [13]). A synthesis process can generate AspectJ components from an analysis of the model and constraints (initial ideas for supporting this have been presented in [16]). This goal fits well with quality of service issues applied to the OMG's Model Driven Architecture (MDA) [12].

8 Concluding Remarks

The main objective of the research described in this paper is to apply the concepts of AOSD to domain modeling. The implementation of this objective has resulted in a means to add aspect modeling to the repertoire of the well-established GME modeling tool. The result of our work is a model weaver framework called the Constraint-Specification Aspect Weaver (C-SAW). Earlier work on aspect modeling has concentrated on important notational issues for extending the UML, whereas the research described in this paper has brought the benefits of aspect-orientation to the modeling process itself. The work described in this paper has been applied to modeling efforts of Boeing Bold Stroke [16, 32]. A model weaver has also been demonstrated with BBN's adaptive UAV project [31], as briefly described in [24].

There are several reasons that would support the adoption of our approach into a general modeling paradigm. It has been discovered that a lack of support for separation of concerns with respect to constraints can pose a difficulty when creating domain-specific models. Constraints may be specified throughout the nodes of a model to stipulate design criteria and limit design alternatives. However, because these constraints are scattered across the hierarchy of a model, they are hard to change. The scattering of constraints throughout various levels of a model makes it hard to maintain and reason about their effects and purpose.

The concept of a domain-specific weaver can be used in many ways beyond the application of constraints. For example, a weaver can be used to distribute any system property endemic to a specific domain across the hierarchy of a model. A weaver can also be used to instrument structural changes within the model according to the dictates of some higher-level requirement that represents a crosscutting concern.

The C-SAW weaver framework serves as a generalized transformation engine for manipulating models. The framework, in conjunction with several code generators and DSLs, is used to provide the adaptability needed to construct new instances of the framework. A core component of this framework is a code generator that translates high-level descriptions of strategies into C++ source code. The conciseness of the ECL, compared to the generated code, provides a measure of the benefit for using DSLs to provide a higher level of abstraction.

Acknowledgements

We would like to thank the following individuals for comments on portions of this paper: Steve Schach, Gábor Karsai, Janos Sztipanovits, and Ákos Lédeczi. Also, discussions with Dave Sharp and other Boeing PCES members have been essential toward improving our understanding of the role of modeling in the development of Bold Stroke. Several comments provided by the anonymous reviewers were beneficial in improving the clarity of the paper.

The DARPA Information Exploitation Office (DARPA/IXO), under the Program Composition for Embedded Systems (PCES) program, funds this work.

References

1. http://www.aosd.net
2. Uwe Aßmann, *Invasive Software Composition*, Springer-Verlag, 2003.
3. Don Batory, Jacob Neal Sarvela, and Axel Rauschmeyer, "Scaling Step-Wise Refinement," *International Conference on Software Engineering*, Portland, Oregon, May 2003, pp. 187-197.
4. Lodewijk Bergmans and Mehmet Aksit, "Composing Crosscutting Concerns using Composition Filters," *Communications of the ACM*, October 2001, pp. 51-57.
5. Siobhán Clarke and Robert J. Walker, "Towards a Standard Design Language for AOSD," *First International Conference on Aspect-Oriented Software Development*, Enschede, The Netherlands, April 2002, pp. 113-119.
6. Paul Clements and Linda Northrop, *Software Product Lines: Practices and Patterns*, Addison-Wesley, 2001.
7. Krzysztof Czarnecki and Ulrich Eisenecker, *Generative Programming: Methods, Tools, and Applications*, Addison-Wesley, 2000.
8. Maja D'Hondt and Theo D'Hondt, "The Tyranny of the Dominant Model Decomposition," *OOPSLA Workshop on Generative Techniques in the Context of Model-Driven Architecture*, Seattle, Washington, November 2002.

9. http://www.htc.honeywell.com/dome/
10. Tzilla Elrad, Omar Aldawud, Atef Bader, "Aspect-Oriented Modeling: Bridging the Gap between Implementation and Design," *Generative Programming and Component Engineering (GPCE)*, Pittsburgh, Pennsylvania, October 2002, pp. 189-201.
11. Robert Filman and Dan Friedman, "Aspect-Oriented Programming is Quantification and Obliviousness," *OOPSLA Workshop on Advanced Separation of Concerns*, Minneapolis, Minnesota, October 2000.
12. David Frankel, *Model Driven Architecture: Applying MDA to Enterprise Computing*, John Wiley & Sons, 2003.
13. Aniruddha Gokhale, Douglas Schmidt, Balachandran Natarajan, Jeff Gray, and Nanbor Wang, "Model-Driven Middleware," in *Middleware for Communications*, (Qusay Mahmoud, ed.), John Wiley & Sons, 2003.
14. Jeff Gray, Ted Bapty, Sandeep Neema, and James Tuck, "Handling Crosscutting Constraints in Domain-Specific Modeling," *Communications of the ACM*, October 2001, pp. 87-93.
15. Jeff Gray and Gábor Karsai, "An Examination of DSLs for Concisely Representing Model Traversals and Transformations," *36th Hawaiian International Conference on System Sciences (HICSS)*, Big Island, Hawaii, January 6-9, 2003.
16. Jeff Gray, Janos Sztipanovits, Douglas C. Schmidt, Ted Bapty, Sandeep Neema, and Aniruddha Gokhale, "Two-level Aspect Weaving to Support Evolution of Model-Based Software," in *Aspect-Oriented Software Development*, (Robert Filman, Tzilla Elrad, Mehmet Aksit, and Siobhán Clarke, eds.), Addison-Wesley, 2003.
17. Wai-Meng Ho, Jean-Marc Jezequel, Francois Pennaneac'h, and Noel Plouzeau, "A Toolkit for Weaving Aspect-Oriented UML Designs," *First International Conference on Aspect-Oriented Software Development*, Enschede, The Netherlands, April 2002, pp. 99-105.
18. Mika Katara and Shmuel Katz, "Architectural Views of Aspects," *2nd International Conference on Aspect-Oriented Software Development*, Boston, Massachusetts, March 2003, pp. 1-10.
19. Gregor Kiczales, Eric Hilsdale, Jim Hugunin, Mik Kersten, Jeffrey Palm, and William Griswold, "Getting Started with AspectJ," *Communications of the ACM*, October 2001, pp. 59-65.
20. Ákos Lédeczi, Arpad Bakay, Miklos Maroti, Peter Volgyesi, Greg Nordstrom, Jonathan Sprinkle, and Gábor Karsai, "Composing Domain-Specific Design Environments," *IEEE Computer*, November 2001, pp. 44-51.
21. Karl Lieberherr, Doug Orleans, and Johan Ovlinger, "Aspect-Oriented Programming with Adaptive Methods," *Communications of the ACM*, October 2001, pp. 39-41.
22. Earl Long, Amit Misra, and Janos Sztipanovits, "Increasing Productivity at Saturn," *IEEE Computer*, August 1998, pp. 35-43.
23. Sandeep Neema, "System Level Synthesis of Adaptive Computing Systems," Ph.D. Dissertation, Vanderbilt University, Dept. of Electrical Engineering and Computer Science, May 2001
(http://www.isis.vanderbilt.edu/publications/archive/Neema_S_5_0_2001_System_Lev.pdf
)
24. Sandeep Neema, Ted Bapty, Jeff Gray, and Aniruddha Gokhale, "Generators for Synthesis of QoS Adaptation in Distributed Real-Time Embedded Systems," *Generative Programming and Component Engineering (GPCE)*, Pittsburgh, Pennsylvania, October 2002, pp. 236-251.
25. Basher Nuseibeh, Jeff Kramer, and Anthony Finkelstein, "A Framework for Expressing the Relationship Between Multiple Views in Requirements Specification," *IEEE Transactions on Software Engineering*, October 1994, pp. 760-773.
26. *OMG Request for Proposal: MOF 2.0 Query / Views / Transformations RFP*, OMG Document: ad/02-04-10, April 2002.
27. David Parnas, "On the Criteria To Be Used in Decomposing Systems into Modules," *Communications of the ACM*, December 1972, pp. 1053-1058.

28. Risto Pohjonen and Steve Kelly, "Domain-Specific Modeling," *Dr. Dobb's Journal*, August 2002.
29. Peter Puschner and Alan Burns, "A Review of Worst-Case Execution Time Analysis," *The Journal of Real-Time Systems*, Vol. 18, Number 2/3, pp. 115-128.
30. Awais Rashid, Ana Moreira, and João Araújo, "Modularization and Composition of Aspectual Requirements," *2nd International Conference on Aspect-Oriented Software Development*, Boston, Massachusetts, March 2003, pp. 11-20.
31. Richard Schantz, Joseph Loyall, Michael Atighetchi, and Partha Pal, "Packaging Quality of Service Control Behaviors for Reuse," *5th IEEE International Symposium on Object-Oriented Real-Time Distributed Computing (ISORC)*, April/May 2002, Washington, D.C., pp. 375-385.
32. David Sharp, "Reducing Avionics Software Cost Through Component Based Product-Line Development," *Software Technology Conference*, Salt Lake City, Utah, April 1998.
33. Dominik Stein, Stefan Hanenberg, and Rainer Unland, "An UML-based Aspect-Oriented Design Notation," *First International Conference on Aspect-Oriented Software Development*, Enschede, The Netherlands, April 2002, pp. 106-112.
34. Janos Sztipanovits and Gábor Karsai, "Model-Integrated Computing," *IEEE Computer*, April 1997, pp. 10-12.
35. Janos Sztipanovits, "Generative Programming for Embedded Systems," *Keynote Address: Generative Programming and Component Engineering (GPCE)*, Pittsburgh, Pennsylvania, October 2002, pp. 32-49.
36. Peri Tarr, Harold Ossher, William Harrison, and Stanley Sutton, "N Degrees of Separation: Multi-Dimensional Separation of Concerns," *International Conference on Software Engineering*, Los Angeles, California, May 1999, pp. 107-119.
37. Jos Warmer and Anneke Kleppe, *The Object Constraint Language: Precise Modeling with UML*, Addison-Wesley, 1999.

The Convergence of AOP and Active Databases: Towards Reactive Middleware

Mariano Cilia, Michael Haupt, Mira Mezini, and Alejandro Buchmann

Department of Computer Science
Darmstadt University of Technology - Darmstadt, Germany
{cilia,haupt,mezini,buchmann}@informatik.tu-darmstadt.de

Abstract. Reactive behavior is rapidly becoming a key feature of modern software systems in such diverse areas as ubiquitous computing, autonomic systems, and event-based supply chain management. In this paper we analyze the convergence of techniques from aspect oriented programming, active databases and asynchronous notification systems to form reactive middleware. We identify the common core of abstractions and explain both commonalities and differences to start a dialogue across community boundaries. We present existing options for implementation of reactive software and analyze their run-time semantics. We do not advocate a particular approach but concentrate on identifying how the various disciplines can benefit from each other. We believe that AOP can solve the impedance mismatch found in reactive systems that are implemented through inherently static languages, while AOP can benefit from the active database community's experience with event detection/composition and fault tolerance in large scale systems. The result could be a solid foundation for the realization of reactive middleware services.

1 Introduction

Software development in the past decade has exhibited several trends:

- monolithic ad-hoc software development is being replaced by service-based architectures relying on customizable generic services;
- crosscutting concerns must be modularized and are often added after a system has been designed;
- the need for asynchronous interactions has been recognized, particularly in the face of mobility and the resulting instability of communications;
- the need for reactive behavior and the ability to handle exceptions are essential for very diverse applications ranging from ubiquitous computing to event-based supply chain management.

Solutions to cope with (some of) these trends have emerged in different communities: the database community has developed active databases, the programming languages community has developed aspect oriented programming, and the middleware community has developed asynchronous notification mechanisms and service-based architectures. Each approach reflects the idiosyncracies of the corresponding community, but they all share a core of common abstractions extended by issues that are important in a given community as shown in Fig. 1.

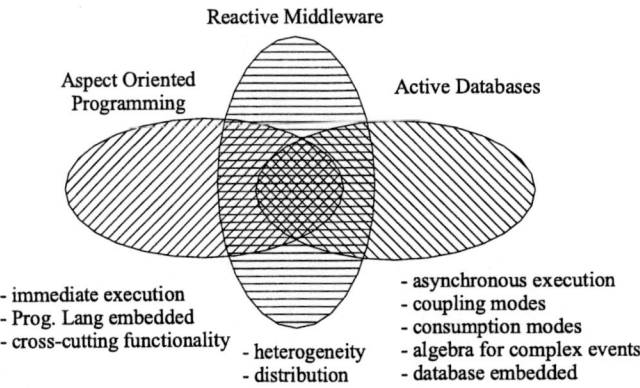

Fig. 1. Technologies in context

It is the goal of this paper to identify the common abstractions, understand both similarities and differences, and start a dialogue across community boundaries. Towards this goal, the first contribution of this paper is to introduce the terminology, to identify the commonalities of the various approaches to reactive software, present experiences and discuss the difficulties. We exploit the fact that each of the authors is thoroughly familiar with at least two of the three areas and has good working knowledge of the third.

The second goal of this paper is to present existing options for implementation of reactive software and to analyze their run-time semantics. The flexibility of reactive systems is determined by the time at which reactive functionality can be added to existing code, how the reactive capability can be activated or deactivated, and how an event, i.e., the occurrence of a happening of interest, is signalled. To this end we introduce a spectrum ranging from compile-time to run-time binding on one dimension, and from non-invasive to invasive situation detection mechanisms. Invasive detection mechanisms require the modification of the underlying code, while non-invasive mechanisms do not.

In this paper we do not push any particular approach but concentrate on identifying how the various disciplines can benefit from each other. We believe that aspect oriented programming can solve the impedance mismatch found in active databases and service based middleware when dynamic capabilities are implemented through inherently static languages. On the other hand, aspect oriented programming can benefit from the experience gained in the active database area with event detection/composition and fault tolerance in large-scale systems.

The result could be a solid foundation for the realization of reactive middleware services and eventually a platform for reactive software.

The remainder of this paper presents in Section 2.1 the underlying technologies and introduces the terminology. Section 2.2 deals with the definition of reactions. Section 2.3 deals with the execution of reactions, i.e., the run-time semantics. Section 2.4 discusses the options afforded by the various run-time environments. Section 3 shows how the technologies converge towards reactive middleware. Finally, Section 4 presents conclusions and a brief summary of our ongoing work.

2 Active Databases and AOP Side-by-Side

2.1 Origins and Basic Concepts

The basic problem that motivated the work in active databases and AOP is modularization of crosscutting concerns and the need to detect relevant situations and react to them efficiently. In the case of monitoring applications that track changes to the underlying (passive) database the problem lies in the need to poll periodically the state of the database to detect changes. This is highly inefficient, not only because many unnecessary queries are executed but also because queries are issued in user space, the queries in their execution traverse several layers of the database management system (DBMS) and monitoring functions (conditions) may be replicated across applications. Active databases solved this problem by defining *Event-Condition-Action* (ECA) rules that are defined in the schema and executed in the DBMS kernel. Whenever an event is detected and a guarding condition is true, the corresponding action is executed. *Aspect Oriented Programming* (AOP) has been motivated by the need to modularize crosscutting behavior, such that new crosscutting behavior can be added in a localized manner and without changing existing code. AOP introduced join points and point cuts to signal situations of interest and advice to react to them. In the remainder of this section we summarize the notions of Active Databases and Aspect Oriented Programming, and introduce the terminology used throughout this paper.

Active Databases: In conventional (*passive*) database management systems data is created, modified, deleted and retrieved in response to requests issued by users or applications. In the mid-80s database technology was confronted with monitoring applications that required the reaction to changes in the database. To avoid wasteful polling, passive database functionality was extended with ECA rules to allow the database system itself to perform certain operations automatically in response to the occurrence of predefined events. Those systems are known as *active DBMSs* [1, 63, 53]. They are significantly more powerful than passive DBMSs since they can (efficiently) perform functions that in passive database systems must be encoded in applications. The same mechanism can also be used to perform tasks that require special-purpose subsystems in passive databases

(e. g., integrity constraint enforcement, access control, view management, and statistics gathering).

Historically, production rules were the first mechanism used to provide automatic reaction functionality. Production rules are Condition-Action rules that do not break out the triggering event explicitly. Instead, they implement a polling-style evaluation of all rule conditions. In contrast, ECA rules explicitly define triggering events, e. g., the fact that an update or an insert occurred, and conditions on the content of the database are only evaluated if the triggering event is signaled.

ECA rules consist of three parts: a lightweight *Event* causes the rule to be fired; an (optional) *Condition* is checked when the rule is fired; and an *Action* is executed when the rule is fired and its guarding condition evaluates to true.

In active relational databases, events were modelled as changes of state of the database, i. e., insert, delete and update operations that could trigger a reaction [31, 59]. This basic functionality is common fare in today's commercial DBMSs in the form of triggers. In object-oriented systems, ECA rules are considered as *first-class objects* [17]. This treatment of ECA rules as first-class entities enables them to be handled homogeneously like any other object. In these systems more general events were defined: temporal, method invocation (with before and after modifiers), and user-defined events [17, 3, 28, 11, 66].

In addition to these events, more complex situations that correlate, aggregate or combine events can be defined. This is done by using an event algebra [28, 67] that allows the definition of *composite or complex events*.

Active database functionality developed for a particular DBMS became part of a large monolithic piece of software (the DBMS). As it is well known, monolithic software is difficult to extend and adapt. Moreover, tightly coupling the active functionality to a concrete database system precludes its adaptation to today's Internet applications, where heterogeneity and distribution play a significant role but are not directly supported by (active) database systems.

Aspect Oriented Programming: The goal of aspect-oriented programming is to facilitate the separation and modularization of concerns whose natural structures are crosscutting [46, 47]. Crosscutting concerns imply different decompositions of the system into modules. The different decompositions yield different models, i. e., sets of interrelated modules. Given two crosscutting models M1 and M2, if we adopt one of them, say M1, as our basic decomposition of the system, then definitions that are modularly captured in M2 will be spread around several modules in M1, causing code scattering and tangling, negatively affecting the extensibility and maintainability of the software. For a technical and an intuitive definition of the term "crosscutting models", the reader is referred to [46], respectively [47].

To avoid such scattering and tangling, with AOP the question is not which criteria to choose for decomposing the system, but how to support the decomposition according to several independent criteria simultaneously. Aspect-oriented languages modularize a system's various crosscutting models into independent aspect modules and provide appropriate means for specifying *when* and *how* they should join the overall definition of the system. By modularizing crosscutting concerns into aspects, behavior that conventional programming would distribute throughout the code congeals into a single textual structure, making both aspect code and the target easier to understand [26]. This promises simpler system evolution, more comprehensible systems, adaptability, customizability, and easier reuse.

The design space of aspect-oriented languages is determined by several factors. First, AO languages may vary in how they represent the modules they support for specifying individual crosscutting models. Second, different approaches can be taken for the specification of *when* crosscutting models join. This specification is expressed using *join points* that can be placed in the source code of different aspects, or they can be points in the object call graph of the running system, yielding the distinction between AO languages with a static versus dynamic join point model. Furthermore, one might distinguish between coarse-grained join points such as method signatures, and fine-grained join points like the access of a variable within the execution of a control flow. Finally, AO languages may also vary in the specification of *how* aspects come together at join points.

Implementation approaches for AO languages can be classified based on two criteria. First, systems may use different ways for detecting/signaling join points. The second criterion regards how actual implementations perform the dispatch to advice code at join points once they are detected.

In the course of this paper, we will refer to the AspectJ system [41, 5] because it offers a rather well-defined terminology for the most important parts of aspect orientation and is the most prominent AO language today.

2.2 Definition of Situations and Reactions

Both AOP and active databases provide mechanisms for describing situations under which specific reactions should be invoked. Although the concepts and mechanisms are surprisingly similar, the two communities use different terminology. In this section we describe the basic detection and reaction primitives from the point of view of their specification and show the convergence of both technologies.

Defining ECA Rules: Primitive or composite events are associated with ECA rules in order to describe the situation that must be detected for the action to be executed. The subsystems of an active database - query processor, transaction and recovery managers, etc. can signal the occurrence of primitive events [9]. These can be data manipulation operations, timer events or explicit events signaled from outside the database, e. g., from the operating system.

The use of method invocation events in the definition of ECA rules can include `before`, `after`, and `instead` modifiers. These are used to explicitly define whether the rule should be executed before or after a method execution or alternatively to the original code.

An event is characterized by having a type and a set of parameters. Parameters are associated to event occurrences with the purpose of describing information about the context where the event was signaled. These parameters are specific to the event type. For instance, an occurrence of a database event of type **insert** carries the following parameters: name of table in question, the involved fields and their corresponding values, transaction identification, timestamp, etc. Both a rule's condition and its action have access to the associated parameter information of an event occurrence.

As mentioned before, events may be composed to form more complex events by using an event algebra. Once a pattern of events being signaled matches an event expression, the associated rule is fired. A variety of event algebras has been defined [17, 30, 28, 13, 67]. Examples of possible event expressions are:

- **Sequence:** The two events must occur in the given order for the expression to match.
- **Alternative:** One of the two events must occur for the expression to match.
- **Closure:** The event may occur multiple times during a transaction, but it is not effectively signaled until the transaction ends or until it has occurred a certain number of times. The event's context information is accumulated.

An important issue must be considered when composing events, specifically when more than one event occurrence is to be consumed in the composition of a complex event. The specification of a *consumption mode* [13] associated to the event part of the rule specification allows the rule processing engine to precisely determine which event occurrences must be considered for consumption. Different consumption modes may be required by different application domains. The two most common modes are **recent** and **chronicle**. In the former, common in sensor-driven applications, the most recent event occurrences of the specified type are used, while in the latter, common in workflow applications, the oldest event occurrences of the specified type are consumed.

Conditions are optional and allow the expression of additional constraints that must be met for the action to execute. If they are missing we speak about *Event-Action (EA) rules*. Conditions can be expressed as Boolean predicates or query language expressions. Also external method invocations can be used. The specification of conditions can involve variables that will be bound at run-time with the content of triggering events.

The action part of an ECA rule may be a sequence of operations related to the database, transaction commands, operations related to the rule management (e. g., activate, deactivate), or the invocation of (external) methods. It is performed only if the condition holds.

For some applications it is useful to delay the evaluation of a triggered rule's condition or the execution of its action until the end of the transaction, for example, when evaluating a consistency constraint that involves several updates. In other cases it may be useful to evaluate a triggered rule's condition or execute its action in a separate transaction. These possibilities resulted in the notion of *coupling modes*[18]. Coupling modes can specify the transactional relationship between a rule's triggering event, the evaluation of its condition and the execution of its action. Coupling modes can be defined when specifying ECA rules. The originally proposed coupling modes include:

- **Immediate:** The condition (or action) is evaluated instantly (synchronously) suspending the execution of the current transaction.
- **Deferred:** Condition evaluation (or action execution) takes place just before the transaction commits or rolls back.
- **Detached:** There are two possible ways to evaluate a condition/action in detached mode. Evaluating it *causally independent* means that the condition/action is evaluated completely asynchronously: a separate transaction is started. *Causally dependent* evaluation also starts a separate transaction, but not before the original transaction has committed or rolled back.

Most active database projects defined their own rule specification language but they share most of the features presented above. A small subset has become part of the SQL standard and is available in commercial DBMSs.

A difficulty in using ECA rules is to predict how the defined rules will behave in all possible scenarios. For some active database rule languages it is possible to perform automatic static analysis on sets of rules to predict certain aspects of rule behavior (i.e., conflicts, termination, or confluence) [65, 2, 40, 7]. Rule analysis techniques are dependent on the semantics of rule execution which are addressed in Section 2.3.

Defining Aspects: The AspectJ system we refer to [41, 5] is an extension to the Java programming language, therefore both base applications and aspectual behavior used to extend them are implemented in Java. Aspectual behavior is applied using information from the weaving description, a precise quantification of when and how aspectual behavior has to be interwoven with the application. AspectJ follows a compiler-based approach, interweaving aspect code with the base application at compile-time.

In AspectJ, aspectual behavior and weaving descriptions are usually expressed side by side in syntactical constructs called *aspects*. An aspect looks much like an ordinary class in that it may define methods and attributes, inherit from other aspects (including abstract ones) or classes and implement interfaces. Apart from that, aspects may contain *pointcuts* and *advice* to define crosscutting behavior, of which AspectJ supports two kinds. Static crosscutting means adding functionality to existing classes, while dynamic crosscutting allows for executing additional functionality at join points.

In terms of Sec. 2.1, AspectJ's join point model is dynamic, join points being nodes in the run-time object call graph. Both coarse- and fine-grained join points are supported, e.g., calls to methods, read or write accesses to objects' attributes or exception handler executions.

AspectJ uses *pointcuts* to quantify aspect applications. Pointcuts are composed of several join points and, optionally, values from the context of these join points that are of interest to aspectual behavior. Due to the dynamic nature of join points, it is possible to take whole partitions of the object call graph into account for quantification of pointcuts. AspectJ's `cflow` (control flow) pointcuts, parameterized with another pointcut, match whenever join points in the control flow of that parameter are met.

Aspectual behavior is defined in units of Java code called *advice*. Advice can be applied `before`, `after`, or `around` pointcuts, the former two plainly meaning that the advice code is executed before or after the code corresponding to a matched pointcut. Around advice are a more powerful instrument, allowing for modifications of the intended original control flow in that they completely *wrap* the code associated with the pointcut. A special statement, `proceed()`, can be used to invoke the original functionality at any point in the advice code.

2.3 Run-Time Semantics

Active Databases: Rule execution semantics prescribe how an active system behaves once a set of rules has been defined. Rule execution behavior can be quite complex, but we restrict ourselves to describing only essential issues here. For a more detailed description see [63, 1].

All begins with event occurrences signaled by event sources that feed the complex event detector that selects and consumes these events according to the specification of consumption modes. In the case of rules that do not involve a complex event, this step is omitted and event occurrences directly trigger the corresponding rules.

Usually there are specific points in time at which rules may be processed during the execution of an active system. The *rule processing granularity* specifies how often these points occur. For example, the finest granularity is "always" which means that rules are processed as soon as any rule's triggering event occurs. If we consider the database context, rules may be processed after the occurrence of database operations (small-granularity), data manipulation statements (medium-granularity), or transactions (coarse-granularity).

At granularity cycles and only if rules were triggered, the *rule processing algorithm* is invoked. If more than one rule was triggered, it may be necessary to select one after the other from this set. This process of *rule selection* is known as *conflict resolution*, where basically three strategies can be applied: (a) one rule is selected from the fireable pool, after rule execution the set of fireable rules is determined again, (b) sequential execution of all rules in an evaluation cycle, and (c) parallel execution of all rules in an evaluation cycle.

After rules are selected, their corresponding conditions are evaluated. The evaluation of the condition is performed according to the specification of transaction dependencies (coupling modes). If a condition evaluates to true, then the action associated with this rule must be performed. Actions can be any sequence of operations on or outside of a database. These operations can refer to attributes of the triggering event. Transaction dependencies are considered here too. This ends with a single execution of the rule processing algorithm. Additionally, rules can be activated and deactivated at run-time.

Aspect-Oriented Programming: Basically, all existing AOP systems with static weaving follow the same approach, as outlined in Sec. 2.1. Code for invoking aspectual behavior is interwoven with the base application's code. Thus, what happens at run-time in an application decorated with statically interwoven aspects is not greatly different from what happens in an application where the aspectual behavior is "hard-wired" into the code—in the end, all behavior that was cleanly modularized in aspects is again tangled with and scattered throughout the application code.

Whenever execution reaches a point where aspectual behavior was inserted by the aspect weaver, that functionality is invoked. The special case of more than one aspect applying to a single location in the code is handled as follows. Around advice are always executed first, followed by before advice, the actual base behavior, after advice and, finally, those parts of around advice that come after an eventual proceed() statement. If more than one advice of a kind are present, aspect domination and inheritance relationships are used to determine an order in which the advice have to be applied. This order is well-defined [41].

2.4 Run-Time Environments

According to the specification of ECA rules and aspects there is the need to signal that an application must produce a primitive event, respectively that a program has reached a join point or that a pointcut matches. The techniques used for this purpose can be characterized as *invasive* or *non-invasive*.

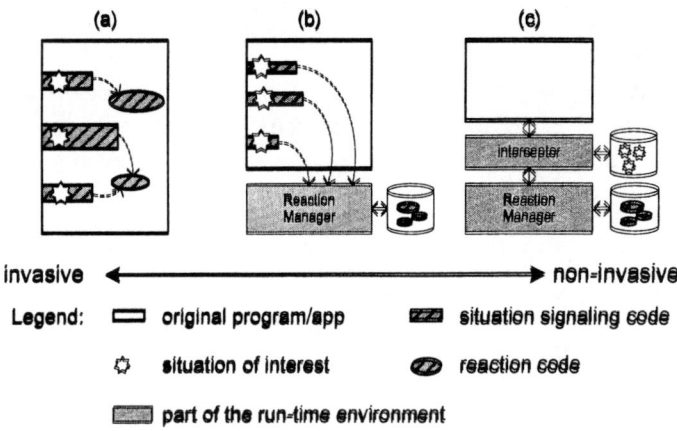

Fig. 2. Spectrum of code modification

In an invasive approach, at least the event signaling logic is mixed with the base application logic. In addition, reaction logic may also get mixed with base application logic. This mixed logic can take the form of instrumented source, byte, or native code, depending on whether the mixer is a pre-processor, a compiler, a byte-code toolkit, or even a just-in-time compiler. In Fig. 2a and b, invasive signaling is depicted by star-shaped wrappers. In Fig. 2a, in addition to the signaling code, the rest of the code that is necessary to execute the reactions is also included in the program. In Fig. 2b, signaling is also invasive but reaction code is separated from the signaling program and administered by a separate entity (which we call "reaction manager" to be domain-neutral).

Non-invasive techniques do not add any logic whatsoever to the base program. Rather the occurrences of situations of interest, e. g., certain operations in active DBMSs or join point execution in AOP systems, are somehow intercepted and, as a consequence, this situation is signaled. There are at least two approaches for doing this. If it is assumed that the application is developed with an interpreted programming language, then the language interpreter must be modified to signal situations of interest [20, 55]. A second possibility of non-invasive event detection is channel snooping [43]. In this approach the communication between client and server is intercepted and interpreted. This is useful when dealing with legacy systems that may not be modified.

Another approach in the implementation spectrum, which is not represented in the figure is one in which applications are programmed from the very beginning to generate events at interesting points. That is, developers are in charge of encoding the signaling of the happenings of interest.

We will now outline various implementation approaches to event detection, signaling and reaction execution in active databases and aspect-oriented programming. Please note that we do not claim either list of systems to be complete.

Active Databases

Invasive Approaches: Most active database systems use variants of the invasive approach. A fundamental difference is whether method wrapping is done manually or by the rule processor, and whether all methods are wrapped or only those methods for which rules are known to exist.

If selective wrapping is done, only those methods are decorated with the signaling code for which it is known that the event is required [28, 21]. This has performance advantages since no events are produced unless they are consumed and the application code is not bloated with unnecessary decorations. The disadvantage of this approach, however, is its inflexibility since new rules requiring new events that are not already produced cannot be added without modifying the application and recompiling it.

The alternative is to wrap automatically every method with a before and an after modifier [8, 66]. The method invocation events are always signaled locally. A fast table lookup is performed and if a subscription to that event exists, it is forwarded, otherwise it is discarded. The benefit is flexibility, since new rules can be added without modifying and recompiling the application code. The cost of this flexibility is acceptable in a database environment where data accesses involve entries in a lock table and accesses to external storage.

A compromise solution was adopted in [12, 10]. It consists in distinguishing between passive objects, reactive objects, and notifiable objects. The interface for reactive objects is modified and only methods in reactive objects are wrapped.

Non-invasive Approaches: Non-invasive approaches are convenient whenever the signaling application is non-cooperative or may not be modified, for example, in the case of legacy systems.

Channel snooping was used in [43]. In this approach a listener is implemented that taps into the communication channel between the client and the server. Since every relevant database operation is transmitted to the server, it can be intercepted, parsed and interpreted. The listener can then signal the occurrence of an event. There are obvious limitations to this approach. For example, events can only be interpreted at the query language statement level, i.e., at medium granularity according to our previous classification. Of course, they may be integrated to the coarser transaction level.

Modification of the interpreter is a powerful non-invasive technique. It was used in [20]. The benefit is flexibility to add new rules. The price is the difficulty of modifying the interpreter (if this is at all possible) and the inherent inefficiency of interpreted languages.

Aspect-Oriented Programming

Invasive Approaches: In terms of Fig. 2, within this category, we distinguish approaches that statically weave reaction code to the points of interest (at the level of source, byte, or native code), and those that only weave signaling code, leaving the reaction to be dispatched at run-time. This corresponds to the distinction between Figures 2a and 2b. AOP approaches corresponding to Fig. 2a directly mix reaction code into the application code before run-time. Hence, there is actually no such thing as situation signaling code. Both Hyper/J [35] and AspectJ [5] fall in this category.

Another class of AOP implementations for Java like EAOP [24, 23, 25], JAC [54, 37] and the *second* generation of PROSE [56, 57] all follow basically the implementation approach that corresponds to Fig. 2b. All three examples modify application classes by inserting hooks and/or wrappers at join points, thereby making the AOP infrastructure environment aware of them.

In more detail, EAOP uses a preprocessor to modify the application's classes before compilation, adding hooks in all places that may be a join point. JAC modifies classes' bytecodes as they are loaded into the virtual machine, inserting hooks in a specified set of places. PROSE 2 uses a modified just-in-time compiler to insert code that checks for the presence of advice at every possible join point in a group of classes that is specified at startup time of the AOP engine. All three approaches do not allow for altering the set of join points that are taken into account at run-time; they either activate all possible join points or only some in a given set of classes. Both approaches are unsatisfying: unnecessarily activated join points lead to – possibly expensive – checking operations, while an unalterable set of activated join points reduces flexibility.

So, on the one hand, the first category of invasive approaches statically binds reaction and disallows for dynamically dispatching of advice. On the other hand, the second category facilitates dynamic reaction dispatch but statically binds the set of join points.

Non-invasive Approaches: Another class of dynamic AOP systems is represented by the *first* generation of PROSE [55]. PROSE 1 does not instrument any code; instead the VM intercepts the execution of join points and dispatches to advice code whenever a join point is encountered that is matched by a pointcut. PROSE 1 makes use of the Java VM's debugging facilities [39, 45] to generate events at join points during application execution and intercept execution there. Hence, it belongs to the category of systems represented by Fig. 2c. This implementation – and probably any other implementation treating events as first-class entities of the run-time environment – suffers from performance overheads introduced by event generation and processing logic. The running application has to be permanently monitored by the run-time environment. However, using infrastructures like JPDA [39] allows for dealing with join points in a very flexible way: they can be arbitrarily activated and deactivated.

Aspect-Aware Runtime Environments: Another category of systems promises to avoid the performance overhead problem of systems like PROSE 1 while preserving its flexibility with respect to extending and reducing the set of activated join points. In this category, we classify approaches that are based on aspect-aware run-time environments. All approaches mentioned so far are characterized by an *impedance mismatch* between their aspect-oriented programming model and their execution model, which is basically that of object-orientation. Truly AOP-supportive approaches have to address this impedance mismatch by being based on an execution model explicitly designed to support the requirements of aspect-oriented programming.

To be aspect-aware, an execution environment must have two prominent features. First, both join points and advice code have to be dynamically bound. In that respect, an aspect-aware execution environment combines the advantages of the two categories of invasive systems mentioned above. A consequence from this requirement is that such an environment allows for weaving and unweaving aspect implementations at run-time. To preserve type safety, this leads to the second consequence that an aspect-aware extension of the type system would be required. The second important feature of aspect-aware execution environments is that the environment must *itself* inherently support weaving.

AspectS [34, 6] and Steamloom [33] are first developments in this category. AspectS is an extension to the Squeak Smalltalk implementation [36, 58], and Steamloom is a Java VM extension based on IBM's Jikes Research Virtual Machine [38]. Both systems fall into the category represented by Fig. 2a, with the important feature that all instrumentation of application code is performed at run-time.

In AspectS, aspects are deployed and undeployed dynamically by sending appropriate messages to instances of aspect classes. For achieving this, AspectS makes use of the powerful meta-level of Smalltalk that provides access to constructs of the run-time system, such as classes' method tables, which are available as normal Smalltalk objects. As such they can be changed on the fly, for example by (un)deployment methods of aspect objects. In terms of our discussion, AspectS only *simulates* an aspect-aware execution model at the application level: the actual execution model is that of the underlying Smalltalk implementation, which is not inherently aspect-aware.

We believe that, by being a new programming paradigm, AOP should be supported directly by the execution model. This is the motivation for our ongoing work on run-time environments, a first outcome of which is the Steamloom VM extension [33]. Steamloom allows for (un)weaving aspects at run-time by recompiling instrumented byte-code fragments that contain calls to advice code at join points.

3 Towards a Reactive Functionality Service

3.1 On the Convergence of Active Databases and AOP

Both aspects and ECA rules improve the separation of concerns and allow the implementation of crosscutting concerns. The discussion so far, has shown that Aspect Oriented Programming and Active Database Functionality present striking similarities, not only in the basic paradigm of reacting to defined situations through the execution of code, but also in the invocation mechanisms and primitives used. In this section, we will summarize these commonalities and will briefly discuss, how we envisage them to converge to what we call reactive functionality. Table 1 summarizes and compares the features and corresponding terms.

Table 1. Terminology in context

	AOP	Active Databases
simple situation	join points	primitive events
complex situation	pointcuts	composite events
[precise] situation	if [AspectJ]	condition
reaction	advice	action
execution	immediate	coupling modes

As described in Sec. 2.2, we have shown that there exist direct correspondences between join points and primitive events, pointcuts and composite events, conditionals in AspectJ and conditions in ECA rules, and advice and actions. An event in an active system denotes the occurrence of a situation that may lead to the execution of an ECA rule's action. In turn, the occurrence of a join point denotes that program execution has reached some specified point at which the invocation of some additional functionality, the associated advice, becomes possible.

Similar to event occurrences, pointcuts carry also additional information such as type and additional information (parameters or context). For instance, pointcuts can be signaled whenever a method m() of a class C is entered or a member x of an instance of T is accessed. Under these circumstances, the type for these join points can be METHOD_CALL or MEMBER_ACCESS respectively. Additionally, the name of the method or variable in question, the execution stack, etc. can be seen as contextual information.

Complex pointcuts in AspectJ are composed of primitive pointcut designators that are combined with logic operators such as && or ||. The only parallel between this kind of composition and that of composite events (as mentioned in Section 2.2) is the *alternative* operator. *Sequences* and *closures* of pointcuts/events are not taken into account, so AspectJ and other existing AOP approaches do not facilitate the composition of pointcuts to form what can be called a *sequential pointcut*.

A sequential pointcut, built using the event sequence operator, is complementary to the AspectJ cflow pointcut designator [41] that is able to match pointcuts occurring in the control flow (call tree) of a method. A sequential pointcut can match pointcuts by taking into account the event history of an application execution [61]. Such sequential pointcuts have the advantage of enabling an aspect to react to far more complex situations.

The task of a condition is to check for circumstances that go beyond the reach of the event—imagine an aspect or a rule that is to become active on the first day of the month only. The AspectJ if() pointcut designator [5] represents an effort to enrich pointcuts by a conditional part. However, the if() condition may only embrace variables that are bound in the pointcut.

As far as execution modes, AOP so far has been concentrating on synchronous execution of aspects, which corresponds to immediate coupling in active databases. We have shown that asynchronous execution of aspects may be a useful execution mode and we postulate that it will be necessary as we move toward a reactive middleware infrastructure. Another point to be taken into account is the concept of *coupling modes*. The question to be asked here is if aspect functionality *really* has to be executed *synchronously*. The common logging aspect usually consists of a call to some code that outputs information to a stream. If this happens synchronously, as with existing AOP implementations, the application decorated with the logging aspect pauses for the amount of time needed for logging. Considering that the output arguments are passed by value, it is possible to actually process the output in a separate thread and asynchronously invoke some entry point to that thread, allowing the actual application to proceed meanwhile.

From the discussion in Sec. 2.3, it becomes clear that the run-time semantics of active databases are richer than the run-time semantics of current AOP approaches, more specifically AspectJ. There are no correspondences to concepts such as processing granularity and processing algorithm in AOP languages. While these concepts as they are found in active databases might be "domain-specific" for the area of databases, it is worthwhile to consider integrating similar concepts in the design space of AOP languages and systems as well.

In Sec. 2.4, we have shown how different run-time environments require a more or less invasive decoration of the code to allow for the introduction of aspects or ECA rules, respectively. We also showed how the different run-time environments support the binding of rules or aspects at different points in time, ranging from compile-time to run-time. It is interesting to observe that the various implementations of today's AOP run-time environments have their correspondence among the implementations of active database systems.

It is part of our ongoing research to determine to what extent the rich semantics of event algebras, event consumption modes, and coupling modes are needed in the AOP context. We believe that some form of algebra for the specification of complex situations will be useful in the AOP context. We further believe that AOP can benefit from previous experience with event consumption and asynchronous execution of reactions. On the other hand we are encouraged by the possibilities that AOP and truly dynamic languages afford us to avoid the impedance mismatch that results when implementing reactive middleware functionality with static programming languages. However, in order for this to come true, AOP language technology should evolve from mainly code transformation techniques toward true run-time support for aspects.

From the predictability point of view and as a consequence of extracting crosscutting concerns conflicts among them may occur. The AOP community has paid little attention to this topic that needs further research.

3.2 Toward a Marriage of Distributed Services and Aspects

The last decade in the development of many areas of computer science, including database technology, middleware, and programming languages, is characterized by moving from monolithic software systems toward systems that are dynamically composed of autonomous, loosely-coupled components or services, as a way to react to changes in the environment.

A cornerstone in this development are asynchronous communication mechanisms. In recent years, academia and industry have concentrated on such mechanisms because they support the interaction among loosely-coupled components. Loosely-coupled interactions promote easy integration of autonomous, heterogeneous components into complex applications enhancing application adaptability and scalability.

For instance, in CORBA event [51] and notification [52] services were introduced to provide a mechanism for asynchronous interaction between CORBA objects. In the Java platform the Java Message Service (JMS) [32] provides the ability to process asynchronous messages. JMS has been part of Java Enterprise Edition (J2EE) [60] since its origin but was incorporated as an integral part of the Enterprise Java Beans (EJB) component model only in the EJB 2.0 specification [19]. It includes a new bean type, known as message-driven bean (MDB), which acts as a message consumer providing asynchrony to EJB-based applications. This formally introduces the possibility to write pieces of software (beans) that react to the arrival of messages.

In the late-90s the active database community has moved toward a service-oriented approach with the purpose to fulfill the requirements of new applications. In particular, the unbundling approach [29] consists in decoupling the active part from DBMSs. Various projects like C²offein [42], FRAMBOISE [27], and NODS [16] have followed this approach. However, they did not address adequately the characteristics of distributed systems, for example, the lack of a central clock and the impossibility to establish a total order of events [44]. This has an enormous impact on the composite event detector and also on the underlying event algebra. A service-oriented approach that supports distribution and heterogeneity has been proposed in [15].

In the aspect-oriented software development research several efforts are being made in developing techniques that postpone aspect weaving ever later in the life cycle of an application [55, 57, 54, 37, 48]. These approaches are valuable experiments to demonstrate the usefulness of late aspect weaving (be that load-time or run-time). However, they all build on top of existing object-oriented language implementation technology, hence, suffer from impedance mismatch. For instance, the work on JAC [54, 37] is based on framework, MOP, and byte-code modification [14] technology, while PROSE 1 [55, 57] builds on the Java Platform Debugger Architecture [39]. The work on Caesar [49] focuses on language design rather than language implementation.

First steps toward solving the impedance mismatch of AO systems are being made [33]. This encourages us to see a new kind of distributed service-oriented systems emerge. They will be the result of marrying aspect-aware run-time environments that support an AO model, as the one we envisaged to be the convergence of AOP and active database systems and which also properly supports distribution and heterogeneity as in [15].

The AOP and the active database approaches need to detect the situation of interest (e.g., the invocation of a method call and the signal of an event respectively). In middleware platforms, like CORBA, .NET and J2EE, service requests and method invocations can be intercepted allowing the possibility of detecting transparently these situations. Interceptors have the ability to enhance an existing framework and the support applications transparently [50, 62]. The container model approach [60, 22] handles this issue by generating code based on configuration files. In this way the application or component can add selected services to its functionality by specifying properties in a configuration file. DADO [64] proposes the use of adaptlets at points where the application interacts with the middleware supporting in this way programming crosscutting concerns in distributed and heterogeneous environments.

4 Summary and Ongoing Work

Aspect Oriented Programming and Active Database Functionality present striking similarities. As far as execution modes, AOP so far has been concentrating on synchronous execution of aspects, which corresponds to immediate coupling in active databases. We have shown that asynchronous execution of aspects may be a useful execution mode and we postulate that it will be necessary as we move toward a reactive middleware infrastructure.

As it was mentioned before, both aspects and ECA rules improve the separation of concerns and allow the implementation of crosscutting concerns. There are different alternatives to allow the introduction of aspects and ECA rules into a run-time environment depending on more or less invasive decoration of the code. It was also shown how the different run-time environments support the binding of rules or aspects at different points in time, varying from compile-time to run-time. It must be noticed that there is an impressive correspondence between the implementation of numerous active database systems and today's AOP run-time environments.

As part of our ongoing work we are developing AORTA (Aspect-Oriented Run-Time Architecture [4]), and a distributed active functionality service [15]. The proof of our hypothesis will come as we implement the distributed active functionality service on an aspect oriented platform.

Acknowledgments

The authors thank the anonymous reviewers for their helpful comments and suggestions.

References

1. ACT-NET Consortium. The Active Database Management System Manifesto: A Rulebase of ADBMS Features. *ACM SIGMOD Record*, 25(3):40–49, 1996.
2. A. Aiken, J. Widom, and J. M. Hellerstein. Behavior of database production rules: termination, confluence, and observable determinism. In *Proc. of ACM SIGMOD*, pages 59–68, San Diego, California, June 1992.
3. E. Anwar, L. Maugis, and S. Chakravarthy. A new perspective on rule support for object-oriented databases. In *Proc. of ACM SIGMOD*, pages 99–108, Washington, D.C., May 1993. ACM Press.
4. AORTA Home Page. http://www.st.informatik.tu-darmstadt.de/static/pages/projects/AORTA/AORTA.jsp.
5. AspectJ Home Page. http://aspectj.org/.
6. AspectS Home Page.
   http://www-ia.tu-ilmenau.de/~hirsch/Projects/Squeak/AspectS/.
7. Elena Baralis and Jennifer Widom. An Algebraic Approach to Static Analysis of Active Database Rules. *ACM Transactions on Database Systems*, 25(3):269–332, 2000.
8. H. Branding, A. P. Buchmann, T. Kudrass, and J. Zimmermann. Rules in an Open System: The REACH Rule System. In *Proc. of RIDS*, pages 111–126. Springer, 1993.
9. A. Buchmann. *Architecture of Active Database Systems*, chapter 2, pages 29–48. In Paton [53], 1999. In Paton, N. 1999.

10. S. Chakravarthy. SENTINEL: An Object-Oriented DBMS With Event-Based Rules. In *Proc. of ACM SIGMOD*, pages 572–575, Tucson, Arizona, USA, May 1997.
11. S. Chakravarthy, V. Krishnaprasad, Z. Tamizuddin, and R. H. Badani. ECA Rule Integration into an OODBMS: Architecture and Implementation. In Philip S. Yu and Arbee L. P. Chen, editors, *Proc. of ICDE*, pages 341–348, Taipei, Taiwan, March 1995. IEEE Computer Society.
12. Sharma Chakravarthy, V. Krishnaprasad, Eman Anwar, and S.-K. Kim. Composite events for active databases: Semantics, contexts and detection. In *Proc. of VLDB*, pages 606–617, Santiago de Chile, Chile, September 1994. Morgan Kaufmann.
13. S. Charkravarthy, V. Krishnaprasad, E. Anwar, and S. Kim. Composite Events for Active Databases: Semantics, Contexts and Detection. In *Proc. of VLDB*, pages 606–617, September 1994.
14. S. Chiba. Load-Time Structural Reflection in Java. In Elisa Bertino, editor, *Proc. of ECOOP*, volume 1850 of *LNCS*, pages 313–336. Springer, 2000.
15. M. Cilia. *An Active Functionality Service for Open Distributed Heterogeneous Environments*. Ph.D. Thesis, Department of Computer Science, Darmstadt University of Technology, Darmstadt, Germany, August 2002.
16. C. Collet. The NODS Project: Networked Open Database Services. In K. Dittrich et.al., editor, *Object and Databases 2000*, number 1944 in LNCS, pages 153–169. Springer, 2000.
17. U. Dayal, A. Buchmann, and D. McCarthy. Rules are Objects Too. In *Proc. of Intl. Workshop on Object-Oriented Database Systems*, volume 334 of *LNCS*, pages 129–143, Bad Muenster am Stein, Germany, September 1988. Springer-Verlag.
18. U. Dayal and et al. The HiPAC Project: Combining Active Databases and Timing Constraints. *ACM SIGMOD Record*, 17(1), March 1988.
19. L. DeMichiel, L.U. Yalcinalp, and S. Krishnan. Enterprise JavaBeans. Technical Report Version 2.0, Sun Microsystems, JavaSoftware, August 2001.
20. O. Díaz, N. W. Paton, and P. Gray. Rule management in object oriented databases: A uniform approach. In *Proc. of VLDB*, pages 317–326, Barcelona, Catalonia, Spain, September 1991. Morgan Kaufmann.
21. K. Dittrich, H. Fritschi, S. Gatziu, A. Geppert, and A. Vaduva. SAMOS in Hindsight: Experiences in Building an Active Object-Oriented DBMS. Technical Report 2000.05, Institut fuer Informatik, University of Zurich, 2000.
22. Microsoft .NET Home Page. http://www.microsoft.com/net/.
23. R. Douence, O. Motelet, and M. Südholt. A Formal Definition of Crosscuts. Technical Report 01/3/INFO, École des Mines de Nantes, 4 rue Alfred Kastler, 44307 Nantes cedex 3, France, 2001.
24. R. Douence and Mario Südholt. A Model and a Tool for Event-Based Aspect-Oriented Programming (EAOP). Technical Report 02/11/INFO, Ecole des Mines de Nantes, 2002.
25. EAOP Home Page. http://www.emn.fr/x-info/eaop/.
26. T. Elrad, R. Filman, and A. Bader. Aspect-oriented programming. *CACM*, 44(10):29–32, October 2001.
27. H. Fritschi, S. Gatziu, and K. Dittrich. FRAMBOISE - an Approach to Framework-based Active Data Management System Construction. In *Proceedings of CIKM'98*, pages 364–370, Maryland, November 1998.
28. S. Gatziu and K. R. Dittrich. Events in an Active Object-Oriented Database System. In *Proc. of RIDS*, Workshops in Computing, pages 23–29. Springer, 1993.
29. S. Gatziu, A. Koschel, G. v. Buetzingsloewen, and H. Fritschi. Unbundling Active Functionality. *ACM SIGMOD Record*, 27(1):35–40, March 1998.

30. N. Gehani, H. Jagadish, and O. Shmueli. Composite Event Specification in Active Databases: Model & Implementation. In *Proc. of VLDB*, pages 327–338, August 1992.
31. E. N. Hanson. An Initial Report on The Design of Ariel: A DBMS With an Integrated Production Rule System. *SIGMOD Record*, 18(3):12–19, 1989.
32. M. Hapner, R. Burridge, and R. Sharma. Java Message Service. Specification Version 1.0.2, Sun Microsystems, JavaSoftware, November 1999.
33. M. Haupt, C. Bockisch, M. Mezini, and K. Ostermann. Towards Aspect-Aware Execution Models. http://www.st.informatik.tu-darmstadt.de/database/ publications/data/ObjectModelDraft.pdf?id=75. Submitted for review.
34. R. Hirschfeld. Aspect-Oriented Programming with AspectS. http://www-ia.tu-ilmenau.de/~hirsch/Projects/Squeak/AspectS/Docs/ AspectS_NODe02_Erfurt2_rev.pdf.
35. HyperJ Home Page. http://www.research.ibm.com/hyperspace/HyperJ/HyperJ.htm.
36. D. Ingalls, T. Kaehler, J. Maloney, S. Wallace, and A. Kay. Back to the Future: the Story of Squeak, a Practical Smalltalk Written in Itself. In *Proc. of OOPSLA*, pages 318–326. ACM Press, 1997.
37. JAC Home Page. http://jac.aopsys.com/.
38. The Jikes Research Virtual Machine. http://www-124.ibm.com/developerworks/ oss/jikesrvm/.
39. Java Platform Debugger Architecture Home Page. http://java.sun.com/j2se/ 1.4.1/docs/guide/jpda/index.html.
40. A. P. Karadimce and S. D. Urban. Conditional Term Rewriting as a Formal Basis for Active Database Rules. In *Proc. of RIDE'94*, pages 156–162, February 1994.
41. G. Kiczales, E. Hilsdale, J. Hugunin, M. Kersten, J. Palm, and W. G. Griswold. An Overview of AspectJ. In J. Lindskov Knudsen, editor, *Proc. of ECOOP*, volume 2072 of *LNCS*, pages 327–353. Springer, 2001.
42. A. Koschel and P. Lockemann. Distributed Events in Active Database Systems - Letting the Genie out of the Bottle. *Data & Knowledge Engineering*, 25(1-2):29–53, March 1998.
43. T. Kudrass, A. Loew, and A. Buchmann. Active Object-Relational Mediators. In *Proc. of CoopIS*, pages 228–239, Brussels, Belgium, September 1996.
44. C. Liebig, M. Cilia, and A. Buchmann. Event Composition in Time-dependent Distributed Systems. In *Proc. of CoopIS*, pages 70–78, September 1999.
45. T. Lindholm and F. Yellin. *The Java Virtual Machine Specification*. Addison-Wesley, 2nd edition, 1999.
46. H. Masuhara and G. Kiczales. A Modeling Framework for Aspect-Oriented Mechanisms. In L. Cardelli, editor, *Proc. of ECOOP*. Springer, 2003.
47. M. Mezini and K. Ostermann. Modules for Crosscutting Models. In *Proceedings of the 8th International Conference on Reliable Software Technologies (Ada-Europe 2003)*, 2003.
48. M. Mezini and K. Ostermann. Object Creation Aspects with Flexible Aspect Deployment. http://www.st.informatik.tu-darmstadt.de/staff/Ostermann/aosd02.pdf.
49. M. Mezini and K. Ostermann. Conquering Aspects with Caesar. In *Proc. of AOSD*. ACM Press, 2003.
50. P. Narasimhan, L. Moser, and P. Melliar-Smith. Using Interceptors to Enhance CORBA. *IEEE Computer)*, 32(7):62–68, July 1999.
51. Object Management Group. Event Service Specification. Technical Report formal/97-12-11, Object Management Group (OMG), May 1997.

52. Object Management Group. CORBA Notification Service Specification. Technical Report telecom/98-06-15, Object Management Group (OMG), May 1998.
53. N. Paton, editor. *Active Rules in Database Systems*. Springer, 1999.
54. R. Pawlak, L. Seinturier, L. Duchien, and G. Florin. JAC: A Flexible Solution for Aspect-Oriented Programming in Java. In *Proc. of Metalevel Architectures and Separation of Crosscutting Concerns (REFLECTION 2001)*, volume 2192 of *LNCS*, pages 1–24, Kyoto, Japan, September 2001. Springer.
55. A. Popovici, T. Gross, and G. Alonso. Dynamic Weaving for Aspect-Oriented Programming. In G. Kiczales, editor, *Proc. of AOSD*. ACM Press, 2002.
56. A. Popovici, T. Gross, and G. Alonso. Just-in-Time Aspects. In *Proc. of AOSD*. ACM Press, 2003.
57. PROSE Home Page. http://prose.ethz.ch/.
58. Squeak Home Page. http://www.squeak.org/.
59. M. Stonebraker, A. Jhingran, J. Goh, and S. Potamianos. On Rules, Procedures, Caching and Views in Data Base Systems. In H. Garcia-Molina and H. V. Jagadish, editors, *Proc. of ACM SIGMOD*, pages 281–290, Atlantic City, NJ, May 1990.
60. Sun Microsystems. Java 2 Enterprise Edition Platform Specification. Technical Report Version 1.3, Sun Microsystems, JavaSoftware, August 2001.
61. R. J. Walker and G. C. Murphy. Joinpoints as Ordered Events: Towards Applying Implicit Context to Aspect-Orientation. In *Proceedings for Advanced Separation of Concerns Workshop*, 2001.
62. N. Wang, K. Parameswaran, and D. Schmidt. The design and performance of metaprogramming mechanism for object request broker middleware. In *Proc. of COOTS'01*, January 2001.
63. J. Widom and S. Ceri, editors. *Active Database Systems: Triggers and Rules for Advanced Database Processing*. Morgan Kaufmann, 1996.
64. E. Wohlstadter, S. Jackson, and P. Devanbu. DADO: Enhancing middleware to support cross-cutting features in distributed, heterogeneous systems. Technical report, Computer Science Dept., University of California at Davis, June 2003. http://macbeth.cs.ucdavis.edu/dado.pdf.
65. Y. Zhou and M. Hsu. A theory for rule triggering systems. In *Proc. of EDBT*, volume 416 of *LNCS*, pages 407–421, Venice, Italy, March 1990. Springer.
66. J. Zimmermann and A. Buchmann. *REACH*, chapter 14, pages 263–277. In Paton [53], 1999. In Paton, N. 1999.
67. D. Zimmer and R. Unland. On the Semantics of Complex Events in Active Database Management Systems. In *Proc. of ICDE*, pages 392–399, Sydney, Australia, March 1999. IEEE Computer Society Press.

A Selective, Just-in-Time Aspect Weaver*

Yoshiki Sato[1], Shigeru Chiba[1], and Michiaki Tatsubori[2]

[1] Dept. of Mathematical and Computing Sciences
Tokyo Institute of Technology
{yoshiki,chiba}@csg.is.titech.ac.jp
[2] IBM Tokyo Research Laboratory
mich@trl.ibm.com

Abstract. Dynamic AOP (Aspect-Oriented Programming) is receiving growing interests in both the academia and the industry. Since it allows weaving aspects with a program at runtime, it is useful for rapid prototyping and adaptive software. However, the previous implementations of dynamic AOP systems suffered from serious performance penalties. This paper presents our new efficient dynamic AOP system in Java for addressing the underlying problem. This system called Wool is a hybrid of two approaches. When a new aspect is woven in, the programmers can select to reload into the JVM a modified class file in which hooks for executing advice are statically embedded, or they can insert hooks as breakpoints in the JVM. Since the two approaches have different performance characteristics, the programmers can select the best one for each join point. Our experimental result shows, under a certain circumstance, Wool runs dynamic AOP application about 26% faster than a traditional static code translation approach.

1 Introduction

Recently, practical demands are being made of dynamic aspect-oriented programming (AOP [14]) systems [17, 18, 2, 20, 19]. Unlike static AOP, a dynamic AOP system allows dynamically weaving and unweaving an aspect into/from a program. Moreover, advice and pointcuts are changeable during runtime. These dynamic features extend the application domains of aspect-oriented programming. Dynamic AOP can make development cycles shorter [7] and it allows for aspects that can adapt the behavior of application software at runtime to follow the changes of the runtime environment and requirements [11, 25, 21].

The most typical technique for implementing dynamic AOP systems is based on static code translation although it is not efficient. This approach statically inserts pieces of code, which we call hooks, into all join points, and these hooks determine at runtime whether or not there is associated advice to be activated at each join point, in contrast to static AOP systems like AspectJ [13]. These runtime checks imply serious performance overhead although they are necessary since dynamic AOP allows turning advice on and off during runtime.

---
* This work was supported in part by the CREST program of Japan Science and Technology Corp.

This paper presents our Java-based dynamic AOP system called *Wool*, which exploits our new implementation technique for addressing the performance problem mentioned above. Wool inserts hooks into a program at runtime *just in time* when the programmer directs the program to start using an aspect. Wool allows the programmers to select from two implementation techniques the best one for each join point. The first one is to insert the hooks as breakpoints handled through the debugger interface of the Java virtual machine (JVM). The other one is to produce a program in which the hooks are embedded as method calls and reload that new program into the JVM. These two techniques do not require a custom JVM, but work with the standard JVM.

The rest of this paper is organized as follows. Section 2 describes a typical implementation technique of dynamic AOP systems and a performance problem of that technique. Section 3 presents our new implementation technique for dynamic AOP. It also shows an overview of the current implementation of Wool. Section 4 compares Wool to other AOP systems. Section 5 presents the results of our experiments. We conclude the paper in section 6.

2 Dynamic AOP

Aspect-oriented programming can be classified into two categories: static AOP and dynamic AOP. The static AOP systems such as AspectJ weave in the aspects at compile time or load time. The woven aspects cannot be removed or reconfigured during runtime. On the other hand, the dynamic AOP systems can weave aspects in at runtime. The programmers can dynamically *plug* and *unplug* an aspect in/from running software. This section shows the benefits of dynamic AOP and typical implementations of AOP systems.

2.1 Need for Dynamic AOP

Dynamic AOP is not just a mechanism that sounds fascinating but useless in practice. It is a necessary mechanism especially, if an aspect implements a non-functional concern cutting across several modules and the requirement of the functionality dynamically changes at runtime. Non-functional concerns are additional features such as transactions, distribution, security, and logging. They are not directly involved with the core logic of the application and thus they are not mandatory for the application software to provide the minimum service.

Profiling a performance of software (or logging) is a good example showing that a dynamic AOP system is useful. It is recognized as a non-functional concern that can be well modularized using AOP [7][9]. Since the code fragments for collecting profiling information tend to be spread over the whole program, they should be modularized into an aspect. However, the performance profiling implemented on static AOP systems is not useful from the programmatic viewpoint. Suppose that the software is a Web-based business application, which must run 24 hours a day. Our scenario is that we first run the software without profiling code and, once it shows performance anomaly, perhaps under heavy load, we insert profiling code. The profiling code should be inserted without shutting down the software since the anomaly may be due to the workload up to that point. If the software is restarted, all the internal data structures are reset and hence the information necessary for analyzing the anomaly would be lost. Furthermore, we would need to interactively plug and unplug various kinds of profiling code until solving the anomaly. Each profiling code would cut across different join points for collecting different profiling information. We thus need dynamic AOP. Although we could use large profiling code that collects all the information, it would imply serious performance impacts. We should use minimal profiling code at a time for reducing performance impacts. To satisfy these requirements, dynamic AOP is a good solution.

Adaptable response cache in a web application is also a good example to show the usefulness of dynamic AOP. The implementation of the response cache includes not only caching the results of method calls but also invalidating the cached results that scatter in the software. Since the response cache is a non-functional and crosscutting concern, it cannot be modularized with object-oriented programming; AOP is necessary [21]. However, to make the response cache adaptable, the software must be able to dynamically switch a number of aspects, in which various strategies are modularized, as the runtime environment changes. Yagoub *et al.* reported that there is no universal caching strategy that is optimal for all web applications and all the configurations [26]. For example, if the cache provided by an aspect shows a low hit ratio, the software should switch that aspect to another. If only part of the cache shows a high hit ratio, the software should remove the aspects that do not provide that part of the cache. The traditional object-oriented techniques like Design patterns never modularize such a crosscutting concern, and still less switch it at runtime. Also, static AOP does not even work in this example. If we use static AOP, all the caching aspects must be statically woven in advance. Note that they are woven at different join points and hence, whenever the program execution reaches one of the join points, they must dynamically examine whether every cache is turned on or off. This runtime check causes a serious performance overhead. On the other hand, if we use dynamic AOP, only the activated aspects can be woven to avoid the runtime check. Dynamic AOP enables efficient implementation of adaptable cache.

2.2 The Implementation of AOP Systems

Typical implementations of object-based AOP systems, including both static and dynamic AOP, insert hooks at a number of execution points such as method calls, field access, instance creation, and exception handling. These execution points are called *join points*. If the program execution reaches join points, the inserted hook intercepts it and executes a piece of code called *advice* if it is included in a set of join points identified by *pointcuts*. Different advice can be associated with each different pointcut. An aspect is a set of pairs of pointcuts and advice.

In most static AOP systems, a hook is usually implemented as inlined hooking code, in which pieces of aspects are directly embedded into a base program by static translations of source code or bytecode. However, several join points cannot be uniquely determined by the pointcuts, such as *cflow* or *this*. Such a set of join points depends on the current execution context and changes dynamically. Thus, hooking code must be embedded into potential join points with conditional statements, which examine if the advice should be executed in the execution context.

Generally, a dynamic AOP system must examine whether any advice should be executed at every join point when the execution of a program passes that point. In dynamic AOP, all the join points are dependent on the execution context, since the set of join points are specified at runtime. Furthermore, the set of join points changes dynamically. Thus, the check whether or not the system should execute advice must continue after the join point has been specified.

2.3 Static Code Translation

There exists a well-known approach that enables every join point to be checked at runtime, and which is supported by static code translation of application programs. For example, JAC [18] and Handiwrap [2] are dynamic AOP systems using a static code translation approach, in which a compiler (or a translator) inserts minimal hooks for all potential join points (Figure 1). They translate the code of a program to a version with inserted hooks. The translation is performed by the source-to-source or binary-to-binary, during compilation or class loading. Most static AOP systems also use static code translation and this is more or less appropriate to their purpose because most intercepted join points are identified statically.

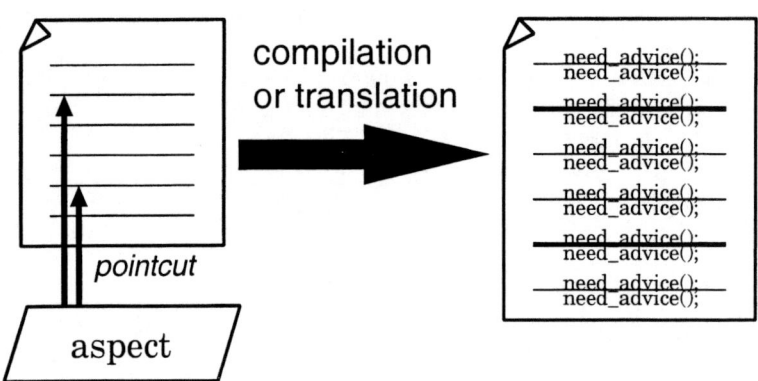

Fig. 1. Static code translation.

Static code translation does not cause much of a performance penalty in advice execution, while involving some overhead in normal operations with no woven aspect. The execution of advice is fast since an inserted hook is represented as just a method call. However, even if no aspects are woven, all checks whether or not the system should execute advice is performed. This results in unnecessary method calls or verbose indirection of object references, which involves overhead in normal operations that cannot be ignored.

Popovici *et al.* [19] have implemented a Just-In-Time (JIT) aspect compiler based on Jikes RVM [1]. Their JIT compiler inserts hooks at all potential join points only at the time of the first just-in-time compilation. Thus, their work can be regarded as a static code translation approach mentioned above. They avoided adding options to the JIT compiler that could recompile bytecode since that would increase the complexity of the JIT compiler support too much. They reported they could limit the overhead due to the hooks since their hooks are implemented using native code, not Java byte code. Unfortunately, the JIT compiler approach is irreconcilable with recent high-performance runtime technologies like Sun's HotSpot(TM) technology or the IBM JIT compiler [23], which involves the mixture of a JIT compiler and interpreter.

3 Wool

We developed Wool, which inserts hooks into the program on demand, in Java. Since the hooks are inserted after all of the intercepted join points are specified, Wool does not insert unnecessary hooks. This section presents the details of our new dynamic AOP system Wool and shows how it enables efficient dynamic AOP.

3.1 An Overview of Wool

Wool is implemented as a Java library that provides dynamic AOP functionality, consisting of APIs to write aspects, a weaver to compose aspects with programs, and a subsystem for accepting a request for weaving from the outside of the running program.

Wool allows the aspect to be woven either locally, from within an application running on the same JVM, or remotely when sent to the subsystem of Wool. The following code shows how the aspect is woven in by Wool.

```
WlAspect azpect = WlAspect.forName("ProfileAspect");
Wool wool = Wool.connect("localhost", 5432);
wool.weave(azpect);
```

In a locally woven case, the aspect instance `azpect` is created in the running program. The weaver instance `wool` is connected to the subsystem of Wool. Weaving runs immediately after the method `weave()` is called. Alternatively in a remotely woven case, the aspect instance is actually created and recomposed outside of the JVM in which it will be woven. It is then serialized and sent over the network to the subsystem of Wool in the target JVM.

3.2 Just-in-Time Hook Insertion

Wool adopts a hybrid approach so that the programmers can choose a suitable hook at a join point considering the entire cost, and which hooks are breakpoints or method calls. In Wool, just-in-time hook insertion is done in two timeframes at runtime, as shown in Figure 2.

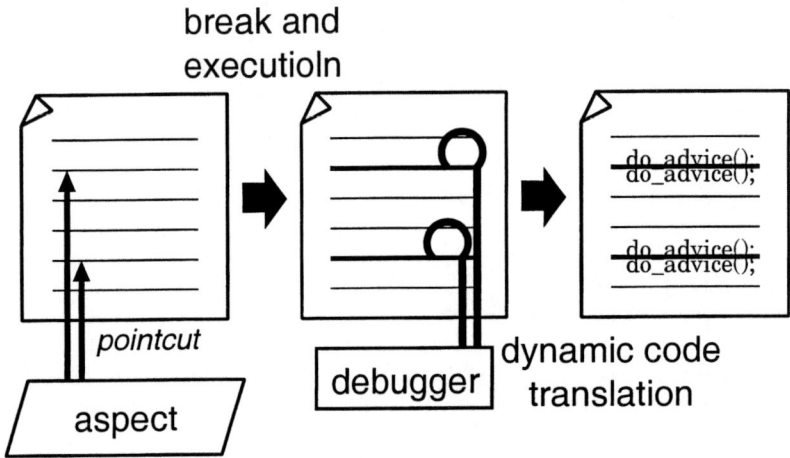

Fig. 2. Two timeframes for hook insertion.

The strategy for deciding at the hooked join point whether advice is executed or embedded into the program is simple. All of the hooks are represented as breakpoints first. At each hooked join point, there are alternative ways, one is executing pieces of advice by using the debugger and the other is embedding hooks into the program using dynamic code translation. If the hooked join point using a breakpoint is judged likely to be intercepted again and again in the future, and if the degradation it causes is estimated to be higher than that caused by dynamic code translation, such a hook should be embedded into the program instead of executing the advice by using the debugger. After the hook is embedded, the breakpoint at the join point is removed.

A comparison of the implementation techniques of dynamic AOP systems is shown in Table 1. Wool is a hybrid of the last two techniques. Unlike static code translation, both of the two techniques that Wool adopts do not insert any unnecessary hooks (Column 1 in Table 1).

As a Breakpoint. The first hook insertion method, which we call breakpoint-based execution, where all the hooks are inserted as breakpoints, which are set at runtime through standard debugger interface in Java called JPDA (Java Platform Debugger Architecture) [24]. The JPDA allows a programmer to register requests for execution events inside a JVM and controls execution for each event notification. These breakpoints are set for all join points specified by a pointcut. If the thread of control reaches one of the breakpoints, it switches to the debugger thread and the advice associated with that join point (breakpoint) is run. Using JPDA doesn't require the modification of the runtime system.

The execution overhead due to breakpoint is not a serious problem since the HotSpot (TM) VM that comes with the Java 2 SDK 1.4 runs a program together with a just-in-time compiler even if any breakpoints are set. In addition, hooks in the form of breakpoints can be inserted into programs so quickly (Column 3 in Table 1). Although programs must be run in a debug mode, it doesn't cause much performance penalty under normal operations without active advice (Column 4 in Table 1).

For frequently executed advice, the overheads for breakpoint-based execution are not negligible (Column 1 in Table 1). The large number of context switches to execute the advice causes the overhead, since advice has to be executed separately in the debugger process.

As a Method Call. The second hook insertion method, which we call dynamic code translation: To reduce the overhead caused by context switches, a frequently invoked join point expressed as a breakpoint is replaced with a modified method in which the hooks are directly embedded. The method body is modified at the bytecode level so that a bytecode sequence for executing the advice is embedded at the join points contained in the method body. At the breakpoint, all join points specified by the pointcut are identified, so hooks can be statically embedded into the programs without garbage (unnecessary) hooks as in other static-code-translation-based dynamic AOP systems.

The runtime replacement of bytecode is done using the hotswap mechanism [8] of the JPDA. The hotswap mechanism allows a new class to be reloaded at runtime while under the control of a debugger. The actual reloading isn't performed immediately when the static code translation is completed, because the cost of such a translation is very large. If there is a method that should be replaced with a hook embedded method, dynamic code translation is forked, the breakpoint-based execution continues until the translation is finished. Therefore, the dynamic code translation stops the application thread for a short time and uses the translation time effectively. After replacing the method, the thread of control does not stop at the join points contained in the method body. The hooks are embedded into the program as simple method calls, and therefore the advice execution is much faster than using the debugger (Column 1 in Table 1).

Dynamic code translation is not efficient under certain circumstances. It causes only a single context switch to embed hooks into the program. However, the cost of the translation and the hotswap performed for every crosscut class is relatively high if advice is rarely executed (Column 2 and 3 in Table 1). In this case, dynamic code translation is just unnecessary as most of hooks are in the static code translation approach in Section 2.3.

Table 1. Comparison of the three approaches. Wool is a hybrid of the last two techniques, which are using breakpoint-based execution and dynamic code translation. Each column indicates the degree of the efficiency of using that approach.

	frequently executed advice	rarely executed advice	hook insertion	normal operation without aspect
Static code translation	O	×	O (statically)	×
Breakpoint-based execution	×	O	△	O
Dynamic code translation	O	×	×	O

3.3 Aspect in Wool

Wool provides the programmers with APIs to define an aspect in Java. It does not provide a special aspect language for easily writing an aspect, which is different from the languages such as AspectJ or any others that are intended to enhance flexibility and abstraction. Using these APIs, an aspect can be instantiated in the Java program. Therefore, the aspect can be composed and changed by a program dynamically. This means that pointcuts and advice can be reconstructed while the target program runs.

The following fragment of a program is a sample profiling aspect described in Java with Wool APIs:

```
1:  public class ProfileAspect extends WlAspect {
2:    Timer timer = new Timer();
3:    int count = 0;
4:    Pointcut timedentry = Pointcut.methodCall("public","FigureElement","paint","*");
5:    public void weave(Wool wool) throws WeaveException {
6:      wool.insert(new BeforeAdvice(timedentry) {
7:        public void advice(Joinpoint joinpoint) {
8:          timer.start();
9:          count++;
10:       }
11:     });
12:     wool.insert(new AfterAdvice(timedentry) {
13:       public void advice(Joinpoint joinpoint) {
14:         timer.stop();
15:       }
16:     });
17:   }
18: }
```

Here, the class `ProfileAspect` inherited from `WlAspect` is used for profiling the bottleneck of a program. In particular, the above example is specified by the `Pointcut` object for profiling the method call that belongs to the class `FigureElement` and named `paint` and that has a `public` modifier. This aspect inserts *before* advice and *after* advice to measure the elapsed time and the number of the method calls. `BeforeAdvice` and `AfterAdvice` represent *before* and *after* advice, respectively. Advice in Wool is inserted by using the method `insert()` in the class of `Wool`.

Aspect. The first step in the use of Wool is to create a `WlAspect` object representing an aspect defined by programmers. This step is for creating the aspect and makes it accessible from a program. In an aspect of Wool, the programmers can define it in the following two ways:

- Define the subclass of `WlAspect`, or
- Add advice to the scratch object of `WlAspect`.

The subclass of `WlAspect` represents an encapsulation of crosscutting concerns. Programmers can define aspect variables in it, which are accessed from advice or aspect methods or introductions such as `timer` and `count` shown in the above example. In addition, it contains initial weaving advice described in the method `weave()`, inherited from `WlAspect`. It is called on the return from the weaver at the time an aspect is actually woven into a program. It is only by using the method `weave()` that the programmers can insert advice into a program in the subclass of `WlAspect`.

To construct and reconstruct an aspect object dynamically, Wool provides another way to create it from scratch. This feature is useful because an aspect, which is the intercepted join point identified by the pointcut or the operation defined by advice, can be formed according to the behavior of the running program. To do this, a `WlAspect` object must be created as follows:

```
WlAspect azpect = WlAspect.scratchAspect();
azpect.add(new BeforeAdvice(log) {
    public void advice(Joinpoint joinpoint) {
      /* some code */
    }
});
```

The created object `azpect` represents an empty aspect that has no advice or introductions although the method `add()` adds advice to the aspect later. If new advice is added to a non-empty aspect like the class `ProfileAspect`, advice inserted in the method `weave()` is left as it is, and the new advice is just added as extra advice.

The added advice is not immediately reflected in the program. In Wool, advice is synchronized with the program only by the method `weave()` or `unweave()`. Thus, the behavior of a running program is changed only when those methods are called.

Pointcut. Wool provides several methods for identifying the set of join points by using the `Pointcut` class. The `Pointcut` class has some static methods to identify a set of join points and some methods to be used for some logical operations. For example, the method `methodCall()` identifies a call to the method with four `String` arguments. Those arguments are used for indicating a modifier, a method name, a declared class, and a signature. Table 2 lists several methods in `Pointcut`.

Table 2. Methods in `Pointcut` for identifying a set of join points.

```
static Pointcut methodCall(String, String, String, String)
    identify a call to the method.
static Pointcut methodExecute(String, String, String, String)
    identify an execution of the method.
static Pointcut fieldGet(String, String, String)
    identify a read of the field.
static Pointcut fieldSet(String, String, String)
    identify a write of the field.
static Pointcut instanceCreate(String, String, String)
    identify a creation of the instance.
static Pointcut exceptionHandle(String)
    identify a handling of the exception.
static Pointcut within(String)
    identify any join point defined in the class.


Pointcut and(Pointcut)
    perform an AND operation.
Pointcut or(Pointcut)
    perform an OR operation.
```

Advice. Wool provides methods for inserting a piece of code called advice into a program by the `WlAdvice` class and its subclasses, such as `BeforeAdvice` or `AfterAdvice`. Advice consists of a pointcut and an advice body. The constructor of the `WlAdvice` class takes as a parameter a `Pointcut` object to identify the join point. In addition, an advice body is described in the method `advice()` declared in the class inherited from the class `WlAdvice`. The object of `WlAdvice` is inserted into a program in the method `weave()` on the `WlAspect` class through the object of `Wool`.

If advice is defined as an anonymous class like a closure:

```
public void weave(Wool wool) throws WeaveException {
  wool.insert(new BeforeAdvice(log) {
    public void advice(Joinpoint joinpoint) {
      /* can access the external variables */
    }
  });
}
```

The code in the method `advice()` can access external variables. Consequently, the scope of the aspect can be made naturally because aspect variables can be accessed from an anonymous class inherited from `WlAspect`. Moreover, the advice is easily changed and modified at runtime.

A parameter of the method `advice()`, the object of `Joinpoint`, contains reflective information about the current join point for the advice to use. It is similar to *thisJoinPoint* of AspectJ. Mainly, this object is used to obtain certain dynamic information such as the currently executing object or the target object or the arguments. The current version of Wool doesn't support obtaining more reflective information such as data structures of the class for the sake of efficiency. However, such an optimization technique as partial evaluation [15] offers the possibility of efficiently providing rich reflective information for programs, since it can statically pack that information only into the advice that requires them.

Introduction. Although the limitations of the JPDA prevent Wool from implementing an introduction directly, it is easy to implement it indirectly. When a class is replaced with a new one, the JPDA restricts the new one to changing the schema like fields and the hierarchy like subclasses or the interfaces and class modifiers and method modifiers, and to deleting methods. Thus, the introduction itself is restricted with the JPDA. However, the introduced method or field is actually referred to only from the advice code. Therefore, by adding a hidden map or a list for the introduction to all of the classes at load-time, then making the advice code use the hidden variable, Wool can allow for the addition of class elements.

3.4 Control of the Weaver

Wool provides an optional function for programmers to control the behavior of a weaver. This function operates at the time when an aspect actually weaves the program, in other words, when the effect of an aspect appears in the running program. In dynamic AOP systems, the timing of the weaving is important because there is a non-determinacy when an aspect is woven from a remote JVM and there is a necessity to care for a paired advice in relation to the activation frames.

This function is implemented by delegating methods related to the weaving operation from Wool to the programmer. A programmer can control Wool by overriding the methods of `WlAspect`, specifically `hook()` and `initWeave()`. The object of `Wool` is passed to the programmer through those two methods as a parameter. Thus, by implementing the weaving operation by hand with several provided methods, the programmer can control Wool and take care of paired advice using dynamic information. Again, the programmer can select the method of hook insertion as described below in detail. Table 3 lists the available methods through the object of `Wool`.

3.5 Implementation of Just-in-Time Hook Insertion

We present the implementation issues of just-in-time hook insertion by describing the details of weaving step-by-step. The order of the weaving process in Wool is:

(1) Scan classes.
(2) Insert hooks as breakpoints.
(3) The programmer selects the most suitable method.
(4)-1 Execute using the debugger, or
(4)-2 Embed the hook and call the advice.

Following are the details of each step.

Table 3. Available methods in `Wool` for the control of Wool.

`void advice(Joinpoint)`
  execute advice associated with the join point.
`void embedHook(Joinpoint, Pointcut or String, `*`optional`*` boolean)`
  embed hooks into the program by using dynamic code translation. Second optional parameter triggers undocking the translation thread.
`int countActivationFrame(String)`
  count the number of activation frames in the context the intercepted program is running in.
`void filterClass(String, boolean)`
  restrict the loaded classes to be effected by an aspect.

Scan Classes. After Wool is attached to the target program, the application threads except for the threads like the garbage collection and JIT compiler threads are suspended for a while. Wool scans all of the loaded classes and finds out the join points specified by any pointcut. The method `initWeave()` is called just before this scan. For example, if some classes are filtered by the method `filtering()` in `initWeave()` as follows:

```
public class ProfileAspect {
  public void initWeave(Wool wool) throws WoolException {
    wool.filterClass("^java.*|^sun.*", false);
  }
```

those classes are excluded from the scanning. then

Insert Hooks as Breakpoints. Wool sets breakpoints to specify each join point in a set of filtered classes. In order to set the breakpoint, Wool use the subclasses of `Hook` (`CallHook`, `GetHook`, etc.) included in the `wool.hook` package that is implemented using the class `BreakpointRequest` in JPDA. At the same time, pieces of any advice represented as a closure is associated with the join point through the objects of `Hook`. Finally, all of the threads that Wool has suspended are resumed.

The Programmer Selects the Most Suitable Method. When any thread of the target program reaches the first join point, it is intercepted by Wool. Wool calls the method `hook()`. A programmer can avoid the executing advice that join point for the paired advice by overriding the method `hook()` in the subclass of `WlAspect`. Wool gives programmers dynamic information about the join point through the object of the functions using `Joinpoint`(`CallJoinpoint`, `GetJoinpoint`, etc.) included in the `wool.joinpoint` package, which are all implemented using the class `BreakpointEvent`. At the same time, the programmer can select whether to activate dynamic code translation by the method `embedHook()` or to execute the advice by the method `advice()`:

```
Pointcut p
  = Pointcut.methodCall("public","FigureElement","paint","*");
public void hook(Wool wool, Joinpoint joinpoint)
    throws WoolException {
    if (wool.countActivationFrame("main") > 0)
      wool.advice(joinpoint);         // breakpoint-based execution
    else
      wool.embedHook(joinpoint, p); // dynamic code translation
}
```

This fragment of a program means that if there is no activation frame at the join point on the thread named `main`, the advice associated with the joinpoint `joinpoint` is activated. Otherwise, dynamic code translation is performed. The method `embedHook()` takes the object of `Pointcut` or the name of the class as a parameter.

Execute Using the Debugger. There are two cases when the debugger executes advice. One is that the method `hook()` is not overridden, which is the default case. The other is that the method `advice()` is called in an overriding `hook()`. Just by calling the method `advice()`, the appropriate advice associated with that join point is executed.

Embed the Hook and Call the Advice. When the method `embedHook()` is called, Wool creates a hook for the class to be installed using Javassist [4], which is a load-time bytecode modification tool, and calls the method `redefineClass()`, which is declared in the class `VirtualMachine` in JPDA, to replace it with the new one. During the translation and replacement, the intercepted program allowed to resume execution. The advice is executed by the debugger substituting the advice as required until the replacement is completed.

Once dynamic code translation has been executed, the control of Wool will not return to the aspect program for the sake of efficiency. Not to adopt dynamic code translation or to insert hooks per thread it is better to continue breakpoint-based execution because hooks can be embedded anytime under the control of Wool.

3.6 Taking Care of Activation Frames

Using just-in-time hook insertion, there is an exceptional case that we have to treat in a special way when substituting a method in which hooks are embedded. This is when the execution of some advice involves a join point contained in the method currently being executed. For example, suppose that a draw method in a Rectangle class is currently being executed and the activation frame associated with that method is on the execution stack. After the class file of Rectangle is reloaded with the hotswap mechanism, however, the execution of the draw method with that activation frame on the stack is still being performed according to the definition of the draw method given by the old class file. Thus, the hooks contained in the new class file are not effective for that execution. The hooks are effective only for the execution of the draw method started after the reloading. However, the draw method might recursively call itself after the class file. To avoid this problem, dynamic code translation is automatically delayed, instead breakpoint-based execution is performed on the activation frame until the activation frame is popped from the stack.

We also have to be careful with the execution of a pair consisting of before and after advice woven at the same join point. If that pair is woven accidentally while the method containing that join point is executed, only the after advice will be executed at the end of that execution. The before advice will not be executed since the method execution had already been started. This behavior might cause a problem if the after advice depends on the results of the before advice. For example, the before advice might record the current time and the after advice can use that value to compute the elapsed time. In this case, after advice must not be executed if the corresponding before advice was not executed. To solve this problem, our technique allows the programmers to select the behavior in that case using the dynamic information at the join point.

4 Related Work

In this section, we discuss some AOP implementations related to our work, and compare them to Wool. Most current AOP implementations are based on code translation performed by a preprocessor at compile-time or by an extended classloader at load-time of the classes. Two extreme dynamic AOP systems have already proposed exceptions to static code translation, where hooks consist of all-breakpoints or all-methodcalls. Both of these systems have drawbacks in their program execution performance. Wool can avoid these performance penalties by taking a suitable approach for each join point according to the programmer's specification.

An earlier version of AspectJ [13] pre-processes the source code of the aspects and produces a base Java program used to generate a pure Java program that includes woven aspects within it. Even though it only supports static AOP, AspectJ is a typical compiler-based AOP system. Since it is a static AOP system, whether to weave the advice at a join point is determined at compilation time. Also, the advice activity never changes during the runtime in AspectJ. This is sometimes a problem for faster development cycles [7] and for adaptable aspects [11, 25, 21].

Several researchers have addressed the problem of compile-time weaving by shifting the timing of aspect weaving to later stages. Approaches using bytecode-modification tools such as BCA [12] and Javassist [4] use a customized Java class loader to allow weaving at load-time. Extensions of a just-in-time (JIT) compiler like OpenJIT [16] allow weaving at the time of dynamic compilation by the JIT compiler. These are useful for faster development cycles. With these approaches, however, the chance of composition of an aspect with a program is restricted to only one time, at load-time or at dynamic compilation. In order to allow the dynamic activity of advice code, we need some tricks like runtime class evolution [10] to decompose the aspects from a program. We employed the hotswap mechanism of the JPDA for that in Wool.

PROSE [20] uses the JVM debugger interface called JPDA to insert a hook as a breakpoint, which is same as Wool when it inserts only hooks as breakpoints. They report that the execution of advice is too slow in their system to be acceptable. However, we think this approach is useful in limited cases. For example, when a system administrator must recover from system failure as soon as possible, a lightweight diagnosis aspect could be helpful. Meanwhile, when Wool inserts all of the hooks as method calls, this is the same as our previous work [6]. Our experiment has shown that dynamic code translation and class hotswapping impose heavy costs in execution time. However, dynamic compilation may amortize such costs in the long term.

5 Experimental Results

This section first shows the result of our preliminary experiments validating the fundamental of Wool approach basing in a debug mode and combining two hooking means in Wool. After that, it reports the result of our application benchmark which compares Wool to other implementation approaches to dynamic AOP systems. We performed all the experiments on the Sun Java 2 SDK v1.4.0 HotSpot^{TM} Client VM / Solaris8 / Sun Blade1000 (CPU:UltraSPARC-III dual 750MHz, RAM:1GB).

5.1 Preliminary Experiment

Debug Mode. Wool forces application programs run in the debug mode but it is not a major problem with Java 2 SDK 1.4. Although [20] reported that this overhead is too large to use the JPDA for implementing a dynamic AOP system, this overhead has been significantly reduced by using Java 2 SDK 1.4. We measured the overhead incurred by a debug mode to show that Wool adopts a realistic method. Table 4 summarizes the relative execution time of the SPECjvm98 [22] benchmarks in the debug mode of Sun Java 2 SDK 1.4. The observed performance loss is less than 5%.

Table 4. The overhead for SPECjvm98 in the debug mode of Sun Java2 SDK 1.4.

Benchmark	overhead
_200_check	103.52 %
_201_compress	99.18 %
_202_jess	104.64 %
_209_db	101.54 %
_213_javac	100.82 %
_222_mpegaudio	101.33 %

Two Kinds of Hooks. To demonstrate the differences of the two kinds of hooks, the breakpoint and the method call, we compared the performance of a join point hooked by a breakpoint with the same one using a method call, both using Wool. In these measurements, the join point was an empty method call, and the advice was empty. These measurements involved 10,000 iterations. The results of these micro-measurements are shown in Table 5.

Breakpoint hooking takes approximately 700 times longer than method-call hooking on average. The elapsed time for breakpoint hooking varies widely depending on the implementation of the process scheduler used in the experimental environment because a breakpoint must be intercepted by a debugger process. Consequently, once a hook is inserted as a method call, it brings about a large performance improvement. The average time of the hook as a method call shown in Table 5 does not include the time elapsed during dynamic code translation in order to measure the pure elapsed time for the hook as a method call.

Table 5. Hooks as breakpoints and method calls in Wool.

Measurement	Average	Minimum	Maximum	Hook insertion
breakpoint	9.956[ms]	9[ms]	103[ms]	
method call	14.3[us]			435[ms]

5.2 Wool Measurements

To demonstrate the effectiveness of the proposed just-in-time hook insertion, we compared the overhead of Wool with other techniques. We picked the `jess` benchmark program from the SPECjvm98 benchmarks and measured the execution time of the program with one of the input data called monkey banana. The `jess` benchmark is the Java Expert Shell System based on NASA's CLIPS expert shell system, which has over 10,000 lines of code and 140 classes.

We provided a before advice code which does nothing and let it woven into all the `public` method bodies in the `jess` program. The methods woven an advice code exists 163 and totally called 87,457 times. For comparison, we measured the execution time of the program with the advice woven varying the underlying systems to the one with static code translation stated in Section 2.3, the one only with dynamic code translation, the one only with breakpoint-based hooks, and Wool. For making use of Wool's hybrid approach, we implemented a simple profiler using Wool APIs as follows:

```
public void hook(Wool wool, Joinpoint joinpoint)
  throws WoolException {
  wool.advice(joinpoint);
  Class clazz =
    ((ExecutionJoinpoint)joinpoint).method().declaringType();
  if (map.increment(clazz) > 100)
    wool.embedHook(joinpoint, clazz.getName());
}
```

Table 6. Elapsed Time [ms] of jess. The results in AspectJ is 1013 ms just for reference.

	Static code translation	Dynamic code translation	Breakpoint-based execution	Wool
pointcut	0	2,428	2,428	2,428
hook insertion	0	3,553	0	1,196
execution	10,938	4,077	398,286	4,514
elapsed time	10,938	10,058	400,714	8,138

Table 7. The numbers of translated classes, inserted hooks, and pointcut test. The numbers in parenthesis represents the comparison to AspectJ.

	Static code translation	Dynamic code translation	Breakpoint-based execution	Wool
translated classes	149 (196%)	76 (100%)	0	15 (20%)
inserted hooks	2,815 (1727%)	163 (100%)	163	163
execution times	1,077,338 (1231%)	87,457 (100%)	87,457	87,457

This means that if a class is being frequently intercepted, the hooks are embedded into this class dynamically. Using this simple profiler and adjusting the threshold, the method for hook insertion was automatically and suitably selected without requiring in-depth knowledge of the application.

Table 6 lists the results of the benchmark execution. The total time consists of the pointcut time (elapsed time for scanning classes), the hook insertion time (elapsed time for runtime code translation and hotswapping) and the execution time (the rest of the elapsed time). Table 7 lists the numbers of translated classes, inserted hooks, and executed pointcut tests, for each hook implementation approach. These results show that Wool ran dynamic AOP application about 26% faster than a dynamic AOP system using static code translation approach. This is because Wool avoided inserting unnecessary hooks. The static code translation inserted hooks into the program 17 times as many as Wool, and thus resulted in 12 times more pointcut tests. Moreover, Wool was about 19% faster than dynamic code translation and about 98% faster than breakpoint-based execution. This is because Wool allowed switching the breakpoint and method call implementations at every join point. The results for dynamic code translation show that compiling extra 61 (76 - 15) classes did not improve the performance against Wool. The compilation cost 2357 (3553 - 1196) msec. whereas the execution time was reduced by only 437 (4514 - 4077) msec. The breakpoint-based execution caused very large performance degradations because of over 87,000 context switches.

According to Table 6, Wool was 4 times slower than the ideal result using AspectJ with respect to the pure execution time excluding time for pointcut and hook insertion. This is mainly because Wool reifies runtime contexts at every join points whereas AspectJ does not unless reifying is explicitly required. In fact, another experiment by us showed that the execution performance of AspectJ was 25-30% slower if advice includes a special variable named *thisJoinPoint* and thus AspectJ reifies part of runtime contexts. Another reason is that hooks are not specialized for the type of each join point. Therefore, the hook code is indirectly invoked at a join point and the context there is indirectly accessed from advice. The overhead by Wool could be reduced if we employ the techniques proposed in [5] and [3].

6 Conclusion

This paper presented a new dynamic aspect weaver called Wool, which makes it possible to implement efficient dynamic AOP systems. Wool is implemented in Java without modifying the existing runtime system. It integrates a technique using breakpoints provided by the debugger interface of the JVM and a technique using the hotswap mechanism, which allows us to reload a class file that has already been loaded. This selective functionality is delegated to programmers with dynamic information about the target program. Furthermore, it provides a framework for taking care of activation frames by controlling the timing of the aspect weaving.

Our experiment showed Wool runs dynamic AOP application about 26% faster than a dynamic AOP system using static code translation approach under a certain circumstance. This is because Wool avoids inserting unnecessary hooks. Moreover, the experiment showed. Wool is about 19% faster than dynamic code translation, and about 98% faster than breakpoint-based execution. This is because Wool allows programmers to select the most suitable hooking means at each joinpoint from breakpoint or method call implementation.

Our first version of Wool requires the programmers to make decisions about the hooks. This manual selection has a high probability of producing good results. However, sometimes the programmer does not know the best combination of hooks as breakpoints and as method calls. In the future, we will implement a sophisticated profiler like that of the HotSpot VM to automatically select the most appropriate hooks.

Acknowledgement

We would like to express our deep gratitude to our shepherd, the anonymous reviewers, and the program co-chairs. Their valuable suggestions and comments helped us revise this paper. We also thank Shannon Jacobs for his great efforts to fix numerous English problems in this paper.

References

1. Alpern, B., Attanasio, C.R., Barton, J.J., Burke, M.G., Cheng, P., Choi, J.D., Cocchi, A., Fink, S.J., Grove, D., Hind, M., Hummel, S.F., Lieber, D., Litvinov, V., Mergen, M.F., Ngo, T., Russell, J.R., Sarkar, V., Serrano, M.J., Shepherd, J.C., Smith, S.E., Sreedhar, V.C., Srinivasan, H., Whaley, J.: The Jalapeno virtual machine. IBM System Journal **39** (2000) 211–238

2. Baker, J., Hsieh, W.: Runtime Aspect Weaving Through Metaprogramming. In: AOSD 2002. (2002) 86–95
3. Braux, M., Noyé, J.: Towards Partially Evaluating Reflection in Java. Proceedings of the 2000 ACM SIGPLAN Workshop on Partial Evaluation and Semantics-Based Program Manipulation (PEPM '00) (2000)
4. Chiba, S.: Load-time structural reflection in Java. In: ECOOP 2000. LNCS 1850, Springer-Verlag (2000) 313–336
5. Chiba, S., Nishizawa, M.: An Easy-to-use but Efficient Java Bytecode Translator. In: Second International Conference on Generative Programming and Component Engineering (GPCE'03), Erfurt Germany (2003)
6. Chiba, S., Sato, Y., Tatsubori, M.: Using HotSwap for Implementing Dynamic AOP Systems. 1st Workshop on Advancing the State-of-the-Art in Run-time Inspection, july, 2003, Darmstadt, Germany held in conjuction with ECOOP 2003 (2003)
7. Davies, J., Huismans, N., Slaney, R., Whiting, S., Webster, M., Berry, R.: Aspect oriented profiler. In: 2nd International Conference on Aspect-Oriented Software Development. (2003)
8. Dmitriev, M.: Towards flexible and safe technology for runtime evolution of java language applications. In: In Proceedings of the Workshop on Engineering Complex Object-Oriented Systems for Evolution, in association with OOPSLA 2001 International Conference, Tampa Bay, Florida, USA (2001) 14–18
9. Easy Software Foundation: ajProfiler - easy java profiler. http://ajprofiler.sourceforge.net/ (2002)
10. Evans, H., Dickman, P.: Zones, contracts and absorbing changes: An approach to software evolution. In: Proceedings of OOPSLA'99, Proceedings of the 1999 ACM SIGPLAN Conference on Object-Oriented Programming Systems, Languages & Applications. Number 10 in SIGPLAN Notices vol.34, Denver, Colorado, USA, ACM (1999) 415–434
11. Joergensen, B.N., Truyen, E., Matthijs, F., Joosen, W.: Customization of Object Request Brokers by Application Specific Policies. In: Middleware 2000 conference. (2000)
12. Keller, R., Hëlzle., U.: Binary component adaptation. In: ECOOP'98 - Object-Oriented Programming. LNCS 1445, Springer-Verlag (1998) 307–329
13. Kiczales, G., Hilsdale, E., Hugunin, J., Kersten, M., Palm, J., Griswold, W.G.: An overview of AspectJ. In: ECOOP 2001. LNCS 2072, Springer-Verlag (2001) 327–353
14. Kiczales, G., Lamping, J., Menhdhekar, A., Maeda, C., Lopes, C., Loingtier, J.M., Irwin, J.: Aspect-oriented programming. In: Proceedings European Conference on Object-Oriented Programming. Volume 1241. Springer-Verlag, Berlin, Heidelberg, and New York (1997) 220–242
15. Masuhara, H., Kiczales, G., Dutchyn, C.: A compilation and optimization model for aspect-oriented programs. In: Compiler Construction, 12th International Conference, CC 2003, Held as Part of the Joint European Conferences on Theory and Practice of Software, ETAPS 2003, Warsaw, Poland, April 7-11, 2003, Proceedings. Volume 2622 of Lecture Notes in Computer Science., Springer (2003) 46–60
16. Ogawa, H., Shimura, K., Matsuoka, S., Maruyama, F., Sohda, Y., Kimura, Y.: OpenJIT frontend system: an implementation of the reflective JIT compiler frontend. In: ECOOP 2000. LNCS 1850, Springer-Verlag (2000)
17. Orleans, D., Lieberherr, K.: DJ: Dynamic adaptive programming in Java. In: In Reflection 2001: Meta-level Architectures and Separation of Crosscutting Concerns. LNCS 2192, Springer-Verlag (2000) 73–80

18. Pawlak, R., Seinturier, L., Duchien, L., Florin, G.: JAC: A flexible framework for AOP in Java. In: Reflection 2001. (2001) 1–24
19. Popovici, A., Alonso, G., Gross, T.: Just in Time Aspects: Efficient Dynamic Weaving for Java. In: 2nd International Conference on Aspect-Oriented Software Development. (2003)
20. Popovici, A., Gross, T., Alonso, G.: Dynamic Weaving for Aspect-Orinented Programming. In: AOSD 2002. (2002) 141–147
21. Segura-Devillechaise, M., Jean-Marc Menaud, G.M., Lawall, J.L.: Web Cache Prefetching as an Aspect: Towards a Dynamic-Weaving Based Solution. In: 2nd International Conference on Aspect-Oriented Software Development. (2003)
22. Spec - The Standard Performance Evaluation Corporation: SPECjvm98. http://www.spec.org/osg/jvm98/ (1998)
23. Suganuma, T., Ogasawara, T., Takeuchi, M., Yasue, T., Kawahito, M., Ishizaki, K., Komatsu, H., , Nakatani, T.: Overview of the IBM Java just-in-time compiler. IBM Systems Journals **39** (2000) 175–193
24. Sun Microsystems: Java^{TM} platform debugger architecture. http://java.sun.com/j2se/1.4/docs/guide/jpda/index.html (2001)
25. Truyen, E., Jrgensen, B.N., Joosen, W.: Customization of component-based object request brokers through dynamic configuration. In: Technology of Object-Oriented Languages and Systems. (2000)
26. Yagoub, K., Florescu, D., Issarny, V., Valduriez, P.: Caching Strategies for Data-Intensive Web Sites. In: In Proceedings of the 24th International Conference on Very Large Databases (VLDB), Cairo Egypt (2000)

An Extension to the Subtype Relationship in C++ Implemented with Template Metaprogramming

István Zólyomi, Zoltán Porkoláb, and Tamás Kozsik

Department of Computer Science, Eötvös Loránd University
Pázmány Péter sétány 1/D H-1117 Budapest, Hungary
{scamel,gsd,kto}@elte.hu

Abstract. Families of independent classes, where each class represents a separate, orthogonal concern are highly attractive for implementing collaboration-based design. However, required subtype relationship between such families cannot be expressed in many programming languages. This paper presents a framework to handle collaborating groups of classes using template metaprogramming based on standard C++ features in the style of `Loki::Typelist`. Our solution provides tailor-made implicit conversion rules between appropriate groups, inclusion polymorphism and a tool for dynamic binding.

1 Introduction

In this paper an extension to the subtyping mechanism of C++ is presented. Subtyping based on inheritance (subclassing) is known to cause many problems. (See e.g. Bruce in [3] for an extensive discussion of such flexibility and type-safety problems). In spite of these problems, most popular object-oriented languages, such as C++, Java, C# and Eiffel use subtyping provided by inheritance. Our extension to subtyping in C++ will not be an exception, as it will be based on multiple inheritance.

Subtyping is explicit in the aforementioned languages: the subtype relationship must be explicitly indicated in the type definitions. For obvious reasons, the subtype relation is made transitive, by defining it as the reflexive and transitive closure of the declared subclassing properties appearing in the type definitions. Multiple inheritance with a disjunctive subtype relation is highly attractive for implementing collaboration-based designs [12]. Each particular class from a family of collaborating classes represents a separate, orthogonal concern. In the same time, the client code must be separated from the knowledge about the exact structure of the family of classes. This client should be able to refer to a subset of supertypes of the collaborating classes.

The subtype relation in C++ and similar languages does not have language support for disjunctivity with respect to multiple inheritance. To clarify disjunctivity look at the classic example given by Stroustrup in [14]. It describes two orthogonal concerns. One is a hierarchy of vehicles with the base class `Vehicle` and derived classes, e.g. `Car` and `Truck` (see figure 1). Here a class like `Car` is a subtype of `Vehicle`; the functionality of `Vehicle` is a subset of `Car`'s. The other concern represents the aspect of an emergency vehicle which e.g. has priority in intersections and is under radio control of a dispatcher. This concern is implemented in class `Emergency`. Cars like a policecar or trucks like a fireengine should have the functionality provided by class `Emergency`, therefore classes `PoliceCar` and `FireEngine` should be subtypes of class `Emergency` and either `Car` and `Truck` respectively. The functionality of `PoliceCar` and `FireEngine` is the union of the functionalities of the collaborating classes. The subset relation between functionalities should be closed under union (disjunction). Assume we have a client code handling generic emergency vehicles as a collaboration of classes `Vehicle` and `Emergency`. The class `EmergencyVehicle` should be a supertype for classes `PoliceCar` and `FireEngine`, but implementing it using multiple inheritance we lose the language support for the subtype relationship between `EmergencyVehicle` and `PoliceCar` (marked with dashed line on figure 1), e.g. no automatic conversion is possible.

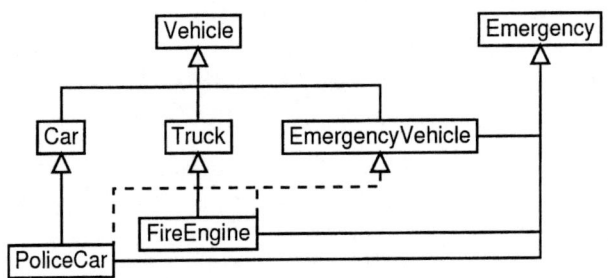

Fig. 1. Class hierarchy for the Vehicle example.

This paper presents a framework that supports a natural way to handle collaborating groups of classes. The framework consists of templates that provide tailor-made implicit conversions between two appropriate groups of collaborating classes in the spirit of our previous example: the class `PoliceCar` defined as `FAMILY_2(Car, Emergency)` is automatically converted to `FAMILY_2(Emergency, Vehicle)`. (Note that the order of the classes in the the groups is irrelevant and we could also apply a hierarchy of emergency levels derived from `Emergency`.) As a part of the increased support for inclusion polymorphism, our framework also provides a tool for dynamic binding of method calls.

2 Applicability

In this section we present a few examples to show our motivation and underline the advantages of our approach. An important advantage of this technique is that we can create our software components with less unnecessary dependencies so we can increase the maintainability of C++ code.

In this paper we will follow through a single example originally introduced by Harold Ossher in [15]. We write an application manipulating expressions consisting of literals and operators. Different manipulations are orthogonal concerns like evaluating, displaying and syntax-checking. We can express Operator as a collaboration of classes OpDisplay, OpEval and OpCheck (see figure 2). Moreover we can express Plus as the collaboration of PlusDisplay, PlusEval and PlusCheck.

```
typedef FAMILY_3(OpDisplay, OpEval, OpCheck) Operator;
typedef FAMILY_3(PlusDisplay, PlusEval, PlusCheck) Plus;
```

Collaborating classes are themselves in inheritance (and subtype) relation: PlusDisplay is subtype of OpDisplay, PlusEval is subtype of OpEval, etc. We would like to have the subtype relation between the collaborating Plus and Operator classes and this is exactly what our FAMILY construct can provide. Remember that if Plus and Operator were created by ordinary multiple inheritance, then Plus would not be a subtype of Operator. This is the example we will refer through the article.

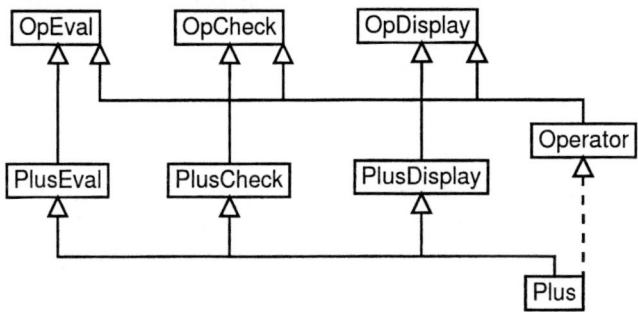

Fig. 2. Class hierarchy for the Operator example.

The next example is related to Grid-computing. Assume that we have Compute Service nodes in a grid offering different computational resources. When a client is started, a Resource Broker will find a Compute Service node where it can be executed. The requirements of the clients can be specified with types (interfaces). A client can run on a node if the required type is a supertype of the offered type. A set of building blocks for constructing the required resources can be BasicTrigonometry (supporting sin, cos, tan), AdvancedTrigonometry (it is a subtype of BasicTrigonometry with sh, ch, arcsin, cotan), ComplexNumbers, ComplexTrigonometry, (child of AdvancedTrigonometry and ComplexNumbers), Derivation, Integration and DifferentialEquations (subtype of Derivation and Integration).

A client can specify its requirements as FAMILY_2(AdvancedTrigonometry, Derivation). The Resource Broker can choose a node offering either FAMILY_2(

AdvancedTrigonometry, Derivation) or FAMILY_3(ComplexTrigonometry, Derivation, Integration) or any similar.

To achieve similar flexibility without our framework one should define all possible combinations of the building blocks declaring the appropriate subtype relationships. This would be very cumbersome to write and impossible to maintain, especially if new computational libraries were to be introduced.

3 Class Hierarchy

A typical group of collaborating classes involves classes usually unrelated to each other. When designing the class hierarchy, we cannot find a common superclass. What is more, introducing such an artificial base class would be misleading both conceptually and technically (it would allow implicit conversions not deducible from the conceptual model). Therefore we did not choose an object-oriented but a generative method to express the required relationships.

The fundamental element in the implementation is structural conversion between groups of collaborating classes. Implementing structural conversion we have to provide a structure holding our collaborating classes together. This may not seem a problem at all because C++ has multiple inheritance, so any combination of classes can be created. However, for implementing the appropriate conversions, we also need the exact map of the inheritance hierarchy of the participating classes. Thus we have to implement a framework that provides all required inheritance information.

A natural way to implement such a framework is to assemble the required structure of classes in a controlled way. Thinking in generative programming terms, we can use template parameters to specify the components of the structure to be built. We want a template class that inherits from all parameter types. Using an ordinary `Mixin` class a naive implementation can be given:

```
template <class Left, class Middle, class Right>
class Family3 : public Left, public Middle, public Right {};
```

This example has an important limitation: the number of components is "hardwired". Extending this implementation philosophy our template should repeatedly be rewritten to support all possible numbers of collaborating classes.

An arbitrary long list of types can be specified using a single template parameter. Introduced by Alexandrescu[1] in [1] a template framework was designed to handle this kind of type lists. We could have written our own template classes, but why to reinvent the wheel? `Loki::Typelist` is a useful, versatile tool at hand and we will rely on it when building our structures.

---

[1] Though similar typelists were also discovered by Jaaki Järvi and they are also introduced in [6] both before [1], it was Alexandrescu who provided a comprehensive library and framework with it.

3.1 Overview of Loki::Typelist

The only role of this class is to hold compile-time information as a list of types in a single class. Its definition is very simple:

```
template <class T, class U>
struct Typelist {
    typedef T Head;
    typedef U Tail;
};
```

Basically this template is similar to a *trait* in that it contains static type information. An example of using this template can be given as:

```
template <class TypeInfo> class RefCountPtr {
    typedef typename TypeInfo::Head counterType;
    typedef typename TypeInfo::Tail pointeeType;
    ...
};
```

```
typedef Typelist<unsigned int, string> MyPtrTraits;
typedef RefCountPtr<MyPtrTraits> MyPtr;
```

One may think that `Typelist` can hold information of only two types. However, using a recursive approach, longer lists can also be written.

```
typedef Typelist< char, Typelist<signed char, unsigned char> >
        CharList;
```

Obviously, the head of the list can be simply referenced as `CharList::Head` when using such a list. To refer to the remaining types a longer expression is needed, but specifying classes like `CharList::Tail::Head` is almost as undesired as hardwiring the number of parameters. Fortunately it is possible to provide a better way.

By convention, a `Typelist` must end with the special type `NullType`. For compile-time algorithms it serves as \0 does for C-strings: it marks the end of a list as an extremal element. Thus indexing and iterating over the list can be implemented without serious restrictions.

Because recursion makes defining a long list really annoying and error-prone, macros are written in Loki to ease this problem. Though we have to specify the exact length of the list and the types to use them, recursion-handling and adding `NullType` are not needed explicitly anymore:

```
#define TYPELIST_1(T1) Typelist<T1,NullType>
#define TYPELIST_2(T1, T2) Typelist<T1, TYPELIST_1(T2) >
#define TYPELIST_3(T1, T2, T3) Typelist<T1, TYPELIST_2(T2, T3) >
...

typedef TYPELIST_3(char, signed char, unsigned char) CharList;
```

3.2 Recursive Inheritance

`Loki::Typelist` has several recursive compile-time algorithms: random access, append, removal of duplicates, etc. All of them are based on partial template specialization (see [14] and [1]) utilizing `NullType` at the end of the list.

Our solution will be very similar to them from this point of view[2]. Now `Family` may have only one parameter type containing all required types to be assembled to a structure:

```
// --- Forward declaration
template <class List> class Family;

// --- Partial specialization for general lists
template <class Head, class Tail>
class Family< Typelist<Head,Tail> > :
    public Head, public Family<Tail>
{};

// --- Partial specialization for lists of one element
template <class Head>
class Family< Typelist<Head,NullType> > :
    public Head
{};
```

The forward declaration is only for safety purposes, there is no implementation for it. The two partial specializations have their own implementations, thus ensuring that a compile-time error will occur if the template is instantiated with any type other than a `Typelist`.

The first implementation inherits from both `Head` and `Family<Tail>`, but — because it is specialized for lists of only one element — no `Tail` remains for the second, therefore it inherits only from `Head`. A sample instance and an according class hierarchy may be seen below and in figure 3.

```
typedef Family< TYPELIST_3(OpDisplay, OpEval, OpCheck) Operator;
```

4 Instantiating Objects

After creating the class hierarchy we construct instances of classes. We need a constructor for our structure. As a consequence of using `Typelist` and recursive inheritance, during our compile time recursions we know nothing about the types in the list: we have only the atomic type `Head` and the remaining list `Tail` of any

---

[2] We could also use classes introduced in [1] like `Loki::GenScatterHierarchy` or `Loki::GenLinearHierarchy` to build our hierarchies, but they are needlessly complex for us. We do not need most of their functionalities so we would rather write a similar, but very simple class from scratch.

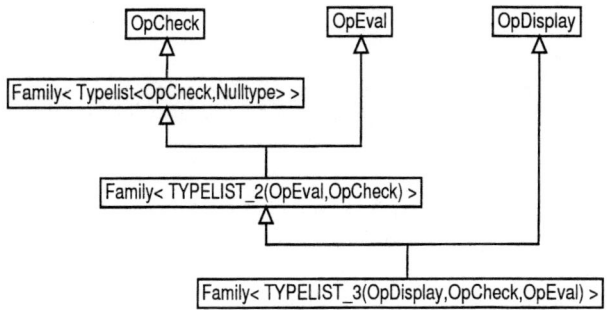

Fig. 3. A sample hierarchy of the `Family` template.

length. Without knowing all list elements, conventional constructor techniques cannot be used.

Our only possibility is continuing with the recursive technique by demanding two constructor parameters of types `Head` and `Family<Tail>`. Hereby our structure still remains quite simple as its base classes can be directly set using member initializer lists. (For a solution of the mixin constructor problem see [7]). Reasonably, we also want a copy constructor for easy initialization:

```
template <class Head, class Tail>
class Family< Typelist<Head,Tail> > :
    public Head, public Family<Tail>
{
public:
    // --- Type name shortcuts
    typedef Family<Tail> Rest;
    typedef Family< Typelist<Head,Tail> > MyType;

    // --- Copy constructor
    Family(const MyType& mt) : Head(mt), Rest(mt) {}

    // --- "Recursive" constructor
    Family(const Head& head, const Rest& rest) :
        Head(head), Rest(rest) {}
};

template <class Head>
class Family< Typelist<Head,NullType> > :
    public Head
{
public:
    // --- All in one constructor
    Family(const Head& head) : Head(head) {}
};
```

After defining the required constructors we are able to create our first collaboration group.

```
typedef Family< TYPELIST_2(PlusEval, PlusCheck) > PlusCalc;
typedef Family< TYPELIST_3(PlusDisplay, PlusEval, PlusCheck) > Plus;

// --- Create a 3-in-1 object
PlusEval add; PlusCheck checkParams; PlusDisplay show("+");
PlusCalc calculate(add, checkParams);
Plus sum(show, calculate);
```

Unfortunately a temporary object sum has to be used for passing a second parameter to the constructor. For a longer list more temporary objects are needed and longer member initialization is done. Though one could write this in a shorter form without variables[3], it is still not an appropriate solution:

```
Plus sum( PlusDisplay("+"), PlusCalc(PlusEval(), PlusCheck()) );
```

Even for this form of instantiation we have to embed constructor calls. It is very similar to the typelist definition problem, where macros were written to linearize the recursion. We can generate macros for our classes and use them in almost the same form as TYPELIST_X:

```
// --- Sample macro definitions for a family of 3 classes
#define FAMILY_3(T1,T2,T3) Family< TYPELIST_3(T1,T2,T3) >

#define FAMILYVAR_3(name, T1, P1, T2, P2, T3, P3) \
    FAMILY_3(T1,T2,T3) name (P1, FAMILY_2(T2,T3) (P2,P3) )

// --- Using a default constructor
FAMILY_3(PlusDisplay, PlusEval, PlusCheck) sum;

// --- Using object for initialization
FAMILYVAR_3(sum, PlusDisplay, PlusDisplay("+"),
    PlusEval, PlusEval(), PlusCheck, PlusCheck());
```

In the last example above sum stands for the name of the variable followed by the parameter types and the actual parameters. Though a default constructor was still not introduced for the Family template, it can be easily implemented for both specializations. We need only two lines of code to be added next to the copy constructors:

```
Family(): Head(), Rest() {}     //for general lists
Family(): Head() {}             //for a list of one element
```

---

[3] This form of constructor calls could be parsed as a function declaration with pointer-to-function type parameters, see [9].

5 Structural Conversions

We have already got class families, but they are still not related to each other. To provide the required subtype relations we need a structural conversion between adequate groups of classes. Unlike the creation of the hierarchy and the objects, we have lots of different ways to implement the conversion.

5.1 Do It in the Naive Way

At first glance the most simple way is a conversion function iterating over all types in the list and convert them to their appropriate base types. Following our compile-time recursion technique, this can be made in two steps: recursively converting the tail of the list first and simply converting the head type at last. We can make use of partial template specialization to implement this function. Because partial template specialization is allowed only for classes, we introduce an auxiliary `Converter` class. We do not want to create any instances of the class `Converter`, hence our function `convert` will be static:

```
// --- Forward declaration
template <class ToList, class FromList> struct Converter;

// --- Partial specialization for general lists
template <class ToHead, class FromHead,
          class ToTail, class FromTail>
struct Converter< Typelist<ToHead,ToTail>,
                  Typelist<FromHead,FromTail> >
{
    typedef Family< Typelist<ToHead,ToTail> > ToType;
    typedef Family< Typelist<FromHead,FromTail> > FromType;

    static ToType convert(const FromType& from)
    {
        // --- Recursion to the rest of list
        Family<ToTail> toTail =
            Converter<ToTail,FromTail>::convert(from);

        // --- Conversion FromHead -> ToHead
        return ToType(from, toTail);
    }
};


// --- Partial specialization for lists with one element
template <class To, class From>
struct Converter< Typelist<To,NullType>,
                  Typelist<From,NullType> >
```

```
{
    // --- Simple conversion From -> To
    static To convert(const From& f) {
        return f;
    }
};


// --- An example using the Converter class
typedef TYPELIST_3(OpEval, OpCheck, OpDisplay) ToList;
typedef TYPELIST_3(PlusEval, PlusCheck, PlusDisplay) FromList;

Family<FromList> sum;

Family<ToList> expr = Converter<ToList,FromList>::convert(sum);
```

This conversion became quite complex, but would be worth the hard work if it was all we need. Unfortunately it is far from that for its highly limited usability. The solution above supports only lists of classes of the same length and the same ancestor-descendent order. When adding a new element to `FromList` or when changing the order of elements in either lists, an error will occur during compilation.

There are still other problems with this construction. Firstly, there is a serious hidden inefficiency in the conversion. The construction of a `Family` object requires time linear in the length of the list of types. This is optimal because each type in the list has to be initialized. Inefficiency comes in sight during conversion: in every call of `convert()` an object is instantiated to return the result of the actual conversion step, which has a linear cost itself. Multiplied with the number of function calls, the total conversion cost becomes $O(n^2)$.

Secondly, there is still an explicit call of a function needed for the conversion. We intend our framework to work completely transparent (i.e. structural conversions should work without explicit function calls).

5.2 Template Constructors

All problems above can be solved by using a different approach. Firstly, we do not assume that the type we want to convert is a `Family` which is accessible by iterating over only `ToList` and ignoring `FromList`. Consequently, the object to be converted can be any user type created by multiple inheritance.

To avoid explicit function calls, we can use either a simple conversion operator or a constructor. Neither of them is suited for recursive solutions. Difficulties arise at generality, because not a single specific conversion is needed: we want all possible conversions to be supported. Both functions have to be implemented as members, so our `Converter` is of no use anymore, we must change to template functions.

To solve the cost problem, we need a radical change in our approach, because a conversion function returning a constructed result by value is not acceptable.

We can avoid copying the temporary results by initializing the adequate part of the resulting structure directly within the converted object.

We need a neat trick to solve the united needs of the two approaches above. Using template constructors may sound a little weird, but constructors are functions, thus they provide a possible solution. Even the essence of our previous conversion may remain the same, only its frame changes. Consider the following code:

```
template <class Head, class Tail>
struct Family< Typelist<Head,Tail> > :
    public Head, public Family<Tail>
{
    typedef Family<Tail> Rest;
    typedef Family< Typelist<Head,Tail> > MyType;

    // --- Good old constructor
    Family(const Head& head, const Rest& rest) :
        Head(head), Rest(rest) {}

    // --- Conversion and copy constructor
    template <class FromType>
    Family(const FromType& from) : Head(from), Rest(from) {}
};

template <class Head>
struct Family< Typelist<Head,NullType> > : public Head
{
    typedef Family< Typelist<Head,NullType> > MyType;

    // --- All-in-one constructor
    Family(const Head& head) : Head(head) {}
};
```

This code is even more simple. It is not obvious to see, but it follows the same conversion steps using the member initialization lists.

To examine this code, see the following example:

```
class Plus: public PlusEval,public PlusCheck,public PlusDisplay{};
Plus sum;
FAMILY_2(OpEval, OpCheck) calculate = sum;
```

As explained above, the converted object does not have to be an instance of Family, a hand made type will do. We can see that no temporary objects were used. The time cost of the conversion is linear since we iterate over the list elements only once.

The conversion is implicit, we did not use any explicit function calls. Since it is implemented as a constructor call, the compiler will silently do these kinds of conversions whenever needed, which greatly improves the ease of use.

Still one additional feature for our class may be desirable: an `operator=` to copy our objects. It can be easily implemented following our previous recursive techniques, similarly to our template constructor:

```
// --- Implementation for general list
template <class FromType>
MyType& operator = (const FromType& from) {
    Head::operator= (from);

    // --- recursive call
    Rest::operator= (from);
    return *this;
}

// --- Implementation for lists of one element
MyType& operator = (const Head& from) {
    Head::operator= (from);
    return *this;
}

// --- Example using our previous object
FAMILY_3(MinusEval, MinusCheck, MinusDisplay) minus;
calculate = minus;
```

6 Dynamic Binding

Now conversion works fine, providing coercion polymorphism for our class families. Like all default conversions in C++, our conversion is done by value, not by reference. We would also like to use dynamic binding, so we will follow the C++ way: build our smart pointer and reference classes to support it.

6.1 Smart Pointers

How can we write a smart pointer? The usual way is to have a referring member (mostly pointer but it also can be a reference) and overloaded operators like `operator->` which do some additional work (e.g. reference counting).

The natural extension of our previous recursive technique would produce an inheritance hierarchy using referring types for bases. We cannot inherit from either pointers or references so a pointer data member for each type in the list will be used instead. We build the following structure:

```
template <class Head, class Tail>
class FamilyPtr< Typelist<Head,Tail> > : public FamilyPtr<Tail>
{
    Head* head;
    ...
};
```

```
template <class Head>
class FamilyPtr< Typelist<Head,NullType> >
{
    Head* head;
    ...
};
```

Thus the structure becomes linear. An example (for the same list of types as shown in figure 3) can be seen in figure 4.

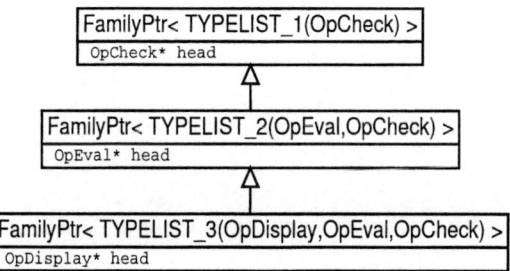

Fig. 4. A sample hierarchy of the `FamilyPtr` template resulting from the same example as that of figure 3.

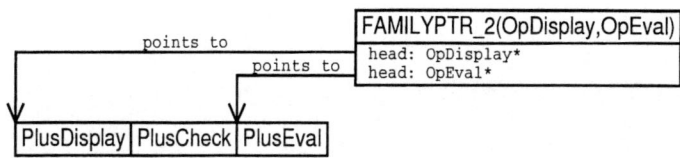

Fig. 5. A sample initialization of pointer members in `FamilyPtr`.

When constructing a `FamilyPtr` instance, every pointer member is set to the adequate part of the referred composite object. (See figure 5).

```
// --- FamilyPtr general implementation for Typelists
template <class Head, class Tail>
class FamilyPtr< Typelist<Head,Tail> > : public FamilyPtr<Tail>
{
    Head* head;
public:
    typedef FamilyPtr<Tail> Rest;
    typedef FamilyPtr< Typelist<Head,Tail> > MyType;

    FamilyPtr() : Rest(), head() {}
```

```
    // --- Conversion and copy constructor
    template <class FromType>
    FamilyPtr(FromType& from) : Rest(from), head(&from) {}

    // --- Simple cast operators
    operator Head& () const { return *head; }
    operator Head* () const { return head; }
};

template <class Head>
class FamilyPtr< Typelist<Head,NullType> >
{
    Head* head;

public:
    typedef FamilyPtr< Typelist<Head,NullType> > MyType;

    // --- Simple default and copy constructors
    FamilyPtr() : head() {}
    FamilyPtr(Head& from) : head(&from) {}

    // --- Simple cast operators
    operator Head& () const { return *head; }
    operator Head* () const { return head; }
};
```

Most of this code should not be a surprise by now, only the cast operators are really new. Because Head is not an ancestor any more, we need a workaround for keeping the possibility of conversion to Head. Overloading operator-> to return pointer head will not do what we need: always the operator-> of the most derived type would be called because of hiding, no better match would be searched for in base types.

Cast operators can provide a solution for this problem. Instead of overloading operators like operator->, we can directly convert our object to a pointer. Unfortunately this solution also has a drawback. By language definition automatic conversions are disabled on the left side of operators like operator-> , so an explicit cast is needed to the required type. See the following example:

```
FAMILY_3(PlusDisplay, PlusEval, PlusCheck) sum;
FAMILYPTR_3(OpDisplay, OpEval, OpCheck) exprPtr(sum);

// --- Function call with explicit cast
static_cast<OpDisplay*>(exprPtr)->show();

// --- In longer form with implicit cast
OpDisplay *displayPtr = exprPtr;
displayPtr->show();
```

This explicit cast can be uncomfortable, but it also can be useful for removing the possibility of ambiguous expressions. It is still not an advantage though, but we could find no better way so we will have to live together with this limitation.

We should also implement a copy operator for our pointers which will be quite similar to the one of Family. A surprising explicit cast is needed though, because a conversion T → U with the cast operators of T does not imply that T* → U* is also possible, because builtin pointer types do not have their own cast operators.

```
template <class Head, class Tail>
class FamilyPtr< Typelist<Head,Tail> > : public FamilyPtr<Tail>
{
    template <class FromType>
    MyType& operator = (FromType& from) {
        // --- No builtin FamilyPtr<T>* -> T* conversion
        // --- allowed so explicit conversion needed
        head = & static_cast<Head&>(from);
        Rest::operator= (from);
        return *this;
    }
};

template <class Head>
class FamilyPtr< Typelist<Head,NullType> >
{
    MyType operator = (Head& from) {
        head = &from;
        return *this;
    }
};
```

As a result, dynamic binding and all conversion facilities of Family are provided by our pointers as structures and pointers are completely interchangeable[4]. No operator* is needed to dereference the pointers, so all conversions are possible between pointers and structures:

```
FAMILY_3(PlusDisplay, PlusCheck, PlusEval) sum;
FAMILYPTR_3(PlusDisplay, PlusCheck, PlusEval) plusPtr = sum;

FAMILY_3(OpDisplay, OpCheck, OpEval) expr;
FAMILYPTR_3(OpDisplay, OpCheck, OpEval) exprPtr = sum;

exprPtr = plusPtr;     // --- pointer -> pointer conversion
exprPtr = sum;         // --- object  -> pointer conversion
expr = plusPtr;        // --- pointer -> object  conversion
```

---
[4] This property is not necessarily an advantage and may need further revision.

When a `FamilyPtr` object is a left value, no objects are copied, only pointer members are set to adequate addresses. This greatly improves speed compared to `Family` which copies whole objects by value.

Apart from the need of the explicit cast to the required builtin pointer type, `FamilyPtr` is able to substitute `Family` much more efficiently. Why would we still use `Family` then? We do not have to, but we had better to do. It is designed to contain several objects and handle them together, without it we would have tons of separate objects and a chaotic resource management. We suggest creating collaborating objects in one `Family` object and then making all conversions using adequate `FamilyPtr` types.

6.2 Smart References

Usually references are preferred to pointers. Using them we can do the same as with pointers without essential changes. The only difference is that pointer members are changed to references, thus no address operator (`operator&`) is needed for initialization and copy. This has a few consequences:

- No default constructor can be made (references have to be initialized immediately when created).
- When using `operator=`, not pointers are set, but whole objects are copied, which may cause loss of dynamic type information. This means that dynamic binding is done only when initializing the reference. (E.g. we have a reference of type `Vehicle&` initialized to a `Car` object. If an object of `SportsCar` is copied to the referenced object using `operator=`, no dynamic binding is provided).

Because its implementation is almost like that of `FamilyPtr`, we omit the necessary program code[5].

7 Robustness and Limitations

An important advantage of our solution is that it relies only on standard C++ template features. Similarly to STL no extension to C++ is required, so (theoretically) any number of collaborating classes could be used with any standard compliant compiler. Effectively compilers do not follow the C++ standard and have finite resources. We have tested some compilers and had the following results:

---

[5] Source code of our whole framework can be downloaded from http://gsd.web.elte.hu/publications/

Compiler	# of classes	Cause of limitation
g++ 3.2	45	Macro parameter limit in precompiler
g++ 2.96	17	Recursion depth limit reached
Intel 7.1	25	Unacceptable compile time on a PIII 750MHz processor, it seems that exponential resources are consumed
VC++ .NET	0	Partial template specializations are not implemented
Borland 6.0	0	Loki does not compile
OpenWatcom 1.0	0	Loki does not compile

Though the number of classes in a family is limited, it's not a serious limitation because at most a dozen of classes are practically enough to express most design issues. Our solution is also completely type safe which is gained by relying on builtin compiler rules and language features. Our structures are converted class by class, so the compiler supports all types of required conversions. On the other hand, a compile time error will arise whenever an invalid conversion is done.

Though our conversions are working properly, they still have a few issues in consequence of certain C++ language rules. They are as follows:

- All required conversions are supported, but sometimes even conversions that were not intended are also introduced. They are valid but undesirable results of a class design error. Just imagine the class std::string in the source list and std::istringstream in the target list. Now an error would be expected, but std::istringstream has a constructor with a string parameter as an initial buffer value, so the conversion is completely legal. Defining our constructors explicit does not help here because explicit constructor calls are made in Family during conversion in the member initializer lists. It can be avoided only by careful class design.
- If a type is added to a list more than once or repeated inheritance occurs in the user object to be converted, a compilation error will arise for type ambiguity.
- If a required method of the class is not present (e.g. there is no copy constructor, default constructor or the conversion to a base class is explicitly forbidden), the code based on the non-existent feature will not compile.

They are not results of our construct, only consequences of the C++ language standard.

8 Related Work

Several discussions were made on the applicability of C++ mixins/mixin layers to solve similar problems (see e.g. Smaragdakis and Batory in [12]). They had shortages either not to cover the whole problem addressed by us or inconveniences at usage.

In languages with structural subtyping (see e.g. [4]) the same problem does not arise: structural subtyping is disjunctive. Our tailor-made conversions can be considered as a tool to make the subtype relation of C++ closer to structural subtyping. We increase the flexibility of subtypes, but "without the loss of the semantic information that hierarchies of type names provide". The goal of Muckelbauer and Russo in [10] is similar, but they start from a language with structural subtypes and propose the addition of "semantic attributes" to types. This way they can express the same semantic dependencies as the inheritance-based type hierarchies for the different concerns in our approach.

Advanced techniques for separation of concerns such as Multi-Dimensional Separation of Concerns [11], Aspect-Oriented Programming [8] or Composition Filters [2] can also aid collaboration-based design. However, these techniques are aiming to solve problems different from the one this paper brought on. For example, in AspectJ [5] or in AspectC++ [13] we can extend a hierarchy of classes with orthogonal concerns (implemented as aspects), preserving the subtype relationships, but this extension applies to whole classes and not to individual objects.

9 Conclusions

C++ supports explicit subtyping based on multiple inheritance. This subtyping mechanism is not flexible enough to express certain subtype relationships which are necessary for implementing collaboration-based designs. Our framework extends the possibilities of the subtyping mechanism in C++: it allows families of collaborating classes to be subtypes of other families. The framework makes the subtype relation disjunctive with respect to multiple inheritance.

In the implementation of our framework we have used standard template metaprogramming tools such as `Loki::Typelist`. If the programmer expresses families of collaborating classes with the help of the templates defined in our framework, (s)he can make use of coercion polymorphism using class `Family` or inclusion polymorphism with class `FamilyPtr`.

References

1. Andrei Alexandrescu. Modern C++ Design: Generic Programming and Design Patterns Applied. Addison-Wesley (2001)
2. Lodewijk Bergmans, Mehmet Aksit. Composing Crosscutting Concerns Using Composition Filters. Communications of the ACM, Vol. 44, No. 10, pp. 51-57, October 2001.
3. Kim B. Bruce. Foundations of Object-Oriented Languages. The MIT Press, Cambridge, Massachusetts (2002)
4. Luca Cardelli. Structural Subtyping and the Notion of Power Type. Conference Record of the Fifteenth Annual ACM Symposium on Principles of Programming Languages, San Diego, California, January 1988. pp 70-79.

5. Eclipse. The aspectj project. http://www.eclipse.org/aspectj/
6. Krzysztof Czarnecki, Ulrich W. Eisenecker. Generative Programming: Methods, Tools and Applications. Addison-Wesley (2000)
7. Ulrich W. Eisenecker, Frank Blinn and Krzysztof Czarnecki. A Solution to the Constructor-Problem of Mixin-Based Programming in C++. Presented at the GCSE2000 Workshop on C++ Template Programming.
8. Gregor Kiczales, John Lamping, Anurag Mendhekar, Chris Maeda, Cristina Videira Lopes, Jean-Marc Loingtier, John Irwin. Aspect-Oriented Programming. Proceedings of the European Conference on Object-Oriented Programming (ECOOP), Finland. Springer-Verlag LNCS 1241, June 1997.
9. Scott Meyers. Effective STL. Addison-Wesley (2001). pp. 33-35.
10. Patrick A. Muckelbauer, Vincent F. Russo. Lingua Franca: An IDL for Structural Subtyping Distributed Object Systems. USENIX Conference on Object-Oriented Technologies (COOTS), http://www.usenix.org/publications/library/proceedings/coots95/
11. Harold Ossher, Peri Tarr. Multi-Dimensional Separation of Concerns and The Hyperspace Approach. IBM Research Report 21452, April, 1999. IBM T.J. Watson Research Center. http://www.research.ibm.com/hyperspace/Papers/tr21452.ps
12. Yannis Smaragdakis, Don Batory. Mixin-Based Programming in C++. In proceedings of Net.Object Days 2000 pp. 464-478
13. Olaf Spinczyk, Andreas Gal, Wolfgang Schröder-Preikschat. AspectC++: An Aspect-Oriented Extension to C++. Proceedings of the 40th International Conference on Technology of Object-Oriented Languages and Systems (TOOLS Pacific 2002), Sydney, Australia, February 18-21, 2002.
http://www.aspectc.org/download/tools2002.ps.gz
14. Bjarne Stroustrup. The C++ Programming Language Special Edition. Addison-Wesley (2000)
15. Harold Ossher, Peri Tarr. Multi-Dimensional Separation of Concerns and The Hyperspace Approach. IBM Research Report 21452, April, 1999. IBM T.J. Watson Research Center.
http://www.research.ibm.com/hyperspace/Papers/tr21452.ps

Concept-Controlled Polymorphism

Jaakko Järvi, Jeremiah Willcock, and Andrew Lumsdaine

Open Systems Laboratory, Indiana University, Bloomington, IN 47405 USA
{jajarvi,jewillco,lums}@osl.iu.edu

Abstract. Concepts – sets of abstractions related by common requirements – have a central role in generic programming. This paper proposes a general framework for using concepts to control polymorphism in different ways. First, concepts can be used to constrain parametric polymorphism, as exemplified by type classes in Haskell. Second, concepts can be used to provide fine-grained control of function and operator overloading. Finally, generic functions can be overloaded (specialized) based on concepts, rather than simply on types. We describe a C++ implementation of a new mechanism, which we call *enable_if*, and its role in concept-controlled polymorphism.

1 Introduction

A definition of generic programming from [17] states that its goal is the expression of algorithms and data structures in a broadly adaptable, interoperable form that allows their direct use in software construction. Fundamental to realizing generic algorithms is the notion of abstraction: generic algorithms are specified in terms of abstract properties of types, not in terms of particular types. Following Stepanov and Austern, we use the term *concept* to mean the formalization of an abstraction as a set of requirements on a type (or on a set of types) [4]. Types that meet the requirements of a concept are said to *model* the concept. Ideally, a generic algorithm is defined only (and exactly) for those argument types that are models of the concepts in its interface; types that do not model the specified concept are *constrained* from use with the function.

Constraining (bounding) polymorphism is one important application of concepts to generic programming. However, concepts can be used to direct the operation of polymorphism in different ways as well, a property we refer to as *concept-controlled* polymorphism. Besides constraining parametric polymorphism, concepts can be used to provide fine-grained control of function and operator overloading. In addition, generic algorithms can be overloaded (specialized) based on concepts, rather than simply on types.

This paper applies results of research on type classes [21, 24, 41] to get closer to the ideal of constrained polymorphism. Type classes were first introduced to Haskell to control ad-hoc polymorphism, and are now found in several languages, including Gofer [19], Isabelle [43], and Mercury [18]. This paper demonstrates that type classes can to a large extent be emulated in C++ as well. Type classes are closely related to concepts in generic programming [4, 28]. Like concepts, type classes encapsulate requirements for a type, or for a set of types collectively. In C++, concepts are merely part of documentation whereas type classes in Haskell are explicit representations of concepts.

The presented type class emulation builds on the work on *static interfaces* in C++ [27]. The main focus of static interfaces is in checking concept requirements for improved error diagnostics, but they also provide a mechanism for concept-based dispatching. This technique uses a generic forwarding function, which dispatches to a set of different implementation functions. Recent findings in the C++ template system let us go further in this direction, allowing concept-based overloading without any forwarding functions. In short, a class template specialization can be augmented with a static metaprogram that examines properties of the template arguments and conditionally enables or disables the specialization. Analogously, such guards can be attached to function templates.

We describe a new mechanism, which we call *enable_if*, for supporting concept-controlled polymorphism in Section 2. Section 3 describes Haskell type classes and means for emulating them in C++. As an application of emulated type classes in C++, Section 4 suggests a replacement for the "Barton-Nackman" technique [5]. Section 5 discusses concept-based overloading using the infamous *swap* function as a motivating example[1]. Related approaches are described in Section 6. Finally, we discuss our conclusions in Section 7.

2 Background

Since the discovery [36] and early applications [38,39] of C++'s template-based sublanguage for *static metaprogramming*, a notable amount of effort has been put into the development of metaprogramming tools and techniques [3,8,14,37], and several C++ template libraries [15,32,33,40] use static metaprogramming extensively. Consequently, C++ has become a popular and readily available platform for generic and generative programming. The primary use of static metaprogramming in generative programming is in the assembly of components; static metaprograms allow fine-grained control over how code fragments are welded together to form concrete components. In this paper, we use static metaprogramming to attain this level of fine-grained control over function overloading.

In C++, a complex set of rules determines which function definition is invoked for a particular function call expression. As a part of these rules, *argument dependent lookup* brings functions from many namespaces into the overload resolution set. Functions from namespaces that define any of the argument types, or any classes that the argument types derive from, are included. For argument types that are instances of a template, the namespaces containing the definitions of the template argument types are considered as well. As these rules apply transitively, the set of functions considered for overload resolution can contain functions defined for unrelated purposes, coincidentally sharing the same name. This can lead to compilation errors due to ambiguous function definitions residing in different, and seemingly unrelated, modules. Worse, the best matching function can be different from what the programmer intended, producing no compiler

---

[1] Allowing a safe mechanism for users to provide a specialized *swap* function to be used by standard algorithms has been a topic of long discussions in the C++ standards committee.

diagnostic but an erroneous program [1]. The term *ad-hoc polymorphism* [35] for function overloading is well justified for C++.

Sensible operation of template function overloading in C++ relies on the *SFINAE* (substitution-failure-is-not-an-error) principle [37]: if an invalid argument type or return type is formed during the instantiation of a function template, the instantiation is removed from the overload resolution set instead of causing a compilation error. This section describes the SFINAE principle and tools to take advantage of it, summarizing the discussion in [16].

When multiple definitions of a function template exist in a program, it is often the case that some of them are invalid for particular argument types. For example, consider the following simple function:

int negate(int i) { return −i; }
int i; ...; negate(i);

Assume further, that another overload defining **negate** for nullary functions exists in some visible namespace:

template <class F>
typename F::result_type negate(const F& f) { return −f(); }

Overload resolution must consider both definitions to select the better match. Attempting to instantiate the latter definition for a call with an argument of type *int* would result in the prototype:

int::result_type negate(const int&);

The return type *int::result_type* is invalid; *int* has no nested types. By applying the SFINAE principle, however, the function definition is removed from the overload resolution set, the error is avoided, and the former definition of **negate** is selected. A template system without SFINAE would be fragile; adding a function template that was never called could break existing working code.

Conditions where the SFINAE principle applies can be created intentionally. SFINAE is a crucial ingredient for many *compile-time reflection* tools in C++. For example, it is possible to check at compile-time whether a class has a given member type, or whether a given type is a class or not [37]. The uses of SFINAE are, however, not limited to compile-time reflection. Any function template can be accompanied with a compile-time predicate that determines whether the function is to be considered as a candidate for the best matching definition [16]. Furthermore, matching partial specializations of class templates is performed with the same set of rules as function template argument deduction. This means that a partial specialization of a class template can only match if template argument deduction does not fail, and thus the SFINAE principle can be exploited to enable and disable class template specializations [34].

The following simple template provides a controlled mechanism to create the SFINAE conditions:

template <bool B, class T = void>
struct enable_if { typedef T type; };

template <class T>
struct enable_if<false, T> {};

The ***enable_if*** template selectively includes or fails to include a member type ***type*** based on the value of the parameter ***B***. If ***B*** is true, the ***type*** member will be defined to be the ***T*** parameter to ***enable_if***. If ***B*** is false, no member will be defined. Thus, a reference to ***enable_if<B, T>::type*** is either valid or invalid depending on whether ***B*** is true or false.

Wrapping the actual return type of a function in the ***enable_if*** template adds a guard to the function. For example, this code defines a function ***foo*** whose condition is always true, and is thus always enabled; and another function ***bar*** whose condition is always false, and is thus always disabled:

template<class T>
typename enable_if<true, T>::type foo(T t) { return t; }

template<class T>
typename enable_if<false, T>::type bar(T t) { return t; }

For any copy constructible argument type, a call to ***foo*** will always succeed, while a call to ***bar*** will always cause an error, because it is not possible to create a valid instance of ***bar*** for any argument type. Instead of constant truth values, the condition can be a compile-time function that depends on the properties of one or more template arguments.

The same ***enable_if*** template can be applied to enabling and disabling class template specializations [34]. One extra template parameter is needed for the guard. Each specialization inserts the guard as the value of this extra argument. The template parameter has a default value ***void*** and thus the guard is not visible for the client of the template. In the following example, we use traits classes ***is_integral*** and ***is_float*** from the Boost type_traits library [26] as the predicates. For example:

template<class T, class Enable = void> class A;

template<class T>
class A<T, typename enable_if<is_integral<T>::value>::type> { ... };

template<class T>
class A<T, typename enable_if<is_float<T>::value>::type> { ... };

Instantiating *A* with any integral type matches the first specialization, whereas any floating point type matches the second one. As with function templates, the condition can be any expression that depends on the template arguments of the class, and that can be evaluated at compile-time.

3 Emulating Type Classes

3.1 Haskell Type Classes

Type classes were introduced to Haskell to allow controlled function overloading [41]. A type class definition contains a set of function signatures (and possibly their default implementations). The type class represents the collection of types for which that set of functions is defined. As an example, the following type class ***Showable*** represents the collection of all types ***t*** for which the ***show*** function is defined (the *instances* of *Showable*):

class Showable t where
    show :: t → String

This is a simplification of the **Show** type class in the Haskell Prelude [23]. The presentation of the various instances of **Showable** is also similar to the presentation in [41].

Types are not automatically instances of **Showable**. Instead, an explicit *instance declaration* is required:

instance Showable Int where
    show i = ...

The ellipsis stands for the definition of the *show* function for **Int** values. The instance declaration thus makes **Int** values **Showable** and attaches an implementation to the *show* function for **Int**s. A single instance declaration can apply to more than one type. According to the following declaration, for any type *t* that is an instance of **Showable**, lists containing elements of type *t* are also instances of **Showable**:

instance Showable t ⇒ Showable [t] where
    show l = ...

Haskell constrains the type arguments of polymorphic functions using type classes. These constraints ensure that the body of the polymorphic function does not refer to any function that is not defined for the argument types. For example, the *print* function below outputs a value of any **Showable** type. The *context* **Showable t**, before the ⇒ symbol, expresses the constraint on the argument type of the *print* function:

print :: Showable t ⇒ t → IO ()
print x = putStr (show x)

Type classes are a rich formalism and provide more features than these simple examples show. Functions declared in type classes can have default implementations, which are applied if no definition is given in an instance declaration. A type class *A* can inherit from one or more other classes: all instances of *A* must first be instances of its superclasses, and also meet the requirements of *A*. Higher-order type classes act as constraints on type constructors (analogous to templates) rather than on concrete types. In addition to these features defined in Haskell 98 [23], widely available implementations include several extensions to type classes. These include *multi-parameter type classes* to allow constraints on multiple related types, and *functional dependencies* that can express a requirement that one type is accessible from another type, serving the same purpose as associated types and traits classes in C++ [22, 24].

3.2 Type Classes in C++

The C++ representation of a type class consists of two separate C++ class templates. The following two templates correspond to the Haskell version of the Showable type class (sans-serif text is used when referring to a type class abstractly, as opposed to its representation as C++ code):

template <class T, class Enable = void>
struct showable_traits { static const bool conforms = false; };

```
template <class T>
struct showable {
  BOOST_STATIC_ASSERT(showable_traits<T>::conforms);
  string show(const T& x) {return showable_traits<T>::show(x);}
};
```

The parameter T in both classes is the actual type class parameter. The first class encodes whether the type T is an instance of the type class; each specialization of this traits class must contain a boolean constant to indicate this. By convention, we name this constant *conforms*. The **Enable** parameter is for compile-time predicates that enable conditional instance declarations. The second class template contains the functions that the instance types must implement. Unlike in Haskell, the existence of implementations for these functions are not checked at the point of an instance declaration.

Note that the functions are not just signatures, but define bodies that forward the calls to the implementation functions which are defined within the instance declarations. This forwarding helps to ensure that generic functions do not accidentally rely on functions not listed in type classes that constrain template arguments. The compile-time assertion (see [25] for the definition of **BOOST_STATIC_ASSERT**) prevents instantiations on types that are not instances of the type class (according to the *conforms* constant). This could be extended to include an invocation of a concept checking library [27, 30, 31] to ensure that the instance declaration contains all of the required functions. Such solutions are not part of our framework yet.

The primary template *showable_traits* defines the *conforms* constant with the value *false*. Thus, the default is that no type is an instance of Showable. As in Haskell, an explicit instance declaration is used to express that a type is an instance of a certain type class. The C++ counterparts for instance declarations are class template specializations. For example, the following specialization declares that *int* is Showable:

```
template <>
struct showable_traits<int> {
  static const bool conforms = true;
  string show(int x) { /*...*/ }
};
```
(3.1)

The *conforms* constant has the value *true*, stating the intent that *int* conforms to the requirements of the Showable type class. The specialization also provides the implementation of all the required functions (just *show* in this example) for integers.

As in Haskell type classes, a single instance declaration can apply to more than one type. C++ can readily express sets of types with one expression, but they are limited to certain kinds of sets, such as all instances of a given template, all pointer types, and all *const*-qualified types. Creating instance declarations that cover such sets of types requires nothing more than partial template specialization. For example, the following instance declaration makes all pointer types showable:

```
template <class T>
struct showable_traits<T*> {
  static const bool conforms = true;
  string show(T* x) { /*...*/ }
};
```

Traditional partial specialization cannot, however, express instance declarations for arbitrary sets of types. Section 3.1 showed the Haskell version of an instance declaration covering all lists where the element type is an instance of Showable. To be able to support instance declarations on such sets of types, the *enable_if* template can be used as a predicate to guard template specializations. This is where the *Enable* template parameter is needed. As a concrete example, the following instance declaration adds *list<T>* to Showable types, but only when the element type *T* is an instance of Showable:

template <class T>
struct showable_traits<
  list<T>,
  typename enable_if<showable_traits<T>::conforms>::type> (3.2)
{
  static const bool conforms = true;
  string show(const list<T>& x) { / ... */ }*
};

Without the predicate, all types of the form *list<T>* would match the specialization, even lists with non-showable element types. The predicate guarantees that the specialization is only considered for lists with showable element types. The instance declaration does not say anything about lists of non-showable elements. Other instance declarations are free to make lists of certain non-showable types showable using a different implementation of the *show* function.

The above definitions create a representation of the Showable type class, and make *int*, all pointers, and all lists with showable element types showable. The Showable type class can now be used to constrain parameters of function templates. The C++ equivalent of the Haskell *print* function shown in Section 3.1 is defined as:

template <class T>
typename enable_if<showable_traits<T>::conforms, void>::type
print(const T& t) {
  typedef showable<T> st;
  std::cout << st::show(t);
}

The enabler causes the function to exist only for types that are showable. An attempt to call it with a non-showable type causes a "no function found" error rather than an error in the function's body. The function gains access to the functions from the Showable type class by instantiating the *showable* class with *T* as the argument. The *print* function uses a *qualified name* in the *show* invocation to ensure that the *show* function defined in the instance declaration *showable_traits<T>* is called. Thus we can avoid all the subtleties of C++ argument dependent lookup of functions [1].

The *print* function can be called without any extra syntax for the user:

int a = 5; print(a);
list<int> b; print(b);

In the first call to *print*, *showable* will be instantiated with *int* as the showable type, and so the instance declaration in Listing (3.1) will be used to define the *show* function. In the second call, *int* is again a showable type, and so *list<int>* is also showable. In this case, the definition of *show* for lists in Listing (3.2) will be used, and each element will be printed using the definition of *show* for integers.

The C++ type class simulation can readily implement many of the advanced features of type classes discussed in Section 3.1. The class templates can have more than one template parameter, thus allowing multi-parameter type classes. It is also possible to use template template parameters to allow the equivalent of higher-order type classes. Defaults can be provided for the implementations of type class functions by providing a class template containing default implementations from which the instance declarations can inherit. Type classes can also inherit from other type classes, which requires that each instance of the subclass first be an instance of the superclass. This can be emulated in C++ by adding another static assertion into the subclass's wrapper class, ensuring that instance declarations for the superclasses have been created. This check occurs only when the instance declaration is used; there does not seem to be a way to ensure that a type is an instance of the superclasses at the time of an instance declaration.

The original type class proposal [41] outlined an implementation where type classes and their instance declarations are translated into "method dictionaries" and functions to access the methods in the dictionary. The C++ type classes are a direct translation of this dictionary technique. Unlike the original Haskell version, however, the C++ type class simulation does not require any extra run-time computation.

3.3 Discussion

The type class emulation in C++ is only partial. Most importantly, C++ type classes lack structural conformance checking. At the point of an instance declaration, no checks are made to ensure that the required functions exist, or that they conform to the required signatures. Errors are thus caught later, at the call sites to the functions defined in the type class. This decreases the quality of error diagnostics. There are library solutions for structural conformance checking [27, 31] which, however, are not yet incorporated into our type classes. Conditional instance declarations, however, remain a problem. Concept checking occurs at the time of instantiating a template with concrete types; conditional instance declarations describe properties of unbounded sets of types, not any particular type, resulting in an unlimited number of concrete instances to check.

The C++ type class emulation is syntactically heavier than Haskell type classes. A generic function in Haskell can call functions defined in other type classes without any extra qualification, whereas in C++ the type class must be explicitly specified. Furthermore, Haskell can infer the type class constraints for a generic function from the uses of the parameters in the body of the function.

C++ type classes provide features not found in Haskell type classes. The conditions on function and traits class overloads in C++ can be any boolean expressions, including negations and disjunctions. Thus, a function overload can be enabled only when some type is *not* an instance of a type class, as demonstrated by the examples in Sections 4 and 5. A C++ type class can contain other kinds of members besides function signatures, including member types and member templates.

In Haskell, each function name must only appear in a single type class, which is a prerequisite for being able to infer type class constraints from expressions in the bodies of functions. In C++, the same function name can occur in more than one type class, even within the same module of the program. Constraints cannot obviously be inferred but, on the other hand, unrelated parts of a program do not need to handle possible name conflicts between function names in type classes. Allowing overlapping type classes adds to the flexibility of the C++ type class emulation. For example, assume the type classes Less Than Comparable with the *less* function, Greater Than Comparable with the *greater* function, and Minimizable with the *min* function. The *min* function can be implemented using either the *less* or *greater* function, but instance declarations to express this cannot be defined in Haskell; a type could be an instance of both Less Than Comparable and Greater Than Comparable, leading to an ambiguity.

Type classes are an explicit, though partial, representation of concepts in generic programming. The relationship of types modeling concepts is represented by the instance relationship between types and type classes, and type class inheritance corresponds to concept refinement. Haskell type classes can only describe requirements on functions, whereas C++ type classes can contain types and class templates. This gives a direct representation for associated types.

4 A Replacement for the "Barton-Nackman Trick"

The "Barton-Nackman trick" [5], also known as the *Curiously recurring template pattern* [7], enables a strategy for creating controlled overloads for functions and operators. In this section we show how type classes provide a simpler and safer alternative to achieve the benefits of the Barton-Nackman technique.

In the Barton-Nackman technique, a template class derives from an instantiation of another template, passing itself as a template parameter to that other template as follows:

class A : public base<A> { ... };

The important application of this technique is to give a common "base template" for a set of template classes. One can overload operators and other non-member functions for the common base template; the derived classes will match the definitions. Because it avoids run-time dispatching, this technique is often used in the numerical domain [11–13,42].

The usage of the Barton-Nackman trick is best explained with an example, which we take from the domain of linear algebra. Matrix types (***dense_matrix***, ***diagonal_matrix***, and ***triangular_matrix***) represent different kinds of matrices. Each of these matrix types has a common interface which can be exploited to define functions and operators that work for any matrix type. In this example, our interface is just one function. We overload the function call operator that gives the syntax *A(i,j)* for accessing the element at row *i* and column *j* of matrix *A*. This interface is defined in the common base template *matrix*:

```
template <class Derived>
class matrix {
public:
  double operator()(int i, int j) const {
    return static_cast<const Derived&>(*this)(i,j);
  }
};
```

The *matrix* template will always be instantiated in such a way that the template parameter *Derived* is the type of a derived class. Note the static cast in the definition of *operator()*. As long as *Derived* is the actual type of the object, this is a safe downcast to a derived class. The function call operator thus invokes the function call operator of the derived class without dynamic dispatching.

Each specialized matrix type must pass itself as a template argument to the *matrix* template and define the actual implementation of *operator()*:

```
class dense_matrix : public matrix<dense_matrix> {
public:
  double operator()(int i, int j) { ... }
  ...
};

class diagonal_matrix : public matrix<diagonal_matrix> {
public:
  double operator()(int i, int j) { ... }
  ...
};

class triangular_matrix : public matrix<triangular_matrix> {
public:
  double operator()(int i, int j) { ... }
  ...
};
```

With this arrangement, one can overload generic functions for the *matrix* template, instead of separately for each matrix type. For example, the multiplication operator could be defined as:

```
template<class A, class B>
typename product_traits<A, B>::type
operator*(const matrix<A>& a, const matrix<B>& b);
```

The *product_traits* template is a traits class to determine the result type of multiplying matrices of types *A* and *B*. Such traits classes for deducing return types of operations are common in C++ template libraries [15,40,42].

We can observe many benefits in this approach. The run-time overhead of virtual function calls is avoided. Several implementation types can be grouped under a common base template, allowing one operator implementation to cover many separate types. We can also identify several problems with the approach:

- One needs to be careful not to slice objects. Taking the matrix arguments by copy in the above *operator** function would not copy the whole object, but only the base class *matrix*. Thus some data would be lost, leading to undefined behavior at runtime when the object was cast to the actual matrix type in the function call operator of the *matrix* class.
- It is difficult to get the desired overloading behavior if some parameters of a function are instances of "Barton-Nackman powered" types, but others are not. For example, one might want to define multiplication between two matrices, and additionally between a matrix and a scalar with the scalar as either the left or right

argument. The straightforward solution is to define three function templates (we leave the return types unspecified):

template<class A, class B>
... operator∗(const matrix<A>& a, const B& b);

template<class A, class B>
... operator∗(const A& a, const matrix<B>& b);

template<class A, class B>
... operator∗(const matrix<A>& m1, const matrix<B>& m2);

The following code demonstrates why this approach does not work:

diagonal_matrix A; dense_matrix B;
A ∗ B; // error, ambiguous call

The third function is not the best match; instead, the call is ambiguous. The first two definitions are both better than the third definition, but neither is better than the other. Thus, a compiler error occurs. Even though the type ***matrix<A>*** is more specialized than ***A***, the actual argument type is not ***matrix<A>*** but ***diagonal_matrix***, which derives from ***matrix<A>*** where ***A*** is ***diagonal_matrix***. Therefore, matching ***diagonal_matrix*** with ***matrix<A>*** requires a cast, whereas matching it with ***A*** does not, making the latter a better match. Thus, the second definition provides a better match for the first argument, and the first definition provides a better match for the second argument; this makes the call ambiguous.

There are two immediate workarounds: providing explicit overloads for all common scalar types, or overloading for the element types of the matrix arguments. The first solution is tedious and not generic because one cannot know all the possible (user-defined) types that might be used as scalars. The second solution is limiting, as it prevents sensible combinations of argument types, such as multiplying a matrix with elements of type ***double*** with a scalar of type ***int***.

– The curiously recurring template pattern is quite a mind-teaser; it significantly adds to the complexity of the code.

Type classes and the ***enable_if*** template solve the above problems. We rewrite our matrix example using type classes. First, all matrix types must be instances of the following type class:

template <class T, class Enable = void>
struct matrix_traits {
  static const bool conforms = false;
};

template <class T>
struct matrix {
  BOOST_STATIC_ASSERT(matrix_traits<T>::conforms);
  static double index(const T& M, int i, int j) {
    return matrix_traits<T>::index(M, i, j);
  }
};

The element access operator ***operator()*** in the type class is renamed to ***index***, because type classes cannot contain non-static member functions. The concrete matrix classes can still use ***operator()***; instance declarations can forward the call to an arbitrary function or operator. The instance declaration for ***dense_matrix*** is (the other matrix types are analogous):

```
class dense_matrix {
  double operator()(int i, int j) { ... }
};

template <>
struct matrix_traits<dense_matrix> {
  static const bool conforms = true;
  static double index(const dense_matrix& M, int i, int j) {
    return M(i,j);
  }
};
```

Now the multiplication operator can be defined on any pair of argument types where at least one is a matrix type. Using type classes, one definition is enough to cover exactly the valid cases:

```
template<class A, class B>
typename enable_if<
  matrix_traits<A>::conforms || matrix_traits<B>::conforms,
  typename product_traits<A, B>::type>::type
operator*(const A& a, const B& b);
```

This operator is only enabled if at least one of the arguments is an instance of the Matrix type class.

Regarding the three drawbacks of overloading based on the Barton-Nackman trick, type classes solve the ambiguity problem. Slicing is also not a problem as ***A*** and ***B*** are unconstrained template parameters that are deduced to the actual types of the function arguments, rather than base classes of these types. Hence, parameter passing could safely be by copy as well. Third, the code is more direct.

Note also, that adding new types to the type class is non-intrusive. The class ***dense_matrix*** contains no reference to the representation of the Matrix type class, and it does not even use the function names required by the type class. Any matrix type supporting element access in some form can be added to the type class without modifications to the definition of the matrix type, giving it all the operators and functions defined for the type class.

5 Concept-Based Overloading

Function enabler predicates can be arbitrary boolean expressions. Functions can thus be overloaded for types that are not members of a given type class. For example, suppose that there is a generic ***swap*** function that works for any type supporting assignment. Certain types can also define a specialized ***swap*** for better efficiency. The traditional approach to this problem, used in the C++ Standard Library, is to define a generic ***swap*** function that uses assignment, and to provide the specialized implementations as overloads. Without *enable_if* and type class emulation, overloading is limited. For example, it is not possible to define a *swap* function for all types that derive from a particular class; the generic *swap* is a better match if the overloaded function requires a conversion from a derived class to a base class (see section 4). Type classes allow us to express the exact overloading rules.

First, two type classes are defined. Assignable represents types with assignment and copy construction (as in the Standard Library), and User Swappable is for types that overload the generic *swap* function:

```
template <class T, class Enable = void>
struct assignable_traits { static const bool conforms = false; };

template <class T>
struct assignable {
  BOOST_STATIC_ASSERT((assignable_traits<T>::conforms));
};

template <class T, class Enable = void>
struct user_swappable_traits { static const bool conforms = false; };

template <class T>
struct user_swappable {
  BOOST_STATIC_ASSERT(user_swappable_traits<T>::conforms);
  static void swap(T& a, T& b) {
    user_swappable_traits<T>::swap(a,b);
  }
};
```

The Assignable requirements are assignment and copy construction, which are not subject to overload resolution, and thus need not be routed via the type class mechanism.

Second, two overloaded definitions of *generic_swap* are provided. The first is for types that are instances of User Swappable. The function forwards calls to the *swap* function defined in the User Swappable type class:

```
template <class T>
typename enable_if<user_swappable_traits<T>::conforms, void>::type
generic_swap(T& a, T& b) {
  user_swappable<T>::swap(a,b);
}
```

The second overload is used for types which are instances of Assignable but not instances of User Swappable. The exclusion is needed to direct types that are both Assignable and User Swappable to the customized *swap*:

```
template <class T>
typename enable_if<
  assignable_traits<T>::conforms && !user_swappable_traits<T>::conforms,
  void>::type
generic_swap(T& a, T& b) {
  T temp(a); a = b; b = temp;
}
```

Thus, the *generic_swap* function can be defined in the most efficient way possible for each type. There is no fear of overload resolution accidentally picking a function other than that the programmer intended.

6 Related Approaches

Our type class approach shares many of the goals with previous work on concept checking, which allows earlier detection of invalid template parameters, and more direct error messages. In particular, the work of McNamara and Smaragdakis uses a system of named conformance using traits classes, as well as structural concept checking [27]. Their work also includes a technique for concept-based dispatching, which is a useful alternative to the enabler-based technique used in this paper. The concept checking library by Siek and Lumsdaine [31] provides pure structural conformance checking, and allows arbitrary expressions as requirements. Either of the structural conformance checking approaches can be added to a type class implementation in the future to check that instance declarations for type classes contain all of the required functions. The work on C++ *signatures* [6] provided a mechanism to specify a set of required member prototypes as an interface as an extension to the GNU C++ compiler. The signature extension was originally intended for object-oriented programming, but could probably serve as a useful form of static interfaces for concept-based overloading as well. Early work suggesting concept-like structures as extensions to C or C++ includes Kind-C++ [29] and Cforall [10].

An alternative to the curiously recurring template pattern is to use friend declarations to force the instantiation of particular non-member functions. The Boost.Operators library applies this technique to provide default definitions for common operators (in terms of other operators) [2]. This technique allows non-member functions to be defined for particular types, but not easily for more than one type at a time, because it normally relies on explicit instantiation of templates.

Tag dispatching, a form of concept-based dispatching is a relatively common technique in C++. This involves a generic implementation of a function which looks up a particular *tag* type in a traits class and passes an object of this tag type together with its original arguments to a set of implementation functions. Concept-based overloading with the *enable_if* template avoids some of the problems of tag dispatching. The dispatcher function must be applicable for all tags, e.g., its return type expression must compute the return type for all cases. Furthermore, the language imposes restrictions on forwarding functions. It is not possible to define a generic forwarding function that accepts both non-const lvalues and rvalues and forwards them unchanged to another function [9]. Tag dispatching commonly uses inheritance relationships among the tags to implement a priority for each overload. McNamara and Smaragdakis proposed a different priority system, which uses a sequence of compile-time *if* statements to select among enumeration values to determine which implementation to use [27]. Our approach is closer to the latter. The *enable_if* approach allows the dispatching logic to be defined within the function definitions, instead of a separate rule set.

Lastly, *qualified types* present a theory for parametric polymorphism constrained using an arbitrary predicate [20]. This work also includes mappings from predicates to program structures, such as the function definitions in a type class instance declaration, that show why a particular predicate is true. This approach is somewhat similar to the use of a traits class by a generic algorithm to look up type class function definitions for a particular instance. On the other hand, [20] does not have sets of functions which are overloaded based on predicate values, as can be done in C++.

7 Conclusion

Concepts are an important idea in generic programming, as they provide the main mechanism for constraining parameters to generic algorithms. Because concepts do not exist explicitly in C++, however, there is no easy way to select function overloads based on concept modeling relationships. This paper provides a technique for controlling function overload resolution based on concept conformance.

Type classes are an existing approach, used in several languages, for concept representation. A type class provides an encapsulation of a set of functions on a particular type, and can thus be seen as an explicit representation of a concept. Instance declarations add types into type classes; they declare that a type models the concept described by the type class. Instance declarations are non-intrusive; a type can be made to be an instance of a type class without modifying the type's definition.

Building on previous work on static interfaces [27] and recent template programming techniques [16], this paper describes a framework for emulating type classes in C++ to provide concept-controlled overloading. Generic functions can thus be defined for exactly those types that model the required concepts. Definitions cannot cause ambiguities with functions overloaded for different concepts. As a concrete application of the type class emulation, we described an improved alternative for library designs based on the curiously recurring template pattern.

The proposed type class emulation does not provide full-fledged support for type classes. Most notably, structural conformance is not enforced at the point of instance declarations. Leveraging on previous work on C++ concept checking, partial support for structural conformance can be added, but conditional instance declarations remain as a problem.

Acknowledgments

We are grateful to Howard Hinnant, Jeremy Siek, and Mat Marcus for their valuable comments and help on this work. This work was supported by NSF grants EIA-0131354 and ACI-0219884, and by a grant from the Lilly Endowment.

References

1. D. Abrahams. Qualified namespaces. Technical Report N1408=02-0066, ISO Programming Language C++ Project, November 2002. http://anubis.dkuug.dk/jtc1/sc22/wg21/docs/papers/2002/n1408.html.
2. D. Abrahams and J. Siek. The Boost Operators library. www.boost.org, 2002.

3. A. Alexandrescu. *Modern C++ Design: Generic Programming and Design Patterns Applied.* Addison Wesley, 2001.
4. M. H. Austern. *Generic Programming and the STL.* Professional computing series. Addison-Wesley, 1999.
5. J. Barton and L. Nackman. *Scientific and engineering C++.* Addison-Wesley, 1994.
6. G. Baumgartner and V. F. Russo. Signatures: A language extension for improving type abstraction and subtype polymorphism in C++. *Software–Practice and Experience*, 25(8):863–889, August 1995.
7. J. O. Coplien. Curiously recurring template patterns. *C++ Report*, pages 24–27, Feb. 1995.
8. K. Czarnecki and U. Eisenecker. *Generative Programming: Methods, Techniques and Applications.* Addison-Wesley, 2000.
9. P. Dimov, H. Hinnant, and D. Abrahams. The forwarding problem: Arguments. Technical Report N1385=02-0043, ISO Programming Language C++ Project, September 2002. http://anubis.dkuug.dk/jtc1/sc22/wg21/docs/papers/2002/n1385.html.
10. G. Ditchfield. *Contextual Polymorphism.* PhD thesis, University of Waterloo, 1994.
11. G. Furnish. Disambiguated glommable expression templates. *Computers in Physics*, 11(3):263–269, May/June 1997.
12. G. Furnish. Container-free numerical algorithms in C++. *Computers in Physics*, 12(3):258–266, May/June 1998.
13. G. Furnish. Disambiguated glommable expression templates revisited. *C++ Report*, May 2000.
14. A. Gurtovoy and D. Abrahams. The Boost C++ metaprogramming library. www.boost.org/libs/mpl, 2002.
15. J. Järvi, G. Powell, and A. Lumsdaine. The Lambda Library: unnamed functions in C++. *Software – Practice and Experience*, 33:259–291, 2003.
16. J. Järvi, J. Willcock, H. Hinnant, and A. Lumsdaine. Function overloading based on arbitrary properties of types. *C/C++ Users Journal*, 21(6):25–32, June 2003.
17. M. Jazayeri, R. Loos, and D. R. Musser, editors. *Generic Programming*, volume 1766 of *Lecture Notes in Computer Science*. Springer, 2000.
18. D. Jeffery, F. Henderson, and Z. Somogyi. Type classes in Mercury. In *Proceedings of the Twenty-third Australasian Computer Science Conference*, pages 128–137, January/February 2000.
19. M. P. Jones. *Gofer.* University of Oxford, 1992. Documentation distributed with Gofer source.
20. M. P. Jones. A theory of qualified types. In B. Krieg-Bruckner, editor, *ESOP '92, 4th European Symposium on Programming*, volume 582, pages 287–306. Springer-Verlag, New York, N.Y., Feb. 1992.
21. M. P. Jones. A system of constructor classes: overloading and implicit higher -order polymorphism. In *FPCA '93: Conference on Functional Programming and Computer Architecture*, pages 52–61, New York, N.Y., 1993. ACM Press.
22. M. P. Jones. Type classes with functional dependencies. In *European Symposium on Programming*, number 1782 in LNCS, pages 230–244. Springer-Verlag, March 2000.
23. S. P. Jones, J. Hughes, et al. *Haskell 98: A Non-strict, Purely Functional Language*, February 1999. http://www.haskell.org/onlinereport/.
24. S. P. Jones, M. Jones, and E. Meijer. Type classes: an exploration of the design space, June 1997.
25. J. Maddock. The Boost static assertion library. www.boost.org/libs/static_assert, 2000.
26. J. Maddock, S. Cleary, et al. The Boost type_traits library. www.boost.org/libs/type_traits, 2002.

27. B. McNamara and Y. Smaragdakis. Static interfaces in C++. In *First Workshop on C++ Template Programming*, October 2000.
28. D. R. Musser and A. Stepanov. Generic programming. In *ISSAC: Proceedings of the ACM SIGSAM International Symposium on Symbolic and Algebraic Computation*, 1988.
29. P. Scheyen, S. Yu, M. Zhang, and Q. Zhuang. Introducing KINDs to C++. Technical Report 366, University of Western Ontario, London, Ontario, May 1993. http://www.csd.uwo.ca/~pete/kc.ps.
30. J. Siek. *Boost Concept Check Library*. Boost, 2000. www.boost.org/libs/concept_check/.
31. J. Siek and A. Lumsdaine. Concept checking: Binding parametric polymorphism in C++. In *First Workshop on C++ Template Programming*, October 2000.
32. J. G. Siek, L.-Q. Lee, and A. Lumsdaine. *The Boost Graph Library User Guide and Reference Manual*. Addison Wesley Professional, 2001.
33. J. G. Siek and A. Lumsdaine. A modern framework for portable high performance numerical linear algebra. In *Modern Software Tools for Scientific Computing*. Birkhäuser, 1999.
34. R. Smith. A default_constructible traits. Thread of Usenet articles in comp.sci.lang.c++.moderated, Jan. 2002.
35. C. Strachey. Fundamental concepts in programming languages. In *Lecture Notes for the International Summer School in Computer Programming*. August 1967. As cited in [41].
36. E. Unruh. Prime number computation. Distributed in the ANSI X3J16-94-0075/ISO WG21-426 meeting, 1994.
37. D. Vandevoorde and N. M. Josuttis. *C++ Templates: The Complete Guide*. Addison-Wesley, 2002.
38. T. L. Veldhuizen. Expression templates. *C++ Report*, 7(5):26–31, June 1995. Reprinted in C++ Gems, ed. Stanley Lippman.
39. T. L. Veldhuizen. Using C++ template metaprograms. *C++ Report*, 7(4):36–43, May 1995. Reprinted in C++ Gems, ed. Stanley Lippman.
40. T. L. Veldhuizen. Arrays in Blitz++. In *Proceedings of the 2nd International Scientific Computing in Object-Oriented Parallel Environments (ISCOPE'98)*, volume 1505 of *Lecture Notes in Computer Science*. Springer-Verlag, 1998.
41. P. Wadler and S. Blott. How to make ad-hoc polymorphism less ad-hoc. In *Symposium on Principles of Programming Languages*, pages 60–76. ACM, Jan. 1989.
42. J. Walter and M. Koch. *The Boost uBLAS Library*. Boost, 2002. www.boost.org/libs/numeric.
43. M. Wenzel. Using axiomatic type classes in Isabelle (manual), 1995. www.cl.cam.ac.uk/Research/HVG/Isabelle/docs.html.

Component-Based DSL Development

Thomas Cleenewerck

Programming Technology Lab, Vrije Universiteit Brussel
Pleinlaan 2, 1050 Brussel, Belgium
thomas.cleenewerck@vub.ac.be
http://prog.vub.ac.be/

Abstract. Domain specific languages (DSLs) have proven to be a very adequate mechanism to encapsulate and hide the complex implementation details of component-based software development. Since evolution lies at the heart of any software system the DSLs that were built around them must evolve as well. In this paper we identify important issues that cause a DSL implementation to be very rigid in which all phases are tightly coupled and highly dependent upon one another. To increase the poor evolvability of current day DSL development environments a new development environment Keyword based programming (KBP) is proposed where DSLs are built by using a language specification to compose and glue loosely coupled and independent language components (called keywords).

1 Introduction

Component-based software development has proven to be a significant improvement over traditional software development methods, and is well on its way to become the dominating software development paradigm. Nowadays, many software systems are assembled out of reusable and stand-alone parts. However, such composition of components is far from an easy task. It requires selecting the most appropriate components, solving data format and architectural mismatches, adapting to the application context, etc [SN99,LB00]. To encapsulate and hide these complex implementation details, domain specific languages (DSL) have been proposed [Sin96,SB97]. Unlike general purpose languages, DSLs are little languages that are expressive over a particular domain. Using DSLs, users can write higher-level, domain-specific descriptions (DSD) or programs using domain terminology. The code generator that produces an executable program out of the DSD contains the actual implementation details, e.g. the most appropriate components, their interface, the composition rules, the code to glue and adapt components, etc.

Unfortunately, developing DSLs is hard and costly. Therefore, their development is only feasible for mature enough domains. Such domains have been extensively analysed, knowledge about it is considered stable, and their components have been proven to be truly reusable and composable. As such, it is believed the DSL can be developed and will remain stable. Examples of those well-established domains are image manipulation, text processing, database interaction, etc. However, it takes a lot of time before a domain is considered stable (it took us more than a decade to reach a relative stable GUI building library [GS94]). And, even then we cannot avoid changes, since it is generally known that evolution lies at the heart of any software system [MM99]. As such, DSLs need to evolve, even when they are developed for mature enough domains.

Although current DSL development technologies have boosted DSL development, they only freed us from tedious tasks like lexing, parsing, pattern matching, manipulating and transforming an abstract syntax tree (AST). At this low level, a developer cannot help but implement a rigid DSL in which all phases are tightly coupled and highly dependent upon one another. As a consequence, the DSL becomes hard to evolve. To alleviate this problem, we need an advanced DSL development environment, that takes evolution into account and allows us to decouple the different phases and remove unnecessary dependencies. The purpose of this paper is therefore two-fold. First, we identify some important issues related to evolution in current-day DSL development environment. Second, we propose adequate solutions to these problems, that allow us to define DSLs that can be evolved in a more easy and straightforward way.

The paper is structured as follows. Section 2 explains the problem statement in more detail. Section 3 introduces the solution we propose to tackle the problems. Section 4 reflects on the proposed approach. Section 5 discusses related work, while section 6 presents our conclusions.

2 Problem Statement

In this section, we will identify the major problems developers are faced with when evolving a DSL. First, we will discuss the general architecture of a DSL development environment. Next, we introduce the running example, that we will use and gradually evolve throughout the paper to illustrate the problems.

2.1 General DSL Development Environment Architecture

In the general development environment architecture for DSLs consists of tree parts:

1. the grammar of the language, specifying the syntax and the set of correct sentences;
2. the library of components described in the target language;
3. the transformations that define the DSL's semantics

The grammar is usually defined using Backus-Naur-Form (BNF) [NAU60] or some of its variants. A parser processes a character stream according to the grammar and produces an abstract syntax tree (AST), representing the parse tree of a program written in the DSL. The transformations transform this AST to the AST of a program written in the target language, that uses the library of components. Usually the target language is a general purpose programming language (GPL), but it can also be a another DSL.

2.2 Running Example

Throughout this paper we will use a single simple example. In this example, a GUI library, written in Visual Basic, will be encapsulated with a DSL. Initially the GUI library contains only one component: a label. Because labels are widgets with a rather complex interface, we want to encapsulate the common usages of this interface in an easier-to-use DSL language. For the moment, the only expression/sentence that we can write in the DSL is the following:

```
label "title"
```

This program defines a label with caption `title`. As can be seen, a developer doesn't need to know which component he has to use, nor how it should be used, how it should be instantiated or how the caption should be set.

To implement this DSL, we need to specify its syntax and the transformations that translate the expression `label "title"` into code in some executable target language. The syntax is specified in the grammar which is often written in some BNF variant. The following two BNF-rules specify the syntax of the 'label' expression:

```
label        ::= "label" labelcaption
labelcaption ::= string
```

They state that the expression must start with the word '`label`', followed by a *labelcaption* sentence. The latter is defined in the second rule, which states that a labelcaption is simply a string.

Based on this grammer, the parser can generate an abstract syntax tree, which is manipulated by the transformations associated with the DSL. We will specify these transformations in pseudo syntax, that is close to existing transformation systems such as ASF+SDF and Khepera [vdBK02,FNP], to abstract away from irrelevant technical details.

Below is the transformation that translated the DSD expression `label "title"` to the target language. It will transform the expression into the equivalent two Visual Basic expression (lines 5 and 8):

```
(1)   transform label
(2)   define
(3)      A arg(1)
(4)   by VBLabel
(5)      Begin VB.Label
(6)         name = "mylabel"
(7)      End
(8)   by VBSub
(9)      Public Sub Form_Load()
(10)        mylabel.caption = %A%
(11)     End Sub
```

Conceptually, the transformation consists of 3 sections:

- The first section defines the node of the AST that can be transformed by the transformation. In this case, line 1 states that all label nodes of the AST tree will be transformed;
- The second section defines the variables that can be used in the target language structure to retrieve information out of the AST node. For example, line 3 defines the variable A and initializes it with the first element of the label node, i.e the string denoting the labelcaption.
- The last section defines the target language structure that will replace the matched node in the AST. In this example, lines 4 and 8 state that the structure of the target language which is generated is respectively a VB.Label and a VB.Form. Lines 5 to 7 and 9 to 11 generate the resulting expression written in the syntax of the target language.

In the following subsections the GUI library will be gradually extended with new features and components. Naturally the DSL will have to keep up and evolve as well. We will explain the problems we encounter.

2.3 Information Exchange

A transformation defines which elements of an AST tree it transforms. The `label` transformation from the previous section, for example, transforms the label node of the source AST. It uses the label caption (stored in variable A) to produce a VB.Label node of the target AST. The caption is stored in the label source AST node and is locally accessible. We call such information *local information*.

When developing more complex DSLs, transformations often need to access information that is not available locally, but is available elsewhere in the AST. Such information is called *non-local information*.

In what follows, we will gradually extend our running example. First, we will show that the evolvability of a DSL is hampered if information is hard-coded into the transformations. Second, we will argue that simply parameterizing the transformation, and passing the information in some way or other, does not resolve the evolvability problem.

Adding Support for Multilinguality, First Try. Suppose we want to extend our GUI library with support for multilinguality. This requires us to add a *translator* component, that translates strings to another language. Naturally, we need to adapt the DSL accordingly, so that it takes this new component into account. In a first stage, the translation will be triggered automatically, so the DSL's syntax is left unchanged: The DSL program itself thus also remains the same:

```
label "title"
```

Clearly, this example once again illustrates that DSLs abstract away from implementation details, which allows the component library to change without affecting DSL programs.

The translation extension requires the introduction of a new transformation, which is implemented as follows:

```
(1)   transform string in labelcaption
(2)   define
(3)      A arg(1)
(4)   by VBExpression
(5)      translator.translate(%A%, "dutch")
```

This transformation will be triggered for every string node inside a labelcaption node (line 1). The string value itself is stored in variable A (line 3). The result of the transformation is an expression (line 5) that calls the **translate** method on a translator component. This method takes two arguments: the string (caption of the label) that needs to be translated and the language of user interface.

When we apply these transformations to our domain-specific program, the following code is generated:

```
Begin VB.Label
     name = "mylabel"
End
Public Sub Form_Load()
       mylabel.caption =  translator.translate("title", "dutch")
End Sub
```

Although this code seems correct, we still identify two major problems with the definition of the above transformation. First of all, the language of the user interface is hard coded in the transformation, and can thus only be changed by changing the transformation. This seriously hampers its evolvability. Second, the translator component that is accessed through the variable **translator**, used in the resulting program. Clearly, this variable should be defined elsewhere in the program, but should be accessible from within the subroutine, according to the scoping rules of the Visual Basic programming language. The translate transformation cannot guarantee this however, since it does not know which code the other transformations generate.

Based on these two observations, we conclude that the evolvability of the DSL is constrained in two ways: the UI language needs to be defined outside the transformation, as is the expression used to access the translator component.

Adding Support for Multiple Languages, Second Try. To avoid hard coding the UI language into the transformation, we can allow the developer to specify the language elsewhere in the DSD. For example the UI language could be retrieved from a configuration file. The file has a standard property bag containing a list of key-value pairs. Such change requires us to extend the DSL with three new BNF rules. The first states that the 'language' expression must start with the **language** literal followed by two strings denoting the file and the property in the file, respectively. The file is a string (second rule) and the property is an identifier (third rule).

```
language ::= "language" file property
file     ::= string
property ::= id.
```

Our example DSL program now becomes:

```
language "config.ini" UILanguage
```

The translator transformation must now retrieve the UI language to be used out of the AST tree of the DSL program. We will refer to this kind of information as *non-local information* because it is located in another node of the AST tree than the node on which the transformation is applied. The code bellow illustrates the approach taken. In this transformation two new variables are defined (lines 3-4) where the variable C is initialized with the property denoting the UI language in the configuration file.

```
(1)   transform string in labelcaption
(2)   define
(3)      A arg(1)
(4)      C (getParent().getChild(language).getChild(Property))
(6)   by VBExpression
(7)      translator.translate(%A%, configfile.getProperty(%C%))
```

The code or expression that locates and retrieves information somewhere in the AST tree is still a stain on the evolvability of the DSL. Such code or such expression depends in most cases heavily of the particular structure of the AST tree. In the translate transformation the configuration file property containing the UI Language is retrieved by the expression on line (7). The expression contains very detailed information about the location of the information and how to traverse the AST to get to this location. Suppose we extend the GUI library with components to make the UI language configurable within the application itself. Because of the addition of new BNF rules and transformations to support this extension in the DSL, the UI language is contained in other AST nodes. Consequently the expression to locate and retrieve non-local information must changed. So whenever the DSL grammar changes and thus the AST tree, the whole set of transformations must be examined and checked to determine if they are affected and possible invalided because of the changes to the DSL.

Transformations are thus tightly coupled with the overall language structure, requiring permanent maintenance and therefore limiting the evolvability of the domain language.

2.4 Composition of Transformations

In the previous section, we have shown how the fetching of non-local information can tightly couple a transformation to the language specification. We will now show how the *scope of the transformation* also introduces tight coupling with the language specification and prevents the arbitrary composition of these transformations. As a result, transformations cannot be reused in different contexts of the language. Once again, this complicates DSL evolution.

The scope of a transformation is the definition of the regions in the AST tree which will be transformed. Consider for example the translate transformation, it translates only strings within (read, in the context of) labelcaptions. This is specified in the first line of the transformation:

```
(1)    transform string in labelcaption
(2)    ....
```

Hence the translate transformation will only be triggered in a labelcaption. When the DSL evolves the translate transformation must be revised and possibly changed against the new grammar. This forms a major obstacle for evolving the DSL and the free composition of transformations. To illustrate this problem, consider an extension of our GUI library with forms which are containers for labels. The DSL will be extended with the following bnf rule:

```
form        :- "form" id "title" string
```

The rule states that a form starts with the form-literal followed by its name, a title-literal and a string. Since the library offers support for multilinguality, the title of the form must be translated as well. Although the DSL already contains the translate transformation, it cannot be reused for this purpose, because its scope is defined and fixed in the transformation itself, and limited to the translation of label captions. Consequently the transformation is tightly coupled to the overall language context, in this case to the part where the labelcaption is a string. To be able to reuse the transformation and let evolve the domain language more easily, the scope of a transformation should be defined *outside* the transformation.

One could argue to just remove the scoping information out of the transformation (as is given below).

```
(1)    transform string
(2)    ...
```

The problem with this transformation is now that all strings of the DSL will be translated wherever they occur in the AST tree. These kind of uncontrolled transformations are certainly not what we want because they can seriously disrupt and corrupt the transformation process.

3   Proposed Solution: Keyword Based Programming

To render the implementation of a DSL language more evolvable the transformations need to be decoupled from the overall language structure and other transformations. Low coupling and high cohesion are the key factors to enable reusable and composable transformations which lead to a more evolvable DSL implementation. To increase the reuse of transformations we need to be able to encapsulate and parameterize them with non-local and other configuration information. To increase the composability of a transformation the scope of a transformation should be defined outside the transformation itself. Let's introduce the general ideas first by showing the stripped version of the translate transformation that is parameterized by the UI language to use (parameter C) and how to obtain the translator service (parameter B). To be able to use this translate transformation you must bound the parameter C to the UI language and bound the parameter B to an expression which returns a component with the translate service and specify the scope the transformation to the different contexts in which it used, e.g. within the label and the form.

```
(1)   transform string
(2)   define
(3)      A arg(1)
(4)      C
(5)      B
(6)   by VBExpression
(7)      %B%.translate(%A%, %C%)
```

The coupling of the translate transformation with the part of the DSL language that specifies the UI language, the component to translate the strings and the definition of the strings which need to be translated have been removed. When the DSL evolves all the transformations don't need to be scanned and checked for consistency with the overall language structure. Instead only the parameters to configure the transformations need to be checked. As you can see, the transformation doesn't contain any information about the DSL language *for which it was defined*. Actually we can now rephrase the last sentence into: the transformation doesn't contain any context information *in which it is used*.

We have developed the *Keyword Based Programming (KBP)* DSL development environment that implements the ideas stated above.

3.1 Architecture

KBP is a DSL development environment (DE) where DSL are built via the composition of language components. The architecture is quite different compared to the architecture of traditional DE and most other DSL DE's that are based on the former (cfr. section 5). The architecture of traditional DE is structured according to the functional layers in the system, e.g. lexing, parsing, generating, transforming and finally code generation. Functional decomposition results in rigid models where language features are scattered across the different functional layers. In contrast, the architecture of the KBP DE (figure 1) reflects a structural decomposition. We followed the component based approach where each component contains the necessary information to recognize and parse its syntax and contains its semantics to transform itself by producing a result. These components, called language components or keywords, are composed and glued together by a language specification that provides the necessary context information to the keywords. Let us discuss the two parts: *the language specification* and the language components called *keywords* in more detail in the next two sections.

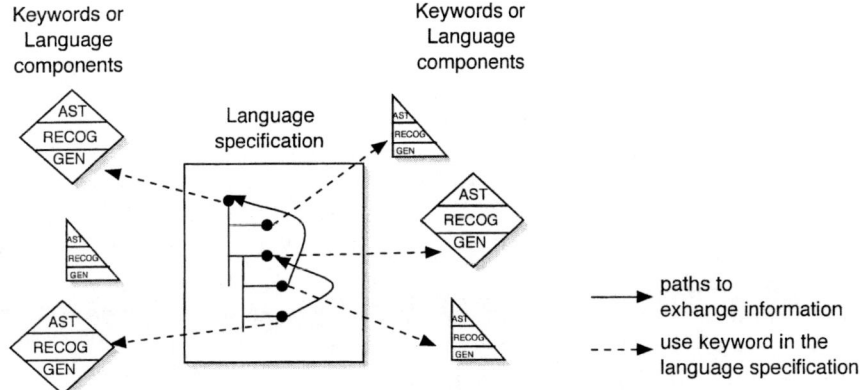

Fig. 1. General overview of the approach. In the middle of the figure the language specification is shown. It composes, glues and configures keywords or language components. A keyword consists of three parts: a definition of its AST node (AST), a recognition pattern describing its syntax (RECOG) and a generator defining its semantics (GEN). The full arrows between the various parts of the language specification symbolizes the paths between the the keywords to exchange non-local information.

3.2 Keywords

Each transformation of the previous section is part of a single keyword in KBP. Keywords are stand-alone components comprising a single fined-grained language feature. The term keyword may be somewhat confusing, but in KBP a keyword doesn't have to start with a reserved word. Keywords can be a Java for-statement, a delimiter e.g a dot or a semi-column, a block-statement, or can have no syntax of its-own like the translator-keyword (i.e. the translator transformation introduced in the previous section will be written as a keyword). A keyword definition consist of four parts: (1) a name, (2) a recognition pattern describing the syntax of the keyword, (3) the AST node that needs to be built during parsing to contain the parsed information and (4) a generator which implements the semantics. The code below is the skeleton of a keyword where: XXX is the name of the keyword (line 1), YYY is the name of the AST node (line 2) and ZZZ (line 5) is the type of the structure that will be returned when generating the keyword.

```
(1) keyword XXX {
(2)     ast { public class YYY { ... } }
(3)     recognition pattern { ... }
(4)     generator {
(5)         public ZZZ generate() {
(6)             return ... ;
(7)         }
(8)     }
(9) }
```

The recognition pattern describes the syntax of the language component. Parsing is done according to this pattern. The pattern is described using a syntax close to regular expressions. During parsing the recognized information is stored in the AST node (the second part of a keyword). The AST node is a java class definition augmented with some new constructs to facilitate the definition, e.g. `keyword c` (which will be further explained in an example). The last part of a keyword is called the generator. The generator is a Java method containing the code that produces a new target language structure, hereby using the information stored in the AST node defined by the keyword. Apart form the java constructs, additional constructs are provided here as well, e.g. `generate c`. In KBP terminology the actual transformation is called a generator because it only produces some results rather than transformations that besides producing, also change the AST tree.

Let's revise the first part of the language that we gradually evolved in the problem statement in KBP. We will not go in all the details of the environment because in this paper we focus on the dependencies inside the transformations. The code below is the definition of the label keyword. Before we go into the details of definition, a keyword can be parameterized with other keywords through keyword parameters defined in the AST, recognition pattern and generator. The label keyword has one parameter `c` which is the caption of the label. To avoid any confusion the expression 'keyword c' is not the definition of the 'c' keyword, but is a formal parameter. In the language specification (which will be introduced later on) keywords can be bound to it.

Let's walk over the definition of the label-keyword step by step. The recognition pattern states that in a DSD one should write the word `label` first followed by an expression that matches the recognition pattern of the keyword in the parameter c. During parsing the AST node (defined right above the recognition pattern) will contain a reference to the AST node defined by the keyword in the parameter c. In the last part of the keyword the generator is defined. The keyword returns a object of type `VB.Label`. First the keyword in the parameter c is generated, which can trigger the generation of a chain of keywords. Its result is stored in the variable A. Note that the variable has type `VB.Expression`. This implies only that the *result* of the generation of the `keyword c` must be a Visual Basic expression. Afterwards a new typed target language structure (`#VB.Label` and `#VB.Sub`) is created which will be returned as the result of the keyword. The target structures that are returned are AST nodes of the target language. To avoid the need to create and initialize them manually e.g.

```
VB.ASTLabel lab = new VB.ASTLabel();
lab.name = "mylabel"
VB.ASTSub sub = new VB.ASTSub();
sub.modifiers.add(Modifiers.PUBLIC);
sub.name="Form_Load";
sub.statements = ...
```

A new construct is added of the form #Language.Type{ ... }. This will create an appropriate AST node of type Type, and parse the content between the curly brackets. During parsing the AST node will be probably initialized. Expressions of the form '%=XXX%' inside the target language structure denote variables that are parameterizing the target language structure, the variables are substituted in to the structure. In the label keyword the expression '%=A%' means that the content of the variable A will be substituted by the result of the generation of the keyword inside the parameter c. You may wonder why the subroutine is nested within the Label. The generator returns a user interface control. In Visual Basic definition of the user interface and the accompanying code is seperated, just like in Java the definition of datamembers and methods is seperated in a class definition. The two AST nodes label and sub may thus not be returned together for example in a single set. To solve this problem, other target structures (AST nodes of the target language) can be hooked to the actual target structure that is returned. The former is called a non-local target structure. The hooking is achieved by nesting the two structures.

```
keyword label {
    ast { public class AST { keyword c; } }
    recognition pattern { ("label", keyword c) }
    generator {
        public VB.Label generate() {
            VB.Expression A = generate c;
            return #VB.Label{
                Begin VB.Label
                    name = "mylabel"
                End
                #VB.Sub{
                    Public Sub Form_Load()
                        mylabel.caption = %=A%
                    End Sub
                }
            };
        }
    }
}
```

3.3 Language Specification

The language specification *glues* the keywords together and *provides information about the overall structure of the language* to the keywords. Below the language specification (LS) for our initial toy language. LS are written in XML syntax. It composes two keywords: a string and a label so that the caption of the label is a string. The `keyword` tag introduces a keyword into the language. Inside this tag other tags can be written to configure the keyword, e.g. the `param` tag. The first line introduces the label keyword (defined above). It has one parameter c in which the `string` keyword is put. This is how the formal parameter c defined in the definition of the `label` keyword gets bound to the `string` keyword.

```
<keyword type="label">
<param name="c">
      <keyword type="string"/>
</param>
</keyword>
```

In KBP (like most other environments) a language implementation consists of two parts: a parser that constructs the AST tree from the DSL program and a transformer to translate this tree to the AST tree of the desired program written in the target language. The KBP development environment generates a parser and a transformer out of the language specification. The parser is built by composing the recognition patterns of the keywords according to the language specification. The transformer is built likewise using the generators of the keywords. After parsing, the transformation is initiated by triggering the generator belonging to the keyword of the toplevel AST node of the AST tree.

In the next two subsections we will discuss the parameterization mechanism of keywords, how these parameters can get values in the language specification and how keywords are scoped through the language specification.

3.4 Information Exchange

The information non-local to a transformation (e.g. the UI language of the translate-transformation) is supplied via the language specification. This information is thus parameterizable, hereby reducing coupling of the keyword with the overall language structure.

To illustrate how in KBP non-local information is obtained we will likewise extend the current language specification with a new `translate` keyword just like we did in the problem statement. The `translate` keyword is parameterized with a keyword-parameter that contains the `string` keyword, and a value to provide the UI language. The latter can be provided to the keywords by means of the value-tag (see the example below). Using this mechanism we are free to determine how to provide the non-local information, the form and the location of the non-local information. One is free to chose how the information can be provided, e.g. a location in the AST tree or a fixed value `<value ...> "english"`

</value> etc. The form denotes which keywords hold the information needed. The location is the location that the information containing keyword(s) have in the grammar.

To locate and retrieve information from other parts of the AST tree a path can be defined between two nodes. In KBP every keyword is a Document Object Model [Whi02] (DOM) element and the AST is thus a DOM tree. This gives us the advantage of being able to reuse many algorithms already available in the java programming language api. One of them was *xpath* [AB02]. With xpath expressions, connections between two or more nodes can be easily established (symbolised by the arrows in figure 1).

To avoid the problems caused by coupling of DSL components to a specific DSL language in which they are used, we specify where the context-information of the component is located with *structure shy paths* [Lie96], [LPS97]. These paths are more robust to changes in the DSL, because they do not contain detailed information about the actual path that needs to be followed to reach the desired AST node. It turns out that xpaths can be used to specify structure shy paths. For example the path //XXX denotes a grand child XXX regardless of the position of the child in the current subtree. These paths are more robust to changes in the specification language than fully specified paths; and thus increase the evolvability of the domain specific language.

```
<keyword type="label">
<param name="c">
        <keyword type="translate">
        <param name="value">
                <keyword type="string"/>
        </param>
        <value name="language" type="String">
                execute("/ancestor::XXX//Language/Property")
        </value>
        <value name="translator" type="String">
                "translator"
        </value>
        </keyword>
</param>
</keyword>
```

The above code shows the language specification for the DSL of the component library that supports multilinguality. The `translate` keyword is put inside the c parameter of the label and encapsulates the `string` keyword. The `translate` keyword is defined below. The information which is provided through the value-tags in the language specification are accessible within the transformation with getter-methods. In the example, the values in the value-tags with the name `language` and `translator` accessible via respectively the `getTranslator()` method and the `getLanguage()` method. Inside the value tag a path `/ancestor ::XXX//Language/Property` to another AST node is executed via the `execute` method. The first part of the path `/ancestor::XXX` locates an ancestor AST node with the name XXX. The second part of the path //Language searches for a Language AST child node somewhere located in the XXX AST node. And finally the third part of the path /Property retrieves the direct Property AST child node of the Language AST node.

In this example no information needs to be passed from the keyword to the language specification, but there is support for it. Making two-way communication possible.

```
keyword translate {
    ast { public class AST { keyword value; } }
    recognition pattern { keyword value }
    generator {
        public VB.Label generate() {
            Object A = generate value;
            return #VB.Expression{
                %=getTranslator()%.translate(
                    %=A%,
                    configfile.getProperty(%=getLanguage()%))
        }
    }
}
```

With this approach the non-local information for a transformation is no longer hard-coded in the transformation itself but is supplied via the language specification. This information is thus parameterizable, and reducing coupling of the keyword with the overall language structure. Furthermore, the code to retrieve and locate information out of the AST defined in the language specification is structure shy, making this code more robust to changes in the language.

3.5 Composition of Transformations

In the previous section we've shown that keywords can be parameterized with other keywords and with configuration information. Although the composability is already greatly improved we identified another important issue concerning the composability of the transformation being the scope of a transformation.

The scope of a transformation is the definition of the regions in the AST tree which will be transformed by the transformation. In KBP the scope of a keyword is defined by its position in the language specification. This is illustrated with the `translate` keyword whose scope is defined through the wrapping around the `string` keyword and the placement inside the `label` keyword (cfr. the language specification above). Therefore the transformation in translate keyword doesn't need to specify where in the source AST tree it must be applied, rendering the keyword more independent and the domain language more evolvable.

Lets revise the extension of the GUI library and DSL from the problem statement to illustrate how the definition of the scope of transformations in KBP increases the evolvability of the DSL. In the problem statement the language has been further extended to support forms i.e. containers for labels. The titles of the forms must also be translated. The extension in KBP is pretty straightforward. The form can be easily added to the language and thereby reusing the both parts of the translate keyword, e.g. the bnf rule and the transformation respectively the recognition pattern and the generator. Because the scope of a keyword is defined in the language specification and there is no further coupling between the translate keyword and overall language structure, the translate keyword could be easily reused. Therefore, in contrast with the situation in the problem section, only the language specification must be changed.

Below is the part of the language specification to support multilingual forms. Recall that a form has a name and a title. In KBP the form will thus have three parameters name, title and body. The title parameter has been bound to the translate keyword which encapsulates the string keyword. The name parameter has been bound to an identifier. The body parameter is bound to the label keyword which has been defined earlier.

```
<keyword type="form">
<param name="title">
     <keyword type="translate">
     <param name="value">
          <keyword type="string">
     </param>
     <value name="language" type="String">
          execute("/ancestor::XXX//Language/Property")
     </value>
     <value name="translator" type="String"> "translator" </value>
     </keyword>
</param>
<param name="name"> <keyword type="ID"/> </param>
<param name="body">
     <keyword type="Label">
     ...
     </keyword>
</param>
</keyword>
```

Recall that the translate keyword must be parameterized with the UI language . The code to retrieve the UI language from the AST was defined using structure shy paths. When the path should become invalid in the context of a form the translate keyword can be easily reused and be redefined, as is presented in the language specification above. When the path remains valid in the context of a form, then the translate keyword must not be redefined but can be referenced a such. This is shown in the code below where the keyword in the parameter title points to the keyword with id translatedstring. In either case the DSL is easily evolvable and the translate keyword is reusable.

```xml
<keyword type="form">
<param name="title">
        <keyword refid="translatedstring"> </keyword>
</param>
...
</keyword>
```

The following illustrates the usages of the form extension in a DSL program.

```
form form1 title "sample form" {
        label "title"
}
```

The definition of the `form` keyword is given below. The recognition pattern and the AST node definition are obvious. The generator creates a form AST node f and return this as its result. First the keywords in the parameters `name`, `title` and `body` are generated. A Form definition contains two parts: a UI part and some code. The name, title and the body are parameterizing the forms definition consisting of a form UI definition and a subroutine Form_Load. The construction and parsing of the AST form node is done by the expression #VB.Form{ ... }). The `label` keyword (when bound to the body parameter through the language specification) returns a label AST node which contains a subroutine AST node. The result is stored in the variable C. The content of the variable is inserted in the UI part of the form, a part where only user interface controls may be inserted. Therefore the subroutine AST node is automatically extracted form the label AST node and placed in the appropiate syntactical area.

```
keyword form {
    ast { public AST {
            keyword name;
            keyword title;
            keyword body;    }
    }
    recognition pattern {
        ("form", keyword name, "title",
         keyword title, "{", keyword body, "}" )
    }
    generator {
        public VB.Form generate() {
            String A = generate name;
            String B = generate title;
            Object C = generate body;
            return #VB.Form{
                Begin Form
                    name = %=A%
                    %=C%
                End Form
```

```
            Public Sub Form_Load()
                %=A%.title = %=B%
            End Sub
        };
      }
    }
}
```

4 Discussion

The keywords in KBP are stand-alone, more reusable and composable language components. Stand-alone because in their definition they contain their syntax representation, AST node to hold information and a generator to implement its effect. Due to the parameterization of keywords with information that is non-local to them keywords are reusable in the sense that when the language in which they are used evolves they remain usable as such. Keywords are easily composable because they are parameterizable with other keywords and their scope is defined through the language specification. Changing the language involves only changing the composition and parameterization of the keywords in the langauge specification.

The DSL is implemented via a language specification that configures, composes and glues the form, label and translate keywords. The following code is an example program written in the DSL:

```
language "config.ini" UILanguage
form form1 title "sample form" {
        label "title"
}
```

which gets translated to

```
Begin Form
     name = "form1"
     Begin VB.Label
          name = "mylabel"
     End
End Form
Public Sub Form_Load()
     form1.title = translator.translate("sample form",
                          configfile.getProperty("UILanguage"))
     mylabel.caption = translator.translate("title",
                          configfile.getProperty("UILanguage"))
End Sub
```

A first prototype of KBP has been implemented in Java supporting all the features and properties introduced in this paper. In addition to those, more experimental features concerning the integration of the results produced by each keyword into a AST, providing defaults values to keywords by reusing other keywords etc. are included. Various DSLs have been implemented, e.g. a metacircular implementation of the system, tuple calculus, small business administration programs, etc. ranging from 10 to 45 keywords.

5 Related Work

The architecture of KBP is quite similar to the one of intentional programming [Sim96], [Sim95] and delegating compiler objects (DCO's) [Bos97]. In both environments DSLs are built out of the composition of language components. However, the granularity of DCO's is more corse grained then keywords. DCO's are actually small conventional compilers which contain lexers, parsers, transformers etc.

The language specification mechanism in KBP is unique. Only the Jakarta Tool Suite (JTS) [BLS98] and DCO's use BNF as a, somewhat limited composition mechanism since it does not allow to configure the parameters of the transformations. This language specification is used to compose, trigger and scope the transformations. Environments without this use some sort of other scheduling and scoping mechanism. The transformations in ASF+SDF Meta-Environment [vdBK02] and XSLT [Cla99] define within themselves which elements of the AST they can transform, rendering them tightly coupled, highly dependent and not reusable in other parts of the language. In intentional programming dependencies can be defined to further aid the scheduling mechanism. Jargons [NJ97], [NAOP99] do not have a language specification, nor sheduling, nor scoping mechanism. A transformation is linked to a syntax description and is triggered where the user has used this syntax.

In each development environment mentioned above there is no explicit support for parameterizing the transformations. In most cases some work-around is possible because either the transformations are written in a GPL allowing proprietary solutions, or either some other feature can be bent to serve for this purpose.

Only in XSLT non-local information between the transformations or language components can be easily exchanged via structure shy navigation expressions. Both KBP and XSLT use XPaths to accomplish this. But due to lack of parameterization in XSLT these expressions are hard coded in the transformations themselves. Intentional programming and JTS does offer some navigation primitives but the resulting code contains detailed information about the structure of the AST limiting severely the evolvability of the DSL language. Retrieving non-local information is not supported in Jargons and in the ASF+SDF environment.

6 Conclusion

Domain specific languages are an excellent mechanism to encapsulate a library of components and hide the complexity of component composition from the library user. However as component libraries evolve, so must their DSLs, which represents an unacceptable cost. In this paper we introduced keyword-based programming as a technology to develop more easily evolvable domain specific languages. Using this technology, developing DSLs for immature libraries has become more feasible.

Keyword-based programming extracts these parts that cause the entanglement from the transformations with the overall language structure and other transformations and introduces a separate language specification which glues the language implementation 'keywords' together. This separation allows to write language features (keywords) that are not tangled with context, non-local and scope information by allowing them to parameterized with configuration information and other keywords. Instead, these are provided by the language specification. The capabilities of KBP allow a developer to implement a DSL which is more easy to evolve and, as such, is more suitable to write a DSL for continuously evolving component libraries.

Structure shy paths are used to exchange information between the various parts of the language (the keywords) allowing the language specification to evolve without invalidating those paths.

Acknowledgements

I would like to thank Johan Brichau and Tom Tourwe for comments on this paper.

References

[AB02]   Don Chamberlin Mary F. Fernandez Michael Kay Jonathan Robie Jërôme Siméon Anders Berglund, Scott Boag. Xml path language (xpath) 2.0 w3c working draft 15 november 2002, 2002.
[BLS98]   Don Batory, Bernie Lofaso, and Yannis Smaragdakis. JTS: tools for implementing domain-specific languages. In *Proceedings Fifth International Conference on Software Reuse*, pages 143–153, Victoria, BC, Canada, 2–5 1998. IEEE.
[Bos97]   Jan Bosch. Delegating compiler objects: Modularity and reusability in language engineering. *Nordic Journal of Computing*, 4(1):66–92, Spring 1997.
[BST+94] D. Batory, V. Singhal, J. Thomas, S. Dasari, B. Geraci, and M. Sirkin. The genvoca model of software system generators. In *IEEE Software*, pages 89–94, September 1994.
[Cla99]   James Clark. Xsl transformations (xslt) version 1.0 w3c recommendation 16 november 1999, 1999.
[Fal01]   David C. Fallside. Xml schema part 0: Primer w3c recommendation, 2 may 2001, 2001.
[FNP]   Rickard E. Faith, Lars S. Nyland, and Jan F. Prins. KHEPERA: A system for rapid implementation of domain specific languages. pages 243–256.
[GS94]   S. Wingo G. Shepherd. *MFC Internals: Inside the MFC Architecture.* Addison-Wesley, 1994.

[JBP89] J.Heering J.A. Bergstra and P.Klint. Algebraic specification. *ACM Press/Addison-Wesley*, 1989.

[LB00] M. Glandrup M. Aksit L. Bergmans, B. Tekinerdogan. On composing separated concerns, composability and composition anomalies. In *ACM OOPSLA '2000 workshop on Advanced Separation of Concerns, Minneapolis*, October 2000.

[Lie96] K. J. Lieberherr. *Adaptive Object-Oriented Software: The Demeter Method with Propagation Patterns*. PWS Publishing Company, 1996.

[LPS97] K. Lieberherr and B. Patt-Shamir. Traversals of object structures: Specification and efficient implementation, 1997.

[MM99] Jan Bosch Michael Mattsson. Experience paper: Observations on the evolution of an industrial oo framework. *ICSM*, pages 139–145, 1999.

[NAOP99] Lloyd H. Nakatani, Mark A. Ardis, Robert G. Olsen, and Paul M. Pontrelli. Jargons for domain engineering. In *Domain-Specific Languages*, pages 15–24, 1999.

[NAU60] Peter NAUR. Revised report on the algorithmic language algol 60. *Communications of the ACM*, 3(5):299–314, May 1960.

[NJ97] L. Nakatani and M. Jones. Jargons and infocentrism. In *First ACM SIGPLAN Workshop on Domain-Specific Languages*, pages 59–74, 1997.

[SB97] Yannis Smaragdakis and Don Batory. DiSTiL: A transformation library for data structures. In *Domain-Specific Languages (DSL) Conference*, pages 257–270, 1997.

[Sim95] C. Simonyi. The death of computer languages, the birth of intentional programming, 1995.

[Sim96] C. Simonyi. Intentional programming - innovation in the legacy age, 1996.

[Sin96] Vivek P. Singhal. *A Programming Language for Writing Domain-Specific Software System Generators*. PhD thesis, 1996.

[SN99] Jean-Guy Schneider and Oscar Nierstrasz. Components, scripts and glue. In Leonor Barroca, Jon Hall, and Patrick Hall, editors, *Software Architectures - Advances and Applications*, pages 13–25. Springer-Verlag, 1999.

[TB00] C. M. Sperberg-McQueen Eve Maler Tim Bray, Jean Paoli. Extensible markup language (xml) 1.0 (second edition) w3c recommendation 6 october 2000, 2000.

[vdBK02] M.G.J. van den Brand and P. Klint. *ASF+SDF Meta-Environment User Manual*. Centrum voor Wiskunde en Informatica (CWI), Kruislaan 413, 1098 SJ Amsterdam, The Netherlands, July 2002.

[vDKV00] Arie van Deursen, Paul Klint, and Joost Visser. Domain-specific languages: An annotated bibliography. *SIGPLAN Notices*, 35(6):26–36, 2000.

[Vis01] Eelco Visser. Stratego: A language for program transformation based on rewriting strategies. *Lecture Notes in Computer Science*, 2051:357–??, 2001.

[Whi02] Ray Whitmer. Document object model (dom) level 3 xpath specification w3c working draft 28 march 2002, 2002.

Towards a More Piece-ful World
Invited Talk

Peri Tarr

IBM Thomas J. Watson Research Center
Yorktown Heights, NY 10598, USA
tarr@watson.ibm.com

Abstract. We envision a world in which we can develop, synthesize, adapt, integrate, and evolve software based on high-quality, perpetually flexible pieces. New pieces may be produced by generation, adaptation of existing pieces, or integration of pieces, and this process of "pieceware" engineering continues–statically or dynamically–until a piece with the desired capabilities and properties is synthesized. The pieces themselves may comprise fragments of requirements, models, architectures, patterns, designs, code, tests, and/or any other relevant software artifacts. Many technologies are critical to achieving pieceware engineering; some have been developed in this community and elsewhere, and others are still required.

Despite the progress in this field, we have encountered two major problems along the way towards realizing the pieceware vision. First, what paradigms, technologies, and methodologies are required to enable full-lifecycle pieceware engineering? Second, how do we provide the necessary tool support?

Our inability to address the second problem has seriously compromised our ability to address the first. The development of tools to realize different pieceware engineering approaches represents a huge investment of time and effort. This is largely because each one must be built from scratch or from low-level abstractions. Consequently, the tools themselves represent isolated point solutions, and rarely have any ability to interoperate or be integrated. This has impeded the development and validation of full-lifecycle pieceware engineering paradigms, technologies, and methodologies.

The Concern Manipulation Environment (CME) represents the first effort to define an open, extensible set of components and abstractions to promote the rapid development and integration of tools that support pieceware engineering. The initial focus is on tools for aspect-oriented software development (AOSD), an emerging technology area that is key to pieceware engineering. This talk describes the pieceware engineering vision, the major issues to be addressed, and the technologies required to achieve it. It then discusses how the CME helps to address many of these issues–illustrated by the use of the CME to enable the evolution of a real-world system–and how it can be leveraged by researchers and developers to produce, experiment with, validate, and integrate new pieceware techologies and paradigms. Finally, we identify some of the key challenges remaining to achieve the vision of pieceware engineering.

References

1. Concern manipulation environment. Web site http://www.research.ibm.com/cme.
2. Peri Tarr, Harold Ossher, William Harrison, and Stanley M. Sutton Jr. N degrees of separation: Multi-dimensional separation of concerns. In *Proceedings of the 21st International Conference on Software Engineering*, May 1999.

A Generative Approach to Framework Instantiation

Vaclav Cechticky[1], Philippe Chevalley[2],
Alessandro Pasetti[3], and Walter Schaufelberger[1]

[1] Institut für Automatik, ETH-Zürich, Physikstr. 3, CH-8092, Zürich, Switzerland
{cechti,ws}@control.ee.ethz.ch
[2] European Space Agency, ESTEC, PO Box 299, 2200 AG Noordwijk, The Netherlands
philippe.chevalley@esa.int
[3] P&P Software, Peter-Thumb Str. 46, D-78464, Germany
pasetti@pnp-software.com

Abstract. This paper describes the *OBS Instantiation Environment*, which demonstrates a generative approach to automating the instantiation process of a component-based framework. The process is automated in the sense that designers configure and assemble the framework components using intuitive visual operations in a GUI-based environment. Their configuration actions are then used to automatically generate the framework instantiation code. Generative techniques for framework instantiation are not new but tend to rely on domain-specific languages or on bespoke specification encoding and compilation techniques. Though effective and powerful, they are comparatively complex and present a high barrier to entry for general users. The distinctive feature of the approach proposed here is instead its simplicity and its reliance on mainstream technology and tools.

1 Introduction

This paper describes the *On Board Software (OBS) Instantiation Environment*, which demonstrates a generative approach to automating the instantiation process of a component-based framework. A software framework is the heart of a product family. It offers the assets from which the applications in the product family are built. In earlier work [1], we conceptualised a software framework as an artefact consisting of three types of constructs: a set of *domain-specific design patterns*, a set of *abstract interfaces* and a set of *concrete components*. The design patterns define the architectural solutions to the design problems arising in the framework domain. The abstract interfaces define the adaptation points where the generic framework architecture is adapted to match the requirements of specific applications. The concrete components support the instantiation of the design patterns and provide default implementations for the framework abstract interfaces.

The process whereby an application is created by specializing a framework is called *framework instantiation*. It takes place in two steps: (1) the application-specific components required by the application are constructed. Their construction is guided and constrained by the need to adhere to the framework design patterns and to implement the framework interfaces; (2) the application-specific components and the framework components are configured and composed together to construct the final application. The instantiation approach proposed in this paper only covers the second step. The paper therefore assumes that the framework provides all the components required to instantiate the target application. This assumption is not unrealistic: a mature framework will normally offer a sufficient complement of default components implementing all or nearly all functionalities required by applications in its domain. This assumption would also typically be satisfied in embedded domains where there is a need to construct several variants of the same basic product. These variants are built from the same pool of components but differ from each other because their components are configured differently.

The problem of framework instantiation has been the object of research for several years. Older solutions [16,17] relied on putting together a body of rules (also known as "recipes") to aid the developer in using the framework. More recent versions of this approach use agents to assist the framework instantiation process [7] but most current work looks at generative techniques [3] as a means to automate the framework instantiation process [11,12,14,20]. Such techniques rely on domain-specific languages (DSL) to specify the target application. Although effective and powerful, these techniques tend to be comparatively complex and to present a high barrier to entry for general users. The distinctive feature of the approach proposed here is instead its simplicity and its reliance on mainstream technology and tools that have the potential of bringing it within the reach of non-specialist users.

The downside of our approach is a certain lack of generality: the OBS Instantiation Environment described in this paper is targeted at one particular framework. The paper however identifies one design pattern and several guidelines that would facilitate its porting to other frameworks. The justification for this way of proceeding is a belief that, given the wide variety of frameworks and the lack of standardization at framework level, there is more practical value in providing a blueprint for the development of a simple, though framework-specific, instantiation environment than there is in constructing a general-purpose, but complex, instantiation environment for a generic framework.

The paper is organized as follows. The next section describes the motivation behind our work. Sections 3 to 6 discuss various aspects of our approach. Section 7 describes its use on a concrete case study. Section 8 addresses the issue of the generalization to other frameworks and section 9 concludes the paper.

The work described here was funded by the European Space Agency under research contract 15753/02/NL/LvH. All its results (including source code) are publicly available through a project web site[1].

2 Background and Motivation

We recently developed the *Attitude and Orbit Control System (AOCS) Framework* [1,2] as a prototype object-oriented software framework for satellite and other embedded control systems. The AOCS Framework exists in three versions: two research prototype versions[2] in C++ and Java and one industrial quality version in C++ commercialized by P&P Software GmbH. The work described here refers to the Java version. Porting to the industrial-quality version may follow in the near future.

---

[1] Currently located at: http://control.ee.ethz.ch/~pasetti/AutomatedFrameworkInstantiation/
[2] Freely available from: http://control.ee.ethz.ch/~pasetti/RealTimeJavaFramework/

The instantiation process for the AOCS Framework consists of a long sequence of instructions that configure the framework components and compose them together. Coding and testing this sequence is a conceptually simple but tedious and error-prone task. We have used abstract factories [5] to simplify the instantiation task but found the simplification thus achieved rather modest. A desire to automate this process was the first motivation for the development of the OBS Instantiation Environment.

The second motivation arises from the target domain of the AOCS Framework, namely embedded control systems. Control engineers have become accustomed to designing their systems in environments like Matlab® that provide easy-to-use GUI-based tools to define the control algorithms and to model and simulate their behaviour together with the dynamics of the system within which they are embedded. The Matlab suite includes facilities to automatically generate code implementing the algorithms defined by the designer. The Matlab approach to control system has gained immense popularity in the control community not least because it holds the promise to allow the software to be directly generated from a model of the control system.

In reality, this promise can only be partially kept. Matlab-like tools excel at modelling control algorithms but the software of a modern control system (see figure 1) is dominated by heterogeneous functions like unit management, command processing, housekeeping data generation, failure detection, failure recovery, and other functions for which Matlab provides no specific abstractions and which it is consequently unable to model effectively. More generally, no single commercial tool offers sufficient abstractions to model all aspects of a complex control system.

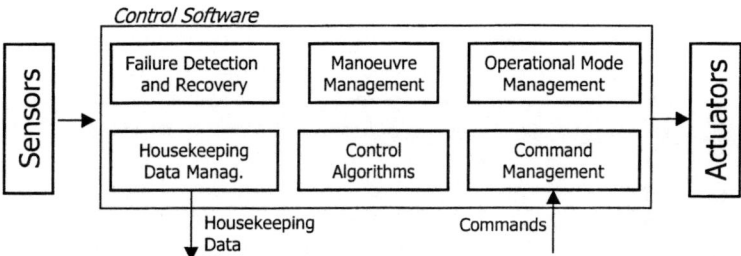

Fig. 1. Structure of typical control software

In our view, a software framework is ideally suited to define the overall architecture for a control application and to provide an umbrella under which components coming from commercial autocoding tools (suitably wrapped) can be combined with each other and with components coming from other sources to build the final application. We therefore see a software framework as complementary to a Matlab-based approach. However, we appreciate that the appeal of the latter largely lies in its GUI-oriented user interface and in the tacit premise that this will allow the control software to be developed directly by the control engineer with only minimal assistance from a software engineer. We believe that a framework-based approach will only be accepted in this community if it can be packaged in a similar way. This is precisely what we are trying to offer with the OBS Instantiation Environment.

Figure 2 shows how the OBS Instantiation Environment fits within the software development process we envisage for a control application. The final application is built by configuring and assembling components. A framework defines the architecture within which they are embedded and assembled and provides a set of default components. Other components are manually coded on ad hoc basis while still others come from wrapping code automatically generated by tools like Matlab. The OBS Instantiation Environment provides the facilities for configuring and linking together these components and for generating the corresponding instantiation code.

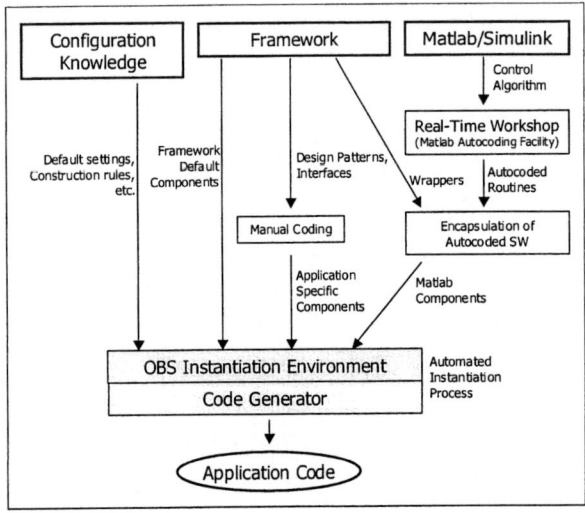

Fig. 2. Development process for embedded control software

Although our work concentrates on control systems, the situation in other domains is similar. Organizations increasingly build their applications by configuring and composing pre-defined blocks [3, 12]. Since these blocks are likely to come from different sources, a framework is required to provide the architectural skeleton within which they can be embedded. The problem then inevitably arises of how the framework is to be instantiated. In many embedded domains, this problem is exacerbated by the fact that the framework is used to build one-of-a-kind applications, which are specified by application engineers who are not software specialists and who therefore are not able or willing to take responsibility for a code-based instantiation process. Since the applications are unique, delegating responsibility for the instantiation process to a group of software specialists has a significant impact on total development costs. There is therefore a need to create an instantiation environment that is sufficiently user-friendly to allow the application specialists to take charge of the development of their software. The OBS Instantiation Environment provides a blueprint of how this objective can be achieved using simple and inexpensive technology.

3 Proposed Instantiation Approach

Three requirements can be inferred from the discussion above for a framework instantiation environment:

1. The environment should be based on mainstream technology. This is the only way to keep its cost low which is in turn essential to its practical adoption.
2. The environment should be easy to use. More specifically, whereas the job of instantiating a framework is traditionally left to a software specialist – and often to a specialist of the framework to be instantiated – the environment should make it possible for this task to be done by end-users. Hence, the environment should be seen as an enabling tool that empowers non-specialist end-users to take direct control of the development of their software.
3. The environment should allow the behaviour of the application under construction to be simulated. The success of environments like Matlab also depends on the fact that they let designers test their design by executing a (possibly incomplete) implementation in order to check its behaviour. An instantiation environment for a framework should offer similar simulation facilities.

The approach taken in the OBS Instantiation Environment to satisfying the above requirements is based on generative programming techniques [3]. Generally speaking, five steps are necessary to develop a generative programming environment for applications within a certain domain:

1. Definition of a formalism for specifying applications in the domain,
2. Definition of a common architecture for applications in the domain,
3. Development of configurable and customizable components to support implementation of a domain architecture,
4. Definition of a formalism to describe the configuration and customization of the components,
5. Development of a code generator to automatically transform an application specification into a domain configuration and to generate a concrete application from the domain configuration.

Step 2 is essentially equivalent to the development of a software framework for the target domain. Some of the components mentioned in step 3 may also be provided by the framework as encapsulation of recurring functionalities in the domain. In other cases, the framework will simply provide wrappers for code coming from other sources (legacy code, automatically generated code, etc). For the sake of simplicity, in this paper we will refer to all these components as *framework components*. This paper concentrates on steps 4 and 5, which are those covered by the OBS Instantiation Environment. Step 1 is discussed in section 6. The provision of simulation facilities is discussed in section 5.

The straightforward way to implement the above five steps is to define a domain-specific language through which the application specification can be expressed, and then to build a compiler that allows these specifications to be translated into source code. This solution, by itself, does not satisfy any of our requirements. The approach we chose is instead based on developing an *environment* where users can express their requirements in an informal manner through graphical means with the aid of context-specific information provided by the environment itself. The environment is then responsible for translating the requirements implicitly formulated by the user into a formal description of the target application and for translating (compiling) this description into an instantiation sequence. The derivation of the application is still done in two steps - formal specification of the target application and its compilation - but these steps are now hidden from the user who only interacts with a user-friendly environment.

Figure 3 shows how our solution is implemented. The figure is annotated with the key technologies behind our implementations. These are: XML for encoding information, XSLT programs for code generation, and Java bean builders for the component composition environment. All three technologies are widely known and well supported thus satisfying our first requirement.

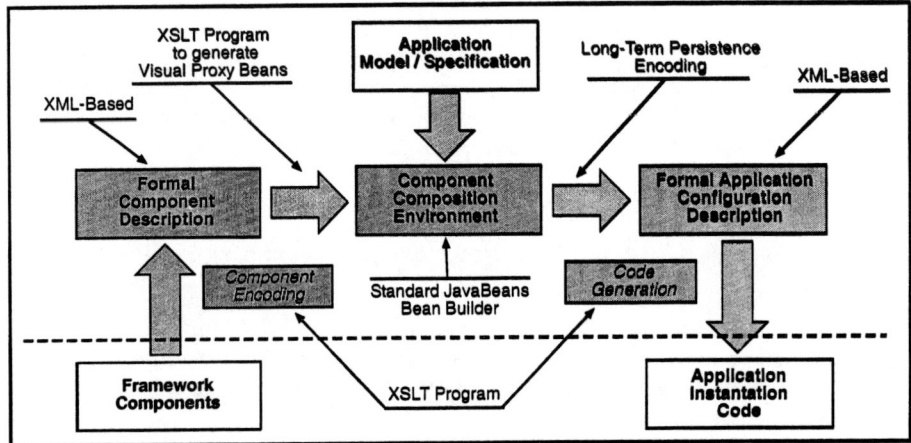

Fig. 3. Generative Approach to Framework instantiation

We use XML to decouple the way the framework components are implemented from the way they are configured (dashed line in the figure). XML grammars are defined to describe the framework components (or, more precisely, those of their characteristics that are relevant to the instantiation process) and to describe the application configuration defined by the user in the component composition environment.

Having selected XML as the encoding standard, we found it natural to use XSLT [4] to perform the code generation process. XSLT is a functional programming language that was developed to transform XML documents into other XML documents. It can more generally be used to manipulate XML-encoded data and to generate from them other textual documents. As already noted by other authors [21] XSLT programs can also act as simple, powerful, and easy-to-use code generators.

We use XSLT programs for two purposes. The designer defines the application configuration in the *component composition environment*. At the end of the configuration process, the selected application configuration is encoded in an XML document. An XSLT program is used to process it and to generate from it the application instantiation code (*code generation process*). This code is ready to be linked with the framework components to form the final application executable.

The second use of XSLT is less obvious. It stems from our choice of component composition technology. The component composition environment is the part of the framework instantiation environment where users configure and assemble the framework components. It represents the interface between the users and the instantiation environment. In order to satisfy our second requirement, it should be GUI-based. Its development is potentially one of the most complex and most expensive parts of a framework instantiation environment.

In order to avoid incurring such costs, we use as component composition environment a standard *bean builder* tool. Bean builders are commercial tools that offer sophisticated graphical environments where JavaBeans components can be manipulated [6]. They cannot be directly used for our purpose for several reasons: the target components may not be visualizable, they may be written in languages other than Java, their instantiation operations may not fit the JavaBeans model, etc.

Since the framework components cannot be imported in a bean builder, we construct *visual proxy components* that model the part of the behaviour of the framework components that is relevant to the instantiation process and that are additionally implemented as JavaBeans. The visual proxy components are then imported in a bean builder tool and designers perform the application configuration upon them. Their equivalence to the framework components (at least as far as the application instantiation process is concerned) means that designers can be given the illusion of manipulating the framework components when in fact they are operating upon their proxies. The second usage of XSLT envisaged in our approach is the automatic generation of the visual proxy components and other support components that support their configuration.

This section has presented the approach we propose from a general standpoint. The next section describes how we applied it to construct the OBS Instantiation Environment as an instantiation environment for the AOCS Framework.

4 The OBS Instantiation Environment

The first step in the construction of a framework instantiation environment must be a precise definition of what is meant by "framework instantiation". In the case of the AOCS Framework, the instantiation of an application from the framework consists in performing an ordered sequence of the following six *instantiation operations*:

1. Instantiation of a framework component,
2. Setting the value of a component property,
3. Setting the value of a static property,
4. Setting the value of an indexed property,
5. Linking an event-firing component to an event-listening component,
6. Adding a component to an *object list* (this is a kind of container component that can hold other components).

Note that the component properties can be either of primitive type or of class type. Thus, the second, third and fourth operations also cover the case of object composition. Note also that, in accordance with the component-based character of the AOCS Framework, all the instantiation operations can be expressed in terms of the methods declared by the external interfaces of the framework components. The instantiation sequence can therefore be encoded as an ordered set of method calls performed upon the framework components.

The *instantiation problem* can thus be defined as the problem of translating a particular application specification into an ordered sequence of instantiation operations which, when executed, will result in the instantiation of an application that implements the initial specifications. The OBS Instantiation Environment solves the instantiation problem for the AOCS Framework.

The primary inputs to the instantiation process are the framework components. When suitably configured, they become the building blocks for the target application. The OBS Instantiation Environment consequently needs to manipulate them and needs to have access to information about them. Since the OBS Instantiation Environment is only concerned with the instantiation process, it only needs information about the part of the framework components that comes into play during the instantiation process.

Given the instantiation model adopted here for the target framework, the only characteristics of the framework components that need to be encoded are: the properties they expose (including static and indexed properties), the events they fire and listen to, the object lists they maintain. This information is encoded using an XML grammar. For each framework component, an XML document describing its instantiation-relevant characteristics is automatically generated by a parser-like facility. Such documents are called *Visual Proxy Descriptor Files*.

The operations exposed by the components of the AOCS Framework adhere to certain naming conventions (roughly similar to those defined by the JavaBeans standard) that, to some extent, allow the semantics of an operation to be inferred from its name. These conventions in particular allow the instantiation operations to be recognized and identified. Hence, the OBS Instantiation Environment can automatically construct the visual proxy descriptor files by parsing the public API of the framework components.

As explained in the previous section, the OBS Instantiation Environment associates to each framework component a visual proxy component. Visual proxies must have two characteristics. Firstly, they must exhibit the same behaviour as their associated framework component during the application instantiation phase. Given the instantiation model adopted here for the target framework, this means that a visual proxy must:

1. Expose the same properties as its associated framework component,
2. Fire and listen to the same events as its associated framework component,
3. Expose the same object lists as its associated framework component.

Compliance with the above means that, for the purposes of application instantiation, a visual proxy component exposes the same API as its associated framework component and, during the instantiation phase, it is essentially equivalent to it. Secondly, visual proxies must be well suited to manipulation in a bean builder. In practice, this means that they must be implemented as visualizable JavaBeans. The OBS Instantiation Environment additionally complements them with beaninfo components, bean editor components and bean customizers. The beaninfos provide meta-information about the components that defines the way they are to be manipulated in the composition environment. The property editors define the way individual attributes of the visual proxy components are to be defined (for instance, they enforce constraints on their values). The bean customizers provide wizards that help the user configure components. Taken together, the visual proxies and their support components implicitly define a model of how the AOCS framework can be instantiated and of the constraints that the instantiation process must satisfy.

The visual proxy components, together with their support components (beaninfos and property editors) are automatically generated by XSLT programs that process the visual proxy descriptor files. Thus, the transition from the framework components to their visual proxies is entirely automatic. Note also that whereas the visual proxies must be implemented in Java, no such restriction applies to the framework components. As already noted, the presence of an intermediate XML encoding separates the framework components from their visual proxies (but see the remark at the end of section 5). The process of construction of the visual proxies is sketched in figure 4 for a sample framework component.

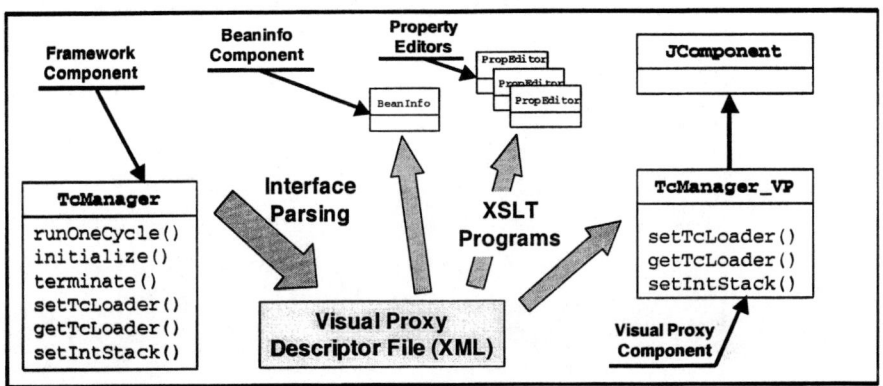

Fig. 4. Visual proxy generation process

The visual proxies are intended to be imported in the *component composition environment* (see figure 3). This is the part of the OBS Instantiation Environment where the designer configures and assembles the target application. In our minimalist approach, this environment is implemented by customizing a JavaBeans bean builder. For the OBS Instantiation Environment, we have used Sun's Bean Builder[3]. Although this bean builder is at present only available as a beta version, it was selected because it implements the long-term persistence mechanism and because it is expected to act, as its predecessor BDK did, as a kind of blueprint for future commercial bean builder products.

Figure 5 shows a screenshot of our composition environment. The top window offers palettes with the framework components. The bottom right window is the composition form where components are displayed and visually manipulated. The connection lines represent composition relationships between components. The component configuration is done using the property sheet in the bottom left window. Wizards (not shown in the figure) are provided to handle non-standard configuration actions (e.g. the additions of items into object lists). The wizards and the property editors are also responsible for enforcing the constraints on the instantiation process (e.g. constraints on the range of values of certain variables).

The operations performed by the designer in the component composition environment result in the definition of an *application configuration*. The application configuration defines which framework components are to be included in the target application and how they are to be configured. The code generation problem is the problem of transforming the application configuration into source code. In the OBS Instantiation Environment, this is done in two steps.

---

[3] Available for free from: http://java.sun.com/products/javabeans/beanbuilder/index.html

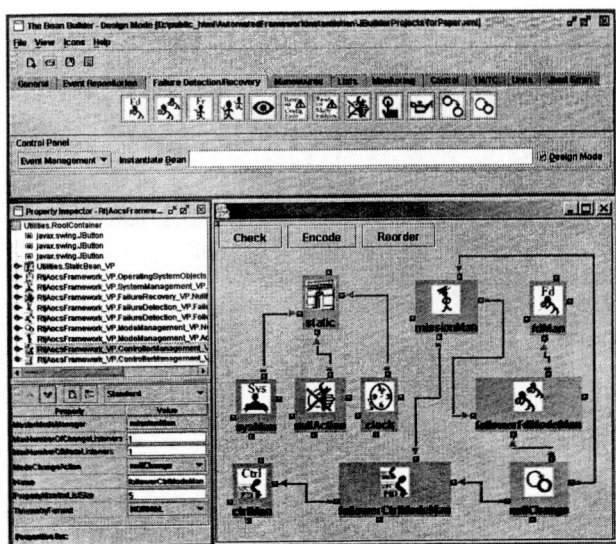

Fig. 5. Screenshot of composition environment of OBS Instantiation Environment

First, the application configuration that is defined through graphical means in the component composition environment must be encoded using some suitable formalism. Then, the encoded configuration description must be processed to generate the source code instantiating the application.

The first step is done using the *long-term persistence mechanism* [18]. This is a new feature of the Java 1.4 platform that allows the state of a set of components to be saved by recording the sequence of instructions that were executed to configure them. This is done by an *encoder* which examines the state of the target components and uses reflection techniques to work out which instructions were performed upon them to bring them to their current state. The relevance of such an encoding mechanism to a generative environment is obvious.

The Java 1.4 platform offers a default implementation of the encoder (the XMLEncoder class). The OBS Environment had to use a specially customized version for two reasons. First, the application configuration is defined by the designer in the component composition environment in terms of the visual proxy components whereas the application configuration must be expressed in terms of the framework components. Hence, the default encoder was extended to perform the translation from the visual proxies back to the framework components. Secondly, the order in which the configuration operations are performed upon the framework components must satisfy certain *ordering constraints*. The persisted image of an application configuration consists of an encoded list of instantiation statements. Enforcement of the ordering constraints is done by sorting this list. The criteria with respect to which the sorting is performed are domain-specific (they depend on the internal structure of the framework components) and can therefore be embedded within the environment. Enforcement of the ordering constraints during the persisting process means that designers are free to specify the instantiation operations in any order in the composition environment. This relieves them of the burden of complying with the constraints and makes it easier for them to move back and forth in the instantiation process by doing and undoing configuration actions.

The codification and enforcing of the ordering constraints was one of the most complex problems we had to solve. At present we use a set of domain heuristics but the problem is conceptually similar to that found in graphical simulation systems where the simulation blocks instantiated by the user must be executed in some predefined order [19]. We plan to extend our environment to implement similar techniques for enforcing the ordering constraints on the instantiation sequence.

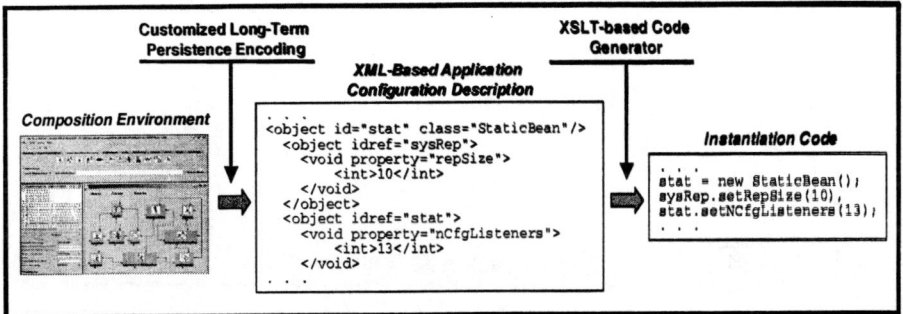

Fig. 6. Instantiation code generation process

The final generation of the source code is straightforward. The long-term persistence mechanism encodes the application configuration using an XML grammar where each element represents an instantiation statement. The XML document is processed by an XSLT program that translates the instantiation statements in Java source code. Translation into another object-oriented language would be equally straightforward. Figure 6 shows the code generation process in schematic form.

5   Simulation

The third requirement of section 3 calls for the instantiation environment to allow for the simulation of the application that is being configured. Simulation is understood here as the selective execution of operations on some of the components within the environment and the monitoring of the resulting change in their observable state. Simulation is seen as a debugging tool to help designers verify whether their configuration actions satisfy their requirements. An important consequence is that it should be possible to simulate an incompletely configured application because debugging is especially valuable *during* the configuration process.

It is noteworthy that current work on framework instantiation does not seem to address the simulation problem. Given the crucial role that simulation plays in commercial tools like Matlab, this is a serious shortcoming. In our view, one of the benefits of a generative approach is that it makes it easy to switch from a model to its implementation and should therefore be easy to extend to cover simulation.

In keeping with the minimalist spirit of our approach, we have built simulation facilities upon existing tools and technologies. We have in particular exploited the capability of JavaBeans-based bean builder to operate in two modes: "design mode" and "run mode". In design mode, the components are configured. In run mode, they are executed. The bean builder used in the OBS Instantiation Environment has a built-in run-mode but this, by itself, is useless because the components it manipulates are the visual proxy components and these have no run-time behaviour associated to them: they just exist to be configured and therefore executing them has no effect.

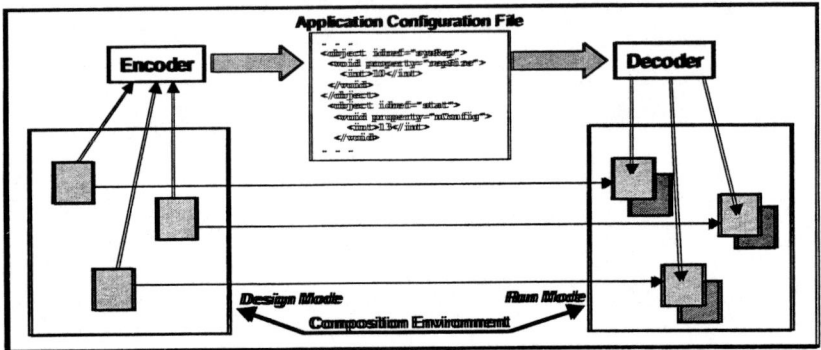

Fig. 7. Simulation concept

The previous section discussed how a customized long-term persistence encoder is used to generate an XML description of the application configuration defined by the user in the composition environment. This description can be used to generate the instantiation code (see figure 6) but it can also be used to dynamically construct and configure the components of the target application. This is exploited as shown in figure 7. When a transition into run-mode is detected, an encoding-decoding process is triggered resulting in the dynamic instantiation and configuration of the framework components (darkly shaded boxes in the figure) that are made to shadow their associated visual proxy components (lightly shaded boxes). The designer can then perform a simulation by asking for a certain operation to be executed upon the application components. The request is intercepted and re-routed to the underlying framework components. The state of the framework components can then be inspected to ascertain the effect of the simulation action.

The fundamental organizing principle of the OBS Instantiation Environment is the preservation of the illusion for the designers that they are manipulating the "real" framework components when in fact they are manipulating their much simpler visual proxies. Our simulation concept complies with this principle in that the simulation actions are ostensibly performed upon the visual proxies but are in fact internally re-routed to the dynamically created and configured framework components.

This simulation concept was demonstrated by endowing the OBS Bean Builder with the ability to perform a so-called "configuration check". All framework components expose an operation through which they can be asked to check their own internal configuration and to report whether or not they are configured. Typical implementations of this operation verify that all the required plug-ins have been loaded, that settable parameter have legal values, that these values are consistent with each other, etc. A configuration check is useful at the end of the instantiation process (to verify that all components are ready to enter normal operational mode) but it is not itself a configuration operation and it is therefore not modelled by the visual proxy components. Thus, performing a configuration check is a simple form of simulation because it involves executing an operation upon the configured application components and observing the result. Other more complex forms of simulations could be built in a similar fashion.

Two remarks are in order. First, the use of XML to encode the framework component properties and the application configuration decouples the implementation of the framework components from that of the visual proxy components (dashed line in figure 3). This decoupling is weakened in the case of our simulation concept because, during a simulation, both the framework components and the visual proxy components exist side-by-side. Second, our simulation concept executes the application in a desktop environment. This introduces inevitable differences (e.g. with respect to timing) with respect to execution in the final embedded environment.

6 Software Development Process

As already noted, current work on generative approaches for framework instantiation tends to put the emphasis on the definition of a DSL. A DSL is useful because it, unlike the implementation language of the framework, "knows" about the framework characteristics (the abstractions it implements, the variation points it offers, the constraints it dictates, etc). For this reason, use of a DSL is probably inescapable in any automated framework instantiation environment. However, DSLs by their very nature tend to be idiosyncratic and thus put off non-specialist users.

Our solution to this dilemma is twofold. First, like many other authors [9, 11, 14, 20], we use XML to encode the framework characteristics and, like some authors [14, 20], we use XSLT to process this information. Both are mainstream technologies and their use helps in fostering acceptance of a generative approach. Secondly, and perhaps more importantly, we try to "hide" the DSL from the user. Conceptually, the composition environment of our OBS Instantiation Environment can be seen as a DSL for its target framework. The components it offers to the user are implementations of the framework abstractions and the environment constrains the operations that the user can perform upon these abstractions. Operations that are not allowed are simply not seen by the user. This is the advantage of using the visual proxies that only model the subset of the operations exposed by the framework components that can legally be used during the instantiation process. Similarly, there are constraints, like for instance the ordering of the instantiation operations, that the user ignores but that are automatically enforced by the environment. Thus, the graphical configuration operations performed by the user in the composition environment are effectively equivalent to writing a specification of the target application in a DSL but the user needs not be aware of this and the formal specification of the target application is automatically generated by the environment itself (it is contained in the application configuration file generated by long-term persisting the configured components in the composition environment).

We have also taken one further step in order to ease the transition of traditional users from manual assembly of the framework components to assembly in a composition environment and automatic generation of the instantiation code. Software development in our domain of interest (embedded control systems for satellite applications) is articulated over three stages. In the first stage, the end-user, an *application engineer*, expresses the requirements to be satisfied by the application using informal English. In the second stage, the *software engineer* translates these requirements into a formal specification. Finally, in the third stage an architecture and an implementation are derived from the specifications.

This development process is somewhat at odds with the development model implied by the approach we propose. One motivation for our approach (see section 2) is to empower the application engineers to directly develop their own software. Given their intimate understanding of their requirements and of their domain, their natural way to operate is to proceed directly to the configuration of the application in the composition environment without first passing through a formal specification phase. This is, for instance, what experienced control engineers do when they use tools like Matlab. The simulation facilities of the environment are used to verify the correctness of the application as it is being constructed.

However, in order to preserve compatibility with the traditional approach, we have endowed the OBS Instantiation Environment with the capability to automatically generate the software specifications from the application configuration. This is done by an XSLT program that processes the XML-based *application configuration file*. The resulting specifications read like structured English text of the kind used in software specification documents in our field of interest. Essentially, the XSLT program associates pre-defined sentence templates to each configuration operation. The templates are user-defined but are intended to be invariant within the framework domain. The values of the template parameters are derived from the XML image of the application configuration. The information in the XML image is obviously formulated in terms of implementation-level concepts (e.g. the names of the interfaces implemented by a certain component). In order to be understandable for a human reader, the specifications must instead be formulated in terms of framework-level concepts (e.g. the name of the abstraction encapsulated by the abstract interfaces). The translation from implementation-level to framework-level concepts is contained in a *domain dictionary* [17] that is associated to the framework and whose purpose is precisely to provide a vocabulary to formally describe applications within the framework domain.

The application configuration file, the software specifications derived from it, and the visually configured components in the composition environment can thus be seen as three views on the same abstract specification of the target application and as three different specifications written in three different but equivalent DSLs.

7   Case Study

The OBS Instantiation Environment is a fully functioning instantiation environment for the AOCS Framework. In order to demonstrate its effectiveness, we used it to develop the control software for a "Swing Mass Model" (see figure 8). This is a laboratory equipment consisting of two rotating disks connected to each other and to a load with a torsional spring. A DC motor drives one of the disks. The goal of the controller is to control the speed and position of the other disk. The instantiated application is representative of a full control system application as conceptualised in figure 1 as it includes the following functionalities:

- Two operational modes,
- Processing of sensor data and stimulation of actuators
- Implementation of control algorithms,
- Failure detection checks on the main system variables,
- Failure recovery actions autonomously executed upon detection of failures,
- Autonomous provision of housekeeping data,
- Processing and execution of operator commands,
- Capability to execute speed profiles.

The instantiation required the configuration and composition of 75 components. The application construction was performed in several stages with intermediate configuration states being saved and then restored. This gave the designer the option to try alternative configuration approaches. The experience of using the environment was a positive one. The environment relieves the designer of much tedious and low-level work and its graphical interface makes its use easy and intuitive. Turn-around time from a configuration to the code implementing it is very short (less than a minute) which facilitates experimenting and prototyping.

The simulation capabilities built into the instantiation environment (the "configuration check", see section 5) proved particularly valuable as they allowed the designer to rapidly identify components whose configuration was still incomplete and which therefore required attention. The instantiation code generated by the environment was highly readable and could easily have been modified by hand if required. A formal description of the application was automatically generated using the facility described at the end of section 6.

Fig. 8. The Swing Mass Model

8 Generalization

The discussion in this paper – and much of the work behind it – is specific to one particular framework, the AOCS Framework, and to one particular generative environment, the OBS Instantiation Environment. However, there are three aspects of our experience that are relevant to the problem of building other generative environments for other frameworks. They relate to the *technologies* we used, to a *design pattern* we applied, and to a number of *framework guidelines*.

Generative techniques have so far failed to find favour with industry. One reason for this failure is their tendency to rely on complex and unusual technology. Automatic configuration of pre-existing components is a natural field of application for generative techniques but industrial applications will come only if ways are found to achieve this aim using standard technologies. In our project, we have found two such technologies that have the potential to make the generative approach attractive to the ordinary software developer.

The first one is the *combination of XML and XSLT*. The suitability of XML as a way to encode the raw information that is to drive the generative process has already been widely exploited [9, 11, 14, 20] and the corresponding power of XSLT to build customizable code generators is attracting more and more attention [14]. Our experience is that once the choice is made to use XML to encode configuration information, XSLT should be the first option for implementing the code generator. It may not always be adequate because it is was devised for other purposes but, when found to be adequate, it will provide an excellent basis upon which to build a code generator quickly and at minimal cost.

The second technology is the *combination of bean builder tools and long-term persistence* as implemented in the Java 1.4 platform. Any non-trivial generative environment for frameworks will need a graphical interface where the user can manipulate the framework components. Bean builders can be useful for this purpose. They provide sophisticated, low-cost, customizable environments for component configuration and manipulation. The facilities offered by older versions of these tools for encoding configuration information were based on Java-style serialization or on rather primitive and poorly-tuneable code generators. The newer versions (of which Sun's Bean Builder, which we used in our project, is a prototype) can be expected to implement the long-term persistence mechanism. This generates an XML-based description of the operations that were executed to configure a set of components. This description is an excellent basis for a simple (and XSLT-based) code generator.

One problem with using standard bean builders as component composition environments is that, in most cases, the framework components cannot be directly imported into a bean builder tool because of language or other incompatibilities. In our project we have used the visual proxy mechanism to overcome this problem. We believe that this mechanism represents a design pattern – we call it the *visual proxy design pattern* – in the sense that the abstract ideas behind it could be beneficial in other contexts.

In general, the visual proxy design pattern is useful when there is a need to manipulate components in a visual environment for the purpose of generating configuration code for them. The components themselves may be awkward to manipulate directly for several reasons: (1) they may be too complex; (2) they may be written in a language that is incompatible with the chosen composition environment; (3) they may not have an "appearance" and may therefore be unsuitable for graphical manipulation. The design pattern calls for the construction of components – the visual proxy components – that only model the part of the behaviour of the original components that is relevant to the instantiation process. These components can be kept simple, can be made visualizable, and can be written in the desired language. Users can then be given the illusion of manipulating their own components when in fact they are operating upon their visual proxies. The illusion can be sustained

ing upon their visual proxies. The illusion can be sustained because the visual proxies and the base components implement the same configuration operations with the same semantics.

The visual proxy design pattern is a second result of our project with general applicability. The third and last one concerns a number of guidelines on how frameworks should be designed in order to facilitate their integration in generative environments for automating their instantiation. In principle, it is always possible to apply generative techniques to the instantiation process of almost any reasonably designed framework. However, one lesson of the work described here is that the cost of doing so can vary a great deal depending on how the framework is designed. More specifically, we have identified four guidelines that should be followed to ensure that a framework is "generative-friendly".

- *Component-Based Instantiation.* The framework should be designed so that the instantiation process can be expressed entirely in terms of configuration operations performed upon the components offered by the framework. This guideline is very natural in the case of a component-based framework. It allows the instantiation process to be expressed only in terms of the public API's of the framework components. This limits the amount of information that must be processed by the automated instantiation environment. Description of the external interfaces of the components is much simpler than description of their implementation and if only the former is needed, there is a clear gain in simplicity.

- *Instantiation Demarcation.* The framework should be designed so that the instantiation operations are clearly separate from the operations that are executed during other phases of the application operation. The point of using the visual proxy components is to replace potentially complex components (the framework components) with other components that, though equivalent to them from the point of view of the instantiation process, are functionally simpler and hence easier to manipulate in an autocoding environment. This approach is feasible only if the behaviour of the framework components can be neatly split between an instantiation-relevant sub-behaviour and another sub-behaviour that is not relevant to the instantiation process. The simplest way to ensure that this split is possible is to design the framework components so that the operations they offer can be separated between operations that are used only during the instantiation process and operations that are only used during the operational phases of the application.

- *Adherence to Naming Conventions.* The framework should be designed so that the names of the instantiation operations conform to some pre-defined naming patterns that allow the semantics of an operation to be inferred from its name. Manipulation of the framework components within an automated instantiation environment requires the environment to find out information about the components. Since the components are manipulated only through the operations they expose, the information the environment needs only concerns these operations. Use of naming patterns for the operations is arguably the simplest way through which this information can be encoded.

- *Instantiation Operation Independence.* The framework should be designed so that the instantiation operations are as far as possible independent of each other. In general, the instantiation sequence will have to satisfy some ordering constraints: some operations can only be performed after some other operations have been performed; or the way some components are configured may be dependent on the outcome of previous configuration actions. This guideline recommends that this type of dependencies be as far as possible minimized. The instantiation sequence is defined by the user in a component composition environment. It is desirable to allow users to specify the instantiation operations individually since this simplifies their task. This means that the instantiation constraints must be imposed by the environment itself. The experience from this project is that imposing these constraints can give rise to significant levels of complexity. This justifies the introduction of this guideline.

It may be noted that most of these guidelines make sense even in the normal case of a framework that must be instantiated manually since they mostly tend to simplify the instantiation process and to clarify the boundaries between operations that must be performed as part of the instantiation process and operations that must be performed as part of the normal operation of an application. Since a framework is often used (i.e. instantiated) by people other than its designer, this type of demarcation can be useful independently of whether a generative approach to its instantiation is foreseen or not.

9 Conclusions and Future Work

In this paper, we propose a generative approach to framework instantiation and we demonstrate it by applying it to a particular framework. We claim that the distinctive feature of our approach is its simplicity and reliance on mainstream technologies. These features are important because they promise to bring a generative approach within the reach of most framework designers and users. In order to substantiate our claim, it is necessary to provide an estimate of how much effort would be required to port our approach to another framework.

The development of the OBS Instantiation Environment – from the start of the project to the execution of the case study described in section 7 – took place over a period of 8 months. The work was done by a senior engineer and a junior engineer allocated to the project at, respectively, 50% and 75% of their time. The total effort was therefore 10 man-months. Since this is a new concept, much of this effort went into false starts and trying out new ideas. Our estimate is that the re-implementation of the concept for a new framework which complies with the guidelines laid down in section 8 would require at most 4 man-months. This is regarded as a rather modest investment but it must be stressed that the estimate is heavily dependent on the way the framework is designed. If a generative approach to instantiation is envisaged, it is essential that this be kept in mind already during the framework development phase.

Our future work will follow two broad directions. On the one hand, we intend to further verify the validity of our approach by applying it to industrial test cases. Our experience to date is restricted to laboratory experiments (see section 7). The results we have obtained encourage us to try a more ambitious experiment where we port the environment to a new framework and apply it to the generation of operational software in an industrial context.

On the other hand, and in a more research–oriented line of work, we are looking at the possibility of extending the capability of the instantiation environment to perform component *customisation* as well as component *configuration*. A component is configured by acting upon it through the operations it declares in its external interface. A component is customized if its internal implementation is modified. The OBS Instantiation Environment is, at present, only concerned with component configuration. The generative effort concentrates on the generation of the component configuration code alone.

We expect that the generation of customisation code will require the use of aspect oriented programming techniques. In particular, an idea we would like to explore is whether we can transform the problem of customizing a set of components with respect to a certain feature into an equivalent problem of configuring a meta-component that describes that feature. This would allow us to preserve much of the current approach that is geared towards component configuration with the important difference that some of the components that are configured in the environment would be meta-components (or maybe their visual proxies) and that the code that is generated from them is component customization code rather than application implementation code.

References

1. Pasetti, A.: Software Frameworks and Embedded Control Systems. LNCS Vol. 2231, Springer-Verlag, 2002
2. Pasetti A., et al.: An Object-Oriented Component-Based Framework for On-Board Systems, Proceedings of the Twelfth Data System in Aerospace (DASIA) Conference, Nice, France, May 2001
3. Czarnecki K., Eisenecker U.: Generative Programming: Methods, Tools and Applications, Addison-Wesley, 2000
4. Kay M.: XSLT – Programmer's Reference, Wrox Books, 2001
5. Gamma E., et al.: Design Patterns – Elements of Reusable Object Oriented Software, Addison-Wesley, Reading, Massachusetts, 1995
6. Englander R.: Developing JavaBeans (Java Series), O'Reilly and Associated, 1997
7. Ortigosa A., Campo M., Moriyon R.: Towards Agent-Oriented Assistance for Framework Instantiation, Proceedings of the Fifteenth Annual Conference on Object-Oriented Programming, Systems, and Languages(OOPSLA 2000), Minneapolis, USA, Oct. 2000
8. Fontoura M., et al.: Using Domain-Specific Languages to Instantiate Object-Oriented Frameworks, IEE Proc.-Soft., Vol. 147, No. 4, August 2000
9. Swe Myat S., Yhang H., Jarzabek S., XVCL: A Tutorial, Proceedings of the Conference on Software Engineering and Knowledge Engineering (SEKE), Ischia, Italy, July 2002
10. Sztipanovits J., Karsai G.: Generative Programming for Embedded Systems, in: Batory D., Consel C., and Taha W. (eds.): Proceedings of the Conference on Generative Programming and Component Engineering (GPCE 2002), LNCS Vol. 2487, Springer-Verlag 2002
11. Czarnecki K., et al.: Generative Programming for Embedded Software: An Industrial Experience Report, in: Batory D., Consel C., and Taha W. (eds.): Proceedings of the 23rd Conference on Generative Programming and Component Engineering (GPCE 2002), LNCS Vol. 2487, Springer-Verlag 2002
12. Czarnecki K., Eisenecker U.: Components and Generative Programming, Proceedings of the Joint European Software Engineering Conference and ACM SIGSOFT International Symposium on the Foundations of Software Engineering (ESEC/FSE'99), Toulouse, France, 1999
13. Bryant B., et al.: Formal Specifications of Generative Component Assembly Using Two-Level Grammar, Proceedings of the Conference on Software Engineering and Knowledge Engineering (SEKE), Ischia, Italy, July 2002

14. Butler G.: Generative Techniques for Product Lines, Software Engineering Notes, Vol. 26, No. 6, November 2001
15. Anastasopoulos M., Gacek C.: Implementing Product Line Variability, Proceedings of the International Conference on Software Engineering (ICSE), Toronto, May 2001
16. Donohoe P. (ed): Software Product Lines – Experience and Research Directions, Kluwer Academic Publisher, 2000
17. Fayad M., Schmidt D., Johnson R. (eds.): Building Application Frameworks –Foundations of Framework Design, Wiley Computer Publishing, 1999
18. http://java.sun.com/products/jfc/tsc/articles/persistence/index.html
19. Giloi W.: Principles of Continuous System Simulation, B. G. Teubner Stuttgart, 1975
20. Oliveira T., Alencar P., Cowan D.; Towards a Declarative Approach to Framework Instantiation, Proceedings of the Workshop on Declarative Metaprogramming, Automated Software Engineering Conference, Edinburgh, Sept. 2002
21. Craig Cleveland J.; Program Generators with XML and Java, Prentice Hall, 2001

Making Patterns Explicit with Metaprogramming

Daniel von Dincklage

University of Colorado at Boulder, Boulder CO 80309, USA
danielvd@cs.colorado.edu

Abstract. Design patterns have been a useful tool for a better understanding of the collaboration between several classes and objects in a program.
One drawback of this approach is the lack of an explicit representation of the patterns used in a program, as the collaboration between classes is normally expressed in the code of the class itself.
In this paper, we present a method for explicitly representing patterns in a program with the help of metaprogramming techniques. The method presented has benefits compared to traditional approaches with respect to documentation and reusability of the program, as well as providing a better separation of the protocol contained in the pattern.

1 Introduction and Motivation

Design patterns are frequently used as a tool to guide and document the design of object-oriented software systems. The benefits of the use of design patterns are broad, as they can be used to abstract from low-level interactions between classes and provide flexible solutions to common problems.

The specification of a design pattern is usually done using a particular template that includes a number of elements required to express the design intent that is to be captured. One of the elements of the specification usually is the classes involved - the approach taken here is to label each class with the role it plays in the whole collaboration. Also specified is the form of collaboration between the participants as required by their specific role. Other elements are quite important in a pattern too - especially the "soft" issues, such as the motivating design problem or design tradeoffs to be made when employing the pattern.

Another part of the pattern is obviously concerned with the method of actual implementation. Often a pattern description will contain some examples and a discussion of issues which are concerned with the implementation phase itself, such as the peculiarities of specific programming languages.

These issues during the implementation of patterns have been analyzed by several authors [1-4]. One of the most common conclusions is that the language or paradigm used affects the implementation effort. It has even been observed that patterns can even "disappear" in the language - the actual use of the pattern becomes completely transparent, as described in [2,3]. One interesting observation is that often dynamic languages provide the possibility of very simple implementations of design patterns.

In contrast to these previous approaches the main goal of this paper is to provide an analysis of the benefits of static metaprogramming when applied to pattern implementation as a single language feature rather than a whole language, as done in [1].

The focus on the pattern "implementation" is also weighed in differently: One issue with design patterns is that they sometimes involve quite large implementation burdens that are largely trivial wiring between classes. An example of this is the Proxy pattern:

For each of the methods present in the public interface of the object proxied, the proxy itself must also provide the same method, with an almost trivial implementation. Writing these routines manually can be very tedious and error-prone, while also complicating maintainance.

To alleviate this problem is one of the goals of this paper. The idea behind the approach is to use a programming technique called Metaprogramming. Metaprogramming is understood as the concept of creating programs that will themselves produce other programs, or manipulate other programs according to their algorithms. Of course, due to this very broad definition there are quite a number of systems that can be classified as metaprogramming systems. Due to this, metaprogramming systems have been categorized with respect to a number of traits [5]. In this paper, the metaprogramming system used is a static one. Static metaprograms are run at compile time of the subject program. They are invoked with the original source program and transform it into another source-level program. The actual nature of the transformation is of course dependent on the metaprogram, as it could insert or delete program statements, procedures or whole classes. These capabilities are important for the goal of this paper - to produce metaprograms that can be used as a form of reusable patterns. As described earlier, it can be very tedious and error-prone to actually implement some of the patterns, work, which could be partially automated. Later, the user only would have to supply the metaprogram with the class the pattern should operate on, and supply some pattern-specific data. This would then be expanded by the metaprogram into the actual code which contains the implemented pattern. This would not only have the benefit of vastly speeding up development and introducing fewer bugs, but would also have advantages with respect to the expressiveness of the code, and thus the documentation as well as making the program more resistant to change. Previously, as the pattern was made up of a lot of hand-written implementation, it was sometimes not necessarily obvious that or which pattern had been used. In contrast to that, if the use of a pattern is expressed in the application code by an explicit invocation of a metaprogram, which receives the important properties of the pattern as parameters, an explicit documentation is present in the code itself.

Although the transformations described in this paper are quite simple and could be performed with any sufficiently expressive metaprogramming system, the system chosen for the actual implementation of the system is Common Lisp with a full object system and meta object protocol [6], as it has very easily usable metaprogramming capabilities.

The main problem with implementing a similar system with other programming languages is that the approach taken to implement the patterns most closely resembles the extension of the original source language with new constructs in such a way that these seamlessly integrate into the original language. These new constructs are then used by the programmer by specifying the appropriate metadata in order to invoke them.

Unfortunately, this prevents the use of purely dynamic reflection systems, such as present in Java, as there is no easy way to communicate the metadata specified by the programmer to the dynamic systems, provided there is no specific support for adding metadata to programs (such as in Eiffel or languages based on the MSIL, such as C#).

However, if there is the possibility to introduce these extensions, such as using a system like ELIDE [7], there is no specific limitation that would prevent the use of languages other can Common Lisp. Especially unproblematic is the use of statically typed languages.

The idea of expressing patterns as meta-programs obviously leads to another question - that of behaviorally similar patterns. As in [8] and similar work, patterns usually have been classified according to their intent, as it is seen by the implementor. This clearly has advantages when choosing the right pattern for a given problem, as each pattern is specifically adapted to its special usage. However, this fails to be helpful when trying to provide the implementations of patterns as metaprograms, as this conventional classification does not provide a taxonomy that is useful for the reuse of the pattern implementations.

2 The Benefits of Metaprogramming for Patterns

As already noted in [2, 3], for some of the GoF-patterns dynamic languages are very appropriate. The best example for this property is some of the creational patterns - As noted there, in some dynamic languages the implementation of these patterns degenerates unto the point where it disappears. These easily implementable patterns are (in GoF-terms) Abstract Factory, Prototype and Singleton

In order to generate a reusable implementation of these patterns with the help of metaprogramming, a possible approach is to create a new metaclass that implements the instantiation protocol specified by the respective pattern. The pattern can then simply be reused by declaring a new class as an instance of the metaclass associated with the pattern.

To now implement the Singleton pattern it is advisable to first analyze the pattern itself. The idea of this pattern is to limit the number of instances of a particular class to one . Usually this is implemented with the help of a language feature - "static" functions in Java or "once" in Eiffel. The actual protocol of the pattern is quite simple: The user calls a predefined function, it then will return the unique instance.

An implementation using CLOS is somewhat different, as it neither uses a special language feature to control the number of instantiations, nor requires a distinct function to return the instance, as shown in listing 1.

```
(defclass singleton-class (standard-class) ((store ::initform nil)))

(defmethod allocate-instance ((class singleton-class) &rest args)
(if (null (slot-value class 'store))
  (setf (slot-value class 'store) (call-next-method class args))
  (slot-value class 'store)))

(defclass shape () () (:metaclass singleton-class))
(make-instance (find-class 'shape))
```

Listing 1: The singleton example

One observation is that the actual code implementing the "singleton" behavior can be expressed regardless of the clients that later use it, as well as the fact that a client adheres to the "singleton"-protocol of instantiation is made explicit by the :metaclass-specification during class definition. Providing such explicit indications of the usage of patterns is the main goal of this paper.

The two other patterns mentioned - Abstract Factory and Prototype are quite similar with respect to their behaviour. In both cases, in order to abstract from the concrete instantiation process, methods are called that will return the instance that should be used by the client. The object instantiation itself is done according to some internal algorithm inside of the called method. Implementing these patterns would be similar to the implementation of the singleton.

One interesting property of these three patterns is that they exhibit a striking similarity between each other, up to a point where all three can be regarded as specializations of a more general pattern "creator" that exposes the instantiation protocol of the programming language used, and thus spans multiple abstraction levels.

With the notion of a more general "Creator" pattern the reason for the simple and similar implementations in dynamic languages of the three patterns mentioned becomes obvious:

As the normal object instantiation protocol is also a specialization of the more general pattern, this special instance of the Creator pattern must already be implemented in every object-oriented language. The advantage of dynamic languages, however, is that exactly this implementation is exposed and easily available to the programmer, allowing the programmer to modify it.

The difficulties that arise when implementing these patterns in more static languages also become understandable - there, the instantiation protocol is usually implemented in the compiler, and thus out of reach of the normal application programmer.

With this example, the advantages of implementing patterns with the help of metaprogramming should have become obvious - both with respect to reusability, documentation and separation of code, as well as conceptual benefits.

3 Devising Metaprograms

As shown in the previous section, it is desirable to have the language already implement parts of the design pattern, as it can save considerable overhead while at the same time producing better code.

Of course, it is an important question how these metaprograms actually work. The idea is that the user can specify the application of the design pattern with a special syntax in his original program. While specifying the application, the user also supplies metadata to the static metaprogram, such as the classes involved in the design pattern.

The benefit of this approach is that, afterwards, the pattern is made explicit in the code, as it is represented in the invocation of the metaprogram. Ideally, the result of the metaprogram itself is another class that then can be processed by additional metaprograms. At first glance, the results of the approach might seem different from the approach taken by the language designers for implementing the Creator pattern, but it certainly is not: The difference is in the actual method of parameterizing the pattern. Whereas the Creator pattern is parametrized implicitly by overloading specific functions, the metaprograms are parametrized explicitly at the time of invocation. The benefit of the latter method is that the parameters are made explicit as such, whereas the former requires knowledge about the instantiation protocol.

A very important part of the actual process is the method used to create the metaprograms. As already mentioned, the metaprograms receive classes and data relating to the pattern, and with that information generate additional behavior in the classes. However, in order to have a useful metaprogram it is desirable to supply it with parameters that express a great deal of information while imposing very little burden on the user; the more information the metaprogram can deduce by itself, the more useful it is. Thus, it is important not to require too much parametrization. A metaprogram that takes two pieces of code, only to execute them in a given order, provides too little benefit to the user to be accepted.

Thus, the question of how a metaprogram can deduce as much information as possible becomes quite important. One key is the actual mode of collaboration used by the participants of the implemented pattern. The more specific this protocol of interaction is, the more data can be deduced by the pattern and thus automatically be implemented. Due to this, it is obvious that the main benefit will be achieved by patterns that rely heavily on objects collaborating according to a strict protocol, whereas patterns that only loosely define interfaces that can vary significantly in terms of behavior will exhibit only minor improvements.

4 The Mediator Pattern

A frequent task handled by a pattern is dispatching requests that are directed by a sender to a number of clients, thus performing the function of a mediator. A central mediator object receives messages from attached objects and processes these messages according to rules and possibly its internal state. Resulting messages are then distributed to the associated objects. Replies are collected and returned to the original sender.

Implementing the Mediator pattern as a reusable piece of software therefore requires three fundamental sets of data that have to be supplied in order to generate a usable mediator class:

- The set of messages the mediator must accept. Each declaration of a message consists of an "uplink" and a "downlink" format. These formats specify the data transmitted in the message. The first format is used for transmission from a colleague or client to the mediator, the second format for transmission from the mediator to the colleagues,
- A set of rules associated with each message to perform the message-processing internal to the mediator and to determine the set of associated objects that should receive the result of the computation by the mediator. If the two formats are different, these rules also have to handle the transformation between uplink- and downlink-format,
- in the case of statically typed languages, the basetypes of the associated objects.

With this information, one can generate a mediator class that will adhere to a specific mediator protocol specified by the user. The meta-program to transform a class into a mediator-class adhering to a specific protocol would work somewhat like this:

- add a new variable to the class to store the colleagues at runtime,
- for each message specified, generate a function with a name specific to the message, accepting messages in the uplink-format, that will:
  - perform optional transformations of the content of the message,
  - filter the list of colleagues according to some internal criteria,
  - distribute the message to the resulting colleagues by invoking a method with a name specific to the message and pass the contents of the message in the appropriate downlink format to it,
  - If the message has a return value, apply a fold function to the results of the clients, in order to generate a possibly distilled version of all return values
- store the properties of each message as a static item associated with the class defined, ideally as part of its type.

Defining the colleague classes corresponding to the protocol that one specific mediator-class adheres to is done in this fashion:

- add a new variable to the class that will store a reference to objects of the type of the corresponding mediator-class,
- for each message defined by the mediator class generate a method, with the name being the one chosen by the mediator as "receiver" name, accepting messages in the downlink format. This method either will discard the message received or forward it to another function specified by the user, in order to be processed,

```
(defmediator the-mediator ()
  ((some-value :accessor some-value :initarg :some-value))
  (:message (:name message-a) (:format (one-arg))
    (:distributor (lambda (x y)
      (print (format nil "Received Message. Data: ~S" y)) y))))

(defmediator-client the-mediator-client ()
  ((color :accessor color :initarg :color :initform 'clear))
  (:mediator the-mediator)
  (:receive message-a #'message-a-handler)
  (:send message-a the-uplink)
  (:autoregister))
```

Listing 2: The mediator example

– for each message specified to be sent from the class to the mediator, define a method to handle that distribution.

This approach will obviously enhance the actual typesafety of the program, as each message is explicitly represented by a set of collaborating methods. Another advantage is the reliance on metadata - the programmer only supplies the messages together with a couple of specific functions. The metaprogram then wires together the logic needed to perform the communication.

Using the implementation of the pattern, a specification of a mediator would look like the one in listing 2 : The mediator shown there understands a message to communicate with clients - "message-a". It is associated with a specific translation procedure that prints the content of the message and returns it to distribute it to all clients. The client is specified to communicate with mediators of type "the-mediator" and, upon instantiation, autoregister with the then specified instance of the mediator itself. As for communication the client announces that it wants to receive messages of type "message-a" with a specific handler and ignore other messages. The client also specifies that it desires to distribute the message by calling its instance method "the-uplink".

An important thing to note is the benefit gained from implementing the Mediator pattern with metaprogramming. Of course, one could implement the pattern with the help of normal classes, but this would incur a design decision - Either the protocol between the clients and the main mediator class is based upon methods or on more dynamic message exchange: While the former approach has the advantage of being typesafe, it is much less maintainable, as new messages require extensive modification. The maintainance issue is not present in the alternative approach, which, on the other hand, is not typesafe. This situation forces the designer to make a decision upfront, which later on could prove problematic.

This problem is not present if the metaprogramming approach is taken, as the methods used for message exchange are added at compile time and can then be checked statically. Also, the programmer does not have to care anymore about the concrete method of message exchange.

5 Specializing the Mediator Pattern

After having defined the Mediator pattern as an explicit metaprogram, it is now possible to analyze different patterns with respect to their similarity in communication protocol with the mediator pattern. When doing this analysis for the GoF-patterns, a large group of patterns can be found to be substantially similar:

When regarding other patterns as specialized versions of the Mediator, it becomes obvious that most of them specialize the Mediator pattern in four different ways:

- **Limiting the direction of communication**
  Many patterns specialize the mediator protocol in such a way that the communication is unidirectional from the mediator to the clients.
  Examples: Observer, State, Decorator, Composite, Adapter, Bridge, Proxy, Chain of Responsibility
- **Limiting the number of clients**
  A number of patterns exhibits a similar communication protocol as Mediator, but limits the number of clients to 1. These patterns usually define the same interface for the mediator and the single client.
  Examples: Adapter, Bridge, Proxy, Decorator, Chain of Responsibility
- **Limiting the message format**
  Frequently patterns define a fixed set and format of messages. This set is usually fixed to a subset of or the whole external interface of the mediator, creating a 1:1 relation between the external methods of the mediator and supported messages.
  Examples: State, Decorator, Chain of Responsibility, Bridge, Proxy, Composite
- **Defining the "distribution selection" method**
  Some patterns specialize the Mediator pattern in a way that they define the method used to select which clients receive messages.
  Examples: State, Chain of Responsibility, Adapter, Bridge, Proxy

5.1 Specializing the Mediator Pattern for "Adapter"

The intent of the "Adapter" design pattern is to offer clients an expected interface, while implementing the functions it contains with the help of a class that exposes a different interface.

The protocol used here is very similar to the one of the mediator: The adapter receives a message from a client, transforms it according to internal rules into one or more messages that then are sent to the adaptee[1].

In fact, the main task of the Adapter pattern is the actual translation between the signature of a method offered by the adapter, and the signature of the corresponding method of the adaptee.

---

[1] We only consider object adapters, as class adapters are merely a performance enhancement.

```
(defclass window-impl () ())
(defclass x11-impl (window-impl) ())
(defclass pm-impl (window-impl) ())

(defbridge window () () (:target window-impl)
 (:bridge (:from drawline) (:to impl-line))
 (:bridge (:from drawtext) (:to impl-text)))
```

Listing 3: The bridge example

As this process corresponds to the translation between an "uplink"-message-format ($\equiv$ the signature of the method in the adapter) and a "downlink"-message-format ($\equiv$ the signature of the method in the adaptee), everything important is already provided in the implementation of the Mediator pattern.

5.2 Specializing the Mediator Pattern for "Bridge"

The intent of the Bridge pattern is to separate concrete implementations of abstractions from the refinements of the abstractions themselves. In an actual implementation this is usually done by constructing two different class-hierarchies, one for the abstractions, and one for the implementation. As the behavior of the refined abstractions is defined in terms of the more general abstractions, it is sufficient for the implementations to implement an interface equivalent to the most general abstraction provided.

While the conceptual idea of the Bridge pattern is somewhat complicated, the actual protocol it adheres to is not: The most general abstraction maintains a reference to a concrete implementation object to which it will forward "primitive" messages.

Expressing this protocol as an instance of the mediator-protocol is very simple - Each method bridged corresponds to one message, the format of which is the same as the arguments of the primitive method. The receiving function is the method to be invoked in the concrete implementation, the sending function the method of the abstraction.

The use of the resulting pattern is shown in listing 3, similar to the example in [8].

5.3 Specializing the Mediator Pattern for "Composite"

The intent of the Composite pattern is to enable the composition of tree structures in order to represent part/whole hierarchies.

The protocol used by this pattern involves a single Composite object that holds references to multiple parts and exports two different interfaces to its clients. The first interface is the part-interface. This interface is common to all the elements of the structure, the composite and the clients. The second interface is special to the composite object, in that it exports routines to manage

```
(defdecorator decoratorA (component) ()
 (:decorate (:name funB) (:target component)
    (:before (lambda (x y) (print "Decorating") y))
    (:after  (lambda (x y) (print "Decorating some more"))))
 (:proxy (:names funA)))
```

Listing 4: The decorator example

the multiple parts the composite holds references to. Messages received by the composite in the part-interface are distributed to all of the parts it currently holds a reference to. Additionally, the composite can execute code before or after the distribution.

The specialization of the "Mediator" pattern to limit the protocol is quite simple - One only has to limit the message filtering function to always let messages through. The system automatically should also generate a message for each routine present in the part-interface, including a sender-function in the composite object itself. As the mediator already implements the possibility of executing code before or after the message distribution, this capability can be directly reused.

5.4 Implementing "Decorator" and "Chain of Responsibility"

The use of the Decorator pattern is to provide an easy way of extending functionality of objects without subclassing these. This is implemented by providing a fixed set of operations in the objects that later on should be able to be extended. The decorators, deriving with the extendable objects from a common superclass, both provide a custom extension to these operations and forward the original request to the object of the type of the common superclass which they extend at runtime.

The protocol this pattern uses for its communication is very similar to the ones already described - The decorator awaits requests from the clients and forwards requests that it chooses not to handle itself to the object it holds as a reference. The main capability of the decorator, however, is to possibly execute code before or after the forwarding of a request, allowing the decorator to dynamically attach code to its client.

The relation of the Decorator pattern to the Composite pattern is quite obvious , the only difference being that the protocol of the Decorator pattern limits the number of parts the composite can hold references to to exactly one.

This specialization does not involve much work - the single difference would be that for the routine possibly executed after the forwarding of the request, it could be desirable to eliminate the fold semantics of the method executed after forwarding the request, as there is only a single client.

The actual usage is done similarly to the program in listing 4, which declares a decorator-class "decoratorA" that will forward function calls to the function funA, but decorate calls to the function funB.

```
(defchain-of-resp elementA (component) () (:target component)
  (:request (:name funB)
    (:handler (lambda (x y) (print "Handling request.") y))
    (:has-handled (lambda (x y z) t))))

(defchain-of-resp elementC (component) () (:target component)
  (:proxy (:names funB)))
```

Listing 5: The chain-of-responsibility example

The Chain-of-Responsibility pattern is very similar to the Decorator pattern with regard to the protocol used. Whereas in the Decorator pattern the request is always forwarded to the "main" object and the decorators attach additional responsibilities to it by executing code, in the Chain-of-Responsibility pattern the interaction is different - here, the attached objects do not execute their own code and then forward the request, but rather only forward the request and stop the forwarding in the event that they have handled the request sufficiently. This leads to a very similar implementation, that almost only differs in the terminology offered to the user, as shown in listing 5.

An obvious extension to this version of the Chain-of-Responsibility pattern would be to also allow decorations by the elements of the chain. In that case, the Decorator pattern could be regarded as a specialization of the thus modified Chain-of-Responsibility pattern.

5.5 Specializing the Mediator Pattern for "Proxy"

The Proxy pattern is used to provide a placeholder object in order to control the way how the "real" object is accessed.

Again, as in the Bridge pattern the protocol used is relatively simple: The proxy object awaits messages, and, upon receiving them, forwards them to the real object. If this protocol is implemented as a specialization of the mediator-protocol, one can use a mapping nearly identical to the one used for the Bridge pattern. This is due to the fact that these two patterns are also structurally very similar - the only major difference being the fact that with the Proxy pattern the "abstraction" and "implementation" hierarchies are put together into one common tree. The one addition very useful for the Proxy pattern is the possibility to provide a single key that will add a transformation for all the routines in a given class with the specified processing involved. This alleviates the problem of having to specify each routine by hand.

In this example there are three classes involved - "picture" as an abstract superclass for all picture-related things, "real-picture" as the concrete implemenetation and "picture-proxy" as a proxy that forwards calls to the method show.

The difference between these classes is first of all the ":target"-directive indicating the class proxied. The ":proxy"-directives are used to specify the routines that actually should be proxied, in this case show. As the actual picture should

```
(defclass picture () ())
(defmethod show ((x picture)) (error "Abstract!"))

(defclass real-picture (picture) ())
(defmethod show ((x real-picture)) (print "A nice picture."))

(let ((fun (lambda (x y)
   (unless (mediator-has-client x)
      (print "Loading picture from disk...")
      (add-client x (make-instance (find-class 'real-picture)))
      (print "Done.")) y)))

 (defproxy picture-proxy (picture) () (:target picture)
  (:proxy (:names show) (:processor fun))))
```

Listing 6: The proxy example

be loaded prior to accessing, a processing function that will do just that is neccesary. One thing to note is that the processing function needs only be defined once, as it can be used in multiple proxying rules.

One can see the ease with which a new proxy can be specified when using the specialized proxy-metaprogram. Next to this there are, of course, several other advantages - such as the improved documentation and better resistance to change. This is mostly due to the fact that the actual specification of the proxied methods is independent of their parameter declaration. A similar argument applies to the specification of the processing-function: This function does not have to be specified for each proxied function separately, and thus can be changed more easily.

5.6 Specializing the Proxy Pattern for "State"

The State pattern is used to ease the modeling of an internal state of a given object. This is done by providing a central context-class that denotes the whole object to the external world. This context-class holds a reference to a current State-object. This object is an instance of one of multiple subclasses of a common State-class. As long as the Context-object retains its state, all appropriate requests will be handled by the currently associated state object. If the state of the Context-object changes, it will replace the current State-object with an instance of a different subclass of the common State-class.

The protocol involved in this pattern is again quite simple - The central Context-object awaits requests and then forwards these to the current state object. This obviously is a simple extension of the Proxy pattern: The proxy has only one client of a set of different classes. This client frequently is exchanged by other clients, while all interesting method calls are forwarded to the current client. In addition to the behavior as defined by the proxy, there is also a sec-

```
(defsubject shape-subject ()
  ((color :accessor color :initarg :color :initform 'clear))
  (:observe (:name color)))

(defmediator-client the-observer () ()
  (:mediator shape-subject) (:receive color #'handler))

(defmethod handler ((l the-observer) slot old new ) [...] )
```

Listing 7: The observer example

ondary part that is responsible for determining the actual class of the "next" state.

The metadata specified by the user in this case would consist of three parts apart from the abstract class that all the states inherit: The first one is the set of functions that need to be forwarded from the central dispatching object to the current state. The second piece of metadata is a transition-function that describes how the states are changed. A start-state also has to be specified .

5.7 Specializing the Mediator Pattern for "Observer"

The usage of the Observer pattern is to automatically update clients of a given object, should certain properties of the observed subject change.

The protocol involved with this communication is quite simple - as soon as the observed event is recorded in the subject, the subject sends a given message to all of its clients who then react accordingly.

As a specialization of the Mediator pattern, it determines the messages exchanged between the observer and the subject by fixing the possible events the observers actually can observe. In addition to the types of messages, the format of the messages themselves is also limited, as one usually will limit the transmitted information to a reference to the subject observed and possibly the new and old value of the data observed.

The actual usage of the generated system is very simple, as demonstrated in listing 7. In this example two classes are defined: first of all the shape-subject class, which will operate as a subject. The user also specifies the actual slots of the class he wishes to observe with the help of the ":observe"-keyword. The system then internally translates this into an appropriate definition for a message of the same name as the observed slot. The system also automatically adds code that is used to determine the (write) access of the slot.

The actual usage of the message is in the definition of the client that will receive the data - here the user specifies the receiving end of the message just as in the Mediator pattern. Of course, the method attached to the message has now a predefined layout, just the same as the sender of the method specifies.

6 Other Patterns

Due to space constraints it is not possible to present an exhaustive analysis of all the GoF patterns. Nevertheless, a short overview of the properties of the remaining patterns shall be provided.

6.1 The Builder, Command, Factory Method and Iterator Patterns

These four patterns share similar problems, as implementing metaprograms for them would not prove very beneficial.

For the Builder pattern this is due to the fact that the specification of the configurable parts of the pattern (the interface of the Builder, the implementation of the Director and the concrete Builder) contains almost all of the work that needs to be done to implement the pattern.

A similiar analysis applies to the Command pattern. As the main work while implementing the Command pattern is reflected in the actions performed by the concrete command objects upon the receivers, there is no substantial benefit to be gained by implementing it as a metaprogram.

With the Factory Method pattern, the user has to supply the metaprogram with data about which subclass of the "Creator" object returns which concrete instance. This data completely covers the semantics associated with the Factory Method pattern, resulting in no real benefit apart from better documentation.

For the Iterator pattern, the intent is to provide access to a collection of objects in an abstract fashion. The main work for implementing the Iterator pattern is to map the interface of the iterator to the one of the datastructure. As datastructures vary, significant change to the iterators is required, although there have been several approaches to solve this problem, such as [9]. Unfortunately, this leads to an insignificant amout of code that can be automatically generated by a metaprogram.

6.2 The Facade Pattern

As already described in [8], the Facade pattern is somewhat similar to the Mediator pattern. The main difference is that the facade object is not known to the object it hides. Additionally, facade objects usually implement little internal logic. These properties can be used to specify a specialization of the Mediator pattern, although the resulting metaprogram is not substantially different.

6.3 Flyweight

When implementing the Flyweight pattern, the relation of it to the Singleton pattern is apparent: For both patterns, the object instantiation plays a crucial role, as a common object is created and returned. An instance of the Singleton pattern can be regarded as a specialization of the Flyweight pattern, in that the singleton object does not require the passing of an external state to its functions.

6.4 The Interpreter Pattern

The implementation of the Interpreter pattern would be simply the same as the implementation used by the Composite pattern, as their structure is essentially equivalent. This result is similar to the one presented by Agerbo [10], who classifies the Interpreter pattern as an application of the Composite pattern.

6.5 The Memento Pattern

The Memento pattern stores the internal state of an object. Despite a simple protocol, one can experience benefits by using a metaprogram. The metadata consists of a description of the partial state of the object the memento object should be created for. From this data, the metaprogram can generate code to save and restore the particular state[2].

6.6 The Patterns Strategy and Template Method

These two patterns are very similar - Both delegate part of the actual work they do to abstract functions. The main work an implementor does for these patterns is reflected in both the interface and the implementations of the different concrete parts of the pattern. As there is no substantial protocol involved that can be derived from metadata, the benefit of using a static metaprogram to implement these patterns is very limited.

6.7 The Visitor Pattern

The Visitor pattern lends itself very well to an implementation as a metaprogram, as its protocol is defined very narrowly. In fact there have been multiple implementations of automatically generated Visitor patterns or similar applications in various systems, such as DJ [11].

7 Related Work

There are multiple areas in which related work has been produced. In particular, the areas work applicable to the material presented in this paper are:

- The creation of pattern libraries or tools to handle design patterns explicitly
- The impact of language features or paradigms upon the effort required to implement patterns
- The classification of patterns, in order to identify relationships between them

---

[2] With the same metadata, one could also generate copy- and comparison-functions.

7.1 Pattern Libraries and Tools

The most direct relation to the work presented in this paper is contained in pattern libraries and tools to handle the implementation of patterns.

Agerbo [12] presents a library of classes that implements their fundamental design patterns and is used by inheriting the library classes. As the pattern itself is reused by simply inheriting it, there is no possibility for the implementation of the pattern to adapt statically to the context of its use by examining the classes operated upon. This prevents any substantial code generation when compared to the approach taken in this article.

In his work, Soukop [13] introduces pattern classes. These classes act as templates that contain the methods used for the specific role of an object in the given pattern. The pattern classes then are woven together with the data contained in the application classes by a special program. As the weaving process can only perform very limited transoformations, such as the introduction of a piece of code that cannot be adapted by information, such as the names of the methods, found in the transformed class, an effective generation of code for many patterns, as presented in this article is not possible.

Tokuda and Batory [14, 15] describe a set of refactorings, which includes the application of a certain set of design patterns. These refactorings can be applied by a user to an existing program which will subsequently be transformed automatically to reflect the explicit occurence of the particular pattern. As this process is mainly concerned with the discovery of design pattern and a subsequent transformation in a more maintainable representation, the relation to the material presented here is somewhat indirect.

The ELIDE System [7] allows the user to introduce additional parametrized modifiers into Java programs. These modifiers are associated with program transformations which can be used to attach code or otherwise modify the initial program. Using this technique, the user is able to implement transformations similar to the ones presented in this article.

Another system was developed by Budinsky [16]. This system provides a web-based user interface that allows different design choices to be made that are appropriate to the design pattern. The system then transforms templates for each design pattern and produces code that then can be integrated into the final application by the user. However, the transformations that can be applied to the various patterns by the system are extremely limited in that they cannot depend on properties of the code which is to be extended by the particular pattern. This severely limits the possible benefit as only very schematic code can be produced.

Alexandrescu [17], with Vlissides in [18] present a technique using C++ templates and inheritance to provide the user with parametrizable patterns. The configurable parts are encoded as template parameters and are resolved during compilation by the C++ compiler. However, as no compile-time access to the structure of manipulated classes is possible, the expansion cannot deduce information from them, forcing the user to configure all aspects.

Bosch [19] describes an object model called LayOM that implements patterns by composing objects of a number of different layers that filter the messages received by the object. Patterns are implemented by defining layers which then can be attached to application classes. While also presenting patterns as first-class entities that can be used by the programmer, the implementation of the pattern depends on the capabilites of the object model provided, thereby limiting the extent of configuring the particular pattern implemented. This is also reflected in problems that arise if one were to implement patterns as specializations of others in the model presented by the author.

7.2 Design Patterns and Language Properties

Work in this area indirectly relates to the material presented in this paper. This is due to the fact that the approach taken here relates to the use of a single feature, static metaprogramming.

Baumgartner, Laufer and Russo [1] analyze implementations of Patterns in common programming languages in order to determine a set of single language constructs that ease the implementation of design patterns. Major constructs determined to be useful include separation of types and classes, lexically scoped closure objects, metaclass objects as well as multiple dispatch.

Norvig [2] and Sullivan [3] both analyze the effects of dynamic languages upon the effort required for implementing design patterns. Both observe that due to certain properties in dynamic languages, such as first-class-types, design pattern implementations can become much simpler, up to the point of them disappearing, should they be captured by language constructs. The impact of certain paradigms upon design pattern implementation has also been analyzed, as done by Hannemann [4]. There the benefits of Aspect-Oriented programming with AspectJ is investigated with the result of substantial enhancement of the modularity of the implementations.

As static metaprogramming is a feature often present in dynamic programming languages, and can also be regarded as a more general form of AOP, the results are interesting when compared to the previous work. One interesting question for further investigation would be which of the actual benefits of the previously analyzed languages and techniques are in fact a direct result of the application of static metaprogramming techniques.

7.3 Classification of Design Patterns

In this paper, the classification of the patterns is based upon the similarities in communication between participating objects in a design pattern, in order to exploit possible specializations in the reusable implementations of the patterns by reusing parts of the communication protocol.

Previous work has been done to classify design patterns according to a broad range of characteristics:

Agerbo [10] classifies design patterns into fundamental patterns, which are not covered by programming languages, and language-dependent design patterns, whose implementation varies with the programming language used.

Another classification is provided by Gil [20], which is done by evaluating patterns by their distance from being actual language features as being either uses of cliches, which are defined to be common language features, idioms which are non-mainstream features of programming languages, or cadet patterns, which are not yet incorporated in programming languages. It is interesting to note that the main work performed in this paper could be viewed as an attempt to turn each design pattern into a part of the language, thus changing its classification.

8 Conclusion

In this article, we have demonstrated the benefits of using static metaprogramming techniques to alleviate some problems common to the implementation of design patterns.

This is done by using static metaprogramming to introduce new constructs that can be used by the pattern implementor similar to elements of the normal language. When using these constructs, the user specifies metadata that provides information about the concrete problem he wishes to solve, using idioms that correspond to the design pattern he wishes to use. By using this approach, the intent of the programmer is made explicit, thereby documenting the approach taken and alleviating the tracing problem.

As shown, the benefit of the implementations of the patterns as metaprograms directly depends on the additional information that can be concluded from or extracted with the help of the metadata supplied by the user. Often, the additional data can directly be devised from the protocol implied by the pattern itself. The more derived data or implied protocol is present in a pattern, the more effective the implementation is in saving work. Due to the approach taken, this method is also, in principle, capable of combining several patterns in one object, if care is taken during the implementation of the metaprogram.

Other conclusions presented include the benefits of using metaprograms to generate code specific for the design patterns, as one can eliminate design decisions in favor of more static type safety while at the same time preventing errors resulting from simple omissions in the manual transcription work.

Another important conclusion is the benefit of grouping patterns by their similarity in protocol, or, more precisely, their method of extracting additional metadata. This grouping helps organize design patterns in a fashion more applicable to direct implementation when compared to the previous classifications. Of additional interest is the specialization hierarchy that can be imposed upon the design patterns, as it results in fewer design patterns as roots when compared with other classifications. With the help of this classification, a better understanding of the properties of particular programming languages or paradigms with respect to implementing patterns is also possible, as one can compare language features with metaprograms, as a language feature directly corresponds to a metaprogram.

However, this classification is purely based upon the structure of the implementation, which can be regarded as being orthogonal to the usual classifications which are based upon the intent which leads to the use of a particular design pattern.

On a more concrete side, the actual implementations of the patterns done in Common Lisp with CLOS should be regarded as a proof-of-concept, as for the sake of simplicity some options and desirable features have been omitted.

References

1. Baumgartner, G., Läufer, K., Russo, V.F.: On the interaction of object-oriented design patterns and programming languages. Technical Report CSD-TR-96-020, Department of Computer Science, Purdue University (1998)
2. Norvig, P.: Design patterns in dynamic programming. (1996)
3. Sullivan, G.T.: Advanced programming language features for executable design patterns. Technical Report AIM-2002-005, MIT Artificial Intelligence Laboratory (2002)
4. Hannemann, J., Kiczales, G.: Design pattern implementation in java and AspectJ. In Norris, C., Fenwick, J.J.B., eds.: Proceedings of the 17th ACM conference on Object-oriented programming, systems, languages, and applications (OOPSLA-02). Volume 37, 11 of ACM SIGPLAN Notices., New York, ACM Press (2002) 161–173
5. Sheard, T.: Accomplishments and research challenges in meta-programming. Lecture Notes in Computer Science **2196** (2001) 2–44
6. Kiczales, G., Rivieres, J.D., Bobrow, D.: The Art of the Metaobject Protocol. MIT Press, Cambridge, MA (1991)
7. Bryant, A., Catton, A., Volder, K.D., Murphy, G.C.: Explicit programming. In: Proceedings of the 1st international conference on Aspect-oriented software development, ACM Press (2002) 10–18
8. Gamma, E., Helm, R., Johnson, R., Vlissides, J.: Design Patterns: Elements of Reusable Object-Oriented Software. Addison-Wesley Professional Computing Series. Addison-Wesley Publishing Company, New York, NY (1995)
9. Kuehne, T.: Internal iteration externalized. In Guerraoui, R., ed.: Proceedings ECOOP '99. Volume 1628 of LNCS., Lisbon, Portugal, Springer-Verlag (1999) 329–350
10. Agerbo, E., Cornils, A.: How to preserve the benefits of design patterns. In: Proceedings of the 13th Conference on Object-Oriented Programming, Systems, Languages, and Applications (OOPSLA-98). Volume 33, 10 of ACM SIGPLAN Notices., New York, ACM Press (1998) 134–143
11. Lieberherr, K., Orleans, D., Ovlinger, J.: Aspect-oriented programming with adaptive methods. Communications of the ACM **44** (2001) 39–41
12. Agerbo, E., Cornils, A.: Theory of language support for design patterns. Master's thesis, Department of Computer Science, Aarhus University (1997)
13. Soukop, J.: Implementing patterns. In Coplien, J.O., Schmidt, D.C., eds.: Pattern Languages of Program Design. Addison-Wesley Publishing Company (1995) 395–412
14. Tokuda, L., Batory, D.: Evolving object-oriented designs with refactorings. In: 14th IEEE International Conference on Automated Software Engineering, IEEE Computer Society Press (1999) 174–182

15. Tokuda, L., Batory, D.: Automating three modes of evolution for object-oriented software architectures. In: Proceedings of the 5th USENIX Conference on Object-Oriented Technologies and Systems (COOTS-99), Berkeley, CA, USENIX Association (1999) 189–202
16. Budinsky, F., Finnie, M., Vlissides, J., Yu, P.: Automatic code generation from design patterns. IBM Systems Journal **35** (1996) 151–171
17. Alexandrescu, A.: Modern C++ Design: Generic Programming and Design Patterns Applied. Addison-Wesley Publishing Company (2001)
18. Vlissides, J., Alexandrescu, A.: To code or not to code. C++ Report **March/June** (2000)
19. Bosch, J.: Design patterns as language constructs. Journal of Object-Oriented Programming **11** (1998) 18–32
20. Gil, J., Lorenz, D.H.: Design patterns vs. language design. In Bosch, J., Mitchell, S., eds.: Object-Oriented Technology: ECOOP'97 Workshop Reader. Volume 1357 of Lecture Notes in Computer Science., Springer (1997) 108–111 Workshop on Language Support for Design Patterns and Frameworks.

Generating Spreadsheet-Like Tools from Strong Attribute Grammars

João Saraiva[1] and Doaitse Swierstra[2]

[1] Department of Computer Science
University of Minho, Portugal
jas@di.uminho.pt

[2] Department of Computer Science
University of Utrecht, The Netherlands
swierstra@cs.uu.nl

Abstract. This paper presents techniques for the formal specification and efficient incremental implementation of spreadsheet-like tools. The spreadsheets are specified by strong attribute grammars. In this style of attribute grammar programming every single inductive computation is expressed within the attribute grammar formalism. Well-known attribute grammar techniques are used to reason about such grammars. For example, ordered scheduling algorithms can be used to statically guarantee termination of the attribute grammars and to derive efficient implementations. A strong attribute grammar for a spreadsheet is defined and the first incremental results are presented.

1 Introduction

"Functional programming is a good idea, but we haven't got it quite right yet. What we have been doing up to now is weak (or partial) functional programming. What we should be doing is strong (or total) functional programming - in which all computations terminate..."
[Tur96]

Attribute grammars (AG) and (lazy) functional programming are closely related, as initially pointed out by Johnsson [Joh87], Kuiper and Swierstra [KS87] and recent work at Utrecht [SA98,Sar99] and Oxford [dMPJvW99,dMBS00,VWMBK02] confirms. However, what the attribute grammar community, like its functional programming counterpart, has been doing up to now is weak attribute grammar programming. There are powerful attribute grammar techniques based on attribute dependencies which statically infer important properties of the underlying attribute grammar (for example, both the circularity test and Kastens' ordered scheduling algorithm [Kas80] infer termination properties of the AG). The fact is that it is common practice in the design of attribute grammars to define (some) inductive computations via semantic functions (to perform look-up operations in an environment, for example). Although some of these computations can be efficiently defined by semantic functions (expressed in a declarative language), by defining them outside the AG formalism, they are not analysed by the standard attribute grammar techniques. Therefore, they are simply copied/translated to the implementation of the AG (the attribute evaluator). As a result, if the semantic functions induce non-termination, then the attribute evaluator will not terminate. To complicate the task of the AG writer, the AG systems will mislead the writer by indicating that the AG is non-circular (in the case that no circularities are induced by the attribute dependencies). But, the fact is that the attribute evaluator does not terminate due to the existence of circular definitions! Indeed, all attribute grammar-based systems [RT89,JPJ+90,GHL+92,MLAŽ02,KS98] extend the AG formalism with a (declarative) language where inductive computations can be expressed. Besides the termination issue, there is a second important reason to express all our computations within the AG formalism. The attribute grammar community has done a considerable amount of work on deriving highly optimized implementations from AGs. For example, the fusion of AG fragments, the scheduling algorithms that minimize the number of traversals of the attribute evaluator, the deforestation techniques, etc. Thus, when the inductive computations are expressed within the AG formalism, we can use such techniques to derive highly optimized implementations for these computations. This is not the case when the computations are expressed as semantic functions.

The purpose of this paper is two-fold:

- First, to introduce the style of strong attribute grammar programming. Within strong attribute grammars all inductive computations are expressed via attributes and attribute equations. In this way, we can reason about our specifications within the AG setting by using well-known techniques. To achieve this style of AG programming, we rely entirely on the higher-order extension of attribute grammars [VSK89]. Within higher-order attribute grammars (HAG) every inductive computation can be modeled through attribution rules. More specifically, inductive semantic functions can be replaced by higher-order attributes. By expressing such functions within the AG formalism, we inherit all the nice properties of AGs, namely the static detection of circularities. On the other hand, within the setting of strong attribute grammars, we limit programming to the use of primitive recursion only, albeit in an effective syntactical manner.
- Second, to show that under this style of design and implementation of attribute grammars powerful tools can be constructed, we present a strong attribute grammar for a spreadsheet-like tool. In the design of this spreadsheet, we do not rely on semantic functions nor any library functions. Actually, all inductive computations are defined through attributes and their equations. Thus, the circularity test statically guarantees that this tool terminates for all possible (finite) inputs.

Spreadsheet-like tools heavily depend on a incremental model of re-evaluation. Efficient and elegant incremental attribute evaluators for HAGs can be obtained by using function memoization [SSK00], which provides an efficient implementation for the spreadsheet by relying entirely on the AG formalism. Furthermore, HAGs provide a component-based style of programming for AGs [Sar02]. We will use this feature of HAGs to glue useful AG components to our tool. We will consider the gluing of a table formatter component (the usual representation of spreadsheets) and a query language (for querying the database).

The style of strong attribute grammar programming can be used under any AG-based system that processes higher-order attribute grammars. We will use the *Lrc* system: an incremental, purely functional, and higher-order attribute grammar-based system [KS98]. Thus, the techniques presented in this paper are implemented in *Lrc* and our spreadsheet-like tool has been produced by this system. We also present results of the incremental behaviour of this tool. When compared with previous results of incremental attribute evaluation [SSK00], these results show that spreadsheet-like tools are a natural setting for incremental evaluation.

This paper is organized as follows: Section 2 introduces strong attribute grammars. Section 3 presents a strong attribute grammar for a spreadsheet-like tool. In Section 3.1 we extend the spreadsheet with a pretty-printing SAG component. Section 4 discusses the specification of a query language within SAG and its embedding in the running spreadsheet example. Section 5 discusses the incremental evaluation of strong attribute grammars and presents the results of the incremental behaviour of the spreadsheet. Section 6 discusses related work and Section 7 presents the conclusions.

2 Strong Attribute Grammars

Strong attribute grammars (SAG) are higher-order attribute grammars where every inductive computation is defined via (higher-order) attributes and their respective equations. Or, in other words, no recursive semantic function definition is included in the AG specification. Strong attribute grammars have four key properties:

- In the first place, the standard AG-based techniques apply directly to HAGs which implies that they also apply directly to strong attribute grammars. Since all inductive computations are specified via attribute and attribute equations, we can then use well-know attribute grammar techniques to statically detect circularities (*e.g.*, the circularity test). This is not the case in classical AGs, where a non-terminating semantic function can be included in the specification. Since standard attribute grammars do not consider semantic functions, the implementation derived for such grammars will not terminate either.
- Second, there are AG-based techniques that automatically derive efficient, highly optimized implementations from a (higher-order) attribute grammar. If we express the inductive computations outside the AG formalism, then optimization will not be applied to such semantic functions by the AG systems.

  For example, when structuring an attribute grammar, it is common practice to separate different semantic aspects into different AG fragments. Then, standard attribute grammar techniques will first fuse such fragments and statically schedule the computation (minimizing the number of tree traversals), before a set of optimized evaluator functions is generated. Consider that one expresses such semantic aspects with semantic functions, like, for example, functional programmers do. In this situation, the semantic functions are just translated to the generated attribute evaluator. These semantic functions will perform several traversals over the tree (actually, one per semantic function), while they could (probably) be tupled so that the number of traversals can be reduced (and the construction/destruction of intermediate gluing

data structures eliminated by using fusion). Such optimised functions can be obtained by applying the tupling, fusion and deforestation techniques [Wad90] which are well-known in the context of functional programming. In this case, we are relying on the compiler of the AG implementation language to perform the optimizations. However, such a compiler may not be available (if it exists at all).
- Third, the attribute grammar writer defines all the required algorithms within a single programming paradigm: the attribute grammar paradigm. No previous knowledge of a different programming paradigm (*e.g.*, functional programming) or programming language is necessary to efficiently and elegantly express these algorithms within SAG. This style of AG programming also makes the understanding, maintenance and updating of the AG specifications much simpler.
- Finally, because there is no need to support inductive semantic functions, the developers of AG-based systems do not have to include in their systems a powerful declarative language (and its complicated processor) to allow their definitions. This makes the systems simpler to construct, and easier to maintain and update.

We omit here the formal definition of higher-order attribute grammars which are the basis of strong attribute grammars. For their formal definition the reader is referred to [VSK89,Sar99] . Let us, however, briefly describe HAG. Higher-order attribute grammars extend classical attribute grammars with *higher-order attributes*, the so-called *attributable attributes*. Higher-order attributes are attributes whose value is a tree. We may associate, once again, attributes with such a tree. Attributes of these so-called *higher-order trees*, may be higher-order attributes again.

In order to show this style of attribute grammar programming we will consider now a motivating example: the design and implementation of a spreadsheet-like tool to manage a database of students and their respective marks.

3 The Students Spreadsheet Strong Attribute Grammar

Suppose that we have a (textual) database of students registered in one course. Each student (*i.e.*, register) has several attributes such as: identification number, name, and a list of marks (pairs containing the mark identification, and the value the student got). A possible (concrete) instance of the database is presented below.

```
33333,"Ana","tm"=16,"p1"=15,"p2"=17
44444,"Eduardo","tm"=12,"p1"=13,"p2"=15
```

The first register expresses that the student with number *33333*, named *Ana* got the mark 10 as theoretical mark (tm), 15 in the first project (p1) and 17 in the second one (p2). This database/language is defined by the following context-free grammar. A production p is denoted as $X_0 = \text{P } X_1 \ldots X_n$, where the name of the production, *i.e.*, p, also indicates the term constructor function P. The type of the constructor function is P :: $X_1 \to \cdots \to X_n \to X_0$ and we say that function P takes as arguments values of type $X_1 \cdots X_n$ and returns a value of type X_0. Roughly speaking, non-terminal symbols correspond to tree type constructors, and productions correspond to value constructors. We focus on the abstract structure of the language and we ignore its syntactic sugar, *e.g.*, punctuation symbols, etc.

Students = CONSSTUDS *Stud Students* 	NOSTUDS *Stud*　　= ONESTUD　　*Int String Marks* *Marks*　= CONSMARKS *Mark Marks* 	NOMARKS *Mark*　　= ONEMARK　　*String Real* 　　　　*Fragment 1*: The abstract grammar for the students database.

Having a database with the information about the students marks, the natural operations we would like to perform on that database are the mapping of a given formula through all the students in order to calculate, for example, their final classification. That is to say that we wish to construct a spreadsheet-like tool. To express a formula we consider a domain specific language (DSL) very much like the desk calculator language presented in [Paa95]. A concrete example of a formula is as follows:

```
"FinalMark" = ("tm" + "pm")/2
    where "pm" = ("p1" + "p2")/2
```

To define the formula that is applied to each student we have two possibilities:

- We may use a straightforward AG approach where the formula is defined as a semantic function, written in the declarative language used to express semantic functions in the AG formalism. As a result, this semantic function will not be analyzed (to infer termination properties) nor optimized by AG techniques. In this approach, the semantic function is part of the AG specification of the tool. As a result, the formula is processed statically and not dynamically. Thus, if we wish to use a different formula, the AG has to be modified, analysed and compiled in order to produced the desired tool.
- We use a key characteristic of strong attribute grammars: as semantic functions are redundant, they are modeled via higher-order attributes. Thus, we model the formula, or, more precisely, that language of formulas as a higher-order attribute of our spreadsheet. This is done as follows: first we define a grammar describing the (abstract) structure of the language of formulas and we extend it with attributes and equations. We introduce an inherited attribute to pass the list of marks as the "argument" of the formula, and a synthesised attribute to deliver the result of "applying" the formula to its inherited/argument. After that we have to "apply" such "function" in the context of every student. To do this, we just introduce a higher-order attribute to represent the abstract formula, we instantiate its inherited attribute (with the marks of a particular student) and we use its synthesised result. So, we define a DSL for formulas as a sub-language of our spreadsheet. Note that in this case the formula is processed dynamically since it is part of the input sentence. As a result, if the spreadsheet user wishes to change the formula, he just changes the part of the input sentence where the formula is defined.

Next we discuss in detail how this latter approach can be implemented in SAG. The structure of the spreadsheet is defined through the following grammar, where non-terminal *Students* is defined in Fragment 1, and non-terminal *Formula* represents the (abstract structure) of the formula under consideration.

SpreadSheet = ROOTPROD *Formula Students*
Formula   = ONEFORM *Exp Decls*

Fragment 2: The abstract grammar for the Spreadsheet-like language.

Let us assume that we have an off-the-shelf AG component whose root non-terminal is *Formula*. This non-terminal has one inherited attribute (representing a finite function mapping variable names to values) and it synthesises one attribute with the value expressed by the formula. Synthesised (inherited) attributes are prefixed with the up (down) arrow $\uparrow$ ($\downarrow$).

$Formula <\downarrow env : Env, \uparrow res : Real >$

We omit here the attribute declaration and equations of the (trivial) definition of this component. Note, however, that in this AG component we need to express an (inductive) lookup function because we have to lookup a particular mark in the inherited environment. Obviously, we define such a lookup function in the style of strong attribute grammars via higher-order attributes. See [Sar99] (page 37) where similar inductive functions are expressed within the AG formalism. To simplify our presentation, we shall consider that this SAG component is included in our specification in order to create a monolithic AG, which is then analised and the respective implementation derived.

In order to map the formula through the database of students, we have to move the (abstract) formula to the context of every student. Thus, we use another characteristic of the HAG, the so-called *syntactic references*, meaning that the abstract tree can be used directly as a value within a semantic equation. That is, grammar symbols can be moved from the syntactic domain to the semantic domain. In our example the "syntactic" symbol *Formula* is used within an equation as follows:

SpreadSheet = ROOTPROD *Formula Students*
          Students.form = *Formula*

Fragment 3: Passing the formula to the students.

Instead of defining attributes and equations to move the (abstract) formula downwards in the tree (*i.e.*, the student list) via trivial *copy rules*, we use a special notation to access a remote attribute (up in the tree). The expression {*Students.form*} refers to the local attribute *form* at the non-terminal *Students* [RT89,Hed99][1]. In our AG-based system the copy rules that are automatically generated corresponding to frequently used monadic structures: reader, writer, and state monads. The AG notation, however, is much easier to use, more aspect oriented, and does not suffer from the fact that monads do not compose well.

Now that we are able to access the formula in the desired context, *i.e.*, in production ONESTUD, we use a higher-order attribute to model the semantic function that "applies" the formula to the list of marks of a student. Note that the inherited attribute *form* is a higher-order attribute: it is a (higher-order) tree that has attributes as well. In order to access those attributes we have to use the higher-order extension to the AG formalism.

---

[1] See [KW94,SAS99] for a survey of special notation for common attribute propagation patterns.

This is done as follows: first, we declare a higher-order attribute, *i.e.*, attributable attribute (*ata*) named *form* of type *Formula*, to represent the formula. Then, we instantiate this attribute with the inherited global formula. After that, we instantiate the inherited attribute *env* of that *ata* with the list of marks of the student (and we use a syntactic reference once again). And finally, we access the synthesised value of the formula. We use a local attribute (*finalMark*) to store the computed value. This attribute value will be included in the pretty-printed representation of the spreadsheet (Section 3.1). In the HAG notation this is expressed as follows:

$Student$ = ONESTUD Int $Name$ $Marks$
    ata $form : Formula$ -- Declaration of the ata
    local $finalMark : Real$ -- Declaration of a local attr.
    $form$ = \{$Students.form$\}   -- Instantiation of the ata
    $form.env$ = $Marks$ -- Instantiation of the inherited attr.
    $finalMark = form.res$ -- Use of the synthesised attr.
    Fragment 4: The formula as a higher-order attribute.

Before we proceed, let us compare this higher-order style of defining such computations with the classical attribute grammar one. In the classical style we could express this inductive computation by defining a (generic) semantic function that accepts as arguments the abstract representation of the formula and the list of marks of the students. It delivers the result of applying the formula to the list of marks. We can write it as follows:

$Student$ = ONESTUD Int $Name$ $Marks$
    $finalMark = evalFormula(\{Students.form\}, Marks)$

where *evalFormula* is the inductive function. This function has to be defined and included in the AG specification. If this semantic function is semantically equivalent to the formula AG component, then, the previous two AG fragment are semantically equivalent as well. Furthermore, this approach also supports the dynamic update of the formula, since its representation is an argument of the semantic function. But, there are two important differences between these two approaches: while in the strong AG one, the AG techniques analyse the attribute dependencies, check for termination properties and, if no circularities are induced, finally, produce an optimized implementation. In the classical AG one, the function is simply translated to the output without any analysis nor optimization. As a consequence, it can cause the non-termination of the attribute evaluator. Moreover, for more elaborate semantic functions, such as pretty printing algorithm that will be presented in Section 3.1, it can be complicated to hand-write such inductive semantic functions.

The reader familiar with the implementation of (higher-order) attribute grammars may have noticed that the AG fragment just presented above corresponds to the structure of the attribute evaluator generated by the AG techniques from the higher-order one.

3.1 A Strong Attribute Grammar for Table Pretty-Printing

Spreadsheets are usually displayed (or, in other words, pretty printed) in a table-like representation. In this section we show how a generic, off-the-shelf pretty-printing SAG

```
<TABLE>                                        |------------------|
<TR><TD> This    </TD> </TR>                   |This              |
<TR><TD> is  </TD> <TD> a </TD> </TR>          |------------------|
<TR><TD>                                       |is        |a     |
   <TABLE>                                     |------------------|
   <TR><TD> This </TD><TD> is </TD></TR>       ||----------||table|
   <TR><TD> another </TD></TR>                 ||This  |is ||     |
   <TR><TD> table </TD></TR>                   ||----------||     |
   </TABLE>                                    ||another|  ||     |
</TD><TD> table </TD> </TR>                    ||----------||     |
</TABLE>                                       ||table  |  ||     |
                                               ||----------||     |
                                               |------------------|
```

Fig. 1. Table formatter.

component can be plugged into our students spreadsheet so as to obtain the desired representation[2]. This SAG component is based on the processor for HTML style tables we have presented in [SAS99]. It computes a pretty-printed textual (ascii) table from a HTML (table) text. An example of accepted input and the associated output is given in Figure 1. In the computed textual table, all the lines have the same number of columns and the columns have the same length. Both features are not required in the HTML language[3].

The abstract structure of nested tables is defined by the abstract grammar shown in Fragment 5.

Table = ROOTTABLE *Rows*
Rows = CONSROW   *Row Rows*
         | NOROW
Row   = ONEROW   *Elems*
Elems = CONSELEM *Elem Elems*
         | NOELEM
Elem = SNAME   *String*
         | NESTEDT *Table*

Fragment 5: The abstract grammar for nested tables.

As we did previously with the formula AG component, we omit here the attribution rules of the table formatter because they are not relevant for this paper. To reuse this

---

[2] Actually, attribute grammar systems provide a special domain specific language (or, in other words, a fixed number of combinators) to pretty-print the syntax tree (usually called *unparsing rules*).

[3] It is easy to see that the processor performs two traversals over the abstract tree that represents the input under consideration. First, it computes the maximal height and width of each row and column, respectively. Then, it passes such values down in the tree to add "glue" where needed. Things get a bit more complicated with the nesting of the tables. As we have shown in [SAS99] it is complex to hand-write this DSL's processor.

grammar we need to know the (above) abstract grammar and its *interface*, *i.e.*, the inherited and synthesised attributes of its root symbol, named *Table*. This table formatter grammar is context-free (it does not have inherited attributes) and synthesises the pretty printed ascii representation (attribute *ascii*). More recently we have extended our original AG in order to synthesise a LATEX, a XML, a VRML, and HTML table representation. Thus, we have a representation for our abstract tables in all these concrete languages. So, the root symbol has an additional synthesised attribute per every mentioned representation.

$Table <\uparrow ascii : String, \uparrow html : Table, \uparrow xml : Xml, \uparrow latex : Table, \uparrow vrml : Vrml>$

The table formatter SAG can be efficiently and concisely embedded in the specification of our spreadsheet as follows: first, we associate new attributes and attribute equations to the non-terminals and productions, respectively, of the spreadsheet abstract grammar (Fragment 2) in order to synthesise a table representation of the spreadsheet. So, we declare a new synthesised attribute, named *table*. The attribute equations simply use the constructors (productions) of the table formatter SAG in order to define the abstract table[4]. The resulting AG fragment looks as follows:

Students $<\uparrow table : Rows>$
Students = CONSSTUDS *Stud Students*
            $Students_1.table = $ CONSROW *Stud.table Students$_2$.table*
            | NOSTUDS
            Students.table = NOROW
Stud $<\uparrow table : Row>$
Stud   = ONESTUD *Int String Marks*
            Stud.table = ONEROW (CONSELEM (SNAME *Int.str*) (CONSELEM (SNAME *String*)
                         (CONSELEM (SNAME *finalMark.str*) NOELEM)))
            Fragment 6: Constructing the abstract table.

---

where *finalMark* is the local attribute declared in Fragment 4, which defines the final mark of a student according to the formula under consideration. By $finalMark.str$ we access its string representation. To make the AG more readable, we explicitly declare the attributes and their types for each non-terminal, although such information can be inferred from the semantic equations.

Having introduced attributes and their equations to define the abstract table representation of the database, we introduce now a higher-order attribute to "apply" the pretty-printing function to that abstract representation.

            $SpreadSheet <\uparrow ascii : String>$
SpreadSheet = ROOTPROD *Formula Students*
            ata *table* : *Table*
            table   = ROOTTABLE *Students.table*
            SpreadSheet.ascii = *table.ascii*
            Fragment 7: "Applying" the table formatter AG component.

---

[4] We explicitly use the constructor function induced by the table formatter grammar. We could, instead, define a set of functions with a more friendly user-defined syntax, like in Haskell.

3.2 The Students Spreadsheet Environment

The *Lrc* system produces a programming environment from a higher-order attribute grammar. Figure 2 displays a snapshot of a spreadsheet-tool produced by *Lrc* from a AG specified using the techniques presented in this paper. *Lrc* includes an attribute grammar component for describing interactive interfaces that is embedded in the specification using the techniques described in this paper. The GUI AG is described in detail in [Sar02]. Such an AG component has standard graphical user interface objects, like buttons that can be pressed, menus that can be selected, etc (see the main window). The second window (with name *Students ascii*) is the result that we obtain (for free) after embedding the table formatter SAG. A single view (*i.e.*, the ascii view) is shown, although the five different views (*e.g.*, HTML, LaTeX, VRML, etc) are automatically computed and can be selected in the menu *Views*. In the background, a frame contains a syntax-editor to edit the pretty-printed formula (actually, we use a list of formulas) and the student database. In this syntax-editor, the user can point to a formula and dynamically change it. The user can also point to a particular student and select it through a mouse button. Then, the information of the student is displayed in a new window, where it can be easily updated. All of these actions are modelled as (abstract syntax) tree transformations, since the *Lrc* system maintains an abstract syntax tree to represent the input under consideration. Indeed, the (pretty printed) text displayed in the environments, corresponds to the textual view of such a tree. The *Lrc* system uses incremental attribute evaluation, in order to provide immediate real-time feedback, after a user action. This will be discussed in Section 5.

4 A Strong Attribute Grammar for Querying Languages

Having specified the students database, the formula to compute their final marks and how such formula is applied to each of the students, we may wish to compute which students got good or bad results. Or, we may wish to compute the students that have a final mark greater than a given number. In other words, we would like to have some mechanism to be able to query our database.

Rather than defining a particular query language for our student database, we want to define a generic query language that can not only be used for querying this particular example, but also to query any other textual database defined within the AG formalism. That is to say that we want to define a domain specific language that can be easily embedded in any AG specification. In order to not introduce yet-another querying language, we will consider the *XQuery* language: a typed, functional language for querying XML, currently being designed by the *Xml* Query Working Group of the World-Wide Web Consortium [Dra02,Wad02]. We choose *XQuery* for two reasons: first, because attribute grammars and *Xml* technology are closely related [Bra98] (both extend the context-free grammar formalism), thus *XQuery* is indeed a suitable declarative language to express queries on AG-based language specifications. Second, a *Xml* combinator library to map abstract grammars (or trees) into *Xml* documents (or *Xml* trees) is already defined (via attribute grammars) in *Lrc*. Thus, we may re-use such a library, firstly to map the abstract grammar of the language under consideration to a *Xml* document, and then to query that *Xml* document.

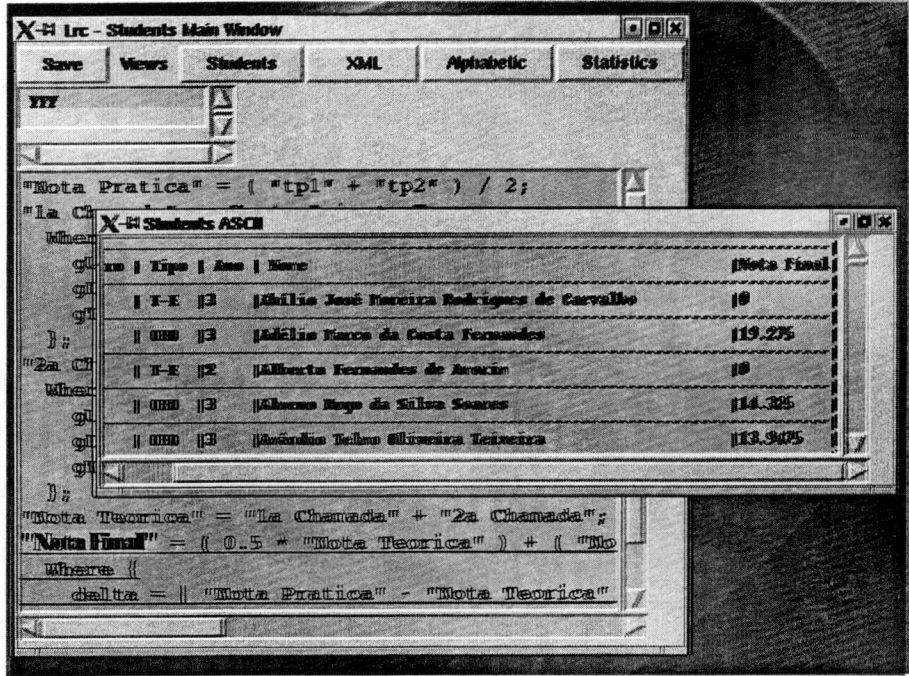

Fig. 2. A (domain specific) spreadsheet-like programming environment.

Before we briefly explain the *XQuery* language, let us present a fragment of the abstract grammar defining the structure of a *Xml* document.

Document = CDOCUMENT *Prolog Miscs Element*
Element = CELEM *Name LstAttribute LstContent*
Content = CELEMENT *Element*
 | CSTRING *CharData*
Fragment 8: The abstract grammar defining *Xml* documents.

XQuery uses *path expressions* that is a mechanism very much like the Unix notation to define paths on its file system. Instead of using the directory names, however, it uses the tags contained in an *Xml* document to indicate the path. Such tags correspond to the production names (or constructors) of the attribute grammar.

To introduce *XQuery*, let us consider some example queries on our student database. To list the students registered in the course we have to write the following simple *XQuery* sentence (see non-terminals and productions on fragments 1 and 2):

```
RootProd/Students
```

To list the students that got a final mark greater than 13 we can write the following query:

```
RootProd/Students/OneStud[//OneMark/@FinalMark.>.13]
```

This query selects the element OneStud (or the subtree constructed with constructor OneStud), that contains as descendent (the double slash // means that the tagged element can be a direct or an undirect descendent) an element OneMark where the attribute FinalMark is defined and it is greater than 13.

To model *XQuery* in the SAG formalism we start by defining the (abstract) structure of this language via a context-free grammar. A fragment of such a grammar is presented next.

$$
\begin{aligned}
Query &= \text{PRODQUERY} \quad AQuery \\
AQuery &= \text{CURRENTCONTEXT} \quad TQuery \\
&\mid \text{ROOTCONTEXT} \quad TQuery \\
&\mid \text{DEEPCONTEXTFROMROOT} \; TQuery \\
TQuery &= \text{PRODBRACKETTQ} \quad TQuery \; XQuery \\
&\mid \text{PRODTAG} \quad XQuery
\end{aligned}
$$

Fragment 9: The abstract grammar defining *XQuery* langauge.

We extend this grammar with attributes and equations in order to synthesise the desired information, that is to say, the answer to the query under consideration. The result of a query is another *Xml* document that contains the elements of the original document that answers the query. Thus, to perform a query is to evaluate a function, say *query*, that takes the query and the *Xml* document as arguments and returns another *Xml* document. In our setting, such a function has type:

$$query :: AQuery \to Document \to Document$$

This is, once again, an inductive function that can be efficiently defined within the style of strong attribute grammar programming, using the techniques presented in Section 3. We omit here the definition of the attributes and respective equations since they are not relevant to understand our technique nor to re-use such a query language AG component.

Now that we have introduced this generic query component, we can embed it in any attribute grammar specification. For example, we can embed it in a bibliographic database processor (*e.g.*, *BibTeX* [Sar99]) to list the books written by a given author. Or, we can embed it in our spreadsheet specification in order to extend the spreadsheet environment shown in Figure 2 with a powerful querying language. Figure 3 displays a new window included in the spreadsheet that provides the user with a syntax editor to interactively query the student database. The query being displayed is the example query discussed above.

5 Incremental Evaluation of Strong Attribute Grammars

A spreadsheet-like system has to react and to provide answers in real-time. Consequently, the delay between the user interaction and the system response is an extremely important aspect in such interactive systems. Thus, one of the key features to handle such interactive environments is the ability to perform efficient re-computations. That is to say that spreadsheets must use an efficient incremental computational model. Implementing an efficient incremental engine from scratch is a complex task.

Generating Spreadsheet-Like Tools from Strong Attribute Grammars   319

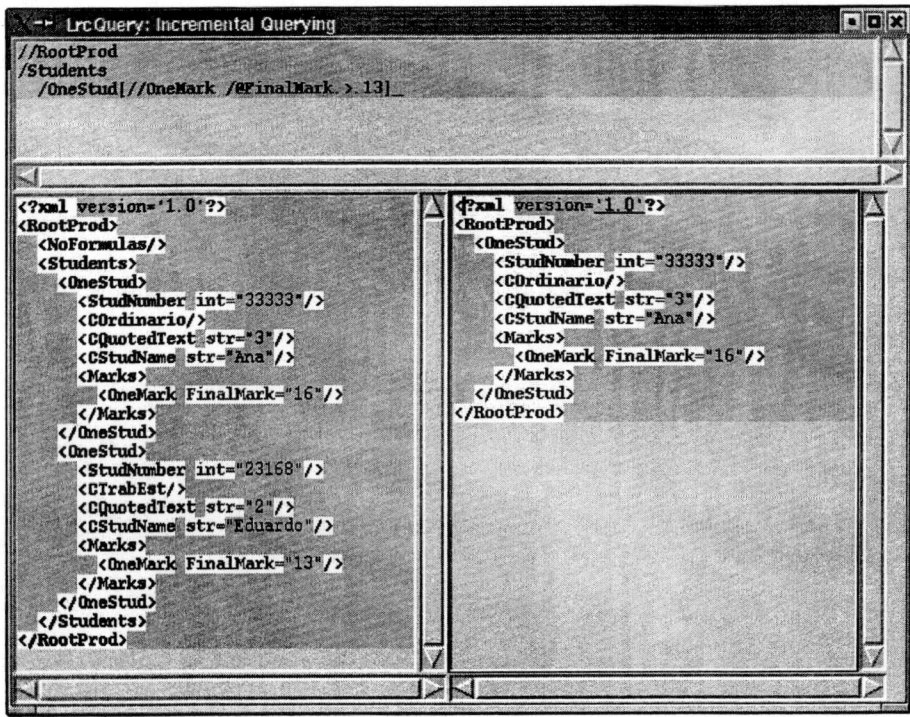

Fig. 3. Querying the students spreadsheet: the top frame displays the query that is performed on the *Xml* representation of the database (frame on the left). The answer to the query is displayed as a *Xml* document on the right frame.

A key characteristic of (higher-order) attribute grammars is that efficient incremental implementations can be automatically derived from them. A simple and efficient incremental model is obtained by standard function memoization techniques: abstract trees are collapsed into directed acyclic graphs and calls to the attribute evaluator's pure functions are memoized [SSK00].

Next, we present results obtained when executing the spreadsheet with a real student database: the database contains the students and all their marks, who followed the compiler construction course at University of Minho where this tool was proposed as the course project. The number of students attending this course was 144 and to each of them corresponds 15 evaluation elements (*i.e.*, partial evaluation marks) wich are used by a list of 7 formulas to compute different aspects of their evaluation (for example, a particular exam, the projects mark, the final mark, etc). This database was constructed and is maintained by the spreadsheet tool. Actually, we have used this tool to manage the course, as opposed to the use of a commercial tool as we had done before.

The table below presents results obtained both with non-incremental evaluation, *i.e.*, without memoization of the calls to the evaluator functions, and with incremental evaluation, *i.e.*, with memoization of the function calls. It shows the number of functions evaluated (*cache misses*), functions reused (*cache hits*), and time (in seconds on an 433

MHz Intel Celeron processor, running Linux Red-Hat 7.2). We consider five different situations: the processing of the database from scratch (*i.e.*, starting with an empty memo table), and the reaction after adding a new formula, editing one, deleting a student and editing a student mark.

	Fun. Evaluated (cache misses)	Fun. Reused (cache hits)	time (secs)
Non-Incremental:			
Scratch	217743	-	32.3
Adding a formula	229553	-	37.2
Editing a formula	217743	-	33.8
Deleting a student	216442	-	34.9
Editing a student mark	217743	-	34.8
Incremental:			
Scratch	14540	5305	5.9
Adding a formula	6375	5494	3.7
Editing a formula	2557	2131	1.9
Deleting a student	1724	1571	1.4
Editing a student mark	1652	1486	0.8

As the above table shows, our incremental model of attribute evaluation produces efficient implementations. Even when processing an input from scratch, the incremental evaluator computes 6.6% as many functions as compared to when no incrementality is used (14540 functions evaluated against 217743, respectively) and is 6 times faster. The reused functions are, in this case, due to the decoration of the same tree (representing the formula) with the same inherited attributes (the same marks). Or, in other words, the reuse of previous evaluations of the formula with the same "arguments". As expected, the tool handles very well updates of the input: adding a new (global) formula requires the re-evaluation of 0.03% of the functions computed with non-incremental evaluation and 44% of the functions if we consider incremental evaluation. Better results are obtained with local changes (*e.g.*, editing a student mark).

We have previously presented results of incremental evaluation in the context of incremental syntax-based editing [SSK00], where the performance of the incremental engine is not as efficient as the one presented here. For example, when processing the input from scratch, the incremental evaluator is 70% slower than the non-incremental one, due to the overhead of the incremental computational model. In the spreadsheet tool what happens is exactly the contrary. Indeed, these results prove that spreadsheet-like tools are a natural setting for incremental evaluation.

6 Related Work

The approach presented in this paper was strongly inspired by David Turner's work on elementary strong functional programming [Tur96] and the Charity programming language [CF92]. Strong functional programming, however, is known to be restrictive in the recursion patterns it allows. Our notion of strong attribute grammars is more flexible: we have the full expressiveness of higher-order attribute grammars. Charity is a polymorphic, strongly-typed language. Programs in this language are built as the composition of combinators (such as anamorphisms, catamorphisms, hylomorphisms, etc). Written in this functional style, any program has a guarantee to terminate, in the sense that it can always be reduced to a head normal form, and, therefore, a result is produced for every (finite) input.

Incremental attribute evaluation can also be achieved by using Thomas Reps' *change propagation algorithm* [RTD83]. Such an algorithm stores attribute values in the nodes of the tree and propagates changes through the tree, re-using the values of non-affected attributes and computing the values of the affected ones. Roughly speaking, this algorithm memoizes results of attribute evaluation locally in the nodes where the computation is performed (while we memoize such values as results of function calls in a global memo table). Change propagation algorithms are known to give non-optimal incremental behaviour for HAG [CP96]. Our spreadsheet-like tool is a good example to show the limitations of this approach. Consider, for example, that a given formula is applied to a student, then the result of such function is memoized in one node of the subtree that represents that particular student. If the formula is applied to other student who has same marks, rather than re-evaluating the function we wish to reuse the previously computed result. Because the result of the previous application is memoized and available in the context of the first student, no reuse can then be achieved. That is to say that, under a change propagation algorithm, our spreadsheet will have a poor incremental behaviour. Reps' change propagation algorithm has been implemented in the synthesizer generator system [RT89]: an attribute grammar based system that generates language-based editors. Unfortunately, we are not able to present results using this approach since the synthesizer generator does not handle the class of higher-order attribute grammars.

7 Conclusions

This paper presented strong attribute grammars. In this style of attribute grammar programming every inductive function is defined within the AG formalism, by modelling it via higher-order attributes. Under this style of AG programming, well-known AG algorithms are used both to guarantee termination of the AG implementation and to derive efficient implementations. Furthermore, the use of attribute grammars has brought a nice aspected-oriented (syntactic) notation to programming with primitive recursive functions.

To prove that powerful tools can be constructed in SAG, a spreadsheet-like tool was constructed. This tool was efficient and elegantly specified within this style of attribute grammar programming. The *Lrc* system processed such a specification and derived a correct and efficient implementation. The results of incremental evaluation show that spreadsheets are a natural context for incremental evaluation. Actually, these results are much better than previous results of incremental evaluation (mainly produced in the context of syntax-based editing).

No inductive semantic function was included in the specification of the spreadsheet. Indeed, strong attribute grammar programming is just programming with attributes and their equations.

Acknowledgements

We would like to thank the students who followed the course *Processamento de Linguagens* in the scholar years 2000/2001 and 2001/2002 at University of Minho for their enthusiasm in discussing the design and implementation of the spreadsheet used as our running example. A special thanks to David Costa and António Faria for developing the query AG presented in Section 4. We also would like to thank the anonymous reviewers for their helpful comments.

References

[Bra98] Neil Bradley. *The XML Companion*. Addison Wesley, 1998.

[CF92] Robin Cockett and Tom Fukushima. About Charity. Yellow Series Report No. 92/480/18, Department of Computer Science, University of Calgary, June 1992.

[CP96] Alan Carle and Lori Pollock. On the Optimality of Change Propagation for Incremental Evaluation of Hierarchical Attribute Grammars. *ACM Transactions on Programming Languages and Systems*, 18(1):16–29, January 1996.

[dMBS00] Oege de Moor, Kevin Backhouse, and Doaitse Swierstra. First-Class Attribute Grammars. In D. Parigot and M. Mernik, editors, *Third Workshop on Attribute Grammars and their Applications, WAGA'99*, pages 1–20, Ponte de Lima, Portugal, July 2000. INRIA Rocquencourt.

[dMPJvW99] Oege de Moor, Simon Peyton-Jones, and Eric van Wyk. Aspect-Oriented Compilers. In *Proceedings of the First International Symposium on Generative and Component-Based Software Engineering (GCSE '99)*, volume 1799 of *LNCS*. Springer-Verlag, September 1999.

[Dra02] W3C Working Draft. *XQuery 1.0: An XML Query Language*, April 2002.

[GHL+92] R. W. Gray, V. P. Heuring, S. P. Levi, A. M. Sloane, and W. M. Waite. Eli: A Complete, Flexible Compiler Construction System. *Communications of the ACM,*, 35(2):121–131, February 1992.

[Hed99] Gorel Hedin. Reference Attributed Grammars. In D. Parigot and M. Mernik, editors, *Second Workshop on Attribute Grammars and their Applications, WAGA'99*, pages 153–172, Amsterdam, The Netherlands, March 1999. INRIA rocquencourt.

[Joh87] Thomas Johnsson. Attribute grammars as a functional programming paradigm. In G. Kahn, editor, *Functional Programming Languages and Computer Architecture*, volume 274 of *LNCS*, pages 154–173. Springer-Verlag, September 1987.

[JPJ+90] Martin Jourdan, Didier Parigot, Catherine Julié, Olivier Durin, and Carole Le Bellec. Design, implementation and evaluation of the FNC-2 attribute grammar system. In *ACM SIGPLAN'90 Conference on Programming Languages Design and Implementation*, volume 25, pages 209–222. ACM, June 1990.

[Kas80] Uwe Kastens. Ordered attribute grammars. *Acta Informatica*, 13:229–256, 1980.

[KS87] Matthijs Kuiper and Doaitse Swierstra. Using attribute grammars to derive efficient functional programs. In *Computing Science in the Netherlands CSN'87*, November 1987.

[KS98] Matthijs Kuiper and João Saraiva. Lrc - A Generator for Incremental Language-Oriented Tools. In Kay Koskimies, editor, *7th International Conference on Compiler Construction, CC/ETAPS'98*, volume 1383 of *LNCS*, pages 298–301. Springer-Verlag, April 1998.

[KW94] Uwe Kastens and William Waite. Modularity and reusability in attribute grammars. *Acta Informatica*, 31:601–627, June 1994.

[MLAŽ02]   Marjan Mernik, M. Lenič, E. Avdičaušević, and V. Žumer. Lisa: An interactive environment for programming language development. In Nigel Horspool, editor, *International Conference on Compiler Construction, CC/ETAPS'02*, volume 2304 of *LNCS*, pages 1–4. Springer-Verlag, April 2002.

[Paa95]   Jukka Paakki. Attribute Grammar Paradigms - A High-Level Methodology in Language Implementation. *ACM Computing Surveys*, 27(2):196–255, June 1995.

[RT89]   T. Reps and T. Teitelbaum. *The Synthesizer Generator*. Springer, 1989.

[RTD83]   Thomas Reps, Tim Teitelbaum, and Alan Demers. Incremental context-dependent analysis for language-based editors. *ACM Transactions on Programming Languages and Systems*, 5(3):449–477, July 1983.

[SA98]   S. Doaitse Swierstra and Pablo Azero. Attribute Grammars in a Functional Style. In *Systems Implementation 2000*, Berlin, 1998. Chapman & Hall.

[Sar99]   João Saraiva. *Purely Functional Implementation of Attribute Grammars*. PhD thesis, Department of Computer Science, Utrecht University, The Netherlands, December 1999.

[Sar02]   João Saraiva. Component-based Programming for Higher-Order Attribute Grammars. In Don Batory, Charles Consel, and Walid Taha, editors, *Proceedings of the ACM SIGPLAN/SIGSOFT Conference on Generative Programming and Component Engineering, GCSE 2002, Held as Part of the Confederation of Conferences on Principles, Logics, and Implementations of High-Level Programming Languages, PLI 2002, Pittsburgh, PA, USA, October 3-8, 2002*, volume 2487 of *LNCS*, pages 268–282. Springer-Verlag, October 2002.

[SAS99]   Doaitse Swierstra, Pablo Azero, and João Saraiva. Designing and Implementing Combinator Languages. In Doaitse Swierstra, Pedro Henriques, and José Oliveira, editors, *Third Summer School on Advanced Functional Programming*, volume 1608 of *LNCS*, pages 150–206. Springer-Verlag, September 1999.

[SSK00]   João Saraiva, Doaitse Swierstra, and Matthijs Kuiper. Functional Incremental Attribute Evaluation. In David Watt, editor, *9th International Conference on Compiler Construction, CC/ETAPS2000*, volume 1781 of *LNCS*, pages 279–294. Springer-Verlag, March 2000.

[Tur96]   D. A. Turner. Elementary strong functional programming. In R.Plasmeijer and P.Hartel, editors, *First International Symposium on Functional Programming Languages in Education*, volume 1022 of *Lecture Notes in Computer Science*, pages 1–13. Springer-Verlag, 1996.

[VSK89]   Harald Vogt, Doaitse Swierstra, and Matthijs Kuiper. Higher order attribute grammars. In *ACM SIGPLAN '89 Conference on Programming Language Design and Implementation*, volume 24, pages 131–145. ACM, July 1989.

[VWMBK02]   E. Van Wyk, O. de Moor, K. Backhouse, and P. Kwiatkowski. Forwarding in attribute grammars for modular language design. In R. N. Horspool, editor, *Compiler Construction, 11th International Conference, CC 2002, Held as Part of the Joint European Conferences on Theory and Practice of Software, ETAPS 2002, Grenoble, France, April 8-12, 2002*, volume 2304 of *Lecture Notes in Computer Science*, pages 128–142. Springer-Verlag, 2002.

[Wad90]   Philip Wadler. Deforestation: transforming programs to eliminate trees. *Theoretical Computer Science*, 73:231–248, 1990.

[Wad02]   Philip Wadler. Xquery: a typed functional language for querying XML. In *Fourth Summer School on Advanced Functional Programming, Oxford*, August 2002.

SynchNet: A Petri Net Based Coordination Language for Distributed Objects

Reza Ziaei and Gul Agha

Department of Computer Science
University of Illinois at Urbana-Champaign, USA
{ziaei,agha}@cs.uiuc.edu

Abstract. We present SynchNet, a compositional meta-level language for coordination of distributed. Its design is based on the principle of separation of concerns, namely separation of the coordination from computational aspects. SynchNet can be used in combination with any object-based language capable of expressing sequential behavior of objects. SynchNet, which is inspired by Petri nets, has a simple syntax and semantics, but is expressive enough to code many of the commonly used coordination patterns. The level of abstraction that it provides allows tools and techniques developed for Petri nets to be readily applied to analysis and verification of the specified coordination patterns.

1 Introduction

To manage the complexity of designing distributed object systems, many proposed frameworks advocate separation of coordination from computational aspects of systems [14]. One distinct group of solutions in this category may be called the *two-level* approach. A two-level framework consists of two languages: a *base* language in which the functionality of application processes and objects is described, and a *meta* language in which the developer specifies the coordination logic that governs the interaction among application level objects. Examples of such frameworks include the Synchronizers of [19], the reflective meta-architecture of [2], and the Two-Level Actor Machine (TLAM) of [22]. The use of 'meta' vs. 'base' terminology reflects the view that meta-level coordination policies are in fact modifications to the interaction semantics of the base application.

Two-level languages usually have an involved semantics. As a result, it may be difficult to understand programs written in these frameworks and it is usually even harder to reason about them. This is especially true when the meta-level components are allowed to access the state of the base-level objects; this creates a source of interference that is difficult to control. To counter these difficulties many proposed solutions disallow meta-level coordination components to access the states of base-level objects.

Frølund [19] has proposed a coordination language and framwework in which a group of distributed objects are coordinated by entities called *synchronizers*. Each synchronizer is responsible for coordination of a group of objects: it decides when a message *may* or *must* be delivered to an object in the group. Synchronizers do not have access to the state of coordinated objects and maintain their own independent state. The decision to approve a message delivery is based on predicates that refer to the state of the synchronizer and the information in the message. The state of the synchronizer is updated whenever an approved message is delivered. Therefore, the state of the synchronizer can be seen as an abstraction of some global snapshot of the states of the objects in the group. With this kind of abstraction, which provides a virtual local view of distributed actions, it is much simpler to solve coordination problems than with a language that only provides asynchronous message passing as a means of communication. Depending on the compiler for the synchronizer language, either centralized or distributed code may be generated.

We propose a new language called SynchNet, which follows the same design principles as Frølund's Synchronizers, but is based on Petri Nets [18]. Petri Nets is a formal modeling language for concurrent systems that has received wide academic and practical interest since its introduction by Carl Adam Petri in 1962 [18]. Its popularity is due to its rich and well-studied theory together with a friendly and easy-to-understand graphical notation. Petri Nets are less powerful than Turing machines, and therefore verification of many interesting properties is decidable [6]. Decidable properties include reachability, which is useful in verification of safety properties such as deadlock-freedom.

Using SynchNet, one can specify a synchronizer coordinating a group of objects. The specification of a synchronizer is translated into a *synchronizing net* or *synchnet*, which is in fact a Petri net. A two-level semantics relates the execution of the synchnet to method invocations in coordinated objects and thus allows enforcement of coordination requirements as specified.

The formal language of Petri Nets allows us to give formal definitions of interesting properties for synchnets. For instance, in the last section of this paper, we define a preorder relation on synchnets that states when it is safe to replace a deadlock-free synchnet with an alternative implementation while preserving the coordination properties of the first synchnet. Using this relation, one can verify the correctness of a synchnet implementation with respect to a more abstractly defined synchnet.

1.1 Related Work

Designing linguistic primitives and styles for distributed coordination, that is coordination of systems in which the primary mode of communication is asynchronous message passing, has a long history. We discuss hightlights of this evolution by first considering low-level mechanisms, and then move towards more abstract and modular constructs.

Most languages for programming communicating processes contain two operations `send` and `receive` that communicate data over *channels* connecting communicating processes. Usually a process executing a `receive` operation on a channel blocks until a message is available on the channel. Sending processes, however, may either block until a receiver is available to receive the message (*synchronous* mode), or proceed with their execution, leaving the message in channel's *buffer* for the receiving process to pick it up later (*asynchronous* mode).

To protect blocked processes from remaining blocked whenever a channel remains empty indefinitely, the *input-guarded command* was introduced. Input-guarded command is an extenstion of Dijkstra's guarded command [5] with added conditions to check availability of messages on a channel. This construct was introduced in the language Communicating Sequential Processes by Hoare [10]. CSP uses synchronous communication, but it is not difficult to conceive of input-guarded commands in a language with asynchronous communication primitives.

A more structured and higher-level construct, which is also based on input-guarded command is Ada's *rendez-vous* mechanism [4]. Rendez-vous hides a pair of message-based communications behind an abstraction similar to a procedure call. Ada combines this procedure-like abstraction with input-guarded commands into an elegant and powerful coordination mechanism.

A practical communication abstraction, which is similar to rendez-vous, but can be virtually used with any procedural language is *Remote Procedure Call* (RPC). RPC was first introduced in the programming language Distributed Processes (DP) by Brinch Hansen [9]. RPC implementations slightly modify the procedure call semantics by translating a call/return into a pair of message communications, somewhat similar to rendez-vous. RPC is less flexible than rendez-vous as it does not allow receiving processes to choose the channel from which to receive messages. The RPC framework would require the programmer to write extensive code to avoid deadlock situtations. Yet, the simplicity and efficiency of RPC has turned it into a widely used mechanism in practice. Inspired by this success, some object-oriented languages, such as Java, extended their method invocation semantics in a similar fashion to a distributed version called *Remote Method Invocation* (RMI).

All the communication and coordination mechanisms mentioned so far suffer from a software engineering deficiency, namely the mix-up of coordination behavior with the compuational aspects of a system. To provide a separation between coordination and computation aspects, there have been many proposals for modular specification [19, 3, 7, 16, 21]. The focus of these works has mainly been on the software engineering benefits obtained from separation of concerns, such as reuse and customizability. Our proposal, while fitting in this category of work, further attempts to limit the expressivity of the language to the extent that available formal tools and theories for analysis and verification become applicable.

A useful aspect of our proposed framework is that the compiler for SynchNets automatically generates distributed code from the specification of a synchronizing net. The generated code, which is interweaved with coordinated objects' code, uses the communication primitives available in the base-language. In this sense our framework can also be placed in the more general scheme of aspect oriented programming [12], in which a separately specified aspect of a program's behavior is automatically "weaved" into the code that implements the basic functionality of the program.

SynchNet can also be used in specifying *synchronization constraints* on the order of method invocation for a single object. It is known, however, that synchronization constraints often conflict with *inheritance* in concurrent object-oriented languages. This phenomenon is generally known as *inheritance anomaly*. Many linguistic solutions have been proposed to counter the inheritance anomaly. Matsuoka and Yonezawa provide a rather comprehensive analysis of the situation and compare various proposed solutions in [15]. They have distinguished three reasons for inheritance anomaly in this paper and show that most proposals fail to consider all. They go on by presenting a complete solution. SynchNets too, seem to successfully avoid the three sources of inheritance anomaly, despite the simplicity of their syntax and semantics.

1.2 Outline

In section 2 we motivate our approach in designing a new coordination language. In section 3 we present the syntax and semantics of SynchNet. We also present several examples to illustrate the expressive power of the language. Section 4 defines a refinement relation that states when it is safe to replace a synchronizing net with another one. Finally, we provide a summary and discuss future work.

2 Coordination of Objects with SynchNets

Our object-based model of distributed computation is inspired by the Actor model [1]. We assume each object is identified by a unique reference. Objects communicate by an asynchronous communication mechanism called ARMI (Asynchronous Remote Method Invocation). Physical locations of objects are not modeled explicitly and hence all communications are uniformly assumed to be remote. In ARMI, the source object asynchronously sends a message specifying the method of the target object to be invoked accompanied by the arguments to be passed. Messages are guaranteed to reach the target object free from error and are buffered in the target object's mailbox. No assumption is made on the order of message arrival. A local scheduler selects a message from the mailbox and invokes the specified method using the message content as arguments. Objects are single threaded and at most one method invocation can be in progress at any moment. According to this model, synchronizers are specifications that dictate the behavior of schedulers.

ARMI is similar to the remote method invocation model used in many distributed object-based languages and platforms such as CORBA [8], DCOM [20], and Java RMI [13]. The difference is that our model of invocation is asynchronous. The usual remote method invocation (RMI) is a rendez-vous like communication mechanism, in which the source object blocks until the method execution is complete and returns with a message containing the result. In ARMI, the source does not even wait for the invocation to begin. When an invoked method reaches the end of its execution, it may choose to send back the result using a separate ARMI. Hence, it is possible to model RMI as a pair of ARMI communications. Therefore, our results can be incorporated into practical platforms that use RMI like communication mechanisms.

We propose a two-level language for coordination of distributed objects communicating via ARMI. The *base* language can be any conventional sequential class-based language such as Java or C++, with the method invocation semantics modified to be ARMI. The meta language is SynchNet. In SynchNet, coordination patterns are specified as modules. Each module is translated into a so called *synchronizing net* or *synchnet*, which is a Petri net with a slightly modified semantics that relates the transitions of the net to method invocations in the base objects. After a brief overview of Petri Nets, we motivate our work via two classical coordination problems.

2.1 Petri Nets

We begin this subsection by an informal introduction to Petri Nets and its graphical notation. A formal definition of the model will be given later. A well-written exposition on Petri Nets can be found in [17]. We also argue why Petri Nets by itself is not a suitable language for the development of distributed systems.

The graphical presentation of a Petri net is a graph with nodes and arcs connecting the nodes. There are two kinds of nodes: *places*, which usually model resources or partial state of the system, and *transitions*, which model state transition and synchronization. Arcs are directed and always connect nodes of different types. Multiple arcs between two nodes are allowed. Figure 1 is an example net.

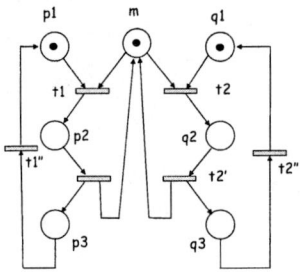

Fig. 1. A Petri Net Example

In a Petri Net, the state of the system is modeled by marking the places of the net with *tokens*. A place can be marked with a finite number (possibly zero) of tokens. For instance, in Figure 1 the token in place m represents the availability of a semaphore. The semantics of transitions determine how the state of the system changes. A transition t is said to be *enabled* in a certain marking if for every arc from a place p to t, there exists a distinct token in the marking of p. For instance, in Figure 1, the two transitions $t1$ and $t2$ are enabled. An *enabled* transition can *fire* and result in a new marking. Firing of a transition t in a marking μ is an atomic operation that subtracts one token from the marking of any place p for every arc connecting p to t, and adds one token to the marking of any place p for every arc connecting t to p. For instance in Figure 1 the transition $t1$ can fire and as a result change the marking of the net by removing one token from m and one token from $p1$ and putting one token in $p2$. It is also possible for transistion $t2$ to fire. The choice is made non-deterministically.

Petri Nets is not a suitable model for distributed object-based programming. In Petri Nets asynchronous computation is represented naturally, but only synchronous communication can be modeled directly. Modeling asynchronous communication requires explicit representation of communication channels. This renders Petri Nets unfit for distributed programming. Almost every distributed programming language hides channel and buffering representations and only provides high-level primitives for communication and synchronization. Another disadvantage is that Petri Nets are not capable of directly expressing creation of new processes or objects (More expressible extensions are available but they lack the nice decidability properties of classical Petri Nets).

2.2 Example I

We state a coordination problem and write a SynchNet module to solve it. A group of transmitters are scattered in a field to transmit sensed data. Transmitters communicate with one another via asynchronous sending of messages. Delivery of messages triggers invocation of methods in the objects that control the transmitters. Each transmitter is controlled by an object with two methods: An on method takes an argument that determines transmission power and turns on the transmitter, and an off method that turns it off. A global requirement is that no two transmitters may be transmitting at the same time. It is therefore necessary that off messages are sent to turn off the transmitters before the next transmission begins. We abstract away the distributed logic that decides on when and to which transmitter on and off messages must be sent, and try to coordinate the global order of message delivery so that two conditions are guaranteed: (I) on and off messages are delivered to each object in alternation, (II) no two transmitters are transmitting simultaneously.

Suppose controller objects are instances of the class TransmitterC and that Transmitters is a list containing references to the identifiers of a collection of controller objects. The following module specifies the two requirements stated above:

```
synchnet TransmitterME(Transmitters: list of TransmitterC)
   init = { ob'.off | ob' in Transmitters}

   foreach ob in Transmitters [with fairness]
      method ob.on
         requires    {ob'.off | ob' in Transmitters}
```

```
           consumes    {ob.off}
      method ob.off
           requires    {ob.on}
           consumes    {ob.on}
end TransmitterME
```

To generate and install a synchnet according to the specification of `TransmittermE` on a collection of objects `G` by issuing the statement `TransmitterME(G)` in the base-language. `G` is a list of object references on which the generated synchnet must be installed.

`TransmitterME` states that an `on` method can be invoked on object `ob` if every transmitter in the group is off. In Petri net terms, it states that `ob.on` may be invoked only when in the state of `TransmitterME` there is one `ob'.off` token available for each object `ob'` in the group. Once the invocation of an `ob.on` is decided the state of the generated ynchnet is modified by adding one token corresponding to the invoked method (`ob.on` here), and consuming the tokens specified in the `consumes` multilist. Note that consuming `ob.off` here guarantees that no other `on` method is invoked unless the object `ob` is turned off again. The only requirement on invocation of an `ob.off` method is that `ob` is turned on. After consuming the token `ob.on` which indicates `ob` is on, other transmitters may get a chance to be turned on. The optional condition [`with fairness`] requires that all pending methods to objects in the group must be given a fair opportunity of invocation.

Figure 2 is the graphical version of the synchnet generated by the expression `TransmitterME({t1,t2})`, which is an instantiation of `TransmitterME` on two transmitters `t1` and `t2`. There is one place for each method of each object in the group. There is one transition for each pair of `requires-consumes` clauses specified for each method. The `requires` clause specifies tokens required for the transition to become enabled. The `consumes` clause specifies which required tokens are actually consumed and are not put back in their corresponding places. Also note that, for every transition, there is an outgoing arc to its corresponding place, and is used to record method invocation that take place.

2.3 Example II

Now we use SynchNet to solve a distributed version of the dining philosophers problem: a group of philosophers are sitting around a round table and spend their time between thinking and eating. Each philosopher needs two forks to eat but every philosopher has to share one fork with the philosopher sitting on the left and share one fork with the philosopher on the right. Philosophers may only eat if they can pick up both their forks, otherwise they have to wait for philosophers next to them to finish eating and put down the shared forks. The problem is to coordinate picking up and putting down of the forks so that every hungry philosopher gets a fair chance of eating and that a deadlock situation does not occur in which every philosopher is holding one fork while waiting for the next philosopher to release the other fork.

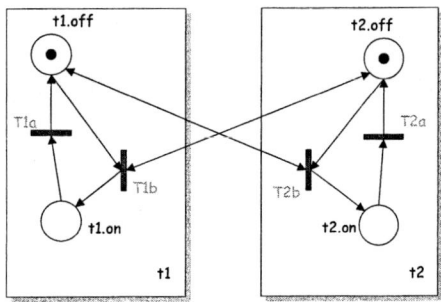

Fig. 2. Diagram of `TransmitterME` instantiated on `t1` and `t2` in its initial state

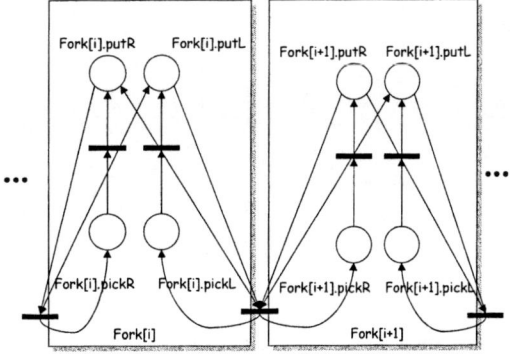

Fig. 3. Partial diagram of `Philosophers`

Suppose philosophers and forks are modeled as objects and communicate via asynchronous remote method invocation. Since we are concerned only with access to forks, we won't worry about the methods in philosopher objects. Each fork may be accessed using one of four methods: `pickL` and `putL` are used by the philosopher on the left of the fork to obtain and release the fork, and `pickR` and `putR` are used by the philosopher on the right. A local requirement is that no two back to back invocations of the form `pickX` or of the form `putX` (where X stands for either L or R) are allowed. There are two global requirements: fairness and deadlock-freedom. The following synchnet is a shared memory solution to this coordination problem. We assume that forks are instances of the class `Fork`. Figure 3 is a diagram of the synchnet `Philosophers`. It only depicts the part of the net corresponding to two adjacent forks. The rest of the diagram consists of similar boxes for the other forks and the whole diagram forms a cycle.

```
synchnet Philosophers(N: int, Forks : array[1..N] of Fork)
    init = {fork.putL, fork.putR | fork in set(Forks)}
```

```
foreach fork in set(Forks) [require fairness]
    method fork.pickL
        requires    {fork.putL, fork.putR}
        consumes    {fork.putL}
    method fork.pickR
        requires    {fork.putL, fork.putR}
        consumes    {fork.putR}
    method fork.putL
        requires    {fork.pickL}
        consumes    {fork.pickL}
    method fork.putR
        requires    {fork.pickR}
        consumes    {fork.pickR}

foreach i in {1 .. N}
    atomic(Forks[i].pickL,Forks[ (i+1) mod N].pickR)
end Philosophers
```

3 Syntax and Semantics of Synchronizing Nets

We first present the concrete syntax, followed by a translational semantics of modules into synchnets which are in fact Petri nets. Then, we present the semantics of the two-level language by relating the firing semantics of synchnets to method invocation in base-level objects. Finally, we define an inheritance mechanism that allows extension of a module with new constraints.

3.1 Syntax of Synchnets

We first present the core syntax of SynchNet. Later, we will introduce more advanced constructs as syntactic sugar. A SynchNet module has the following general form:

```
synchnet ⟨id⟩ ( ⟨param-list⟩ ) is
   init = ⟨token-list⟩
   ⟨method-clauses⟩
   ⟨atomicity-clauses⟩
end ⟨id⟩
```

where $\langle id \rangle$ is a programmer supplied identifier used to refer to the defined synchnet. $\langle param\text{-}list \rangle$ is a list of formal parameters along with their types:

$$\langle param\text{-}list \rangle ::= \langle var_1 \rangle : \langle type_1 \rangle, \ldots, \langle var_n \rangle : \langle type_n \rangle$$

All $\langle var_i \rangle$'s must be distinct. $\langle type_i \rangle$s can be any type that is available in the base language, including both simple types and aggregate types such as lists or arrays. In particular, they can include class types if $\langle var_i \rangle$ is supposed to an object. ⟨*param-list*⟩ acts as a binder for the specified variables, with their static scope being the body of the synchnet

The body of a module consists of a clause specifying the initial state of the corresponding synchnet and a collection of guard-transitions. Syntactically, the state of a synchnet is represented as a multilist of *tokens*. Tokens correspond to the methods of the objects whose references are passed to the synchnet and are supposed to be coordinated by the synchnet. The syntax of tokens and multilists of tokens is specified as

$$
\begin{aligned}
\langle token \rangle &::= \langle var \rangle.\langle method \rangle \\
\langle token\text{-}list \rangle &::= \{\langle token \rangle, \ldots, \langle token \rangle\} \\
&\quad | \ \{\langle token \rangle \,|\, \langle predicate \rangle\} \\
&\quad | \ \langle token\text{-}list \rangle \ \texttt{union} \ \langle token\text{-}list \rangle \\
&\quad | \ \langle token\text{-}list \rangle \ \texttt{intersect} \ \langle token\text{-}list \rangle
\end{aligned}
$$

where ⟨*var*⟩ must be a variable whose type is a class and ⟨*method*⟩ must be a method identifier belonging to that class. ⟨*predicate*⟩ is a predicate over object references. Predicates consists of equality or inequality constraints over variables whose types are classes, composed with the usual boolean operators. The collection of tokens inside the brackets in the expression { ⟨*token*⟩, ..., ⟨*token*⟩ } must be treated as a multiset, that is, the order of tokens is irrelevant, and the same token may appear more than once.

The body of a module consists of two kinds of coordination behavior. The first kind, ⟨*method-clauses*⟩ consists of a collection of *method clauses*. Each method clause has a header and a body. The header of the clause consists of a variable (with a class type) and a method identifier belonging to that class. The body of a method clause consists of a list of guard-transitions. A guard-transition has two parts: A *guard*, which is the condition required for the method to be invoked, and a *transition* that specifies how the state of the synchnet must change if the method is invoked. Each method clause is written as

```
method ⟨var⟩.⟨method⟩
     requires  ⟨token-list⟩
     consumes  ⟨token-list⟩
or   ...
or
     requires  ⟨token-list⟩
     consumes  ⟨token-list⟩
```

A syntactic requirement is that the consume list must be contained in the require list extended with an additional token corresponding to the method for which the require-consume pair is specified.

Atomicity is another kind of coordination requirement that can be specified in the body of a module. Atomicity requirements are represented as constraints called *atomicity clauses*. Each atomicity clause has the following format:

$$\langle atomicity\text{-}list \rangle ::= \texttt{atomic}(\langle var_1 \rangle.\langle method_1 \rangle, \ldots, \langle var_n \rangle.\langle method_n \rangle)$$

where all ⟨var_i⟩s must refer to distinct objects.

To avoid repetitive declarations, we introduce a universal quantification operator as syntactic sugar.

foreach ⟨var⟩ in ⟨var-set⟩
 ⟨clauses⟩

where all clauses in ⟨clauses⟩ use the variable ⟨var⟩ in their headers. ⟨var-set⟩ is a subset of variables specified as formal arguments to the synchnet. The variable must be of class type or of aggregate types such as arrays or lists with elements being of class type. This syntactic form is equivalent to a list of clauses obtained by making copies of clauses in ⟨clauses⟩ each having ⟨var⟩ replaced with some variable in the set ⟨var-set⟩.

3.2 Translating SynchNet Modules to Synchnets

Let's first formalize the Petri Net model introduced in Section 2.1.

Definition 1. *Formally, a Petri net N is a four-tuple (P, T, I, O) where P is a finite set of places, T is a finite set of transitions. P and T are disjoint. $I : T \to P^\infty$ is a mapping from transitions to multisets of places. Similarly, $O : T \to P^\infty$ is a mapping from places to multisets of transitions.* □

The following is the formal definition of the graph of a Petri Net:

Definition 2. *The graph of a Petri Net $N = (P, T, I, O)$ is a bipartite directed multi-graph $G = (P \cup T, A)$ where $A = \{a_1, \ldots, a_n\}$ is a multiset of directed arcs of the form (p, t) or (t, p) for $p \in P$ and $t \in T$.* □

Now we can formalize the notions corresponding to execution of a Petri Net.

Definition 3. *A marking μ of a Petri Net (P, T, I, O) is a multiset of places. That is $\mu \in P^\infty$. A transition $t \in T$ is enabled in a marking μ if $I(t) \subseteq \mu$. An enabled transition t fires by subtracting $I(t)$ from μ and adding $O(t)$. That is, firing of t results in a new marking $\mu' = (\mu - I(t)) \cup O(t)$. Where $-$ and $\cup$ are taken to be multiset operations.* □

A synchnet is a Petri net and is generated when an expression of the form $S(\mathcal{O})$ is evaluated in the base language, where S is the name of a module specified in the SynchNet language and $\mathcal{O}$ is a collection of base-level object references. Now, we formally define the Petri net that constitutes the synchnet generated by evaluating the expression $S(\mathcal{O})$ given the specification of module S in SynchNet. We need to make a few assumptions before we describe the construction of a synchnet.

To avoid aliasing problems, all object references $\mathcal{O}$ passed in $S(\mathcal{O})$ must be distinct. This includes all the references contained in aggregate data structures such as arrays and lists. This sanity condition can be checked at run-time when the synchnet instance is generated. Let $\mathcal{O}$ be the collection of all object references used to create an instantiation of the module S specified in the general form below.

```
synchnet S ( V1 : T1,..., Vn : Tn ) is
   init = I
   ...
   method Vi.Mj
      ....
   or
      requires Rijk
      consumes Cijk
   or
      ...
   ...
   AC
end S
```

For simplicity of presentation, let's assume that all $T1,\ldots,Tn$ are class types. In the general case, we ignore parameters which have a non-class type, and we expand aggregate parameters into a collection of class-type variables. The type system of the base language can be used to verify that for every pair of the form $Vi.Mj$ the method Mj actually belongs to the class Ti. We further assume that an environment $\eta : \{V1,\ldots,Vn\} \to \mathcal{O}$ is given that maps variable names to actual object references passed during the creation of the synchnet instance. For a multiset of tokens Tok, we let $\eta(Tok)$ be the multiset obtained by renaming every occurrence of $V_i.M \in Tok$ by $\eta(V_i).M$.

With these assumptions, we construct a synchnet for $S(\mathcal{O})$ in two steps. First we ignore atomicity clauses and define a Petri Net $SN = (P,T,I,O)$. If AC is non-empty, we modify SN to obtain a net $SN' = (P,T',I',O')$ that incorporates atomicity constraints specified by the list of atomicity clauses AC.

For a module S with the general form described above, let the net $SN = (P,T,I,O)$ be defined as follows. We assume that the environment η binds formal parameters (Vi) of S to object references given in $\mathcal{O}$.

- For every pair of variable V_i and method M that belongs to the class of V_i we consider a place $o.M$ with $o = \eta(V_i)$. That is $P = \{\eta(V_i).M | 1 \leq i \leq n$ and M belongs to $Ti\}$.
- T is the smallest set such that for every pair of require-consume clause $(Rijk, Cijk)$ that belongs to a method $Vi.Mj$, there exists a transition $t \in T$ such that

$$I(t) = \eta(Rijk) \text{ and } O(t) = (\eta(Rijk) - \eta(Cijk)) \cup \{\eta(Vi).Mj\}$$

If there are no require-consume pair specified for a method $Vi.Mj$ we assume there is a transition $t \in T$ such that

$$I(t) = \{\} \text{ and } O(t) = \{\eta(Vi).Mj\}$$

we call these transitions *simple* and we say the simple transition t *corresponds to* the singleton $\{\eta(Vi).Mj\}$.

If the body of the module S contains atomicity clauses $AC_1, \ldots, AC_n$. We obtain a sequence of nets by gradually merging simple transitions into *tuple transitions*. We also keep track of merged simple transitions as the set $MT \subseteq T$, to remove them from the set of transitions after all atomic clauses are processed. Let $SN_0 = SN$ and $MT_0 = \emptyset$. For every atomicity clause AC_i ($1 \leq i \leq n$) of the form

$$\texttt{atomic}(V_1.M_1, \ldots, V_l.M_l)$$

we modify the net $SN_j = (P, T_j, I_j, O_j)$ to obtain $SN_{j+1} = (P, T_{j+1}, I_{j+1}, O_{j+1})$ in the following way. Let T_{j+1} be the smallest set containing T_j such that for every collection of transitions $t_i \in T$ where $1 \leq i \leq l$ and t_i corresponds to $V_i.M_i$, we have a *tuple* transition $(t_1, \ldots, t_l) \in T_{j+1}$. We say that $(t_1, \ldots, t_l)$ corresponds to the set $\{\eta(V_1).M_1, \ldots, \eta(V_l).M_l\}$. We further let I_{j+1} and O_{j+1} be identical to I_j and O_j, respectively, on transitions in T_j, and for a new transition $(t_1, \ldots, t_l) \in T_{j+1}$, let $I_{j+1} = I_j(t_1) \cup \cdots \cup I_j(t_l)$ and $O_{j+1} = O_j(t_1) \cup \cdots \cup O_j(t_l)$. Finally, let $MT_{j+1} = MT_j \cup \{t_1, \ldots, t_l\}$.

By repeating the above process, we obtain $SN_n = (P, T_n, I_n, O_n)$ and MT_n. Now, let $SN' = (P, T', I', O')$ where $T' = T_n - MT_n$ and I' and O' are restrictions of I_n and O_n to T'. This completes our translation and we have SN' as the Petri net of the synchnet S.

The operational semantics of a synchronizing net $SN = (P, T, I, O)$ is a labeled transition system $(\mathcal{M}, \mathcal{L}, \mathcal{T})$ where $\mathcal{M} = P^\infty$ is the set of possible markings of SN, $\mathcal{L} = 2^P$ the set of labels with each label being a finite set of places, and $\mathcal{T} \subseteq \mathcal{M} \times \mathcal{L} \times \mathcal{M}$ defined as the smallest ternary relation such that if $t \in T$ is enabled in marking μ, t corresponds to the set of methods L, and μ' is the marking that results after t fires in marking μ, then $(\mu, L, \mu') \in \mathcal{T}$. We write $\mu \xrightarrow{L} \mu'$ for such a triple.

It is possible to extend SynchNet to support disjunction of atomicity constraints. Extending the synchnet construction to account for this extension is straightforward and is similar to the construction for disjuction of require-concume clauses. Due to space limitation we do not provide the construction in this paper.

3.3 Semantics of the Two-Level Language

The specification of a synchnet S is akin to a class declaration in class-based languages. To coordinate a group of objects, a synchnet must be created by the base-level program. To allow this, we extend the base language to include expressions of the form $S(Params)$. Such expressions can be added as statements if the base language is imperative or as function applications if the language is functional. The evaluation or execution of such an expression creates a new instance of S and uses $Params$ to initialize and set up the Petri net corresponding to S. In general, $Params$ would include references to newly created objects. A sanity check guarantees that references included in $Params$ are all distinct. We require this to generate a synchnet unambiguously.

We now present the operational semantics of the two-level language. We use SI to refer to a created synchnet and assume that $\mathcal{O}$ is the set of object references coordinated by SI. Suppose μ_S denotes the state of a SI (a net marking), and σ_o the state of an object $o \in \mathcal{O}$. As stated before, we expect the base language follow the asynchronous remote method invocation protocol for communication. We don't make any assumption about the representation of the state of objects in the base language, but we assume that its formal semantics is defined as a labeled transition system with labels being either $o.\tau$ referring to some internal computation by the object o, or $o.l(v_1, \ldots, v_n)$ where o is an object reference, l is the label of some method that belongs to object references by o and $v_1, \ldots, v_n$ are actual values. The transition corresponds to the invocation of method l of object o with $v_1, \ldots, v_n$ passed as arguments. We will use the abbreviation $\tilde{V}$ for the list of values $v_1, \ldots, v_n$.

The semantics of object execution in the two-level language is defined as a labeled transition system. Suppose a synchnet SI coordinates a group of objects $\mathcal{O} = \{o_1, \ldots, o_n\}$. We let $\mathcal{S} = \{(\sigma_{o_1}, \ldots, \sigma_{o_n}, \mu)\}$, where σ_{o_i} are the local states of objects o_i $1 \le i \le n$ and μ is a marking of SI, be the set of global states of objects o_i coordinated by SI (we will also use the abbreviation $(\tilde{\sigma}, \mu)$). Let $\mathcal{L}_i$ be the set of transition labels that are either $o_i.\tau$ (silent or internal transition by o_i) or correspond to invocations of o_i's methods in the base language. We define a labeled transition system on global states as a triple $(\mathcal{S}, \mathcal{L}, \mathcal{T})$ where $\mathcal{L} = \mathcal{L}_1 \times \cdots \times \mathcal{L}_n$ and $\mathcal{T} \subseteq \mathcal{S} \times \mathcal{L} \times \mathcal{S}$. We use the abbreviation $\tilde{l}$ for $(l_1, \ldots, l_n)$, where $l_i \in \mathcal{L}_i$. We also write $s \xrightarrow{\tilde{l}} s'$ for $(s, \tilde{l}, s') \in \mathcal{T}$. The transition relation $\mathcal{T}$ is defined as the smallest relation satisfying the following rules

$$\frac{\sigma_{o_i} \xrightarrow{o_i.l(\tilde{V})} \sigma'_{o_i} \quad \mu \xrightarrow{o_i.l} \mu' \quad l_j = \begin{cases} o_j.\tau & \text{if } j \ne i \\ o_j.l(\tilde{V}) & \text{if } j = i \end{cases}}{(\ldots, \sigma_o, \ldots, \mu) \xrightarrow{\tilde{l}} (\ldots, \sigma'_o, \ldots, \mu')}$$

$$\frac{\forall 1 \le i \le n \ . \ \sigma_{o_i} \xrightarrow{o_i.l(\tilde{V})} \sigma'_{o_i} \quad \mu \xrightarrow{o_i.l} \mu'}{(\tilde{\sigma}, \mu) \xrightarrow{\tilde{l}} (\tilde{\sigma}', \mu')}$$

$$\frac{\forall 1 \le i \le n \ . \ \sigma_{o_i} \xrightarrow{o_i.\tau} \sigma'_{o_i} \quad l_i = o_i.\tau}{(\tilde{\sigma}, \mu) \xrightarrow{\tilde{l}} (\tilde{\sigma}', \mu')}$$

In words, a message $l(\tilde{V})$ sent to object o can result in invocation of $o.l$, only if the synchnet is in a state that permits the invocation. Furthermore, if the invocation takes place, the state of the synchnet changes accordingly.

3.4 Composition of Synchronizers

We can extend a synchnet specification by relaxing or further constraining the constraints specified in it. We do so via an inheritance mechanism. Suppose $S1$ is a synchnet specification, we write

```
synchnet S2 ( Params ) extends S1 is
   init = I
   ...
   method V.M
      ...
   or
      requires    [ intersect | union ] R
      consumes    [ intersect | union ] C
   or
      ...
   ...
   atomic(V1.M1,...,V1.Ml)
   ...
end S2
```

as the specification of a synchnet $S2$ that extends the specification of $S1$. Parameters of $S1$ must be exactly the same as those of $S2$. $S2$ may refer to the initial state of its parent synchnet by the expression Super.init. Therefore, I can be either a multiset of tokens or the union or intersection of Super.init with a new multiset of tokens. The optional operators intersect or union can be used in require-consume clauses to relax or further constrain the requirements of the parent synchnet. If neither intersect nor union are specified, the multisets replace those of the parent multisets.

An independent specification for $S2$ can be obtained by a simple substitution: Super.init is replaced with the initial multiset of tokens defined in $S1$, and every pair of require-consume clauses of the form

```
   ...
   or
      requires    X R
      consumes    Y C
   ...
```

that belongs to method $V.M$, and where $X, Y \in \{\text{intersect}, \text{union}\}$ we replace it with

```
   ...
   or
      requires R1 X R
      consumes C1 Y C
   or
      requires R2 X R
      consumes C2 Y C
   or
      ...
```

```
    or
      requires Rn X R
      consumes Cn Y C
    or
      ...
where
    method  V.M
      requires  R1
      consumes  C1
    or
      ...
    or
      requires  Rn
      consumes  Cn
```

is the complete set of require-consume clauses of $V.M$ in $S1$. The set of atomicity clauses of unwinded $S2$ is the union of atomicity clauses in $S1$ and those specified in $S2$.

3.5 More Examples

Here we present some examples to illustrate how our language may be used to modify the interactive behavior of single objects and create more familiar coordination mechanisms such as sempahores.

Example 1. In this example, we show how synchnets may be used to implement semaphores, another coordination mechanism. Suppose ob is some object with two methods put and get. For instance, ob can simply be a variable, with its content accessed via get invocation, and updated with invocations of put. The following synchnet will turn this object into a semaphore, in the sense that the number of times the put method is invoked always exceeds the number of times get is invoked. In other words, put will behave like the V operation of a semaphore and get like the P operation.

```
synchnet Sem(of : Variable)
    init = { }
    method of.put
        requires {}
        consumes {}
    method of.get
        requires {of.put}
        consumes {of.put}
end Sem
```

The guard-transition for method of.get indicates that every invocation of get requires a distinct invocation of put to occur in the past. As every invocation of either methods put or get adds a new token to the corresponding places, the consume clause of **get** guarantees that the number of invocations of **get** would not exceed the number of invocations of **put**. However, because **put** does not require any tokens, **put** maybe invoked any number of times regardless of how many times **get** is invoked. This is the usual invariant requirement for semaphores, which can be intuitively verified through the simple semantics of the synchronizer language. Adding fairness to the semantics allow definitions of fair semaphores.

Example 2. A *k-bounded semaphore* has the property that at most k processes can issue a V operation that is not matched by a P operation. A 1-bounded semaphore can be defined easily by further constraining the behavior of a general semaphore.

```
syncnet  OneSem(ob : Variable) extends Sem
  init = {ob.get}
  method ob.put
     requires {ob.get}
     consumes {ob.get}
end OneSem
```

This synchronizer states that the method **put** may be invoked only if **get** had been invoked once in the past. To allow for the first **put** to go through we have modified the initial state to include a token of type **ob.get**. When this synchnet is installed on a single element variable, it turns the variable into a single-element buffer.

A *2-bounded semaphore* can be defined similarly:

```
synchnet TwoSem(ob : Variable)
   init = {ob.get,ob.get}
   method ob.put
      requires    { ob.get }
      consumes    { ob.get }
   method ob.get
      requires    { ob.put }
      consumes    { ob.put }
end TwoSem
```

Alternatively the same semaphore can be expressed using synchnet inheritance:

```
synchnet TwoSem(ob : Variable) extends OneSem
    init = {ob.get, ob.get}
end TwoSem
```

Only the initial state is modified. The rest of the synchnet specification is inherited from **OneSem**.

Example 3. Synchronizers for inherited objects may be defined compositionally using synchnet inheritance. Suppose a new class of objects **InfBuf2** is defined that adds a new method `get2` to an infinite buffer such that two elements of the buffer may be fetched at one time. The required coordination for the new class can be specified modularly and compositionally as the following synchronizer:

```
synchnet TwoBuf(A : Buffer) extends OneSem is
  init = Super.init
  method  A.get2
      requires   {A.put, A.put}
      consumes   {A.put, A.put}
end TwoBuf
```

TwoBuf does not modify the synchronization requirements on put and get methods and hence does not suffer from *inheritance anomaly* which many coordination mechanisms for concurrent object-oriented programming suffer [15].

4 A Preorder on Simple Synchronizers

Freedom from deadlock is an important safety property that we usually desire a collection of interacting objects to have. We define deadlock as the situation in which the state of one or more synchnet disables certain methods forever. This definition, of course, also includes the extreme case of a synchronizer disabling the invocation of all methods of an object; regardless of the behavior of the environment, this is an obvious deadlock situation.

One can verify deadlock-freedom of a synchnet by performing a reachability analysis. However, since reachability of Petri nets has non-elementary complexity, we introduce an alternative formal method for development of deadlock-free synchnets. We define a preorder relation on synchnets that allows "safe" substitution of a synchnet with an alternative implementation. In other words, we introduce a preorder relation $\leq$ over synchnet instances that is deadlock-freedom preserving: $S \leq S'$ implies that whenever S' does not deadlock in an environment E, using S' in environment E would not result in deadlock either.

The formal framework that we develop here is along the lines of the theory of failure equivalence of CSP processes presented in [11].

Definition 4. *A* trace *of a synchnet S with initial state I is a path in the labeled transition systems of the net with the root I.* □

Next we define the *failure* of a synchnet S. Intuitively, a failure describes an environment that allows S to reach a state in which all of the messages offered by the environment are blocked. A failure, therefore, consists of a pair (t, L) meaning that S can follow the trace t and end up in state μ such that none of the methods in the set L would be enabled in μ.

Definition 5. *A* failure *of a synchnet S with initial state I is a pair (t, L) where t is a trace of S starting with the marking I and ending at state μ, and L is a set of method tags such that for all $o.M \in L$, $o.M$ is not enabled in μ.*

The failures of a synchnets S with initial marking I is written as failures(S) and is the set of all failures of S starting at I. □

We are now ready to define the preorder relation on synchnets.

Definition 6. *For two synchnets S and S' that are instantiated with the same set of objects, we say $S \leq S'$ whenever failures(S) $\subseteq$ failures(S').*

We also write $S \equiv S'$ whenever $S' \leq S$ and $S \leq S'$. □

It is not difficult to see that substituting S' with S when $S \leq S'$ would not cause further deadlock situations than S would. Therefore, if synchnets are always substituted according to this preorder, a non-deadlocking synchnet would never be substituted with a one that deadlocks.

5 Discussion and Future Work

We have proposed the use of Petri Nets as a simple meta-level language to specify coordination requirements of a group of distributed objects. When this meta-level language (SynchNet) is combined with an object-based language with asynchronous remote method invocation semantics, we obtain an expressive distributed object-based language. To keep things simple, our coordination language only refers to the labels of methods. As a result, coordination requirements that discriminate between messages containing distinct values cannot be expressed in our currently proposed language. We have observed that, despite this limitation, our language is still expressive enough to represent many interesting coordination patterns.

Since synchnets are in fact Petri nets, we can benefit from the rich and well studied theory of Petri Nets. The theory includes formal characterizations of many interesting properties along with decision algorithms to decide those properties. Automatic analysis tools have made these theories accessible to practitioners.

Our compiler for SynchNet automatically generates distributed code. The current implementation uses a naive distributed shared memory protocol and therefore suffers from low performance. Currently, we are working on a new algorithm that, by exploiting the structure of synchnets, would hopefully generate distributed code with efficiency comparable to the best distributed solutions available.

Considering that most modern distributed systems operate in open and dynamic environments and that coordination requirements usually evolve throughout the lifetime of a system, it is generally desirable to have development systems that allow dynamic customization of coordination aspects. Our proposed two-level model provides some support for dynamically evolving systems: It is possible to dynamically create new objects (and threads that execute their scripts), and instantiate new synchnets to coordinate the newly created objects. More flexibility would be achieved if one could replace or modify a running synchnet on the fly. Even though our current model does not support this level of dynamic customizability, its simple and formal semantics should simplify the study of such issues.

References

1. G. Agha. *Actors: A Model of Concurrent Computation in Distributed Systems*. MIT Press, Cambridge, Mass., 1986.
2. Mark Astley, Daniel Sturman, and Gul Agha. Customizable middleware for modular distributed software. *Communications of the ACM*, 44(5):99–107, 2001.
3. Juan-Carlos Cruz and Stéphane Ducasse. Coordinating open distributed systems. In *Proceedings of International Workshop in Future Trends in Distributed Computing Systems'99*, Cape Town, South Africa, 1999.
4. U.S. Department of Defence. *Reference Manual for the Ada programming language*. DoD, Washington, D.C., January 1983.
5. E.W. Dijkstra. Guarded commands, nondeterminacy, and formal derivation of programs. *Comm. ACM*, 8:453–457, August 1975.
6. Javier Esparza and Mogens Nielsen. Decidability issues for petri nets - a survey. *Inform. Process. Cybernet.*, 30:143–160, 1994.
7. Holger Giese. Contract-based component system design. In *HICSS*, 2000.
8. Object Management Group. *Common Object Request Broker Architecture*. OMG, 1999.
9. Per Brinch Hansen. Distributed processes: A concurrent programming concept. *Comm. ACM*, 21(11):934–941, November 1978.
10. C.A.R. Hoare. Communicating sequential processes. *Comm. ACM*, 21(8):151–160, August 1978.
11. C.A.R. Hoare. *Communicating Sequential Processes*. Prentice-Hall, 1985.
12. Gregor Kiczales, John Lamping, Anurag Menhdhekar, Chris Maeda, Cristina Lopes, Jean-Marc Loingtier, and John Irwin. Aspect-oriented programming. In Mehmet Akşit and Satoshi Matsuoka, editors, *Proceedings of the European Conference on Object-Oriented Programming*, volume 1241, pages 220–242. Springer-Verlag, Berlin, Heidelberg, and New York, 1997.
13. I. Kumaran and S. Kumaran. *JINI Technology: An Overview*. Prentice Hall, 2001.
14. A. Lopes, J.L. Fiadeiro, and M. Wemelinger. Architectural primitives for distribution and mobility. In *SIGSOFT 2002/FSE-10*, pages 18–22, Nov 2002.
15. Satoshi Matsuoka and Akinori Yonezawa. Analysis of inheritance anomaly in object-oriented concurrent programming languages. In Gul Agha, Peter Wegner, and Akinori Yonezawa, editors, *Research Directions in Concurrent Object-Oriented Programming*, pages 107–150. MIT Press, 1993.
16. Naftaly H. Minsky and Victoria Ungureanu. Law-governed interaction: a coordination and control mechanism for heterogeneous distributed systems. *ACM Transactions on Software Engineering and Methodology*, 9(3):273–305, 2000.
17. J. Peterson. *Petri net theory and the modeling of systems*. Prentice-Hall, 1981.
18. C.A. Petri. *Kommunikation mit Automaten*. PhD thesis, University of Bonn, Bonn, West Germany, 1962.
19. Frølund S. *Coordinating Distributed Objects: An Actor Based Approach to Coordination*. MIT Press, 1996.
20. R. Sessions. *COM and DCOM: Microsoft's Vision for Distributed Objects*. John Wiley and Sons, 1997.
21. Sander Tichelaar. A coordination component framework for open distributed systems. Master's thesis, University of Groningen, 1997.
22. Nalini Venkatasubramanian and Carolyn L. Talcott. Reasoning about meta level activities in open distributed systems. In *Symposium on Principles of Distributed Computing*, pages 144–152, 1995.

Partial Evaluation of MATLAB

Daniel Elphick[1], Michael Leuschel[1], and Simon Cox[2]

[1] Department of Electronics and Computer Science
[2] School of Engineering Sciences
University of Southampton
Highfield, Southampton, SO17 1BJ, UK
{dre00r,mal}@ecs.soton.ac.uk, sjc@soton.ac.uk

Abstract. We describe the problems associated with the creation of high performance code for mathematical computations. We discuss the advantages and disadvantages of using a high level language like MATLAB and then propose partial evaluation as a way of lessening the disadvantages at little cost. We then go on to describe the design of a partial evaluator for MATLAB and present results showing what performance increases can be achieved and the circumstances in which partial evaluation can provide these.

1 Introduction

Scientific computing is moving away from hand-coded, hand-optimised codes, written in low to medium level languages like FORTRAN, towards codes written in a general way in high-level programming languages or using problem solving environments, e.g. MATLAB, Maple, MATHEMATICA.

With the current diversity of computer architectures (due to differences in cache configurations, speeds and memory bandwidths as well as processor types), it is becoming increasingly difficult to produce near optimal code without expending excessive time. Even then the code ties the developer to one architecture, which is no longer ideal in an era of heterogeneous systems. One effort to tackle this problem has been the ATLAS project, which produces a BLAS (Basic Linear Algebra Subroutines), automatically tuned to the architecture on which it is being used [21]. MATLAB itself uses ATLAS for its linear algebra operations.

The use of high level languages allows rapid prototyping to ease development. Producing optimal code in the initial stage is not so important as actually producing something which solves the problem. This often leads to general solutions which can be applied to a wide variety of problems albeit slowly due to their generality.

One way to address these issues is to transform general programs written (or produced by other programs) in high level languages such as MATLAB into specialised programs that executes more quickly using partial evaluation and other high level code optimisations. To this end we have developed a partial evaluator called MPE (MATLAB Partial Evaluator).

In Sect. 2, we examine existing work on partial evaluation as well as work on improving MATLAB program performance using parallelisation and compilation. In Sect. 3, we examine the MATLAB programming language, looking at its grammar and performance issues. Sect. 4 presents a formal analysis of the type system used in MPE. The design and implementation details of MPE are given in Sect. 5. In Sect. 6, we demonstrate the effectiveness of automatic partial evaluation by applying our tool to several test programs and comparing timings. Sect. 7 gives our conclusions based on the results and also describes future work that could enable further improvements.

2   Optimising MATLAB

MATLAB is a problem solving environment sold by The Mathworks and currently used by around 500,000 people around the world [20]. It is controlled using a language also known as MATLAB. From now on when we refer to MATLAB, we are referring to the language unless otherwise stated. MATLAB is a dynamically typed imperative language which is normally interpreted. Variables do not need to be declared and can change type. Matrices and arrays are not of fixed size but are reshaped when assignments are made to subscripts outside the current bounds.

The Mathworks provides a compiler called MCC, which translates MATLAB into C. This C code is then compiled by the native compiler to produce an executable. The code produced consists mostly of function calls and very little attempt is made to use native C types, as dynamic typing means that a variable can contain anything from a matrix to a function handle.

Another compiler is FALCON, which produces Fortran 90 code [17]. This uses extensive type inferencing at compile time to produce code which does very little type checking. Initial results showed FALCON outperforming MCC, but no recent comparisons have been reported by its authors.

Following on from FALCON, Almási has developed MaJIC, a MATLAB *just-in-time* compiler as part of "an interactive frontend that looks like MATLAB and compiles/optimises code behind the scenes in real time, employing a combination of just-in-time and speculative ahead-of-time compilation." [1] Because MaJIC compiles code in an interpreted environment, it has information about the parameters used to call functions and attempts to produce more appropriate code. When compiling *just-in-time* it eschews most optimisations in favour of fast compilation times and so cannot easily perform the types of aggressive optimisation seen in offline compilers and partial evaluators. MATLAB 6.5 has also recently introduced *just-in-time* compilation as part of its normal operation, although we have not yet examined its effectiveness.

An example of work on array shape determination is MAGICA, which "takes a MATLAB program as input and statically infers each variable's value range, intrinsic type and array shape." [11] Unlike the research compilers discussed above, MAGICA can handle multi-dimensional arrays, although its approach is different to ours.

Other approaches to speeding up MATLAB execution have involved parallelisation. Mostly this involves adding parallels extensions to the language, like MultiMATLAB [12] or the DP toolbox [15]. However Otter is an attempt to translate MATLAB scripts into C programs targeting parallel computers supporting ScaLAPACK [16]. This approach produces varying results depending on the sizes of matrices and the complexity of the operations performed on them.

Partial Evaluation. "Partial evaluation is a technique to partially execute a program, when only some of its input data are available." [13] In other words, to take a program, for which some of the inputs are known prior to full execution, and execute as much of the program as possible. In cases where programs are executed many times with few parameters changing, dramatic savings can be made as many calculations are performed just once during partial evaluation. Partial evaluators normally perform aggressive optimisations like loop unrolling and inlining which, while also possible in traditional compilers, are less easy to control or see the effects of when the transformation is not source to source. A program generated by partial evaluation is called a *residual* program.

Traditionally partial evaluation has been mostly applied to declarative languages, like Scheme [7] or Prolog [10]. But there are also partial evaluators for C [3], Java [19] and Fortran [8].

We believe that partial evaluation has a potential for scientific applications in general and MATLAB code in particular. For example, in some of our MATLAB code to solve partial differential equations, the same mesh structure is used over and over again, and we believe that we might gain speedups by partially evaluating the code for a given mesh structure.

There are two main forms of partial evaluation, online and offline. In *offline* partial evaluation, *binding-time analysis* is performed first which parses the input and determines which parts are static and which parts are dynamic. This data is then embedded in the source file in the form of annotations which are used by the partial evaluator to produce the final result. In *online* partial evaluation, there is no binding-time analysis step but instead decisions about static vs. dynamic expressions are made as late as possible, and it is thus, in principle, more precise. In general, offline partial evaluators can be made more efficient and predictable while online partial evaluators are typically slower but more precise.

Due to the non-static nature of MATLAB (no static types, types of variables can change) and the presence of complicated elementary operations (e.g., multiplication of multi-dimensional matrices), we have chosen to use the online approach.

3 Overview of MATLAB

For the purposes of this project we intend only to look at a subset of MATLAB. In this section the structure of MATLAB will be discussed in order to give a better understanding of the later sections.

MATLAB code is always stored in a file with a .m extension, called an m-file. An m-file is either a script or a function, depending on whether the file starts with the `function` keyword. Scripts are executed within the current scope whereas functions execute within their own scope.

Functions are declared using the `function` keyword. They can return zero or more values and take zero or more parameters. We have chosen to exclude functions that can take a variable number of parameters. Any values stored in the return variables at the end of the execution of the function are returned. E.g.

```
function [a,b] = f(x,y)
```

MATLAB statements are either separated by new lines or semi-colons, although in matrices, these also delimit rows. A MATLAB statement must be one of the following: an expression, an assignment, an `if` statement, a `for` loop, a `while` loop, a `switch` block, or a `global` variable declaration. Note that we can have a multi-value assignment for use only with functions which return multiple values. To simplify matters, we require that global variable declarations come immediately after the function declaration and cannot appear later.

MATLAB allows the creation of complex expressions in a very intuitive way. The basic construct is the array, of which matrices, vectors and scalars are special cases. The only other data type we consider is the string. Apart from standard matrices which are two dimensional, MATLAB also has n-dimensional arrays. Matrices can be either real, complex or logical. Logical arrays are returned from boolean operators and built-in functions like `isreal` and `isinf`. While generally they will have the values 0 or 1, they can have any real value.

It is possible to index into a matrix using more dimensions than the matrix has, as long as the extra indices are equal to 1. If fewer dimensions are used then the dimensions that are not explicitly specified are flattened, so that the final index can be used to access all of them. For example matrices can be indexed linearly.

MATLAB allows more than just scalars as indices; any appropriately sized matrix can be used. In particular, ranges can be used to extract parts of matrices. Indices start at 1 and `end` can be used to get the last element along a particular dimension. If the index is ':', it indicates all elements along a given dimension should be extracted. Finally, if an index is logical it predicates which part of the matrix should be extracted. Below, for example, the first row of a is retrieved and stored in b and then all elements in b not equal to 2 are displayed.

```
>> a = [1 2 3; 4 5 6; 7 8 9];
>> b = a(1,:)
b =
         1       2       3
>> b(b ~= 2)
ans =     1       3
```

There are several MATLAB features that we do not yet consider, such as function handles, `try-catch` statements, cell arrays and persistent variables. By limiting the set of MATLAB features that we can handle we limit the number of

MATLAB programs with which we can initially work. However we have to make a pragmatic decision to ignore certain features that are not critical to testing our hypothesis that partial evaluation is a viable technique for the optimisation of MATLAB programs. In the future, it is hoped that these features could also be added to our tool.

4 Abstract Domains

MATLAB has a complicated type system which has evolved over time from just representing two dimensional matrices to N-dimensional arrays, cell arrays, structures, strings and function handles. We have chosen to exclude cell arrays, structures and function handles in the current work and just handle arrays (including matrices). In this section, we formalise the abstract domains our partial evaluator uses to capture information about arrays. The notation and methodology is based on [1] and [4].

4.1 Abstract Type System

A MATLAB array can have the following types: *real*, *complex*, *logical* or *character*. These types are not exclusive, as *logical* and *character* arrays are also real. There is no single `gettype` function, but there are various boolean functions that determine the properties of an array: `isreal`, `islogical` and `ischar`. An array of type *real* is made up from double precision floats. A *logical* array is identical to a *real* array except that it has a flag indicating that it is logical. *Complex* arrays use twice the memory of real ones, in order to store the real and imaginary components. *Character* arrays are just like arrays except that the elements are two byte characters. Some example types are shown in Fig. 1.

```
>> [isreal([1 pi]), islogical([1 pi]), ischar([1 pi])]
ans =     1       0       0
>> [isreal(3 == 2), islogical(3 == 2), ischar(3 == 2)]
ans =     1       1       0
>> [isreal('abc'), islogical('abc'), ischar('abc')]
ans =     1       0       1
>> [isreal(3 + 2i), islogical(3 + 2i), ischar(3 + 2i)]
ans =     0       0       0
```

Fig. 1. Examining MATLAB types (Non-zero values indicate true)

We cannot always reliably make assumptions about types in MATLAB for several reasons. For one, it is possible to add two complex numbers together and get a real number as the result. A compiler would almost certainly assume the result was complex and allocate enough storage for that. MATLAB allocates the extra space only when it determines that the result is actually complex. It is also possible to force the creation of a complex type with no imaginary component using the `complex` built-in. The `isreal` built-in indicates whether storage has been allocated for an imaginary component, not whether it is really real.

To handle these types, an inclusive type system is required, which indicates what possible types an array might have. This would have three trinary flags, which indicate *true*, *false* or *unknown*. The *unknown* value is actually equivalent to $\top_b$ in a lattice and so we shall write that from now on. These values all form the set **B**, given in Definition 1. There is also nominally another value, $\bot_b$, which denotes an *invalid* type. The three flags are *real*, *logical* and *character*. While in theory this would allow 3^3 possible types, in practice the value of one flag can dictate the value of another flag, as for instance logical arrays cannot be complex. There are in fact only 12 valid combinations including the *invalid* type, which are shown in Fig. 2.

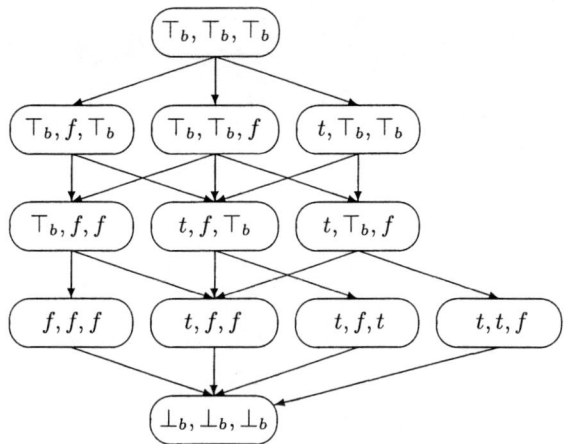

Fig. 2. Visualisation of the type lattice $\mathfrak{L}_t$, of valid triples (*real, logical, complex*) $\in$ **B** × **B** × **B**, where the arrows indicate the partial ordering

Definition 1. $\mathbf{B} = \{\top_b, true, false, \bot_b\}$ is the extended boolean type, with an associated partial order $\sqsubseteq_b$ defined by $\bot_b \sqsubseteq_b false \sqsubseteq_b \top_b$ and $\bot_b \sqsubseteq_b true \sqsubseteq_b \top_b$. $\mathbf{T} \subset \mathbf{B} \times \mathbf{B} \times \mathbf{B}$ is the following set of all valid triples of **B**:

$$\mathbf{T} = \{\langle \top_b, \top_b, \top_b\rangle, \langle \top_b, false, \top_b\rangle, \langle \top_b, \top_b, false\rangle,$$
$$\langle \top_b, false, false\rangle, \langle false, false, false\rangle, \langle true, \top_b, \top_b\rangle,$$
$$\langle true, \top_b, false\rangle, \langle true, false, \top_b\rangle, \langle true, false, false\rangle,$$
$$\langle true, false, true\rangle, \langle true, true, false\rangle, \langle \bot_b, \bot_b, \bot_b\rangle\}$$

The partial order $\sqsupseteq_t$ associated with **T** is depicted in Fig. 2. Finally we define the lattice $\mathfrak{L}_t = (\mathbf{T}, \bot_t, \top_t, \sqsubseteq_t, \sqcup_t)$ where $\top_t = \langle \top_b, \top_b, \top_b\rangle$, $\bot_t = \langle \bot_b, \bot_b, \bot_b\rangle$, and where $\sqcup_t$ and $\sqcap_t$ are defined in the usual way (cf., Fig. 2).

4.2 Dimension Information

The above abstract domain captures the types of arrays. As matrix manipulations are the backbone of MATLAB, to enable advanced optimisations, we need to capture abstract information about the shape of matrices. As loops are frequently controlled by the size of a matrix dimension, knowing the matrix shape can allow loop unrolling.

Arrays have a number of dimensions, which is always greater than or equal to 2 and is returned by the ndims function. Each dimension then has a value greater than or equal to 0. The size function us used to get the dimension sizes. Requesting a dimension beyond the number of dimensions always returns 1. The shape of an array is defined initially in Definition 4 and Definition 5.

Definition 2. *We define the extended set of non-negative integers $\mathbb{Z}^\omega = \mathbb{Z}^* \cup \{\omega\}$, We extend the ordering $<$ on $\mathbb{Z}^\omega$ by stating $\forall n \in \mathbb{Z}^\omega, n \leq \omega$ and also $\omega \leq n \Rightarrow n = \omega$.*

Definition 3. *A range is a tuple $\langle l, u \rangle$, where $l, u \in \mathbb{Z}^\omega$ and $l \leq u$. l is called the lower bound and u the upper bound of the range. We define the set $\mathbf{R}$ to contain all possible ranges with the addition of the $\bot_r$ element to indicate an invalid range ($\mathbf{R} \subset \mathbb{Z}^\omega \times \mathbb{Z}^\omega \cup \{\bot_r\}$). The top element is the least constrained range possible, i.e. $\top_r = \langle 0, \omega \rangle$. We define two functions: $low(\langle l, u \rangle) = l$ and $up(\langle l, u \rangle) = u$. We also define join ($\sqcup$) and meet ($\sqcap$) operations on this set.*

$$\langle l_1, u_1 \rangle \sqsubseteq_r \langle l_2, u_2 \rangle \iff l_1 \geq l_2 \text{ and } u_1 \leq u_2$$

$$\langle l_1, u_1 \rangle \sqcup_r \langle l_2, u_2 \rangle = \langle \min(l_1, l_2), \max(u_1, u_2) \rangle$$

$$\langle l_1, u_1 \rangle \sqcap_r \langle l_2, u_2 \rangle = \begin{cases} \langle \max(l_1, l_2), \min(u_1, u_2) \rangle & \text{if } l_1 \leq u_2 \wedge l_2 \leq u_1 \\ \bot_r & \text{otherwise} \end{cases}$$

We use ranges to represent the possible values a shape characteristic might have. Note that ω is used for ranges without an upper bound.

Definition 4. *The number of dimensions is a range (Definition 3), except that the minimum value is 2, as an array always has at least 2 dimensions. This is given by the set, $\mathbf{N} = \mathbf{R} - \{\langle i, j \rangle \mid i \in \{0, 1\}, j \in \mathbb{Z}^\omega\}$. The top element in $\mathbf{N}$ is $\top_n = \langle 2, \omega \rangle$. The partial ordering $\sqsubseteq_n$ and operations $\sqcap_n$ and $\sqcap_r$ are equivalent to $\sqsubseteq_r$, $\sqcap_r$ and $\sqcup_r$ respectively.*

Definition 5. *The list of dimensions is a sequence of ranges, $\langle r_1, r_2, \ldots, r_n \rangle \in \mathbf{D}$, where $\mathbf{D} = \mathbf{R}^*$. We also define two functions $low(i, d) = low(r_i)$ and $up(i, d) = up(r_i)$. The length of a list, d, is given by $|d|$. The join and meet operations ($d \sqcup_d d' = \langle r_1 \sqcup_r r'_1, \ldots, r_n \sqcup_r r'_n \rangle$ and $d \sqcap_d d' = \langle r_1 \sqcap_r r'_1, \ldots, r_n \sqcap_r r'_n \rangle$) and the partial ordering, $d \sqsubseteq_d d' \iff \forall i \in \mathbb{Z}^+, i \leq |d|, r_i \sqsubseteq_r r'_i P(\sqsubseteq_d)$, are defined for dimension lists of the same size, where $d = \langle r_1, r_2, \ldots r_n \rangle$ and $d' = \langle r'_1, r'_2, \ldots r'_n \rangle$.*

$$dim(i, n, d) = \begin{cases} \bot_r & \text{if } n = \bot_n \vee d = \bot_d \\ \langle low(i, d), up(i, d) \rangle & \text{if } i \leq |d| \\ \langle 0, \omega \rangle & \text{if } |d| < i \leq up(n) \\ \langle 1, 1 \rangle & \text{otherwise} \end{cases} \quad (1)$$

The function in (1), given $i \in \mathbb{Z}^+$, $n \in \mathbf{N}$ and $d \in \mathbf{D}$, gives the range representing the ith dimension. If the range is in the dimension list, this is returned; else if the dimension number is less than the number of dimensions, the dimension size is unknown so $\top_r$ is returned; otherwise the dimension is beyond the number of dimensions and its size is 1. Not all values of n and d give meaningful values for (1) and we will describe the constraints in Sect. 4.4.

4.3 Definedness

We also need to consider that a variable may not be defined. When a function is called, it does not need to be passed as many parameters as there are in the function signature. As a result some of the parameters may be undefined. Variables can also be undefined if they are only set on one branch of a conditional statement. In this case, it would be unknown whether the variable was defined. The *defined* flag is $\delta \in \mathbf{B}$. It is an error to use an undefined variable, but the built-in function `exist` takes a variable name and returns whether the variable exists.

4.4 Putting It All Together

The full type of an array could be described by $\mathbf{T} \times \mathbf{N} \times \mathbf{D} \times \mathbf{B}$, but components of the type are not entirely independent. It is possible to produce many $n \in \mathbf{N}$, $d \in \mathbf{D}$ which give the same values of $dim(i, n, d)$ for all $i \in \mathbb{Z}^+$, for instance:

$$n_1 = \langle 2, 2\rangle, d_1 = \langle\langle 1, 1\rangle, \langle 1, 1\rangle\rangle, \quad n_2 = \langle 3, 3\rangle, d_2 = \langle\langle 1, 1\rangle, \langle 1, 1\rangle, \langle 1, 1\rangle\rangle$$
$$n_3 = \langle 2, 3\rangle, d_3 = \langle\langle 5, 10\rangle, \langle 2, 2\rangle\rangle, \quad n_4 = \langle 2, 3\rangle, d_4 = \langle\langle 5, 10\rangle, \langle 2, 2\rangle, \langle 0, \omega\rangle\rangle$$
$$n_5 = \langle 2, 3\rangle, d_5 = \langle\langle 5, 10\rangle, \langle 2, 2\rangle, \langle 0, \omega\rangle, \langle 1, 1\rangle, \langle 1, 1\rangle\rangle$$

In the above examples, $\langle n_1, d_1\rangle$ and $\langle n_2, d_2\rangle$ represent the same shape. However MATLAB would return 2 as the value of `ndims` and so n_2 is wrong. The same values of dim would also be given for $\langle n_3, d_3\rangle$, $\langle n_4, d_4\rangle$ and $\langle n_4, d_4\rangle$ so clearly redundant information is present in d_4 and d_5. Finally if $n = \langle 2, 2\rangle$ and $d = \langle\langle 1, 1\rangle, \langle 1, 1\rangle, \langle 2, 2\rangle\rangle$, then clearly n and d contradict, as there are 3 dimensions. In order to compare types, we need a concrete description of each type with no ambiguity. In addition if a variable is undefined, it is meaningless for it to have shape or type. If the definedness is unknown, it can still have shape and type as might be the case when a variable is defined in only one branch of a conditional statement. The constraints on the type are given below:

1. The shape, $s \in \mathbf{S}$ ($\mathbf{S} \subset \mathbf{N} \times \mathbf{D}$), must be in the canonical form described in [5].
2. If an array, with full type $\langle t, s, \delta\rangle$, is undefined, e.g. $\delta = \textit{false}$, then the values of t, n and d can only be $\bot_t$, $\bot_n$ and $\bot_d$ respectively.

We have thus defined a canonical form for our type system (along with the abstract interpretation concretisation functions), which allows us to compare two shapes and compute their least upper bound. Full details are given in [5]. All of this is then used by our data flow analysis and our partial evaluator proper, as described later in the paper.

5 Design of a Partial Evaluator

We wish to perform optimisations based on the characteristics of arrays such as shape and type. For example, while the exact value of a matrix may be unknown, the dimensions and whether it is real or complex could well be known. In this case built-in functions which try to determine these properties can be replaced by the actual values, which might lead to speed-ups due to loop unrolling and the removal of conditionals.

5.1 Overview

Below we give an overview of the stages of our partial evaluator:

1. Parse main source file to be partially evaluated (Sect. 5.2).
2. Insert the static values (given at the command line) by creating assignments within the parse tree of the main source file (Sect. 5.3).
3. Convert placeholders in the parse tree of the first function from the main source file.
   (a) Whenever a function is encountered, load and parse the function, while adding it to the list of functions called by the current function.
   (b) Repeat step 3 for all the functions in the list created in step 3a.
4. Partially evaluate the parse tree of the main function obtaining a new parse tree (Sect. 5.4).
5. Post-process the new tree, removing dead code.
6. Write out the final tree as MATLAB source code.

Each of these stages will be described in more detail in the following sections.

Our MATLAB partial evaluator (MPE) was written for GNU/Linux systems in C++, but only uses the MATLAB runtime libraries aside from the core libraries and so should be easy to port to other platforms on which MATLAB is supported. It is invoked from the command line and in its basic mode of operation takes one file and partially evaluates the functions found within it. It does not currently partially evaluate the whole system and currently does no polyvariant specialisation. Its effectiveness is therefore currently limited to functions that do not call other functions with dynamic parameters. Function calls with fully static parameters can be evaluated and so the results can be embedded directly into the partially evaluated function. Whether this is always desirable will be discussed later.

5.2 Lexical Analysis and Parsing

MATLAB was designed more to allow mathematicians to read it than for simple parsing. This leads to ambiguous constructs that are fairly simple for a human to understand as they can more easily make contextual judgements, but a lot harder for a lexical analyser. Problems occur because in matrices, spaces can be column delimiters or white space. Outside matrices new lines are treated as an end of command indicator, but inside they are treated as row separators. Fortunately `flex` can be made stateful thus avoiding the need for a hand-written lexical analyser.

Due to difficulties in disambiguating variables and function calls, identifiers that could represent either are stored initially as placeholders. In the following stage, these will be replaced with either variables or function calls.

5.3 Converting Placeholders

This stage is necessary because the distinction between variables and functions is not immediately determinable unlike in C (assuming macros are not used). Variables do not have to be declared but are created as required by assignments. Variables can also shadow the names of both built-in and ordinary functions. This means that an identifier could be used to indicate a function call at one point in a function and then later be used to access a variable if there is assignment to the variable in between. This also needs to be done by all MATLAB compilers and is discussed in [18] and [2].

The end result of this stage is one parse tree where all placeholders have been replaced with either variable, subscript or function call identifiers, for each function in all m-files in the system.

5.4 Partial Evaluation

In this pass, we try to evaluate as much of the function as possible. This stage takes a list of MATLAB statements and a table mapping variables to values and returns a new list of statements. This can be applied recursively to lists of commands within control flow statements like `for` loops.

For every expression, we have a structure which stores what information we have for it. In some cases the value will be known, in which case full substitutions can be performed. In the case where the actual value of an expression is not known, we store all relevant information that can be inferred about it. This corresponds to the full type described in Sect. 4.4.

There are two types of partial evaluation that are carried out by our tool. In one, a function is evaluated as much as is possible in conjunction with a list of variables and information about their contents, in the end producing a final table containing the values of variables at the end of a function. The other mode of operation also produces a new parse tree for the residual code as it goes along. Evaluation without producing code is required for dealing with function calls as well as for iterating over loops, which will be described later in Sect. 5.4.

For each kind of statement discussed in Sect. 3, we will now give a description of how they are partially evaluated.

Expressions. Expressions are stored in a binary tree structure. Our implementation performs a depth first traversal of the tree evaluating wherever possible.

Most binary operations in MATLAB are called *element-wise* binary operations. These either operate on two arrays with equal dimensions, one non-scalar and a scalar or two scalars. They always result in an array of the same shape as the non-scalar operand or a scalar in the case of two scalars. These include addition, subtraction, array multiplication (as opposed to matrix multiplication), left and right array division, array power, relational operations and logical operations. The operations that have non-array alternatives (multiplication, division and power) are prefixed with a full stop to differentiate them (e.g. .*, ./, .\ and .^). While the values of these of operands will frequently not be known it is often possible to make inferences about the dimensions of the operands and thus infer the dimensions of the result of an operation. We use the following scheme for $c = a \oplus b$, (a, b and c have shapes $s_a, s_b, s_c \in \mathbf{S}$. $s_s \in \mathbf{S}$ is the shape of a scalar and $\oplus$ is an element-wise binary operator):

- If a is a scalar ($s_a = s_s$), c will have the same shape as b ($s_c = s_b$). If b is a scalar ($s_b = s_s$), c will have the same shape as a ($s_c = s_a$). If both are scalars ($s_a = s_b$), c will also be a scalar ($s_c = s_s$).
- If there is complete information about the shape of a and b and they have identical shapes ($s_a = s_b$), c will also have the same shape ($s_c = s_a = s_b$).
- If incomplete information is known about the shapes of a and b, but they are definitely not scalars ($s_a \sqcap s_s = \bot_s \land s_b \sqcap s_s = \bot_s$) and their shapes do not conflict ($s_a \sqcap s_b \neq \bot_s$), then the shape of c will be the meet of the two shapes ($s_c = s_a \sqcap s_b$). E.g. a has 5 rows and is added to b which has 3 columns; the result will therefore have 5 rows and 3 columns.
- If a can be a scalar but b cannot ($s_a \sqcap s_s = s_s \land s_b \sqcap s_s = \bot_s$), use the shape of b ($s_c = s_b$), or if b can be a scalar but a cannot ($s_a \sqcap s_s = s_s \land s_b \sqcap s_s = \bot_s$), use the shape of a ($s_c = s_a$). E.g. a has 2 rows and 2 columns is added to b which has 1 column but an unknown number of rows. The only way the operation can be valid is if b has 1 row and is thus a scalar, in which case the result would have 2 rows and 2 columns.
- If both a and b can be scalars ($s_a \sqcap s_s = s_s \land s_b \sqcap s_s = s_s$), use the join of the two shapes ($s_c = s_a \sqcup s_b$). E.g. If a has between 1 and 3 rows, b has between 0 and 2 rows and both have one have column, then the result will have between 0 and 3 rows as either a or b could be a scalar.
- If both are definitely not scalars and there are conflicting dimensions ($s_a \sqcap s_s = \bot_s \land s_b \sqcap s_s = \bot_s \land s_a \sqcap s_b = \bot_s$), give an error.

The scheme above assumes that user code has no errors as it could hide errors by inferring valid shapes for operands when complete information is not available. This is discussed further in Sect. 7. Currently information is never passed backwards meaning that information, about the operands themselves, is never updated, but this change is planned for the future.

There are several non-array binary operations, matrix multiplication, division and power. These operations only work on two dimensional matrices and each has different dimension requirements.

- Matrix multiply : a * b
  The number of columns in a must match the number of rows in b. The result of the operation will have the same number of columns as b and the same

number of rows as a. The exception here is that if either a or b are scalars then the result will have the same dimensions as the other.
- Left matrix division : `a \ b`
  a must have the same number of rows as b, in which case the result will have as many rows as a has columns and as many columns as b. The exception is if a is scalar, in which case it is equivalent to array division of b by a.
- Right matrix division : `a / b`
  a must have the same number of columns as b, in which case the result will have as many columns as b has rows and as many rows as a. The exception is if a is scalar, in which case it is equivalent to array division of a by b.
- Matrix power : `a ^ b`
  Either a or b must be a scalar and the other must be a square matrix. The result will have the same dimensions as the matrix.

There are two types of function calls that we have to deal with in expressions: built-in functions and m-files.

Built-in functions that have static parameters can usually be executed directly via the MATLAB runtime libraries. There are however some built-in functions that cannot be executed directly as they require context. Examples include `exist`, which can be used to determine the existence of variables as well as files and functions, I/O functions, graphing functions and timing functions.

Some built-in functions like `exist` can be evaluated but indirectly by examining our symbol table. It makes little sense to evaluate timing functions while partially evaluating as the intention would usually be to time the final program. I/O functions are discussed in Sect. 7.

Built-in functions that cannot be evaluated directly are handled by the partial evaluator internally. For each built-in function we extract as much information as possible about the return values based on the input passed to it. In the case of functions like `size` and `ndims`, we can fully evaluate them if we have sufficient shape information. If insufficient information is available, an entry, describing what we can determine of the shape and type of the returned value, is returned.

Functions stored in m-files are evaluated using the partial evaluation process without code generation. Later we plan to implement polyvariant specialisation where new specialised functions are created when some of the parameters are fixed. Currently functions are evaluated as completely as possible and if the final result is static then the function call can be removed and a constant substituted for it. If this is not possible, then any shape or type information garnered by evaluating the function is retained.

Assignments. Simple assignments discard the old value of the target variable and are relatively easy to handle. If the new value is known, it is stored in the symbol table, otherwise we store inferred information such as type, shape and rank. With assignments to subscripts, the target variable is changed but not replaced. If the indices are outside the bounds of the matrix, then the matrix is resized to allow the assignment.

Functions with multiple outputs are more complicated. If the function can be fully evaluated, it is removed and replaced with several assignments. E.g.

```
[a,b] = size(c);
```

If the shape of c is known then two assignments to a and b are substituted, but if only one dimension is known, we would have to use a function call. E.g.

```
a = size(c,1);
b = 1;
```

This is more expensive than the original as there are two assignments and a function call, but post-processing could eliminate the assignment to b. It is easy to transform the size function into multiple assignments, but most function calls are not so simple and so we do not perform this kind of transformation.

for **Loops.** There are two cases to consider with for loops: the loop bounds are either static or dynamic. In the static case, the number of iterations is immediately determinable without data flow analysis as we do not consider break or return statements. Unrolling is achieved by partially evaluating the body of the loop for each iteration, setting the value of the loop variable as appropriate. Indexed assignments, to the loop variable in the loop body, require an explicit assignment to be written out. At the end of the loop, an assignment may be required to ensure the final value of the loop variable is available to the rest of the program. If the loop bounds indicate that the loop body is never executed, the entire loop is deleted.

If the loop bounds are dynamic, the loop is retained in the residual program. To find the least upper bound of the loop state, we iterate over the loop body evaluating its statements, comparing the state of the symbol table after each iteration. Note the loop variable is reset to dynamic before each iteration, although its shape and type is inferred if possible. A separate final state table is maintained with which the results are merged each time. If, as a result of a merge, the final state table is left unchanged, iteration ceases. This is almost certainly not an optimal approach and could, in the case of nested loops, lead to excessive computation but this will be refined later. This approach detects variables left unchanged after every iteration and preserves their values.

If the loop might not execute even once (due to its bounds), the final state table of the loop is merged with the symbol table that would be obtained if the loop did not execute, possibly leading to information being lost; therefore it is important to examine the loop bounds first in case this merge can be skipped.

while **Loops.** No attempt is made to unroll these loops apart from removing while loops that are never executed. A fix-point iteration is performed for shape and type analysis as described above for for loops.

if **Statements.** If the condition expression is static, the conditional statement is removed and replaced with an appropriate set of commands depending on whether or not the condition expression evaluated to zero. Otherwise, both sets of commands are partially evaluated with the same initial conditions and the resulting symbol tables merged, meaning that if both branches set a variable to the same value, it will have that value after the loop. If the value is different, but the type or size of the matrix are the same, then this information is retained instead as the least upper bound for the shape and type is calculated.

switch Statements. As with **if** statements, if the condition is static the entire statement is removed and replaced with the appropriate set of commands. Otherwise cases that cannot match are removed, thus reducing the number of comparisons required. If the exact control flow cannot be determined, each branch of the **switch** statement needs to be partially evaluated in parallel and the results then merged, skipping branches that can never be reached.

Annotations. In addition to standard MATLAB language constructs, our tool recognises annotations which guide the partial evaluation. These always begin with %# and are ignored by MATLAB as comments. There are two types of annotations: variable annotations and function annotations. Variable annotations specify the type, shape and definedness of a variable.

```
%# x size [1 1]
%# x complex
%# y undefined
```

Function annotations describe how the function has been called. They specify the values returned by built-in functions like **nargin** and **nargout**, which return the number of parameters and the number of return values respectively.

```
%# nargin 2
%# nargout 1
```

5.5 Post-processing

In this phase dead code is removed. A statement is considered dead if it has no side-effects and does not affect the final result. We will use a simple approach, which is to work backwards through a function marking variables which are used so that the last assignment before it can be marked as live. As noted by Knoop [9], removing dead assignments or expressions can change the program semantics as the dead code could generate a run-time error. Multiplying two matrices with incompatible dimensions or raising a matrix to the power of another matrix is illegal and will halt execution. Problems like this are discussed further in Sect. 7.

Expressions. If an expression is on a line on its own and it is terminated with a semi-colon then it has no side-effects and can be safely removed. If there is no semi-colon, then the result of evaluating the expression will be printed to the screen. Expressions, containing function calls that have side effects, cannot be removed.

Assignments. If the assignment is to a variable whose value may be required for a later statement, it is considered live. If nothing depends on the variable being assigned then it is dead and can be removed in the same way as expressions above depending on the presence of semi-colons.

If the assignment is to multiple variables, but only some of those variables are live then ideally we would transform it into an assignment which only assigned to the relevant variables, but as with the partial evaluation of assignments, the transformation is tricky and so we do not attempt it. As with stand-alone expressions, we must be wary of removing assignments involving expressions containing function calls with side effects.

Loops. Our simple approach of moving backwards through the code will not work for loops. E.g.

```
function y = f(x)
a = 1;
y = 1;
for n = 1:x
  y = n * a;
  a = a + n;
end
```

Moving backwards with y as the only live variable would result in the second assignment to a being removed, even though the previous line is dependent on it. To avoid this, the loop dependants must first be found and treated as live variables before working backwards. In this case n and a would be marked live and the assignment to a would be left intact. Since removing a statement can change the loop dependants, the two steps need to be iterated until no changes are made.

In the previous example, x could be less than 1, meaning that the loop body would never be executed. If the loop body is never executed then the value of y would remain 1, but moving backwards naively assuming the body of the loop is executed would lead to the removal of the initial assignment leaving y undefined. Unless we can guarantee that $x \geq 1$, we must assume that the loop might not be executed, in which case the live variable information from the loop must be merged with the live variable information from after the loop to ensure that correct code is generated.

This is not a perfect algorithm, but it is quite simple to implement. For instance an assignment which only creates new values for dead variables will not be removed. Muchnick [14] describes an algorithm that deals with even these assignments using UD and DU chains. Knoop [9] describes partial dead code elimination which allows assignments to be moved to the code blocks in which the assigned variables are live, speeding up the execution for alternate code blocks.

Conditional Statements. A simple conservative approach to dealing with conditional statements is to post-process all code blocks in parallel and then merge the lists of live variables. Later code motion may be used to perform partial dead code elimination [9].

Annotations. These are just removed from the final output.

6 Results

In this chapter we will evaluate the effectiveness of our partial evaluator on several source programs. The code for these tests is a mixture of code developed inside the Computational Engineering and Design research group at the University of Southampton, code come from partners from other universities and code found in code repositories on the internet. All of the timings were taken using the MATLAB 6.1 interpreter.

Experiment 1. The first code tested was a function for the generation of Chebyshev polynomials, which, like power series, are used to approximate functions by summing terms. As with power series, using more terms leads to better approximations. This function has two parameters, a m-by-n matrix, c of coefficients for calculating m functions with n terms and a vector, x, as input to the functions. Table 1 shows the relative timings for the chebyshev function (iterated 5000 times to get measurable results). Timings are shown where the function has been partially evaluated where just n is fixed, c is fixed and lastly where c is fixed along with the size of x. The timings are further subdivided according to whether post-processing was used. The results show a steady increase in performance as more information is fixed, with the final function running in half the time of the original. Partial evaluation has been previously been successfully applied to Chebyshev approximation previously [6].

Table 1. Relative timings for the Chebyshev functions with $m = 3$ and $p = 3$, relative to original function (p.p. is post-processing)

size(c,2)	Original	n fixed		c fixed		c and size of x fixed	
		No p.p.	With p.p.	No p.p.	With p.p.	No p.p.	With p.p.
2	1.00	0.90	0.89	0.81	0.77	0.60	0.48
4	1.00	0.94	0.92	0.84	0.81	0.59	0.50
6	1.00	0.94	0.93	0.85	0.82	0.58	0.51
8	1.00	0.94	0.94	0.85	0.83	0.57	0.52
10	1.00	0.95	0.95	0.86	0.84	0.57	0.52

Experiment 2. The second test function, when given a set of points from a function, computes the Lagrange interpolating polynomial that passes through them and returns a set of points on the curve. The MATLAB code is comprised of two nested loops both dependent on the number of points to interpolate

Table 2. Relative timings for the Lagrange functions with values of n

		n fixed		x-coordinates fixed	
n	Original	No postproc	Postproc	No postproc	Postproc
2	1.00	0.73	0.67	0.67	0.58
4	1.00	0.82	0.79	0.68	0.64
6	1.00	0.85	0.83	0.67	0.65
8	1.00	0.86	0.84	0.68	0.66
10	1.00	0.87	0.86	0.68	0.66

Table 3. Timings in seconds for the Gaussian Hypergeometric differential equation solver (iterated 8000 times). (Relative times are given in brackets)

n	Original	Partially Evaluated	Post-processed
4	1.17	0.85 (0.73)	0.72 (0.62)
6	1.47	1.07 (0.73)	0.94 (0.64)
8	1.77	1.30 (0.73)	1.17 (0.66)
10	2.08	1.54 (0.74)	1.40 (0.67)

Table 4. Timings for the computational fluid dynamic solver in seconds. (Relative times to the original are shown in brackets)

Original	After mpe	After mpe with postproc
67.91	54.64	52.77
67.88	54.54	52.71
67.97	54.55	52.74
67.92	54.58 (0.80)	52.74 (0.78)

followed by a third loop also dependent on the number of points. We specialised this function by first fixing the number of points, n, (and thus the number of x and y coordinates) resulting in all of the loops being unrolled and then further specialised it by fixing the x coordinates. Again, timings were taken with and without post-processing. Table 2 shows the improvements we achieved including at least 50% speed increases when the x coordinates are completely fixed.

Experiment 3. The next example function solves the Gaussian Hypergeometric differential equation, $x(1-x)\frac{d^2y}{dx^2} + c - (a+b+1)x\frac{dy}{dx} - aby = 0$, using a series expansion. The main work is done by a single `for` loop which calculates the series terms. To get more accurate results, higher order series terms are required and thus more iterations. The number of terms is the parameter that we have chosen to specialise. As can be seen from Table 3, partial evaluation with post-processing is very effective at speeding up the function, showing a 62% performance increase over the original function.

Experiment 4. Our final set of results in Table 4 are for a computational fluid dynamic solver in our research group. The main function is very general allowing users to choose what parameters they want to optimise. After some initial set up code which can be fully evaluated when specialised, it consists of a main loop that cannot be unrolled and an inner loop which can be, leading to the removal of many conditional statements and allowing the full evaluation of several function calls. This function would benefit from many traditional optimisation techniques but since MATLAB does not perform these and our partial evaluator does, we can see some improvements.

The code we have examined in this section was chosen because it was in the subset of MATLAB that we can handle and because it had control flow structures that would benefit from unrolling. We have not examined highly vectorised codes with few control flow structures as we conjecture that partial evaluation can do little without making code non-vectorised, which would hurt performance. The code we have examined has shown promising results. Inferring shape characteristics has allowed loop unrolling in many cases, but the large performance increases in experiment 1 and experiment 2 came from knowing the actual values stored in these matrices.

7 Future Work and Conclusion

The results show that partial evaluation can give large performance increases for relatively simple functions like those in experiments 1 to 3, but also for larger programs as in experiment 4. The results we have seen are encouraging and show that partial evaluation can achieve performance increases for MATLAB code. Unfortunately the number of functions that we could assess was limited by the subset of MATLAB that we currently handle. The omission of support for functions taking variable numbers of parameters, cell arrays and control flow change keywords like `return`, `break` and `continue` means that many functions, that could have benefited from partial evaluation, had to be discarded. Below are other areas where we plan to expand the capabilities of our tool.

While Loops. Currently while loops are not unrolled at all except for in the trivial case where the loop condition can never be met and so it can be deleted. Data flow analysis will be required to determine whether the loop condition will be static throughout the loop.

Assignment Amalgamation. As a result of unrolling the partial evaluator generates large series of assignments, either overwriting the same variable again and again while using its value as an operand or by writing to different subscripts of a variable. Many of these cases can be combined into single assignments in the preprocessing stage giving performance increases. Compilers for many languages optimise these away and so partial evaluators for these languages do not need to perform this optimisation themselves. Unforunately MATLAB does not do this (even when using the compiler).

Asserting Assumptions. When confronted with operations on operands for which only incomplete shape information is known, our implementation assumes that the program is bug-free and still attempts to infer shape and type information. Function calls using only this information could be fully evaluated and the original operation could then be removed, changing the semantics of the program in the case of programmer error. We plan to offer options to automaticall insert into the residual code assertions to check for these cases.

Widening. Currently MPE can loop infinitely on input containing loops which steadily increase shape values. Checks needs to be carried out to find these cases and widen the shape value to prevent further iteration.

I/O operations. As mentioned in Sect. 5.4, we currently do not support loading in data with I/O commands like fopen, fscanf and fclose. To be effective with mathematical codes, we must handle data sets that are loaded from files.

Polyvariant specialisation. This is very important for getting speed increases from large programs rather than the fairly simple functions examined in this work. For instance, most MATLAB functions check to see that they have been passed enough parameters and that their dimensions are valid. A significant advantage of polyvariant specialisation should be the prevalidation of parameters thus simplifying many functions.

We have presented the first partial evaluation system for MATLAB. We have shown how to deal with MATLAB data structures, notably how to store shape information about partially specified matrices. This is of utmost importance for scientific MATLAB code, as knowing the shape of a matrix often enables one to perform loop unrolling (and it is less common to statically know the full values of an entire matrix). We have presented our implementation and have shown on several non-trivial, practical examples that our system has achieved a significant speed increase.

References

1. G. Almási. *MaJIC: A MATLAB Just-In-Time Compiler.* PhD thesis, University of Illinois at Urbana-Champaign, 2001.
2. G. Almási and D. Padua. MaJIC: compiling MATLAB for speed and responsiveness. In *Proceeding of the ACM SIGPLAN 2002 Conference on Programming language design and implementation*, pages 294–303. ACM Press, 2002.
3. L. O. Andersen. *Program Analysis and Specialization for the C Programming Language.* PhD thesis, DIKU, University of Copenhagen, 1994.
4. P. Cousot and R. Cousot. Abstract interpretation and application to logic programs. *Journal of Logic Programming*, 13(2-3):103–179, 1992.
5. D. Elphick. Implementation of a MATLAB partial evaluator. Technical Report DSSE-TR-2003-4, University of Southampton, 2003.
6. R. Glück, R. Nakashige, and R. Zöchling. Binding-time analysis applied to mathematical algorithms. In *System Modelling and Optimization*, pages 137–146. Chapman & Hall, 1995.
7. N. D. Jones, C. K. Gomard, and P. Sestoft. *Partial Evaluation and Automatic Program Generation.* Prentice Hall, 1993.
8. P. Kleinrubatscher, A. Kriegshaber, R. Zöchling, and R. Glück. Fortran program specialization. In G. Snelting and U. Meyer, editors, *Semantikgestützte Analyse, Entwicklung und Generierung von Programmen. GI Workshop*, pages 45–54, Schloss Rauischholzhausen, Germany, 1994. Justus-Liebig-Universität Giessen.
9. J. Knoop, O. Ruthing, and B. Steffen. Partial dead code elimination. In *SIGPLAN Conference on Programming Language Design and Implementation*, pages 147–158. ACM Press, 1994.

10. M. Leuschel and M. Bruynooghe. Logic program specialisation through partial deduction: Control issues. *Theory and Practice of Logic Programming*, 2(4 & 5):461–515, July & September 2002.
11. MAGICA website. http://www.ece.northwestern.edu/cpdc/pjoisha/MAGICA/.
12. V. Menon and A. E. Trefethen. MultiMATLAB: Integrating Matlab with high performance parallel computing. In *Supercomputing '97 ACM SIGARCH and IEEE Computer Society*, pages 1–18, 1997.
13. T. Æ. Mogensen and P. Sestoft. Partial evaluation. In A. Kent and J. G. Williams, editors, *Encyclopedia of Computer Science and Technology*, volume 37, pages 247–279. Marcel Dekker, 270 Madison Avenue, New York, New York 10016, 1997.
14. S. Muchnick. *Advanced Compiler Design & Implementation*. Morgan Kaufmann Publishers, 1997.
15. S. Pawletta, T. Pawletta, W. Drewelow, P. Duenow, and M. Suesse. A MATLAB toolbox for distributed and parallel processing. In Moler C. and S. Little, editors, Proc. of the Matlab Conference 95, Cambridge, MA. MathWorks Inc., October 1995.
16. M. Quinn, A. Malishevsky, N. Seelam, and Y. Zhao. Preliminary results from a parallel MATLAB compiler. In *International Parallel Processing Symposium*, pages 81–87. IEEE CS Press, 1998.
17. L. D. Rose. Compiler techniques for MATLAB programs. Technical Report UIUCDCS-R-96-1956, University of Illinois at Urbana-Champaign, 1996.
18. L. D. Rose, K. Gallivan, E. Gallopoulos, B. A. Marsolf, and D. A. Padua. FALCON: A MATLAB interactive restructuring compiler. In *Languages and Compilers for Parallel Computing*, pages 269–288. Springer, 1995.
19. U. P. Schultz, J. L. Lawall, C. Consel, and G. Muller. Towards automatic specialization of Java programs. In *European Conference on Object-oriented Programming*, volume 1628 of *Lecture Notes in Computer Science*, pages 367–390, 1999.
20. The MathWorks, Inc. - About Us.
http://www.mathworks.com/company/aboutus.shtml.
21. R. C. Whaley, A. Petitet, and J. J. Dongarra. Automated empirical optimizations of software and the ATLAS project. *Parallel Computing*, 27(1-2):3–35, Jan. 2001.

An Easy-to-Use Toolkit for Efficient Java Bytecode Translators[*]

Shigeru Chiba and Muga Nishizawa

Dept. of Mathematical and Computing Sciences
Tokyo Institute of Technology
{chiba,muga}@csg.is.titech.ac.jp

Abstract. This paper presents our toolkit for developing a Java-bytecode translator. Bytecode translation is getting important in various domains such as generative programming and aspect-oriented programming. To help the users easily develop a translator, the design of our toolkit is based on the reflective architecture. However, the previous implementations of this architecture involved serious runtime penalties. To address this problem, our toolkit uses a custom compiler so that the runtime penalties are minimized. Since the previous version of our toolkit named *Javassist* has been presented in another paper, this paper focuses on this new compiler support for performance improvement. This feature was not included in the previous version.

1 Introduction

Since program translators are key components of generative programming [5], a number of translator toolkits have been developed. For the Java language, some toolkits like EPP [9] and OpenJava [18] allow developers to manipulate a parse tree or an abstract syntax tree for source-level translation. Other toolkits, such as BCEL [6], JMangler [13], and DataScript [1], allow manipulating a class file, which is a compiled binary, for bytecode-level translation. The ease of use and the power of expressiveness are design goals of these toolkits. The latter goal means what kinds of translation are enabled. The former goal is often sacrificed for the latter one.

The bytecode-level translation has two advantages against the source-level translation. First, it can process an off-the-shelf program or library that is supplied without source code. Second, it can be performed on demand at load time, when the Java virtual machine (JVM) loads a class file. A disadvantage of the bytecode translation is, however, that the toolkits are difficult to use for developers who do not know detailed specifications of the Java bytecode.

To overcome this problem, a few researchers have proposed bytecode translator toolkits that provide higher-level abstraction than raw bytecode. For example, our toolkit named *Javassist* [4] provides source-level abstraction based

---

[*] This work was supported in part by the CREST program of Japan Science and Technology Corp.

on the reflective architecture. The application programming interface (API) of Javassist is designed with only source-level vocabulary like *class* and *method* instead of bytecode-level one like *constant pool* and *invokevirtual*. Javassist interprets the program transformation written with the source-level vocabulary and executes an equivalent transformation at the bytecode level.

So far Javassist has allowed only limited modification of a method body for performance reasons. Other reflection-based translator toolkits enable inserting a hook at an interesting execution point such as method invocation in a method body so that the execution can be intercepted to change the computation at that point or to append extra computation there. The execution contexts at that point are converted into regular objects and passed to the intercepting code. If the intercepting code modifies these objects, then the modifications are reflected on the original execution contexts. The former conversion is called *reify* and the latter one is called *reflect*. Although this modification mechanism still restricts a range of possible program transformation, a number of research activities have revealed that it covers a wide range of application domains. Also, the idea of this mechanism has been also adopted by aspect oriented programming systems such as AspectJ [11, 12]. However, the reify and reflect operations are major sources of runtime overheads due to the reflective architecture. Existing reflective systems such as Kava [19] and Jinline [17] always perform these operations and thus imply not-negligible runtime overheads.

This paper presents our solution of this performance problem. We developed it for a new version of Javassist, which now allows the users to modify a method body as other reflection-based translator toolkits. To reduce runtime penalties due to the reify and reflect operations, Javassist suppresses unnecessary part of these operations as much as possible. A compiler specially developed for Javassist enables this suppression. It can compile source code written in Java with extensions for reification and reflection. Javassist uses this compiler for compiling intercepting code into efficient bytecode.

In the rest of this paper, we first show a performance problem of the previous implementations of the reflective architecture in Section 2. We next present our solution developed for Javassist in Section 3. We mention the results of our micro benchmark in Section 4. Related work is discussed in Section 5. We conclude this paper in Section 6.

2 Modifying a Method Body

Jinline [17] is a typical translator toolkit that is based on the reflective architecture and enables modifying a method body. From the implementation viewpoint, it is a Java class library developed on top of Javassist by a research group different from ours. With Jinline, the users can develop a bytecode translator that substitutes a hook for a specific expression in a method body. For example, it can substitute hooks for all the accesses to the fields in a Point class. The hooks can call the methods specified by the user so that the methods perform the altered behavior of the field-access expressions. In the case of Jinline, the call to this method is inlined in the method body containing the replaced expression; this is why the toolkit is called Jinline.

The Jinline users can define a method that implements new behavior of the hooked expression and then they can specify that method to be called by the hook. However, the definition of that method must be subject to the protocol provided by Jinline. For a simple example, we below show a translator for enforcing the Singleton pattern [8]. Suppose that the translator guarantees that only a single instance of a class is created if the class implements an interface named **Singleton**.

First, the Jinline users prepare the following class for runtime support:

```
class Factory {
  static Hashtable singletons = new Hashtable();

  Object make(Object[] jinArgs) {
    String classname = (String)jinArgs[2];
    Class c = Class.forName(classname);
    Object obj = singletons.get(classname);
    if (obj == null) {
      Constructor cons = c.getDeclaredConstructor(...);
      obj = cons.newInstance((Object[])jinArgs[3]);
      singletons.put(classname, obj);
    }
    return obj;
  }
}
```

Then, they write a translator program using the Jinline toolkit. Since Jinline can notify the program whenever an interesting expression is found in the given method body, the program can have only to receive an object representing that expression and examine whether a hook must be substituted for that expression. To examine it, the program can use the lexical contexts supplied by Jinline. If a hook is substituted, the program must specify the method called by the hook. For the example above, we must specify the **make** method in **Factory** if the expression is the creation of an instance of a singleton class.

The parameter jinArgs to make is constructed by the hook at runtime. jinArgs[2] is the class name of the created object and jinArgs[3] is an array of **Object** representing the actual parameters to the constructor of the created object. The make method uses these runtime contexts to implement the Singleton pattern. For example, it uses jinArgs[3] for creating an object through the standard reflection API of Java [10]. The value returned by make is used as the result of the original expression. The type of the return value is converted by the hook into an appropriate type.

Constructing jinArgs and converting the type of the return value correspond to the *reify* and *reflect* operations of the reflective architecture. Exposing runtime contexts of the hooked expression through jinArgs is significant since they are needed to implement the altered behavior. It also makes the make method generic enough to deal with the instantiation of any class. Suppose that the hooked expression is "`new Point(3, 4)`". If the hook did not perform the reify operation, it would directly pass the constructor parameters 3 and 4 to the make method. The make method would have to receive two int parameters and thus it could not be generic since it could not deal with instantiation with different types of parameters. A different make method would be necessary for every constructor with a different signature.

However, the reify and reflect operations are major sources of runtime penalties. If a parameter type is a primitive type, then these operations involves conversion between the primitive type such as int and the wrapper type such as java.lang.Integer. Since these operations are performed whenever the hooked expression is executed, this overhead is not negligible.

3 Javassist

Javassist [4] is a reflection-based toolkit for developing Java-bytecode translators. It is a class library in Java for transforming Java class files (bytecode) at compile time or load time. Unlike other libraries that are not based on reflection, it allows the users to describe transformation with source-level vocabulary; the users do not have to have detailed knowledge of bytecode or the internal structure of Java class file.

The Javassist users can first translate a Java class file into several objects representing a class, field, or method. The users' programs can access these "meta" objects for transformation. Introducing a super interface, a new field, and so on, to the class is performed through modifying these objects. The modifications applied to these metaobjects are finally translated back into the modifications of the class file so that the transformation is reflected on the class definition. Since Javassist does not expose internal data structures contained in a class file, such as a constant pool item and a method_info structure, the developers can use Javassist without knowledge of Java class files or bytecode*. On the other hand, other libraries such as BCEL [6] provide objects that directly represent a constant pool item and a method_info structure.

Javassist allows the users to modify a method body as Jinline does. To avoid the performance problem, Javassist lets the users explicitly specify when the reify and reflect operations should be performed. Several meta variables and types are available for specifying this in the code executed by a hook. Javassist analyzes the occurrences of these meta variables and types and it thereby eliminates unnecessary reify and reflect operations.

3.1 Structural Reflection

The CtClass object is an object provided by Javassist for representing a class obtained from the given class file. It provides the almost same functionality of

---

* For practical reasons, Javassist also provides another programming interface to directly access the internal data structures in a class file. However, normal users do not have to use that interface.

Table 1. Part of methods for modifying a class

Methods in CtClass	Description
void setName(String name)	change the class name
void setModifiers(int m)	change the class modifiers such as public
void setSuperclass(CtClass c)	change the super class
void setInterfaces(CtClass[] i)	change the interfaces
void addField(CtField f, String i)	add a new field
void addMethod(CtMethod m)	add a new method
void addConstructor(CtConstrutor c)	add a new constructor

Table 2. Part of methods for modifying a member

Methods in CtField	Description
void setName(String n)	changes the field name
void setModifiers(int m)	changes the field modifiers
void setType(CtClass c)	changes the field type
Methods in CtMethod, CtConstructor	**Description**
void setName(String n)	changes the method name
void setModifiers(int m)	changes the method modifiers
void setExceptionTypes(CtClass[] t)	sets the types of the exceptions that the method may throw
void setBody(String b)	changes the method body

introspection as the java.lang.Class class of the standard reflection API. Introspection means to inspect data structures, such as a class, used in a program. For example, the getName method declared in CtClass returns the name of the class, the getSuperclass method returns the CtClass object representing the super class. getFields, getMethods, and getConstructors return CtField, CtMethod, and CtConstructor objects representing fields, methods, and constructors, respectively. These objects parallel java.lang.reflect.Field, Method, and Constructor. They provide various methods, such as getName and getType, for inspecting the definition of the member. Since a CtClass object does not exist at run time, the newInstance method is not available in CtClass unlike in java.lang.Class. For the same reason, the invoke method is not available in CtMethod and so forth.

Unlike the standard reflection API, Javassist allows developers to alter the definition of classes through CtClass objects and the associated objects (Table 1 and 2). For example, the setSuperclass method in CtClass changes the super class of the class. The addMethod method adds a new method to the class. The definition of the new method is given in the form of String object representing the source text. Javassist compiles the source text into bytecode on the fly and adds it into the class file. The addField method adds a new field. It can take source text representing the initial value of the field. Javassist compiles the source text and inserts it in the constructor body so that the field is appropriately initialized.

The setName method in CtClass changes the name of the class. To keep consistency, several methods like setName perform more than changing one attribute field in a class file. For example, setName also substitutes the new class name for all occurrences of the old class name in the class definition. The occurrences of the old class name in method signatures are also changed.

3.2 Behavioral Reflection

The new version of Javassist allows the users to modify a method body as other reflection-based toolkits. The users can develop a bytecode translator that inserts a hook at the beginning or end of a method body. The bytecode translator can also substitute a hook for a specific expression in a method body. The hook executes intercepting code specified by the users in the form of source text. The intercepting code can be a single Java statement or several statements surrounded by {} and it can directly execute the altered behavior of the hooked expression or call another method for indirectly executing the altered behavior. The code is inlined in the hook and thus executed in the same scope as the original expression. It can access private fields of the object although it cannot access local variables.

The following example substitutes the hooks for the caller-side expressions that invoke the move method in the Point class if the expressions belong to the Graph class:

```
CtClass cc = ClassPool.getDefault().get("Graph");
cc.insrtument(new ExprEditor() {
  public void edit(MethodCall m) {
    if (m.getClassName().equals("Point")
        && m.getMethodName().equals("move"))
      m.replace("{ System.out.println(\"calling move()\");"
              + "  $_ = $proceed($$); }");
  }
});
```

The hook executes the code printing a log message. The variable cc is the CtClass object representing the Graph class.

The instrument method in CtClass receives an ExprEditor object and scans the bodies of all the methods declared in the class, in the case above, the Graph class. If an interesting expression is found, the edit method is invoked on the given ExprEditor object with a parameter representing the expression. The edit method can be invoked if a method call, a field access, object creation by the new operator, an instanceof expression, a cast expression, or a catch clause is found. The parameter is a MethodCall, FieldAccess, NewExpr, Instanceof, Cast, or Handler object, respectively. These objects provide various methods for inspecting the lexical contexts of the expression.

The edit method can inspect the given parameter to determine whether a hook must be substituted for the expression. If the hook must be substituted, the replace method is called on the given parameter. It replaces the expression with the hook that executes the given Java statement or block. For the example above, the hook executes the following block:

```
{ System.out.println("calling move()");
  $_ = $proceed($$); }
```

The second statement in the block is written with special variables starting with $, which are extensions to Java by Javassist. It executes the original method-call expression.

Besides the instrument method, insertBefore, insertAfter, and addCatch methods are available in the CtMethod and CtConstructor classes. They receive source text as a parameter, compile it, and insert the hook executing the compiled code at the beginning or end of the method. The addCatch method inserts the hook so that the hook will be executed when an exception of the specified type is thrown in the method body. The hook executes the code given to addCatch as a parameter.

3.3 Meta Variables and Types

The reify and reflect operations have been major sources of runtime overheads in the reflective architecture. They are operations for converting runtime contexts to/from regular Java objects so that the program can access and modify them. Since other toolkits like Jinline use a regular Java compiler for compiling the code executed by a hook, the code must be written as a regular Java method, which must take the reified object as a parameter and return an object to be reflected on the runtime contexts. Thus, the hook must always perform the reify and reflect operations before/after invoking the method even though they might be often unnecessary.

To avoid this problem, Javassist uses a Java compiler specially developed for compiling the intercepting code. The compiler interprets several symbols in the source text of that code as *meta* variables or types (Table 3). These symbols are used to access the runtime or lexical contexts of the expression replaced with the hook. If necessary, this access involves the reify and reflect operations. From the implementation viewpoint, these symbols are macro variables expanded to context-dependent text at compile time.

The meta variables enable Javassist to perform the reify and reflect operations on demand. Javassist does not perform these operations if the code executed by the hook does not need them. If only part of the runtime contexts must be reified or reflected, the compiler produces optimized bytecode to minimize runtime penalties due to the reify and reflect operations.

We below show details of some significant meta variables and types.

- $0, $1, $2, ...

  They represent method parameters if the hooked expression is method call. $0 represents the target object. The types of $0, $1, ... are identical to the types of the corresponding parameters. If the value of $1, $2, ... is updated, the value of the corresponding parameter is also updated.

Table 3. Meta variables and types

$0, $1, $2, ...	parameter values
$_	result value
$$	a comma-separated sequence of the parameters
$args	an array of the parameter values
$r	formal type of the result value
$w	the wrapper type
$proceed(..)	execute the original computation
$class	a java.lang.Class object representing the target class
$sig	an array of java.lang.Class representing the formal parameter types
$type	a java.lang.Class object representing the formal result type
$cflow(..)	a mechanism similar to cflow of AspectJ

If the hooked expression is object creation, then $1, $2, ... represent the actual parameters to the constructor. If it is field assignment, then $1 represents the assigned value. The other variables like $2 are not available.

- $_

The meta variable $_ represents the result value of the hooked execution. If a new value is assigned to this meta variable, then the assigned value becomes the result of the method call, field read, object creation, and so on. The type of $_ is identical to the type of the result value of the original expression. If the result type is void, then the type of $_ is Object.

- $$

The meta variable $$ is interpreted as a comma-separated sequence of all the actual parameters. For example, if the hooked expression is a call to a method move(int, int, int), then $$ is syntactically equivalent to $1, $2, $3. move($$) is equivalent to move($1,$2,$3). This meta variable abstracts the number of parameters from the source text so that the source text can be generic.

- $proceed

This is a meta method. If it is invoked, then the original computation of the hooked expression is executed. For example, if the expression is a method call, then the originally called method is invoked. If the expression is field read, then $proceed() returns the value of the field. Typical usage of this meta method is as following:

$_ = $proceed($$);

This executes the original computation with the current runtime contexts, which may be updated through the meta variables.

Note that the types of the parameters of $proceed is the same as those of the original ones. The result type is also the same. If the expression is field read, then $proceed does not take a parameter. If the expression is field assignment, then $proceed takes a new value of the field as a parameter. If the expression is object creation, then $proceed takes the same parameters as the constructor.

- $args

  The meta variable $args represents an array of all the parameters. The type of this meta variable is an array of Object. Whenever this meta variable is read, a new copy of the array is created and the parameters are stored in the array. Note that $args is different from $$; $args can be used as a regular Java variable whereas $$ is syntax sugar used only with a method call.

  If the type of a parameter is a primitive type such as int, then the parameter value is converted into a wrapper object of that primitive value. For example, an int value is converted into a java.lang.Integer object to be stored in $args.

  If an array of Object is assigned to $args, then each element of that array is assigned to each actual parameter. If a parameter type is a primitive type, the type of the corresponding array element must be a wrapper type such as java.lang.Integer. The value of the element is converted from the wrapper type to the primitive type before it is assigned to the parameter.

- $r and $w

  These are meta types available only in a cast expression. $r represents the result type of the hooked expression. If the expression is a method call, then $r represents the return type of the method call.

  If the result type is a primitive type, then ($r) converts the value from the wrapper type to the primitive type. For example, if the result type is int, then

```
Object res = new Integer(3);
$_ = ($r)res;
```

converts res into the value 3 and assigns it to the meta variable $_ of type int.

If the result type is void, then the type cast operator with ($r) is ignored. If the type cast operator with $r is used in the return statement, then that statement is regarded as the return statement without any return value. For example, if res is a local variable and the result type is void, then

```
return ($r)res;
```

is regarded as:

```
return;
```

This specification is useful for the generic description of the intercepting code.

($w) converts the value from a primitive type to the wrapper type. For example, in this program:

```
Integer i = ($w)5;
```

the cast expression converts the int value 5 to the java.lang.Integer object. If ($w) is applied to a value of Object type, then ($w) is ignored.

3.4 Compilation

The hook produced by Javassist does not prepare an object corresponding to jinArgs of Jinline. Rather, the prologue of the hook stores the runtime contexts in local variables without any data conversion. If the hooked expression is a method call, all the parameters pushed on the operand stack are popped and stored in the variables. The epilogue of the hook reads the value of $_, which is implemented as a local variable, and pushes it on the operand stack as the resulting value of the hooked expression. The intercepting code executed by the hook is inlined between the prologue and the epilogue.

The local variables containing the runtime contexts are accessed through the meta variables. If $args is read, the runtime contexts are obtained from the local variables and the parameters are converted into an array of Object. This conversion is the reify operation. Javassist does not perform the reify operation until it is explicitly required by the meta variables such as $args.

Since the programmers can use the meta variables for explicitly specifying when and what runtime contexts must be reified or reflected, Javassist can minimize runtime penalties due to the reify and reflect operations. If these operations are not required, Javassist never performs it. For example, if the source text of the intercepting code is only "$_ = $proceed($$);", then no reify or reflect operations are performed. $proceed is compiled into the bytecode sequence for executing the original computation. For example, if the hooked expression is a method call, the parameters are loaded from the local variables onto the operand stack and the method originally called is invoked by the invokevirtual instruction. The resulting value on the operand stack is stored into $_. The overheads are only extra costs of load and store instructions.

3.5 Example

In Section 2, we showed an example of the use of Jinline. For this example, we substituted a hook for an expression for creating an object so that the Singleton pattern would be enforced.

This example can be implemented with Javassist as well. We must specify that the hook will execute the following intercepting code:

```
Object obj = Factory.singletons.get($class);
if (obj != null)
  $_ = ($r)obj;
else {
  $_ = $proceed($$);
  Factory.singletons.put($class, ($w)$_);
}
```

This intercepting code is generic; it covers all the singleton classes.

Factory.singletons is a hashtable containing the singleton objects that have been created. The intercepting code first searches this hashtable and, if it finds an object of the target class, then it returns that object. Otherwise, the code creates the object by $proceed and includes it in the hashtable. Note that the meta types $r and $w are used in cast expressions since the type of $_ (the resulting value) is the class type of the created object.

4 Experiment

To measure the runtime overhead of the hook substituted by Javassist, we executed micro benchmark tests. We used Javassist to replace a method-call expression with a hook that executes the following intercepting code:

```
{ $_ = $proceed($$); }
```

This only executes the original computation, which is a method invocation with the original parameters. We measured the elapsed time of executing this hooked expression. The body of the called method was empty. The measured time represents the overhead of Javassist in the best case where no reification or reflection is required.

For comparison, we also measured the elapsed time with the hook that invokes the originally called method through the standard reflection API of Java. The given code is:

```
{ $_ = ($r)method.invoke($0, $args); }
```

Here, method is a static field containing a java.lang.reflect.Method object. It represents the originally called method. Note that $args is used for obtaining the parameter list and ($r) is for converting the type of the result value. They are the reify and reflect operations. The measured time represents the minimum overhead of the previous implementation technique of the reflective architecture, which always performs the reify and reflect operations. Furthermore, we measured the time with the behavioral reflection system included in the Javassist toolkit. The system enables typical runtime reflection as Kava [19] does. In this measurement, a metaobject trapped the method call and only executed the body of the originally called method. The measured time includes the cost for handling the metaobject as well as the reify and reflect operations.

Table 4 lists the results of our measurement using Sun JDK 1.4.0_01 for Solaris 8. The listed numbers are the average of four million iterations after one million iterations. We measured for several combinations of the return type and the parameter types of the null method called by the hook. Reflection API means the standard reflection API and Behavioral means the behavioral reflection system. If Javassist was used, the elapsed time of all the combinations except one was less than 10 nanoseconds. Since the pair of call and retl machine instructions takes about 10 nanoseconds, these results mean that the overhead was negligible and thus the method invocation was inlined by the JVM. On the other hand, the other experiments showed the overheads were about 500 to 1,300 nanoseconds.

5 Related Work

This work is not the first work on improving the runtime performance of reflective systems. The technique of partial evaluation [7] has been actively studied

Table 4. The elapsed time of a null method call (nsec.)

Return type Parameter types	void no	void String	String String	String String×2	void int	int int	int int×2	double double×2
Javassist	*	*	*	*	*	*	*	20
Reflection API	500	550	560	630	760	880	1,110	1,290
Behavioral	560	620	620	700	820	930	1,200	1,370

Sun Blade 1000 (Dual UltraSPARC III 750MHz, 1GB memory), Solaris 8, Sun JDK 1.4.0_01
* indicates the time was less than 10 nsec.

in this research field [14, 2]. However, since partial evaluation involves relatively long compilation time, it is not appropriate for bytecode translators, which may be used at load time. Compile-time reflection [3] can improve the runtime performance but it makes runtime contexts difficult to access from the program.

The pointcut-advice framework of the AspectJ language [12] is similar to the programming framework of Javassist. It allows programmers to insert a hook in a method body for executing the code given as *advice*. Like Javassist, AspectJ does not perform the reify operation unless they are explicitly requested through the special variables such as thisJoinPoint. However, AspectJ is not a bytecode translator toolkit but an aspect-oriented programming language and it does not well support the reflect operation. On the other hand, Javassist supports both of the reify and reflect operations. For example, assignment to $args updates the runtime contexts.

The problem of Jinline mentioned in Section 2 is included in other aspect-oriented systems that provide the pointcut-advice framework but are implemented as a class library. For example, JAC [15] always reifies the runtime contexts before passing them to the wrappers. PROSE [16] allows choosing whether the runtime contexts are reified or not but, if they are not reified, the description of advice cannot be generic. Our compiler-based solution will be applicable to those systems.

6 Conclusion

This paper presented a new version of our Java-bytecode translator toolkit named *Javassist*. It allows the programmers to modify a method body according to the reflection-based framework. A unique feature against other reflection-based toolkits like Jinline is that Javassist uses a customized compiler for reducing runtime penalties due to the reify and reflect operations, which are fundamentals of the reflective architecture. These runtime penalties have been disadvantages of reflection-based toolkits while ease of use by the high-level abstraction has been an advantage. Javassist reduces the runtime penalties while keeping the ease of use. The version of Javassist presented in this paper has been already released to the public and getting widely used. Applications of Javassist include product-quality software like the JBoss EJB server.

References

1. Back, G., "DataScript — A Specification and Scripting Languages for Binary Data," in *Generative Programming and Component Engineering (GPCE 2002)* (D. Batory, C. Consel, and W. Taha, eds.), LNCS 2487, pp. 66–77, Springer, 2002.
2. Braux, M. and J. Noyé, "Towards Partially Evaluating Reflection in Java," in *Proc. of Symposium on Partial Evaluation and Semantics-Based Program Manipulation (PEPM'00)*, SIGPLAN Notices vol. 34, no. 11, pp. 2–11, ACM, 1999.
3. Chiba, S., "A Metaobject Protocol for C++," in *Proc. of ACM Conf. on Object-Oriented Programming Systems, Languages, and Applications*, SIGPLAN Notices vol. 30, no. 10, pp. 285–299, ACM, 1995.
4. Chiba, S., "Load-time structural reflection in Java," in *ECOOP 2000*, LNCS 1850, pp. 313–336, Springer-Verlag, 2000.
5. Czarnecki, K. and U. W. Eisenecker, *Generative Programming*. Addison Wesley, 2000.
6. Dahm, M., "Byte Code Engineering with the JavaClass API," Techincal Report B-17-98, Institut für Informatik, Freie Universität Berlin, January 1999.
7. Futamura, Y., "Partial Computation of Programs," in *Proc. of RIMS Symposia on Software Science and Engineering*, LNCS, no. 147, pp. 1–35, 1982.
8. Gamma, E., R. Helm, R. Johnson, and J. Vlissides, *Design Patterns*. Addison-Wesley, 1994.
9. Ichisugi, Y. and Y. Roudier, "Extensible Java Preprocessor Kit and Tiny Data-Parallel Java," in *Proc. of ISCOPE '97*, LNCS, no. 1343, 1997.
10. Java Soft, "Java[TM] Core Reflection API and Specification." Sun Microsystems, Inc., 1997.
11. Kiczales, G., J. Lamping, A. Mendhekar, C. Maeda, C. Lopes, J. Loingtier, and J. Irwin, "Aspect-Oriented Programming," in *ECOOP'97 – Object-Oriented Programming*, LNCS 1241, pp. 220–242, Springer, 1997.
12. Kiczales, G., E. Hilsdale, J. Hugunin, M. Kersten, J. Palm, and W. G. Griswold, "An Overview of AspectJ," in *ECOOP 2001 – Object-Oriented Programming*, LNCS 2072, pp. 327–353, Springer, 2001.
13. Kniesel, G., P. Costanza, and M. Austermann, "JMangler — A Framework for Load-Time Transformation of Java Class Files," in *Proc. of IEEE Workshop on Source Code Analysis and Manipulation*, 2001.
14. Masuhara, H. and A. Yonezawa, "Design and Partial Evaluation of Meta-objects for a Concurrent Reflective Languages," in *ECOOP'98 - Object Oriented Programming*, LNCS 1445, pp. 418–439, Springer, 1998.
15. Pawlak, R., L. Seinturier, L. Duchien, and G. Florin, "JAC: A Flexible Solution for Aspect-Oriented Programming in Java," in *Metalevel Architectures and Separation of Crosscutting Concerns (Reflection 2001)*, LNCS 2192, pp. 1–24, Springer, 2001.
16. Popovici, A., T. Gross, and G. Alonso, "Dynamic Weaving for Aspect-Oriented Programming," in *Proc. of Int'l Conf. on Aspect-Oriented Software Development (AOSD'02)*, pp. 141–147, ACM Press, 2002.
17. Tanter, E., M. Ségura-Devillechaise, J. Noyé, and J. Piquer, "Altering Java Semantics via Bytecode Manipulation," in *Generative Programming and Component Engineering (GPCE 2002)* (D. Batory, C. Consel, and W. Taha, eds.), LNCS 2487, pp. 283–298, Springer, 2002.
18. Tatsubori, M., S. Chiba, M.-O. Killijian, and K. Itano, "OpenJava: A Class-based Macro System for Java," in *Reflection and Software Engineering* (W. Cazzola, R. J. Stroud, and F. Tisato, eds.), LNCS 1826, pp. 119–135, Springer Verlag, 2000.
19. Welch, I. and R. Stroud, "From Dalang to Kava — The Evolution of a Reflective Java Extension," in *Proc. of Reflection '99*, LNCS 1616, pp. 2–21, Springer, 1999.

A Case for Test-Code Generation in Model-Driven Systems

Matthew J. Rutherford and Alexander L. Wolf

Department of Computer Science
University of Colorado
Boulder, Colorado, 80309-430 USA
{rutherfo,alw}@cs.colorado.edu

Abstract. A primary goal of generative programming and model-driven development is to raise the level of abstraction at which designers and developers interact with the software systems they are building. During initial development, the benefits of abstraction are clear. However, during testing and maintenance, increased distance from the implementation can be a disadvantage. We view test cases and test harnesses as an essential bridge between the high-level specifications and the implementation. As such, the generation of test cases for fully generated components and test harnesses for partially generated components is of fundamental importance to model-driven systems. In this paper we present our experience with test-case and test-harness generation for a family of model-driven, component-based distributed systems. We describe our development tool, MODEST, and motivate our decision to invest the extra effort needed to generate test code. We present our approach to test-case and test-harness generation and describe the benefits to developers and maintainers of generated systems. Furthermore, we quantify the relative cost of generating test code versus application code and find that the artifact templates for producing test code are simpler than those used for application code. Given the described benefits to developers and maintainers and the relatively low cost of test-code development, we argue that test-code generation should be a fundamental feature of model-driven development efforts.

1 Introduction

A primary goal of generative programming and model-driven development is to raise the level of abstraction at which designers and developers interact with the software systems they are building. During initial development, automatic generation of software artifacts from high-level specifications offers many advantages to system developers, including increased productivity, enhanced source-code consistency, high-level reuse, and improved performance of the generated system [2]. However, increased distance from system implementation can be a disadvantage during testing and maintenance phases. Testing must be performed to certify initial systems and to help cope with future changes, both planned and unexpected; this does not change because the bulk of a system is automatically generated.

With model-driven systems, one might assume that framework and generated software have been debugged and certified elsewhere, and that testing the instantiated code is redundant and wasteful. While it is most likely true that framework and generated software have been tested, the question remains: in what context? In practice, any previous testing can be seen as irrelevant; the only context that truly matters is that of the particular system being created.

Testing artifacts serve as an essential bridge between the high-level specifications and the specific instantiation of a model-driven system. In the event of an error or failure, their existence provides a road map through the potentially vast amount of unfamiliar, generated code. Testing artifacts are particularly important in data-driven distributed systems, where software is deployed in potentially heterogeneous environments with complicated interactions across multiple tiers. In these systems, there are many layers surrounding the generated software that can be independently altered to conflict with the set of assumptions that were made at generation time. Although assumptions may be listed in the documentation of the abstract models or generators, the test cases (provided they give good coverage) are an *executable* form of these assumptions.

With an appropriate level of detail in the interface specifications of domain-specific components, it is possible to automatically generate some or all of their test cases. In fact, test cases can be specified and generated in parallel to the specification and generation of components. Of course, many model-driven systems are not completely generated. Instead, the "cookie-cutter" code is generated, and some crucial domain-specific components are hand written. Thus, these domain-specific components can only be fully tested by hand-coded test cases. Nonetheless, generation technology still has a role to play: In the same way that domain-specific components are constrained by the generated code surrounding them, test cases for these components are also constrained by generated code. The scaffolding that is generated to surround the domain-specific test cases is the *test harness*. Test harnesses are intended to handle as much test setup and cleanup as possible, allowing the developer to concentrate on the logic to perform the actual tests.

In this paper we describe our experience with a generative approach to test-case and test-harness development. Collectively, we refer to test cases and harnesses as *test code*, and show how we generate the test code in parallel with the system it is meant to test.

Our experience is based on the use of a model-driven generative programming tool called MODEST (Model-Driven Enterprise System Transformer), developed by the first author while at Chronos Software, Inc.[1] All systems generated by MODEST have the same basic architecture and design. The systems differ in their domain-specific data and logic, and some features can be enabled and disabled, leading to generated variations on a basic theme. MODEST does not implement OMG's Model Driven Architecture (MDA) standard [12]. However,

---

[1] http://www.chronosinc.com/

there are enough similarities that many of the lessons learned could be readily applied to MDA-compliant tools.

In describing MODEST, we carefully distinguish among three roles: the developer, the customer, and the (end) user. A *developer* uses MODEST in the creation of a system tailored to the needs of a *customer*; the outcome of this activity is the structured system specification that serves as one of the inputs to MODEST. The developer repeatedly adjusts the code templates that serve as the other inputs to MODEST. Lastly, the developer implements domain-specific operations and the test cases for them. Once development is complete, the developer delivers both the application code and the test code to the customer. During maintenance, the customer has the ability to execute test code and adjust application and test code as needed. However, it is important to note that the customer does not have access to the generative capabilities of MODEST. Finally, the customer makes the system available to a *user* who interacts with the system at run time to achieve some business purpose.

MODEST represents a structured description of the system to be generated as an XML document. This document captures the domain-specific data model, the interfaces of domain-specific logic components, dependencies on third-party libraries, and characteristics of the deployed system. Artifact generation in MODEST is accomplished by a series of XSL transforms. Initially, the system specification is used to generate a customized build script for the entire system. This build script includes targets to generate all of the other artifacts that comprise the generated system. MODEST generates Java source code, database management scripts, and Enterprise JavaBean (EJB) deployment descriptors.

Systems developed using MODEST are intended to be delivered to customers who need to maintain and extend their system without access to MODEST's generative capabilities. This requirement has several far-reaching consequences, one of which, in fact, is the need to provide test code. To make this practical, the decision was made to try to generate as much of the test code as possible.

While the initial decision to provide test code was not made for technical reasons, the presence of the test code turned out to greatly enhance the development process of the underlying framework and the generation templates. In particular, by requiring template developers to think also about test-code generation, they became more familiar with the code being generated. Furthermore, when underlying infrastructure software (e.g., the database, application server, and the like) was changed, the test code enabled developers to quickly certify existing systems. On the other hand, there is a cost associated with the generation of test code. In this paper we attempt to quantify the complexity of code-generation templates, and compare the complexity of templates for test-code generation with templates for application-code generation. Given the benefits to developers and maintainers and the relatively low cost of test-code development, we argue that test-code generation should be a fundamental feature of model-driven development efforts.

In the next section we describe the important aspects of MODEST and the salient characteristics of the family of systems it generates. Section 3 explains the strategy used by MODEST to generate test code. Section 4 presents an evaluation of our experience with MODEST, and also compares the complexity of test-code templates with application-code templates. Section 5 outlines related research, and Section 6 provides some concluding remarks.

2   An Overview of MODEST

MODEST is a model-driven code generation tool developed to streamline the programming activities of a small software consulting company. By generating "cookie-cutter" code from a structured representation of a customer's requirements, MODEST allows developers to concentrate on understanding the customer's needs, developing domain-specific logic, and adding to the corporate knowledge base. At the end of a development cycle, the customer receives delivery of a complete, self-contained system that satisfies their initial requirements. Obviously, this is an idealized version of the process, but the notion that the end product is self contained, ready for use or extension by the customer, is key.

Figure 1 depicts the three major conceptual elements of the tool: the domain specification, artifact templates, and the generative engine. Of these, the domain specification is the only customer-driven entity. From an engineering perspective, all systems generated by MODEST have the same architecture and design, which are embodied in the artifact templates. The variability of each system comes entirely from the different domain models that can be represented by the domain specification.

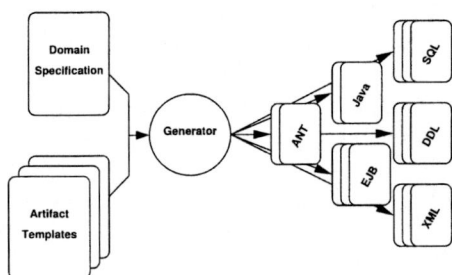

Fig. 1. Conceptual Elements of MODEST

The domain specification uses an XML document to represent a conceptual model of a customer's domain of interest, including the data model and the interfaces of any domain-specific business objects that are needed. The domain specification does not include engineering details, which are captured entirely by the artifact templates and the generator control script. The generator control script is itself created automatically.

The artifact templates are written in XSL, and are used by the generator to create different kinds of artifacts, including build scripts, Java source code,

Enterprise JavaBean deployment descriptors, and database creation and management scripts. During the generation of a given system, a particular template will be used separately for each instantiation of the artifact that it describes, as dictated by the system build script.

The generator is simply the Xalan XSLT engine wrapped inside an ANT task. It is controlled by ANT build scripts, the first of which contains the targets to generate the system-specific build script that, in turn, is used to control the generation of all other artifacts.

2.1 Domain Specification

Figure 2 contains a high-level view of the important sections of the MODEST domain specification. The figure is organized hierarchically to help convey the nesting of the XML elements. The domain specification is the only place within the MODEST environment that a customer's requirements are explicitly maintained.

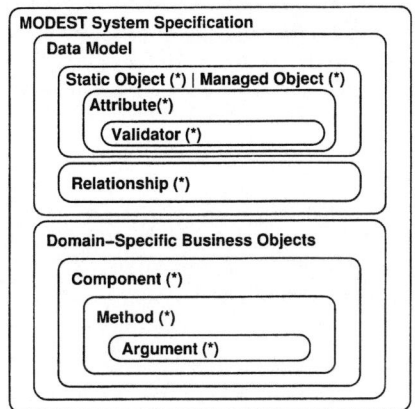

Fig. 2. Organization of the Domain Specification

The data model for the domain of interest is captured by specifying *static objects*, *managed objects*, their *attributes*, and the *relationships* among them. Static objects are those entities that are not intended to be changed by users of the system. Typically, static objects are used to model ancillary objects that exist to support the core domain entities. The attribute values for all instances of static objects must be detailed in the domain specification. The static object data are used to populate reference tables within the database, and flyweight pattern [5] classes are generated for use in the software.

Figure 3 shows a sample specification for the automobile domain. In this case, Make has been modeled as a static object with one attribute. Two instances of Make are available: SUBARU and FORD. The customer, after receiving the system generated from this domain specification, can add further instances.

```
<domain-specification>
  <static-object name="Make">
    <attribute name="name" type="String" unique="true" required="true">
      <validator type="string-length" min="1" max="64"/>
    </attribute>
    <instance name="SUBARU" key="10">
      <attribute-value name="name">Subaru</attribute-value>
    </instance>
    <instance name="FORD" key="10">
      <attribute-value name="name">Ford</attribute-value>
    </instance></static-object>
  <managed-object name="Car" type-key="20">
    <attribute type="String" name="id" unique="true" required="true">
      <validator type="string-length" min="1" max="128"/>
      <validator type="alphanumeric-string"/></attribute>
    <attribute name="make" static-object="Make" required="true"/>
  </managed-object>
  <managed-object name="Driver" type-key="30">
    <attribute type="String" name="name" required="true">
      <validator type="string-length" min="1" max="128"/>
      <validator type="alphabetic-string"/></attribute>
    <attribute type="Integer" name="age" required="true">
      <validator type="range" min="16" max="110"/>
    </attribute></managed-object>
  <relationship src="Car" dest="Driver" type="1-n"/>
  <business-object name="IdGenerator">
    <business-method name="nextId" return="String"/>
  </business-object></domain-specification>
```

Fig. 3. Sample Domain Specification

A *validator* in a domain specification is used to describe the range of values that are valid for a particular attribute. The validator details are used at run time to guard attribute values, and they are also used in the generation of data for unit and integration tests. In Figure 3, for example, a validator is given for the name attribute of the Model static object. For efficiency reasons, attribute values of static objects are not validated at run time, so development-time testing of instance attribute values is important. Furthermore, instances of static objects represent a software feature that has a high likelihood of being changed by customers after delivery, so the generated test cases are crucial to maintaining high-quality software.

Managed objects are those entities that can be created, updated, and deleted by the user during the operation of the system. Aside from the basic data types, managed objects can also have attributes of any declared static object types. Managed objects require more support code than static objects; since they represent persistent changeable data, they need to be stored and retrieved from a database, and they typically have relationships with other managed objects or static objects. Additionally, because attributes of a managed object are dynamic, the managed object must use validators to ensure that its internal state is always consistent.

The system modeled by the specification shown in Figure 3 contains the managed objects Car and Driver. For managed objects, the attribute validator properties are used to instantiate representative test data for the system. Values that would pass validation are used to test the functional operation of the system, and invalid values are used to test error handling. Because managed objects represent the core persistent data processed by the system, test cases that exercise this aspect of the system are vitally important to the customer.

Relationship elements model a "has" relationship among managed objects. The three supported relationship cardinalities are one-to-one, one-to-many, and many-to-many. Figure 3 includes a one-to-many relationship between Car and Driver.

2.2 Generator

Code generation in MODEST is a straightforward instance of using XSL to transform XML documents into other XML documents and plain text files. The XML/XSL combination was used because the Chronos developers already had familiarity with the Xalan XSLT engine, and because decent tool support for creating XML documents already exists. Following the terminology of Czarnecki and Eisenecker [2], the MODEST artifact generator is a *transformational* generator that performs *oblique* transformations.

The structures that are used in the domain specification are significantly different from those that are embodied in the generated artifacts. In most cases the template that creates a particular artifact pulls data from many different parts of the specification. Figure 4 shows an augmented data-flow diagram for the MODEST code generator. The XSL transformer is controlled by two different build scripts, the *bootstrap control script* and the *generated control script*. The bootstrap script contains only the targets and dependencies needed to invoke the XSLT engine for the creation of the system build script. Once the system build script has been generated, it contains the dependencies and targets needed to generate all the other artifacts in the proper order.

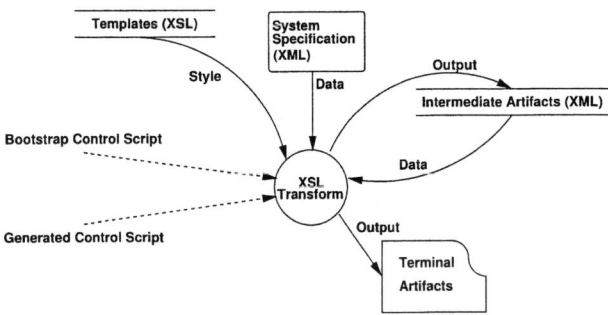

Fig. 4. Data Flow in MODEST

Several artifacts needed for the final system are generated using a multi-stage process. Figure 4 shows this as a distinction between *terminal artifacts* and *intermediate artifacts*.

2.3 Artifact Templates

All of the design and implementation decisions that go into the creation of the end product are codified in the artifact templates, which are XSL style sheets. There is a different artifact template for each type of artifact that is generated. For example, there is an artifact template that generates a Java class to encapsulate a managed object, and this template is parameterized by the intended name of the managed object. For a given system, a particular artifact template might be used multiple times, once for each instance of the artifact called for in the domain specification. The domain specification shown in Figure 3 contains two managed objects. Thus, the generated build script contains two transformations that use the managed-object template, one for `Car` and one for `Driver`.

2.4 System Family

From an engineering perspective, all systems generated by MODEST have the same design. Figure 5 provides a high-level view of the MODEST family of systems. Architecturally, the scope of MODEST is restricted to the application logic and data storage tiers of a standard three-tier architecture. The scope is further restricted in that MODEST systems are designed to operate within the Enterprise JavaBean (EJB) distributed object framework. This represents the target environment for code generation.

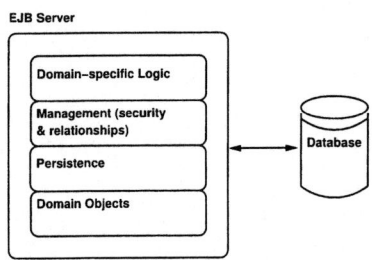

Fig. 5. MODEST System Family

The simplest classes generated by MODEST are those that encapsulate the attributes of managed and static objects. These simple classes are labeled "Domain Objects" in Figure 5.

The top three layers shown in Figure 5 all consist of EJB components. Both Java code and deployment descriptors are generated for these.

The components in the persistence layer are implemented as entity EJBs that contain the logic for storing and loading managed-object values to and from the database. There is a different entity EJB for each managed object in the domain specification. The persistence layer is not visible to external clients;

its functionality is only available to the management and domain-specific layers above it in the system architecture.

Next is the management layer whose objects are implemented as session EJBs. The objects perform relationship management, and authorization and authentication for clients. These components are used by client code to create, update, and delete managed objects as needed by the user. A separate EJB is generated for each managed object in the domain specification.

At the highest level in Figure 5 are the components that provide domain-specific logic. The interfaces for these components are described explicitly in the domain specification, and their implementation is performed manually by developers. However, deployment descriptors, remote interfaces, and framework code can all be generated directly from the domain specification. Framework code that allows these objects to interact properly with the security model is encapsulated in generated base classes through which all method calls are passed.

For example, consider the business object `IdGenerator` shown in Figure 3. This object has a single method with signature `String nextId()`. The remote interface for this object is as follows.

```
interface IdGenerator extends EJBObject
{
    String nextId( SecurityToken st ) throws AuthorizationException,
                                             ServerException,
                                             RemoteException;
}
```

The signature of the `nextId` method has been augmented with a standard parameter and standard exceptions. The generated base class contains the augmented method that is actually called by clients. This method wraps a call to the abstract method `nextIdImpl()` in code that checks the client's authorization and deals with logging and error handling in a standard way. The developer is responsible for providing a derived class that implements `nextIdImpl()` with the correct semantics.

By wrapping the methods of domain-specific logic objects in this way, MODEST ensures that security, logging, and error checking are handled in a consistent manner, allowing the developer to concentrate on the complexity of the business logic, not on the complexity of the MODEST framework. However, this scaffolding also makes it harder for the developer to test their hand-written logic directly, since they would have to understand quite a bit about the MODEST framework to be able to create an integration test case for it by hand. For this reason, it is critical that equivalent scaffolding be generated for the testing of the domain specific logic.

Beneath all of the application logic sits the database. MODEST generates a schema creation script that can be used to create all of the tables and views needed to efficiently handle the data requirements of the managed and static objects that are outlined in the domain specification. Additionally, this creation script creates other database objects that are needed to enforce MODEST's security model and to validate data as much as possible.

3 Test-Code Generation

Test code is generated by the MODEST system in parallel with the main application code. Test code is generated for two major reasons.

1. To validate and certify development-time activities.

   Even given the generative capabilities of MODEST, development of distributed component-based systems is a complicated undertaking. Subtle, unexpected interactions among components, that are not present in simple domains, crop up in complicated domains. Additionally, implementation of a customer's domain logic is often complicated, and the existence of test harnesses and test cases reduces the chances that unexpected side effects will result from the hand-written portions of the system.

2. To provide a framework for supporting long-term maintenance activities.

   As described in Section 2, the systems generated by MODEST are delivered to customers under the assumption that maintenance and extension are going to be performed by customers without the benefit of MODEST's generative capabilities. The generation of test harnesses and test cases is an important piece of this business model, and it gives potential customers confidence that the software they receive is operational, and that it can be maintained and extended in a rational manner so that it remains operational.

In MODEST, test-code generation consists of four major aspects: generation of code to instantiate representative static and managed objects; generation of test cases for validating static-object implementations; generation of test cases for validating managed-object implementations; and generation of test harnesses for facilitating the testing of domain-specific logic.

3.1 Representative Object Instances

All test cases need access to representative data to exercise the functionality of the system. In MODEST, the lowest-level domain-specific classes are those that simply wrap the attributes of static objects and managed objects. In Section 2.4 these are referred to as "domain objects". Representative instances of these objects are needed throughout the generated test code for use as method parameters and the like. To accomplish this, a class that provides methods for instantiating representative domain objects is generated and used by other test cases.

For the domain specification shown in Figure 3, the base test-case class would have the following methods.

- newMake(): randomly chooses one of the Make instances.
- newDriver(): randomly populates attribute name based on its validators.
- newCar(): randomly populates attribute id using newMake() to pick a Make.

As mentioned above, the validators for managed objects are used as guidelines for choosing valid attribute values. The algorithms to select these values probabilistically generate null values, boundary condition values, and mid-range values to attempt to get adequate test coverage.

3.2 Test Cases for Static Objects

As mentioned in Section 2.1, static objects represent immutable data that play a supporting role to managed objects. They are implemented as reference tables in the database, and as flyweight pattern classes in software. Each static object type is supported by a factory that provides lookup methods and access to collections of flyweight classes. Both unit tests and integration tests are generated to validate their implementations. The static object Make contained in the domain specification shown in Figure 3 and its supporting factory, MakeFactory, is used as an example below.

Unit Tests. The implementations of static objects are validated with unit tests. All valid instances of static objects are enumerated in the domain specification, and these data are used to exhaustively test the software. Unit tests ensure the following properties.

1. All instances are present. This means that Make.SUBARU and Make.FORD are available and found in the MakeFactory.all() collection.
2. equals() and compareTo() work properly for each instance. The test cases would compare Make.SUBARU and Make.FORD to themselves and then to each other, and verify that the results were correct based on the data in the specification.
3. Attribute values match what is listed in the domain specification. The test cases would verify that Make.SUBARU.getName() == "Subaru".
4. Lookup methods on factory classes work properly for each attribute of each instance. The test cases would verify that MakeFactory.findByName("Subaru") == Make.SUBARU.

Integration Tests. Integration tests are needed to ensure that the generated implementation matches the data that are contained in the reference tables in the database. For efficiency purposes, there are no run-time checks of data consistency, so development-time checking is especially important. This is accomplished by selecting all the data from the database reference table, and ensuring that its contents match that of the MakeFactory.all() collection.

3.3 Test Cases for Managed Objects

Managed objects represent the core domain entities that comprise a particular domain. The managed-object instances are stored in the database, and their values can be changed, and instances can be deleted. Because they are the central entities in the system, and because they can be modified and deleted, they are guarded by a security model ensuring that a user is properly authenticated and authorized before a particular action is performed. There is code to deal with managed objects in three of the layers shown in Figure 5: domain, persistence, and management. Both unit tests and integration tests are needed to test the implementation effectively.

Unit Tests. Unit tests are generated to validate the domain-object implementation. These tests ensure that the validation code is working properly for each class by verifying that invalid attribute values cannot be used in constructors or mutator methods, and that randomly generated valid data can be used. There are also tests to ensure that standard methods such as `equals()` and `compareTo()` are implemented properly.

For the `Car` managed object shown in Figure 3, these tests would ensure that `Car` could not be instantiated without a valid value for the `id` attribute, and that it could not subsequently be changed to something invalid. The unit tests would also ensure that properly instantiated `Car` objects could be compared properly.

Integration Tests. Integration tests are generated to test the implementation of the persistence and management layers. The persistence layer implementation for each managed object is tested to ensure the following.

1. Managed-object data are replicated perfectly in the database after a store operation.
2. Managed-object data are replicated perfectly in the software after a load operation.
3. Two separately loaded copies of the same data compare properly.
4. Data are replicated perfectly in the database after an update operation.
5. Data are removed from the database after a remove operation.

Because of the design decision that managed objects cannot have invalid internal state, it is not necessary to test invalid data values at this level.

Integration tests are generated at the management level to ensure that relationships among managed objects are properly maintained. This involves ensuring that any required relationships are satisfied in the proper order and that invalid relationships are not permitted. For the `Car` object from Figure 3, this would mean ensuring that a valid `Driver` object existed before a `Car` was created, and that `Driver` objects could not be deleted if that would result in an unsatisfied `Car` relationship.

3.4 Domain Logic Test Harnesses

As described in Section 2, domain-specific logic is captured in the specification through business objects. The interfaces to these business objects are captured in the specification, but the semantics are not. Although the implementations of the actual business methods cannot be automatically generated, much of the scaffolding and supporting code can. For application logic, this means that the developer only has to concentrate on the complexity of the business rules and not the complexity of the MODEST framework. A similar approach is taken for the generation of test harnesses.

The goal of the generated test harness is to allow the developer to operate at the same level of detail at which the business method is implemented. This implies that the scaffolding code should handle any setup that is needed to interact with the business method, and wrap the domain-specific testing logic properly to handle exceptions that are generated by the framework. For the `IdGenerator` business object shown in Figure 3, an abstract test case, `IdGeneratorTestCase`, would be generated that had the following methods.

- `setUp()`: performs authentication and authorization setup that is needed to have permission to call the business method.
- `nextId()`: proxy method used by the hand-written test code. Within this method, the actual call to the business method is performed with the appropriate security ticket and error handling.
- `tearDown()`: performs any clean up related to `setUp()`.

Developers are then responsible for extending this class and implementing the actual tests, using `nextId()` as a proxy for the remote EJB object.

4 Discussion and Evaluation

This section describes the benefits of test-code generation and quantifies its costs. Initially, we summarize some observations made during the development of the first few prototype systems. Next, we present an example in which generated test code is used to identify and debug a subtle integration problem. Finally, we analyze the relative complexity of creating test-code templates versus application-code templates.

4.1 Utility of Generated Test Code

This section contains some observations and analysis of the utility of test-code generation during development and maintenance activities.

Test Cases for Static Objects. The code generated to handle static objects is relatively simple. Since its initial development, few bugs have been found in the implementation. This is due partly to the simplicity of the code, and partly to the exhaustive nature of the generated test cases. For these reasons, static object test cases do not add a lot of value at development time.

Conversely, the real utility of the static-object test cases is to help ensure consistency during system maintenance. This is due to two factors: (1) a common way for customers to extend their system is to manually add new static-object instances for items that were overlooked initially and (2) proper implementation of the static objects requires that changes are made to two disconnected locations, the software classes and the database. The existence of exhaustive integration tests ensures that the two implementations are always consistent.

Test Cases for Managed Objects. The generated implementations of managed objects are fairly complicated and must be consistent across three different layers of the resulting system. These factors ensure that the generated test cases are used often during system development to track down subtle bugs and inconsistencies in the generated implementations and specifications. The situation presented in Section 4.2 provides a concrete example of this.

A common maintenance activity performed by the customer is to augment existing managed objects with additional attributes. This simple extension of the system involves a significant number of changes, not only to the software, but also to the EJB configuration scripts, and the database table definitions. In order to test their changes, the customer augments the generated test code to account for the new attributes. The existing test cases provide a framework within which the customer can add new tests, adding significant value during maintenance. The presence of test cases also provides a well defined way for the customer to certify the system on new platforms.

Domain Logic Test Harnesses. The presence of test-harness scaffolding saves time during development. Developers are able to ignore the details of how the framework alters the signature of the business methods and how the security model must be initialized for testing, thereby reducing the barrier to manual test-code creation.

Also, business rules are pieces of a system that often change after initial development. The presence of existing domain-logic test cases (written by the initial developers) encourages their maintenance in parallel with changes to business rules, increasing the chance that the entire system will be tested as it evolves.

4.2 Development-Time Benefits of Generated Test Cases

Above, we describe the benefits that generated test code provides during development activities and during maintenance activities. In that context, maintenance activities are defined as being those that occur after a generated system is delivered to the customer and, in fact, performed by the customer, not the developer. The bulk of our experience with systems generated by MODEST is with development activities performed during the creation of a few prototype systems.

As the design of the family of systems matures and the artifact template code stabilizes, the subtlety of bugs being found increases. Additionally, as MODEST supports more advanced features, occasionally these features interact in subtle ways when operating in domains with higher complexity.

One such advanced feature is support for cascading deletes in the management EJB layer (see Figure 5). This feature allows a managed-object instance and all other instances reachable from it across explicit relationships to be deleted with a single method call. For example, in the domain specified in Figure 3, a `Car` instance and all of the `Driver` instances associated with it can be deleted by a single cascading delete operation. During an atomic delete operation, logic in the management layer ensures that an object cannot be deleted if it will leave a parent object with an unsatisfied relationship. However, during cascading deletes this check is disabled, since it is known that the parent object will be deleted immediately after the child object is deleted. One of the prototype systems has a fairly complex domain model, and initially the integration tests that exercise cascading deletes failed. By making incremental changes to the domain specification, regenerating the system, and rerunning the integration tests, developers traced the problem back to the section of the management EJB artifact template that disabled the relationship checks during cascading deletes.

Without the generated test code being a standard part of the system, this bug might not have been found during development. Furthermore, the ability to rapidly regenerate test cases from modified domain specifications provides an invaluable tool to aid in debugging.

4.3 The Cost of Generating Test Code

Above, we present the benefits of test-code generation. However, to developers of generative tools there are costs associated with the generation of test code. The principal cost is the additional effort required of developers to create and maintain the artifact templates that generate test code. In order to evaluate this effort, we have used some simple metrics to measure the size and complexity of artifact templates. The values of these metrics are presented in tables 1 and 2. By examining these metrics we can get a feel for the relative level of effort in artifact template creation and maintenance for the test code compared to the effort needed to create and maintain the templates for application code.

Table 1. Average Relative Complexity of MODEST Test-Code Templates

Type	Sub-Templates	XSL Elements	Parent Queries
Test Code (10)	4	92	1
Application Code (27)	9	184	1
Unit Tests (6)	3	52	2
Integration Tests (3)	6	177	0
Test Harnesses (1)	5	77	0

The three measures of artifact template size and complexity presented in tables 1 and 2 are: (1) the number of sub-templates; (2) the number of XSL elements; and (3) the number of XPath parent queries.

XSL style sheets process XML documents by matching sub-templates against the structure and data contained in the XML document[2]. Sub-templates can also be named and called as functions. The number of sub-templates gives some indication of both the size and complexity of an artifact template, since they

---

[2] In this paper we refer to the entire XSL style sheet as the template; this corresponds to the top-level `xsl:stylesheet` element. Sub-templates correspond to the `xsl:template` elements that are children of `xsl:stylesheet`.

Table 2. Total Relative Complexity of MODEST Test-Code Templates

Type	Sub-Templates	XSL Elements	Parent Queries
Test Code (10)	42	927	17
Application Code (27)	247	4968	41
Unit Tests (6)	18	317	16
Integration Tests (3)	19	533	1
Test Harnesses (1)	5	77	0

represent the basic data-processing unit of an XSL style sheet. The numbers for these are shown in the second column of tables 1 and 2.

XSL style sheets are themselves XML documents containing special XSL elements intermingled with elements from the output XML document. XSL processors handle the special elements, which contain both control instructions and data-expansion instructions, and pass through the output elements without interpretation. The second metric, XSL element count, gives an indication of the amount of parameterization of the output document, and hence the complexity of the template. The numbers for XSL element counts are shown in the third column of tables 1 and 2.

The third metric, XPath parent queries, is another way to measure the complexity of the XSL template. XPath is a language for querying paths in an XML document. XPath expressions are used extensively in XSL documents for matching templates against parts of the input document, and for selecting parts of the input document to which templates should be applied. Since input documents to an XSL transform are always XML documents, they are inherently hierarchical. In the simplest case the output document has the same hierarchical decomposition as the input document, which means that the transformation can proceed in a top-down fashion. As the output document structure diverges from the input document structure, XPath queries that move up the hierarchy are needed. We refer to these as XPath *parent queries*. They begin with the XPath parent axis shortcut "..". We use a count of these XPath parent queries to represent the level of structural difference between the input and output documents. Keep in mind that when generating Java source code, MODEST employs a two-stage transformation process in an effort to reduce the complexity of artifact templates, principally by removing the need for extensive XPath parent queries.

The first two rows in tables 1 and 2 show the values of our metrics for test code and application code, respectively. These data are intended to provide a feel for the relative complexity of test-code templates compared to application-code templates. The remaining three rows of the tables break down the values for the three different kinds of test code. The number in parenthesis in the first column of both tables is the number of style sheets that were analyzed to come up with the numbers in each row.

Table 1 presents the average metric values. These data represent the relative level of complexity of a single artifact template of each of the representative template types. These data show that, on average, the size and complexity of test-code templates is less than that of application-code templates. It also shows that out of the three test-code template types, the integration test-case templates require the largest number of XSL elements to generate their desired output.

Table 2 shows the total metric values. This is intended to represent the total effort required to generate templates of the various types. The high-level result shown by these data is that test-code templates are seemingly smaller and simpler than application-code templates. Assuming that our metrics are a reasonable measure of a template's complexity and size, this implies that test-code generation is a fraction of the overall effort required to generate all of a system's code.

5 Related Work

The work described in this paper lies at the confluence of some well-established areas of software engineering research and practice. In this section we briefly review related work in the areas of OMG's Model Driven Architecture, model-based testing, and enterprise Java code generation.

5.1 Model Driven Architecture

At a conceptual level, the design of MODEST shares a number of similarities with the OMG's Model Driven Architecture (MDA) [12]. The basic idea of the MDA is that enterprises can insulate themselves from the volatile nature of the commercial middleware market by focusing their energies on creating Platform Independent Models (PIMs) of their business functions and relying on standard mappings and/or platform experts to map their PIMs into Platform Specific Models (PSMs). The models discussed in the MDA specification are UML models. In the MODEST system, the domain specification is platform independent, but much more restricted than a generic UML model.

Much of the MDA approach is centered around transformations and mappings between UML models at different levels of abstraction, and between PIMs and PSMs. The following mappings have been enumerated.

- PIM to PIM: enhancing, filtering, or specializing models without introducing any platform-dependent details.
- PIM to PSM: projecting a sufficiently refined PIM onto a model of the execution environment.
- PSM to PSM: refining a platform-dependent model.
- PIM to PSM: abstracting existing implementation details into a platform independent model.

MODEST employs the first three mapping types, which can all be viewed as refinement mappings. The generalization mapping, PIM to PSM, is not utilized in MODEST, since there is a very clear distinction between which artifacts are generated and which must be produced manually. In MODEST, manually generated artifacts often have to conform to interfaces that are generated. However, there is no mechanism for changes to the structure of manual artifacts to be propagated back up to the higher-level models.

Gervais [6] outlines a methodology that is based on both MDA and the Open Distributed Processing Reference Model (RM-ODP) [1]. Gervais proposes a process for modeling the domain-specific features of a system in a "Behavioral Model" and the high-level technological features of the system in an "Engineering Model". These would be merged into a platform-specific "Operational Model", which could then be used as the basis for generating implementation artifacts. While MODEST's domain specification fills the same role as Gervais' behavioral model, its artifact templates are too low level to even be considered an operational model. Future plans for MODEST include higher-level models for engineering features similar to what Gervais proposes.

5.2 Model-Based Testing

Due to the time-consuming nature of test-case and test-data creation, there have been many studies aimed at generating them automatically. Many approaches focus on the use of high-level formal specifications as the input to their test-generation schemes.

A framework for conducting performance tests of EJB applications is introduced by Liu et al. [10]. Their primary objective is to be able to compare the performance trade offs that are present in different J2EE-compliant servers in the absence of significant application-level logic. Interestingly, the testing they perform is somewhat model driven, since their test-case selection is driven by a common model of the trade offs that are expected to exist within the common feature sets present in J2EE servers.

Grundy, Cai, and Liu [7] discuss the SoftArch/MTE system. This system enables the automatic generation of prototype distributed systems based on high-level architectural objectives. Their emphasis is on performance testing, not on application functionality testing. Many of the generative techniques used in MODEST are similar, in particular the use of XML/XSL to generate code, database schemata, deployment descriptors, and build files.

Dalal et al. [3, 4] present a model-based approach to application functionality testing. In their studies, formal specifications of functional interfaces to various telecommunications systems were made available by a software development team. A combinatorial approach was used to generate a set of covering test-data pairs, which was used to find several failures that were not discovered by the existing testing infrastructure.

Mats [11] and Gu and Cheng [8] present two approaches to the derivation of test cases for communications protocols specified using SDL, while Gupta, Cunning, and Rozenbilt [9] discuss an approach to generating test cases for embedded systems. These approaches differ from ours in that they derive test cases for a particular system from formal specifications, as opposed to creating templates that can generate test code for any system instance.

5.3 Enterprise Java Code Generation

Generation of code for Enterprise Java systems is a fairly common activity. A popular approach is to generate the Home and Remote EJB interfaces, deployment descriptors, and stubs for an EJB implementation, all from a simple description of a database table[3]. The majority of these simple code generators are *compositional* generators, in which the descriptor contains the modular decomposition that the generator needs to amplify. The approach used by MODEST is to allow for domain-specific modeling at a higher level than the software components. The modular decomposition is embedded in the generated build script and the XSL style sheets that comprise the bulk of the MODEST system.

6 Conclusion

In this paper we presented our experience in generating test code in parallel with application code, using a model-driven generator of component-based, distributed systems targeted at the EJB framework. Our experience and evaluation suggests that the level of effort required for the test code is only a small fraction of the overall effort, and brings with it significant benefits. We believe that test-code generation should become a common feature of all model-driven generative systems.

While MODEST is a useful tool that achieves the business goals laid out for it, it only raises the level of abstraction a few small steps above the implementation. A future goal for our work is to use higher-level models for both domain and engineering features. Additional work is aimed at utilizing MODEST's generated test code to experiment with design and implementation trade offs, similar to the approach outlined by Grundy, Cai, and Liu [7] for testbed generation, except that our target would be to evaluate full-featured systems.

Acknowledgments

The authors would like to thank Dan Weiler, President of Chronos Software, Inc., and co-developer of MODEST.

This work was supported in part by the Defense Advanced Research Projects Agency under agreement number F30602-00-2-0608. The U.S. Government is authorized to reproduce and distribute reprints for Governmental purposes notwithstanding any copyright annotation thereon. The views and conclusions contained herein are those of the authors and should not be interpreted as necessarily representing the official policies or endorsements, either expressed or implied, of the Defense Advanced Research Projects Agency or the U.S. Government.

---

[3] EJEN, http://ejen.sourceforge.net
Jenerator, http://www.visioncodified.com

References

1. ISO IS 10746-x. ODP reference model part x. Technical report, International Standards Organization, 1995.
2. K. Czarnecki and U.W. Eisenecker. *Generative Programming: Methods, Tools, and Applications*. Addison-Wesley, 2000.
3. S.R. Dalal, A. Jain, N. Karunanithi, J.M. Leaton, and C. M. Lott. Model-based testing of a highly programmable system. In *Proc. 9th International Symposium on Software Reliability Engineering (ISSRE '98)*, 1998.
4. S.R. Dalal, A. Jain, N. Karunanithi, J.M. Leaton, C. M. Lott, G.C. Patton, and B.M. Horowitz. Model-based testing in practice. In *Proceedings of the 1999 International Conference on Software Engineering (ICSE '99)*, 1999.
5. E. Gamma, R. Helm, R. Johnson, and J. Vlissides. *Design Patterns*. Addison-Wesley, 1995.
6. M.P. Gervais. Towards an MDA-oriented methodology. In *Proceedings of the 26th Annual International Computer Software and Applications Conference (COMPSAC 2002)*, 2002.
7. J. Grundy, Y. Cai, and A. Liu. Generation of distributed system test-beds from high-level software architecture descriptions. In *Proceedings 16th Annual International Conference on Automated Software Engineering (ASE 2001)*, 2001.
8. Z.Y. Gu and K.E. Cheng. The derivation of test cases from sdl specifications. In *Proceedings of the 30th Annual Southeast Regional Conference*. ACM Press, 1992.
9. P. Gupta, S.J. Cunning, and J.W. Rozenbilt. Synthesis of high-level requirements models for automatic test generation. In *Eighth Annual IEEE International Conference and Workshop on the Engineering of Computer Based Systems (ECBS '01)*, 2001.
10. Y. Liu, I. Gorton, A. Liu, N. Jiang, and S. Chen. Designing a test suite for empirically-based middleware performance prediction. In *40th International Conference on Technology of Object-Oriented Languages and Systems (TOOLS Pacific 2002)*, Sydney, Australia, 2002.
11. L. Mats. Selection criteria for automated TTCN test case generation from SDL. In *Second IEEE Workshop on Industrial Strength Formal Specification Techniques*, 1998.
12. J. Miller and J. Mukerji. Model driven architecture (MDA). *OMG Document ormsc/2001-07-01*, July 2001.

Author Index

Agha, Gul 324

Bapty, Ted 151
Buchmann, Alejandro 169

Calcagno, Cristiano 57
Cechticky, Vaclav 267
Chevalley, Philippe 267
Chhokra, Kumar Gaurav 138
Chiba, Shigeru 189, 364
Cilia, Mariano 169
Cleenewerck, Thomas 245
Consel, Charles 1
Cox, Simon 344

Danvy, Olivier 117
Dincklage, Daniel von 287

Eames, Brandon 138
Elphick, Daniel 344

Fuentes, Lidia 118

Gokhale, Aniruddha 151
Gray, Jeff 151

Hamdi, Hedi 1
Hammond, Kevin 37
Haupt, Michael 169
Huang, Liwen 57

Järvi, Jaakko 228
Johann, Patricia 97

Kästner, Daniel 18
Kozsik, Tamás 209

Ledeczi, Akos 138
Leroy, Xavier 57
Leuschel, Michael 344
Lumsdaine, Andrew 228

Mezini, Mira 169
Michaelson, Greg 37
Muntz, Richard R. 77

Natarajan, Balachandran 151
Neema, Sandeep 151
Nishizawa, Muga 364
Nordstrom, Steve 138

Pasetti, Alessandro 267
Pinto, Mónica 118
Porkoláb, Zoltán 209
Pu, Calton 1

Réveillère, Laurent 1
Rutherford, Matthew J. 377

Saraiva, João 307
Sato, Yoshiki 189
Schaufelberger, Walter 267
Schmidt, Douglas C. 151
Shetty, Shweta 138
Singaravelu, Lenin 1
Sprinkle, Jonathan 138
Swierstra, Doaitse 307

Taha, Walid 57, 97
Tarr, Peri 265
Tatsubori, Michiaki 189
Troya, Jose María 118

Wang, Zhenghao 77
Willcock, Jeremiah 228
Wolf, Alexander L. 377

Yu, Haiyan 1

Ziaei, Reza 324
Zólyomi, István 209

Lecture Notes in Computer Science

For information about Vols. 1–2730
please contact your bookseller or Springer-Verlag

Vol. 2731: C.S. Calude, M.J. Dinneen, V. Vajnovszki (Eds.), Discrete Mathematics and Theoretical Computer Science. Proceedings, 2003. VIII, 301 pages. 2003.

Vol. 2732: C. Taylor, J.A. Noble (Eds.), Information Processing in Medical Imaging. Proceedings, 2003. XVI, 698 pages. 2003.

Vol. 2733: A. Butz, A. Krüger, P. Olivier (Eds.), Smart Graphics. Proceedings, 2003. XI, 261 pages. 2003.

Vol. 2734: P. Perner, A. Rosenfeld (Eds.), Machine Learning and Data Mining in Pattern Recognition. Proceedings, 2003. XII, 440 pages. 2003. (Subseries LNAI).

Vol. 2735: F. Kaashoek, I. Stoica (Eds.), Peer-to-Peer Systems II. Proceedings, 2003. XI, 316 pages. 2003.

Vol. 2736: V. Mařík, W. Retschitzegger, O.Štěpánková (Eds.), Database and Expert Systems Applications. Proceedings, 2003. XX, 945 pages. 2003.

Vol. 2737: Y. Kambayashi, M. Mohania, W. Wöß (Eds.), Data Warehousing and Knowledge Discovery. Proceedings, 2003. XIV, 432 pages. 2003.

Vol. 2738: K. Bauknecht, A M. Tjoa, G. Quirchmayr (Eds.), E-Commerce and Web Technologies. Proceedings, 2003. XII, 452 pages. 2003.

Vol. 2739: R. Traunmüller (Ed.), Electronic Government. Proceedings, 2003. XVIII, 511 pages. 2003.

Vol. 2740: E. Burke, P. De Causmaecker (Eds.), Practice and Theory of Automated Timetabling IV. Proceedings, 2002. XII, 361 pages. 2003.

Vol. 2741: F. Baader (Ed.), Automated Deduction – CADE-19. Proceedings, 2003. XII, 503 pages. 2003. (Subseries LNAI).

Vol. 2742: R. N. Wright (Ed.), Financial Cryptography. Proceedings, 2003. VIII, 321 pages. 2003.

Vol. 2743: L. Cardelli (Ed.), ECOOP 2003 – Object-Oriented Programming. Proceedings, 2003. X, 501 pages. 2003.

Vol. 2744: V. Mařík, D. McFarlane, P. Valckenaers (Eds.), Holonic and Multi-Agent Systems for Manufacturing. Proceedings, 2003. XI, 322 pages. 2003. (Subseries LNAI).

Vol. 2745: M. Guo, L.T. Yang (Eds.), Parallel and Distributed Processing and Applications. Proceedings, 2003. XII, 450 pages. 2003.

Vol. 2746: A. de Moor, W. Lex, B. Ganter (Eds.), Conceptual Structures for Knowledge Creation and Communication. Proceedings, 2003. XI, 405 pages. 2003. (Subseries LNAI).

Vol. 2747: B. Rovan, P. Vojtáš (Eds.), Mathematical Foundations of Computer Science 2003. Proceedings, 2003. XIII, 692 pages. 2003.

Vol. 2748: F. Dehne, J.-R. Sack, M. Smid (Eds.), Algorithms and Data Structures. Proceedings, 2003. XII, 522 pages. 2003.

Vol. 2749: J. Bigun, T. Gustavsson (Eds.), Image Analysis. Proceedings, 2003. XXII, 1174 pages. 2003.

Vol. 2750: T. Hadzilacos, Y. Manolopoulos, J.F. Roddick, Y. Theodoridis (Eds.), Advances in Spatial and Temporal Databases. Proceedings, 2003. XIII, 525 pages. 2003.

Vol. 2751: A. Lingas, B.J. Nilsson (Eds.), Fundamentals of Computation Theory. Proceedings, 2003. XII, 433 pages. 2003.

Vol. 2752: G.A. Kaminka, P.U. Lima, R. Rojas (Eds.), RoboCup 2002: Robot Soccer World Cup VI. XVI, 498 pages. 2003. (Subseries LNAI).

Vol. 2753: F. Maurer, D. Wells (Eds.), Extreme Programming and Agile Methods – XP/Agile Universe 2003. Proceedings, 2003. XI, 215 pages. 2003.

Vol. 2754: M. Schumacher, Security Engineering with Patterns. XIV, 208 pages. 2003.

Vol. 2756: N. Petkov, M.A. Westenberg (Eds.), Computer Analysis of Images and Patterns. Proceedings, 2003. XVIII, 781 pages. 2003.

Vol. 2758: D. Basin, B. Wolff (Eds.), Theorem Proving in Higher Order Logics. Proceedings, 2003. X, 367 pages. 2003.

Vol. 2759: O.H. Ibarra, Z. Dang (Eds.), Implementation and Application of Automata. Proceedings, 2003. XI, 312 pages. 2003.

Vol. 2761: R. Amadio, D. Lugiez (Eds.), CONCUR 2003 - Concurrency Theory. Proceedings, 2003. XI, 524 pages. 2003.

Vol. 2762: G. Dong, C. Tang, W. Wang (Eds.), Advances in Web-Age Information Management. Proceedings, 2003. XIII, 512 pages. 2003.

Vol. 2763: V. Malyshkin (Ed.), Parallel Computing Technologies. Proceedings, 2003. XIII, 570 pages. 2003.

Vol. 2764: S. Arora, K. Jansen, J.D.P. Rolim, A. Sahai (Eds.), Approximation, Randomization, and Combinatorial Optimization. Proceedings, 2003. IX, 409 pages. 2003.

Vol. 2765: R. Conradi, A.I. Wang (Eds.), Empirical Methods and Studies in Software Engineering. VIII, 279 pages. 2003.

Vol. 2766: S. Behnke, Hierarchical Neural Networks for Image Interpretation. XII, 224 pages. 2003.

Vol. 2768: M.J. Wilson, R.R. Martin (Eds.), Mathematics of Surfaces. Proceedings, 2003. VIII, 393 pages. 2003.

Vol. 2769: T. Koch, I. T. Sølvberg (Eds.), Research and Advanced Technology for Digital Libraries. Proceedings, 2003. XV, 536 pages. 2003.

Vol. 2773: V. Palade, R.J. Howlett, L. Jain (Eds.), Knowledge-Based Intelligent Information and Engineering Systems. Proceedings, Part I, 2003. LI, 1473 pages. 2003. (Subseries LNAI).

Vol. 2774: V. Palade, R.J. Howlett, L. Jain (Eds.), Knowledge-Based Intelligent Information and Engineering Systems. Proceedings, Part II, 2003. LI, 1443 pages. 2003. (Subseries LNAI).

Vol. 2776: V. Gorodetsky, L. Popyack, V. Skormin (Eds.), Computer Network Security. Proceedings, 2003. XIV, 470 pages. 2003.

Vol. 2777: B. Schölkopf, M.K. Warmuth (Eds.), Learning Theory and Kernel Machines. Proceedings, 2003. XIV, 746 pages. 2003. (Subseries LNAI).

Vol. 2778: P.Y.K. Cheung, G.A. Constantinides, J.T. de Sousa (Eds.), Field-Programmable Logic and Applications. Proceedings, 2003. XXVI, 1179 pages. 2003.

Vol. 2779: C.D. Walter, Ç.K. Koç, C. Paar (Eds.), Cryptographic Hardware and Embedded Systems – CHES 2003. Proceedings, 2003. XIII, 441 pages. 2003.

Vol. 2781: B. Michaelis, G. Krell (Eds.), Pattern Recognition. Proceedings, 2003. XVII, 621 pages. 2003.

Vol. 2782: M. Klusch, A. Omicini, S. Ossowski, H. Laamanen (Eds.), Cooperative Information Agents VII. Proceedings, 2003. XI, 345 pages. 2003. (Subseries LNAI).

Vol. 2783: W. Zhou, P. Nicholson, B. Corbitt, J. Fong (Eds.), Advances in Web-Based Learning – ICWL 2003. Proceedings, 2003. XV, 552 pages. 2003.

Vol. 2786: F. Oquendo (Ed.), Software Process Technology. Proceedings, 2003. X, 173 pages. 2003.

Vol. 2787: J. Timmis, P. Bentley, E. Hart (Eds.), Artificial Immune Systems. Proceedings, 2003. XI, 299 pages. 2003.

Vol. 2789: L. Böszörményi, P. Schojer (Eds.), Modular Programming Languages. Proceedings, 2003. XIII, 271 pages. 2003.

Vol. 2790: H. Kosch, L. Böszörményi, H. Hellwagner (Eds.), Euro-Par 2003 Parallel Processing. Proceedings, 2003. XXXV, 1320 pages. 2003.

Vol. 2792: T. Rist, R. Aylett, D. Ballin, J. Rickel (Eds.), Intelligent Virtual Agents. Proceedings, 2003. XV, 364 pages. 2003. (Subseries LNAI).

Vol. 2794: P. Kemper, W. H. Sanders (Eds.), Computer Performance Evaluation. Proceedings, 2003. X, 309 pages. 2003.

Vol. 2795: L. Chittaro (Ed.), Human-Computer Interaction with Mobile Devices and Services. Proceedings, 2003. XV, 494 pages. 2003.

Vol. 2796: M. Cialdea Mayer, F. Pirri (Eds.), Automated Reasoning with Analytic Tableaux and Related Methods. Proceedings, 2003. X, 271 pages. 2003. (Subseries LNAI).

Vol. 2798: L. Kalinichenko, R. Manthey, B. Thalheim, U. Wloka (Eds.), Advances in Databases and Information Systems. Proceedings, 2003. XIII, 431 pages. 2003.

Vol. 2799: J.J. Chico, E. Macii (Eds.), Integrated Circuit and System Design. Proceedings, 2003. XVII, 631 pages. 2003.

Vol. 2801: W. Banzhaf, T. Christaller, P. Dittrich, J.T. Kim, J. Ziegler (Eds.), Advances in Artificial Life. Proceedings, 2003. XVI, 905 pages. 2003. (Subseries LNAI).

Vol. 2803: M. Baaz, J.A. Makowsky (Eds.), Computer Science Logic. Proceedings, 2003. XII, 589 pages. 2003.

Vol. 2804: M. Bernardo, P. Inverardi (Eds.), Formal Methods for Software Architectures. Proceedings, 2003. VII, 287 pages. 2003.

Vol. 2805: K. Araki, S. Gnesi, D. Mandrioli (Eds.), FME 2003: Formal Methods. Proceedings, 2003. XVII, 942 pages. 2003.

Vol. 2807: V. Matoušek, P. Mautner (Eds.), Text, Speech and Dialogue. Proceedings, 2003. XIII, 426 pages. 2003. (Subseries LNAI).

Vol. 2810: M.R. Berthold, H.-J. Lenz, E. Bradley, R. Kruse, C. Borgelt (Eds.), Advances in Intelligent Data Analysis V. Proceedings, 2003. XV, 624 pages. 2003.

Vol. 2812: G. Benson, R. Page (Eds.), Algorithms in Bioinformatics. Proceedings, 2003. X, 528 pages. 2003. (Subseries LNBI).

Vol. 2815: Y. Lindell, Composition of Secure Multi-Party Protocols. XVI, 192 pages. 2003.

Vol. 2816: B. Stiller, G. Carle, M. Karsten, P. Reichl (Eds.), Group Communications and Charges. Proceedings, 2003. XIII, 354 pages. 2003.

Vol. 2817: D. Konstantas, M. Leonard, Y. Pigneur, S. Patel (Eds.), Object-Oriented Information Systems. Proceedings, 2003. XII, 426 pages. 2003.

Vol. 2818: H. Blanken, T. Grabs, H.-J. Schek, R. Schenkel, G. Weikum (Eds.), Intelligent Search on XML Data. XVII, 319 pages. 2003.

Vol. 2819: B. Benatallah, M.-C. Shan (Eds.), Technologies for E-Services. Proceedings, 2003. X, 203 pages. 2003.

Vol. 2820: G. Vigna, E. Jonsson, C. Kruegel (Eds.), Recent Advances in Intrusion Detection. Proceedings, 2003. X, 239 pages. 2003.

Vol. 2821: A. Günter, R. Kruse, B. Neumann (Eds.), KI 2003: Advances in Artificial Intelligence. Proceedings, 2003. XII, 662 pages. 2003. (Subseries LNAI).

Vol. 2822: N. Bianchi-Berthouze (Ed.), Databases in Networked Information Systems. Proceedings, 2003. X, 271 pages. 2003.

Vol. 2823: A. Omondi, S. Sedukhin (Eds.), Advances in Computer Systems Architecture. Proceedings, 2003. XIII, 409 pages. 2003.

Vol. 2824: Z. Bellahsène, A.B. Chaudhri, E. Rahm, M. Rys, R. Unland (Eds.), Database and XML Technologies. Proceedings, 2003. X, 283 pages. 2003.

Vol. 2825: W. Kuhn, M. Worboys, S. Timpf (Eds.), Spatial Information Theory. Proceedings, 2003. XI, 399 pages. 2003.

Vol. 2827: A. Albrecht, K. Steinhöfel (Eds.), Stochastic Algorithms: Foundations and Applications. Proceedings, 2003. VIII, 167 pages. 2003.

Vol. 2830: F. Pfenning, Y. Smaragdakis (Eds.), Generative Programming and Component Engineering. Proceedings, 2003. IX, 397 pages. 2003.

Vol. 2832: G. Di Battista, U. Zwick (Eds.), Algorithms – ESA 2003. Proceedings, 2003. XIV, 790 pages. 2003.

Vol. 2834: X. Zhou, S. Jähnichen, M. Xu, J. Cao (Eds.), Advanced Parallel Processing Technologies. Proceedings, 2003. XIV, 679 pages. 2003.

Vol. 2836: S. Qing, D. Gollmann, J. Zhou (Eds.), Information and Communications Security. Proceedings, 2003. XI, 416 pages. 2003.

Vol. 2837: N. Lavrač, D. Gamberger, L. Blockeel. Todorovski (Eds.), Machine Learning: ECML 2003. Proceedings, 2003. XVI, 504 pages. 2003. (Subseries LNAI).

Vol. 2838: N. Lavrač, D. Gamberger, L. Todorovski, H. Blockeel (Eds.), Knowledge Discovery in Databases: PKDD 2003. Proceedings, 2003. XVI, 508 pages. 2003. (Subseries LNAI).

Vol. 2839: A. Marshall, N. Agoulmine (Eds.), Management of Multimedia Networks and Services. Proceedings, 2003. XIV, 532 pages. 2003.